THE GENTLE PURITAN

A Life of Ezra Stiles

1727-1795

Ezra Stiles, age forty-four, 1771, by Samuel King. Courtesy of Yale University Art Gallery.

THE
GENTLE PURITAN

A Life of Ezra Stiles, 1727-1795

BY EDMUND S. MORGAN

Published for the
Institute of Early American History and Culture
at Williamsburg, Virginia
by The University of North Carolina Press
Chapel Hill

for

ALICE BRAYTON

Preface

I FIRST BECAME ACQUAINTED with Ezra Stiles through the note-book he kept on the Stamp Act Crisis, in which I discovered information about the subject that I had found nowhere else. Stiles was an assiduous recorder of events and ideas, both his own and other men's. Beside the Stamp Act notebook in the vault of the Yale University Library stood a mass of other Stiles papers that had hitherto been used by scholars, as I was using the notebook, for the study of particular topics or episodes, but not for a comprehensive investigation of their author and his times.

In 1949 I began such an investigation. Since then I have read and reread the papers several times, along with newspapers, pamphlets, books, and collections of papers by other New Englanders of the day. The result has been that I now know Ezra Stiles more intimately than I know most of my contemporaries and more fully in some ways than he knew himself or than I know myself. I have tried not to mistake this familiarity for omniscience. Though Stiles put more of himself on paper than most men do, he also withheld much, consciously and unconsciously; and I am sure that I have often missed the significance of what he did put down. Moreover, in spite of the great volume of his surviving papers, many are missing (see bibliographical note). But I have tried to convey the man as I found him in the papers that remain.

As I found him, he was an intellectual, and I have focused my attention principally on his intellectual growth, his adventuring in ideas. He was not an original thinker, and his impact on his times was not great, though in his role as president of Yale it was not negligible. But his intellectual curiosity was omnivorous, and precisely because his mind was more receptive than creative, this book is as much a study of the times as it is of the man. The Stiles papers furnish, I believe, a unique access to the intellectual life of eighteenth-century New England. Whether I have made good use of it the reader must judge.

If I have not, it is not for want of assistance and encouragement. My wife, Helen M. Morgan, has worked with me from the beginning and knows Ezra Stiles as well as I do, probably better. This book is as much hers as mine.

Together we enjoyed the hospitality and help of another friend of Ezra Stiles, Miss Alice Brayton of Portsmouth, Rhode Island, who first showed us Stiles's Newport and read an early draft of the chapter on Newport. Her penetrating comments brought the eighteenth-century town to life for us.

Lewis Stiles Gannett, of West Cornwall, Connecticut, a direct descendant of Ezra Stiles, has assisted us not only by his generous gifts of Stiles papers to the Yale Library but by allowing us to examine his remaining holdings and by entertaining us several times while we did so.

Miss Marjorie G. Wynne, custodian of the Stiles Papers at Yale, has always helped us above and beyond the call of duty. When we began work on the project, she arranged for the microfilming of most of the papers, so that we could work on them away from Yale. Since then she has cooperated cheerfully with our repeated reexaminations of the originals. Other custodians of manuscripts in the Yale Library, Miss Jane W. Hill, Mrs. Zara Jones Powers, and Mr. Howard Gottlieb, have been equally helpful in making other manuscripts available, and Miss Josephine Setze of the Yale Art Gallery offered expert advice about Stiles portraits.

The librarians of the Newport Historical Society, the New Haven Colony Historical Society, and the Connecticut Historical Society, the only other repositories on whose manuscript holdings we have drawn extensively, have also offered us every assistance and convenience.

Like most historians today, I am indebted to a variety of institutions that support modern scholarship. The Institute of Early American History furnished a grant in 1949, which enabled us to begin calendaring the Stiles papers. Brown University, where I was then teaching and which will always have my affection, admiration, and gratitude, did everything possible to encourage me: it unhesitatingly paid for my microfilms, furnished secretarial assistance, provided me (and the other junior members of its faculty) with teaching loads that made research possible, and gave me a sabbatical leave in 1952–53.

In that year the Henry E. Huntington Library awarded me a fellowship that enabled me to spend the entire year in research and writing and provided a congenial place in which to work. The Library's holdings of eighteenth-century books, together with my microfilms of the Stiles papers, made it possible for me to write most of the first draft of the book during that year at San Marino.

Finally I am indebted to Yale University, now my academic home, which has honored Ezra Stiles in the name of one of its new colleges and which has assisted me in numerous ways during the past six years.

E. S. M.
New Haven, Connecticut   *August 14, 1961*

Contents

Illustrations

Ezra Stiles, age forty-four, 1771, by Samuel King. Yale University Art Gallery. In his Diary (*Lit. Diary*, *1*, 131–33), Stiles gives an extensive description of this portrait and explains the significance of the "emblems," which were evidently included in it at his direction and which he says "are more descriptive of my mind, than the Effigies of my Face." The globe in the upper left-hand corner represents Stiles's view of the universe (see pp. 74–77), while the circle and ellipse on the pillar at the left represent sun, planets, and comets.

Frontispiece

I

The Meaning of New England

"SEPT. 9TH AD 1742. Ezra Stiles was Examined per Mr. Chauncy Whittelsey and Mr. John Worthington tutors of Yale College and was Accepted." The new freshman, a small, sober boy, with a long nose and an open, guileless face, wrote it carefully in his notebook.[1] He was fifteen years old. He came from North Haven. He knew arithmetic, Latin, and a little Greek. He was going to Yale.

Yale was where he belonged, because he was the oldest boy in the family and because his father was a minister, had been to Yale himself, and might be expected to send at least one son to college. It need cost the family nothing, for his mother, who died four days after he was born, had left him some property in Glastonbury that would more than pay his board and tuition. She had been the daughter of a minister, so that from both sides of the family he gained a claim to a collegiate education. As far as ability went, he had no worries; he knew his Latin well enough to have been admitted three years before and only stayed out because his father thought him too young.

Now that the time had come to leave home, he approached it eagerly. He did not exactly dislike his father, but there was no getting around the fact that Isaac Stiles was hard to live with.[2] Repining

---

1. He used the notebook as a commonplace book during his early years at college. This and all other manuscripts referred to, unless otherwise indicated, are located in the Stiles Papers, Yale University Library.

2. The account of Isaac Stiles is taken mainly from a manuscript memoir of him by Ezra Stiles, June 15, 1760. Most of the specific facts in the present chapter, except where otherwise indicated in text or footnotes, are drawn from this source.

and querulous, Isaac was always reproaching everyone in the family for the most trifling faults. Though there was never enough money, he would not lift a finger to get more. He had made one attempt, while Ezra was still an infant, to carry on some sort of business along with his ministerial duties, but it had come to nothing, and since then the family had been obliged to get along on his £60 yearly salary and on whatever else could be gained from the hundred-acre farm on which they lived.

It was a valuable piece of land, adjoining the southwest corner of the North Haven green, and the house, which stood until 1850, was as good as any in the neighborhood.[3] But somehow the Stileses did not live as comfortably as a minister's family was supposed to. Isaac knew nothing about farming and made no effort to learn. Though in 1739 he purchased a Negro couple to do the field work, he neither knew enough nor cared enough to direct them. That task, along with every other one except preparing sermons and visiting his parishioners, was left to his wife, Ezra's stepmother. Fortunately she knew more about farming than her husband, and in the course of a lifetime built the family fortunes to a respectable sum; but Isaac could always find something wrong with the way she did it.

Sometimes he belabored his own faults, though not his most obvious ones, as when he confessed in a scrap of diary preserved among his son's papers, that he "did not embrace an opportunity to Discorse with a neighbor: which is a grif to me the Lord pardon my sins of omission"; and that he was "much beset with wicked thots saturday night." He did not say what the thoughts were, or what he meant by "about home not so well Employd as I ought."

This humility, whatever it meant, he reserved for his diary and for God. Within the family someone else was always wrong, and the children came to expect angry or sullen words whenever he emerged from his study, his head held high, his back very straight, and "his small, black, piercing Eye" ready to pin one of them to the wall. His ill temper disappeared only when he came into the presence of men

3. On Isaac's farm, in addition to the Memoir of Isaac Stiles, see William T. Reynolds, *An Historical Address on the One Hundredth Anniversary of the Town of North Haven, Delivered Oct. 21st 1886* (n.p., n.d.), p. 20; Sheldon B. Thorpe, *North Haven Annals* (New Haven, 1892), pp. 31–34, 60–61, 93; and Franklin B. Dexter, ed., *Extracts from the Itineraries and other Miscellanies of Ezra Stiles* (New Haven 1916), p. 183.

whom he considered his superiors. Then those black eyes would flash, and he would be witty and altogether charming for a time. Perhaps his trouble was a lack of assurance. He did not have the advantage his children enjoyed, of being born to the scholarly life. His own father had been—and still was—a plain farmer in East Windsor, and he himself had been trained to become a weaver. Isaac was already twenty and ready to practice his trade when the Reverend Timothy Edwards saw the signs of something bigger in him and prepared him for college. Perhaps Timothy Edwards spoiled a good weaver (it was said that Isaac could weave fourteen yards in a single day) to make an unhappy minister. Though he received his degree in three years instead of the usual four, he never was quite at home in the world of scholarship where a minister had to live. Isaac's son, at any rate, never thought highly of his father's learning: "He read much, but digested almost nothing. His mind was stored with rich and valuable Ideas, but classed in no Order, like good Books thrown in Confusion in a Library Room." [4]

Writing these words in 1760, at the age of thirty-two, Ezra Stiles found it easy to dismiss his father's erudition. He did not, however, belittle the man's achievements. Like many New Englanders before and since, Ezra Stiles maintained a consuming interest in his ancestry and took pains to record his impressions not only of his father but of all his close relatives. When he compared his father and other Stileses of his father's generation with the preceding one, he had to acknowledge that they had all come a long way. [5]

The preceding generation was personified, for Ezra, in Grandfather John Stiles—"an honest Man, tho' of a low Capacity and Understanding . . . naturally rather dull, and cloudy Make, his passions quick tho not often disturbed—at Times melancholly tho often social yet something in a low tho' innocent Manner." Grandfather Stiles had no ambition to be more than a simple farmer. He was neither active nor indolent; if he could lay up enough in summer to feed his family in winter, that was enough for him. In short, "Tho' he had little Evil about him, yet he had nothing extraordinary Good." Ezra used to ask

4. Memoir of Isaac Stiles.

5. The ensuing account of the Stiles and Bancroft families and of Kezia Taylor is based primarily on a memoir by Ezra Stiles written in a commonplace book originally belonging to the Rev. Edward Taylor. The book is the property of Lewis Stiles Gannett and is now on deposit in the Yale University Library.

his grandfather how old he was, but always received evasive answers, perhaps because the old man, after outliving two wives, went to courting again when he was easily seventy-five. Ezra later discovered that John had been born in 1665 in Windsor, Connecticut, where his family were among the first settlers (in 1636), coming from Milbroke, Bedfordshire, by way of Dorchester, Massachusetts.

The best thing that Grandfather Stiles ever did was to marry Ruth Bancroft. She was his first wife, and she bore him fourteen children, to all of whom she communicated something the Stileses had lacked —fire. The Bancrofts were "of a brisk, smart, quick, sensible and lively Cast," and Ezra quickly recognized that his aunts and uncles as well as his father all possessed a manifest superiority of mind to Grandfather Stiles. They also possessed, however, what he experienced only too often in his father, "Violence of Passion," that is, quickness of temper: "not one but was quick and passionate to a high Degree," and this "Boisterousness, Impetuosity and Ungovernableness of their passion involved them in many Trials, which Men of more Meekness and Condescention had avoided."

The family were all small of stature, Isaac being the tallest; but even he was of only a little more than "middling" height. And they all had one further common characteristic: they were good at telling jokes (unfortunately nowhere recorded). The fact that Grandfather Stiles had no such talent made Ezra conclude that this trait, too, came from the Bancrofts, who had "a Turn for Story telling of the innocent and humorous kind." All in all, Ezra took pride in the recent Stileses and their Bancroft endowments, and especially in his father, who with all his faults "was in every Respect superior to all the Family in every Branch of Family Character and Disposition."

About his mother and his mother's family Ezra learned less, though he used to inquire of the neighbors in North Haven about her. They had known Kezia Taylor Stiles for only two years before she died of bearing him, her first child. They remembered her as a bride of twenty-three, tall and slender, "of a delicate soft Make," and addicted to the polite pastimes of young ladies, such as needlework and painting. She was evidently all that a minister's wife should be, with none of her husband's violent temper, for even those members of the parish who were not fond of Isaac spoke highly of her.

Her father, the Reverend Edward Taylor of Westfield, Massachusetts, held a position of respect, though not of eminence, in New England. Kezia was a child of his old age, and he survived her by less than two years, so that her child never really knew him. Ezra used to talk about him with Uncle Eldad Taylor, Edward's son. From these conversations and from the family papers which he eventually inherited, Ezra could tell that Edward Taylor had possessed an inquiring mind. He had been much interested in some large bones (presumably those of a mammoth) dug up near Albany, New York. Taylor had taken them to be relics of a giant, a supposition in which Ezra Stiles readily followed him.[6] Ezra could also tell that Taylor had been a man of principle in the old Puritan line, for he had left England in 1668, when the Restoration had made Puritanism unpopular there.[7] Ezra carefully saved the Taylor papers (using the blank pages of a commonplace book to record his own comments on the Stiles family) and thereby preserved the best poetry written in colonial America. But it is doubtful that Ezra ever fully appreciated the poetic genius of his maternal grandfather.

His grandfather's wife, however, he knew to have been a fine woman. Though she died in the same year as her husband, so that he could not have remembered her either, she was a Wyllys, and everyone in Connecticut knew the Wyllyses were successful and honorable. Ezra liked to think that his mother "had the Delicacy and Humanity and Elegance of the Wyllys Family, with the mechanic Ingenuity and Curiosity of her Father, with the rational and sober sincere Piety of both."

Ezra was born on November 29, 1727 (o.s.), and upon his mother's death was nursed by a neighbor, Mrs. Abigail Ray, who perhaps influenced him more than he knew. Throughout his childhood he

6. Taylor composed a poem on the subject of the giants, of which the manuscript is now in the Yale University Library, along with that of his other poems. See also *Itineraries and Miscellanies*, pp. 81–83, 206; Stiles to Thomas Jefferson, June 21, 1784, Stiles Papers in Massachusetts Historical Society; Stiles to Thomas Hutchinson, March 25, 1765; Franklin B. Dexter, ed., *The Literary Diary of Ezra Stiles* (3 vols. New York, 1901), *1*, 366–67. Taylor's poetry was not printed until the present century, when a selection was edited by Thomas H. Johnson (*The Poetical Works of Edward Taylor*. Princeton, 1943) and the complete poems by Donald Stanford (*The Poems of Edward Taylor*. New Haven, 1960).

7. "The Family of the Rev. Edward Taylor A.M.," manuscript by Ezra Stiles, Stiles Papers.

loved her for her "native Sweetness of Temper Pleasantness and Kindness and Piety." [8] Probably as soon as he was weaned, Mrs. Ray's place was taken by the new mother whom his father married before the boy was a year old. She was Esther Hooker, daughter of Samuel Hooker of Farmington, great-granddaughter of Thomas Hooker, the founder of Connecticut. She was what people at the time called a good economist, for when Isaac died in 1760 he left a clear estate of more than £1400.[9] The credit for this must go to her, for he had the talent neither to accumulate money nor to preserve any that may have come to him as dowry with his two wives. Esther was less delicate than Ezra's mother had been, for she bore children regularly; and on one occasion when her husband fainted, she was able to carry him in her arms to his bed. But if she was stronger than Isaac in many ways, hers was the yielding personality. Though Ezra sympathized with her in the difficulties of running the household, he and all the rest of the family bent to Isaac's commanding will. Isaac was unquestionably the dominant influence in the early shaping of his son's mind.

New England could scarcely have found a better instrument for teaching the young mind to see what it ought to see and hear what it ought to hear. Since Isaac was something of a parvenu in the world of ideas, he probably set more store than another man would have on the dogmas, large and small, conscious and unconscious, of the time. His son, no rebel and no poet, looked at North Haven and Connecticut and New England, and saw what his father taught him to see.

When the boy was thirteen, a horde of locusts descended on North Haven, and he noted meticulously: "They Came about the time strawberrys began to ripen and when the strawbery were gone they went:

8. Edward Taylor Commonplace Book.

9. According to an inventory in the Stiles Papers, the estate was valued at £1,626 5s. 6d., with debts amounting to £238 0s. 6d. But the probate records (Connecticut State Library) show inventories amounting to £1,645 4s. 0d. The largest item was the house lot of 126 acres at North Haven, valued at £567. The figures are in "Lawful Money," sometimes called "Proclamation Money" (after a royal proclamation of 1704) which was supposed to stand to sterling in the ratio of 4 to 3; that is, an amount of silver worth £1,000 L.M. was worth £750 sterling. Throughout Ezra Stiles's papers, however, he calculates the difference in the ratio of 3 to 2. His father's salary, for example, which was £60 L.M., he considered to be worth only £40 sterling. See Henry Bronson, *A Historical Account of Connecticut Currency* (New Haven, 1863), pp. 23–26, 74.

they were not so many in the Plains as in the woods they would seem to Cover the Bodies of walnuts trees—but did not much hurt in the orchard. On Each one's Wings there was a plain W about this bigness: and it is said that when they came before (i.e. 17 years ago) they had P which Letter (some supposes) Denotes P for peace then and W for War now (they are Call'd the 17 year Locusts)." [10]

Would he have seen the "W" or called it that if someone had not said that it stood for war? It may not have been his father who suggested the observation, but his father and everyone else would have taught him to look through the locusts to a higher power that could have marked their wings with a "W" now and with a "P" seventeen years before. Isaac Stiles was not versed in the "new philosophy" of Locke and Newton, so that he could not instruct his son in the advantages of accurate observation of the world. But Isaac knew how to look through nature up to God, and his son could not avoid learning—from the daily Bible reading during family worship, from homely parental platitudes, and from sermons such as the one Isaac put into print in 1742, the year that Ezra entered college, "The Earth (no less than the Heavens) with all its Appurtenances; its useful Atmosphere and all its beautiful Apparatus and rich Furniture; the winged Choristers which sing among the Branches . . . every Beast of the Forrest and the Cattle upon a thousand Hills; the Finny Nations and whatsoever passeth through the paths of the Seas, these all loudly proclaim the Wisdom, the Power and the Goodness of their Munificent Creator. *O Lord, how manifold are thy works! in wisdom hast thou made them all: The Earth is full of thy riches.*" [11]

There is no suggestion here that Isaac Stiles had ever listened to a winged chorister or held a member of the finny nations wriggling on the line. The son would understand better than the father the importance of firsthand observation, but behind everything he observed he would still see God—wise, powerful, and munificent. At the age of eleven he calculated that God had made the world 5,700 years before. Looking at the great cliff of East Rock as he rode into New Haven, he could be sure that the Deluge had washed over it exactly 4,032 years ago in the time of Noah. Watching a strange light in the

10. From a notebook, the only surviving manuscript by Stiles that antedates his matriculation at Yale. Hereafter referred to as First Commonplace Book.

11. Isaac Stiles, *A Prospect of the City of Jerusalem . . . Preach'd at Hartford . . . May 13th, 1742* (New London, 1742), p. 3.

northern sky on the evening of July 20, 1741, he might wonder how it came there, but he knew that however it came, God made it.[12]

Just as he learned to recognize God's fingerprints on the landscape and on the animals that wandered in it, so among men too. Here it was even easier to see what he was taught to see. People were obviously different from one another in many ways, and it required no straining of the eyes to see that God had made some better and more important than others. For one thing, the people of New England were better than other people, because God had singled them out for special favors, just as he had once done with the Jews. Within New England the people of Connecticut had been specially favored because God had arranged matters so that they still selected their own governors, whereas their more pretentious neighbors in Massachusetts had lost that privilege in 1685. Inside Connecticut the governor and his council and the members of the General Assembly commanded respect, because governments were the work of God and these were His appointed agents. Ministers, too, were important and entitled to honor and dignity, and parents were more important than children, and rich men than poor men. Ezra Stiles heard his father intoning the aphorisms of this creed to the General Assembly at election time in 1742: "God is to be seen in Raising up, Qualifying and Improving, Counselling and Assisting, Prospering and Succeeding those whom he advances to Place, Power and Dignity above others. . . . He first Inspires them therewith, and then makes use of their Wisdom, Piety, Justice, Magnanimity, Zeal, &c. in promoting the publick Weal and the Upbuilding of Jerusalem." [13]

The main outlines of the system were obvious enough, but the details required close attention. One must know, for example, the limits of subordination. When Ezra Stiles was growing up, slavery was still within the limits, though cruelty to servants, slaves, or children was not. Tyranny by kings or governors was definitely outside the limits. The execution of Charles I had caused no mourning in New England, and Connecticut had actually harbored the regicides. There were doubtless old men living in North Haven who could have shown Ezra Stiles where they were hidden from the king's agents after the Restoration. Now, of course, the House of Hanover occupied the throne and ruled without infringing the rights of the

12. First Commonplace Book.
13. Isaac Stiles, *Prospect of the City of Jerusalem*, p. 29.

subject. The people of Connecticut owed allegiance to George II, though he was far enough away that no one need inquire too closely what allegiance meant.

Within the colony, however, one must learn where everyone belonged; distinctions not drawn in so many words must be inferred from a look, a gesture, the tone of a voice. Isaac Stiles was a good instructor, for his own insecurity made him demand a careful deference from all his inferiors, and Ezra could gather from his father's manners with a man exactly how far below or above him that man belonged.

There were, of course, points at which even the initiated might hesitate. Isaac Stiles obviously owed deference to his father, for all children did to their parents. On the other hand, his father was only a farmer, and he was a minister. According to Ezra, Isaac resolved this difficulty in his own favor: though he was extremely scrupulous in honoring his superiors, he never included his father among them. When Ezra grew up, his own attitude toward Isaac likewise became a problem. Ezra had the assurance of the second generation, and while he maintained the semblance of honor toward his father, he did it with condescension. He was borne out, of course, by the opinion of the society around him. At Yale, where entering students were ranked within their class according to a complex system involving both individual merit and family background, Ezra profited by his father's rise in Connecticut society. While Isaac had been next to last in the class of 1722, Ezra made third place in the class of 1746.[14]

The social scale within a town was easily mastered; one learned it almost automatically as one grew up. But ministers and other persons in the upper brackets frequently had a wide range of acquaintance outside their own town. Anyone who moved in these higher circles must know who was who throughout the colony and be able to weigh a Hall of Wallingford against a Hubbard of New Haven or a Fitch

14. On the class lists at Yale in the eighteenth century the pioneer work was Franklin B. Dexter, "On some Social Distinctions at Harvard and Yale before the Revolution," in American Antiquarian Society, *Proceedings*, new ser., *9* (1893–94), 34–59, and *A Selection from the Miscellaneous Historical Papers of Fifty Years* (New Haven, 1918), pp. 203–22. Dexter's views have been revised and corrected by Samuel E. Morison, "Precedence at Harvard College in the Seventeenth Century," American Antiquarian Society, *Proceedings*, new ser., *42* (1932), 371–431; and by Clifford K. Shipton, "The Mystery of the Ages Solved, or, How Placing Worked at Colonial Harvard and Yale," *Harvard Alumni Bulletin*, *57* (1954), 258–63.

of Norwalk—not to mention a Bancroft or a Taylor against a Stiles. Since western Massachusetts fell within the range of Connecticut society, one had also to sort out the various Williamses and Stoddards and Dwights. Moreover, one had to be sensitive to the alliances of blood and marriage that tied them all together. Most people tried to marry on their own level or, if possible, higher. In the case of the best people this might mean marrying outside their own town, so that the whole of Connecticut and western Massachusetts was enmeshed in a network of family ties. The Stileses were caught up in it, as Ezra well knew, though not on the highest level. Isaac Stiles, after climbing to the ministry, had anchored his social standing when he married Kezia Taylor and, after her, Esther Hooker.

Merely knowing who had married whom was not enough to guide a man safely through Connecticut society, for families that were allied by marriage might be estranged by politics or religion or by some nameless grudge that they all understood but never discussed in public. The Whittelseys and the Halls were connected by two marriages, but it was an open secret that they hated each other. There was something dark between the Edwardses and the Williamses, and there was even something between the Edwardses and the Stileses. It could hardly be supposed that these feuds were part of God's plan in disposing honor and rank among men, but family alignments were easily clothed with religious or political principle, and no young man headed for Yale could afford to ignore them.

This is not to say that the people of Connecticut were hypocrites. Their concern with religion was genuine and urgent. Growing up in the eighteenth century, a man needed religion to make life bearable, or rather to make death bearable, for death was the most familiar fact of life. Ezra Stiles met it early. His own mother had died of bearing him, and his stepmother presented him with a succession of half brothers and sisters who also died with fearful regularity. When he was six, he watched his baby brother expire as his mother was wrapping him to go to meeting. Of the ten children she bore, only four lived beyond their teens. Other families fared much the same. In the late 1730s New England children died by the hundreds from an epidemic of diphtheria and scarlet fever known as the throat distemper.[15] Ezra Stiles was sick enough to fear the end himself on at least two occasions before he was grown, and the death rate continued

15. Ernest Caulfield, *A True History of the Terrible Epidemic Vulgarly Called the Throat Distemper* (New Haven, 1939).

throughout his lifetime. A letter from his father written after he left home suggests what an epidemic meant in a small town like North Haven:

> We of North haven have been the Latter End of the summer past in great tribulation. Many were weak and sickly among us and many slept the sleep of Death. Old Serjt. Samuel Brocket's wife is Dead, James Barns is dead, Samuel Brocket Junior Lost 4 children and but one surviving, and so it happend to David Jacobs, Seth Heaton also buried 4 of his children. James Humeston's wife is Dead a very pious valuable woman and one of his children, Jonathan Sanford Lost one child, his brother Moses two, Enos grannis one; James Turner one, nor have I as I suppose enumerated all that dyed of the same distemper and about the same time. but to this number must be added your Dear and darling sister she likewise is gatherd to the Congregation of the Dead. O Ruth my Daughter, my Daughter, my Daughter Ruth, my dear and pleasant Child, would god thou mightest have outlived me! [16]

In order to look death in the face so regularly, one needed to look with something more than the naked eye. God, of course, was behind it all, but a God who had so little regard for human life needed explaining. Everyone in New England knew how important it was to get the right explanation. New England had been founded so that children like Ezra Stiles should know the truth about God and live their dangerous lives accordingly. As soon as he was old enough to recognize death, perhaps sooner, Ezra Stiles began to learn how to look at it.

It was, in fact, his father's business to teach not only him but everyone else in North Haven. Every Sunday morning men and women rode in from their scattered farms to hear the Reverend Mr. Stiles. After the service they retired to the green for lunch, and in winter warmed themselves and their food at an open fire in a "sabbaday house" (a small shelter set up for the purpose) before trooping back to the cold meetinghouse for another sermon. They evidently liked what they heard, for they came in such increasing numbers [17]

16. Mar. 25, 1760, Stiles Papers.

17. By the time Isaac died in 1760, his congregation had grown from 50 or 60 families to 175 or 180 (about 1,000 persons): Thorpe, *North Haven Annals*, p. 92; *Lit. Diary, 1,* 177.

that it was necessary to set up a new and larger meetinghouse. Ezra recorded in his commonplace book: "Aug. 2, 1741 last meeting in old meetinghouse / Aug. 9, 1741 first meeting in new."

In the old meetinghouse and the new, as well as in the circle of the family, Ezra learned the facts of life and death. Death, he discovered from his father's sermons, was not so total a transformation as it seemed to the hand or the eye, nor was life on this earth so dear as the heart would have it. A better world awaited, and a worse one—for whom? Because of Adam's sin and the consequent corruption of all mankind, every man deserved the worst (if Adam had obeyed, all men would have enjoyed eternal bliss). God, however, of his infinite mercy, did not condemn all men. Instead he came to the world Himself in the person of Christ and in the name of Christ saved a few men for heaven. Those few He did not select out of any regard for their merit; in fact He had chosen them from eternity before Adam had committed the original sin. It was impossible, therefore, for anyone to influence His prior and unchanging decision. A man could not go to heaven by wishing nor yet by working at it.

What connection, then, could there be between this world and the one to come? Not a causal one certainly. Nothing that a man could do of his own free will would affect his future. But he who looked at himself and the world with care might at least gain some hint of what was in store for him. God's choice of a man for salvation would be manifested in this world by faith in Christ and also by good conduct. Since the fall of Adam it was impossible for anyone to be completely virtuous; but there were degrees of sin, and God's chosen few would sin in a lesser degree than other men: their faith would be evidenced in their works or, in other words, by their decent behavior. It was possible, therefore, to make a reasonable guess in this world whether you were destined (or predestined) for salvation in the next, though no one supposed that human faculties were entirely trustworthy in this respect.

Seen in this way, life was supposed to interest those who lived it chiefly as an index of their eternal condition. To become attached to it simply for itself was to lose all perspective, the sign of a doomed soul. From our own unregenerate point of view it is obvious that these ideas must have induced a strong tendency toward asceticism in those who wished themselves among the elect. And when we read their books and journals and letters today, we are apt to think that the people of New England were all too successful in preferring another world to this. They would scarcely have agreed, for in spite of their efforts they found the world too good.

They knew the joys of the flesh, of hard work by day and good company by night, the differing warmths of rum and fire and sunlight. They knew all the beauties of the New England landscape, and more intimately than we do. But they had not come here to enjoy the scenery. Death was on hand every day to remind them of the other world they should be seeking, and their ministers hammered home the lesson on Sundays and on all other occasions they could find, whenever there was a funeral or a fast, a thanksgiving or an execution.

The lesson needed constant repetition, because it was not only unpalatable but difficult to comprehend: the minister must urge his people to seek salvation, yet warn them that successful seeking was really the result, and not the cause, of finding. In thousands of sermons he would describe the steps by which God transformed a man into a saint, and then urge the listener to take these steps. The feet of the man who trod them would be moved by God, but God operated through means, and one of his principal means was the exhortation of preachers. Ministers considered and rejected the obvious comment that their teachings must result in despair or indifference: "If I am not elected may a person say, to what purpose are all my endeavours for salvation? I can never attain to it by them. And if I am elected, why should I strive and labour, when my salvation is made sure by the immutable decree of God?" This, said the preachers, somewhat uneasily, was a preposterous way to reason. "God's decree does not at all take off the use of our endeavours . . . If any are or- dain'd unto eternal life, it is also ordain'd that they *shall be awakn'd* to a sence of their sin and misery, to earnest prayer to God for recovering and renewing grace; and to a diligent waiting on him in the ways of his appointment, until that he have mercy on them." [18]

Even when a man had been converted—that is, when he had felt the entrance of recovering and renewing grace in his soul—he could not rejoice in the assurance of salvation. It was true that God's elect could not relapse into hell any more than the reprobate could work their way to heaven. The difficulty was that no saint could be abso-

18. William Cooper, *The Doctrine of Predestination unto Life, Explained and Vindicated* (Boston, 1740), pp. 97–99.

lutely certain of his sainthood, for he might be mistaken about his conversion. The devil could fool a man. In fact one of the signs of damnation was a feeling of security; and ministers generally used the word "secure" only in an ironical sense, to describe the deluded condition of sinners who thought they were saved. The true saint could never rest, but must constantly review and assess his life, hoping to find purity of heart and deed but never daring to find enough to warrant that peace of mind which might be labeled secure. Only in death could he rest.

Death, then, was the end of earthly striving and the beginning of heavenly peace. Saints must greet it joyfully for themselves and without excessive grief when it came to their friends and relatives. It was the judgment of charity when a godly man died, that he was gone to eternal bliss. The loss of his advice and example might be mourned as a visitation of God's wrath on those who were left behind, but it was proper to suppose that he himself had been raised to a better world. As for ungodly persons, or those who had shown no signs of saving grace, the most that could be hoped was that they had received it in their last moments.

In the case of infants the problem was more difficult. Ezra Stiles was confident that his mother "slept in Jesus," but what of the brother he saw die at the age of ten weeks? He might take refuge in the fact that the child's mother and father were probable saints, and that the chances of salvation were therefore good (God's promise to Abraham had included his offspring). But God presumably rejected more than he chose, and unless one assumed that all who died in infancy were among the elect, then clearly some children who had scarcely lived to draw a breath were eternally damned. Old Michael Wigglesworth in his *Day of Doom* had allowed these babes the easiest room in hell. In spite of a general tough-mindedness, New England ministers were never very happy with this solution, but they could not find a better one within the limits of orthodoxy.

In the eyes of its adherents the great merit of this creed was that it made no impeachment of God's glory and omnipotence for the sake of human pretensions. If the logic of God's omnipotence demanded the damnation of infants, then they were damned. If man could do nothing toward his own salvation, then it was no good suggesting that he could. In the sixteenth century John Calvin had spelled out the details of the system with relentless consistency, and New Englanders still honored his name. Before New England was settled, Calvin's doctrines had been challenged by a seventeenth-century Dutchman named Jacob Arminius, who maintained that mankind was not hopelessly depraved and that human efforts might produce saving faith. It was partly because Arminian influence had penetrated the English church that the Puritans left England for America.

In coming here they hoped to worship God in His unlimited majesty, and they warned their children against the errors of their Dutch and English brethren, until the word "Arminian" became a term of abuse for anyone who deviated from the strict dogmas of predestination. And yet the New England Puritans brought with them in the very vocabulary of their theology the suggestion of another Arminianism. They thought of God as dealing with man through a covenant or agreement in which God offered eternal life in return for faith. It was a covenant in name only, for in fact God fulfilled both parts of the bargain: no man could have faith unless God gave it to him, and God gave it only to his eternally elect. Nevertheless the doctrine of predestination when stated in terms of a covenant did sound less rigorous than it was, and unless a preacher was careful to emphasize that faith was the free gift of God, it might sound to the listening sinner as though he could actually reach heaven by pulling on his own bootstraps.[19]

The idea of the covenant was embedded in the theological writings that New England most admired. Calvin himself made use of it, and his successors gave it a central place in their writings. At the time when Ezra Stiles entered Yale, students were still studying the tracts written in the early seventeenth century by William Ames, an English clergyman who was one of the principal expounders of the doctrine. It was a rare sermon that made no mention of the covenant of grace. Every generation was thus exposed to a vocabulary that invited Arminianism. At the same time English divines who had traveled the whole road from predestination to Arminianism were publishing subversive tracts to entice others along the same route. As a result, the New England ministers found it necessary to maintain a continuous posture of attack, though some of them, even while shouting loudest against Arminianism, were themselves gliding unconsciously toward

19. On the place of the covenant in New England theology see Perry Miller, *The New England Mind: The Seventeenth Century* (New York, 1939), and *Errand into the Wilderness* (Cambridge, Mass., 1956), pp. 48–98.

it. Generally, however, before they reached the fatal position itself they heeded their own warnings and affirmed the absolute power of God.

Arminianism was, in fact, something of a New England bogy man. He lurked in the shadows of theology to trap incautious Calvinists, but he seldom got them. Though a few laymen doubtless succumbed, no one could point to a minister who had. If there were Arminians among the New England clergy, apart from the handful of Anglicans, they did not defend their ideas in public.[20] Not, that is, until 1722, when the bogy man came briefly to life, and of all places at Yale, the citadel of orthodoxy, which had been founded only twenty-one years before, in order to provide a safe education at a time when Harvard was thought to have departed from the straight and narrow way.

It happened at the commencement when Isaac Stiles graduated, five years before Ezra was born, but the reverberations resounded throughout his lifetime, and he must have heard the story often when the Reverend Mr. Hall of Cheshire or Samuel Whittelsey of Wallingford stopped at North Haven for an evening of gossip and conversation with the Stileses. The whole episode was an object lesson in the danger of Arminian books. In 1714 Jeremiah Dummer, a former New Englander, sent the college a collection of new books which he had solicited in England. Hitherto, according to one of the tutors, Yale had been scraping along on dog-eared volumes whose authors were dead before the first settlers of New England landed. As the crates were unpacked, a new world opened, peopled by new men: Locke, Newton, Boyle, and Sydenham in science, Addison, Steele, Defoe, and Butler in literature, and, more ominously Patrick Whitby, Barrow, Tillotson, Stillingfleet, Scott, and Sherlock in theology.[21]

During the next few years as the tutors, the rector, and several of

20. Jonathan Edwards was fond of denouncing Arminianism, and his widely read strictures have often led historians to assume, erroneously, that there were large numbers of avowed Arminians among the New England clergy in the first half of the eighteenth century. Before 1740 there were probably none in Connecticut. See *Lit. Diary*, 3, 361; manuscript entitled "Itineraries," 5, 186 (in 6 vols.; not to be confused with the published *Itineraries and Miscellanies*). The best study of the growth of Arminianism in New England is Conrad Wright's *The Beginnings of Unitarianism in America* (Boston, 1955).

21. On the Dummer gift see Anne S. Pratt, Louise May Briant, and Mary Patterson, in *Papers in Honor of Andrew Keogh* (New Haven, 1938), pp. 7–44, 423–92.

the local ministers made themselves familiar with these names, the leaven of Arminianism began to work. Samuel Johnson, originally one of the tutors, was so absorbed with his study that he took a position as minister of West Haven simply to be near the library and the college. As he and his friends read and talked, they became dissatisfied not only with the strict doctrine of predestination but also with the congregational organization of the church, and discovered that the Anglican Church suited their new ideas better both in doctrine and in polity.[22]

Aware of how their opinions would be greeted and not entirely sure of themselves, the group kept as quiet as possible, but in the spring of 1722 it was rumored that "Arminian Books are cryed up in Yale Colledge for Eloquence and Learning, and Calvinists despised for the contrary; and none have the courage to see it redressed." [23] By commencement time in September the rumor had grown to alarming proportions; and as people from all over the colony flocked to New Haven for the event, the air was tense. When the rector closed his commencement prayer with the Anglican form, "And let all the people say, amen," everyone recognized that the rumor had been, at least in part, confirmed. The next day the trustees met in the library with Rector Timothy Cutler, Tutor Daniel Browne, and the Reverends John Hart, Samuel Whittelsey, Jared Eliot, James Wetmore, and Samuel Johnson, all pastors of nearby churches. To the consternation of the trustees and indeed of all New England, these gentlemen confessed that they doubted the validity of Congregational or Presbyterial ordination, and some of them declared themselves fully persuaded that the Anglican way was the true one. The shock could not have been greater if they had announced that they had sold their souls to the devil.

In the course of the next month Hart, Whittelsey, and Eliot were talked out of their position. The others were adamant: Cutler, Browne, and Johnson, followed shortly by Wetmore, resigned their positions and sailed for England to take holy orders. The Yale trustees re-

22. Herbert and Carol Schneider, eds., *Samuel Johnson of King's College: His Career and Writings* (New York, 1929), *1*, 7–13.

23. Franklin B. Dexter, ed., *Documentary History of Yale University under the Original Charter of the Collegiate School of Connecticut 1701–1745* (New Haven, 1916), p. 225. The ensuing account of the defection of 1722 is based principally on this volume, pp. 225–34, and on Schneider, *Johnson*, pp. 14 ff.

sponded with a rule requiring all future officers of the college to demonstrate "the Soundness of their Faith in opposition to Armenian and prelatical Corruptions" (they neglected, however, to padlock the library).[24] They had some difficulty in finding a new rector but finally prevailed upon Elisha Williams, a Harvard graduate whom Ezra Stiles later recalled as a "man of splendor." [25] Splendid or not, Williams had his troubles in restoring Yale's reputation, particularly after Samuel Johnson, returning to Connecticut as an Anglican missionary, persuaded Bishop Berkeley to donate another collection of books to the library. But Williams took every opportunity to remove the suspicion of Arminianism and, when he had the chance to preach before the legislature, gave the members as strong a dose of Calvinism as anyone could ask for.[26]

The impact of these events on Isaac Stiles is hard to assess. He was one of the students who heard Arminian books cried up, and he had great respect for the men who cried them. Since his own learning was strongest in the Latin classics, he was especially impressed with Timothy Cutler's abilities in that language. When he began to prepare Ezra for college, he used to call the boy to his study and read aloud to him in Latin in the way that he remembered Dr. Cutler reading.[27] But Isaac Stiles stayed orthodox. He was well enough satisfied with Congregational ordination to accept the parish at North Haven which James Wetmore had vacated (he also got Wetmore's house and land), and one may be sure that the elders examined him pretty sharply about his views before they took him on. They had liked Wetmore. If they had had any sympathy with his conversion, they might have followed him in it, but only one family was ready to do so; the others stuck to Calvinism and Congregationalism.

As in North Haven, so in the rest of Connecticut and in Massachusetts. Congregationalism, nurtured by the government, was still the religion of the people a hundred years after the colonies had been planted. Other sects were insignificant in number. Even the Anglicans, whom the Congregationalists dared not repress for fear of reprisals by the home government, had only scattered churches ministered to

24. Dexter, *Documentary History*, p. 233.

25. *Lit. Diary*, 2, 336.

26. See Elisha Williams, *Divine Grace Illustrious in the Salvation of Sinners. A Sermon Delivered in the Audience of the General Assembly* (New London, 1728).

27. *Lit. Diary*, 2, 340.

by missionaries paid from England. Ezra Stiles, in later years when
the religious complexion of New England had changed, nostalgically
recalled his boyhood and the unchallenged Calvinism of those days:
"I was educated to love those Doctrines and that preaching which
was calvinistic, not so much as party principles, as Truth. So I was
accustomed to esteem the congregational Worship above Episcopal,
as scriptural, not because I was heated with party, for neither Arminianism nor Episcopacy were conversant in my Fathers parish, more than
Anabaptism or Romanism. . . . When Ministers came to my Fathers I found by their Discourse, calvinism was their Favorite, and so
it became mine." [28]

In retrospect the picture was almost idyllic. The great defection of
1722 was a thing of the past, useful only to conjure up the dangers of
Arminianism, which became once more a bogy man. The locusts came
and went, and so did the great snow, and the northern lights and the
throat distemper. Mothers and brothers died, and everyone worried
about salvation. But still God was in His heaven and made the earth
move and the winged choristers sing. One's father was a Calvinist, and
so were all the neighbors, and so were the other ministers who came
to call, and Calvinist was the right thing to be.

Then, two years before he went to college, the idyll was broken.
People were at the house from morning till midnight arguing with
his father. They called him an Arminian. And they called the other
ministers he knew Arminians too. They went off to hear strange new
preachers and cried out like madmen.

The Great Awakening had begun, and no one in the Stiles family
was very happy about it.

28. Manuscript entitled "Another Review," Nov. 21, 1769, bound with Birthday
Reflections, Stiles Papers.

2

The Great Awakening

THERE IS DUST EVERYWHERE. It hangs in the October air, suffocating, nauseating. Men and women dismount from panting lathered horses. The riders are dirty, their faces streaked with sweat. Sneezing, coughing, choking, stamping their feet, brushing at their clothes, they hurry toward the meetinghouse, where hundreds are already gathered. From the rising ground one sees ferry boats, heavily loaded, hurrying back and forth across the broad river, and from all directions the dust rises in yellow ribbons converging on the meetinghouse.

> *I saw before me a Cloud or fogg rising; I first thought it came from the great River, but as I came nearer the Road, I heard a noise something like a low rumbling thunder and presently found it was the noise of Horses feet coming down the Road and this Cloud was a Cloud of dust made by the Horses feet; it arose some Rods into the air over the tops of Hills and trees and when I came within about 20 rods of the Road, I could see men and horses Sliping along in the Cloud like shadows and as I drew nearer it seemed like a steady Stream of horses and their riders, scarcely a horse more than his length behind another, all of a Lather and foam with sweat, their breath rolling out of their nostrils every Jump.*[1]

1. An account of George Whitefield's visit to Middletown, Conn., October 23, 1740, by Nathan Cole: L. W. Labaree, ed., "George Whitefield Comes to Middletown," *William and Mary Quarterly*, 3d ser., 7 (1950), 588–91.

Finally there are 4,000 people treading uneasily before the meet-inghouse, waiting with hushed expectancy, looking toward the scaffold-ing that has been hastily thrown up. A slim young man climbs it and begins to speak, his voice carrying clear to the outer edge of the dusty crowd. He moves about rapidly on the platform, bending toward them and leaning back, raising his arms and pointing this way and that. He is talking about their awful danger. You think you deserve well of God, you think you are different from the rest, that you have done many good things in your life and that somehow or other God will recognize your merit. But you have no merit. You are utterly damned. No place but hell is fit to receive you. Your only hope is Christ, and there is no reason, no reason at all why He should help you. The preacher, a man named Whitefield, has said it to thousands before and will say it to hundreds of thousands again. And there will be many like him to follow, who will keep saying it until all New England has heard.

Some of the people who have hurried desperately through the dust this morning will go away changed for life. *And my hearing him preach, gave me a heart wound; By Gods blessing: my old Founda-tion was broken up, and I saw that my righteousness would not save me.*[2] As the movement spreads, some will be so frightened by the vision of their danger that they will groan or faint or cry out in agony. And why not? *If we should suppose that a person saw himself hang-ing over a great pit, full of fierce and glowing flames, by a thread that he knew to be very weak, and not sufficient to bear his weight, and knew that multitudes had been in such circumstances before, and that most of them had fallen and perished, and saw nothing within reach, that he could take hold of to save him, what distress would he be in? How ready to think, that* now *the thread was breaking, that now* this minute, *he should be swallowed up in those dreadful flames? And would not he be ready to cry out in such circumstances?*[3]

Some will reach beyond despair and find themselves in the arms of a Redeemer, and as they had been overcome by grief before, will now give way to an overpowering joy and lie in a trance for days at a time. *Noah Chappel and Mary Webster aet about 12 were at Night both in a kind of Trance and so remained for near 2 Days and 2 Nights*

2. Ibid.

3. Jonathan Edwards, *Works*, ed. Sereno E. Dwight (10 vols. New York, 1829–30), *3, 563*.

. . . calm and still, with their eyes open seeming as if they were writing or reading . . . had a vision of Christ and read in the book of Life in Golden Capitals several names. Mr. Whitfield's first, than Mr. Whelocks, Mr. Pomeroy's, Mr. Rogers, Mr. Warren.[4]

All New England appears to be seized with this religious frenzy. The taverns are emptied. The young people no longer spend their time in frolics and games but come together only for religious discussion. The churches are filled. The people cannot contain their joy. *Nay, han't it been common in some Parts of the Land, and among some Sorts of People, to express their religious Joy, by singing through the Streets, and in Ferry-Boats?* [5] What more need be said, when New Englanders sing in the streets?

Ezra Stiles was twelve years old when it began, not too young to have taken part. But he was not among those who fell into a trance—he was not the kind of boy for ecstatic visions. Indeed his only mention of the affair in the notebook he was keeping at the time was a simple record: "Octr. About the Latter End A:D: 1740 the Renound Revd. Mr. George Whitefield Came to New Haven on a thursday Night." [6]

The notebook is only a fragmentary series of jottings, small help in forming an idea of what sort of boy Ezra was at this time. But the fact that he reported Whitefield's arrival, together with the fact that he was not among those awakened in the ensuing revival, was characteristic. Throughout his life Ezra Stiles stood close to important events, watched them with intense interest, recorded them, and had his life profoundly affected by them, but somehow managed to remain more a spectator than a participant.

In the Great Awakening, however, no one could be wholly a spectator. If you cared about religion (and what New Englander dared not to?) this was the great event of the century, the landmark by which men set their courses for at least two generations to come. The Stileses were no exception. In the 1740s, as all New England divided into New Lights (supporters of the Awakening) and Old Lights (opposers), they had to take sides; and Isaac, with his violence of passion, was not slow about it.

4. *Historical Magazine*, new ser. 5 (1869), 33.
5. Charles Chauncy, *Seasonable Thoughts on the State of Religion in New England* (Boston, 1743), p. 126.
6. First Commonplace Book.

He had his reasons for what he did; and his son, as he came to understand them, heartily approved. But Isaac's decision had more than reason behind it, and to make it as early as he did—"From the the Beginning of Whitefieldianism," as Ezra remembered it, "he commenced an Old Light and a violent Opposer" [7]—was a dangerous and daring thing to do. For the Great Awakening at first appeared to be the answer to a hundred years of prayer.

The founders of New England had scarcely got their houses built and their fields planted before they began to notice that their children were not turning out quite as they had hoped. They were growing up respectable and law-abiding but were not enjoying the priceless experience known as conversion, which came to a man when God signalized his election to eternal salvation. Without such an experience a man faced the prospect of hell; and unless a substantial number of the rising generation enjoyed it, New England churches would dissolve and religion perish, for church membership was restricted to the converted. Everyone in a town must attend church, but only "visible saints" could belong, with the privilege of communion and of baptism for themselves and their children.

By one means or another the churches were kept alive. Standards of membership were lowered; the meaning of conversion was diluted; and every possible argument was used to persuade young and old to join. Natural catastrophes, especially earthquakes, were found to have a happy effect, and preachers rose to new heights of eloquence in efforts to take advantage of such events. New England sermons, originally rather dry expositions of doctrine, became more passionate and more explicit in application. Some ministers found that hell-fire, depicted vividly enough, might be as useful as a genuine earthquake in scaring their congregations into church membership. Isaac Stiles was himself an adept at this. According to his son, "None could give more animated Descriptions of Heaven and Hell, the Joys of the one and the damnation of the other." [8]

The Great Awakening, which swept people into the churches in numbers never before known, seems to have arisen simply from a new method of preaching this kind of sermon. Among the original exponents of the method was an old acquaintance of Isaac's, Jonathan Edwards. Jonathan, the son of Isaac's old teacher, Timothy Edwards,

7. Memoir of Isaac Stiles.
8. Ibid.

was pastor of the church at Northampton, Massachusetts, where he had succeeded his illustrious grandfather, Solomon Stoddard. Stoddard had been famous for the hell-fire revival sermons which had made the church at Northampton one of the most flourishing in New England. In 1735 Edwards exceeded his grandfather with a revival at Northampton that caused a small sensation as it spread to neighboring towns, with reverberations as far as New Haven.

After it was over, Edwards explained how he had done it.[9] The object of his preaching had been to make sinners aware of their total dependence on Christ. It had been understood before this that sinners might be prepared for saving grace by inducing in them a thorough conviction of their own sinfulness. Hitherto, however, it had been common to utilize such a conviction to effect a greater moral striving toward a Christian life. By behaving as though he were already converted, it was thought, a sinner might prepare himself for conversion.

To Edwards the implication of this view was Arminian: it suggested that a good life on earth was a means of reaching heaven, that a sinner might do something toward his own salvation. Edwards attacked sin in a different way. His object was to produce a conviction of such utter humiliation and helplessness, that the sinner would have no place left to put his hope except in Christ. He must be frightened, not into respectability but into dependence on Christ. Edwards emphasized that God was under no obligation to give grace simply because a sinner achieved conviction, but as an observer he was bound to report that in large numbers of persons conviction of this kind was followed by conversion.

The lesson of Northampton, then, was simple: intensify the preaching of terror, but direct it entirely toward conviction, toward the simple creation of despair. Perhaps if preachers could learn this technique, the great revival that New England had been waiting for and almost ceased to expect might actually come. Hitherto, young ministers had been told that their sermons should "smell of the lamp," that they ought not to extemporize but give the people their money's worth of learning.[10] Perhaps this was wrong, and to prove it word be-

9. In *A Faithful Narrative of the Surprising Work of God*, in Edwards, *Works, 4,* 5–74.

10. See, for example, Israel Loring, *The Duty of an Apostatizing People* (Boston, 1737). Cf. John Jennings, *Two Discourses* (Boston, 1740), in which the new techniques are described by an English minister.

gan to arrive in 1740 of the great success of George Whitefield, who combined a thoroughly commonplace mind with an uncanny talent for moving large audiences.[11] Traveling from place to place, preaching sermons without a trace of erudition, Whitefield was making converts by the score wherever he went. When he reached New England in September of 1740, at the age of twenty-five, his cherubic face beaming complacently at the admiring throngs that attended him, it seemed that not only New England but the whole world was at his feet. Only those who had heard him knew why, and even they could not quite explain it. But it was clear that the effect of his preaching was to create conviction and that conviction was generally followed by conversion.

To produce conviction Whitefield had a whole bagful of oratorical tricks. He would alternately denounce and caress his listeners. He would pretend to see Christ on the cross beside him and describe His agony in vivid detail. He would assume the position of Christ at the last Judgment and hand down awesome sentences on the sinners before him. When they were ready to weep, he could start the tears running by a perfectly timed flow from his own eyes. "You blame me for weeping," he would say, "but how can I help it, when you will not weep for yourselves, though your immortal souls are upon the verge of destruction, and, for aught I know, you are hearing your last sermon, and may never more have an opportunity to have Christ offered to you." [12]

Whitefield did not stay long in one place. Part of the effectiveness of his performances came from the fact that they had been tried again and again on different audiences and all the defects ironed out. When he rode off to New York in a blaze of glory after a six-week tour, he left New England reeling in religious intoxication, all but a few, like Isaac Stiles and his son, convinced that God had begun a great outpouring of His spirit. As winter closed in, the coldest one that anybody could remember, people tramped gladly through deep snow to spend morning and afternoon in meetinghouses where the only

11. On Whitefield see John Gillies, *Memoirs of Rev. George Whitefield*. Originally published in 1772, this was considerably expanded in later editions. I have used that published in New Haven, 1834. See also Luke Tyerman, *The Life of the Rev. George Whitefield* (2 vols. New York, 1877). There is no adequate scholarly biography of Whitefield. On his career in New England see Edwin L. Gaustad, *The Great Awakening in New England* (New York, 1957).

12. Gillies, *Memoirs*, p. 274.

heat was furnished by their own visions of hell. Not content with one Sabbath a week, they demanded week-day and evening lectures.[13]

In the midst of these frigid ecstasies, as if New England ministers were not learning the new technique quickly enough, another self-appointed messenger of God descended on them from New Jersey and by even more extravagant activity in the pulpit whipped them into a greater frenzy than Whitefield had done. Gilbert Tennent had none of the unctuous quality of Whitefield. A great boor of a man, sloppily dressed, boisterous of manner, he flung himself at his audience with the clumsy but effective fury of an enraged bull. After hearing Tennent, Whitefield himself confessed that his own methods were too soft, and that he should be more "careful not to comfort overmuch those that are convicted." [14] It was becoming more and more apparent that conviction was the way to conversion and that mitigation of a sinner's distress was fatal to his ultimate safety. The crowds of people who wallowed through the snow to hear Tennent did not come to be comforted. They came to shudder under the force of his imprecations. When they had sunk low enough, they would rise again to joy unutterable. Tennent himself set them the example by roaring with hearty, but presumably holy, laughter when he heard of a soul suffering under conviction.[15]

When New England ministers heard Whitefield weep and Tennent laugh, they were impressed by the effect on their congregations, and many adopted the method with similar success. Ezra Stiles found it a little surprising that his father did not, for the new technique was only a variation of the methods that Isaac already employed. Indeed, according to Ezra, Isaac was "so warm a Man in his preaching, that Mr. Hall of Cheshire used to say if Mr. Stiles had turned New Light, there would have been no standing before him, and that he would have exceded the warmest New Lights in preaching Terror." [16]

But Isaac evidently sensed at an early date some of the implications of the new technique. It was obvious, for one thing, that the new preaching did not depend for its effectiveness on erudition, and this raised the question as to what did make a good minister. Whitefield

13. *Boston Weekly News-Letter* (Jan.–Apr. 1741), passim.

14. Richard Webster, *A History of the Presbyterian Church in America* (Philadelphia, 1857), p. 389.

15. Chauncy, *Seasonable Thoughts*, p. 127.

16. Memoir of Isaac Stiles.

and Tennent both had an answer: the one indispensable qualification for a minister was that he be himself a converted man.[17] Actually the New England clergy *were* converted men, and the importance of their conversion was often stressed in ordination sermons.[18] But it had not hitherto been supposed that a man's preaching would be worthless if his conversion was illusory. Whitefield disagreed. Unregenerate ministers, he said, could lead their people only into hell; and he went on to affirm with all the confidence of omniscience that most of the ministers in New England were unregenerate.[19]

Thousands of people who had gone through the most important experience of their lives under Whitefield's hand were ready to look upon his words as infallible. If he said their ministers were unregenerate and leading them into hell, it must be so; and proof enough lay in the fact that years of preaching had never affected them while Whitefield had done the job in a few hours. Thus a wedge was driven between ministers and people, and it did not take many blows to send it home. Where the minister welcomed the Awakening and reformed his preaching, he was often rewarded by a stronger and more devoted church. Where he hesitated or drew back, the wedge drove deeper until his church might be split.

Isaac Stiles was one of the first to experience this danger. Fifteen or twenty families in his church were struck hard by the Awakening, and when he expressed his skepticism about "the great and good work," as its devotees called it, they were immediately up in arms. Ezra remembered that during one whole summer "they came and visited my father incessantly and he conversed with them from Breakfast to 12 o'Clock at Night. That is when one Company was gon away, another came till it was usually late at night. Sometimes he reasoned with them coolly—but generally with heated Zeal against Extravagancy." That, of course, was Isaac's way: he did not suffer

---

17. George Whitefield, *A Continuation of the Reverend Mr. Whitefield's Journal* (Boston, 1741), pp. 70–71, 85, 90, 94. Gilbert Tennent, *The Danger of an Unconverted Ministry* (Philadelphia, 1740). Chauncy, *Seasonable Thoughts*, pp. 140–41, 147–49.

18. See, for example, Nathanael Eells, *The Ministers of the Gospel* (Boston, 1729); Nathanael Appleton, *Gospel Ministers Must Be Fit for the Master's Use* (Boston, 1735); and Ebenezer Turell, *Ministers Should Carefully Avoid Giving Offence* (Boston, 1740).

19. Whitefield, *A Continuation of the Reverend Mr. Whitefield's Journal*, p. 95. Chauncy, *Seasonable Thoughts*, pp. 140–41.

fools gladly, or as his son put it, "He was not calculated to convince Gainsayers with Gentleness." He could not oppose extravagance except in an extravagant manner.[20]

Before very long, however, it became obvious where the real extravagance lay. Since the New Lights held that regeneration was the essential qualification for a minister, some of them declared that it mattered little whether he had a formal education. Enthusiastic laymen, overloaded with zeal and confident of their own salvation, set themselves up as preachers and seized the burden which they thought their ministers unworthy to carry. But this was not all. Whitefield's pontifical pronouncements on the condition of the New England ministry were only part of a larger assurance with which he endowed some of his followers, namely that it was possible to determine with certainty, in this world, who was saved and who was not. A true believer could ascertain both his own condition and anyone else's as well. Those who accepted this doctrine thought it necessary to return to the old high standards of church membership. Not only must the minister be assuredly regenerate, but every member must be likewise. True saints must not remain in impure churches where persons merely pious and respectable were admitted to baptism or communion, but must either expel such unworthy members or else separate and form pure churches of their own. New churches and new heresies appeared with increasing frequency: it was wrong for the unregenerate even to pray; the true believer never doubted his salvation; faith was not evidenced by works.[21]

As separatism rent the churches and heresies multiplied, Isaac Stiles saw his skepticism justified, and other New Englanders began to join him in it. Among them, to Isaac's delight, was the rector (a title later changed to president) of the college where Ezra would shortly be going. Thomas Clap had been inducted on April 2, 1740, half a year before Whitefield hit New England. A thick-set, domineering individual, Clap had come to Yale from the ministry of Windham with a reputation as a champion of orthodoxy. He had as much violence of passion as Isaac did; Ezra Stiles later said of him that if he

---

20. Memoir of Isaac Stiles.

21. On the proliferation of heresies in the Awakening see Ellen Larned, *History of Windham County, Connecticut* (Worcester, Mass., 1874), *1*, 393–485; and Chauncy, *Seasonable Thoughts*, passim.

had been a cardinal he would have used the Inquisition to support his views.[22]

Clap did not have the Inquisition, but he did have Yale College, and he had ideas about college education that made him a formidable ally of Isaac Stiles. Though he expected most of his students to become ministers and was concerned that they should be orthodox in religion, he did not think that conversion was the only qualification for the ministry, and he did not confuse the function of the college with that of a theological seminary. One of his first steps as rector was to prepare a catalogue of the library, arranged by subject matter in the order that he expected students to follow in their academic progress. His advice in the preface reflects the curriculum over which he presided at Yale: ". . . in the First Year to Study principally the Tongues, Arithmetic and Algebra; the Second, Logic, Rhetoric and Geometry; the Third, Mathematics and Natural Philosophy; and the Fourth, Ethics and Divinity." Although he wanted the students to use their knowledge "to obtain the Clearest Conception of Divine Things," he obviously believed that a thorough grounding in the traditional liberal arts should precede the study of divinity.[23]

When Whitefield first passed through New Haven in October 1740, Clap welcomed him as an ally in the great cause of converting sinners. Whitefield seasoned his sermons at New Haven with a caution "against mixed dancing and frolicking of males and females together; which practice was then very common in New England"— this on the testimony of Samuel Hopkins, a student in his senior year.[24] Clap doubtless approved such a wholesome admonition; it might help keep the boys at their studies. In the following March, Gilbert Tennent burned up New Haven with seventeen sermons in the course of one week. According to Hopkins, thousands were awakened. The students, who heard Tennent preach two or three times in the college hall, were particularly hard hit. Several of them felt the call to play preacher to their classmates, and "discoursed freely and with the

22. *Lit. Diary*, 2, 336. On Clap see Clifford K. Shipton, *Biographical Sketches of Those Who Attended Harvard College (Sibley's Harvard Graduates)* (Cambridge, Mass., 1873–), 7, 27–50.

23. [Thomas Clap] *A Catalogue of the Library of Yale-College in New Haven* (New London, 1743), preface.

24. Samuel Hopkins, *Works* (Boston, 1852), 1, 15.

greatest plainness with each one." [25] Not everyone appreciated the freedom and plainness which these minor prophets took upon themselves, but Hopkins was himself converted by their efforts and lived to become the greatest disciple of Jonathan Edwards. Others were equally moved, and it became common both in college and town for small groups to meet together for religious discussion.[26]

This was all very well, but it was scarcely conducive to the close study of Latin or geometry. When a number of students followed Tennent on his way, to hear one last sermon, Clap fined them for their absence.[27] Even before Tennent there had been evangelists of one sort or another, exhorting at private meetings in New Haven; and the students, after attending them, became dissatisfied with the sermons they had to hear from the Reverend Joseph Noyes in the New Haven church. When Clap called one of them to account for missing regular Sunday service, the boy had the audacity to say that he had stayed away "because of the Coldness of the air and of the preacher." [28] The students were obviously coming to value heat more than solid learning in a minister, and the rector was approaching the conclusion that the Great Awakening itself was more a matter of heat than of light. If he needed more persuasion, he got it in April 1741, when the students invited Ebenezer Pemberton, a New York minister and adherent of Whitefield, to come to New Haven. Pemberton, a Harvard graduate with a good reputation, must have seemed safe enough, for Clap let him preach in the college hall. Only when he began to talk did it become apparent how far the current enthusiasm had weakened his judgment.

He had taken his text from I Corinthians 2:2: "For I determined not to know anything among you, save Jesus Christ, and him crucified." His interpretation was literal: the only kind of knowledge worth having was that which came from conviction of sin and a regenerate heart. Even the study of divinity was of doubtful value, for "Many who have had their understandings inlightened with divine truths, have had their hearts fill'd with inveterate enmity against the power of Godliness." Knowledge as such might even be a hindrance. It "puffs up the mind, raises the natural vanity." It is "specious

25. Ibid., p. 16.
26. Ibid., pp. 16–18. Dexter, *Documentary History*, p. 357.
27. Edwards, *Works*, *10*, 50.
28. Shipton, *Harvard Graduates*, 7, 37.

ignorance, and is esteem'd by God no better than foolishness." Study
of the arts and sciences may advance your credit among men, but it
will never give you a title to heaven.[29]

It is not hard to guess what effect such doctrines would have on a
group of college students, always disposed to question the usefulness
of useless knowledge and already keyed up to high enthusiasm for
"experimental" knowledge of Christ. How thoroughly they approved
of Pemberton's pious nonsense was demonstrated when all but three
of them contributed to the cost of publishing it.[30]

By the time he heard Pemberton on April 19, 1741, Clap had probably seen Whitefield's remarks about New England colleges. The
great evangelist kept a journal of his travels, and not being troubled
by modesty, made a practice of publishing it in installments whenever
he had accumulated a sizable number of pages. When the portion
dealing with his tour of New England came off the Boston presses
on April 6, Harvard and Yale got a jolt. Both colleges, it seemed,
were in pretty bad shape: their light had become darkness, and the
saintly itinerant prayed that they might be purified.[31]

For the moment Clap said nothing in reply, but he began to gather
his forces. When the New Haven County Association of Ministers
met in May 1741 he was gratified by passage of a resolution aimed at
itinerants: "That in ordinary cases it is not well for any minister to
preach in any parish which is not his own charge, unless with the
countenance and approbation of the settled minister of the said parish
first had and obtained." [32]

This, of course, was merely an expression of opinion and had no
effect in law. It did not in any case prevent the arrival, less than
two months later, of James Davenport, who exemplified everything
that men like Clap and Isaac Stiles found objectionable in the Awakening. Davenport was minister of Southold, Long Island, and un-
happily a graduate of Yale. In the summer of 1741 he felt the call
to cross the sound and carry the gospel to Connecticut. Before long

29. Ebenezer Pemberton, *The Knowledge of Christ Recommended, in a Sermon Preach'd in the Public Hall at Yale-College in New Haven April 19th, 1741* (New London, 1741), pp. 5, 7, 17.

30. Franklin B. Dexter, *Biographical Sketches of the Graduates of Yale College* (6 vols. New York, 1885–1911; New Haven, 1912), *1*, 662.

31. Whitefield, *A Continuation of the Reverend Mr. Whitefield's Journal*, p. 96.

32. Dexter, *Biographical Sketches, 1*, 662.

the air above New London and Lyme and other Connecticut towns
was rent with shrieks and groans and holy laughter, as Davenport
made his way up and down the coast, singing hymns in the streets as
he came, gathering a flock behind him like the Pied Piper.

When Davenport preached, he seemed to count his success by the
outcries of agony or joy in his audience. He was most impressive at
night, when one could see him on the platform, his face lit by flicker-
ing, smoking candles, waving his arms, stamping his feet, screaming
with rage or joy, the audience swaying before him, as now one person
and then another fell to the floor and rolled or jerked in helpless
spasms, or leapt for joy and embraced his companions, while a chorus
of animal sounds rose up on all sides. Davenport could keep it up for
hours until the people went home overcome with holiness or disgust.
He was not squeamish about pointing out which ministers were unregenerate. He would burst in upon a parsonage and, after subjecting
the occupant to a few minutes' interrogation, pronounce him damned
and tell his people to cast him off. Wherever he went, he left a trail
of schisms.[33]

Davenport arrived in New Haven early in September 1741, just
before commencement, when ministers from all over the colony were
gathering there. Ezra Stiles heard him—presumably he rode down
with his father—and was shocked at the "indecent mad and blasphemous religion" that Davenport preached.[34] Isaac was shocked too,
not merely at Davenport's religion but at his treatment of a family
friend, the Reverend Joseph Noyes. Mr. Noyes, Davenport decided,
was dead of heart, a blind leader of the blind: Mr. Noyes, it seemed,
had once tried to comfort a woman who came to him under conviction, thus placing an obstacle in the way of saving grace.[35] While
the visiting ministers strolled in to watch Davenport's daily and
nightly performances, he denounced the New Haven pastor and
advised the congregation to leave him, which a substantial number
promptly did. The New Light students, who had already found
Noyes cold, were jubilant to have their judgment confirmed, and
Clap saw further problems of insubordination ahead. There was as

33. On Davenport see Chauncy, *Seasonable Thoughts*, pp. 151–68; *Boston Weekly
News-Letter* (June 24–July 1, 1742); and Diary of Joshua Hempstead, New London
Historical Society, *Proceedings*, *1* (1901), 379 ff.

34. Stiles to Chauncy Whittelsey, Mar. 6, 1770.

35. Leonard Bacon, *Thirteen Historical Discourses* (New Haven, 1839), pp. 215 ff.

yet no way of stopping this itinerant lunatic, but Clap and the ministers who made up the Yale trustees determined that the students at least should no longer set themselves up as judges of their betters. On September 9, commencement day, they voted "that if any Student of this College shall directly or indirectly say, that the Rector, either of the Trustees or Tutors are Hypocrites, carnall or unconverted Men, he Shall for the first Offence make a publick Confession in the Hall, and for the Second Offence be expell'd." [36]

The action of the Yale trustees, though it was not a repudiation of the Awakening, showed that the area of neutrality was narrowing. But New England at this moment was not looking to the trustees for leadership. It was waiting for the commencement sermon. Jonathan Edwards had been asked to deliver it. Everyone knew his account of the revival of 1735 in his own church at Northampton, and almost everyone accepted it at face value. What would he say now? After the ravings of Davenport, and the multiplication of church schisms, would he repudiate the present Awakening as a gigantic mistake, the work of overheated passions and oratorical tricks? Everyone recognized that the Awakening had reached a critical point, and they looked to Edwards for guidance when he rose to speak about "the Distinguishing Marks of a work of the Spirit of God, applied to that uncommon operation that has lately appeared on the minds of many of the people of New-England." His text was the first verse of the fourth chapter of John: "Beloved, believe not every spirit, but try the spirits, whether they are of God, because many false prophets are gone out into the world." [37]

To the ministers who had watched James Davenport the night before (those who had not watched could scarcely have escaped hearing him) the applicability of the text was obvious. At least Edwards was not going to dodge the issue, and as he began to "open" the passage, men like Joseph Noyes, who had felt the sting of Davenport's wild accusations, breathed a sigh of relief. This grandson of Stoddard, this sober, dispassionate young man who knew more about revivals at firsthand than any other New Englander, was saying that counterfeit revivals were common even in the apostolic age, that the devil could mimic "both the ordinary and extraordinary influences of the Spirit of God." With that incredible simplicity of language which no one

36. Dexter, *Documentary History*, p. 351.
37. Edwards, *Works*, 3, 559–612.

else could quite approach he explained that the church must "be furnished with some certain rules, distinguishing and clear marks, by which she might proceed safely in judging of the true from the false without danger of being imposed upon." It was his purpose that day to examine the Scriptures and discover these rules, these "true, certain and distinguishing evidences of a work of the Spirit of God." And to begin with he would clear the ground by showing "what are *not signs* or evidences of a work of the Spirit of God." [38]

At this point most of the audience must have supposed that Edwards was about to denounce the preaching of men like Davenport as the work of the devil. Of course he would not mention names—that was not the Edwards manner—but surely he was about to delineate the excesses of the Awakening as signs that it was no work of God. In the next breath he destroyed the illusion: he was not going to do what they thought at all. The signs he was going to describe were those which "are no argument that the work is not of the Spirit of God." [39] Suddenly he had slipped in another negative and put himself squarely on the other side of the fence. He proceeded with a description of all the unhappy features of the current revival, an exhaustive catalogue of horrors; and as he examined each shocking detail, he concluded that it meant nothing, that it was *no* sign that the work was *not* of God: tears, trembling, groans, outcries, visions, indecent behavior in church, censuring others as unconverted, all were compatible with a genuine outpouring of the spirit of God. Even the presence of counterfeit saints and delusions of the devil was no reason for condemning the work as a whole; Satan was always extraordinarily active during such a time. "Yea the same persons may be the subjects of much of the influences of the Spirit of God, and yet in some things be led away by the delusions of Satan, and this be no more of paradox than many other things that are true of real saints, in the present state, where grace dwells with so much corruption, and the new man and the old man subsist together in the same person." [40]

By the time he was through with the negative signs, it was clear where Edwards stood. The positive signs which proved a work to be of God were sufficiently general so that he could safely apply them to the present revival: esteem for Christ, hatred of sin, respect for the

38. Ibid., pp. 559–61.
39. Ibid., p. 561.
40. Ibid., p. 574.

Scriptures, belief in the truths of Christianity, love of God. It was no surprise when Edwards announced his conclusion "that the extraordinary influence that has lately appeared, causing an uncommon concern and engagedness of mind about the things of religion, is undoubtedly, in the general, from the Spirit of God." [41]

Only at the close of his sermon, and with a mildness that seemed wholly disproportionate to the offense, did Edwards rebuke the errors of the New Lights. He warned them against spiritual pride, against anticipating the day of judgment by judging here and now of who was saved and who was damned, against mistaking impulses for revelation. "They who leave the sure word of prophecy—which God has given us as a light shining in a dark place—to follow such impressions and impulses, leave the guidance of the polar star, to follow *a Jack with a lantern.*—No wonder therefore that sometimes they are led into woeful extravagances." [42]

As time went on, Edwards would find the extravagances more and more woeful, but right now he had given the revivalists the strongest endorsement they could have asked for. Many of the ministers who heard him agreed heartily with his conclusions; his sermon, quickly printed, became the rallying point for friends of the revival. But not everyone, and particularly not Isaac Stiles, was willing to dismiss the current horrors as irrelevant and incidental accompaniments of a work of the spirit of God. Though Stiles had not been one of Davenport's targets, he had seen what damage the Awakening could do to a church, what heresies could grow out of the new preaching; he had seen Yale College rocking under its impact, his friend Joseph Noyes and other faithful ministers subjected to a cruel attack. And then there was the fact that Jonathan Edwards had started the whole business and was now defending it. The Great Awakening, for Isaac Stiles more than for most other New Englanders, was one of those religious disputes that became inextricably entangled with dark and unspoken feelings toward another family.

Isaac Stiles and Jonathan Edwards had known each other as long as two people of their respective ages could. Stiles was six years old when Edwards was born, the only boy in the Reverend Timothy Edwards' houseful of girls in East Windsor. It was a small town, where no one could escape knowing everyone else, and the minister's only

41. Ibid., p. 588.
42. Ibid., p. 606.

son was doubtless the subject of close scrutiny by the other children. Isaac Stiles, of course, was too old to play with him, but what did he think of this boy who kept so much to himself and led his schoolmates to build a booth in the woods where they could pray? Even in a religious age it probably seemed to the older boy that the minister's son was laying it on a bit thick. After Jonathan's father discovered Isaac Stiles's talents and transformed him from a weaver into a college student, he began his freshman year, aged twenty-one, with Jonathan, the infant prodigy, a mighty junior.[43]

College had not altered Jonathan's temperament. While other students at Yale distinguished themselves by occasional rowdiness, Jonathan had no time for such foolishness. There must have been a touch of condescension in his dealings with Isaac; and the latter, already sensitive about his late start in scholarship, doubtless found it hard to take, especially from a mere boy. When Isaac was examined for admission, young Jonathan investigated his performance and wrote home complacently: "I have diligently searched into the circumstances of Stiles's examination, which was very short, and as far as I can understand was to no other disadvantage than that he was examined in Tully's Orations; in which, though he had never construed before he came to New-Haven, yet he committed no error in that or any other book, whether Latin, Greek, or Hebrew, except in Virgil, wherein he could not tell the *Preteritum* of *Requiesco*." In spite of Isaac's age and lack of social standing, Jonathan was able to report: "He is very well treated among the scholars, and accepted in the college as a member of it by everybody, and also as a freshman; neither as I think, is he inferior as to learning, to any of his classmates." [44] All this, of course, was intended more as a testimony to Timothy Edwards' teaching than to Isaac Stiles's learning.

After becoming a graduate student, young Jonathan continued to take a fatherly interest in Stiles. He evidently attempted to secure the position of college butler for him and was particularly distressed when Isaac joined with a number of other students in one of the perennial rebellions against the food served in college commons. Edwards again wrote back to his father about it: "As Soon as I Understood him to be One of them, I told him that I thought he had done exceedingly Unadvisedly, and I told him also what I thought the

43. Ola E. Winslow, *Jonathan Edwards* (New York, 1940), pp. 28–73.
44. Edwards, *Works*, *1*, 31–32.

Ill Consequences of it would be, and quickly made him sorry that he did not take my advice in the matter, I am apt to think that this thing will be the Greatest Obstacle of any to Stiles's being Butler. I must needs say for my Own part, that although the Commons at some-times have not been sufficient as to quality, yet I think there has been very little Occasion for such an Insurrection as this." [45] But this was the man who improved himself by "self-denial in eating, drinking and sleeping." [46]

That the other students did not share his feelings is evident from the fact that they were discovered, at least by his report, to have been guilty of stealing "Hens, Geese, turkies, piggs, Meat, Wood &c." During Stiles's junior year Edwards thought that the students had reached a new high pitch in "Unseasonable Nightwalking, Breaking People's windows, playing at Cards, Cursing, Swearing, and Damning, and Using all manner of Ill Language." If Edwards thought the scholars unbearably wicked, they doubtless thought him a hopeless prig, and did what they could to make life miserable for him. In the letter describing Isaac Stiles's failure to measure up to the Edwards standard, he adds: "There has no new quarrels Broke Out betwixt me and any of the Scholars, though they still Persist in their former Combination, but I am not Without Hopes that it will be abolish'd by this meeting Of the Trustees." [47]

Probably Isaac Stiles did not join in this combination against his pastor's son, but probably, too, he shared the prevailing feelings about Edwards. Nor could his attitude have been improved by two episodes that occurred after graduation. Shortly after Stiles took his degree in 1722, Edwards received a call from the church at Bolton, Connecticut. The congregation's second choice was Isaac Stiles. [48] Edwards took several months to make up his mind to accept, and then, after postponing his induction several months longer, changed his mind and went to become tutor at Yale. Meanwhile Isaac, unable to wait, went to Westfield, Massachusetts, as schoolmaster. [49] If he had not gone there, he probably would not have married Kezia Taylor, Ezra's

45. Winslow, *Edwards*, p. 71.
46. Edwards, *Works*, *1*, 78.
47. Winslow, *Edwards*, p. 71.
48. Dexter, *Biographical Sketches*, *1*, 264–65.
49. Memoir of Isaac Stiles. Memoir of Stiles Family in Edward Taylor Commonplace Book belonging to Lewis S. Gannett.

mother, but the Bolton pastorate was a better job, and if Edwards had only refused it at once, it would have been his.

The other incident occurred after Isaac was installed with his new bride at North Haven. In September 1725, right after Yale commencement, Edwards fell ill as he was preparing to leave for his father's house in East Windsor. Hoping to get home anyhow, he started out, but felt worse with every mile he rode and soon drew up at the door of his friend's house in North Haven. He did not leave for several months. His mother came down from Windsor for a few weeks to help care for him, but most of the time this task fell to the Stileses. Timothy Edwards wrote to his wife: "Forget not to thank Mr. Stiles and Mistress for any kindness they have showed to you and for their Care of him, and put Jonathan in Mind to pay Mr. Stiles for their Entertainment." [50] But there is no way to pay for the irritation that comes from having a sick intruder in the house for several months, especially right after your marriage, even if you know (and Stiles did not) that he is a genius.

A lot had happened since that winter, but as Isaac Stiles listened to Edwards on commencement day of 1741, some of the old irritation doubtless rose to reinforce his already fervid hostility to the Awakening, and to prod him to action. He and Edwards had not maintained close relations, and all of Stiles's friends seemed to be on the other side of the question. Since he lived close to New Haven, he was well aware of how the students' morale had been undermined by the people whom Edwards was now defending. There could be no doubt that the effect of Edwards' sermon, despite the gentle admonitions at the close, would further encourage the students in their contempt for learning. Ezra would be going to Yale in another year, and unless something were done to stem the tide, he might well become infected with the enthusiasm and return home a New Light.

During the next year, as the time for Ezra's matriculation approached, the opposition to the Awakening began to solidify under the leadership of the ministers in New Haven County. Partly at the instigation of Rector Clap, a General Consociation of all Connecticut churches came together at Guilford on November 24, 1741, and after acknowledging that God had been extraordinarily active recently, condemned roundly the unauthorized preaching of itinerant ministers and the introduction into the ministry of unlearned men.[51]

50. Edwards, *Works*, *1*, 96. Winslow, *Edwards*, p. 342.
51. Connecticut Historical Society, *Collections*, *11* (1907), 5–10.

Inside Yale, Clap cracked down hard. When it was reported to him that David Brainerd, a junior and an ardent New Light, was saying that Tutor Chauncy Whittelsey had no more saving grace than a chair, Clap promptly expelled Brainerd.[52] Since Clap's methods always savored of tyranny, it is likely that the other students resented this piece of discipline. At any rate, by April 1742 they had all left college and either gone home or taken to the road as itinerant preachers without degree, license, or ordination.[53]

Perhaps Clap contributed to their extravagance by playing the martinet. But Isaac Stiles and most of the other ministers in New Haven County were ready to back him up. Even the governor of Connecticut, Jonathan Law, became alarmed and brought the matter before the Assembly. On May 13, 1742, a committee, appointed to investigate, returned a report that recited the various woes of the college—students defying their teachers, setting themselves up as itinerant preachers, attending Separate meetings, and neglecting their studies. As a remedy the committee urged full support to the rector and trustees in reclaiming the wayward and expelling the incorrigible.[54]

The day on which the Assembly heard and accepted this report was the annual election day, when the new governor, deputy-governor, and assistants were chosen. The most important part of the ceremony —the balloting was usually a foregone conclusion—was the sermon preached by some outstanding minister. In 1742 it was Isaac Stiles, and this was the opportunity he had been waiting for. Though he spoke the traditional clichés which the occasion demanded, he applied them pretty closely to the minister of Northampton and the other supporters of the great religious debacle.[55]

Edwards had begun his sermon as though he were going to attack the Awakening but had shown very soon that he was on the other side. Stiles kept his audience in suspense much longer, while he enunciated some of the typical sentiments of orthodox Calvinism, particularly the absolute power of God in dispensing grace. There was a large gathering, for it was open to the public; and the New Lights were soon convinced that they had gained another champion. One woman even cried out in apparent conviction (one can imagine the

---

52. Edwards, *Works*, 10, 50–51.

53. Benjamin Colman to George Whitefield, June 1742, Mass. Hist. Soc., *Proceedings*, 53 (1920), 214–15.

54. Dexter, *Documentary History*, pp. 356–58.

55. Isaac Stiles, *Prospect of the City of Jerusalem*.

withering look from the speaker).[56] When he began discussing the wickedness of those who turn their backs on God, the New Lights doubtless supposed that he was describing the opposers of the Awakening, but as he proceeded, the truth became apparent: "They will not endure *sound Doctrine,* but after *their own Lusts heap to themselves Teachers, having itching Ears,* they now turn *away their Ears from the Truth,* and are turned *unto Fables:* Come not to *the Law and to the Testimony,* and thence neither speak nor act according *to this Word:* Whence 'tis Evident that (how much so ever *New Light* they may have) they have *no true Light in them.*" [57] It was the New Lights who neglected the means of grace offered by the ministers of God and went awhoring after their own hearts' lusts. And he prepared a shaft especially for Edwards: "Now they withdraw from and forsake those *burning and shining Lights,* in whose Light they were willing *to Rejoice for a Season,* and follow *wandring Stars:* Or if I may borrow a simile from a celebrated Author, *They leave the Pole-star to follow Jack with a Lanthorn.*" [58] The sarcasm was crude but effective.

Isaac directed the next part of his sermon to the governors of the colony, first flattering them with the usual talk about their being agents of God, and then giving them specific directions about their duty in the present crisis: bridle the tongues of the imposters, halt the separations which are devastating the cause of God. He was as thankful as anyone "for all the genuine fruits of the Spirit visible among us." But he warned, "We have all reason to tremble *for the Ark of God;* if some Irregularities and Extravagancies which are grown rife and bare-fac'd and but too notoriously known, be not timely suppress'd." [59] The ministers he advised to go on saving what souls they could, and to ignore the contempt of those "whose throat is an open Sepulchre and their tongue an unruly Evil, full of deadly Poison, and set on fire of Hell." [60] After all, "The world hated Christ before it hated his Ministers." [61]

Turning to the large assembly of ordinary people, Stiles told them that he would probably never see most of them again and therefore

56. Memoir of Isaac Stiles.

57. *Prospect of the City of Jerusalem,* p. 23.

58. Ibid., pp. 23–24.

59. Ibid., p. 47.

60. Ibid., p. 52.

61. Ibid., p. 53.

they might heed what he said as his dying counsel: "Beware of that
Luciferian Pride and Arrogancy, which prompts some to invade the
Divine Prerogative . . . to Censure and Condemn even those as
Unconverted and Hypocrites, *of whom the world is not worthy.*" Shun
the evil counsellors who cause divisions in the church. Meddle not
with them that are given to change. Separate meetings "are subversive of *Peace, Discipline and Government:* [they] Lay open the
Sluices and make a Gap to let in a Flood of Confusion and Disorder;
and very awfully portend the Ruin of these Churches, unless a Stop
be put to them. Should this spirit and practise generally obtain and
be in Vogue . . . This would soon be an *Habitation of Dragons,* and
a *Court for Owls*— Wherefore let us beware lest we throw the House
out at the Windows, or pull it down upon our Heads." [62]

This was the first public attack on the Great Awakening in New
England, and it proved to be the cue for a widening of the opposition.
The Connecticut Assembly went into session and enacted a law following Stiles's advice: any minister who invaded another's parish
without permission would be deprived of state support for his salary.
A lay exhorter or itinerant who did so would be treated as a vagrant.[63]
A couple of weeks later, when Davenport appeared again in Connecticut, he was taken up at New Haven by the sheriff, on a warrant issued
by the General Assembly itself. In spite of direct orders from Davenport, God failed to strike the sheriff dead, and Davenport was brought
to Hartford, where the Assembly decided that he was "under the
influences of enthusiastical impressions and impulses, and thereby disturb'd in the rational faculties of his mind, and therefore to be pittied
and compassionated, and not to be treated as otherwise he might be." [64]
They sent him back to Long Island, and Connecticut licked its wounds.
In spite of madmen like Davenport and geniuses like Edwards, Isaac
Stiles had turned the tide of battle. He could reasonably hope that
by the time Ezra reached Yale in the fall, Clap would have the college once more under control. But he must have known that neither
he nor anyone else could undo the last two years. The world that he
knew had dissolved in the laughter of Tennent and the tears of Whitefield. New England religion would never be one again, and fifty years
later his son would still mourn the division.

62. Ibid., pp. 55–58.
63. Charles J. Hoadly, ed., *The Public Records of the Colony of Connecticut*
(Hartford, 1850–90), *8,* 454–57.
64. *Boston Weekly News-Letter* (June 24–July 1, 1742).

3

Yale

WHEN COLLEGE OPENED in the fall of 1742, most of the students returned to New Haven and submitted to the dominion of the rector. The irreconcilables took themselves to New London, where Timothy Allen (Yale 1736) opened a seminary called the Shepherd's Tent, for training those who wanted to know nothing but Christ.[1] This was probably a blessing in disguise for Yale, because it drained off the most radical students, but the Connecticut Assembly saw subversive tendencies in it and legislated it out of existence. Though Allen set up shop again over the border in Rhode Island, he could not make a go of it,[2] ar.d Clap was left in undisputed possession of the field. He consolidated his position three years later by procuring a new charter. "Yale College" now became the institution's legal title, and the governing body was transformed from "Trustees" to "President and Fellows." The greater dignity of the title "President" was not only in the name. Where the rector had been merely the agent of the trustees, the president was an essential member of the new corporation, and in the ensuing years Clap sometimes acted as though he were the only member. Under his firm, if arbitrary, dominion Yale returned in the fall of 1742 to the routine of scholarship and to the traditions which every college, however young, takes care to nourish.

1. Frances M. Caulkins, *History of New London* (New London, 1895), p. 453. Dexter, *Documentary History*, p. 370. Diary of Joshua Hempstead, New London Hist. Soc., *Proceedings*, *1*, 379 ff.
2. *Boston Weekly News-Letter* (Nov. 12, 1742). Dexter, *Biographical Sketches*, *1*, 552.

The new freshman class was not a large one, only thirteen boys. None of them, Ezra Stiles included, left much record of what his life as a student was like, but a few things are obvious.[3] With sixty-six upperclassmen towering above them in awesome seniority, the handful of freshmen must have been kept on the run, for they had to do errands for their betters whenever required and to show "due Respect and Distance" at all times. There was plenty of opportunity to show respect, for all the students, except those who had special permission to room elsewhere, lived in the long (22 x 165 feet) three-story frame building, which also contained the college hall and the library. The tutors lived in the building too, and the rector's house was right across the street.

Ezra found the life of a college student closely regulated. He rose by six in the morning and hurried to the hall, where he and the other students waited for the rector. As the great man entered, they bowed to him and took their seats for morning prayers and reading of the Scriptures. Only when these ceremonies had been concluded was it time to breakfast, on a quarter-loaf of bread, and enjoy a half-hour of freedom before classes began. No freedom for a lowly freshman, however. At this time Ezra might be fetching wood or water or carrying messages for the upperclassmen, though not outside the college yard. Inside the yard every student must be sure to take off his hat if the rector or any of the tutors appeared, and not call loudly to any other student in their presence. Lectures and recitations occupied the morning; dinner came at noon, consisting of meat, bread, beer, and "sauce" (vegetables or fruit); in the afternoon there were more classes and study and then evening prayers at four, followed by supper of apple pie and beer. From supper until nine o'clock freedom again, and the opportunity to visit friends in college or town, or more errands for any freshmen unskilled in dodging them.

If one went outside the college yard, it was necessary to wear hat, coat, and gown, and not to go more than two miles, or go hunting or fishing or sailing without the rector's permission. All students must

3. This and the two ensuing paragraphs are based largely on the College Laws of 1726 and 1745, Dexter, *Biographical Sketches*, *1*, 347–51; *2*, 2–18, corrected from the manuscript copy (made by Ezra Stiles), Yale Univ. Lib. On the college building see Dexter, *Documentary History*, pp. 82–83, 146; and Edwin Oviatt, *The Beginnings of Yale 1701–1726* (New Haven, 1916), pp. 353–56. On the meals see Dexter, *Biographical Sketches*, *1*, 663; *2*, 141.

"behave Themselves inoffencively blamelesly and justly toward the People in New-Haven: not unnecessarily Frequenting their Houses, or Intresting Themselves into any Controversey among Them." No student was to drink strong liquor in a tavern or bring it to his room without permission, or play cards or dice, or "Play at Swords, Files or Cudgels," or jump out of the college windows or over the board fences, or "be Present at any Court, Election, Town-Meeting, Wedding, or Meeting of young People for Diversion or any Such-like Meeting which may Occasion Mispence of precious Time without Liberty first obtain'd," or fire a gun in the college yard, or "wound Bruise or Strike" the rector or tutors. After nine o'clock in the evening all students were to be in their own rooms, and the rector or one of the tutors made a tour of inspection to see that they were there.

College custom and student pride demanded that these rules be broken occasionally, say by ringing the college bell at night, or playing hooky in a sailboat on Long Island Sound, or by drinking parties like the one that took place in Peter Curtiss' room in 1738:

> Last night some of the freshmen got six quarts of Rhum and about two payls fool of Sydar and about eight pounds suger and mad it in to Samson, and evited every Scholer in Colege in to Churtis is Room, and we mad such prodigius Rought that we Raised the tutor, and he ordred us all to our one rooms and some went and some taried and they geathered again and went up to old father Monsher dore and drumed against the dore and yeled and screamed so that a bodey would have thought that they were killing dodgs there.[4]

The rooms of the "College," as the building was called—the institution took the name from the building—were already hallowed by such escapades as this, as well as by the activities of Brainerd and his pious friends, before Ezra Stiles arrived. Brainerd was gone now, but his brother John and his cousin Elihu Spencer had taken his place, and there were many other New Lights still left in other classes. The rector was watching them like a hawk, but they knew they were beaten and hung their heads in holy despair at the wickedness of their opponents. John Maltby, a nephew of James Davenport and Stiles's roommate during their junior year, wrote home: "Christians are

4. Dexter, *Biographical Sketches*, *1*, 598.

dreadfull dead here. The children of God sink down there seems to be no strength in a great many of them. The opposers seem to reign and have the upper hand of the blessed children of God." [5]

Maltby and Brainerd and Spencer knew that the chief of the opposers, the rector excepted, was Isaac Stiles, and they would have been correct in ranking the son with the father. Ezra, though often irritated by his father's domestic tyranny, never doubted the correctness of Isaac's position in the Great Awakening. Years later, when he understood the issues better, he still thought his father was right: "tho' he was intemperately warm and zealous, yet I look upon it that he herein signally served the Cause of Christ." [6] The difference between Ezra and his father was that Ezra would never be intemperately warm and zealous about this or anything else. On the other hand he was no cold fish. He took a friendly interest in everything and everybody. Though he did not make close friends among his New Light classmates, he did not make enemies of them either. After they had graduated, he received occasional letters from them, always in friendly terms.

His principal friends, however, were among the students who later chose careers, as he himself intended to, outside the ministry: Peletiah Webster, a Lebanon boy; Thomas Fitch of Norwalk, whose father later became governor; and John Morin Scott of the New York Scotts, who became a lawyer and politician and achieved fame in the pre-Revolutionary agitation. The letters which these friends sent him shortly after graduation are even more effusive in their expressions of affection than was customary in an age when politeness was sometimes equated with flattery. Scott begged him in the most importunate terms to correspond with him, so that he should not be wholly deprived of the company which he said "has been of the greatest comfort to me and support to my drooping spirits in all the broils we have been engaged in while we were members of Colledge." [7] Webster, who tried to keep up his Latin by writing to Stiles in something resembling that language, called him "Pars altera mei," and signed himself "tui Amantisimus, et observantissimus Pelatias Webster." [8] Webster asso-

5. November 18, 1742, in James D. McCallum, *Eleazar Wheelock, Founder of Dartmouth College* (Hanover, N.H., 1939), pp. 12–14. *Lit. Diary, 1,* 181.
6. Memoir of Isaac Stiles.
7. Scott to Stiles, Sept. 13, 1746.
8. Webster to Stiles, Nov. 4, 1747.

ciated his college studies so closely with Stiles that he could not bear to calculate a solar eclipse, he said, because it brought back such strong recollections of the days they had spent together.[9]

There must have been some special warmth in Stiles's person to elicit these tributes. Throughout his life he made friends quickly wherever he went. They nicknamed him "Uzz'd" at Yale. Though the origin and significance of the name are not apparent, it was used affectionately (after he was married and began to have children, Webster congratulated him on the growth of many little Uzz'ds).[10] The most impressive tribute to his personality was the fact that he kept his friends in spite of being a teacher's pet. The rector naturally felt well disposed toward the son of the man who had faced up to the New Lights and told them off in public, and the boy himself earned Clap's approval and affection. "President Clap was my Friend," Stiles later wrote, "and by procuring offices favored me so much that my four years Education at College exclusive of my Apparel did not cost my Father Fourty Pounds sterling," [11] (and the forty pounds doubtless came out of the estate his mother left him). Stiles did not say what offices he performed, but probably he served as monitor, noting down absences from chapel, a task which must have posed a severe test to his popularity.

Stiles also formed a strong attachment for his tutors, Thomas Darling and Chauncy Whittelsey, both of them big men, both of them Old Lights, and both of them somewhat more judicious in temperament than Clap, or for that matter than Ezra's father. They were, as was normally the case, recent graduates, not much older than the boys whose recitations they heard. And though the college hierarchy was strict, it was possible for close friendships to spring up between tutors and students. Ezra Stiles retained an affectionate respect for both men throughout his life.

His association with the rector must have been embarrassing at times, since Clap was not handsome in victory. Though the New Lights were now having a rough time of it outside the college as well as inside, Clap never relented. In 1744 when Stiles was a junior, the two Cleaveland brothers, John and Ebenezer, were expelled for at-

9. Ibid., Sept. 2, 1748.

10. Ibid., Sept. 28, 1765. *Itineraries and Miscellanies*, p. 580.

11. Autobiographical fragment in manuscript Memoirs of the Family of Stiles, begun by Ezra Stiles in 1762.

tending a Separate meeting with their parents during the vacation.[12] It is likely that the two boys were unpleasantly sanctimonious and not popular with the other students. The year before Stiles entered Yale, John Cleaveland, then a freshman, confided to his diary the horror he felt when the other students joined in what he called a "coris," presumably some sort of glee club. "O the desolation of Sion," he sighed, and what was worse, the rector allowed them to use his house for it! When Isaac Stiles preached for Mr. Noyes one Sunday, John recorded laconically, "I did not Lik him." [13] No correspondence between either of the Cleavelands and Ezra Stiles has survived, and probably there was none. Ezra's taste in friends may have been not quite broad enough to include these two, who were not in his class anyhow. Still, they received something less than justice at the hands of the rector. When Clap called them before him, they argued modestly but firmly and convincingly that they had broken no law of the college. Under these circumstances their peremptory dismissal must have gone considerably against the irenical disposition of Ezra Stiles; but he evidently managed to swallow his objections, for he remained the friend of the rector—and of Maltby and Brainerd and Spencer.

The experience he gained in dealing with people of opposing opinions and temperaments was perhaps the most important part of Ezra Stiles's four years as an undergraduate. This would bear fruit for the rest of his life. Though his catholicity may have been a necessary outcome of his natural temperament, he could scarcely have put it to a more severe test than it endured at Yale.

Ecclesiastical diplomacy, however, was not a formal part of the curriculum. While he was learning to handle people, he had also to study his lessons, the lessons that had been so endangered by the Awakening and that Yale had now been made safe for.

These lessons and the ways of teaching them were described in an edition of the college laws which Clap issued in 1745: freshmen studied languages (Latin, Greek, and a little Hebrew) and logic; sophomores rhetoric, geometry, and geography; juniors natural philosophy, astronomy, and mathematics; seniors metaphysics and ethics. On Saturdays, but only on Saturdays, all classes studied divinity. Each

12. Dexter, *Documentary History*, pp. 367–72. Shipton, *Harvard Graduates*, 7, 38. Larned, *History of Windham County*, 1, 419–22.

13. Diary of J. Cleaveland, photostat in Yale Univ. Lib.

of the lower classes was taught by a tutor, the senior class by the president. Instruction consisted mainly of recitations in assigned textbooks; but juniors and seniors also engaged in prepared debates or "disputations" twice a week, and every undergraduate took his turn on Fridays in delivering a "declamation" to the entire college.[14]

This curriculum, as prescribed in the college laws, was substantially the same as the curriculum at Harvard or at Oxford or Cambridge during the preceding centuries. The seven liberal arts, with the few additions and revisions made in the sixteenth and seventeenth centuries, still furnished the labels for the subjects studied and disputed and declaimed in the 1740's. But beneath the cover of the old terminology a revolution was taking place at Yale as elsewhere.

When Samuel Johnson was an undergraduate (1710–14), all the books available to him were 100 to 150 years old. At least that was how Johnson remembered it many years later; [15] and his memory could not have been far off, since his college notebook of "Technologia" shows that he was taught the old system of philosophy and logic that had prevailed before the introduction of Locke and Newton.[16] The basic assumption of this older scheme, which developed out of the logic of Petrus Ramus, was that everything in the world represents some idea in the mind of God. The aim of logic was simply to discover these ideas, and Technologia was the ideas set down in black and white. Though the whole thing was full of jargon and encumbered with innumerable divisions and subdivisions, it was nevertheless overwhelmingly simple: it could put the mind of God in 1,267 propositions.

The arrogance of such a system escaped its advocates. Only after Locke and Newton had exploded it did its absurdity become apparent, and at Yale no one knew this had happened until Jeremiah Dummer's collection of books arrived in 1714. Even after this time, it appears, Yale was slow to absorb the new learning. Though Samuel Johnson explored it at once, as did Jonathan Edwards a few years later, Isaac Stiles, who went to Yale still later (class of 1722), did not. Ezra Stiles apparently believed that Newtonian science was not taught at

14. Dexter, *Biographical Sketches*, 2, 5–6, corrected from the manuscript, Yale Univ. Lib.

15. Schneider, *Johnson*, 1, 6–7.

16. Ibid., 2, 55–186. On Technologia see Miller, *New England Mind: the Seventeenth Century*, chaps. 5–7.

Yale in his father's day, for he wrote, "The Newtonian Science had not passed the Atlantic then; and after its Arrival he had no Taste or Genius for more than a superficial Knowledge of it." Ezra also implied that the system of Technologia was still taught at Yale in Isaac's time, when he said, "The old Logic, Philosophy, and Metaphysics he read, but never understood, because unintelligible." [17]

This testy dismissal of the Technologia as unintelligible could indicate that Ezra himself suffered from exposure to it, a possibility suggested also by the appearance in one of his college notebooks of a proposition reading "Quanto Dignior est Finis alicujus Artis, Tanto Dignior est Ars ipsa" (the more worthy the end of an art, the more worthy the art itself).[18] This was a typical proposition of Technologia, and it is properly labeled "Thesis Technologiae." But by Ezra's time little but the name survived from the old system. One may watch its disintegration in the commencement programs which announced the theses (propositions in each of the arts and sciences) that members of the graduating class were prepared to defend. Even after Ezra Stiles was in his grave these continued to include, at the head of the list, a number of "theses technologicae," but by the 1730s the form had begun to lose its substance. Instead of the precise formulations of the Ramist system, the propositions became general statements about the nature and purpose of the liberal arts. Occasionally, to be sure, a thesis technologica will sound like something from the old days, but the appearance is deceptive. The thesis which Stiles wrote in his notebook, and which found a place at his own commencement, would have made sense in the seventeenth century but not the same kind of sense it made in 1746. By then words like "art" and "end" had lost their special Ramist meaning. Old graduates reading them might hark back to the time when they had worked through the complicated, satisfying propositions, but the young bachelors who stood ready to defend the thesis would not have employed Ramist logic. For them Locke and Newton had rendered the old meaning of the words ridiculous.

One might suppose, then, that Locke and Newton, having driven out Technologia, would form the central core of what Ezra Stiles studied at Yale. Theses derived from Locke begin to appear on the

17. Memoir of Isaac Stiles.

18. Stiles Papers. The statements in the remainder of this chapter about what Stiles studied at Yale are based primarily on these notebooks.

commencement programs, under the heading of Logic, in 1728, and theses derived from Newton a year before that. Moreover, there is evidence that by 1750 at the latest Locke's *Essay Concerning Human Understanding* was a principal text for the junior or senior year. It is somewhat surprising, therefore, to find only a few entries from Locke in the notebooks which Stiles kept as an undergraduate at Yale, and not one entry from Newton.[19] It may be, of course, that the notebooks have not all survived, but those which have, containing his reading notes and outlines of declamations, give no evidence of close acquaintance with either Locke or Newton. Though he learned to praise these great names, what Stiles read at Yale for the most part was not the old books which Samuel Johnson had been obliged to put up with, nor yet the new ones which Jeremiah Dummer had sent over, but still newer ones. The Yale Library had continued to grow after the Dummer gift, more than doubled by contributions from Bishop Berkeley in 1733 and from Isaac Watts throughout his life.[20] It was mostly the books they sent which Stiles studied and abstracted in his notebooks.

If the notebooks are an accurate index of what was studied at Yale, this must have been a time of considerable uncertainty, for Stiles was reading a strange conglomeration of the first-rate and the third-rate. Books which went beyond Locke and which could scarcely be understood without a thorough grounding in his works as well as in Newton's are listed in his notes side by side with relics of scholasticism and with books so elementary as to be childish. Although this disorder probably represents in part the indiscriminate extracurricular reading of a studious undergraduate, the confusion was not solely Stiles's. When Locke and Newton destroyed the old learning, no one was quite sure what had happened. How much of the old system could be salvaged? The proper answer was very little, but only hindsight could give it. In the 1740s Clap and the Yale tutors, like most

19. Stiles's notes of his work as a tutor in that year show that he was teaching Locke. One of his notebooks, acquired by the Yale Lib. in 1960 from Mrs. Katherine D. Foote, shows a number of "theses" derived from Locke and some from Henry Pemberton's *View of Sir Isaac Newton's Philosophy* (London, 1728). The latter is a digest of Newton's thought by a personal friend of Newton's. But neither this nor Locke is included in the lists of books "quos perlegi" which Stiles wrote in this and other notebooks.

20. Dexter, *Biographical Sketches*, 1, 471. Anne S. Pratt, *Isaac Watts and His Gifts of Books to Yale College* (New Haven, 1938).

of the rest of the world, were still groping in the rubble, trying to find some of the familiar landmarks, and at the same time gazing in admiration at the new structures which more enterprising hands were beginning to raise. They clung, for example, to the old study of rhetoric, defining it in the commencement programs in good Ramist terms as *ars ornate dicendi*, but teaching it from an Aristotelian text first published in 1633, Thomas Farnaby's *Index Rhetoricus*.[21]

Stiles was exposed in his sophomore year both to this volume and, as he later remembered it, to Isaac Watts's *Logick* (London, 1725), a volume in which the hymnist adapted Lockean epistemology and Aristotelian logic to the common sense of tender minds. In his junior year he went on to read Watts on *The Art of Reading and Writing English* (London, 1722). Whether this was part of the regular curriculum is doubtful. Certainly it would have done little credit to any college to adopt Watts on English. Written for use in a charity school in England, his book was concerned almost wholly with spelling and punctuation. One need not belittle the attempt to impose standards on spelling which the book represents, but it is strangely elementary for a college student in his third year.

The same may be said of another work by Isaac Watts, of which Stiles made copious summaries and extracts, *A Short View of the Whole Scripture History* (London, 1732). This was simply an outline of the Bible in a catechetical form. In the preface Watts points out that the Bible is a very large book, "and tho' it ought to be read (at least many Parts of it) by Persons of all Characters and Conditions, yet the reducing of the several things contained in it to a short and narrow View by way of Abridgment is so exceeding *useful*, that I had almost called it *necessary*, at least for Youth, and for Persons in the lower Ranks of Life, who have fewer Conveniencies and Advantages of Knowledge." Watts recommends that copies be placed in the nursery, the parlor, and the servants' quarters. An excerpt will indicate that these were perhaps more appropriate places for it than Yale College.[22]

Q. Who were Adam's first Children? A. Cain and Abel, Gen. 4.
1, 2.

---

21. On Ramist vs. Aristotelian rhetoric see Miller, *New England Mind*, chap. 11.
22. The copy given by Watts is missing from the Yale Lib. Quotations are from the 3d ed. (London, 1745) pp. vii, 9.

Q. What was Cain? A. Adam's eldest Son, and he was a Tiller of the Ground, Gen. 4. 1, 2.

Q. But what Mischief did Cain do? A. He killed his brother Abel, who was a Keeper of Sheep, Gen. 4. 2, 8.

Q. Why did Cain kill him? A. Because his own Works were evil, and God did not accept his Sacrifice; but his Brother's Works were righteous, and God gave some Token that he accepted him, Gen. 4. 4, 5. I John 3. 18.

Q. Whither went Cain when God reproved him for this Murther?

And so on. If all the books studied by Yale students had been of this caliber, we might suppose that the new learning had simply proved too much for Yale, and that the college had reverted to a grammar school. Happily this was not quite the case. In the mathematical sciences and what was called "natural philosophy," Stiles's reading was more respectable. As a sophomore he studied elementary mathematics, probably in John Ward's *Young Mathematician's Guide* (London, 1709) and in the three-volume work by Edmund Wells entitled *The Young Gentleman's Course of Mathematics* (London, 1714), and at the same time went through part of Euclid. With this preparation he began the study of astronomy in the junior year. Here again the textbook was by Isaac Watts, who must have appeared to Yale students as the universal genius of the age. In 1738 Watts had made the college a gift of two large globes, one terrestrial and the other celestial.[23] Yale responded by adopting the text which was designed to go with the globes: *The Knowledge of the Heavens and the Earth Made Easy: or, The First Principles of Astronomy and Geography Explain'd by the Use of Globes and Maps* (London, 1726). Though this was an elementary work, it was several cuts above the other books of Watts which Stiles was reading. It was designed not as an introduction to Newtonian astronomy but simply as a course in the mathematics of the globe and the celestial sphere. Watts expressed in the preface a hope that his readers might be tempted to go on "to the higher Speculations of the great Sir Isaac Newton and his Followers on this Subject"; but he also warned that "there should

23. Pratt, *Isaac Watts*, p. 1. Thomas Clap, *Annals or History of Yale College* (New Haven, 1766), p. 17.

be a due Limit set to these Inquiries too, according to the different Employments of Life to which we are called: For it is possible a Genius of active Curiosity may waste too many hours in the more abstruse Parts of these Subjects, which God and his Country demand to be apply'd to the Studies of the Law, Physick or Divinity, to Merchandize or Mechanical Operations."

There is no evidence that Clap or anyone else at Yale endorsed this view. Astronomy was Clap's special interest, and he constructed for his students an orrery, representing the motions of the solar system.[24] The purpose of the instrument was to show in their true relation the positions which the students calculated on their globes with the assistance of Watts's textbook. The orrery depicted the orbits of the planets in relation to the ecliptic and also the motion of the moons and of Saturn's rings. With this instrument, crude though it was by comparison with the more elaborate ones constructed in Europe, Clap could take his students beyond what they learned in Watts. Among other things he could show them how Venus and Mercury would sometimes transit between the earth and the sun, and in October of Ezra Stiles's junior year they were able to observe through a telescope the transit of Mercury. On the orrery and the globes they could predict a transit of Venus, visible to the naked eye in 1761. Clap also showed them how to calculate longitude from the eclipses of Jupiter's moons, an operation which Watts mentioned but made no effort to describe, apparently considering it beyond the scope of his book.

In observational astronomy, then, the students at Yale were given a taste of something better than Watts. Yet none of this required an understanding of Newton. On all sides they heard the praises of Newton, but how close an acquaintance they made with his ideas is a matter of some doubt. Forty years later Stiles thought that the textbook of natural philosophy which he recited in his junior year was Willem Jacob van 's Gravesande's famous introduction to Newtonian science, entitled *Mathematical Elements of Natural Philosophy* (trans. J. T. Desaguliers, London, 1720–21). His recollection is supported by the fact that several of the theses physicae on the commencement program of 1746 seem to have been taken from Gravesande. On the other hand, Stiles's notebooks show that he used the book in teaching the junior class after he became a tutor in 1749, but they do

24. See the letter by Chauncy Whittelsey in *The Boston American Magazine* (Jan. 1744), 202–03.

not show that he studied it as an undergraduate. Whether he used it or not, one thing is certain: his introduction to Newton was tempered by a number of other books in which the Newtonian principles were domesticated and reconciled to the world that men had known and understood before they knew Locke and Newton. In the old days everything had a purpose assigned it by God: "the end of the Sunne, Moone, and Starres is, to serve the Earth; and the end of the Earth is, to bring forth Plants, and the end of Plants is, to feed the beasts." [25] When Newton appeared, it was impossible to take quite so simple a view of things, but only a few concluded—and Newton himself was not one of them—that purpose had been driven from the world. "The more worthy the end of an art, the more worthy the art itself," wrote Ezra Stiles. As earnest men later worked to reconcile Darwin with nineteenth-century theology, so now there appeared a host of writers to reconcile Newton with eighteenth-century theology. It was not Newton but these admirers of Newton whom Ezra Stiles read at Yale: William Whiston,[26] a close friend of Newton's; William Derham,[27] an Anglican minister and amateur scientist; and Bernard Nieuwentijdt, a Dutch mathematician and physician, whose three-volume work demonstrating the existence of God from the new science had been translated into English the year after its appearance in Holland.[28] In these books Ezra Stiles learned that Kepler's third law was a proof of God's close control of the universe, because it showed that "every Body throughout the whole Creation is, as far as it is possible for us to observe, set at such a due Distance, as not only to avoid all violent Concourses, but also so as not to eclipse or shade one the other, wherever it may be prejudicial, or indeed not useful and convenient, or so as to hinder one anothers kindly Influences, or to prejudice one another by noxious ones." [29]

The Newtonian system as expounded by these interpreters showed God to be far more glorious than had hitherto been supposed. Former superlatives were reduced to mediocrity as the boundaries of the universe were pushed out, and the fixed stars, instead of being feeble

25. John Preston, quoted in Miller, *New England Mind*, p. 218.

26. *Astronomical Principles of Religion* (London, 1717).

27. *Astro-Theology: Or a Demonstration of the Being and Attributes of God, from a Survey of the Heavens* (London, 1715).

28. *The Religious Philosopher: or the Right Use of Contemplating the Works of the Creator*, trans. J. Chamberlayne (3 vols. London, 1718–19).

29. Derham, *Astro-Theology*, pp. 51–52, 56–57.

lights for the earth, became new suns, the centers of countless worlds. The very grandeur of this vision was itself a proof of its correctness. That the stars should be centers of other solar systems was "a far more probable and suitable use for so many Suns, so many glorious Bodies, than to say they were made only to enlighten and influence our lesser, and I may say inferior, Globe; which another Moon or two, or one or two of those very Suns set nearer to us, would have better done, than all the whole train of Heavenly Bodies now doth." [30] Even the comets, which were now found to be part of the solar system, helped to bolster the old theology; for the descriptions of hell in Scripture "exactly agree with the Nature of a Comet, ascending from the Hot Regions near the Sun, and going into the Cold Regions beyond *Saturn*, with its long smoking Tail arising up from it, through its several Ages or Periods of revolving, and this in the Sight of all the Inhabitants of our Air, and of the rest of the System." [31] The law of gravitation, needless to say, was reduced, or magnified, to the sustaining providence of God.[32]

Thus Newton was assimilated to the teleological views which had fathered the Technologia. The Technologia itself was swept away, but if there was a contradiction between the new science and the old theology, it would seem that no one at Yale perceived it. On Saturday the students recited the *Medulla Theologiae* of William Ames, blissfully indifferent to the fact that it was constructed on Ramean logic. On Monday they might be studying the size of the Newtonian universe, and on another day—and here one gets a new jolt—they might be reading Bishop Berkeley. Ezra Stiles read at least three works of Berkeley at Yale, *De Motu, An Essay toward a New Theory of Vision*, and *Three Dialogues between Hylas and Philonous*. Since Berkeley was Yale's principal benefactor, it is perhaps not a matter for surprise that students should have read his books, but Berkeley's philosophy was incompatible with Newton's, and the *De Motu* in particular was written to disprove Newton's theory of absolute motion. Moreover, Berkeley was not read in a perfunctory way. Ezra Stiles argued before the rector in the hall on March 12, 1744, the proposition that judgment of distance is the product of experience, and his arguments were taken directly from Berkeley's *New Theory of Vision*. On November

30. Ibid., pp. 35–36.
31. Whiston, *Astronomical Principles of Religion*, p. 156.
32. Ibid., pp. 111–14.

19 he made extracts from the *Dialogues*, proving that heat does not exist in fire. On November 16 he demonstrated that there is no such thing as absolute motion.

Did Stiles and his teachers realize that these ideas would not square with Newton or with the Technologia or with Aristotle? If so, they gave no indication of it. The students were not presented with opposing views and asked to choose between them. Instead they were expected to assimilate Aristotelian rhetoric, Ramist theology, Berkeleyan metaphysics, and diluted Newtonian physics. These were all incompatible in varying degrees and on different levels, and no specific alternative was offered for any one of them: no rhetoric based on Locke, no logic based on Ramus, no theology based on Berkeley. In 1746 it would have required real genius merely to ascertain the precise points of conflict among the various parts of the Yale curriculum.

What was happening at Yale was not unique. Students everywhere were undergoing the same kind of experience. The old curriculum of the seven liberal arts was breaking up, and a new one was not yet devised. The arrival of Jeremiah Dummer's books in 1714 had signalized the beginning of the end for the old learning at Yale, but here, as elsewhere, the end was a long time in coming. You could not close down the college while you retooled for the new model of learning, particularly when you had the specifications for only a few parts of it. The best you could do was to teach the old and the new together, and hope that truth in its greatness would somehow prevail.

This curriculum, for all its faults, was what Clap had fought the New Lights to preserve, and he never doubted that the fight had been worth while. He probably did not perceive, for his temper was wholly dogmatic, that the confusion might have positive virtues, but at least one student emerged from the course with a new kind of excitement, which the old system would probably not have produced. Though Ezra Stiles graduated from Yale without the comfortable certainties of the Techonologia, he somehow acquired, or developed, the one quality that is indispensable in the search for truth—curiosity. The indigestible and incompatible chunks of learning had not dulled his appetite for more but merely whetted it. If he had known where everything belonged, he might have been content to put the various pieces together according to the prescribed pattern, and let it go at that. Or if he had felt the thrill of that other kind of certainty, familiar to the New Lights, he might have been content to know nothing but Christ. Instead he had gained an inkling of how little he knew and how much more there was to know. The Yale Library had some 2,600 books, most of them new. Somewhere in their pages he might be able to find the key to the mysteries that he now saw all around him. Like Samuel Johnson, thirty years before, he resolved to stay near those books.

4

Infidelity

NEW HAVEN in the 1740s was not much larger in population—unless one counted the outlying districts—than North Haven. The town had begun in 1638 as a separate colony, with large amounts of capital invested by merchants who hoped to make it a thriving port. The investment had not succeeded, and a hundred years later New Haven was merely one town in Connecticut, not as large as several others. Little commerce entered the harbor, which was so shallow that ships at the wharf rested on bottom at low tide. In the compact portion of the town some 150 houses clustered around the green, a rough, treeless field where the inhabitants pastured their cows, buried their dead, built their churches, and jailed their criminals.[1]

As small towns went, it had its attractions, quite apart from the college. For Ezra Stiles as an undergraduate it was just far enough from home so that he could make his own new friends. Though Yale students were forbidden to visit "unnecessarily" the houses of the townspeople, they made a habit of necessity and appeared regularly where hospitality was offered, to court the daughters or simply to enjoy civilized conversation. Among the houses where Ezra Stiles seems to have knocked fairly often was that of Captain David Wooster

1. On the appearance of New Haven at this time see H. T. Blake, *Chronicles of New Haven Green* (New Haven, 1898); Thomas R. Trowbridge, "History of the Ancient Maritime Interests of New Haven," New Haven Colony Historical Society, *Papers, 3* (1882), 85–204; Franklin B. Dexter, "New Haven in 1784," in *A Selection from the Miscellaneous Historical Papers of Fifty Years* (New Haven, 1918), pp. 116–32; *Itineraries and Miscellanies*, pp. 2, 104, 265; "Itineraries," 2, 514; 3, 230, 233

(Yale 1738), a classmate of Chauncy Whittelsey, and son-in-law of President Clap. Wooster evidently considered Stiles a reliable man to have about, even reliable enough to leave his wife with (she was two years younger than Stiles); for shortly after Stiles graduated, when the Captain went off to fight the French in King George's War, he invited Stiles to live in his house. Stiles, abandoning a job as schoolmaster in Cheshire, leaped at the opportunity. After Wooster returned in 1748, Clap enabled his protégé to continue in New Haven by procuring him the office of college butler.[2]

The butlership entitled him to sell cider, strong beer, loaf sugar, pipes, and tobacco at the "buttery" (the students could buy cider and beer nowhere else). The butler also attended the president at prayers, brought candles into the hall as needed, kept a record of all fines inflicted on students for misbehavior, and rang the college bell for breakfast, dinner, and study time. The job was demanding, but Stiles's notebooks show that he still found plenty of time for reading.

It was not unusual for serious young men to prepare themselves for the ministry or even for some other profession by staying on at college as Stiles did. Until they received the master's degree they enjoyed the title of "Sir" (attached to the last rather than the first name) and ranked somewhere between the faculty and the seniors. The degree itself was a perfunctory honor, regularly awarded at the commencement three years after graduation to those who returned to college prepared to argue certain approved *quaestiones*. It required no residence at college, no courses, no examinations. Stiles became a "master" at commencement in September 1749, but for him the honor was more than perfunctory. He was chosen to give the valedictory oration which closed the commencement ceremonies. At his own commencement three years before he had been similarly honored, when he was chosen to defend publicly the proposition: "Jus regum non est jure divino haereditarium" (the hereditary right of kings is not by divine authority). In 1749 he spoke on the more general topic of liberty and the benefits to be found in the free pursuit of knowledge.

Stiles had already in the previous April found a way to continue his pursuit of knowledge beyond the master's degree, by climbing to the other side of the academic fence as tutor. The office gave him a

2. Abiel Holmes, *The Life of Ezra Stiles* (Boston, 1798), 15–16. Manuscript entitled "Series of Occurrences in My Life," written Dec. 28, 1767, and Memoirs of the Family of Stiles, begun by Stiles in 1762. Yale Corporation Records, Aug. 19, 1748.

room in the college and £23 sterling a year—£30 when he became senior tutor the next year. He held the office until 1755 and thus was able to remain at Yale for a total of nine years after graduation, enjoying the company of books and bookish men "cum summa voluptate." [3]

During those years, at Captain Wooster's or in his room at the college, Stiles was mainly engaged in exploring the implications of his religious inheritance. The four years at Yale as an undergraduate had left no perceptible mark on his religion. Loyalty to his father and to President Clap, as well as natural temperament, had insulated him from the Great Awakening. On the other hand, he felt no urge to become a champion of their views. The fact was that he took his religion pretty much for granted. He held all the views he was expected to hold, considered himself a Calvinist, deplored the wild accusations of Arminianism that were leveled against his father, and interested himself in astronomy and physics. Most of his friends were headed for secular careers, and, as far as he knew, he was too. Nothing he had seen of his father's life made him want one like it. According to his later recollections, he "read no Divinity" in college.[4] Though this was not strictly true, for he had to recite Ames's *Medulla*, he certainly gave the subject as little attention as possible. When President Clap introduced the study of Hebrew, mainly for the benefit of future ministers, he learned no more than the alphabet and got away with it.[5]

But Stiles's rejection of the ministry was no rebellion. In spite of chronic irritation with his father, he was not one of those ministers' sons who feel compelled to spend their lives in extravagant demonstrations of worldliness. As if to confirm his maturity in this respect, two months after graduation he joined his father's church as a member in full communion. Fifty years before, such an act would probably have meant that he had undergone a profound religious experience, a moment of illumination when he cast off all dependence on his own merit and found assurance of salvation in Christ. There is no evidence that Ezra Stiles had any such experience. Isaac Stiles seems to have

---

3. Latin manuscript entitled "Vita Ezra Stiles S.T.D.," dated Aug. 2, 1766, included in the manuscript Memoirs of the Family of Stiles. Yale Corporation Records, Apr. 20, 1749 (appointed tutor), May 25, 1749 (inducted as tutor). Yale Univ. Lib.

4. Manuscript entitled "Another Review," Nov. 21, 1769, bound with Birthday Reflexions.

5. "Memoir concerning my learning Hebrew," May 12, 1768.

run his church according to the principles of Solomon Stoddard: anyone who lived a blameless moral life and professed belief in the orthodox doctrines of Christianity was entitled to full membership, including the privilege of the sacraments. Children baptized in infancy were provisional members. When grown to maturity they were expected to "own" the covenant in which they had hitherto participated through their parents, and perhaps also to subscribe to a confession of faith. Each church had its own covenant and confession of faith, the wording of which was often the product of long and heated discussion. The confession of faith to which Ezra Stiles gave his assent in North Haven on November 23, 1746, committed him to believe in the Trinity, original sin, and justification by faith. The covenant was more general. As he stood before the church his father intoned the words of it:

> You do now in the awful Presence of the dread Majesty of Heaven and Earth before Angels and Men, with Seriousness and as you hope with Sincerity of Soul, avouch the Lord Jehovah to be your Sovereign Lord and supreme God thro' Jesus Christ, and solemnly devote and give up yourself to his fear and service; and engage yourself, by his Grace assisting, in the most sacred Ties, to observe all Gods Commandments, seeking his Glory, and to walk in christian Fellowship and in the conscientious Performance of Xtian Duties in all the Ordinances to be enjoyed in his Church, and in this particular Church, so long as God in his providence shall continue you here.[6]

This form was designed to cover those who felt an inward movement of grace in their hearts as well as those who only hoped for it and held themselves in readiness by a conscientious performance of Christian duties. Presumably Ezra Stiles believed at this time that the supreme experience was still ahead of him. As he settled down to his reading at Yale, he found that he was worried. Would the experience ever come? Would he be among the elect when the trumpet of doom sounded or among the far greater number who might populate the surface of the comet Whiston described, alternating between eternal frost and unbearable fire? When he pondered the question and examined his soul for evidence of its condition, as three generations of New Englanders had done before him, he reached a conclusion

6. *Lit. Diary*, 2, 408–09.

which would scarcely have satisfied his forbears: "When unable to determine myself of the happy Number elected to Mercy, I came to an instant conclusion, which has abode with me ever since, that if predestined to misery yet that misery would be less, the less I sinned and the more earnestly I sought the divine Favour. From this Time I more vigorously resolved to refrain from Sin, if not to obtain heaven of which I saw no prospect, yet to mitigate and lessen the Torments of Damnation." [7]

Though at the time he would have disavowed the title, these sentiments smelled strongly of Arminianism. He was still within the bounds of orthodoxy, because he saw no prospect of heaven resulting from his efforts, but he was aiming at good works without reference to saving grace. In the eyes of a strict Calvinist eternal damnation was so overwhelming a thing that it hardly admitted of degrees. Stiles was ignoring heaven and trying to regulate his conduct in such a way as to put limits on the wrath of God. Such boldness seemed to argue an indifference to the supremacy of saving grace. An experienced theologian might have anticipated that before long this young man would extend his reliance on good works, and instead of merely warding off the hottest fires of hell would expect to climb to heaven by his own efforts. That Stiles was moving in this direction is apparent from a number of resolutions he drew up for himself about this time:

1. In every action and station of life, act with judgment, prudence, calmness, and good humour of mind.

2. Endeavour to make the business of your life your pleasure, as well as your employment. *Labor ipse voluptas.*

3. Be contented with whatever condition and circumstances providence shall allot you in the world; and therein endeavour, some way or other, to be useful to your fellow-men.

4. Persuade yourself, that to live according to the dictates of Reason and Religion is the surest, and indeed the only way to live happily in this world, and to lay a foundation of happiness in the other.

5. Extirpate all vicious inclinations; cultivate and improve the mind with useful knowledge, and inure it to virtuous habits;

7. Holmes, *Life*, p. 34. "Birthday Reflexions 1767. Aet. 40."

think, live, and act, rationally here, that you may be progressively preparing for heaven. *Nulla dies sine linea.*[8]

These resolutions, especially the last, implied a rejection of the usual Calvinist conception of human depravity, a rejection made more explicit two years later in a notation that "if man is not to be rewarded in the future World for His Virtue, neither can I see any Reason why punished for Vice."[9] Anyone hearing Stiles utter sentiments of this kind in 1749 would have recognized him at once for an Arminian. How did he get that way, this young man whose father had taught him to love Calvinism? The surprising answer seems to be that his father was responsible. In his junior or senior year his father and a number of his father's friends began to read what Stiles called "the new Authors in Divinity," men whose writings had become synonymous, in New England at least, with Arminianism.[10] Perhaps the accusation Isaac Stiles and the Old Lights met so often had awakened their curiosity. When they opposed the Awakening, they had immediately been accused of Arminianism. They had always supposed that Arminianism was a bad thing—they had been brought up to despise it—but if the New Lights hated it so much, it might be worth examination. They may have been encouraged in their investigation by the Reverend Charles Chauncy of Boston, who had attacked the New Lights in an exhaustive analysis of the Awakening. Though Chauncy had carefully said nothing in favor of Arminianism, it was known in New Haven that he regarded some of the newer English writers with favor. Chauncy had once spent six weeks visiting the Reverend Samuel Whittelsey at Wallingford (Mrs. Whittelsey was Chauncy's aunt). Chauncy's influence, Ezra Stiles says, "very much begun a liberal Inquiry with Mr. Whittelsey. Conversation and Reading diffused it to several of his Acquaintance and my Father among the rest."

According to Stiles none of the group, which also included Joseph Noyes of New Haven, Samuel Hall of Cheshire, Thomas Ruggles of Guilford, and Jonathan Todd of East Guilford (all ministers), ever

8. Holmes, *Life*, pp. 16–17.

9. Manuscript entitled "Quest. are Mankind really to blame for Adam's Sin?" Apr. 20, 1749.

10. This statement and those in the next two paragraphs are based mainly on the Memoir of Isaac Stiles.

became an outright Arminian, but they were nevertheless pleasantly
surprised by what they found in the new authors. They read "Taylor,
Scott, Benson, Pierce &c.," [11] and though they could not bring themselves to abandon the doctrines on which they were raised, it was
easy enough, by shifting emphasis here and there, to make more room
for the kind of moral effort favored by the new authors. Stiles even
admitted that his father "altered his Sentiments in some Things in
latter part of Life." Though Stiles seems to have been aware of the
theological explorations of this group, he took no active interest in
them during his undergraduate years. At that time he knew only that
the Yale tutors, Chauncy Whittelsey (son of Samuel) and Thomas
Darling, had the reputation of being Arminians and Clap of being
a Calvinist. As far as he could see, they all believed the same things,
so he assumed the charge of Arminianism was another piece of New-
Light irresponsibility.[12] After graduation, however, he must have
become more closely identified with the group, for looking back in
1760 he spoke of them as "we." [13]

However that may be, in his room at college he read the same
kind of books that his father was studying at North Haven. They
probably all got their books from that mine of heresy, the Yale
Library. But while his father only altered his sentiments in some
things, Ezra was more deeply shaken. His resolution to mitigate the
torments of damnation by a moral life carried him not merely to
Arminianism but beyond it.

The route he took was so obvious that it is surprising more New
Englanders had not already found it, for the entrance was plainly
marked out, to all who attended college, by a traditional part of
the curriculum. At Yale, as at Harvard from the time of its foundation, ethics was taught as a subject separate from theology. William
Ames, the leading Puritan theologian, whose name was more revered
in New England than that of any other thinker, had insisted that
ethics had no place outside theology. On this one point New Eng-

11. Probably John Taylor (1694–1761), author of *The Scripture Doctrine of
Original Sin* (London, 1740); John Scott (1639–95), author of *The Christian Life*
(London, 1681) or Joseph Nicoll Scott (1703–69) author of *Sermons* (London,
1743); George Benson (1699–1762) author of *The Reasonableness of the Christian
Religion* (London, 1743); and James Peirce (1674?–1726), author of *A Vindication
of the Dissenters* (London, 1717).

12. "Another Review," Nov. 21, 1769, Stiles Papers.

13. Memoir of Isaac Stiles.

landers refused to listen to him.[14] They studied his theology,[15] but
they also studied ethics as a separate discipline, at first from Aristotelian textbooks and later from the *Enchiridion Ethicum* by the
Cambridge Platonist Henry More, which was still in use at Yale when
Isaac Stiles was there.[16]

New England practice grew out of an unbounded confidence in
the reasonableness of Christianity; for the conception of ethics as a
separate discipline hinged on the assumption that God's moral laws
were recorded not only in the Scriptures but in His created world,
from which they could be extracted by observation and reason. The
student traveling by the route of nature and reason would arrive
at the same ethical principles as if he had gone by the more direct
biblical path. Although human reason was weak and corrupt, although
it would never disclose the great truths of man's fall and redemption,
would never lead to salvation, it could nevertheless serve as a flying
buttress to Christian morality.

By the eighteenth century perceptive minds might have begun to
see that reason was becoming the rival rather than the ally of revelation. Perhaps it was such an insight that led Cotton Mather to renew
Ames's objection to the study of ethics, but Mather's views, though
they, too, carried great authority in New England, were no more
heeded than Ames's had been.[17] The danger that these men anticipated took shape when Clap came to Yale and introduced a new
textbook: *The Religion of Nature Delineated,* by William Wollaston.[18] Wollaston, an English minister, professed to be talking
not about ethics but about religion. Behind the religious terminology,
however, was merely another discussion of ethics, without any real
effort to relate the subject to Christianity. Clap's Calvinism was so
firmly rooted that he could afford to admire this austere exposition
of rational morality and to read into it a new support of Christian
morality. But a student with no religious fervor to prohibit him might
easily substitute Wollaston's religion of nature for the religion of
Christ. Wollaston himself made no such proposal, but many of his

14. Samuel E. Morison, *Harvard College in the Seventeenth Century* (Cambridge,
Mass., 1936), *1*, 260–61. Miller, *The New England Mind*, pp. 196–97.

15. Dexter, *Documentary History*, p. 32.

16. *Lit. Diary*, *2*, 349. Morison, *Harvard in the Seventeenth Century*, *1*, 263.

17. Morison, *Harvard in the Seventeenth Century*, *1*, 263.

18. London, 1725.

ideas came perilously close to those of a group of European thinkers who did. Wollaston sounded very much like a deist, one who believed in God but rejected the whole scheme of Christianity.[19]

By putting the seal of approval on William Wollaston, Clap cleared the way for Ezra Stiles to a number of other books on what he termed "moral Philosophy." Some of these were the work of avowed deists.[20] The first one that Stiles examined (in 1747)[21] was Samuel Clarke's *Demonstration of the Being and Attributes of God*.[22] Clarke's rationalism was more moderate than Wollaston's, for instead of relying wholly upon reason Clarke insisted that revelation was essential to the discovery and enforcement of moral precepts, and he directed a large part of his book specifically against the deists. But the change of tone from the seventeenth century was obvious: revelation was now brought in to support reason instead of the other way round. In the following year Stiles read with great enthusiasm Shaftesbury's *Characteristics* and Pope's *Essay on Man*, committing large sections of the latter to memory and reciting them to himself in his room or as he walked abroad. Shaftesbury's delineation of natural religion he did not recognize as deism and was so impressed with it that in preparation for his master's degree he drew up a number of *quaestiones* derived from it.[23] The quality he admired in all these works was their rationality. Though his study of Newton in college had been at secondhand, he had learned that Newton's method was "to discard the authority of great Names and ingenious Hypotheses in philosophy." Why not do the same in religion? The ethical and religious

19. Clifford G. Thompson, *The Ethics of William Wollaston* (Boston, 1922), pp. 13–14.

20. This statement and those in the next five paragraphs (including quotations) are based on notes kept in notebooks, 1747–49, and on "Birthday Reflections 1767," and "Memoirs of the Family of Stiles," and "Review of the Authors I read and admired during the Rise Height and Decline of my Scepticism, Dec. 12, 1768"—all in Stiles Papers.

21. The "Birthday Reflexions 1767" says 1747; the Autobiographical Fragment in Memoirs of the Family of Stiles, written in 1762, says 1748; Stiles's notebooks include notes on the book taken in 1747.

22. London, 1705.

23. These are recorded in a notebook with the notation "comm. 1749." But the proposition he finally chose to defend was not among them. It was "An quilibet Sanctus in Caelis, singulas Actiones humanas, hoc Mundo peractas, penitus cognoverit" (Whether any saint in heaven will have completely understood individual human actions undertaken in this world).

writings of a Shaftesbury seemed to proceed on this principle: Shaftesbury looked to no man for authority but argued his case from pure
reason.

When Ezra Stiles examined traditional religious beliefs in the
light of these ideas, he decided that the Westminster Confession of
Faith, drawn up by an assembly of English ministers in the 1640s
and generally regarded in New England as the best statement of
Christian doctrine, was "no authoritative Standard of Truth." New
Englanders knew, of course, that the Westminster Confession was
not a product of divine inspiration, but in rejecting the authority of
the Confession Stiles seemed to be lining up with the Arminians, who
likewise rejected it, though for different reasons. The Arminians were
not worried about the authority of great names; they merely disliked
the Calvinistic doctrines and thus rejected the Confession for the same
reason that orthodox New England accepted it. Stiles's position was
more radical, and it brought him inevitably to a fundamental skepticism. None of the books he had read, in spite of their rationalism,
made an outright attack on revelation. But if you rejected the West-
minister Confession, why accept the Bible?

An "ingenious deist" in New Haven, whom Stiles never identified,
suggested this question to him in 1749, and it was three or four years
before he could bring himself to an acceptable answer. The standard
answer, that the Bible was the word of God, required a good deal of
examination before it would satisfy a young man who had turned his
back on the authority of great names. Though he never, even at the
height of his skepticism, doubted the existence of God, that the Scriptures were the word of God required more proof than the mere say-so
of the men who recorded them.

During the next few years, as Stiles struggled with this question,
he did not read the attacks on revelation by men like Tindal, perhaps
because he was concentrating on the Scripture itself, but probably, too,
because he knew what conclusion he wanted to reach. He did, he tells
us, read Taylor,[24] Scott,[25] Butler,[26] and more of Isaac Watts. From

24. Probably the Taylor identified in note 11 above.
25. Possibly the John Scott identified in note 11, for Stiles made notes on his *Christian Life* in 1748, but probably Joseph Nicoll Scott, whose *Sermons* he also read in
that year and greatly admired.
26. Probably Joseph Butler (1692–1752), author of *The Analogy of Religion*
(London, 1736). But Stiles had earlier read Samuel Butler's *Hudibras*.

all these writers and from the Bible, he reached the opinion "that Revelation was a most rational and sublime Scheme far exceeding natural Religion. I only wanted to see that it was true and positively of divine Original."

By comparing the Scriptures with other historical sources, he convinced himself that they contained authentic accounts of actual historical events. Even the resurrection of Christ seemed to be confirmed by the inner consistency of the New Testament, for "the apostles could not have conspired in so uniform a Testimony of the Fact, in opposition to Jews and Idolators, at different Times and Countries, when separate and together, in all circumstances, without betraying contradictions of Facts, and absurd Representations of their Master's Doctrine."

The resurrection together with the fulfillment of the Old Testament prophecy of the dispersion of the Jews, formed the evidence on the basis of which he finally accepted the Bible as divinely inspired. His reasoning remained true to the Newtonian method as he conceived it. "At first," he says, "and in the Depth of Scepticism, I found myself ready to demand too much. I wanted to have displayed before me Demonstration that every Word, or at least every Sentiment in the Scriptures was [inspired by God]; and was liable to have my Faith of the whole overset, if I found one insuperable Difficulty. Newton tho't, whether the power by which a stone falls to the Ground might not retain the Moon in her Orbit; and then went on and investigated the law of Gravity demonstrably obtaining in the solar system and probably thro'out the stellar universe. In like manner, some one principle may be a basis upon which the whole system of Revelation may be firmly supported. Such is the fulfilment of prophecy respecting the Jews. Such is the Fact of the Resurrection of Jesus."

Though Stiles's doubts were not fully resolved until 1755 or 1756, and perhaps not even then, he was able by 1752 to complete a creed which he had begun in 1749, before his skepticism. The statements may have been somewhat tentative at the time, but with a few exceptions they represented fairly the beliefs he continued to hold for the rest of his life.

A Creed—January 11. 1752

I believe there is one God, the Creator and Governor of the World.

I believe his infinite Wisdom formed the Plan of the Universe: Omnipotence gave it Existence: and supports it in Harmony and Glory.

I believe the Moral World is composed of Intelligences, of various Orders, succeeding in a most beautiful Gradation in the Scale of Being, from infinite to nothing.

I believe that in the universal Conformity of Moral Beings of every Order, to those Truths and Laws, which arise from their respective Circumstances of Being governed by a supreme Reference to the Will of the Almighty, consists Virtue and Piety; and thence results the highest Perfection and Happiness of the Moral World—which is the ultimate End of Being; whence arises, or in which consists, the Glory of God as it arises from his Creation.

I believe the Deity as our Creator and Preserver, and Lord of the moral World justly claims and is the only proper Object [of] supreme Worship, and universal Homage.

I believe Man by Disobedience has forfeited the favour of God.

I believe that by Adams Sin, we are justly subjected to those Tryals and Afflictions in Life, which dont immediately arise from actual Sin, and finally to the Death of the Body.

I believe the Necessity of a Revelation to ascertain the Principles of Natural Religion, and Rules of Virtue, and to instruct us in the Methods of Mercy.

I believe the Scriptures of Old and New Testaments to be a Revelation from Heaven.

I believe that Belief in the Messiah, Repentance, and unfailing Resolutions for future Amendment in Life, will intitle to Forgiveness of Sin, which, according to the Plan of the Gospel I believe, is Effect of the Atonement of Jesus Christ.

I believe the Influences of the Spirit are necessary to form within us a Moral Renovation of Mind, to enable us to perfect the Principles of Holiness, and persevere in the divine Life.

I believe the future State of Rewards and Punishments, in which righteous shall be rewarded with Immortality and Glory; but the wicked with Moral Destruction.

I believe the Resurrection of the Dead, as a purchase of the Redeemer.

I believe Christ has instituted the Christian Church: and his Will is, that Officers be appointed for the special Services of the Sanctuary.

I believe tis proper that they be consecrated by the ministerial Order.

I believe the Gospel is a moral Means to bring Men to Religion and Virtue, and thus the Reformation and Perfection of human Nature.

I believe God has afforded every Man sufficient Assistance to attain Salvation and future Happiness.

I believe that a Man may be saved without any Knowledge of Christ, even by Christ's Merits—and that the Heathen, which have but one Talent, may attain future Happiness.

I also believe that no Infants and Idiots, dying in Infancy and Idiotism, will be miserable.

I believe that so long as Men have different Geniuses, and Education, they will necessarily have different Sentiments in Religion both in Speculation and Practice. And therefore that Uniformity in Opinion, Modes of Worship and Church Discipline is not necessary to constitute a true Christian Church.

Tis my Opinion that the Church have no Business to admit Persons: but that this ought to be left to the Minister to lead Persons to a public Profession of Christianity—The Members only to inform of Person's Moral Character. The admission I now speak of, is into the catholic or universal Church:—In Admission to Privileges of particular Churches the Members have a Right to act; sed Quaere.

I believe that as there is but one supreme *Independent* Mind and Being in the Universe so all other Beings are subordinate and dependent upon him: and therefore Jesus Christ is not strictly an *Independent* Being.

I believe that God has a power at any Time actually to create the most perfect of all possible Creatures.

I believe that God can create a Being with Capacity of infinite Knowledge, Power, Wisdom, Goodness &c i.e. Capacity of actually knowing all Things knowable—doing all doable discerning supreme Fitness, and whatever wisest and best to be done in all possible Circumstances and thus acting from highest sense of Goodness: and in Nothing differing from the *Supreme,* except in *Independency,* and perhaps Eternal Existence *a Parte ante.*

I believe that God has actually created such a Being, which is Jesus Christ the Messiah of God unto Men.

I believe that Jesus Christ created this World perhaps the whole Universe, redeemed Men, and will govern this part of the Moral World till he resign it to the father, at the final adjustment of human Affairs: when perhaps he will be appointed President Royal of the whole Moral World to Immortality.[27]

Stiles's creed shows that his period of skepticism was over and that the concern for morality which had led him into skepticism survived. His views of morality however had not remained static. When he joined his father's church in 1746 he had been attracted to Christianity more by the rational perfection of Christian morality than by its divine origin. ("After all I became a Christian rather as a Believer in a well imagined and most beautiful moral System than as feeling the Evidence of a certain real derivation from God.") [28] Now he accepted Christian morality not merely as a dictate of reason but also as a divine command. He even denied the ability of human reason to ascertain the "Rules of Virtue" without the aid of revelation.

His skepticism, though gone, had left lasting marks upon him. He retained a breadth of view that would have been wholly unacceptable to New Lights and somewhat dubious to Old Lights or even to Arminians. The salvation of the heathen, for instance, and of all infants and idiots were debatable propositions; one of his statements sounded like universalism; and his view of Christ was nearly Arian.

27. Stiles Papers.
28. Autobiographical Fragment, in Memoirs of the Family of Stiles.

Moreover, though he now accepted the inspiration of Scripture, he continued to reject the authority of all subsequent glosses on the text. Where the Reformation scholars had made the rediscovery of the Bible an occasion for the reconstruction of theology, Stiles all but abandoned theology in favor of what he took to be the simple clarity of Scripture:

> I seldom found much difficulty in understanding the Scriptures and I read very little in theological Systems, tho' I was not wholly unacquainted with them—but I found more satisfaction in recurring at once to the Original. My Deistical Turn gave me a very thoro' Disgust against the Authority of Councils and Decretals— when any one argued from the Scriptures I was pleased, but for protestants to adduce the opinions of fallible Men in Support of infallible Truth, did ever disgust me: and my alledging the authority of the Catholics as of equal Weight with the protestants, my friends were apt to suspect it only artifice to cover Heresy— whereas I was little concerned about Calvinism or Arminianism or any other *Ism*. This was perfectly consistent with a sceptical state of Mind, that at most rested alone in Scripture. I wished to see the Bible true, before I could feel any sollicitude about any of the various Christian Sects or Writings. From the cursory View I made of Ecclesiastical History, I thot all the protestant Churches as well as all the Xtian Churches since the first Age, had many Usages and Doctrines which I did not find in the Bible —yet I found sincere good men in all Churches catholic and protestant. Hence I adopted and professed an extensive and universal Charity: I readily saw the Mode of Worship in the New England Churches was as conformable to the Bible as any in the World, and I thot more so.[29]

This universal charity, which in some measure embraced even the Jews, was the most beneficent remainder from Stiles's skepticism. His talent for getting along with people was now coupled with a rational acceptance of other men's religions. Without hypocrisy he was able to appreciate almost anyone's point of view in religion; as a result we shall find him making far more friends than we can keep track of.

29. Ibid.

While learning to think of Christianity in the broadest terms and to welcome variations in belief, Stiles was also adjusting his philosophical ideas. The seventeenth century had endowed New England with a fierce love of liberty, a liberty which Governor Winthrop had described as the right to do that which is good, just, and honest. When Stiles delivered the valedictory oration for his master's degree in 1749, he paused to apostrophize liberty in somewhat different terms, terms which ring more of the eighteenth century. "Tis Liberty, my friends, tis the Cause of Liberty we assert—a Freedom from the Biass of a vulgar Education, and the Violence of prejudicate Opinions —a Liberty suited to the Pursuit and Enquiries after Truth—Natural and Moral. This is the Advantage of Education, and this the Emolument of the Liberal Discipline." [30]

The liberty Stiles extolled was the right to follow wherever reason in pursuit of truth might lead, even into forbidden territory. This concept was another aspect of his rejection of councils and decrees, and it became another lasting souvenir of his period of skepticism. It was also, of course, self-justification for the subversive intellectual explorations he was embarking on. Though Stiles rejected the theological reasoning that transformed "ingenious Hypotheses" into dogma, he was quite ready to construct such hypotheses for himself in his effort to pull together into a coherent system some of the diverse elements of knowledge he was first exposed to as an undergraduate.

It was not easy to reconcile Locke and Berkeley and Newton and Wollaston and Isaac Watts. At the distance of two centuries we may be tempted to take the measure of Stiles's intellect from the fact that he ranked Watts as high as any of these, but at the time Watts was much more than a hymn-writer to most people, and Stiles was guilty only of accepting the judgment of his contemporaries. If he took Watts more seriously than we do, he took Locke and Berkeley seriously too, and the picture of the world he finally settled on owed as much to Berkeley as to any other single thinker, though he did not consider himself a Berkeleyan.

What, Stiles asked himself, is the world that man finds around him? On August 7, 1750, he set down the beginnings of an answer. "The Universe," he wrote, "is composed of two Worlds, vizt. the

---

30. "Valedictory Oration," June 15, 1749 (presumably the date of composition, delivered at commencement in September).

Natural and *Moral,* both closely connected and conjoyned by that almighty Power, on which they depend." By the natural world he meant what we would call the physical world, including earth, sun, and stars, "or according to the Berkeleian Hypothesis, that Establishment of General Laws according to which perceptive Beings are affected regularly with sensible Perceptions, or Perceptions from without." [31]

By the moral world Stiles meant "the various Kinds of perceiving Beings which God has made and constituted both above and below Man, as well as man." [32] Presumably he used the word "moral" to imply that all beings were subject to the moral commands of their Creator. But his speculations about the moral world did not concern moral precepts. These were thoroughly delineated in the Bible and in treatises on ethics. He was interested, rather, in the various levels of moral beings and the relations between them. In 1752 he elaborated his ideas in a little treatise which he called "The Universe or Moral View of the Intellectual World and the Analogy of Nature." [33] It is a synthetic rather than an original work, but it furnished him with a philosophical framework for his future education. Like most young men addicted to scholarship he needed some sort of cosmic hatrack on which to hang his ideas, and this was what he built for himself.

The central doctrine of the treatise is that of the "sensible world" or sensible worlds surrounding every living being. Every man lives in five such worlds, corresponding to his five senses. There is no substantial connection between these worlds, but experience teaches us that a change in one is frequently accompanied by a change in another: for example, we both see and feel the movement of an arm. Stiles seems to have believed at times that these sensible worlds have a real existence outside the mind of the perceiver, but he evidently could find no answer to the Berkeleyan arguments and therefore tried to cast his formulation in terms which would not be subject to attack from that direction. Accordingly he never affirmed directly that there is a connection between different sensible worlds outside the mind. Such a connection within the mind, however, either the mind of God or of his creatures, was the means of communication between different

31. "The Universe No. 1," August 7, 1750.
32. Ibid.
33. Stiles Papers. The remainder of the chapter, except where otherwise noted, including quotations, is based on this document.

beings, whether human, angelic, or divine. We find by experience that
changes of various sorts are constantly taking place in our sensible
worlds: changes which have no dependence on our own volition, such
as the growth of vegetation or the movement of heavenly bodies;
changes produced by other minds like our own, or at least by what
appear to be other minds like our own, such as the voices we hear
when others speak; and changes resulting from, or identical with, our
own actions. By producing changes in other persons' sensible worlds,
we communicate with them, and in the same way they communicate
with us.

Ultimately all these changes depend on God, "the common *Sensorium* of the Universe," where all these sensible worlds meet. God
is not only immanent but constantly active. When a man lifts a stone
in defiance of the law of gravity, he is exerting not his own power but
God's. Since God offers this power through regular channels, man has
only to learn the channels, which are nothing less than the laws of
nature, in order to take advantage of the unlimited power of God.
Though human life is short, we can profitably spend it in learning
as much as possible about these laws. "The greater our Insight into
Nature and its Laws, the Greater will be our Power over its Laws,
in altering, suspending, or counteracting them, and the more enlarged
will be our sphere of activity." There is no limit, within the bounds
of our five sensible worlds, to the power that knowledge can bring.
All power is from God, and he does not withhold any of it from
our grasp, not even creative power.

The history of the universe as Stiles conceived it was progressive,
with the rate of an individual's progress depending on the industry
with which he set about to enlarge his "sphere of activity." As a freshman in college Stiles had been much impressed with Isaac Watts's
vision of the varying occupations which men of different capacities
and education would enjoy in heaven.[34] The end toward which his
own theory of the universe proceeded was to encourage the kind of
life in this world which would produce the greatest benefits in the
next. The upper links in the great chain of being were not fixed.
Men and angels move upward as they enlarge their spheres of activity,
or in other words, in proportion as they grow in understanding and
knowledge. Those who have attained great wisdom in this world

34. In a notebook on Apr. 21, 1743, he copied the passage on p. 102 of *Death and
Heaven; Or The Last Enemy Conquered* (London, 1722).

will have a head start on their more ignorant companions in the next. Stiles was obliged to allow, of course, that salvation could be attained only through Christ; but if saved, a man's best equipment for the life hereafter would be an extensive knowledge of the operation of God's laws, natural and moral.

The connection between this world and the next, Stiles admitted, can be inferred only from analogy, but since the same God rules both, the analogical method is a fair one. In the first place we may assume that there are different orders of beings from men, unbodied creatures such as angels or seraphim, whose sensible worlds may include our own but who have additional senses as well, of a type that we can only imagine. It is perfectly possible that we can effect changes in their worlds and they in ours, though we cannot perceive the changes that we make in theirs. This may be understood if we take the example of a man born blind. Since, as Locke demonstrates, simple ideas cannot be communicated, the blind man can never form an idea of color or of any kind of vision. Yet we can see him and read the emotions on his face, without his even being aware of it. If we wish to communicate with him, however, we may do so through his audible world. In like manner, all our activities may produce changes in the sensible worlds of angels without our awareness.

When we die, the curtain is drawn aside which conceals from humans the sensible worlds of higher orders of being. Death, unlike sleep, does not diminish the activity of the mind but heightens it. We take temporary leave of our present sensible worlds until the resurrection, when they are returned to us. In the meantime we live without bodies and perceive through senses as yet unknown to us.

When the resurrection comes, we will reassume the five senses enjoyed before death without losing those acquired after it. The bodies reassumed will be different from the old:

> The Sphere of Action will probably be much enlarged—nor the Body confirmed to so narrow a Compass:—but, unsubjected to the Law of Gravity, a *Volition* may transfer the Vehicle of Sensation, to the most distant parts of the visible Universe—disclose new and surprizing Things among the starry Worlds and their Inhabitants;—infinite Perfection of the adorable Author of Nature, in Creation and Moral Government! How glorious, how expeditious these Journeyings of the Mind, up and down, thro' the spacious, the boundless Regions of Immensity!

This was the closest that Ezra Stiles ever came to a beatific vision. The universe which Newton had discovered for him, and which Whiston and Derham had peopled with countless created beings, would be opened to his inspection. By studying the laws of nature and of nature's God, he would fit himself for interplanetary travel in a scholarly eternity.

Stiles thus arrived at a position of religious and philosophical equilibrium from which he could map out the good life: a life devoted to the industrious pursuit of knowledge. People might call him an Arminian, and from the standpoint of orthodox New England Calvinism (if there was any such thing after the Great Awakening) they might be right, but Stiles could reject the title in all sincerity, not so much because it was wrong as because it was irrelevant. He was no Arminian; he was rather, though he might not have recognized the word, a *philosophe*, a somewhat hesitant *philosophe* to be sure, still clinging to the forms of Christianity, but with his heart dedicated to truth in a way that the *philosophes* understood. What the Yale Library had produced this time was not an Arminian nor yet an Anglican, but something more, a child of the Enlightenment.

5

Abigail

THE YALE LIBRARY, like all libraries, was friendly to skepticism and heresy; but outside its libraries, New England was a lonely place for a skeptic, and while he was groping toward a socially acceptable creed Ezra Stiles was a lonely man. As he remembered it later, there was no one with whom he could talk freely except the ingenious deist who had first raised his doubts and for whose intelligence he had no high regard.[1] In the back of his mind he probably suspected—and unquestionably hoped—that his doubts would be resolved, as they finally were. In the meantime there was no use getting the wind up and ruining his reputation. Were it known that he entertained doubts of any kind about revelation it would be imperative for the college to drop him at once. Yale had had too many scrapes with heresy to risk another.

The fact that everyone was expecting him to enter the ministry did not help matters. After receiving the A.B., most graduates left college to engage in trade or teaching or reading for the bar, often having a go at several careers before settling down. Those who remained at college generally studied theology and were assumed to be heading for the ministry. Though he still had no such intention, Ezra Stiles covered his confusion by obtaining from the New Haven County association of ministers on May 30, 1749, a license to preach.[2] This was the normal first step toward a ministerial career, to be fol-

1. "Birthday Reflexions 1767."
2. *Lit. Diary, 1*, 178; *2*, 524.

lowed by occasional sermons at the invitation of churches with vacant
pulpits. Stiles probably obtained his license before his skepticism had
extended from Calvinism to revelation, so that he could take the step
with a clear conscience, knowing that many ordained ministers held
the same views he did. A trial run at the ministry was considered as
legitimate as a fling at any other career; and, though for him it was
chiefly a means of marking time, he did enjoy preaching, perhaps because of the opportunity it gave him to display his new erudition. Unfortunately, as his skepticism deepened, invitations to preach became
embarrassing occasions when he had either to find excuses for refusing or to pick some topic which would not reveal his infidelity.

With his students, too, he had to exercise great care. Though he
taught them mostly subjects that were remote from the danger zone,
the implications of his skepticism were far-reaching, and a quick-witted
student might easily pick up the trail. A tutor did not ordinarily lecture; that was the business of the president or of a professor if there
should be one (Yale had none). A tutor took charge not of a particular
subject but of a particular class, like a teacher in an elementary school
today.[3] His teaching consisted principally of drilling the students in
the assigned texts. A good tutor might enliven the class with his own
views on a subject, but this was not necessary. His job was merely to
see that the students learned what was in the books.

There was another phase of teaching, however, where a tutor's
ideas might be exposed, and one incidentally which rescued college
education from the mere memorization of predigested knowledge.
The curriculum during the junior and senior years included "disputations" in the hall twice a week, for which the tutor appointed some
students to prepare arguments on the negative and others on the
affirmative side of an assigned proposition. We can only guess what
part the tutor played in helping students prepare these disputations—
probably very little—but he certainly set the topics they argued, and
this in itself might be revealing. What did Mr. Stiles have in mind,
say, when he had students discuss the question "An Peccatum Adami
Posteris suis imputetur" (Whether Adam's sin be imputed to his pos-

3. Ezra Stiles had the junior class in 1749–50 and in 1750–51. In 1751–52, when
he was sick a good part of the year, he seems to have had the freshmen part of the
time and the juniors another part. In 1752–53 he taught the freshmen; 1753–54, the
sophomores; and 1754–55, the juniors. On his activities as a tutor discussed here and in
the next paragraph, see the journal he kept on this subject, May 25, 1749—Sept. 1755.

terity) or "Nullus Actus Dei est arbitrarius" (No act of God is arbitrary)? The tutor also received the written discourse after it was presented and presumably went over it with the author to point out any flaws in his reasoning or expression. In such interviews a student might learn a lot about the way his tutor's mind worked. The relationship was doubtless a pleasant one, and Stiles's pupils expressed their affection for him by annual gifts, of a watch or a gown or even a sum of money, which he accepted with no more hesitation than a schoolteacher today might show. in receiving a polished red apple. But when students went home and started repeating some of the clever things that Mr. Stiles had said, parental ears might pick up implications the children had missed. In spite of all precautions, word began to get around that Ezra Stiles was not altogether sound. Probably no one knew how far he had gone, but he was certainly suspected of Arminianism.

He found out about his reputation in the course of an episode that taught him a lesson he had often heard but never before so fully understood. It was also an exciting experience, moving him in unstirred recesses whose existence he had only half suspected. It began early in 1750 when he received an invitation to come to Stockbridge, Massachusetts, and preach a few sermons.[4] The proposal must have piqued his curiosity, for Stockbridge was a novel settlement, where English and Indian were trying to live together in arcadian harmony. John Sergeant, a Yale graduate of 1729, had conceived the idea and together with Timothy Woodbridge, a gifted schoolmaster, had persuaded the General Court of Massachusetts to found a township where the Indians might receive continuous instruction in Christianity and civilization, by living side by side with white men. Instead of listening to occasional harangues from a missionary, they would live like white men, and cooperate with white men in church, town, and

4. Ephraim Williams to Stiles, Feb. 26, 1750; Timothy Woodbridge to Stiles, Feb. 28, 1750. On the history of Stockbridge and the disputes there see, besides the Stiles Papers, the following: *Boston News Letter*, Aug. 30–Sept. 6, 1739; Samuel Hopkins, *Historical Memoirs Relating to the Housatonic Indians* (Boston, 1753), reprinted in *The Magazine of History*, Extra No. 17 (1912); Edwards, *Works*, *1*, 449–541; Winslow, *Edwards*, pp. 268–92; Perry Miller, *Jonathan Edwards* (New York, 1949), pp. 247–50; letter of Gideon Hawley, July 31, 1794, Mass. Hist. Soc., *Collections*, 1st ser. *4* (1795), 50–67; Electa F. Jones, *Stockbridge Past and Present* (Springfield, 1854); and Sarah Cabot Sedgwick and Christina Sedgwick Marquand, *Stockbridge 1739–1939, a Chronicle* (Great Barrington, Mass., 1939).

school. It was an appealing experiment and became more appealing to those who heard of it in direct proportion to their distance from the scene. The General Court of Massachusetts, sitting comfortably in Boston, was ready to give it legal sanction, and Bostonians contributed a small amount to carrying it out. Three thousand miles away, in London, eager philanthropists embraced the scheme and supported it through the Company for Propagation of the Gospel in New England and by special donations for the maintenance of Indian schools. The Housatonic Indians, after expressing skepticism about this belated interest in their spiritual welfare, moved into Stockbridge to give it a try, and a number of Mohawks from across the Hudson were persuaded to join them.

A few white families agreed to participate, perhaps because the land they would receive looked like a good investment, and by 1739 the town was incorporated under a board of selectmen consisting of two Indians and one white man, with a church gathered under John Sergeant and a school established under Timothy Woodbridge. The white selectman was Ephraim Williams, who had arrived in 1737 with his son Ephraim, Jr., and his daughter Abigail. The whole thing had the character of a romance, and Abigail set out to be the heroine. She was fifteen when she arrived and an uncommonly pretty girl. By the time she was seventeen she had married John Sergeant, and people began to notice, as the saying went, that the gray mare was the better horse. The Williamses were apparently going to take over Stockbridge.

Ten years later, when John Sergeant died, the philanthropists were still pouring in money, and the Williamses were still determined to run the town, but they were finding it a bigger job than they had supposed. There were a dozen English families there now, and 218 Indians (about fifty families). The community, English and Indian alike, was split into hostile camps, one led by the Williamses and the other by Timothy Woodbridge. The divisions had come almost as soon as the experiment started, and it is all but impossible to tell at this distance who was at fault. From the Williams' accounts Timothy Woodbridge was the villain of the piece, aided and abetted by certain apostate Indians, who decided that the good life was not as much fun as the drunken one, and who spread wicked reports about Colonel Williams and the Reverend Mr. Sergeant when those two worthies tried to prevent the tavern keeper from furnishing them with liquor.

The other side of the story consists of accusations against the Williamses as thieves, bent on cheating the Indians of their lands and the philanthropists of their money.

As might be expected, the controversy involved religion. John Sergeant seems to have had a disposition much like that of Ezra Stiles. He liked to be considered "catholic" in his views; he admitted members to his church on the Stoddardean plan. He subscribed to Charles Chauncy's denunciation of the Great Awakening.[5] In short he was an Old Light, and this was sufficient incentive, where the community was already divided on other grounds, to bring out accusations of Arminianism.

When Ezra Stiles was approached by both Woodbridge and Williams to preach at Stockbridge, he probably knew nothing of what had been happening there, and agreed to come up in April for a couple of Sundays. The trees were still bare when he rode over the hill from Great Barrington and, looking down, saw the church and fifteen or twenty crude houses, interspersed with occasional wigwams, stretching out along the winding Housatonic River. As he came down the trail and trotted his horse past silent savage figures, he must have felt that this was the last outpost of civilization.

Riding as he was directed, toward the church at the end of the village, he came upon a house which spoke a more familiar language. Here, as though the other buildings were meant to serve as a foil for it, was a modest but undeniably beautiful little house with as fine a doorway as any back in New Haven. It had been the home of John Sergeant, and his widow was living there now. If you knew her, you recognized that the house was hers more than his. Stiles did not know her; but it had been arranged that he should stay here, and as she came to meet him, he saw a handsome woman. Twenty-seven years old now, Abigail was at the height of her beauty, but her charm was far more than physical. Stiles discovered that she had all the qualities he admired—sympathy, understanding, vigor, and a brilliance of mind he had never seen in a woman. In the week he stayed with her she told him about her husband's heroic labors with the Indians, and he told her as much as he dared of his own religious problems.

He felt instinctively that she was the kind of woman he could trust, and after he left he found himself writing back to her about "the

5. Chauncy, *Seasonable Thoughts*, p. 15. On Sergeant, besides references in note 4 above, see the transcript of his journal, 1739, in the Stiles Papers.

pleasant week I spent at your house; when sorrow itself appears beautiful: and Virtue in Distress supporting itself on God and Immortality, strike the Mind with Delight and Surprize." [6] Before a year was
up he would be suggesting to her how much he needed a wife, and
the kind of wife he needed sounds, not surprisingly, like his vision of
Madam Sergeant: "One I mean, of a refind Genius Education and
Tast to relish and communicate in the Noble Researches of Science
and Wisdom: whose agreeable Humour should dispel Melancholly,
enliven invigorate and diffuse a Chearfulness thro' the Mind, which
would help to wear out this Span of Life in Tranquillity." [7] Abigail,
he thought, was just this kind of woman. To her he could unburden
himself on the beauties of philosophy and the joys of immortality
as he was beginning to picture them and on the progress of the soul
through knowledge and moral truth. He could condole with her on
the bigotry of those who measured her dead husband's merits by
Arminianism or Calvinism. The catholic spirit of John Sergeant en-
veloped them both.

When Stiles went to Stockbridge, he knew that they were trying
him out as Sergeant's successor. The actual appointment would have
to be approved in Boston by the Commissioners of the Company for
Propagation of the Gospel, but the Commissioners would rely heavily
on reports from Stockbridge. After his visit in April the Williams
faction was certain they had found the right man. Stiles was affable
and agreeable; he seemed to have the right views in religion; and he
was obviously taken with Abigail. The only problem was Timothy
Woodbridge and white families who sided with him. They were
evidently New Light in religion and could not be expected to take
readily to the kind of ideas that Stiles expounded from the pulpit.
But perhaps the young man's winning personality would prevail.

Stiles himself was intrigued with the prospect. Under the spell
of Abigail's charm Stockbridge had taken on a different and much
more attractive appearance than he had found as he first rode through
it. His charges would be mostly Indians, and the principal concern
of a minister to the Indians would be to improve their morals. That
was one aspect of religion, or of ethics if you preferred, that he understood and believed in. He wrote to Ephraim Williams, expressing
what sounded like conventional doubts about his qualifications for so

6. Stiles to Abigail Sergeant, July 16, 1750.
7. Ibid., Jan. 8, 1751.

important a task, and adding: "I can't say I am intirely discouraged but would put on the best Resolution, the Armour of Light, and wade thro' the Tryals of but a short Scene of Usefulness at Longest— Indeed what do we live for but, by endeavouring to do good, to cultivate and discipline our Minds for Immortality?" [8] This was the kind of pious platitude that Stiles's skepticism about revelation and his conviction about morality would permit him. He knew, however, that one could not preach indefinitely to New Englanders on this theme without becoming suspect. The majority of his parishioners at Stockbridge would be Indians, but there were also English, from whom he would ultimately be unable to hide his doubts. Though he was accumulating an increasing body of evidence to persuade himself that the Scriptures were divinely inspired, he was still not convinced. Until he had determined this crucial question, he did not wish to ascend a pulpit regularly every Sunday. And yet Stockbridge offered many attractions.

While he was trying to make up his mind, Ephraim Williams showed up in New Haven with a letter from Dr. Ayscough, Chaplain of the Prince of Wales, conveying the encouraging news that the prince had promised forty pounds a year toward the support of Sergeant's successor. He also had a note from Abigail, just a few lines scratched out while her father paused at her house to light his pipe. "We have had a story," she told Stiles, "that all the Principle Gentlemen at Newhaven are Arminian Deists. if you are able to understand such Cristian Language, in a word we have Old [Nick?] to pay here." [9]

Stiles knew what she was talking about. Timothy Woodbridge was having doubts about his orthodoxy and had evidently communicated them to the Commissioners, who had immediately sent Samuel Hopkins of Springfield to inquire into the matter. Hopkins had arrived in New Haven just before Williams, who probably came in order to ward off this counterattack. Stiles was understandably alarmed by the prospect of an examination of his religious beliefs. He had not revealed the full extent of his skepticism even to Abigail, and he knew how little his beliefs could stand examination. Evidently he and Williams were able to put off an inquiry at this time, but he replied to Abigail with a resoundingly hollow affirmation of his own integrity: however his character might be traduced, he would bear it with calm-

8. Stiles to Williams, July 16, 1750.
9. Abigail Sergeant to Stiles, July 27, 1750.

ness and intrepidity. On the other hand he saw that "there is much *Legerdemain* at Bottom. —and am sometimes therefore half of the mind, that should the Commissioners send to me I should decline it—but," he added coyly, "You know, 'tisn't worthwhile to deny before one's askt." With regard to the rumor about the gentlemen of New Haven being Arminian deists, he could reassure her. Since the two words were incompatible, it was honest enough to say that "That contradictious, antichristian, irreconcilable Character of *Arminian Deists* is not to be found in N.H. nor College. nor any where else but in the Land of *Nod.*" [10]

This would satisfy Abigail Sergeant, who was already counting on him as her husband's successor, perhaps in more ways than one, but it would not do for the Commissioners at Boston. Shortly after Williams' departure, Stiles received a letter asking him to come to Boston for an interview at their expense. Williams, hearing of the invitation, dashed off a note of warning: "it is probable you will be desired to preach, for the Pious and good Dr. Sewell that is I Suppose in principe strictly Calvinistical—the old saying is a word to the wise is Sufficient." [11] Williams was telling him that Sewall was a New Light, and that he had better preach a sermon that would not offend New Lights. Abigail, reacting to Stiles's apparent pique over the aspersion of his character, and not suspecting his real vulnerability, wrote soothingly that she thought the Commissioners had acted honorably thus far. He must remember that their ears were "filled with Arminian, Heteradox and what not,—the world semes to be full of nothing Else, and if some of our O[rthodo]x Gentlemen are not indeavoring to establish there own Characters upon the Ruins of others it is well." [12]

Instead of removing Stiles's fears, this only confirmed them. His was precisely the kind of character the ruin of which would be useful to the orthodox. His catholicity went too far. At this point there was only one person with whom he could trust his predicament—his father. Isaac Stiles, wiser in these matters than his son, immediately perceived what was up. If Ezra went to Boston, the Commissioners would extract enough evidence of his infidelity to ruin his reputation in New England forever. Even if he got by the Commissioners and

10. Stiles to Abigail Sergeant, July 30, 1750.

11. Andrew Oliver to Stiles, Aug. 4, 1750. Williams to Stiles, Aug. 1750 (received Aug. 24). Joseph Sewall was minister of Old South Church.

12. Abigail Sergeant to Stiles, Aug. 10, 1750.

went to Stockbridge, Timothy Woodbridge would smoke him out sooner or later, with the same result. Accordingly Ezra wrote the Commissioners that his father was utterly unwilling for him to consider the post at Stockbridge. The Commissioners would therefore excuse him from putting them to the needless expense of his trip to Boston.[13]

It was not so easy to explain his decision to Abigail. In a brief note written in the hubbub of commencement (September 14) he used the lame excuse of the aspersion on his character, which, he said, made his father think it best for him "intirely to lay aside the Tho'ts of Stockbridge." [14] Abigail never received the letter, but she read with horror a similar one addressed to her father.[15] She was totally unprepared for it. She had interpreted Ezra's show of reluctance as conventional modesty or coyness, which it certainly sounded like, and never doubted that he would accept in the end. She sent back a blistering letter, tempered only by an appeal that he change his mind. She accused him of putting worldly comfort ahead of the noble calling of a missionary. He must have been asleep or in a fit of hypochondria when he made such a decision. She did not know that she could ever forgive him. She gave a hint too, of the predicament in which he left her and her friends: "I am extremely Concerned for the Consequences of your Conclutions at this unhappy juncture. I have reason to fear a Certain Gentleman here would readely imbrace an opportunity to Push in as indifferent a Person as poseble, for reasons I leve you to Guess." [16] The certain gentleman she referred to was Timothy Woodbridge, and the "indifferent" person was none other than Jonathan Edwards, who had just been dismissed from his church at Northampton, after a controversy in which his bitterest enemies had borne the name of Williams. In the religious controversies of New England there were always wheels within wheels.

Stiles, who was still yearning for Abigail if not for the job, wrote back at some length, attempting to excuse himself and going as far as he could toward disclosing his true reasons:

> I am young, especially in Character, and unable to confront the disingenuous Calumnies of designing Mortals, unless in some

13. Stiles to Andrew Oliver, Sept. 17, 1750.
14. Stiles to Abigail Sergeant, Sept. 14, 1750.
15. Stiles to Williams, Sept. 17, 1750.
16. Abigail Sergeant to Stiles, Oct. 6, 1750.

inferior Station in Life: Whereas Mr. Sergeant's Character for Wisdom and Piety was so well established as that in a few years, he would have made his Enemies a most cheap and easy Triumph. —And it may be a Question, if it is not altogether impracticable for one who believes no other Religion but that of *Nature* and the *Bible*, to pass thro' all the preparatory Submissions and Approbations for Stockbridge, and preserve a Conscience void of Offence both towards *God* and *Man*. Had I went to Boston, a most strict Examination would doubtless have been most strenuously insisted upon, not by the Commissioners only, but I believe I might add our P———t [President Clap], not that he suspects my Orthodoxy, but from a Principle of Friendship and good Nature to clear up my Reputation. I could say further that Things had got to such a Crisis at College, that hadn't I stood stock still, I must inevitably have &c. There are in our Israel who drive hard for an *Inquisition*, tho' very much under Covert; and Heaven only knows, if it were in their Power, whether they might not again revive the *Marian Fire and Faggot!* [17]

Abigail accepted the apology, still hoping against hope that he would change his mind, and wrote him of the desperate situation resulting from his refusal. Her letter revealed the morass which he had so narrowly escaped:

> I cannot forbear telling you that or [our] worthy Deacon [Woodbridge] is going forth with to Push Mr. Edwards imeadeately into the mission, all though he has Ben intreated Sufficiently to forbear My father Captain Kellogg Mr. Jones &c are very Bitterly against it. . . . it is shameful to mention it but he [Woodbridge] has told the Indian[s] as they say that they must not have a young man, if they do he will likely marry in to my fathers famely and then Be under his Direction . . . you may thank him for the suspecians the Commissioners have obtained about you, he told Mr Bromfeild with his own mouth, that one of your Pupels declared to him that you went ful Length with Mr Tailor [18] in denighing Original Sin and this he told me leve-

17. Stiles to Abigail Sergeant, Oct. 25, 1750.

18. John Taylor of Norwich, England, a dissenting clergyman, whose Arminian work, *The Scripture Doctrine of Original Sin* (London, 1740) Stiles had actually been reading the year before, though he never finished it. See "Review of the Authors I read and admired."

ing out his auther and said if so he Desired to Be Delivered. I told him I beleved nothing of it.[19]

After reading the letter, Ezra Stiles was in a quandary. He could not tell the girl that Woodbridge was right about his heresy, and he did not need to tell her that Woodbridge was also right about the likelihood of at least one young man marrying into the Williams family. If Stiles had gone to Stockbridge, he would almost certainly have married Abigail and spent his life in a local feud. As it was, Jonathan Edwards came to Stockbridge and for four years dueled with Abigail, until he succeeded, with Woodbridge's assistance, in putting an end to the whole Williams faction in Stockbridge. A branch of the Williams family had driven him from his church in Northampton; in Stockbridge he turned the tables, and the account he gives of the Williamses and particularly of Abigail, whom he recognized as his most dangerous antagonist, is a good deal different from the story that came to Ezra Stiles.[20] We need not decide here which was correct, though it is difficult to escape the conclusion that Edwards was. But the Stileses had done a little dueling with Edwards themselves, and Ezra's sympathies lay with Abigail, whom he continued to admire throughout his life. He forfeited his chance to marry her when he turned down the Stockbridge job (two years later she married Joseph Dwight, an ardent advocate of Edwards, and transformed him at once into Edwards' most bitter opponent), but he held her friendship and continued to correspond with her for some time. Looking over her old letters many years later, he wrote across the margin of one of them: "A Woman of a most surprizing Genius." [21]

She was all of that, and his flirtation with her and with Stockbridge had taught him something. He knew now how closely his religious principles would be watched as soon as he stepped out from the shelter of the college. The struggle between New Lights and Old Lights was still a hot one after ten years of running warfare. Though the heat was generated as much from old family feuds as from religion, the two were effectively fused in the minds of the antagonists. There was

---

19. Abigail Sergeant to Stiles, Nov. 6, 1750.

20. Winslow, *Edwards*, pp. 268–92, Sedgwick and Marquand, *Stockbridge*, pp. 49–71.

21. Abigail Sergeant to Stiles, Aug. 6, 1750. In a letter written twenty years later (May 4, 1770) Abigail asked Stiles to destroy her letters or write out orders for their destruction after his death, but they remain among his papers.

not much room in New England for a man whose catholicity could embrace both sides, and no room at all for a man who ventured into the arena without a thorough understanding of who was on which side and for what reasons.

6

Academic Dignity

THE STOCKBRIDGE EPISODE showed Ezra Stiles that he had better get on with some other career than the ministry. Though he was enamored of moral truth and would gladly preach it to an appreciative audience, he was not prepared either intellectually or emotionally for the kind of infighting that evidently went with the office of a pastor. Realizing, however, that he could not remain a Yale tutor all his life (the position was normally a temporary one), he decided to prepare himself for a career in the law.

Preparation consisted of reading the great law reports by Holt, Coke, Raymond, and Salkeld; Coke's *Institutes;* Wood's *Institutes;* and Hale's *History of the Common Law.* It also meant learning the proceedings of the Connecticut courts and something of those in the other colonies.[1] Stiles nowhere says who was his instructor in these studies, but a later letter suggests that it was Jared Ingersoll, a New Haven attorney whom he probably met through his father's friend, the Reverend Joseph Noyes.[2] Noyes, himself an Old Light of catholic taste, was a good friend to Ezra too, especially during his years as a tutor. Ingersoll was one of Noyes's staunch supporters against the New Haven New Lights and would have been glad to help any friend of his. Since the law was not so specialized a profession then as it is today, Stiles was able to qualify for admission to the New Haven bar by November 13, 1753.[3]

1. Autobiographical Fragment, in Memoirs of the Family of Stiles.
2. Stiles to Ingersoll, August 16, 1756.
3. He recorded the date in his journal of activities as a tutor: Stiles Papers. See also Records of New Haven County Court, Conn. State Lib., *4, 620.*

He did not abandon his work at Yale. Though he may have participated in some of Ingersoll's cases—he says he practiced until 1755 [4] —he remained a tutor, and he pursued his other studies without interruption. The rationale of continuing education which he outlined in his essay on the universe gave him all the justification he needed for indulging his expanding curiosity, which was now ranging over every branch of natural science. He was not a profound or original scientific thinker, but in that age of universal geniuses his was a receptive intelligence, quick to see the importance of new ideas in every field. As early as 1747, the year after his graduation, he read with excitement, and recorded in his notes, Halley's directions for calculating solar parallax at the transits of Venus, which were due to occur in 1761 and 1769. He also read Halley's observations on human mortality and began to think about the laws of population.[5] He took the college theodolite and practiced with it on the New Haven green, noting that the surface of the ground by the college foregate was eighteen and one-half feet higher than that at the old meetinghouse.[6] When he heard—presumably from Jared Eliot, a Yale trustee, minister, and scientist—of Benjamin Franklin's discovery that northeast storms come from the southwest, he immediately set about checking it.[7]

He learned, too, of Franklin's experiments in electricity before they were made public. Using apparatus that Franklin himself had contributed, he and the other Yale tutors repeated the more spectacular experiments, all of which were performed by charging a glass tube with static electricity and discharging it in such ways as to excite the wonder and admiration of an audience.[8] Stiles described the Yale experiments in a letter to Pelatiah Webster:

4. Autobiographical Fragment.

5. The 1747 notation is in his notebook for 1743–44; the notation on population is dated Feb. 18, 1754, among miscellaneous notes made 1753–54.

6. Note dated July 5, 1753, in miscellaneous notes 1753–54.

7. See Franklin to Eliot, February 13, 1750, Leonard W. Labaree, editor, Whitfield J. Bell, Jr., associate editor, *The Papers of Benjamin Franklin* (New Haven, 1960–), 3, 463–66; Stiles to Samuel Hopkins, Jr., July 17, 1750, Stiles Papers.

8. Franklin donated electrical apparatus to Yale in the spring of 1749. He must also have communicated his electrical writings to someone at Yale or perhaps to Jared Eliot, for Stiles on Feb. 20, 1749/50, wrote a summary, with extensive quotations, of the Franklin letter on thundergusts, and he began the experiments described below on Mar. 18, 1748/49, according to a notebook he kept of them. Franklin's letter on thundergusts is dated Apr. 29, 1749, but it was not published until 1751 in the first edition of his *Experiments and Observations on Electricity*. For Franklin's writings on

We have communicated the shock sensibly to 52 persons at once—
We frequently fire not only spirits of Wine, but common
Rum. We increase the Force of the Electrical Kiss to a prodi-
gious Degree of Intenseness. We suspend counterfeit spiders, and
by the Repelling and Attraction excited by the Attrition, they
play incessantly to and from the Tube, in a manner so natural
that they [have] frequently been taken to be alive— We represent Lightning, by Electrifying the gilt lines upon the Edges of
the Covers of Books.[9]

Stiles was so impressed by these phenomena that he went on to
state his conviction that "Electricity is a far more extensive and General Law, than *Gravity:* which indeed is one Property of Electricity:
and that as a greater Variety of Phenomena, so perhaps all the Phae-
nomena in the Universe, may hereafter be found, originally to proceed from and be effected by it." [10] This observation, had it been made
the basis of new experiments, might have been fruitful indeed, but
Stiles seems to have had little genius for pushing back the frontiers of
knowledge. All the electrical experiments he described to Webster
had been performed before, and his observation of them disclosed
nothing new. What he and his students gained was an experimental
understanding of what Franklin and others had discovered. He was
the learner and the teacher, insatiable in his thirst for more knowledge—time enough to start pushing into the unknown when he had
mastered everything that others already knew.

During these years, while he was exploring the new worlds of
science and law and satisfying his doubts about revelation and Christianity, his health had not been good. In the summer of 1751 an attack
of dysentery brought him near death.[11] His father's slave Phillis cared
for him so well that he sent her home after his recovery with a note
saying she had saved his life, "and altho' an Oethiopian Servant, I

electricity, see I. B. Cohen, ed., *Benjamin Franklin's Experiments* (Cambridge, Mass.,
1941). For Stiles's summary of the thundergust letter, see Stiles to Abel Stiles, Feb. 20,
1749/50. For his notations on the experiments, see his astronomy notebook, begun
1745, the next to the last signature.

9. May 8, 1749.
10. Ibid.
11. Holmes, *Life,* p. 23. Autobiographical Fragment. Letters from Abel Stiles,
Oct. 7, 1751, and from Abigail Sergeant, Oct. 29, 1751.

hope you'll treat her with Kindness." [12] In 1752 he was prostrated by another illness, which left him weakened for two years to come. When he had recovered sufficiently to stand moderate exercise, he decided to try extensive horseback riding as a restorative. After a trial run of 200 miles to Deerfield and back in May 1754, he rode in July to Boston via Newport and in September to Philadelphia.[13]

It was an American version of the grand tour. Instead of the galleries of Paris and Florence there were Mr. Smibert's paintings in Boston, and Smibert himself displayed his virtuosity for the young man by playing on the spinet. There was also an evening concert at Mr. DeBlois'. Instead of the Coliseum he had to be content with Faneuil Hall; and the wax works at Boston were the nearest he came to the sculptures of Greece and Rome. It was sad enough by comparison with what the young nobility of England were doing, but for a young tutor from New Haven it was glory.

Characteristically he determined to make the experience as broadening as possible. Wherever he went, he sought out gentlemen of the law, in order to learn as much as possible of the local legal procedures. The lawyers, he found, tended to be of a deistical turn of mind, and perceiving that he was not antagonized by their skepticism, they aired their views freely to him, so that he also had "an Opportunity of collecting the whole Force of Deism." With ostentatious catholicity he attended services at the churches of different persuasions in the towns he visited: Quaker at Newport and Philadelphia, Episcopal at New York and Boston; Dutch Calvinist at New York; Roman Catholic at Philadelphia. There were not enough Sundays to make room for others, but at the New Jersey College commencement, where George Whitefield received an honorary degree, he listened to the great evangelist preach and wrote off his humble manner as a pretentious covering for vanity.[14]

The journeys gave a considerable impetus to Stiles's own vanity, which had been developing for some time. Everywhere he went he

12. Stiles to Isaac Stiles, Sept. 1751.

13. The journal of his tour to Boston is in the Stiles Papers; that of his tour to Philadelphia is not but is published in Mass. Hist. Soc., *Proceedings*, 2d ser. 7 (1891–92), 339–44. My account of the tours, except where otherwise indicated, is based on these journals, on the Autobiographical Fragment, and on entries in his commonplace books.

14. Stiles to Edward Wigglesworth, Jan. 12, 1755.

found that his status as Yale graduate, tutor, and attorney gave him a
ready introduction. At Harvard commencement President Holyoke
conferred a master's degree upon him free of charge. After the ceremony he dined with Professor John Winthrop, apart from Franklin
the most eminent American scientist of his day, and spent the night
with tutor Joseph Mayhew. The next day he called on the president
and took dinner with Dr. Wigglesworth, the professor of divinity. In
Boston he visited Charles Chauncy, the nemesis of the New Lights and
Samuel Cooper, pastor of the famous Brattle Street Church. In New
York he found his old classmate John Morin Scott and many other
Yale men whom he had known as student or tutor. William Living-
ston, the future governor of New Jersey, had him to dinner with a
group of New York lawyers, where they "settled politics over a generous bottle." At Newark, Aaron Burr, president of New Jersey College (later Princeton) received him, and Francis Alison, rector of
the Philadelphia Academy, who had come to Newark for commencement, wrote out letters of introduction for him to people in Philadelphia. He met William Franklin, son of Benjamin (who was away
inspecting his post offices); Ebenezer Kinnersley, Franklin's partner
in the electrical experiments; William Smith, later provost of Philadelphia College; William Allen, chief justice of Pennsylvania; Dr.
William Shippen, the famous physician; and Joseph Galloway, Benjamin Chew, and Jasper Yeates, all eminent names in Pennsylvania
politics and business.

It was a heady experience for a young man to be noticed by so
many of the great. Nor was this the first evidence he had had of his
stature in society. The Stockbridge episode, alarming as it was, had
shown him that people on both sides considered him a man to reckon
with. Since other people seemed to take him pretty seriously, it is not
surprising that he began to take himself so. This appeared first in
letters to the family. Ezra's tone toward his father was always condescending, as when he sent him instructions for his younger brother's
education: "I am extreamly desirous Job should have a Liberal Edu-
tion; and next to his being perfected in Reading and Writing, would
have him early entered into the Rudiments of Language." [15] To his
sister Ruth, aged six, who was visiting her uncle, he wrote an avuncu-
lar letter, admonishing her: "If you cant read all my Writing at first,

15. Stiles to Isaac Stiles, May 22, 1751.

ask Uncle, and read it over and over 'till you can. Keep all my Letters by you safe, and dont let them be lost." [16]

This tendency to exaggerate his own importance gave rise at various times during his life to elaborate schemes for ensuring him undying fame. The first of these he drew up on July 13, 1752. Though his worldly estate at the time could scarcely have exceeded £100, he drafted a tentative will, establishing a public library in New Haven, with a group of proprietors to be chosen from among the gentlemen of the town. Stiles outlined the constitution of the organization, guaranteeing life membership without dues to his father, brothers, and cousins. There were to be annual meetings at which one of the members should address the company on "Moral Philosophy or History, Politics, Medicine, Natural Philosophy or any other Subject as they please—except the Controversial Points of Divinity"; and a president and council were to "cultivate a Correspondence with Gentlemen of Learning in any part of the World," in order to keep up with new discoveries in the republic of letters and also in order to beg books for the library.[17]

Needless to say, nothing came of this scheme, but the touch of pomposity which prompted it found ready outlets in academic life. Stiles himself cultivated a correspondence with gentlemen of learning, partly because it flattered his vanity but more specifically to beg books for the Yale Library. Without benefit of introduction he wrote to William Warburton, later Bishop of Gloucester; to Francis Ayscough, the former chaplain of the Prince of Wales, who had helped support the Stockbridge mission; and to William Whiston, the friend of Newton, whose books had held a large place in his own education. An enterprise of this kind required brass, and Stiles at this time seems to have had all that was needed. To Whiston he sent an astonishing request for "a few Plans, Draughts, Schemes of Solar Eclipses, Transits of Mercury and Venus over the Sun, or any Representations of the Celestial Motions, Phenomena of the Planets, Comets &c especially the Comet of 1758 And since the Periods of this Comet have been very unequal, you'd oblige me with your Judgment when it will next be in its Perihelion." [18]

16. June 10, 1753.
17. Stiles Papers.
18. May 9, 1751.

Stiles was doubtless gratified but not surprised to get most of what he asked for; and once he hit upon a generous source of supply he continued to work it for all it was worth, multiplying his requests for books by other authors, and for "philosophical apparatus" (an air pump was much needed), and would the learned doctor or the reverend sir supply him with introductions to other men of learning in England and Europe? When Yale gave Benjamin Franklin an honorary master's degree in 1753, Stiles gained another correspondent, one who could supply him with many foreign contacts. At the same time he was maintaining his correspondence with the most interesting of his classmates and former pupils and with many of the people he had met on his travels. As a correspondent he was tireless but seldom tiresome, for his enthusiastic pursuit of knowledge furnished him with something to say to everyone, and as his reputation expanded so did that of Yale.

Within the college, too, he found opportunities for feeding or sublimating his vanity. In his first year as tutor he persuaded President Clap to make a ceremony of the examination of candidates for the degree. The examination itself seems to have been perfunctory at this time, with the candidates and examiners enjoying a convivial bottle and pipe together in the college hall. Stiles saw in the occasion an opportunity for academic pomp of a more austere variety and, in spite of Clap's dislike of ceremonial, persuaded him to change the procedure. From 1751 onward the candidates were examined by the tutors without wine, tobacco, or "merry talk," and after the examination the whole group marched upstairs to the library, where the senior tutor presented the candidates in a formal Latin address to the president, who was seated in state before a portrait of the king.[19]

It was evidently recognized that Stiles had a gift for ceremony. Whenever there was occasion for an oration he was called upon to deliver it. In his own senior year he had delivered the Cliosophic oration, which followed the examination just mentioned. In 1749, when he took his master's degree, he gave the valedictory oration, and from this time on, scarcely a year passed without a Latin oration of some sort from Tutor Stiles. In 1750 it was a funeral eulogy of Governor Law, in 1752 an oration in celebration of Yale's first half-century, in 1753 on the death of Yale's benefactor, Bishop Berkeley, and in 1755 in praise of Benjamin Franklin, on the occasion of a visit to New

19. Stiles's journal of activities as a tutor.

Haven by the great electrician, whom Stiles addressed as *"Philosophiae princeps."* [20]

The academic life fairly bristled with opportunities for gratifying the ego of a young tutor. In the orderly hierarchy of collegiate rank the senior tutor (Stiles's position from 1750 to 1755) stood next to the top, and the whole authority of the college was exerted to maintain the respect of every rank for those above it. Even the dignity of sophomores was protected by solemn judgments of the president and tutors against freshmen who dared to violate it. When Samuel Cary was called before a group of sophomores and left the room saying "I sware I will not stay here any longer," he was found guilty of violating the laws of God and the college, and suspended (but restored four days later after a public confession of his crime before the whole college). If the authority of the sophomores was a matter for such vigilance, one can imagine the kind of subordination the senior tutor could demand, especially when he was a trifle pompous and very much aware of his growing reputation.

Fortunately the records show that Yale students were not as thoroughly cowed as the tutor might have wished. In a notebook containing the "Acts and Judgments of the President and Tutors of Yale College" [21] for the years 1752–58 there is an entry that records what one must consider a salutary event in Stiles's career:

At a Meeting of the President and Tutors of
Yale College Jan. 21. 1752

Whereas last Evening, before Nine o'Clock, there was a considerable Noise in Spalding's Chamber, and Mr. Stiles, who was with sundry Gentlemen in the Room below, sent up a Freshman and ordered the Noise to cease. Not long after which the Noise was more violent than before; whereupon Mr. Stiles went up and found Goodrich, Wiggins and Spaulding with sundry other engaged in a disorderly Noise, and gave them a particular Reprimand, and peremptorily ordered them to be still.—They ceased for a few Minutes, and soon began again, but not long after they left the Chamber and rushed in an impetuous and violent Man-

20. Stiles records these honors in the Vita, the Autobiographical Fragment, and *Lit. Diary*, 2, 524. The texts of the orations are among his papers. The oration on Law was printed (*Oratio Funebris* . . . , New London, 1751).

21. Yale Univ. Lib.

ner down the Stairs, hollooing and jumping, 'till they came into
the Chamber over Mr. Hopkins, where they continued their
disorderly Rout, and by stamping and jumping brake down the
Plaistering in Mr. Hopkins' Chamber. Whereupon Mr. Hopkins
went up and ordered them to be still; but they continued their
disorderly Noise sometime; then went into the Room under
Mr. Hopkins, and made a horrible Noise by hallooing, screaming
and jumping. Mr. Stiles, being then in Mr. Hopkins' Chamber,
stamped in Order to silence them, yet they either heard nothing
of it, or if they did, contemptuously disregarded it.

Upon which the Tutors went down, but with Difficulty stilled
them by their presence. And as the Tutors were coming down
Stairs, one of the Company halloo'd "put out the Candle," which
Mr. Stiles, when he came into the Room, ordered to be lighted
again; but none could be found, till one was ordered from the
adjacent Room.—When a Candle was bro't, Mr. Stiles ordered
one of them to hold it for him, till he had taken their Names:
Wiggins thereupon took the Candle, and while he held it, behaved in a most indecent and disrespectful Manner; which Mr.
Stiles reproved him for, but he would not cease, 'till ordered to
set down the Candle, nor even then. At the same Time Goodrich
and Spalding behaved with great Levity and Disrespect, by
smiling, laughing, Walking, odd Bowing &c. Mr. Stiles after
taking their Names, ordered them to be still, and tarry in that
Room, 'till he should send for them.

After Mr. Stiles was gone, they, instead of ceasing, went on with
the same disorderly Riot: and Spaulding shoved up the Window,
and halloo'd, "Who has any Thing to give the poor Prisoners."

After a little Space, the Tutors sent for them: and as they came
up Stairs jum[p]ing and hallooing in a violent Manner, so when
they came before the Tutors, they behaved with the utmost Insolence, Contempt and Disrespect—Wiggins, by appearing without any Gown or Hat, and by unseemly, disrespectful Gestures—
Spalding by odd Bowing, Stepping too and fro &c—Porter, who
appeared without his Wigg or Cap, stood back, picking Chips
and Barks from the Wood, and throwing them about Mr Hillhouse's Chamber; who, tho' reprimanded thrice by Mr. Hill-

house and Mr. Stiles, did not cease till ordered to another Place. Upon Examination, Mr. Stiles observing that such Disorders, if persisted in, must finally terminate in Expulsion, Spaulding said, "I dont much matter that."

After the Tutors had dismissed them, they gave them a special Charge to go to their Chambers, with particular Orders to avoid the like Noise for the future. Instead of which, some that were thus dismissed, went into Spaulding's Chamber, and continued the same unsufferable Noise. Whereupon Mr. Stiles went and informed the President of them as incorrigible. And during these Transactions, the Bell was frequently rung—

Upon Examination before the President and Tutors, it appeared that the Transactions before related were a series of violent, riotous, and rebellious Conduct, contrary to the Laws of this College, and in Contempt of the Authority thereof, and the express repeated Orders of the Tutors; a scandal to this College, and of very ill Example to other Students. And that Spaulding, Wiggins and Goodrich were the principal Actors in this Riot: and violated the express Orders of the Tutors 4 or 5 several Times.

And whereas the Students have been generally too much addicted to making a Noise; and there have been several Instances of such Riots heretofore, which have not been suppressed by lesser Punishments.

It is therefore considered by the President, with the advice of the Tutors, that the said Porter, for the Crimes beforementioned, particularly his contemptuous Behaviour towards the Tutors, shall be deprived, and he is hereby deprived of the Liberty of sending Freshmen, 'till the Spring Vacation: and all Freshmen are hereby prohibited from going any Errands for him, and from treating him with any more than civil Respect. And that Goodrich and Wiggins, for the Crimes beforementioned more especially for their being Actors in this Riot, for their repeated Violations of the express Orders, as well as disrespectful and contemptuous Treatment of the Tutors, be suspended, and they are hereby suspended, from all the Privileges of this College; and are hereby prohibited from coming within the Limits of the College Yard. And that Spalding, for the Crimes beforementioned, more especially his being a principal Actor in the Riot aforesaid, his repeated Violations of the express Orders of the Tutors, his disrespectful and contemptuous Treatment of them, his hallooing out at the Window, and for his making light of an Expulsion as before related, and for disrespectful Carriage towards the Tutors at other Times, be immediately Expelled.

On the face of it the tutors would seem to have had the last laugh, but the students doubtless knew that the sentence was not as severe as it seemed. In a Puritan community it had to be taken for granted that the flesh was weak, and misdemeanors must be forgiven when the offender showed a proper remorse. In less than three weeks all the culprits had confessed their wickedness in the college hall and returned to the fold without further penalty.

The episode was not an isolated one. The senior tutor's researches into the orbit of a comet, or the history of China, or the authenticity of the Scriptures, his correspondence with the learned world and with Abigail Sergeant were frequently interrupted by wild ringing of the college bell, students cavorting half-naked in the college yard, breaking the windows of Mr. Noyes's meetinghouse, and battling with the apprentices who were working on the new college house (begun in 1750 and not entirely finished until 1757). This was an inescapable part of college life, part of the price of being a tutor, and it took the edge off the somewhat grandiose vision of himself that Stiles was developing.

A more effective solvent of his vanity, however, was Uncle Abel, his father's younger brother, pastor of a church in Woodstock. Abel was an extraordinary man with a sharp tongue, a lively wit, and a full measure of the Bancroft temper. Ezra characterized him as "A man of little Stature, a most passionate, impatient and unhappy Temper—full of Fire Sarcasm, and Satyr which He dealt unmercifully to all around him especially Those who excited his Resentment." [22] If Ezra spoke ruefully, it may have been because Abel knew how to exercise his sarcasm and satire on his nephew's pretensions. Abel was extremely fond of the boy—it is a tribute to Stiles's human warmth

22. Memoir in the Edward Taylor Commonplace Book, belonging to Lewis S. Gannett.

that most people liked him in spite of his vanity—but Ezra knew that condescension would get him nowhere with Uncle Abel, who frankly told him "your College employment can give you but an imperfect Idea of human nature, compar'd with what you will gain elsewhere." [23]

In an obvious attempt to display his new learning Ezra wrote his uncle long accounts of his philosophical explorations, explaining Franklin's theory of thunderstorms and his own ideas about the orbit of Venus and the aurora borealis.[24] Abel politely read them but failed to show the expected admiration. "I am So terrestrial a Creature," he wrote back, "as to know but little about the Stars, tho I verily believe the smallest of them is Larger than a Lanthorn, and made for some other purpose than once in a while to Twinkle." He wished his nephew all happiness in his studies, but reminded him that "We are Creatures highly Indebted, Creatures dependent and accountable, and to act as such is a thing great and good." [25] He was not more explicit at this time, but as Ezra continued his studies, Abel wondered whether he was making the best use of his time. Perhaps Ezra had not explained how he hoped to prepare for a glorious future by acquiring as much learning as possible in this world; or perhaps he had, and Abel was not impressed. At any rate the uncle began to make his letters more pointed. "You mention," he wrote, "the pleasures of Literary acquisitions &c by which your accademic Life is rendered highly delightsome. I trust these pleasures are somewhat higher Than what are Called amusements," and he went on to warn his nephew against the enticements of mere literature, lest he have occasion to mourn on his deathbed, like the great Grotius, "Alas, I have Thrown away my life, in doing nothing with a Great deal of pains." [26]

Although his own experience in the ministry was troubled by dissension and schism in his church at Woodstock, Abel had his heart set on the ministry for Ezra. When the boy began to prepare for the bar, Abel made no attempt to hide his disappointment and brushed off all Ezra's attempts to defend the profession: "You yourself own the

23. Abel Stiles to Stiles, Jan. 1, 1754.

24. One letter, Feb. 20, 1749/50 is in the Stiles Papers, but Abel's reply (see note 25) refers to two more on the same subjects, dated Mar. 2 and Apr. 3.

25. May 1, 1750.

26. May 14, 1751.

Court is not only a busy but also a noisy Scene, and I wish you might keep Clear of That noise." [27] Evidently Ezra did not dare tell his uncle the real reason for his reluctance to enter the ministry and simply avoided the subject in his letters, endeavoring instead to get Abel started on the story of his own ecclesiastical difficulties. But Abel refused the bait: "To attempt an history of our affairs, would Swell, yea Burst the Belly of an Epistle—not Cadrus himself Could tell a Story more lengthy or more dull, Ergo I conclude the history, with not so much as beginning it." [28] Instead he supplied a few reflections on eternity, which differed sharply from the comfortable views that Ezra had developed.

It is hard to say how much Abel's persistence affected Ezra's final choice of a career. Certainly there were other forces compelling him to give up the happy combination of tutorial and legal life he was enjoying in New Haven. While he was fighting his way through skepticism, Yale was in the throes of a transformation almost as painful as his own, and in the end more disturbing to his peace of mind.

27. Feb. 12, 1753.
28. June 25, 1753.

7

The Calling

THE CHANGES that made Yale a less and less congenial place for Ezra Stiles in the 1750s were changes in New England more than in Yale. When Ezra entered college in 1742, his father was allied with Clap and Joseph Noyes in combating the follies and extravagance of the Great Awakening. Most of the ministers in New Haven County were with them, and the tide had turned against enthusiasm. But Clap and his friends were a little too successful; their repressive measures subjected the New Lights to a minor martyrdom which not only won them sympathy and support but consolidated them into a growing and highly effective political unit. As the first great wave of religious emotion subsided, their unconventional behavior subsided with it, and people who had been offended by James Davenport's ravings began to be attracted by the more orderly zeal which now appeared. Even in New Haven the New Lights grew so rapidly that the group which split from Joseph Noyes's church in 1742 won over a majority of the town by 1757.[1]

The Old Lights meanwhile, many of them at least, were taking the road to Arminianism that Isaac Stiles and his friends had begun to travel in 1745. The charges which the New Lights leveled against their opponents were a good deal better supported by 1752 than they had been ten years before.

These developments presented President Clap with a problem. He was close to the group that read the new authors in divinity and related to some of them by marriage, but he did not participate in their ses-

1. Bacon, *Thirteen Historical Discourses*, p. 236.

sions. He was and remained a rigid Calvinist. As the New Lights abandoned their more extravagant ideas and the Old Lights skirted closer to Arminianism, he came to see that there was less danger to orthodoxy from the New Lights than from the Old. He also saw that the growing strength of the New Lights would pose a growing threat to Yale, unless Yale could do something to win them over. Since they seemed to act in concert, they might make a general decision to send their children to the newly opened College of New Jersey, where New Lights were in control. If they did that and if they continued to grow, Yale might find itself without enough students to keep going. Clap had failed in an attempt to get the Old Lights of the middle colonies to send their children to New Haven,[2] and he could count on only a few boys from New York and western Massachusetts to supplement his Connecticut constituency. Moreover, it looked as though the New Lights would soon have a majority in the Connecticut Assembly. They already constituted so well organized a minority that the Assembly omitted the laws against them from the revised statutes of 1750.[3] If they gained control of the legislature, they might cut off Yale's annual subsidy from the state. For a variety of reasons, then, a rapprochement with the New Lights seemed desirable, and Clap told himself that by joining forces with them he might even persuade them away from the minor errors that they still espoused.[4]

The way he went about winning them was characteristic. Since 1746 he had been planning to establish a professorship of divinity (hitherto Yale had had no professors) and had set aside a small bequest for that purpose. Nothing further had been done about it until September 1752, when at Clap's behest the corporation voted to look for more funds. Though the Assembly refused assistance, one Gershom Clark of Lebanon, who died two months after the corporation's decision, left a sum amounting to £33 10s. sterling to help endow the chair. The corporation then named one of their number, the Reverend

2. Dexter *Biographical Sketches*, 2, 72. L. J. Trinterud, *The Forming of an American Tradition* (Philadelphia, 1949), p. 136.

3. George C. Groce, "Benjamin Gale," *New England Quarterly*, *10* (1937), 701.

4. On Clap's reasons for joining the New Lights, the best analysis is some loose Latin notations in the Stiles Papers, probably written at the time of Clap's death. These are much more explicit than "The Literary Character of President Clap," which Stiles wrote as an obituary at that time, and of which there are several copies in his papers.

Solomon Williams of Lebanon, as professor of sacred theology, his duties to begin as soon as there were funds to support him. The action was premature, since there was still not nearly enough money; but it showed what Clap was up to, for Solomon Williams was a New Light. He was, to be sure, a moderate: he had been instrumental in persuading James Davenport to recant and apologize for his errors; he had espoused liberal views of church membership; he got along well with the Old Light majority of the Yale Corporation. He was, nevertheless, unmistakably a New Light.[5]

Clap's strategy was not difficult to discern. By appointing Williams to the professorship he might heal the breach. With one of their own number in the professorial chair, the New Lights in the Connecticut Assembly might exert themselves for a state grant to complete the endowment. At the very least they might open their own pocketbooks, and surely they would continue to send their sons to Yale. Even Ezra Stiles was impressed by the president's statesmanship: but when he told his uncle about it, Abel was unimpressed. "You seem to speak with pleasure Concerning the Gentleman Elected Professor," Abel wrote him. "You tell me you Imagine the Choice to be very politic and Judicious—and now I'll take my turn at Imagination, for I Can Imagine and do Imagine, the Issue of that Election will be little more than Imagination." [6]

Abel was right. The Assembly again refused to appropriate money for the professorship, though it authorized a voluntary collection in the churches of the colony.[7] The Assembly had apparently lost confidence in the orthodoxy of Yale College. At a corporation meeting on

5. On the establishment of a professorship of divinity at Yale and the controversy that followed, see Dexter, *Biographical Sketches*, *2*, passim; Bacon, *Thirteen Historical Discourses*, pp. 211–42; Shipton, *Harvard Graduates*, 7, 41–44; Groce, "Benjamin Gale," pp. 697–716; and James H. Trumbull, "The Sons of Liberty in 1755," *New Englander*, *35* (1876), 299–313. The contemporary pamphlet literature of the controversy is voluminous and may be found by consulting Evans's *American Bibliography* for the appropriate years, under the names of Thomas Clap, Thomas Darling, Benjamin Gale, John Graham, and Noah Hobart. Some of the literature is analyzed in Lawrence C. Wroth, *An American Bookshelf, 1755* (Philadelphia, 1934). See also Edmund S. and Helen M. Morgan, *The Stamp Act Crisis: Prologue to Revolution* (Chapel Hill, 1953), pp. 220–37.

6. Abel Stiles to Stiles, Feb. 12, 1753.

7. Dexter, *Biographical Sketches*, *2*, 321. Corporation Records, Nov. 21, 1753. C. J. Hoadley, ed., *The Public Records of the Colony of Connecticut . . . 1751–1757* (Hartford, 1857), p. 213.

November 21, 1753, President Clap outlined a new strategy to recover Yale's reputation. His proposal must have caused a few gasps: the trouble, as Clap saw it, was the preaching of the Reverend Joseph Noyes, whose sermons the scholars attended every Sunday and who was sitting before the president recording the minutes of the meeting. How could Yale's reputation be restored? The professor of divinity, when he should be installed, would not only lecture to the students, but would preach to them on Sundays in the college hall. Since it was imperative to withdraw them from harmful influences at once, there would be no further waiting for funds; the president, assisted by the members of the corporation, would assume the duties of the professor until funds sufficient to support the office could be collected. Clap did not shrink from the implications of his action: he intended to set up the college as an independent congregational church.

As further evidence of Yale's concern for orthodoxy, Clap had the corporation pass a series of resolutions signifying their own adherence to the Westminster Catechism and Confession of Faith and the Saybrook Platform. They also voted that all future officers of the college, including fellows of the corporation, should make a similar subscription. And if any should subsequently depart from these doctrines, he should be obliged to resign his post.[8]

Thanks to the force of his arguments and of his personality, Clap was able to push his measures through the corporation, but his gesture of peace toward the New Lights had taken the form of a declaration of war on the Old Lights. He had outraged several members of his corporation, especially the two senior members, Noyes himself and Jared Eliot, who from here on fought him bitterly. Eliot, the minister of Killingworth, who had become a good friend of Ezra Stiles, was perhaps the most distinguished member of the corporation, with an international reputation for his agricultural experiments.[9] Eliot also brought to the lists his peppery son-in-law Benjamin Gale, a Killingworth physician, who became one of the most indefatigable controversialists of eighteenth-century Connecticut. Though Gale was not a member of the corporation, he was influential in Connecticut politics and an ardent writer of inflammatory pamphlets and letters to the newspapers.[10]

While alienating the Old Lights through his intemperate attack on

8. Dexter, *Biographical Sketches*, 2, 321–22. Corporation Records, Nov. 21, 1753.
9. Dexter, *Biographical Sketches*, 1, 52–56.
10. See Groce, "Benjamin Gale."

Noyes, Clap at the same time went out of his way to offend another group hitherto friendly to the college. Just before removing the Yale students from Noyes's church he declined a request by Ebenezer Punderson, the minister of New Haven's recently erected Anglican Church, to permit his two sons (students) to attend Sunday worship in their own church instead of in the Congregational church with the rest of the college.[11] Ever since the great defection of 1722 Yale had always had a few Anglican students, and had enjoyed great benefits from Anglican gifts, such as those from Bishop Berkeley. Ezra Stiles in soliciting gifts from England had made much of the catholic spirit prevailing at Yale: "Though our College is not upon the Episcopal Establishment," he wrote to Francis Ayscough, a prominent Anglican divine, "yet the Sons of Churchmen and Dissenters are admitted with equal Freedom: and I hope we entertain an unbigotted, generous, and benevolent Esteem and Veneration for the Virtuous Character of every Denomination."[12] Clap had now given the lie to these statements. Though Anglican threats of an appeal to England forced him to reverse his decision a few months later, Yale could look for no further support from Anglicans.

All these measures might have justified themselves, from a tactical point of view at least, if they had won over the New Lights, and if the New Lights had proved as powerful a force as it had seemed that they would. As it turned out, Clap was wrong on both counts. The New Lights did eventually gain control of Connecticut politics, but not until 1766, when Yale was all but ruined. Clap underestimated the continuing strength of the Old Lights; in fact his attack on Noyes furnished the occasion for a resurgence of their power. The first gentlemen of New Haven, men like Jared Ingersoll, Thomas Darling (Stiles's former tutor and Noyes's son-in-law) and John Hubbard (who had served his apprenticeship as a physician with Eliot) joined together to harass the president, and cooperated with Benjamin Gale, who was filling the book shops with pamphlets against Clap. In 1755 Gale and his associates persuaded the Assembly to withdraw the annual subsidy paid by the state to Yale. Clap thus brought on the very evil he sought to avoid.[13]

11. Punderson to Clap, Nov. 3, 1753. Clap to Punderson, Nov. 5, 1753. See L. L. Tucker, "The Church of England and Religious Liberty at Pre-Revolutionary Yale," *William and Mary Quarterly*, 3d ser., *17* (1960), 314–28.

12. May 9, 1751.

13. Dexter, *Biographical Sketches*, 2, 356–58. Morgan, *Stamp Act Crisis*, pp. 225–27.

His New Light friends made no attempt to protect him, because
they were not his friends. They had not forgotten his treatment of
Brainerd and the Cleavelands, and his ostentatious change of heart
left them cold. After all, if he believed what he said, why did he retain such suspicious characters as tutors, Isaac Stiles's son for example?
Why indeed? Ezra later recorded in a memorandum his opinion that
"the New Lights would not for a long Time believe the President
that he was sincere because he had Arminian nay Arian Fellows and
Tutors." [14] Stiles neglected to mention that he was talking about
himself.

Stiles's view of Clap's measures was tempered by his feeling of
gratitude toward the man who had befriended him during his undergraduate days and then made it possible for him to continue his studies
as a tutor, even while under the cloud of Arminianism. Perhaps because Clap's own religious beliefs had not crystallized completely
until the age of twenty-five [15] (and, as he boasted, never changed
since), he was wise enough to let young men like Stiles, who was
still in his twenties, find their way through the skepticism of youth
and kind enough to protect them while they did. Stiles never forgot
the debt. When Clap died, he wrote his friend Chauncy Whittelsey,
"You and I knew him perfectly—he was once a good friend to us.
From 1742 to 1752 I found him my best friend tho' upon his political
Conversion his love waxed cool, yet I still honour the Memory of my
once Maecenas." [16]

It was impossible, then, that Stiles should become an enemy to the
president, yet his sympathies in the dispute unquestionably lay with
the Old Lights. Joseph Noyes had been a good friend too during
his years in New Haven, and Stiles's theological views were much
closer to Noyes's than to Clap's. For as long as possible Stiles tried to
straddle the widening rift and chafed at the exasperating futility of
the whole business. He knew that Clap was not really a New Light
but an old-fashioned Calvinist, and that his measures were dictated
more by fear of New Light hostility to Yale than by a genuine concern about Noyes's preaching. And yet, as far as Stiles could see,
Clap accomplished precisely nothing. True, there was no wholesale
exodus of Connecticut boys to the College of New Jersey, but Clap

14. *Itineraries and Miscellanies*, p. 6; notes dated July 10, 1761.
15. Stiles to Chauncy Whittelsey, Mar. 6, 1770.
16. Ibid., Mar. 7, 1767 (begun Jan. 20, 1767). *Itineraries and Miscellanies*, p. 461.

scarcely deserved credit for that, because the New Lights continued
as hostile to him as ever. It merely showed that his fears had been
groundless in the first place.

As Clap moved relentlessly on his catastrophic course, Stiles was
desperately trying to conclude what he recognized as a phase of his
own intellectual development. By 1755, when it seemed impossible to
continue longer at Yale, he had still not finished. Though he had
reached a satisfactory conclusion about the authenticity of revelation,
he did not view the divinity of Christ in quite the orthodox Athanasian
sense. For that reason the law still seemed the most appropriate
career, but people continued to seek him for the ministry. In 1751 he
had refused a call to the church at Kensington.[17] The next year he received an overture from the Anglicans, who had been fishing successfully in New England's troubled waters ever since 1740. From their
point of view Stiles's reputation for Arminianism was not a liability;
catholicity was what they themselves espoused as firmly as he. Many
sober people had already turned to them out of disgust with the harsh
doctrines of the New Lights or the sordid squabbling between New
Lights and Old, and Ezra Stiles seemed a likely candidate, particularly after President Clap turned the whole dispute upside down.
With his growing repute in the learned world, Stiles would be as great
a conquest as Samuel Johnson had been in 1722.

The Anglicans' first try came in 1752 when Stiles undertook a trip
for his health to Newport, Rhode Island. Here he found Jeremiah
Leaming, an old college friend, who had been converted to Anglicanism while at Yale and was now ensconced as master of the Anglican
school at Newport and assistant pastor of Trinity Church. The pastor,
James Honeyman, had died in 1750, and since then Leaming had
been filling in for him, but the vestry had not offered him a permanent
appointment. Instead, when they heard of Stiles's visit, they instructed
Leaming to do everything possible to persuade him to take the post.
They knew that the Church, in the larger sense, had had eyes on Stiles
for some time, and this was an appropriate opportunity to capture him.

17. Holmes, *Life*, p. 23, says 1752, and so does the Autobiographical Fragment.
But the letters and notations on the subject in the Stiles Papers are dated Dec. 11, 13,
16, 1751. A transcription from the Kensington church records gives Dec. 11 as the date
when the church voted to offer him the post. In an almanac for 1751, now in the possession of Lewis S. Gannett, Stiles has noted Nov. 24, 1751, as the "first sabbath I
preached at Kensington." Though he later refused a permanent offer, he had evidently been willing to preach on trial.

It was appropriate because Stiles could not fail to be impressed by Newport, the largest city he had ever seen and unquestionably the most beautiful. It had mansions with landscaped gardens overlooking the sea and fine ships in the harbor, some just returned from every corner of the world and others ready to depart (what an opportunity for correspondence with foreign savants!). It had churches of every denomination, with none of the narrow, hemmed-in feeling of New Haven's religious landscape. It had gentlemen who knew the language of philosophy, gentlemen who had actually smoked their pipes and lifted their mugs with Bishop Berkeley, a name to conjure with, for Ezra Stiles at least. It had the Redwood Library, where a man could continue his education indefinitely. And Trinity Church! This Anglican congregation was the largest in New England and boasted a building which surpassed anything that Stiles had seen before, with its fluted columns and magnificent organ. Jeremiah Leaming conducted Stiles to the schoolhouse, dismissed the scholars for the afternoon, and told him how far they were willing to go in order to get him. They offered £200 sterling a year (his father's salary amounted to £40 sterling); and money was no object, for the Newport church was rich and they had formed so high an opinion of his abilities and reputation that they would not scruple any sum to get him. It was past midnight when the two men left the schoolhouse and Stiles went to lodge with Leaming. The next day, perhaps because he felt the temptation too strongly, Stiles left town, having first persuaded his host "that all his Art and Address and fine offers were ineffectual." At this time he was still much inclined toward deism, but he was sure that if any form of Christianity was true, it was not the Anglican form. All the same it was a flattering offer. He was proud of having received it and even prouder of rejecting it.[18]

A little more than two years later, when the Anglicans approached him again, he was more certain than ever that they were wrong, but he could not resist the temptation to toy with their proposal, or at least to show it a proper respect, as he told himself. They offered him the church at Stratford, vacated by America's leading Anglican, Samuel Johnson, who had just accepted the presidency of King's College (later Columbia) in New York. They would give him "£100 sterling per annum with a handsom Church and genteel Organ, and 1000 pretty Things besides as even to be a Bishop in America before I had done."

18. Autobiographical Fragment.

They stressed the disadvantages which the "extensive charity" of his religious views would place before him in a Congregational or Presbyterian church. When he told them that his charity would be too extensive for them too (he would preach that salvation was as readily attainable in Presbyterian as in Episcopal churches), they were only a little dismayed and continued to press him for an acceptance. The fact that they seemed to care so little about the substance of his religious views and dangled so many worldly honors and rewards before him confirmed his reluctance. On January 11, 1755, he returned a categorical refusal of the offer.[19]

After this final rejection of Anglicanism, Stiles felt that he was pretty firmly committed to a career at the bar. His friends evidently thought otherwise. When the Second Congregational Church in Newport lost its minister and wrote to Jared Eliot for advice about another, the old man immediately thought of Ezra Stiles, caught in the maelstrom at Yale and about to commit himself to the law. James Searing, who had preached at the Second Church until his death, had displayed the same dislike of bigotry that Eliot found in Stiles, and the Second Church liked it. Eliot used to visit Newport occasionally and knew the people there. In spite of any lingering heresies that Stiles might still have about him, Eliot was sure that he and the Second Church would hit it off. He wrote them both and waited for results.[20]

Stiles was reluctant. When the messenger of the church approached him, he agreed to preach for a couple of weeks in May, but said that he would go simply for the sake of the journey and out of respect for Dr. Eliot, with no real intention of settlement. Still, the letter he wrote to the church, like those he had written to the people at Stockbridge, suggested that he might change his mind if they persuaded hard enough.[21]

When he arrived in Newport the charm of the place struck him again with full force, and his own charm struck the Second Church. They were not disconcerted in the least when he preached to them on "The Excellency of the Christian Religion" without once men-

19. Ibid.

20. I infer this fact from the subsequent correspondence of Stiles with the committee of the Newport church (the letters are not in the Stiles papers), from the Autobiographical Fragment, and from Eliot to Stiles, Mar. 24, 1756.

21. Stiles to Messrs. Gardner, Chesebrough, and Wilson, the Committee of the Newport Second Church, Apr. 21, 1755.

tioning Christ. Though he could not explain to them his philosophy of the universe in a single sermon, they listened contentedly to his praise of moral virtue and his vision of eternity where the good man, apparently without assistance from the Redeemer, could "joyn in Society with superior Minds, the pure part of the Intellectual World: and with Them to contribute and communicate in a more extensive Manner to Harmony of the M[oral] World, during the innumerable Scenes of Being from thence to Immortality." [22] The Second Church could not have understood everything that Stiles meant by these words, but they must have recognized that by all the accepted standards the man was an Arminian—and yet they went out and decided unanimously to ask him to settle.

As he told it later, he was unmoved by the offer and still determined to continue at the bar.[23] But he was impressed by the unanimity of the vote, given in the face of a sermon that had fallen little short of deism. Instead of two weeks he stayed a month in Newport, employing himself with calculating the latitude of the place, inquiring into the history of the Narragansett Indians, composing sermons, and visiting the library, the stocking factory, and the shops. There were goldsmiths and silversmiths in Newport, and he was able to get half a dozen teaspons made for his mother, necklaces for his sisters, and a ring for Kate Saltonstall (not a gift—she gave him money for it).[24] He took advantage of Newport's trade with Holland to send off a letter giving his latest thoughts on electricity to Profesor Van Muschenbroek, the famous scientist of Leyden.[25] There was no doubt that Newport had its attractions, not the least of which was its cosmopolitanism and opportunities for communication with the world.

When he got back to New Haven, his friends gave him varied advice. His father said little but made it plain how much he hoped his son would take the job. He knew how his uncle felt, and many other "valuable friends" were pressing him to accept. He does not say who advised otherwise, but doubtless his legal friends wished him to stick with the law. He wrote Dr. Chauncy, whom he had met in Boston, and whom all his friends, Clap excepted, esteemed highly.

22. The sermon, dated Newport, May 11, 1755, is in the Stiles Papers.
23. Autobiographical Fragment.
24. A notebook containing memoranda and a journal of the trip is in the Stiles Papers.
25. May 28, 1755.

Chauncy's concern with morality resembled his own, and Chauncy urged him on moral grounds to accept, the temptations of the ministerial life being not "so powerful, nor so dangerous to Virtue, nor so apt to corrupt the Moral Sense," as those of a lawyer. Stiles in reply offered his own opinion of the clergy in "the holy Land of New England," who were more corrupted in the moral sense and preached doctrines more dangerous to the morals of a people "than either the Temptations of a Lawyer, or his most flagitious Practice." But Stiles was weakening. By the time he decided to try another visit to Newport in July it was really just a question of salary.[26]

The Church had offered him £1,000 a year, Old Tenor, which amounted to little more than £50 sterling, and in the course of continued depreciation might mean less. Moreover, they did not propose to contract for this amount but merely recorded the offer as a vote of the church. His legal training made Stiles suspicious of so infirm an agreement, and though he realized that a pastor's relations with his congregation would be ruined if he had to collect his salary in a law court, he thought it only proper that the Church should make a more binding agreement. At present he was a bachelor and the £1,000 might support him, though barely, but if he married and raised a family it would not be nearly enough, and his health would not permit him to undertake extra employment. Besides, one attraction of the ministry was the leisure it afforded for further study. Without a sufficient salary there would be no leisure.

He must have thought wistfully of the £200 sterling that Trinity Church had offered. Chauncy told him that he could always return to the law as a last resort, but he knew that it takes time to build up a practice and to build one's own skill. Six or eight years hence, with greater financial commitments, it would be too late to break away from one career and begin another. In a quandary he wrote letter after letter to the Church and threw them aside unsent.[27] Finally, late in July, he made another trip equipped with commissions which his family and friends wished him to undertake for them in the big

26. Autobiographical Fragment. Stiles to Chauncy, July 20, 1755. Neither Stiles's original letter nor Chauncy's reply is in the Stiles Papers, but the letter of July 20, written from Newport, rehearses the former two.

27. But he characteristically kept them. See the drafts of letters to the committee and to Gardner, Chesebrough, and Ellery individually, dated June 25, and July 11, 1755.

city ("get Cagg of Claret also get 3 lbs. of Spermaceti, if not above 30/ per pound"). The congregation showered him with attentions. Ex-governor Ellery presented him with a bound copy of Dr. Mayhew's sermons (a suggestion, perhaps, that Mayhew's views, which resembled Stiles's in their liberality, were acceptable to the Second Church). They took him to visit Fort George; they took him to "La belle Assemblée" in the Redwood Library, where Henry Marchant and Ebenezer Flagg entertained him with "oratorical Rehearsals" in the best collegiate fashion. After he had preached to them four Sundays, the bargaining began, and on the twenty-third of August he agreed to come to Newport for a salary of £65 sterling a year plus wood (for fuel) and a house.[28]

Stiles's motives were varied: "partly my Friends and especially my Father's Inclination and Advice, partly an agreeable Town and the Redwood Library, partly the Voice of Providence in the Unanimity of the people, partly my Love of preaching and prospect of Leisure and Books for pursuing Study more than I could expect in the Law." [29] He went back to New Haven for commencement in September and resigned the tutorship he had held for six and a half years. His education at Yale had come to an end, but he had found a corner of the world where he might continue his intellectual and moral progress indefinitely, until he should be summoned to a higher sphere of activity, "in the pure part of the Intellectual World." Besides, Newport was an agreeable town.

28. Journal of trip to Newport, July–Aug. 1755.
29. Autobiographical Fragment.

8

Newport

NEWPORT was three or four times larger than New Haven, but it was more than size that made the town agreeable. Perhaps it was the magic of being on an island. Perhaps it was the attractive setting on a gentle slope that commanded a view of the harbor. Perhaps it was just the obvious aliveness of the place. You could stand on Long Wharf and watch it move, the forest of masts and spars weaving in and out, swaying easily, here a ship heading out under sail, there another letting down her canvas to dry after last night's rain, while her holds were filling with fish or candles or cheeses to be eaten or burnt a thousand miles away.[1]

Though New Haven commerce had begun to come to life before Stiles left, Newport put three or four vessels to sea for New Haven's one; and they went everywhere, to London, Africa, the West Indies, the Baltic, and every port on the coast of North America, wherever merchants or captains could find a chance to make goods change hands —it made no difference what kind of goods. Rhode Island did not produce enough to fill the ships of Newport. It was necessary to find places where men were too busy or too lazy to ship their own goods, do it for them, and bring the profits back to Newport.[2]

---

1. On Newport in the eighteenth century see in general Antoinette F. Downing and Vincent J. Scully, *The Architectural Heritage of Newport, Rhode Island* (Cambridge, Mass., 1952); Carl Bridenbaugh, *Peter Harrison, First American Architect* (Chapel Hill, 1949); *Cities in Revolt* (New York, 1955); Edward Peterson, *History of Rhode Island and Newport* (New York, 1853).

2. On the commerce of Rhode Island in the eighteenth century see James B. Hedges,

Some exchanges were especially profitable, like the hauling of rum (distilled in Newport from West Indies molasses) to Africa to be exchanged for slaves. This was a grim traffic, for the slaves were packed in the ships so closely that a 10 per cent loss from disease during the voyage was normal. Whenever an opportunity presented, they were liable to rebel, and one might read in the newspapers of wholesale slaughters at sea, when the captain and crew killed their profits in order to stay alive.[3] Occasionally, instead of taking the slaves to the West Indies, a ship would bring a cargo to Newport, and the inhabitants could go down to the wharf and buy a man as one might buy a horse.[4] It was not a common thing, but common enough so that there were many more Negroes in Newport than Ezra Stiles had ever seen in New Haven.

But Newport did not specialize in the slave trade. Her vessels were constantly probing for new opportunities, and found them not only in trade but in fishing and whaling. When war came, as the great French and Indian War did, shortly before Stiles arrived, the sailors mounted guns on their decks and tried their hands at privateering. You might walk down Thames Street and hear the auctioneer on one of the wharves crying the goods or the ship that some lucky captain had brought in. It might be *Le Semidore,* which Walter Chaloner captured in 1758, full of flour, wine, brandy, pork, candles, soap, and oil. At nearby Taylor's Wharf rode the *Defiance,* the brigantine in which he took her, with sixteen carriage guns and twenty-four swivels, recruiting men for another voyage: "All Gentlemen Sailors and Others, have now a fine Opportunity to distinguish themselves and make their Fortunes." Perhaps. Job Easton in a much smaller ship made fourteen captures in seven months, but Michael Ryan, in a four-months' cruise, came back empty-handed, with three men killed and two wounded.[5]

It was a risky business, but then so was every business. You might send a cargo on what looked like a good voyage and find yourself ruined because the market was glutted. You might go after whales

---

The Browns of Providence Plantation (Cambridge, Mass., 1952); on the commerce of Newport in particular see Bruce M. Bigelow, "The Commerce of Rhode Island with the West Indies before the Revolution," dissertation, 1930, Brown University.

3. *Newport Mercury,* Nov. 18, 1765.
4. Ibid., June 23, 1761; Aug. 24, 1762.
5. Ibid., Jan. 2, 1759; Dec. 13, 1762.

and come back with your barrels full in two weeks, or you might spend six months without so much as sighting one.[6] The sea itself might rise up and destroy you. But the stakes were high and the odds favorable. Though many a well-known name could be found in Newport's record of bankruptcies, the town itself was evidence that most voyages succeeded. The crowded shops on Thames Street or along the Parade were emblems of prosperity.

So were Newport's fine craftsmen. The cabinet-makers on Easton's Point could cut as tight a joint as the best of them and carve pineapples for gate posts, Corinthian pilasters, and twisted balusters. Silversmiths and pewterers promised to do their work as well as it could be done in London or Boston, and leather dressers would make a pair of buckskin breeches in the best Philadelphia manner. Watchmakers and clockmakers would keep clocks clean and in good condition for a dollar a year. There was even a "mathematical instrument-maker," one of Stiles's parishioners, who could fit a ship with a binnacle and compass and furnish her captain with a sextant to guide him as far as a man could go. And of course there were shipyards, ropewalks and sail lofts.[7]

Ezra Stiles loved Newport from the start, and in the twenty years he lived there he learned to know it well, not just as a matter of course, but deliberately. He paced off the length of the streets and made a map, on which he marked every building and every wharf. He knew that there were 888 dwelling houses (in 1761), that there were 439 warehouses and other buildings, 16 stills, 6 windmills, 177,791 superficial feet of wharf, 3,780¼ tons of vessels, 77 oxen, 353 cows, 1,601 sheep. He knew how many ships belonged to the town and who owned each of them. He knew the exact distance between all the principal points.[8]

He came to know the island almost as well as the town. It was a delight to ride through—he bought a horse on his first trip to Newport—and he often did so, on errands of one sort or another, to accompany parting visitors on the way, or simply for the fun of it.

6. Ibid., Oct. 5, 1762; May 15, 1769.

7. Carl Bridenbaugh, *The Colonial Craftsman* (New York, 1950), pp. 81–82, 86, 94–95. Downing and Scully, *Architectural Heritage*, pp. 72–85. Advertisements in *Newport Mercury*, passim.

8. Notes made Sept. 13, 1761, and other undated notes. *Itineraries and Miscellanies*, pp. 40–41. Downing and Scully, p. 29.

Everyone who came to Aquidneck (the island of "Rhode Island") admired the rolling open fields with cattle grazing winter or summer and hay stacked in picturesque mounds, the trim stone fences and windmills, the well-kept orchards (Rhode Islanders drank a lot of cider), and the handsome groves of trees, resembling those planted on the great estates of England. Naturally and without design the island had much the same appearance that the English landscape gardeners were trying to create artificially. Aquidneck had estates too. Abraham Redwood, who had made a fortune in the West Indies trade and endowed the Redwood Library before he was forty, had a country seat with extensive gardens and artificial ponds and a German-trained gardener to watch over greenhouses filled with exotic tropical fruits. Closer to town, near Easton's Point, Godfrey Malbone presided over a red stone mansion that commanded a sweeping view over terraces, gardens, and canals down to the town and harbor beyond.[9]

There had been nothing like this in New Haven, and though Stiles was never as impressed as his father by mere wealth or social rank, he was fascinated by men like Redwood and Malbone, who had been spectacularly successful in business without losing their humanity. Malbone had been at sea for most of two decades, from his twentieth to his fortieth year, and when he came ashore to stay he was worth about £50,000 sterling. Once when he and Stiles were walking through his gardens, he told the young minister that the country place had been a kind of whim, a whim which Stiles calculated at between £3,000 and £4,000 sterling, exclusive of the land.

There was something grand about whims on this scale; and when Malbone died in 1768, Stiles wrote an account that expressed much of what he felt about Newport. The Colonel, he wrote—for that was the title Malbone had preferred—

> spent the most of his Time at the Coffee House, which he always left late in the night or rather after midnight. His constant manner was to walk from his seat to Town in the Morning, take a

9. On the appearance of the island and of the Malbone and Redwood estates see Carl Bridenbaugh, ed., *Gentleman's Progress: The Itinerarium of Dr. Alexander Hamilton, 1744* (Chapel Hill, 1948), pp. 101–03, 150–58; James Birket, *Some Cursory Remarks*, ed. C. M. Andrews (New Haven, 1916) pp. 26–31; descriptions by Robert Melville and Arthur Brown in *Rhode Island Historical Magazine*, 6 (1885–86), 42–47, 161–73; and article on Redwood by Edith R. Blanchard in *Dictionary of American Biography*.

Turn along the Street, take Snuff and inquire News, and turn
into the Coffee House. Perhaps another airing in the Afternoon,
when he took his Seat for the Evening, he was greatly addicted
to Cards and Gaming, and yet was no Artist: he delighted in
midnight meat suppers at which he ate heartily, and with no
Injury. At two or 3 o Clock in the Morning his Servant lighted
him home with a Lanthorn, when he walked a Mile to his Seat,
generally with his Jacket unbuttoned and open Breast. He seldom slept more than three hours in Twenty four, and often not
above two. . . . And as he died in seventy Third year of his
Age, it is supposed and often remarked that he has been awake
more Time than any man living in the World. . . . He was
of a firm Constitution and an easy Mind, he was perfectly well
natured and pacific, never engaged in Broils and always promoted
Peace and gentlemanly Harmony. Even Cards and Ill Luck
seldom broke in upon the constitutional Disposition to good
nature, peace and Tranquility. Let him have Coffeehouse Company, his Cards, Bottle, Snuff and a good supper and it was the
summit of his Desires his Elysium. He loved to hear news and
chat a little upon Politics and the Church: his Connexions fell
among those that were high in both, but in general it was indifferent to him whether Pompey or Caesar ruled the World. And
had it been in his power, he would have never trespassed on the
happiness of any, would have made all the World happy, if leaving them to their own Desires and Liberty could have made them
so. He would have made the most gentle, easy, human and merciful King upon Earth.[10]

If there had been nothing like Malbone's estate in New Haven,
neither had there been men like Malbone. In fact, the whole atmosphere of Newport was typified in the Colonel's easy tolerance.
Perhaps history had made the difference, for while New Haven was
settled by the orthodox and continued to worry about orthodoxy,
Newport was settled by heretics; and the right to heresy somehow
survived, so that now there were ten different churches, whose members mingled with each other on amiable terms. The minister of the
Second Congregational Church could visit a pillar of the Anglican
Church like Malbone, or walk about the streets with the Chuzzan

10. Stiles Papers in the library of the New Haven Colony Historical Society.

of the Jewish Synagogue, and no one was scandalized. What was more, the minister of the Second Congregational Church could be a young man with slightly unorthodox views, still not quite recovered from an attack of deism.

The spirit of tolerance extended well beyond religion. Newport had a dancing assembly—something New Haven was still not ready to tolerate twenty-five years later—where young ladies and gentlemen learned the pleasant rituals appropriate to their station in life.[11] A few years after Stiles arrived, traveling theatrical companies began to appear, and instead of the frowns that would have greeted them elsewhere in New England there was "universal pleasure and satisfaction" in Newport.[12] In 1769 The Beggar's Opera was performed (with a one man cast!) at Mary Cowley's assembly room.[13] Spurs for fighting cocks were sold at a store belonging to a member of Stiles's congregation.[14] A game of cards could always be had at one of the fifteen or twenty taverns. Horse races were common, and once there was even a kind of circus.[15] Jacob Bates, who traveled through the colonies in the seventies giving exhibitions somewhat like those in our wild-west shows, appeared at Newport in 1773, whereupon Christopher Gardiner, a local boy, got up a similar show, performing "on one, two, and three horses, nearly all the parts which were exhibited here by the celebrated Mr. Bates." [16]

On some occasions everyone broke loose in festivity—election day, or the king's birthday, or especially when news of a great victory over France arrived. Then the bells would ring and the cannon fire all day long. In the morning there might be a thanksgiving sermon by Mr. Stiles, hurriedly composed for the occasion, in which, though he might warn against rioting and intemperance, he would close with an appropriate benediction from the words of the wisest of preachers: "Go thy Way, eat thy Bread with Joy, and drink thy Wine with a merry

11. Rhode Island Historical Society, *Collections 23* (1930), 56–59. *Newport Mercury*, Oct. 28, 1765 and passim.

12. *Newport Mercury*, Nov. 3, 1761.

13. Ibid., Sept. 4, 11, 1769.

14. Advertisement by Jacob Richardson, *Newport Mercury*, June 26, 1759.

15. Ibid., Dec. 23, 1765.

16. Letter of William Ellery, Nov. 14, 1773, quoted in Edward T. Channing, "William Ellery," *The Library of American Biography*, ed. Jared Sparks, 6, 103–04. Peterson, *History of Rhode Island*, p. 62.

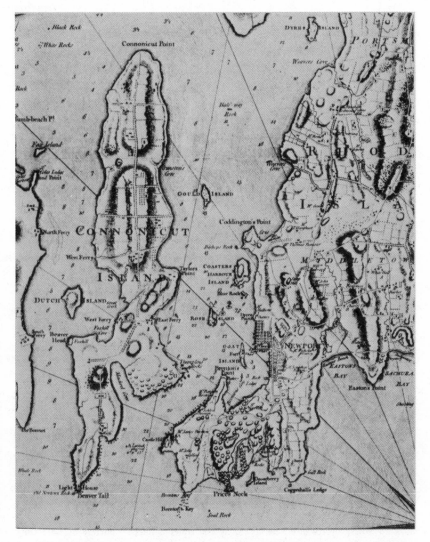

1. Newport and Vicinity, 1777, from *A Topographical Chart of the Bay of Narraganset*, by Charles Blaskowitz.

2. Ezra Stiles, age twenty-nine, 1756, by Nathaniel Smibert. Courtesy of Yale University Art Gallery.

Heart; for God now accepteth thy Works." [17] As the afternoon wore on, there would be many merry hearts; and by evening the town might begin to look as though the conquering army had arrived, with guns and pistols resounding through the streets, sky-rockets taking off everywhere, and knots of celebrators weaving drunkenly down Thames Street and hanging on the posts that lined the sides.[18]

Neither Stiles nor most other Newporters approved of these excesses, but they were part of the general light-heartedness of the place, a light-heartedness that found more innocent expression in the continual outings and excursions that the young people organized. There was always the possibility of a picnic in the country with saddle horses or coach, and frequently a ship from southern waters would arrive with the makings for a "turtle feast" on Goat Island, lasting far into the night, the whole company singing as they sailed back across the harbor and serenaded each other home through the streets.[19]

It would have been hard not to like these people, and Stiles was all but carried away by them. He had never taken delight in mortifying the flesh, but he now began to let himself go as never before. He bought a wig; he bought lace to add to his jacket; he bought gold buttons; and a cobbler in his congregation trimmed his pumps with fur as a gift. When one of the best painters then practicing in America, Nathaniel Smibert, came to Newport, Stiles sat before him in three sittings and paid him two guineas for a portrait, from which he looks out upon us very much the successful young man, dressed in a robe of yellow brocade—perhaps the one donated to him by the admiring ladies of the congregation.[20]

There had been admiring ladies in his life before, and his own

17. Sermon dated Oct. 15, 1759 (Thanksgiving day for victory at Quebec).

18. *Newport Mercury* Aug. 14, Oct. 23, 1759; Sept. 21, 1762. On the appearance of Thames Street see George G. Channing, *Early Recollections of Newport, R.I.* (Newport, 1868), pp. 242–43.

19. Ibid., pp. 155–57. Letter of Sam. Freebody, Dec. 23, 1752, *Magazine of American History*, 6 (1880), 455. Arthur Brown in *Rhode Island Historical Magazine*, 6 (1885–86), 173.

20. This paragraph is based on annotations in almanacs belonging to Mr. Lewis Gannett (hereafter referred to as Gannett Almanacs) and on a brief journal of Stiles's first months at Newport, Stiles Papers, in which are listed both disbursements and gifts. He acknowledged the gift of a gown in a letter dated Oct. 22, 1755. On the Smibert portrait see H. W. Foote, *John Smibert, Painter* (Cambridge, Mass., 1950),

admiration for Abigail Sergeant had even led him to hint about marriage. But as long as he remained a tutor at Yale, he probably considered his career too unsettled to do more than hint. In Newport, however, he had found his niche, and the church had agreed to build him a house, with the expectation, no doubt, that he would find a wife to live with him in it. During his first year at the new job, while boarding with Mrs. Searing, the widow of the former pastor, Stiles watched the house go up on Clarke Street, opposite his church. On June 2, 1756, he noted in an almanac, the house was "raised," and in the following months he recorded the successive stages of its completion: July 10, it was covered; August 10, chimneys finished; September 29, two chambers plastered; October 23, bedroom and hall; October 29, kitchen and "keeping room," November 2, entry (and on November 16, five barrels of cider stored in the new cellar); December 14, cellar cleaned and partitions made; December 29, keeping room and bedroom primed; January 4, 1757, kitchen primed.[21]

Long before the house was finished, Stiles had picked out the girl he wanted to bring there. Abigail, who was not one to dally with laggard lovers, had married again long since; but before he had left Yale, Stiles had been paying visits to Elizabeth Hubbard, the daughter of his friend, Colonel John Hubbard, a New Haven physician. The gay young girls of Newport did not make him forget her, and he may have recognized that Elizabeth Hubbard was the right woman to keep him on the track in this heady new environment. She was more sober than most Newporters but not offensively so, pious but not sanctimonious, meticulous in honoring the distinctions of this world but scornful of those who thought—in case her future husband should —that they could storm heaven in a wig and gold buttons.[22]

She was an Old Light, and her father had been a bulwark of the New Haven group in their stand against President Clap. She was a member of Joseph Noyes's church in full communion, but like most New Englanders she never felt a clear assurance of salvation and worried about it all her life. With Ezra Stiles she shared the view that all religion was pretense if not accompanied by a virtuous life, and she took pains to make her own that way.

---

p. 273, and Josephine Setze, "Portraits of Ezra Stiles," *Bulletin of the Associates in Fine Arts at Yale University*, 23 (1957), 3–10.

21. Gannet Almanacs.

22. On Elizabeth Hubbard see *Lit. Diary*, 1, 563–65.

Elizabeth was no Abigail Sergeant. She had no urge to move in a man's world, no talent for pulling strings behind the scenes. Though she had learned much about medicine from her father—very useful for the wife of a minister, who must constantly be visiting the sick—she had no curiosity about the learned matters that occupied a Yale tutor. Even simple arithmetic she found too tedious to endure, and her brother Leverett used to twit her about it. In a letter to Ezra ten years after her marriage Leverett wrote, "I suppose sister is still learning the multiplication Table. I would not have her discouraged, she will get through by the time she is 50 or 60." [23]

The courtship was a long one. The only surviving letter from Ezra to his future wife was written in January, 1755, two and a half years before the marriage and quite obviously before he had learned that she did not share his scholarly tastes. The letter is about the moon and its effects—not on lovers but on the tides. The only sentiment is packed into the opening "My Dear" and the closing "Your affectionate Philosopher." [24] It was hardly the sort of thing to sweep a girl off her feet, and perhaps Ezra's denseness in perceiving that astronomy was not the way to Elizabeth's heart had something to do with the length of the courtship.

However that may be, by the time his house was finished she was ready to marry him. The wedding took place on February 10, 1757, apparently in Newport, for it is recorded in the town records there. On March 8 they began housekeeping (presumably having traveled or boarded with Mrs. Searing until then).[25] A week after they moved in, Elizabeth's father wrote in a jocular vein to Ezra: "I suppose by this you have got to Housekeeping. I fancy a Journal of the first Week or two would be very entertaining." [26] No such journal has survived, but Stiles by this time had acquired a compulsion for jotting things down. Though he kept no regular diary until some years later, he could not refrain from scrawling little notations in almanacs or on folded sheets of paper that were later sewn together. Sometimes they were utilitarian, notes of how much he spent on this or that, who

23. Sept. 2, 1766, Stiles Papers, New Haven Colony Historical Society.

24. Jan. 18, 1755; in I. M. Calder, ed., *Letters and Papers of Ezra Stiles* (New Haven, 1933), pp. 1–4.

25. Gannett Almanacs. *Newport Historical Magazine*, 2 (1881–82), 214, gives the Newport record of the marriage. The vital records of New Haven do not record it.

26. Mar. 15, 1757, *Itineraries and Miscellanies*, p. 505.

owed him what sums of money and whom he owed. But often they were simply facts that he came across or measurements he had made, how many rings on a tree stump he saw, how tall the steeple of a church, how many sheep in New Haven, who came to town that day. Though in making these notes his home life was not his most consuming interest, he did record enough to give us a picture of the household economy of an eighteenth-century minister during the nineteen years he and Elizabeth lived in the house on Clarke Street.

The £65 sterling per year that he had bargained for was paid him in installments through the year by the deacons of the church. Unlike many ministers he never had occasion to quarrel with his church over this or any other matter. Though they never increased his salary beyond the original £65, he was able to get along comfortably on that. Even after his family grew and his expenses increased, he did not ask for more and thus avoided the rock on which many a pastoral relation foundered. His foresight in having the figure expressed in sterling was partly responsible, for every year the amount he received in the depreciating currency of the colony grew larger.[27]

Though his regular salary was his principal source of income, it was not the only one. Every time he married a couple he received a dollar or two as a wedding fee. Occasionally he undertook a little teaching, one or two boys at a time, probably to prepare them for college, as Isaac had prepared him and Timothy Edwards had prepared Isaac.[28] A more important supplement to his salary was the gifts with which the different members of his congregation showered him. He methodically recorded them in a special notebook,[29] with an estimate of their value, and was generally able to calculate at the end of the year that his total income had amounted to more than £100 sterling. The gifts varied from a quart of nuts to a suit of clothes. He was given a cow, a calf, a milking pail, a load of hay, a velvet cloak for his wife, a "Roquelo" coat for himself, a cradle for his baby, a cheese, a turkey, a side of beef, a bridle, a wig, a dollar, a guinea, a stiver, a pistareen.

Since his congregation included several merchants and sea captains, he occasionally had the opportunity to invest a little extra cash in one of their voyages. For example, in 1763 he sent fifteen gallons of spirits (presumably rum) to South Carolina and received 769 pounds of rice in return. Whether the family ate the rice or whether he sold it, he

27. He kept a record of his income in a separate notebook.
28. Gannett Almanacs.
29. Stiles Papers.

does not say. His most significant investment of this kind was in 1756, before he married. In that year he put a hogshead of rum (106 gallons) aboard a ship commanded by Captain William Pinnegar and bound for Guinea on the coast of Africa. Captain Pinnegar brought him back a ten-year-old Negro boy, to whom he gave the name "Newport." [30]

It might be supposed that a man who made a religion of morality would have found something wrong with the slave trade. To Stiles's discredit, as yet he did not. He was no more drawn to novelty in morals than in science, and though it would have been no great novelty to condemn slavery, few people in New England did. It was not uncommon for ministers to own slaves. His father did, and so did Jonathan Edwards.

Stiles's financial transactions might not altogether satisfy modern morality on some other accounts either. There was something of the gambler in him, though no more so than was common at the time. There is no evidence that he ever played cards, but he regularly bought tickets in lotteries, not merely those held in Newport to raise money for paving the streets or building a market but also in Boston, Philadelphia, and New Haven lotteries for similar purposes (lotteries were a regular method of financing public works). In a small way he also speculated in land. The dramatic multiplication of American population fascinated him, and like other shrewd investors he saw that it was accompanied by the rapid rise in value of land. The trick was to know which land would rise the fastest. Stiles bought for rather trifling sums, usually a few dollars apiece, proprietary rights of doubtful validity in a number of relatively unsettled areas, most of them in the region east of Lake Champlain claimed by Colonel John Henry Lydius. He also invested in the Susquehannah Company, an enterprise based on the assumption that the northern part of Pennsylvania belonged rightfully to Connecticut. Had the Susquehannah Company made good its claim (which it never did), his one and three-quarters shares would have entitled him to 8,565 acres. When his father died in 1760, he came into actual possession of thirty acres in North Haven, 100 acres in Harwinton, and 340 in Cornwall, which he rented to tenants.[31]

30. Journal of first months at Newport. Gannett Almanacs.

31. The records of Stiles's speculations are scattered through his miscellaneous papers; see especially the interleaved almanacs 1762–64, Yale Univ. Lib.; "Itineraries," *1*, 650–51; *Itineraries and Miscellanies*, pp. 183–84.

None of Stiles's investments was large, for he needed most of the money he earned to support the family that he and Elizabeth began to raise as soon as they were married. The first child, named for her mother but always called Betsy, was born April 17, 1758, and Ezra, Jr., followed on March 11, the next year. Thereafter Elizabeth bore six children in ten years: Kezia Taylor (named after Ezra's mother) on September 29, 1760; Emilia, April 21, 1762; Isaac, August 10, 1763; Ruth, August 20, 1765; Mary (usually called Polly) August 25, 1767; and Sarah, July 14, 1769.[32]

All except Sarah grew to maturity, an unusual record in those days. Their father meticulously noted their growth, first on a scrap of paper, then on some blank pages of Edward Taylor's commonplace book, and later in a diary. With his customary passion for measurement he weighed them at birth and took their heights and weights fairly regularly thereafter (they weighed between eight and nine pounds at birth, except for Kezia, 9¼, and Emilia, 10¼). On March 11, 1766, he weighed them before breakfast and after dinner, finding a difference of a pound or so, and then could not refrain from adding up the total weight of the six of them before breakfast at 223 pounds.

If we may judge from some sketches of the family made in 1781,[33] the children all had their father's long nose and slightly receding chin, a fact that must have proved no advantage to the girls. Ezra, Jr., with schoolboy humor described himself as "bearing rampant a pair of huge legs tho tolerably shaped a head for a crest coverd with a mop of hair part pendant and part couchant a mole skin with a nose that might well be taken for the broad sword of a Highlander." [34] Isaac, to judge by the picture, was somewhat better looking. A lock of his hair, tucked into the spine of Edward Taylor's commonplace book, is sandy red.

One is forced to discover the children from such scraps of information, because their father wrote down far less about them than he did about the transit of Venus or the aurora borealis or the Narragansett Indians. He was interested in seeing that they learned to read and

32. The records of the children's births are given in several places but most completely in the Edward Taylor Commonplace Book.

33. These are on two pages of the Literary Diary, formerly missing (see *Lit. Diary*, 2, 496) but recently restored through the generosity of Lewis Gannett. See Fig. 5.

34. Ezra Stiles, Jr., to David McClure, Feb. 17, 1778, McClure papers, Conn. Hist. Soc.

write, and probably taught them himself, but also sent them to different persons in Newport for instruction, usually in May. Once they
had learned to read, he started them in the Bible, a little each day,
and noted each time they read it through. He also read the Bible
to them during family prayers, which he conducted both morning
and evening. Indeed he and his wife and children all read the Bible
individually, collectively, and continuously. As soon as they finished
the New Testament, they began again with the Old.[35]

But apart from this and the regular measuring and weighing, Stiles
did not think it worth while to write down much about his children
or what they did. About himself he reported only a few statistics. In
1760 he measured 31½ inches around the waist. In 1766 his waist
measurement was the same, and he weighed 137 pounds.[36] Five years
later he was down to 128 pounds and seems to have remained rather
spare.[37] Conspicuously absent from all these figures is anything about
the weight or height or measurement around the waist or anywhere
else of his wife. Apparently Elizabeth drew the line at that.

Elizabeth came to her marriage well prepared to run the Stiles
household. She was only thirteen when her mother died, and she had
run her father's house from that time until he found a new wife, some
years later. At Newport she had the assistance of the slave boy and
usually of a maid servant (the turnover seems to have been pretty
rapid), and sometimes she hired a woman to do washing or a nurse
to care for the new baby during her lying in. As the children grew
older they were probably assigned chores, for it was a large household
and often made larger by guests. A minister was usually expected to
put up any fellow minister who happened to be passing through, not
to mention other dignitaries and numerous relatives. Newport being
an attractive town, and travel to and from it somewhat difficult by
reason of the island location, people often stayed several days when
they did come. Uncle Eldad Taylor might drop in for a week, or
Ezra's father for three.[38]

35. *Lit. Diary*, *1*, 555–56 and passim, and notations in the Bible (London, Baskett
and Baskett, 1744) originally belonging to Elizabeth Hubbard Stiles, given to Betsy
in 1785 and by her to Abiel Holmes in 1795. Now in the library of Lewis Gannett.

36. Edward Taylor Commonplace Book.

37. *Lit. Diary*, *1*, 174.

38. Gannett Almanacs, and almanacs in Yale Univ. Lib. The ensuing account of
household economy is based primarily on notations in these almanacs.

Though Newport was a good-sized city as cities went in the eighteenth century, and though the house on Clarke Street was near the
center of it, only a stone's throw from the courthouse, family economy
involved many activities that have since become associated with country living. There was a stable on the house lot, but the horse was often
put out in a rented or donated pasture. Stiles usually kept a cow at
home, had her served by a bull in September, and milked her until
a couple of weeks before she calved. In the spring he killed the calf
for meat, and since the cow gave more milk than the family used, he
sold a pint or two a day to neighbors.

There were butchers in Newport, but it was evidently the practice
to buy meat in what we would consider wholesale quantities and to
preserve it with salt or smoke. Every December Stiles noted the
killing of a hog or two, some of which he had fattened and some
of which he bought ready for slaughter. About December, too, he
would buy beef, as much as 500 pounds, and put a "round" of it up
the chimney to be smoked and then hung beside the gammons. From
time to time, and usually in large quantities, he also bought mackerel,
mutton, lamb, oysters, and fowl. As the meat was used and fat accumulated, along with ashes, there would be soap to make, a barrel
full at a time.

The Stileses bought cider in large quantities too, for they drank about
a barrel (20 or 30 gallons) a month. They also drank claret, metheg-
lin, rum (with limes), and tea—a pound of it every three weeks or
so. Flour came by the barrel and butter by the firkin or tub, 80 or 90
pounds at a time. They used about three-quarters of a pound of butter
a day in 1758, when there was only one child (an infant at that).
Sometimes they bought cheese, sometimes it was given to them, and
sometimes they had it made from the extra milk. A cheese usually
weighed about thirty pounds, and they ate about one pound a day.

They grew their own vegetables in great variety (corn, beans, peas,
cabbages, squash, cucumbers, beets, carrots, radishes, turnips, lettuce,
asparagus, onions, and parsnips), sowing several times between early
April and June. When the crops turned out well, Stiles was as proud
as any other gardener to be able to write "radish 11¾ Inches round"
or "Pulled Beet abo't 4 Bush." Like other gardeners too, he had his
troubles: on June 26, 1757, "Cow eat corn."

The house was heated by fireplaces. The Newport climate, because
of the proximity of the Gulf Stream, was somewhat warmer in winter

than most of the rest of southern New England, but even Newport could be very cold, as in the winter of 1765, when the ice was five inches thick at the end of Long Wharf and the harbor froze over except for a small opening. That winter the wood went fast, but in a normal year the Stileses burned about twenty-three cords, a cord a month even in summer (for cooking). The church furnished it all, in addition to Stiles's salary, and he sawed it, or had it sawed, and stored it in his cellar. The slave boy was doubtless kept busy bringing it up to the different fireplaces.

It was not an easy life, especially for Elizabeth, but it was secure and serene, with Ezra's salary coming in regularly, a cellar stocked with cider, a round of beef up the chimney, and a town full of friendly people. Stiles valued every part of it—the substantial comforts of a house of his own, an agreeable wife, a growing family. Another man might have immersed himself in the daily satisfactions of such a life, but for Ezra Stiles these were simply a happy condition that freed him for further exploration of the "moral and intellectual world."

9

A Library of Unwritten Books

WHEN STILES chose the ministry as a likely profession in which to continue his education, he chose well. In spite of eighteen or twenty pastoral visits every week and in spite of the hours required for preparation of sermons and lectures, he found time to indulge his curiosity in a bewildering variety of intellectual adventures. New Haven after thirteen years had lost much of the power to stimulate him that it once possessed, and the community's preoccupation with guessing President Clap's next move had become a major distraction. In Newport there were fresh minds to rub sparks off his own—hard, mature minds too instead of the adolescent ones he dealt with as a tutor. He reached out eagerly for the friendship of men who could tell him things he never learned in the Yale Library.

What the merchants, for example, had to say about the peculiar properties of rum started his mind working on the "philosophy" of the subject, by which he did not mean what a modern minister might be expected to. William Ellery, the former governor of the colony told him that rum stored in a cold cellar would lose its strength but regain it when placed in the sun. And some traders who took rum to Africa in 1756 found it below strength when they arrived, with oil floating on the top. They had to sell it at a discount, and they brought the oil home in bottles as evidence of the fraud committed by the distillers, who had discovered that a little oil added to diluted rum and mixed vigorously would raise the proof. When the spirits were allowed to stand for a time, the oil separated and the proof went down.[1]

1. Notes dated July 31, Aug. 15, 1758; Mar. 6, 1759.

Ezra Stiles, intrigued by these discoveries, though for different reasons than the distillers, carried their experiments further. He tried mixing other substances, some acid and some alkali, with rum, and found that some lowered, while others raised, the proof. He concluded finally that water and spirit have a mutual repulsion, or at least a weak adhesion, "so that in common Rum made of Water and the Spirit of Melasses, the Water is not impregnated with the spirit in a strong Union." Hence substances which have a strong repulsion to either spirit or water when added to rum will weaken or strengthen the apparent proof. Oil, for example, having a stronger repulsion to water than to spirit, will mix with the spirit and bring it quickly to the top, leaving the water below, "even if violently stired and mixt before the proof Glass is put in." "This," he concluded, "is the Philosophy of the Oyl and Rum." As for the philosophy of the sun on Governor Ellery's hogsheads, the heat expanded the spirit more than the water and thus raised the proof.[2]

Stiles, of course, had no interest in making things easier for dishonest distillers. He advised his merchant friends to develop a new type of proof glass that would draw fluid from both top and bottom of a barrel and thus prevent the use of foreign substances to bring the spirits to the top or the water to the bottom. In the course of his investigations he did discover a fact that troubled him a little, namely that the traders who took rum to the Guinea Coast made a practice of diluting it. He explained the philosophy of this too, but rather less satisfactorily: the practice, he noted, was so regular that the Negro buyers expected it: they bought the diluted rum "as we buy Punch; we dont buy punch for pure Rum; nor do the Traders sell dashed Rum for pure Rum: And indeed it is best for the Negroes that the Rum should be mixt with Water and adulterated." He must have recognized that this last argument smacked of hypocrisy, for he added as an afterthought, "Perhaps at first the Thing was a Fraud." [3] But that was as far as the thought went.

The ship captains and sailors were full of information for him. Who knew the world better than they? Captain Collins told him how sailors knew when shoals were near by the color of the water, long before the sounding line would touch.[4] He quizzed Captain Newton Cox

2. Ibid.
3. Ibid.
4. Notes dated Sept. 21, 1759.

about Quebec, and Captain Simon Newton about Surinam. They also explained to him how water which went bad at sea could be purified by putting an iron "crow" in it—another problem in "philosophy." [5]

There were always newcomers in Newport, people who had come to settle there or tourists up from the south to escape the summer heat, especially from South Carolina.[6] He pumped them for information about the southern colonies. James Lucena, from Portugal, could speak no English, and he and Stiles pronounced Latin so differently that they could not understand each other, but they made shift by writing out their remarks in Latin and thus Stiles discovered that deism had made strides in the universities on the Continent as well as at Oxford, which Lucena had visited before coming to Newport.[7] A Birmingham manufacturer who could not furnish all the information Stiles wanted about the English dissenters in his region went home with two pages of questions to present to the local ministers.[8]

Of course, his opportunities were not all so casual. Several young men of his congregation became his intimate friends and companions in intellectual adventures. William Vernon, a merchant who bought the house three doors from him on Clarke Street, was a man of broad interests, a big man in every sense (the indefatigable measurer even weighed him—199 pounds!). Stiles used to visit him often, and Vernon as a token of friendship and respect gave him a copy of Hippocrates. William Ellery, the son of the old governor, was another man of more than ordinary intellectual stature, and so was Henry Marchant, a lawyer, whom Stiles had first met on his journey to Philadelphia. Both became prominent political figures: Ellery was to be one of the signers of the Declaration of Independence and chief justice of Rhode Island; Marchant served as Rhode Island's agent in England in 1771–72 and as attorney general in 1771–76. Marchant, and probably Ellery and Vernon too, participated in a small group (the "social few") who gathered at the Stiles house of a Sunday evening, after their sabbath had ended, to pursue the pleasures of conversation.

A more formal group that met regularly for philosophical discus-

5. Notes dated Aug. 3, 1759, Aug. 13, 25, 1761.

6. Carl Bridenbaugh, "Colonial Newport as a Summer Resort," R.I. Hist. Soc., *Collections*, 26 (1933), 1–23.

7. Notes dated Nov. 1759.

8. Notes dated Mar. 30, 1762, of questions delivered to Jonathan Scott.

sions was the Redwood Library Company, which honored Stiles by making him librarian the year after he arrived.[9] This enabled him to get books whenever he wanted. If the library lacked a volume he needed, he already had experience in begging from well-disposed English patrons. Age did not deprive him of his brashness in this respect. And as if one library were not enough, he joined with other Rhode Island ministers to found an ecclesiastical library, for which he also begged. Once when he learned of a new book on the history of Hindustan, he wrote the author asking for a free copy for the Ecclesiastical Library, and in case the author could not comply, presented him with a list of nine questions he would like answered.[10]

His correspondence must have occupied a large share of his time. He kept in contact with most of his acquaintances in Connecticut, especially Jared Eliot, John Hubbard, Benjamin Gale, and Chauncy Whittelsey. In the Boston region his principal friends were Professor John Winthrop and Charles Chauncy; in Portsmouth, New Hampshire, Samuel Langdon, later president of Harvard; in New York, John Rodgers; and in Philadelphia, Francis Alison and Benjamin Franklin. The last was as often as not in London and probably furnished him with introductions to correspondents there.[11] He wrote letters in Latin to scholars at Copenhagen and Petersburg, sending them through Franklin or through Newport ship captains bound for the Baltic.[12] There are no answers to these among his papers, but there is a large correspondence with dissenting ministers in England and Scotland.[13] He plied them all with questions and frequently with requests for their publications. Sometimes they rebuffed him—Nathaniel Lardner thought some of his questions "too curious" [14]—but mostly they an-

9. Notes dated July 31, 1765. George C. Mason, *Annals of the Redwood Library* (Newport, 1891), p. 46.

10. Notes dated Oct. 30, 1766. Stiles to Nathaniel Lardner, Nov. 22, 1763, and various dates thereafter; to Alexander Dow, Dec. 27, 1769; and correspondence of various dates with John Barnard, Jared Eliot, Charles Chauncy, Samuel Chandler, and Catherine Macaulay.

11. Stiles to Franklin, Feb. 20, 1765.

12. Stiles to Mikhail Vasilievich Lomonozow, Jan., Mar. 1765; to Joseph Braun, May 1765; to the prefect of the University of Copenhagen, May 1765.

13. See correspondence with Nathaniel Lardner of London; Thomas Wright of Bristol; Philip Furneaux of Clapham, Surrey; James Stirling of Glasgow; and Patrick Cuming of Edinburgh.

14. Lardner to Stiles, Aug. 20, 1764.

swered patiently and added to the encyclopedic fund of knowledge
he was building.

To follow Stiles in his enthusiastic pursuit of fact is a bewildering
experience. Because his curiosity was so inclusive, not to say diffuse, his
learning took on a character which in the present age of specialization
must appear extremely miscellaneous. During his twenty years at
Newport he became one of the most learned men in America. One
often gets the impression in reading through the fragmentary but
enormous bulk of surviving papers that he was a monstrous warehouse
of knowledge, spreading his interests so widely and devoting so much
time simply to garnering information, that he left no room for his own
development. The impression is not wholly just, for all during this
period he was growing, both intellectually and morally, and he was
frequently able to bring his learning to bear on the problems of his
growth. But it is impossible to relate all his interests to his personal
development. His curiosity, justified by his philosophy of the universe, followed every path it came to (and so many paths began in
Newport!), and dissipated so much energy in the sheer joy of learning that there was little left for adding up the facts and reshaping
them into something larger for the world to read.

Stiles, in short, was one of those scholars who never cease to gather
materials for a book but cannot bring themselves to write it. Though
his reputation for learning remained enormous during his lifetime,
and deservedly so, he left behind a pitifully small number of publications to sustain it after his death. To understand the man and the
world he lived in, we must attempt to understand the many books
he did not write as well as the few he did. Though the range of his
interests was limited only by the quality of his imagination, it is possible to single out certain areas where he concentrated attention. The
relevance of these to what he found happening in eighteenth-century
America will become apparent in later chapters. For the moment we
may survey them simply as parts of the intellectual and moral world
which he explored for clues to the mind of their Creator and Director.
Here then are some of the books he failed to write.

The Temperature of North America

Benjamin Franklin may have been responsible for stimulating
Stiles's interest in temperature. Before leaving for London in 1757,
Franklin wrote a long letter on heat and cold to John Lining of

Charles Town, South Carolina, and sent Stiles a copy.[15] Franklin's observations were mostly concerned with the different capacities of various substances for conducting heat. Stiles answered with an equally long letter, in which he speculated on the possibility that cold might be a separate element and not simply an absence of fire. Both he and Franklin assumed fire to be an invisible fluid, capable of penetrating all bodies to a greater or lesser degree and thus accounting for different degrees of heat.[16] Stiles suggested that cold might also be such a fluid, "a species of subtle Matter that freely permeates Bodies, Fluids &c." As was often the case, Stiles was exploring one of the blind alleys of science, but his interest in the subject led him to a more fruitful study. Franklin, returning from London in 1762, brought him a good thermometer, and with it he began to keep a record of the temperature.[17] Dr. Thomas Moffat, a Scotch physician residing in Newport, had one too, and he and Stiles sometimes compared notes. After Moffat left town, another physician, John Bartlett, took his place, and Stiles gained a friend whose enthusiasm for recording temperatures equaled his own.[18]

The benefits to be gained from the simple but exacting task were real and obvious: a record of the temperature in a region would show what crops could be grown there and how long the growing season was. According to medical beliefs of the time, it would also show what symptoms of a disease might be expected to appear. Stiles published some of his early observations in the *Newport Mercury* with a plea to gentlemen in other colonies to make similar observations for a period of at least a year.[19] When Franklin returned to London again, Stiles asked him to persuade the Royal Society to spread thermometers among philosophical gentlemen all over the American continent.[20] Assuming that others would share his zeal, he also sent off letters to scientists in Europe, asking them to furnish him with observations from their localities.[21] Unfortunately neither the Royal Society nor the Euro-

15. Franklin to Lining, Apr. 14, 1757, copy enclosed in Franklin to Stiles, June 2, 1757. See Albert H. Smyth, ed., *The Writings of Benjamin Franklin* (New York, 1905–07) 3, 383–90.

16. Stiles to Franklin, July 12, 1757.

17. Franklin to Stiles, Dec. 19, 1762.

18. Bartlett to Stiles, Sept. 6, 1780. *Lit. Diary, 1,* 47.

19. *Newport Mercury*, Jan. 7, 28, Feb. 18, 1765.

20. Stiles to Franklin, Feb. 20, 1765.

21. Stiles to Lomonozow, Mar. 1765; to ———, at Surinam, Apr. 1765.

pean scientists thought it worth while to take up his project, but this did not deter him. For the rest of his life he made his readings and set them down or, when Betsy grew old enough, let her do it for him. There are six volumes covering the years from 1763 to 1795. They give the temperature at several different times each day, the direction of the wind, and usually an indication of whether it was fair, cloudy, raining, or snowing. Though Stiles never turned his observations into a book, they still constitute an extremely valuable record for students of meteorology.[22]

The Indians of North America

Stiles's interest in the Indians dates at least from his visit to Stockbridge. This was probably not the first time he had seen an Indian, but they were not common around New Haven. When he went to Newport for his trial sermon in May 1755, one of the memoranda he jotted down in his notebook was to remind him to inquire about the origin of the Indians then living in the Narragansett country across the bay from Newport. He got the answer too: they were descendants of the tribes which had remained neutral in King Philip's War. Arriving in Narragansett on a Saturday, he took time, before crossing to Newport, to visit the scene of the great Swamp Fight, "and got some Bones which we dug up out of the grave where numbers were buried." [23] After he settled in Newport, he used to take the ferry across the bay to visit the Indian villages, where he made a census (how many families, how many children, adults, widows), and drew diagrams of the wigwams and how the Indians placed the furniture inside them. He read about Indians in Hubbard's account of the Indian Wars, and in Oldmixon, and Ferdinando Gorges, and Johnson's *Wonder-Working Providence,* and he copied extracts about them from old letters and manuscripts. He asked friends in different parts of the country to collect information for him, especially missionaries in the western regions. Did the western Indians ever write, or record events by the use of characters? How many were east of the Mississippi? Were there any traditions of their having been more populous? Were their "Powaws" hereditary? Did they use idols? Jared Eliot thought he was too credulous in receiving information on these and

22. Stiles Papers.
23. Journal of trip to Newport.

other subjects from anybody and everybody, but Stiles did not necessarily believe everything he heard.[24]

By scooping up all the information he could, he at least avoided
one error made by a more conventional investigator. Thomas Hutchinson, in writing the *History of Massachusetts Bay*, recorded the ex-
termination of the Pequot tribe in the War of 1637. Hutchinson was
relying on contemporary accounts, and subsequent historians have
repeated his error in taking them too literally. Stiles was able to inform him that there were three hundred members of the tribe still living in 1765.[25]

Though he did not attempt to master the Indian languages, he
studied them enough to recognize that a squaw he met at Barnstable
spoke the same language as the Pequots he had talked with at Groton,
Connecticut.[26] Language was of interest not only as a key to the
identity of different tribes but also as a clue to their origin. Like others
of his time Stiles was intrigued by the possibility—though he dis-
counted it—that the Indians might be descended from one of the lost
tribes of Israel. When he heard rumors of an inscribed rock in the
wilderness somewhere between the Mississippi and the Atlantic Ocean,
he requested a missionary to obtain a copy of the inscription and to
record any legends or stories of the Indians about it. He also wanted
a rubbing of the stone in order to get the exact size and shape of the
characters, so that he could see whether they bore any resemblance to
Hebrew. He doubted that they would. If they did, it might prove that
the Indians were descended from the tribe of Judah that returned
to Babylon, not from the lost tribes, who would have used Samaritan
script rather than Hebrew.[27]

No one was able to find the inscribed rock for him, though he continued to make inquiries about it. When he heard of marked rocks
in the vicinity of Newport, he sought them out himself and found
some at Assonet and some on the shore at Job Almy's farm in Ports-

24. John Devotion to Stiles, Nov. 27, 1761. Stiles's notes on Indians are scattered
throughout his papers.
25. Stiles to Hutchinson, Jan. 8, 1765. Thomas Hutchinson, *The History of the
Colony and Province of Massachusetts-Bay*, ed. L. S. Mayo (Cambridge, 1936), *1*, 71.
26. *Itineraries and Miscellanies*, p. 169.
27. Stiles to Samuel Kirtland, Nov. 4, 1767. Eleazar Wheelock to Stiles, Jan. 19,
1768. David McClure to Stiles, Nov. 11, 1771. Stiles to ———, Dec. 28, 1771.

mouth. It was not easy to converse with Almy, who was deaf, but since Stiles was always armed with paper and pencil he contrived to write out his questions:

> Please to tell me how I may find the Rock markt with Characters in your Farm.
> Do you know any other?
> How long ago? 1762?

And then he recorded the kind of answer that antiquarians learn to receive with patience: "Cut it up for Whetstones and sent to Nova Scotia." [28]

There was another rock nearby, at Dighton, which still puzzles modern investigators. Stiles visited it but did not attribute the markings to the Indians, at least not to Indians of recent times. He thought they were probably Phoenician—the Indians, too, might be of Phoenician origin—but also considered the possibility of a Gaelic origin and wrote to England for information on Irish and Welsh palaeography.[29] Stiles's success in eliciting information from the Indians themselves was doubtless facilitated by the tolerance which he tried to maintain in all situations. Where an earlier generation of Puritans had been content to forbid powaws, he was ready to inquire into the details of the ceremony. The book he never wrote would have devoted a large section to the Indians' beliefs and tribal ceremonies, for he made copious notes on these subjects. He had, however, none of the modern anthropologist's zeal for the preservation of native cultures. He thoroughly approved of all missionary efforts and maintained that the Indians must be converted to the white man's way of living before they could be successfully Christianized. This had been the foundation of John Sergeant's scheme at Stockbridge, and Stiles found confirmation for it in the records of a similar experiment by the Jesuits

28. "Itineraries," 2, 345. See also *Itineraries and Miscellanies,* pp. 230, 233.

29. Stiles visited Dighton Rock in 1767 and carried on correspondence about it with several people in 1767 and 1768. See especially letters to John Winthrop, June 1, 15, 1767, to John Hubbard, July 31, 1767, and to Thomas Wright, Sept. 1, 1768. Cf. unaddressed letter, dated Dec. 14, 1792. Stiles believed that the American continent had been discovered several times before Columbus, and he constantly sought for remains and evidence of early visitors. The fact that he never mentioned the now famous Newport tower in surviving notes and correspondence would suggest that no one in his day attributed a Norse origin to it.

in Paraguay.[30] (Ultimately he changed his mind about this, but not because of any desire to preserve Indian customs.) The failure of the Indians to maintain their numbers he attributed to a combination of early promiscuity and an extreme disapproval of children born out of wedlock. The Indians showed him a place in Narragansett known as the bastard rocks, because girls disposed of their illegitimate off-spring there. The only way for the Indians to survive, he thought, was to establish Christian marriage among them. How rapidly they were disappearing he found by comparing the numbers of a census taken in 1698 on Cape Cod and one he took himself in 1762: they had fallen from 4,168 souls to 1,573 in sixty-four years.[31]

These figures, along with many other vital statistics, would doubt-less have appeared in any book by Stiles on the Indians, but they would also have been included, more impressively, in the following.

The Science of Population

Though Stiles was by no means the first person, even in America, to consider the growth and decline of population as a subject worthy of study, probably no other American before him studied it so assidu-ously or so objectively. In considering the decline of the Indian popula-tion, he observed that it could not be accounted for simply by losses in war. The diminution of the Indians held a direct relationship to the increase of the English and must be studied in that connection. "And here," he noted,

> I cannot but remark that Population; or the Laws of human in-crease and degeneracy are as properly a subject of systematical Science, as botany, the theory of agriculture, or raising and im-proving stock—and like all other branches of philosophy is to be founded on experiments. These experiments in all their variety are already made to our hands in the sufficiently authentic history of the last 3000 years in different parts of the world. There re-mains the classing and generalizing of experiments or facts, and pursuing their obvious inductions to certain general Laws: with which we may be prepared for useful and interesting applica-

30. Stiles to Charles Chauncy, Dec. 25, 1761.
31. Notes dated Dec. 25, 1761. *Itineraries and Miscellanies*, pp. 144–47. Undated notes ca. 1762.

tions. These researches will not only [be] very pleasurable, but lead to several Things of great moment, hitherto little attended to by politicians, philosophers, or divines.[32]

Relatively early in his researches Stiles found it possible to classify his facts and arrive at a few tentative generalizations. He could compute the period of doubling for New England—the length of time, that is, required for the population to double in size (about twenty years)—and calculate how large a population might be expected within a given number of years. He could also compute the relative growth, by natural increase, of different groups within the population. He published some of these observations because of their incidental relevance in *A Discourse on the Christian Union* as early as 1761.[33] The little he had learned by this time was sufficient to make his ephemeral remarks useful to Malthus after Stiles was dead,[34] but Stiles himself, in this field as in others, never acquired all the information he wanted for a complete study. Throughout his life he sought figures with avidity and ingenuity. He got them from books, tax collectors, registers of baptism, bills of mortality, and visitors who came to Newport and found themselves obliged to sit down in the study on Clarke Street and estimate the statistics for their home region. When he himself traveled he was forever counting noses and houses, and leaving behind instructions with his hosts for further counts. He made genealogies of his friends to compute the issue of a single couple in the course of a given number of generations. He studied tombstones and the incidence of disease on population growth. He even quizzed the local midwives to get the annual number of births.[35]

This indiscriminate gleaning of information of course laid him open to the danger of error, particularly if he relied on information extracted from harassed visitors, who may have tossed him a few numbers simply to get away. But when he estimated population figures

32. Undated note, probably 1761, written as a marginal note to be added to the *Discourse on the Christian Union* but not included in the published edition.

33. Boston, 1761, pp. 102–23.

34. *An Essay on the Principle of Population* (London, 1798), pp. 105–06. Malthus obtained Stiles's observations at second hand, through citations in Richard Price, *Observations on Revisionary Payments* (London, 1771), pp. 203–06.

35. These observations are scattered throughout his papers. Many are printed in *Itineraries and Miscellanies*.

on the basis of all the information he had at his command, his figures were surprisingly good by comparison with those which can be made on the basis of subsequent, more systematic surveys. Where contemporary estimates were apt to exaggerate, Stiles preferred to err, if necessary, on the side of conservatism. Modern investigators would find fault with his acceptance of Old Testament enumerations of the tribes of Israel, but his estimate of the Indian population of North America east of the Mississippi at no more than 100,000 cannot be far off; and his figure of two million and a half inhabitants for North and South America may be compared with modern estimates of twelve or thirteen million and a contemporary one of one hundred and fifty million.[36]

Though he did not publish anything on the subject except for the few pages in a sermon referred to above, he found his research of real use, not only in grappling with ecclesiastical and political problems but also in calculating the probable increment in value of the lands he speculated in. He even found that his studies had a bearing on theology, for when he numbered the souls of a place, he was conscious that souls were immortal. Reading over his essay on the universe in 1765, he noted that with the ascent of souls to higher spheres of activity after death, there would be vacancies left below, to be filled by new creations. Thus the universe would be "perpetually enlarging." [37] How seriously he considered this theological expanding universe may be judged from a few rough calculations he made on February 7, 1767. As he watched the people passing up and down the Parade (Newport's public square), he boldly estimated the population of the world from beginning to end at an average of eight hundred million persons per generation. If there were 150 generations from the creation to the day of judgment, a number he considered reasonably probable, this would mean a total of one hundred and twenty billion souls to be judged; and since he was toying with omniscience, he went on to guess that ninety billion of these would be saved, of whom two-thirds would be infants, for he still repudiated the traditional New England belief on this matter and consigned to glory all who died in infancy. There would thus be ninety billion on

36. Stiles made many estimates and calculations at different times, all of them conservative. The ones given are from a letter to Jedidiah Morse, Feb. 18, 1794.
37. Note dated May 15, 1765.

Christ's right hand and thirty billion on his left, "An immense and awful Assembly," he concluded.[38] Perhaps he would not have put these speculations in his book; but it was characteristic of him to make them. They gave precise dimensions to the thoughts that a New Englander always carried with him.

The Wisdom of Israel

When Stiles was at Yale, not intending to enter the ministry, he made no effort to learn Hebrew. At Newport, as he studied the Old Testament, though he regretted the deficiency in his theological training, still "the Delight of other Studies, and the Drudgery of learning a dead Language" conspired to continue his neglect. But Newport had ways of stimulating his interest in this subject too, for it contained a small colony of Jews, who in 1762 completed the building of a synagogue on Griffin Street, just off the Parade and only a couple of blocks from his house. He used to slip over often to watch the ceremonies. There was no regular rabbi, but a chuzzan, Isaac Touro, whom Stiles plied with his usual queries, occasionally getting help from him too in interpreting passages of the Old Testament.[39]

By 1767 his sense of shame at not knowing the language and his curiosity about subjects that it would open to him led him to begin a cursory study of it. He studied the alphabet for a few days and then took a turn around the Parade with Touro, learning the proper pronunciation. Once or twice after that he spent an evening with Touro and whenever possible visited services at the synagogue, but he knew that his pronunciation would never be "just and accurate." What he wanted was a reading knowledge, and he got it mostly by himself. Beginning with the Psalter, and devoting his mornings to it, he was able within a few weeks to read ten pages an hour. Though he had not intended to become a master of the language, it came so easily to him that in a little more than three years he had translated the whole of the Hebrew Bible. Meanwhile, finding Semitic languages so easily come by—a fact that must remain unaccountable to others who have struggled with them—he went on to master the variations: Chaldee, Syriac, and Arabic.[40]

His new knowledge enabled him to take full advantage of the op-

38. Notes dated Feb. 7, 1767, bound with miscellaneous notes on Jewish history.
39. "Memoir concerning my learning Hebrew," May 12, 1768.
40. Ibid.

portunities for conversing with the rabbis who occasionally visited the Newport synagogue. Some of them he found surprisingly ignorant, but one, Haijm Isaac Karigal, earned his unbounded admiration. Karigal had spent his life—he was not quite forty—in study and travel. He was a handsome man, "like Joseph of a comely aspect and beautiful Countenance." He was familiar with all the countries of Europe and the Near East; and his conversation had an eastern graciousness that both fascinated and moved a man like Stiles, who perhaps saw in the rabbi an exotic version of himself. After meeting him, Stiles wrote him a letter in Hebrew discussing the Hebrew and Samaritan characters and the question of which were used in the first versions of the Old Testament.[41] Karigal's answer was prefaced by a greeting that read strangely in Newport, as though a Mediterranean warmth had been carried there by the Old Hebrew words. When Stiles had translated it, he read:

> There shone in the house of my Residence a great Light, an Epistle written by the work of thy Hands, to the glorifying and filling the whole House with Light. Blessed be the Mother that bear thee. And I rejoyced with great Joy to behold the strength of thy Wisdom and Tongue. A learned Man art thou. Thy love is engraved in the inmost Thots of my heart that Volumes of Book [sic] would not suffice to write a thousandth part of the eternal Love with which I love you.[42]

This was a little embarrassing, and Stiles actually asked the man when he saw him how he could use such extravagant language. But if this was the way one must write in Hebrew, Stiles would do the right thing. Although he could not quite match the rabbi's effusiveness, he did as well as a Congregationalist could be expected to do. In his next letter, after Karigal had left for Barbados, he wrote, "I remember with great pleasure thy Society and Conversation which was more sweet to my Taste than Honey, and much more pleasant than the spicy Incense and perfume of the High Priest." [43]

41. *Lit. Diary*, *1*, 354–400 passim. Stiles to Karigal, May 24, 1773. Stiles's Hebrew Oration, written 1778, delivered at Yale, Sept. 12, 1781.

42. Karigal to Stiles, dated the 8th day of the month Sivan in the year 5533 of the Creation [May 29, 1773].

43. Stiles to Karigal, dated the first day of the month Nisan in the 5534th year of the Creation.

He kept up a pleasant correspondence with Karigal until the latter's death, discussing subjects which the knowledge of Semitic languages had enabled him to investigate. One of these was the discrepancy in chronology between the Hebrew Pentateuch and the Septuagint. More important was the prophetic revelation of the Messiah he found in the Talmud and in the Cabalistic writings, particularly the Zohar.[44] After he had satisfied himself that the Bible was divinely inspired, he was ready to believe that there might also be divine revelation in the oral traditions that were collected in the Talmud and the Zohar. He even accepted the idea that the massoretic points, which he believed to antedate the birth of Christ, contained a system for discovering a hidden allegorical meaning in every sentence of the Old Testament. This system, he thought, was irrecoverably lost, but much of what it must have revealed was still available in the Talmud and the Zohar. These, therefore, were worth study for what they might contain of revelation; for if there had been an age of revelation, as he now believed, human knowledge must have been deteriorating ever since, and in order to restore it one must proceed not only by experimental observation of the world and its surroundings, but by attempting to recover whatever scraps of revelation could be identified.[45] Though Christianity stood firm on the Old and New Testaments, the scope of our understanding of these might be considerably increased by subsidiary works, among which the Hebrew writings seemed the most promising. As he told Karigal, "Much of this antient Knowledge is gone to ruin, being swallowed up and polluted in other streams that have issued forth from corrupt fountains. But as Gold mixt with reprobate Silver, or the Iron in the Image of Nebuchadnezzar which mixeth indeed but will not unite and cleave to the Clay; so a great deal of this pure Knowledge may be preserved among the Traditions and in the Caballa of the Nations." [46]

Though Stiles's studies in this field never bore fruit, he prosecuted them intensively throughout the rest of his life, and one may surmise from the notes he took that his book would have dealt extensively

---

44. For some of Stiles's notes on the Zohar, with comments by a modern Hebraist, see George Foot Moore, "Ezra Stiles' Studies in the Cabala," Mass. Hist. Soc., *Proceedings*, 51 (1917–18), 290–306.

45. Notes on Jewish history, various dates 1765–73. Hebrew Oration delivered at Yale, Sept. 12, 1781. Stiles to Sir William Jones, Jan. 8, 1794.

46. Stiles to Karigal, July 19, 1773.

with a number of topics, including the chronology of the Old Testament, the doctrine of the Trinity and of the Messiah as found in the Talmud and the Zohar (he was particularly impressed by the evidence he found that the Messiah would suffer), the government of the universe as described in the Zohar, the use of different Semitic characters in the writing of different portions of the Old Testament, and the history of rabbinical learning. On all these subjects he was something of an expert.

The Ecclesiastical History of New England

Among his contemporaries Stiles's ecclesiastical history was probably better known than any of his other projects. Scarcely a minister in New England escaped his inquiries, for he gathered data about every church in the region. When was it founded? What ministers had served it and at what dates? What were its covenant and creeds? How many members? Edes and Gill, the printers of the *Boston Gazette*, clamored to publish the work.[47] Charles Chauncy kept asking if it was not about ready for the press now, and Thomas Hutchinson said he would not have begun his history of Massachusetts if he had known that Stiles was engaged in an historical project.[48] It was just as well that Hutchinson went ahead with his writing, for Stiles never completed his task. Though his papers abound with compilations of data and one rough outline—it can scarcely be called a draft—of the first chapters, nothing more has survived.[49]

Part of the trouble was that he could never settle on the limits of his work. At one time it was to be a history of the world; at another it was to cover the entire history of the British colonies in America, or at least in New England, beginning with the migration and following through "the civil, military, comercial, rural, Ecclesiastical Changes and Revolutions, to the late memorable and glorious War, less glorious Peace, and I fear more inglorious Loss of Charter Privileges." [50] Even after Stiles had decided to limit himself to an ecclesiastical history of New England, his omnivorous appetite for information would

---

47. Edes and Gill to Stiles, July 26, 1762.

48. Chauncy to Stiles, July 25, 1769, May 16, 1772. Hutchinson to Stiles, Feb. 15 1764.

49. The outline is in the Library of the Mass. Hist. Soc. See Bibliographical Note at the end of this book.

50. Stiles to Hutchinson, May 7, 1764.

not allow him to concentrate his efforts. We find him writing in 1768 to John Joachim Zubly in Georgia, asking for biographical information to use in his history.[51]

Stiles was doubtless less disturbed than others by his failure to get anything written. Although other people might be eager for publication of the information his book would contain, he had the information and was constantly getting more; and that, after all, was what interested him. He knew that the writing of history must be something more than the mere compilation of facts, and he would not have been content simply to summarize the materials he had collected. As he told Hutchinson, "Fidelity in narrating *Facts* is a great and principal thing: but then only is this species of writing perfect, when besides a well digested series of authenticated Transactions and Events, the motives and *Springs of Action* are fairly laid open and arise into view with all their Effects about them, when characters are made to live again, and past scenes are endowed with a kind of perpetual Resurrection in History." [52] Moreover, he saw the desirability of treating a subject in a comprehensive and coherent form: "A roomful of books thrown together in a confused heap is no library. The same of history. . . ." [53] For this reason he urged Hutchinson to treat all New England, because the separation of Massachusetts from the rest of New England was artificial and must leave the structure of the work incomplete. He thought, too, that only a friend to New England's charter liberties could do justice to her history, for liberty had been the guiding genius of that history: the period from the founding to his own day would in the future be distinguished as the "Period of Liberty." [54]

Any history written by Stiles would have reflected the views of his age as strongly as that of Bancroft reflected the age of Jackson. It might also have reflected some of Stiles's tolerance and catholicity, if we may judge from the mild rebuke he gave Catharine Macaulay for the perfectionism which he found implied in her history of England. When she presented a copy of her work to the Redwood Library, he wrote her a long and gracious letter, expressing his agree-

51. Stiles to Zubly, Aug. 26, 1768.
52. Stiles to Hutchinson, Nov. 26, 1767.
53. *Itineraries and Miscellanies*, p. 51.
54. Stiles to Hutchinson, May 7, 1764.

ment with her love of liberty, but suggesting that she had "too pure and fine a Taste to write the History of Man."

Not a Character on Earth can stand the principles of your Tribunal. Unsullied and perfect Characters only, and Administrations conducted with unerring Wisdom, please you. If you shd look over all the Empires on Earth, and attend to their policies and the men who from age to age have conducted them, you would be justly disgusted; perhaps at length displeased even with yourself, to have written one page on human Folly, or to have immortalized so inglorious a period as the best in all the Annals of History. Wise policies and designs defeated by actors interfering with the public good, public peculation, mixt and broken characters the monuments of Instability—among the Great and those at the Summit of Empires: Tumult Groans oppression and intestine Distress—among the people—are the materials of the political history of this world. Human Nature is in Ruins.[55]

These were proper sentiments for a New Englander. We are left to wonder how they would have found expression in the history of New England.

The Silkworm in New England

The year after he moved into the house on Clarke Street, Stiles set out three mulberry trees in the garden. Little two- or three-year-old whips they were then, but by 1763 two of them were thirteen feet high. There is no way of telling whether he had silk in mind when he planted them, but when he was returning from a visit to New Haven in 1763, his father's old friend Jonathan Todd, in East Guilford, gave him a packet of silkworm eggs. Todd had a single mulberry tree, about ten or twelve years old, and had raised 20,000 worms on it the preceding year. Unfortunately the tree had not furnished enough leaves for the last stages before cocooning, when the worms eat voraciously, so Todd had not got much silk. He had come near enough, though, to get the fever. Silk culture in America from the time when the first settlers arrived in Jamestown, was a kind of El Dorado to lure the prudent and industrious as surely as others were lured by a fast horse or a legend of gold in the hills. A hundred and fifty years of

55. Stiles to Catharine Macaulay, Nov. 13, 1772.

failure in the southern colonies had taken none of the shine off the
vision, and Ezra Stiles returned to Newport with all the excitement
of an explorer.[56]

It takes about six weeks to raise silkworms from the egg to the
cocoon. This was one of the attractions of silk culture: it would occupy
a man for only a short season and might thus be carried on along with
other occupations. Stiles began to hatch his worms on the last of May;
and for the next six weeks he spent most of his spare time with them.
To him the production of a quantity of silk was only an incidental part
of the business, for, with his passion for information, he must record
the whole process in detail, and try to determine whether silk culture
was practicable in New England and how it ought to be carried on.
Dividing his eggs into four batches, which he labeled A, B, C, and D
(totaling some 3,000), he kept minute records of the growth of each
batch, how many hatched each day, how many leaves they ate, how
large they were, when they entered each stage of their growth, and
so on. Besides these statistics, he entered other miscellaneous observations in a journal which frequently ran to several pages a day. A few
selections will suggest how much time he devoted to this experiment:

> June 15, 1763. Both A and B generally very sleepy to day
> hitherto—neither eat half their Allowance of Leaves in the Morn-
> ing: Now at Noon they seem to revive a little. Some of C droop
> and have lost their Stomach. At III ½ Aft. about 20 more of A
> shed, and two of B. the rest of A and B asleep and nodding and
> past Eating and some the Shudders. I gave 9 Leaves to C
> which eat pretty well—Therm. 72 ½—at V h. Therm. 71. gave
> one Leaf to A another to D.—a Thunder Gust arising and thun-
> der pretty hard—the Worms are so dozy that I cant tell whether
> they are affected. At VI gave C 3 Leaves.—The newfledged ones
> of A have not their Probosis hard eno' to eat, tho' skinned already
> Twelve Hours. Thundered incessantly for half an Hour and
> one very hard Clap—I dont perceive the Worms much affected—
> D seemed a little dull—Many of C are caught of the Initia of
> their sleep, and the rest of them eat feebly. At VII ½ fed, gave

56. Stiles made notations about silk culture in many different papers, but he put
the great bulk of them in a special notebook of "Observations on Silk Worms and the
Culture of Silk A.D. 1763. Being the Journal of an Experiment made in Newport,
Rhode Island in the summer of A.D. 1763 in raising about Three Thousand Silk
Worms." Facts and quotations cited are from this journal.

A 17 B 29 C and D 3 Leaves: A and B eat almost nothing. [This
is only about half the entry for this day.]

June 18 I have been diligently employed all day, except from
I to III PM, in taking care of them— . . . Hope they have got
their Belly full today, having received 741 Leaves, from one to
4 and 5 Inches.

June 23. . . . went out of Town and left wife to take Care
of the Worms . . . My Wife says she was four hours yesterday
forenoon cleaning and feeding the Worms: and an hour and a
half towards Evening.

So closely did he watch the worms that he could recognize many of
them individually and named the two largest ones General Wolfe and
Oliver Cromwell. When some of them seemed to take sick, he became
anxious:

June 17. This has been a terrible Day to the Worms. They lost
Appetite became livid or rather purple, and seemed irrecoverably
lost till near noon. My Wife and self spent three hours from X
to I in cleaning removing and nursing placing upon fresh Leaves
—they would then eat a little at first, but soon cloyed and many
semed to give themselves up to die. Whether the Disorder came
to a Crisis or thro' the Warmth of the Afternoon Sun, I know not,
but they begun to eat more voraciously about IV h or Middle
Afternoon, to my great Satisfaction. And I am in hopes they will
get over it tolerably—tho' I expect their Silk will feel the Effect
of this *uncommon* Sickness.

As they grew larger, Stiles's own mulberry leaves were nowhere
near enough to feed them. Fortunately there were many other mulberry trees in the gardens about town, and the owners gladly gave the
parson permission to use them. He and his Negro slave could be seen
every day except Sunday assiduously plucking leaves, a peck from
Benjamin King's tree and a quart from Governor Ward's and another
from Colonel Malbone's. By July 5 the worms were eating five bushels
of leaves in a day, and it was all Stiles and his man could do to keep up
with them. The next week they began to cocoon, and the ordeal was
over.

From all this labor Stiles extracted 6⅔ pounds of cocoons, enough
to make less than a pound of raw silk; and raw silk was worth about

£1 sterling per pound. He kept up his journals and his experiments until 1771 and produced enough silk so that by purchasing a little more, he had enough material woven to make a silk gown for his wife. The weaving cost £2 14s. 6d. sterling, and the extra silk 11s. 6d., so that the total cost was £3 5s. 9d., not counting a small amount he paid a filature for winding his cocoons. The cost of the same material if purchased in a store would have been £5 5s. 0d., so that Stiles made less than £2 sterling by the operations of several years.

One might suppose that this would be conclusive proof of the impracticability of silk culture in New England, yet Stiles remained an ardent advocate of it, and for reasons that were not without cogency at the time. He had found that silk requires a great deal of labor, but unskilled labor concentrated in a short period of time, labor that could easily be done by women and children. Silk culture was therefore best suited to areas of dense population and large families. The British government had made the mistake of attempting to establish silk culture by bounties in the young province of Georgia, where the population was sparse. The place for silk was in the area north of Maryland, particularly New England, where, Stiles's researches had shown him, the greatest concentration of population existed and would continue to exist.

In a letter which seems to have been intended for Richard Jackson, a London agent of the Connecticut government, Stiles explained these facts and suggested a plan for the promotion of silk culture in New England. A society must be formed with representatives in every county. These men would be entrusted with mulberry seeds, enough to grow 5,000 trees in every parish. (He had already found that 556 mulberries contain 16,510 seeds, weighing one ounce and occupying 5 cubic inches.) After four or five years the society would distribute forty or fifty sapling mulberries to every family that would set them out, and in six or eight years more would distribute eggs. Within twenty years, if half the families in New England participated and every family raised ten pounds of silk annually, New England might produce a million and a half pounds, which would be worth the same number of pounds sterling. It was likely that individual families would have bad luck with their worms—from disease, or the cat might eat them as Stiles's did in 1765—but the total output of the region could be maintained in spite of individual calamities. No family would be dependent on their silk, for it would be only a part-time occupation cared for by the women and children (though there is no evidence that any of the Stiles children were enlisted in their father's attempt), but the region as a whole could count on a staple export of £1,000,000 a year and thus redress the unfavorable balance of trade from which it suffered in its commerce with Great Britain.[57]

Though Stiles did not publish his journals, he argued for his scheme not only in the letter to Jackson but in the columns of the newspapers.[58] After the Revolution, when he was living in New Haven, he even made an attempt to carry it out.[59] Nearly fifty years after his death, the manuscript of his journals, deposited in the Yale Library, continued to inspire other seekers of the silken El Dorado, for one of them attached a long testimonial to it in 1843. Anyone who reads the journals today, when the chemistry laboratories have finally dispelled the vision of a nation of silk-growers, must still be impressed by the meticulousness of the observations. Though the journals are a monument to a hopeless effort, they deserve to be considered also as the record of an experiment carried out with scientific rigor; and one may add that more than one scientist, both before and since, has made experiments with equal pains and no greater results.

The Dimensions of the Universe

After his travels of 1754 Stiles seldom strayed far from home. An occasional visit to friends in Connecticut, a trip to Yale or Harvard commencement, an ordination at Meriden or Plymouth—these were the limits of his wandering. But if he traveled little in the world, he traveled far in Newport. It was not just that he could reach across the globe to ask a Russian about the temperature in Siberia or a Mexican about the position of a comet, but rather that his philosophy of the universe, however naive it may sound to us, gave him a perspective that few persons possess even today. The universe for us has taken on proportions that surpass the limits of imagination. In Stiles's time this immensity was only beginning to be grasped; infinity was not yet so overwhelming but what a man could hope to encompass it. Standing in Newport, Stiles could look at the sun and stars with the same kind of curiosity that made him investigate the philosophy of watered rum.

57. Stiles to ———, Sept. 21, 1764.
58. *New York Gazette* (Parker), Mar. 5, 1767. A copy of the letter is in the Stiles Papers.
59. See below, Chap. 26. See also Parker to Stiles, Jan. 8, 1767.

The universe was expanding—by the creation of new souls—but not exploding. It was there for him to understand and thereby widen his sphere of activity in the scale of being. He may even have thought to facilitate his future as a disembodied spirit by providing himself with a celestial road map. The same passion for understanding by measurement that led him to pace off the streets of Newport and map the site of every building led him to study the heavens and try to mark the dimensions, if not of the universe, at least of the solar system.

It must be confessed that astronomy, though it engrossed a large part of his attention, was not Stiles's forte. He knew enough mathematics, thanks to President Clap, to handle the necessary calculations, but he seems to have lacked the kind of imagination necessary to perceive all the variables with which he must deal. Though the orrery at Yale had contained a wire with which to demonstrate the path of a comet, he had to write President Clap in 1757 in order to get assistance in calculating the orbit.[60] Halley's famous comet of 1682 was about to reappear at this time, and Stiles had become interested in the variations of its periods. He filled pages with calculations and conjectures, the result of which he communicated to Professor Winthrop. Stiles had concluded that the effects of Jupiter and Saturn on the comet would about equalize each other. As he put it in his notes: "Saturn seldom meddles much with Comet, when on this Side his Trajectory, till Jupiter has done with him: and the like may be observed on 'tother side, in the Ascent. Jupiter dont act strongly 'till Saturn has done." [61] His conclusion from this was that the variations in period could not be due to the influence of Jupiter or Saturn. Winthrop quickly set him right by showing that he had neglected to consider the difference in exposure to gravitational pull from the planets, arising from the acceleration of the comet as it approached them, and the retardation as it receded.[62]

The fruitlessness of his labors on this comet might have dampened the enthusiasm of a less dedicated scholar. Some of Stiles's friends, like Francis Alison of Philadelphia, thought he was foolish to waste his time on a matter that would be settled "with certainty and less trouble" in another world. Alison preferred to wait until he could

60. Clap to Stiles, Sept. 1, 1757. Stiles's letter to Clap is missing.
61. Notes dated Sept. 10, 1757, in notebook headed "On Comet 1758."
62. Winthrop to Stiles, Oct. 3, 1757, July 10, 1758, Mar. 6, 1759.

"converse with Newton, Halley, Whiston, and Flamstead and some others of the same complexion, if these great names be alowd to shine in one constellation in heaven." [63] If Stiles did not relax his interest in comets, it was not because he rejected Alison's vision. In fact he frequently delighted himself with such musings, and before receiving Alison's letter he had already expressed much the same sentiment in a letter to Professor Winthrop: "We shall be able to form a more just Idea of the State of Man a thousand years hence— when we shall have left these Regions of incarnate spirits, and entered into the intellectual World or Abodes of unbodied Minds—not only renew our Acquaintance with departed Friends, but personally converse with Moses, Isaiah, Paul, Plato, Cicero, Newton, Locke, and contract new Acquaintance with exalted Minds assembled from all parts of the moral Dominions of Jehovah—and feel our Souls open into the most sublime, generous and expanded Benevolence." [64]

Stiles, however, had no mind to wait for such exalted instruction and went on collecting data on comets the rest of his life, making a catalogue of them from observations he found in books or solicited from friends. Whenever a new one appeared, he would rise in the dark and look at it through his telescope from a bedroom or study window, frequently peering through the glass until daylight obliterated the view. Then he would take his notes and plot its course from the celestial maps of the great Flamsteed. He observed the aurora borealis, whenever it occurred, in the same way, and he and John Winthrop tried to plot its height by simultaneous observations from Cambridge and Newport.[65] Measurement was the great thing in astronomy for Stiles; and though he will never rank as an astronomer, he did participate in observing the most important astronomical phenomenom of his century—the one which gave the greatest promise of revealing the unknown dimensions of the solar system—the transit of Venus across the sun's disc.

The first man ever to observe Venus crossing the sun was James Horrocks, an English clergyman, who predicted and observed the transit of 1639. At the time of Horrocks' observation, it had not occurred to astronomers that the phenomenon could be used to meas-

---

63. Alison to Stiles May 27, 1759.

64. Stiles to Winthrop, Apr. 2, 1759.

65. Stiles to Thomas Wright, Sept. 1, 1768, to Winthrop, Sept. 1, 1768, Dec. 6, 1768, Aug. 1, 1769. Winthrop to Stiles, Jan. 9, Apr. 23, 1769.

ure the distance of Venus, but in 1679 and again in 1716 Edmund Halley pointed out how the next transits (in 1761 and 1769) could be used to provide the data for calculating the distance of both Venus and the sun and by consequence the exact dimensions of all the planets and their orbits. Johann Kepler had already determined the proportions of the solar system with such exactitude that a single linear dimension accurately obtained (together with what was already known of the size of the earth), would give every dimension in the system. If the distance of Venus could be found, astronomers would then know not only the distance of the sun and of the other planets but their size as well. A more vital astronomical discovery could scarcely be hoped for. Since Venus passes visibly between the earth and the sun only twice in a period of more than a century, and sometimes only once, the transit of 1761 was awaited with considerable excitement.

Astronomers all over the western world were preparing to follow Halley's directions which (stripped of much relevant detail) amounted to observing the tiny black dot travel across the face of the sun and noting with extreme care the exact length of time the passage took. The location of Venus' path across the sun's disk would vary according to the location of the observer on earth. From some observation stations Venus would seem to cross near the sun's diameter, from others to cut across only a small slice. The length of time the transit would take naturally depended on the length of the path. The duration would also be affected by the earth's rotation, which speeds an observer on the equator at 24,000 miles an hour but at gradually decreasing rates toward the poles. By knowing the exact duration of the transit at two observation stations and also the exact longitude and latitude of both, the distances of Venus and the sun from the earth could be mathematically computed. A second method called for computing, before the event, how long the transit should take at a particular place, if the distance of Venus was a certain "guessed" figure. When the transit actually occurred, the observed time could be compared with the calculated time. The difference between the two would indicate exactly how far off one's best guess at the distance of Venus and the sun had been. The guess could thus be corrected and transformed into an exact, reliable figure.[66]

66. There are several secondary accounts of the significance of this observation; see, for example, R. A. Proctor, *Transits of Venus* (London, 1874), pp. 93–96; Simon Newcomb, *Popular Astronomy* (New York, 1878), pp. 173–78; Brooke Hindle,

The problem of the astronomer, then, was seemingly simple: he must determine the longitude and latitude of his place of observation, then observe the exact time when the transit began and ended. And this is what men of learning like Ezra Stiles were preparing to do, both in Europe and America, as the time of the transit drew near. For a number of reasons, including the weather, the transit of 1761 was a disappointment. The transit of 1769 was therefore awaited with even more excitement, for there would not be another until 1874.

As the day (June 3) approached, Stiles assembled a team of eight friends to assist him: William Vernon, William Ellery, Henry Marchant, Benjamin King (a maker of nautical instruments), Christopher Townsend (a cabinet maker), Caleb Gardner (a ship captain), Edward Thurston (the colony's official sealer of weights and measures), and Punderson Austin (of New Haven, temporarily filling the pulpit of the First Congregational Church). They had two clocks, two telescopes, and a sextant.

Stiles's record of the enterprise, occupying 268 pages, is an illuminating if sometimes ludicrous account of the pitfalls that beset the best scientific endeavors in eighteenth-century America.[67] To begin with, the clocks, which had to be exactly synchronized, behaved in a most erratic fashion. It was necessary to check them by daily observations of the meridian. Stiles and Marchant contrived a device for doing this by pendant threads hung from two garret windows with weights at the bottom immersed in tubs of water. School boys discovered them and took a good deal of pleasure in pulling them down when the astronomers were engaged in more pressing business. For the measurement of latitude Stiles had relied on a large sextant made by Benjamin King for the colony and deposited in the Redwood Library, but ten days before the transit another group of observers in Providence got an order from the government to have it delivered to them.[68] Before it was sent, King and Peter Harrison, Newport's talented architect,

---

The Pursuit of Science in Revolutionary America (Chapel Hill, 1956), pp. 146–65. For the purposes of this chapter, however, I have found most useful the volumes from which Stiles and his contemporaries worked: Halley's paper in Henry Jones, *The Philosophical Transactions Abridged*, 4 (London, 1749), 214–20; and James Short in *Philosophical Transactions*, 52, Pt. II (1762), 611–28.

67. My account is based on this notebook.

68. Moses Brown to Stiles or Henry Marchant, May 22, 1769. Darius Sessions et al to Librarian of the Redwood Library, May 23, 1769.

took the latitude of Newport with it; but King apparently made sextants better than he read them, for Stiles later found that their calculations were ten minutes off.

The worst trouble came on the day of the transit itself. The group had not had enough practice together to work well as a team, and at the crucial moment they all became so flustered, Stiles included, that they forgot their previously agreed signals. According to their plan, four of them were to watch the two clocks inside the house and record the times of contact as shouted out by the observers at the telescopes and sextant outside. The signal for the beginning of the transit was the word "now." As it happened, Stiles himself was the first to observe the event. Since he was slightly near-sighted, it had been arranged that Marchant should stand at the reflecting telescope and Thurston at the refractor, with Stiles serving as a kind of director over the whole. Stiles was spelling Marchant after a long period of watching, when he caught sight of the first indentation in the sun's disk. He was so overcome with excitement that he called out "Take notice," instead of "now." Marchant, perceiving what he meant, immediately went to the window of the house and asked the observers at the clocks if they had noted his signal. They had heard it but not recorded it, and now they, too, became so rattled that they could not agree on when they had heard it.

Actually the external contact, which Stiles thought he had seen the precise beginning of, was generally held by astronomers to be less easily determined and less reliable than the internal contact (when Venus should be wholly inside the sun). But the Newport observers were unable to agree about the precise moment of either.

When the transit was over, Stiles went to work on the results to see if anything could be made of them, estimating this error and balancing it against that. He kept taking observations and altitudes for the rest of the summer in order to calculate the error in the clocks and determine Newport's longitude and latitude exactly. Though he devoted almost his whole time to it (even the silkworms were neglected and died), the total result seems to have been nothing. He had published the best estimate of his observations in the *Newport Mercury* immediately after the transit; but he never was able to satisfy himself about them. It is only fair to add that other observations conducted under more auspicious circumstances also showed a great variety of results, so that the transit proved less rewarding than everyone had hoped. Stiles's failure to publish any calculations of the dimensions of the solar system may have been the mark of superior wisdom. It certainly did not mean that he had lost interest in the possibilities of astronomy, for he continued a devotee until his death, one may at least hope, furnished him the means of verifying his results without the need of Benjamin King's ingenious instruments.

I O

Dreams of Glory

THERE WERE several other books which Stiles failed to write, and
a few, to be noticed in due course, which he did, but his reputation
in both America and Europe rested mainly on the learning just described. In spite of its failure to reach fruition in print, it won him
considerable fame among his contemporaries. We catch a glimpse
of the awe with which he was regarded in a letter sent to him in
1762 from Amenia precinct in upstate New York. One Thomas Young
wrote for information about the validity of certain land titles in that
region, because he had heard, he said, "that yourself was an Industrious Enquirer into the Natural and Political State of your Country
—that you transmitted frequently your Observations to the Board of
Trade &c and therefrom obtain'd in return all the Desiderata relative
to Our American affairs." Stiles answered modestly and honestly that
he had no connection with the Board of Trade, but he must have been
impressed with the compliment implied, for he was never a man to
dismiss honors lightly.[1]

In the eighteenth century, as today, one of the principal insignia
of merit was the honorary degree, and Stiles showed how much he
valued this badge when he pulled strings to obtain it for deserving
friends. The most coveted degree for an American was one from a
European university, because it indicated an international reputation.
Even more highly prized, for men of science, was membership in the
Royal Society. Stiles's friend Franklin won both these honors, and
Stiles more than once solicited him to procure them for other Ameri-

1. Thomas Young to Stiles, Dec. 5, 1762; Stiles to Young, Feb. 15, 1763.

cans. Franklin respected his requests too—it was Stiles who urged him to get John Winthrop elected to the Royal Society [2]—and Franklin demonstrated his own high opinion of Stiles by obtaining for him in 1765 the degree of S.T.D. from the University of Edinburgh, even though the principal of the University thought that theology was of all the sciences the only one in which Stiles was not perfectly sound.[3] Because he had never so much as hinted that he wished such a degree for himself, Stiles was both surprised and extraordinarily happy to receive it. Ever after he was known as "Doctor Stiles" and cherished the title not a little. It was partly the sense of mortification at being a Doctor of Theology without knowing Hebrew that led him to begin his studies in that subject.[4]

Stiles's restless mind projected several schemes which would both aid and honor learning in America. As early as 1763 he proposed to John Winthrop the founding of an American philosophical society. Winthrop thought the time was not yet ripe, that it would be better to keep communications between American scholars on an informal basis, with Stiles, who had the widest correspondence, serving as a sort of clearing house.[5] Stiles forbore proceeding with the idea at this time, but it kept recurring to him. A few months later he had picked out a president and senate for the society, which he now called the Societas Eruditorum Stilensiana.[6] The president was to be Ezra Stiles, and the senate would be drawn from the most eminent and learned gentlemen of New England. In 1765, after receiving his degree from Edinburgh, he refined and elaborated the scheme, removing the grossest element of vanity by calling it the "American Academy of Sciences." In 1766 he changed the name to "The Newtonian Academy of Sciences in America," and in 1767 he toyed with the "Platonic Academy," and "The Selden Academy of Sciences in New England in America." The last title was intended to honor John

2. Stiles to Franklin, Feb. 5, 1762, Feb. 20, 1765; Franklin to Stiles, July 5, 1765.

3. Franklin sent copies of his correspondence with the University to Stiles: William Robertson to William Strahan (Franklin's London friend, the printer, who seems to have initiated the correspondence), Feb. 18, 1765; Franklin to William Robertson, Mar. 4, 1765; Robertson to Franklin, Apr. 1, 1765; Franklin to Robertson, June 2, 1765; Franklin to Stiles, July 5, 1765.

4. "Memoir concerning my learning Hebrew," May 12, 1768.

5. Winthrop to Stiles, Jan. 18, 1763. Stiles's letter to Winthrop is missing.

6. Notes dated Aug., 1763. The successive schemes described below are delineated in documents dated Aug. 15, 1765, Nov. 24, 1766, Jan. 7, May 6, 1767.

Selden, the famous antiquary, whose name was selected for another society 120 years later. With his usual attention to detail Stiles drew up a constitution to regulate the government of the society, opening the ranks to all who could contribute to knowledge but confining the direction to a select council of twelve, to be headed now by John Winthrop, as president, Chauncy Whittelsey as vice president, and himself as secretary. The council would be self-perpetuating and might make its headquarters at any place between the Penobscot and the Hudson. In order "to preserve the Distinction due to all the Subordinations of Worth and Utility," the members should be classified either as fellows or in three ranks of honor: eminentes, eminentiores, and eminentissimi. And the specific field of a man's eminence was to be distinguished by one of fifteen titles, as follows:

The Newtonian—comprehending natural Philosophy and chronology
Platonic—such as Dr. Henry More, Plotinus, Marcel Ficinus, Locke, Berkeley
Livian—Historians, Polybius, P. Paul, Burnet, Dupin, Sleidan, Rapin
Pitt—eminent Legislators, Bacon, Lycurgus, Grotius, Sidney
Selden—Civilians and Lawyers, Harrington, Spelman, Holt, Raymond, Cambden
Theologian—Divines, Erasmus
Boerhavian—Physicians, Chymists, Sendivogius
Franklinian—Authors of Inventions, as Dr. Eliot, Inventor of Sand Iron, Linnaeus
Addisonian—Poetry and belles Letters, Pope, Rollins, Watts, Young, Voltaire
Liberty—Its advocates and intrepid Defenders, Cato, Ld. Russel, Pitt
Palladian—Architecture
Titian—Painting and Sculpture
Corelli—Musick
Marlborough—Military Atchievments, excellent Generals
Naval—Admirals &c.

In this learned dream—for it never amounted to more than that— Stiles refrained from his earlier self-glorification by not indicating where he would place himself. He did prescribe, however, the subjects which the society should investigate, and once again the list is a reflection of the extraordinary range of his curiosity:

celestial observations of Eclipses of Jupiters Satellites, stellary appulses and Occultations, Meteors or terrestrial Comets, Mete-

orological Registers of the Thermometer and Barometer, Effects
of Lightning and whatever may assist toward perfecting the
theory of the Electrical pointed Rods; Earthquakes and their
Species; Facts illustrative of the Inquiry whether Clearing and
settlement moderate the Intense Cold of the Continental Win-
ters? Whether the Northern Climates on the West side warmer
than on E. side of Amer. Continent—the Botany and Mineralogy
of America—collection of rare Fossils, Animals, plants:—Facts
in verification or Refutation of the Theory of the 10fold Ratio
of Deaths in smallpox, while in natural smallpox one out of 7
or 8 may die, in simple Inoculation may die one in 60 or 70 and
in Mercurial Inoculation die one only in 7 or 800.—ann. or
septennial accounts of Deaths and Births in districts of 100 or
more Families in different parts of America with the age of settlement; the public Numerations or Census of provinces at different Times; and the numbers of settlers as they arrive from
Europe into any part of the Continent, and the deaths among
the two first years and their subsequent Increase; in what parts
population has arrived to its akme, and whether a stagnated or
degenerating population in any place be ever revived and melio-
rated by the mixture of foreign or very distant Accessions—
whether Changing or mixing the Breed be not as necessary for
all species of animals as for sheep and whether particular Clusters
of human kind would not pejorate after a period of rapid Increase, unless revived and fermented by distant Mixtures:—to
collect Accounts of American Colonization and a Number and
Variety of Facts thereon sufficient for the Induction and Investigation of the whole Theory of Population:—also to collect Accounts of the period of Degeneracy and means of Recovering
Orchards of apple and all Fruit Trees, Cattle Hogs Horse Poul-
try, Indian Corn, English Grain, Silk Worms, vines, and in
general, such facts as will suggest the Laws of Degeneracy and
Melioration of the animal and vegetable Kingdoms, Cases in
medical practice and Chyrurgery.

It was characteristic of Stiles to draw up complete plans for this
venture, but to do nothing toward putting them into effect. Though
he was tireless in planning organizations, it was a kind of day-dreaming
for him, a secret life in which he rose to heights of glory as the pre-

siding maestro of American scholarship (headquarters: New England). When it came to bringing the dream alive, he drew back, instinctively suspicious of the element of vanity he discerned in it. Perhaps the degree from Edinburgh helped to restrain him. Such tangible recognition may have relieved the need to display his merits and his talents, whether in print or in the resounding titles of a learned society. But the struggle was always with him, before he received the degree and after. He never dared let himself go. Even in the dream he had finally shrunk from standing forth as the president of his organization. This honor he would reserve for his friend Winthrop, though somewhere in his mind there must have been the thought that everyone would know he was the founder of the society, the man who really ran it. Whatever he thought, he left it to others to embody the dream, which in spite of the element of self-exaltation was a worth-while enterprise. When the American Academy of Arts and Sciences was actually founded in 1780, he did not hesitate to accept membership in it.

Another organization which Stiles projected in 1762 was even more revealing of the touch of vanity in his character, and reminiscent of his earlier dreams at Yale. This was a union of all his descendants, to be celebrated by a family meeting every four years from the year of his marriage, 1757, until the crack of doom, an event that he expected within 350 years. The headship of the family was to be in the male line by primogeniture, and the incumbent would hold the title of prince. Collateral heads of families would be known as chiefs, but the quadrennial assemblies were also to choose, by democratic suffrage, a President of the Issue. When the family grew large enough there might also be a representative assembly to handle affairs between the quadrennial reunions.

Stiles spent a great deal of time drawing up "family constitutions" [7] (rules) to guide the destinies of the family into eternity. They were to be engrossed on parchment by the founder himself and their authenticity attested to at every generation by four witnesses of their transfer from one head of the family to the succeeding one. In the year 1860 they were to be published and a copy presented to every member of the family then alive and to all future members thereafter.

The family constitutions were also to be read aloud at each of the

7. The documents thus headed are dated Mar. 10, 14, 17, May 28, Aug. 6, 8, 25, Dec. 20, 1762, Jan. 12, 17, 1763; see also related documents dated Mar. 26, 1764, and Jan. 23, 1765.

quadrennial reunions, so that the assembled throng might be reminded of the ripe wisdom of their ancestor (attained at the age of thirty-five). They would hear that they ought to marry young and out of the family, so that the breed might be improved by new blood. They were to choose mates from robust and industrious families, having regard to virtue rather than wealth. If, however, any were so unhappy as to select a small or sickly partner, there would be this consolation, that "I myself their common Ancestor am a Man of small Stature but 5 feet and 4 Inches in hight, slender and of thin Habit, of light Complexion, subject to constant Weaknesses and Infirmities." All the more reason, though, to choose healthy husbands and wives. The members of the tribe should seek always the rural life as opposed to the urban, for cities are nurseries of vice and prodigality. They should stay out of politics, plant mulberry trees, and get children as fast as possible. It was to be hoped that they would remain Congregationalists, but they should have charity toward all sects, not excepting the Catholics. A hundred and twenty years after the death of their ancestor, they should choose a family historian, to perform the task which is attempted under somewhat different auspices in this volume, and also to record the history of the family since the death of the founder.

Though the fundamental purpose of this detailed family organization was plainly the gratification of Stiles's ego, he did not, at the time, perceive this. His ostensible purpose was to inculcate virtue among his descendants, and he admonished them to "pay a strict Regard to these Institutes of your Ancestor which you must know proceed from the sincerest Affection to his Offspring." His exposure in Newport to the fact that "cities are nurseries of Vice" may even have sparked the whole grandiose plan. It had long been a truism in New England that the best means of curbing vice was strong parental discipline. In its absence, the Puritans had maintained, civil government must be ineffective. For as long as anyone could remember, however, family discipline had been declining, and virtue had suffered accordingly. Stiles may have thought to restore good family government (and with it virtue) by the simple expedient of establishing it firmly among his own offspring; for his demographic researches assured him that if his descendants followed his injunction to get children as rapidly as possible, they would in a relatively short time inherit the earth.

Stiles seems to have attached a good deal of importance to the numerical increase of the family. By the tenth generation, he hoped, it would amount to nine million adults, nearly half the population he anticipated for New England at that time. As the millennium could be expected by then, the family, by their attachment to the virtuous principles of their ancestor might "become a Subject worthy the peculiar Favor and protection of the most High." And this would have been accomplished without any sacrifice of temporal blessings, for the family constitutions would also "render the family inconceivably useful to the World, bring upon them an accumulated Honor, and distinguish them to eternal Ages in distant regions of the moral World with a name above all the Families of this Earth, not excepting even the Family and natural offspring of Abraham." When the millennium did arrive, "if I should be so happy as to be of the number of the saints who shall return with Jesus at his second coming, perhaps I may be appointed your head to take the Conduct of the family in the millennial state under the prince of peace."

Lest this immortal glory should fail, there was provision for a vicarious immortality, not only in the existence of the organization itself but in the tangible form of a fifty-foot monument, to be erected a hundred years after the founder's death. In laying plans for it, Stiles let his imagination run riot. It was to consist of a shaft about fifty feet in height, set on a pedestal eleven feet high and seven feet square, the whole to be made of stone, preferably marble. Each side of the pedestal was to contain an inscription: on one side a map of the American colonies, with the number of inhabitants; on another the New England colonies only, "somewhat in Resemblance of the Ancyran Marble of Augustus Caesar"; the third side would have a diagram of the solar system, including one or two comets; and the fourth side must be "charged with the Number of my Posterity and the Names of the Chiefs and Heads of Branches, with the Increase of each respective Branch, with the Date of this Institution and the Age of the Family." The column itself was also to be covered with inscriptions, dealing with the principal events of New England history and the increase of the family, with room left to record further increases in the future.

The site of the monument was to be a tract of some hundred acres with a river running through it, preferably in Windsor, Connecticut, the cradle of the Stiles family in America. The obelisk would be surrounded by twelve or fifteen hundred mulberry trees laid out to represent the orbits of the planets and the trajectory of a comet, except that the innermost planet Mercury should be represented by a thick stone wall ten feet high. The rest of the grounds were to be laid out in avenues of mulberry and fruit trees. At the opposite end from the obelisk two buildings would stand, one a "small plain Country seat" for the prince of the family (whose children would tend the silk worms); the other an assembly hall and library, containing paintings and busts of the chiefs, where the quadrennial reunions would be held and a school kept for the youth of the family, "unless they should chuse to be at the Expence of a College Education." In order to pay for all this a thousand acres of the family lands might be sold, lands bequeathed by the founder, which by that time would be worth enough to bear the expense.

The whole thing was a little pathetic. What redeems it is its innocence and the fact that Stiles himself could discern the motives behind it and abandon it before he betrayed himself. Nine years later he wrote on a page of the "Family Constitutions":

> In 1762 I was carried away with this Family Projection. Now 1771 Aet. 44. I am so sick of this pleasing Vanity that I have for years laid it aside and neglected to finish the Plan. And I purpose to destroy all the papers that respect this Institution, after I shall have had Leisure to select a few Things from them. The most that I now desire is.
>
> I. That a record should be kept of all the Births &c in the Family for 5 or six hundred years—as a specimen of american population, and of Diffusion of Blood.
>
> II. That real Holiness and the Love of Jesus may be the portion of as many as possible.

He did not, of course, destroy the papers, but he never resumed this pleasing vanity. Perhaps the second wish he expressed in 1771 may suggest why. His rejection of the plan was not merely a sober second thought; it was the result of a development that had been taking place in him during the years at Newport. While he had been firing his intellectual blunderbuss at every piece of knowledge that came his way, he had been growing—not just filling up with facts but growing intellectually and morally, learning to penetrate the disguises that his vanity assumed in order to trick him, learning to crush it down before it grew to the absurd proportions of the family constitutions, learning, above all, to value real holiness and the love of Jesus.

I I

Puritanism Enlightened

BEFORE EZRA STILES became minister of Newport's Second Congregational Church, he had persuaded himself that the Scriptures were authentic, that he must believe the principal doctrines of Christianity as he had outlined them in his creed. Nevertheless he entered the ministry with a good deal of trepidation. Though his acceptance of Scripture was genuine, he recognized that something was missing, that he lacked the firmness of conviction generally expected of a minister. A letter to his old friend and mentor, Jared Ingersoll, discloses a still lively skepticism after almost a year of preaching: "The substance of Christianity," he wrote, and added parenthetically, "if there is any Thing in it." Then, on second thought, he scratched out this unbecoming sentiment and went on with the affirmation that the substance of Christianity "is as old as Creation." [1] The statement was not incompatible with Christianity, but it was obviously a reflection of Matthew Tindal's famous deistic treatise *Christianity as Old as the Creation*, [2] which Stiles had just been reading.

If Tindal could be, as he claimed, a Christian deist, then Stiles would appear to have been a deistic Christian. It was still the moral aspect of Christianity that attracted him, and he still believed that intellectual progress would lead him to greater opportunities of knowledge in the world to come. "I please myself" he told Ingersoll,

> with the Prospect of hereafter conversing with our good Friends that have left us, and are, I hope 'ere now settled peaceably in

1. Stiles to Ingersoll, Aug. 16, 1756.
2. London, 1730.

other Moral Climes—I intend hereafter to visit them, and make 'em tell me a Thousand New Things. I intend, when I have got a little more *moral Cash* to travel largely in the Almightys Dominions. . . . I should be glad to converse with Father *Abraham* (tho' I dont think the Old Fellow knew more than you and I when here) and *Paul* (for I dont question but he is a boon Companion) and the Prince Royal of the Moral World, if I may be permitted this last Honor; who can readily tell us whether he ever paid a Visit to this disordered World, and what kind of Orders he gave &c &c.

The moral cash which would pay the way to such pleasant intercourse in eternity could evidently be earned by all who were willing to work for it. Virtue was an art, Stiles had decided, and "I am persuaded tis to be learnt, just as any other Art is to be learnt, by Application to *my Master* and by Industry: to this great Master I go, with the same Freedom, I used to go to Master *Ingersoll*."

The assurance of this letter was betrayed by the postscript, "Dont let any Body see this." In reality Stiles had much less confidence in his own position than he admitted. He had talked himself into accepting the Scriptures. What if he should talk himself out of it? The thought bothered him so much that he needed a continuous flow of arguments to keep up his courage. Jared Eliot, to whom he presented his problems from time to time, helped to supply him,[3] and Stiles himself kept busy studying the compilation of both Old and New Testaments, looking for signs of divinity. Since he had not yet learned Hebrew, he had to rely on secondary accounts, from which he acquired such a store of arguments in favor of revelation that he put them together in a sermon.

Upon the "earnest Importunity" of his listeners he prepared a version of it for the press, some 140 manuscript pages in length,[4] but

3. Stiles to Eliot, Apr. 5, 1757; Eliot to Stiles, Apr. 12, July 14, 27, 1757; July 26, Nov. 4, 1758.

4. "A Discourse on the Study of the Scriptures, Delivered at an Evening Lecture in Middletown, R.I. Jan. 19, 1758." Among the works consulted by Stiles were Joseph Butler, *The Analogy of Religion* (London, 1736); Humphrey Prideaux, *The Old and New Testament Connected* (London, 1716–18); Richard Simon, *Critical History of the Old Testament* (London, 1682); John Weemes, *The Christian Synagogue* (London, 1623); and William Whiston, *The Genuine Works of Flavius Josephus* (London, 1737).

before going ahead with publication he submitted it to William Vinal, Newport's other Congregational minister. How far Stiles had previously confided in Vinal is not clear, but Vinal's comments reminded him that the dangers he had so narrowly escaped at Stockbridge still lay in wait. Vinal saw at once that his acceptance of Scripture was the product of reason alone, and that this might prove a frail reed: the authenticity of the Scriptures must "be evinced *chiefly by their own Divinity,* which is so conspicuous that an inattentive Reader can scarce miss of seeing it." In other words the proposition that Stiles was laboring to prove was self-evident to any true believer. By calling up such a host of supporting evidence, he only displayed his own (too great) reliance on mere scholarship. "Would it not be proper," Vinal suggested, "to insert some thing *emphatically* to let your Readers know that the Evidence of the Authenticity of the Scriptures is not deriv'd from thence?—Is there not much depending on your Manner of treating this important Subject, in such a place as this? Are there not many captious? Can you therefore be too much on your Guard . . . ?"[5]

Stiles never sent the sermon to the printer. Perhaps he feared that he had indeed been off guard. But there was probably another reason, namely that he was coming around to Vinal's point of view. He was beginning to see that his arguments would never bring more than a rational acceptance of Scripture, while the true Christian had something more than that. The true Christian had what might be called, for lack of a better term, positive knowledge that the Scriptures were inspired.

It is not clear how or when Ezra Stiles acquired such knowledge. Presumably it was by a gradual process, for there is no evidence that he underwent any sudden conversion of the kind that the New Lights gloried in, but within two years of his arrival at Newport his sermons began to assume an evangelical tone which had hitherto been missing from his whole make-up. When he first accepted Christianity it was as a moral system; his first sermon at Newport, on the excellency of the Christian religion, was a eulogy of Christian morality; and the letter to Ingersoll shows that he still retained this point of view in 1756. By the summer of 1758 he was telling his people that virtue was not enough: though obedience to moral principles would bring great rewards in this world, it would not bring "heavens peculiar Care here-

5. Vinal to Stiles, Sept. 2, 1758.

after, unless by the Grace of God in Christ." [6] Hitherto he had been much taken up with the prospect of enjoying the company of angels and departed friends in the world to come; now he reminded himself and his congregation that however sweet this intercourse might be, it was not to be obtained by human merit (as he had told Ingersoll) any more than by the intercession of saints and angels, but only by the free gift of God. The Arminian tendency which had often characterized his writing was giving way to an insistence upon human corruption and the atonement of Christ.

From 1758 onward this new understanding of Christianity was growing in Ezra Stiles. It can be discerned not only in his sermons, where it found most direct expression, but also in his attitudes toward a number of things. It seems to be reflected in the abandonment of his grandiose plans for a family organization, in his remark that all he wanted for his children was that "real Holiness and the Love of Jesus may be the portion of as many as possible." [7] "I dispise myself," he wrote in 1770, "for at any Time feeling the relish of human Glory. . . . There is a Glory after which I aim, under the lively Anticipations of which I at Times find all this World annihilated." [8] The change is also reflected in a new opinion about missionary efforts. As late as December 25, 1761, he was telling Charles Chauncy that the only way to bring Christianity to the Indians was to civilize them first, the way John Sergeant had done.[9] By January 26, 1768, he had changed his mind, ostensibly because of an account he had read of the United Brethren in Greenland, who had had great success not by teaching moral improvement "but by the Doctrines of Grace—human nature in ruins, Justification by the imputation of the vicarious Righteousness of the crucified Emanuel." [10] It seems probable that his change of mind resulted not merely from the supposed success of the United Brethren, but also from a reduced estimate of the value of moral excellence and a new understanding of the doctrine of saving grace.

6. Sermon 222. This sermon is undated, but the one immediately preceding, number 221, was first preached on July 16, 1758.

7. "Family Constitutions" (note dated June 11, 1771).

8. Stiles to Chauncy Whittelsey, Mar. 6, 1770.

9. Stiles to Chauncy, Dec. 25, 1761.

10. Stiles to Eleazar Wheelock, Jan. 26, 1768. See also note appended in 1786 to letter cited in n. 9, above.

And what are we to make of the extraordinary notation on the margin of a letter to his father, dated November 24, 1755? The letter describes the sermon he has just preached on the recent earthquake of November 18. This was the quake which caused a great controversy in Boston between the Reverend Thomas Prince and Professor John Winthrop, Prince maintaining that earthquakes were a direct judgment of God and Winthrop attributing them to the regular operation of natural forces.[11] Stiles expressed Winthrop's view before he had even heard of it. Describing his sermon to his father, he wrote: "among other Things [I] observed, that I *didn't* apprehend it a *Judgment* in the moral Government of God, as twas manifestly effected according to the Laws of Nature, as much as violent Tempests, *Thunder* or *Comets*, all of which I judg'd of beneficent Influence in the Universe." When he read over his copy of this letter sixteen years later—he seems to have reviewed his correspondence and notebooks at frequent intervals—he wrote pregnantly in the margin beside this passage: "Herein I was mistaken—1771."

Another manifestation of Stiles's religious growth may be found in his change of taste in English authors. In 1759 he still admired the antideist writers whose books he had used in preparing his own defense of revelation. He complained to Jared Eliot that the English philosophers and mathematicians "spend most of their Time in familiarizing the Newtonian philosophy to the Capacities of Boys and Ladies" (the books he had read at Yale!), but he found the English disquisitions on revelation to be "most learned and truly great." [12] In 1766 he wrote to an English Presbyterian condemning such defenses of the rationality of revelation. The period of deism was nearly at an end, he now thought, not merely in himself but in the world at large. It would therefore be well to cease marshaling arguments (as he had done in his sermon) to prove that revelation could bear up under rational investigation and instead preach up the great doctrines of Christianity: "human Nature in Ruins, the Divinity Incarnation and Atonement of the Redeemer, Justification thro Affiance in his Righteousness and vicarious Sacrifice, Regeneration by the Spirit, the

11. Thomas Prince, *Earthquakes the Works of God* (Boston, 1755); *An Improvement of the Doctrine of Earthquakes* (Boston, 1755); John Winthrop, *A Lecture on Earthquakes* (Boston, 1755); *Boston Gazette*, Jan. 26, 1756; and John Winthrop, *A Letter to the Publisher of the Boston Gazette* (Boston, 1756).

12. Stiles to Eliot, Sept. 24, 1759.

nature precepts and motives of Sanctity and Virtue, Immortality and its Retributions." The English Presbyterian ministers, Stiles feared, "tho exemplarily learned and pious, have suffered these Doctrines a little too much to give place to a less pathetic and what is called a more rational and polite manner of preaching." They should resume "those *evangelical Doctrines* for which their learned and pious Ancestors were eminent, and especially that close manner of Address the *powerful Preaching*." They should get more hell-fire into their sermons, and depict "the tremendous Torments of Damnation." [13]

From the time of Solomon Stoddard hell-fire sermons had been common in New England. But since 1741 this type of preaching had been associated with the New Lights, while their opponents had tried to emphasize the rationality which Stiles was now deploring. If I know God's will, Stiles told his English friends, "be it eno' whether I can enter into the Rationale of it or not." [14] He did not go to the extreme of saying that a man should know nothing but Christ, nor did he relax in his own pursuit of knowledge, but there can be no doubt that he had become a different man from the one who preached on the excellency of the Christian religion without mentioning Christ.

The measure of his departure from his former positions can be taken also by the reactions of his old friends. Heresy in New England was usually a matter of emphasis, not always easy to detect. This breadth had enabled Stiles to become a minister while holding views that bordered on infidelity. Now his beliefs had reached the point where they seemed a trifle embarrassing to his more rationalistic friends. In 1764 he had an argument with his father-in-law, John Hubbard, on the extent of human depravity.[15] This was merely a straw in the wind. The real surprise came six years later, when Samuel Hopkins came to Newport as minister of the First Congregational Church.

To those who could remember what happened thirty years before, this event must have recalled the duel between Isaac Stiles and Jonathan Edwards. The Great Awakening was a memory now, but the divisions it had caused lived on, not only in civil and ecclesiastical politics but in theology as well. Though Jonathan Edwards was dead, he had left behind him a group of disciples who erected his doctrines

---

13. Stiles to Thomas Wright, Nov. 18, 1766; Dec. 22, 1767.
14. Stiles to Joseph Jennings, Jan. 20, 1767.
15. Stiles to Hubbard, Nov. 14, 1764.

into a new canon of orthodoxy. The New Divinity, it was called, and Samuel Hopkins was its high priest.[16] An unbending, ponderous, fearless man, Hopkins carried his notions of divine omnipotence and human depravity to the point where he denied that the unregenerate could or should pray. He refused to baptize children unless their parents could give proof of conversion; he argued that men should take joy in their own damnation, since it contributed to the glory of God. By delivering these dreadful doctrines in the dullest possible manner he alienated so large a portion of his church at Great Barrington that he found it necessary to leave them.

When Ezra Stiles's friends heard that Hopkins was leaving Great Barrington and about to descend upon Newport, they were indignant that the son of Isaac Stiles should be compelled to live face-to-face with the most extreme disciple of Jonathan Edwards. Charles Chauncy, who had as low an opinion of the New Divinity as he had had of the New Lights, told Stiles, "I'm sorry, with my whole soul, that Mr. Hopkins is like to settle at Newport. . . . He is a troublesome, conceited, obstinate man—He preached away almost his whole congregation at Barrington, and was the occasion of setting up the Church of England there. He will preach away all his congregation at New-port, or make them ten-fold worse than they are at present." [17] From New Haven Chauncy Whittelsey wrote in the same terms: "His Notions of Baptism will increase the Church of England, or your Congregation, perhaps both." [18]

Stiles's friends thought that he ought to do everything in his power to prevent the Newport First Church from electing Hopkins. When he did not lift a finger to do so, the rumor went round Connecticut that Hopkins had him in his pocket; [19] and when Stiles went so far as to preach the sermon at Hopkins' ordination, even his friends were ready to believe it. The sermon appearing in print shortly after, they scanned it closely for evidence of his defection.[20] Those who were looking for heresy found it, for Stiles had allowed himself a much

16. On the New Divinity see F. H. Foster, *A Genetic History of the New England Theology* (Chicago, 1907), and Joseph Haroutunian, *Piety versus Moralism* (New York, 1932).

17. Chauncy to Stiles, Nov. 14, 1769.

18. Whittelsey to Stiles, Sept. 17, 1769.

19. John Devotion to Stiles, Feb. 16, 1770; Chauncy Whittelsey to Stiles, Feb. 26, 1770.

20. *A Discourse on Saving Knowledge* (Newport, 1770)

stronger expression of human helplessness and divine omnipotence than his friends were willing to accept. In particular they objected to a passage in which he argued that human reason is incapable of apprehending the holiness of God. The other attributes of divinity, he said, could be "learned by reasoning and deduction from God's works or his word,—but this idea must be poured down upon the human intellect, as an emanation into the soul directly from God himself." [21] In this matter reason was helpless to act and equally help-less to refrain from acting, for God could "raise divine Illuminations, and spiritual influences, to a degree of irresistibility." [22]

Now irresistible grace and human passivity were the language of the New Divinity, and Stiles's friends were dismayed by these pas-sages. "This approaches nearer the new divinity than I apprehended your sentiments led you," wrote one of them.[23] "All acknowledge Dr. Stiles Scholarship," said another, "but every One is surprised at his Doctrine and Lament the Publication of the Piece." [24] When Stiles wrote to his father-in-law, attempting to defend himself, he only got in deeper. "To create us anew in Christ Jesus," he said, "to renew the divine Image and Nature within us, can only be done by God." [25] Surely this was a statement which every Christian should accept, but Hubbard did not: "Is it not absurd," he returned, "to ascribe an Effect to God as the sole efficient (which is necessarily included in the idea of creation) which Effect cannot possibly exist without the pure Volition of the Subject, upon which it is supposed to be operated?" [26]

There was no doubt that Stiles's views had changed. In a letter to Chauncy Whittelsey he admitted as much, denying only that he had altered any of his fundamental beliefs. In fact he reminded Whittelsey that anyone who uses his head must change:

> We always accounted it Weakness in Mr. Clap to plume himself on fixing his principles at 25 aet. and never getting any new Knowledge after he took his 2d Degree. It is happy if at 25 aet. we possess the radices or Semina which by Culture unfold into

21. Page 10.
22. Page 42.
23. James Dana to Stiles, ——, 1770.
24. John Devotion to Stiles, Jan. 21, 1771.
25. Stiles to Hubbard, Mar. 18, 1771.
26. Hubbard to Stiles, Apr. 25, 1771.

the Tree of Knowledge bearing various Fruit. When all the
World around us are imbibing good with Ill, Error with Truth,
why should we, let me say we never did, think ourselves exempted. And it becomes the Candor of liberal Inquiry, it becomes
the Reverence we owe to our own understanding to alter and
change Sentiments *intirely*, if we see reason for it.[27]

Stiles had not actually changed his sentiments entirely: he did not
in fact hold any of the peculiar principles of the New Divinity. He
joined Hopkins in ascribing a greater power to God, and a larger
degree of corruption to man, than the Old Lights did, but here the
resemblance ceased. Where Hopkins reached the conclusion that the
unregenerate cannot and ought not to do anything toward their own
salvation, Stiles thought that the greater part of Scripture was "addressed to perishing sinners," with a design to lead them toward the
salvation that might await them.[28] Where Hopkins all but drove
the unregenerate out of his church, Stiles tried to sweep them in.
Throughout his career as a minister he consistently offered the sacraments to all persons who lived without scandalous offenses. New
Divinity clergy excluded from the Lord's Table all who failed to
demonstrate conversion. Stiles also rejected the New Light doctrine,
still retained by some exponents of the New Divinity, that unconverted ministers can do no good to their people. This question was
still agitating the Presbyterians of the middle colonies, who wrote
him for advice about it in 1761. He answered that as far as New
England was concerned, the examination of a minister's religious
experiences was wholly unknown before Whitefield's time and had
been abandoned even by most New Lights since then. His own opinion
was that inquiry into a minister's or any other person's conversion
was an invasion of the divine prerogative, "for it is really impossible
for us to judge of the Heart. The blameless and sober Life, is all
we can judge of." [29]

What Stiles had done, and what set him off both from the Old
Lights and from the New Divinity, was to reach back to the evangelical faith of the seventeenth century. "I am in principle with the good
old Puritans," he told Abigail Dwight in 1770, when she asked him
what he thought of the New Divinity, and he did not think the New

27. Stiles to Whittelsey, Mar. 6, 1770.
28. Stiles to Madam [Dwight], Nov. 30, 1770.
29. Stiles to Francis Alison, Aug. 16, 1761.

Divinity approached close to the Puritan principles.[30] Where Hopkins had developed his peculiar ideas out of the theology of Jonathan Edwards, Stiles developed his out of the writings of an earlier generation. His conception of church membership resembled that of Jonathan Edwards' grandfather, Solomon Stoddard, the most evangelical of the latter-day Puritans. Of the earliest New England divines Stiles thought that Thomas Hooker had "a Penetration, Depth of Thot and Solidity of Judgment beyond them all." As it happens, Hooker was also the most evangelical of this group.[31]

By 1775 Stiles's antiquarian studies in the history of the New England churches led him to the writings of a still earlier Puritan, William Perkins, who had been the principal teacher, at Cambridge University in England, of most of the first ministers to emigrate to New England. Stiles conceived for Perkins an admiration even surpassing what he felt for the man's students.[32] It was high time, he thought, that New England ministers returned to the evangelical preaching of men like Perkins, and he urged his professional friends to do so before it was too late. To Edward Wigglesworth, the Professor of Divinity at Harvard, he wrote:

I fear also a Loss of the Evangelical Doctrines the Doctrines of Grace as held by the good Old Puritans and by our Ancestors. They have evanished from the Church of England since Archbishop Laud, they are evanishing apace from the Churches of Scotland and even Holland, and from the Dissenters in England: and System (like that of Dr. Priestly) little better than Deism is taking place. It will be your Care, my Dear sir, in your important Office, to use your most vigorous Endeavors to prevent a like Leaven spreading among the American Churches. I greatly wish that you may be instrumental, in your Day, of making such a Sett of Ministers as those made by the Tuition of that eminent Man of God Mr. Perkins of Cambridge. The Writings of that excellent Divine are worthy the Attention of every Student in Divinity, not for any Systematic order in them, but for the Perspicuity and Justness of his theological Principles. A general Approbation of any author, is always with Exceptions. It is this

30. Stiles to Madam [Dwight], Nov. 30, 1770.
31. *Lit. Diary*, *1*, 133.
32. Ibid., pp. 525, 528, 529, 533; Stiles to Edward Wigglesworth, Mar. 30, 1775; to Samuel Wilton, Apr. 13, 1775.

kind of Divinity that has been blessed to m[any? *torn*] good
Men in all Ages:—and the Ministers of [every? *torn*] Denomination, who have imbibed the good old puritan Doctrines of
Grace, especially that of *Justification,* have been the Ornaments
of the Churches, and I doubt not have had a better Account to
give up to God than those whose Preaching might as well have
been formed on Texts out of Seneca or Antoninus as the Old
and New Testament.[33]

Stiles was not without grounds when he claimed to be maintaining
the old religious traditions of his country. The theological position
he had been taking up in the 1760s and 1770s was much closer to
that of the Puritans of a hundred years before than either the New
Divinity of a Hopkins or the new rationalism of a Chauncy could
claim to be. He had gone back to the views of human depravity and
redemption which his rationalist friends had all but abandoned and
which Hopkins was unconsciously reducing to absurdity. He was, he
thought, truly an old Puritan.

It was a pleasing orientation for a man who revered the past. But
if it began in antiquarian scholarship, it had grown into something
more than that. In identifying himself with the old Puritans, Stiles
was unconsciously masking his own growth under the cloak of tradition and filial piety. His Puritanism was in fact a compound of the
old piety and the new enlightenment. When he looked back on his
Puritan heritage, his enlightened eyes saw only those colors which
looked well under the warm illumination of the eighteenth century.
A hundred and fifty years had seen a noble growth of human liberty,
and Stiles freely, perhaps gratuitously, gave his Puritan ancestors the
credit for it. "I inherit," he said, "from my Ancestors who came out
of England among the first Accessions of the last Century, an ardent
and inextinguishable Love of *Liberty civil and religious*—which I
pray God may overspread America, and be perpetuated into the millennial Ages." [34]

Though the genealogy was dubious, it was a noble error. And seen
from the proper perspective it was perhaps not an error at all. How
democracy and liberty could grow so quickly in a land peopled by
Puritans has long puzzled historians. Some have alleged that these

33. Stiles to Wigglesworth, Mar. 30, 1775.
34. Stiles to Samuel Wilton, Apr. 13, 1775.

rare fruits grew spontaneously, in spite of Puritan efforts to extirpate them, in the free air of the American wilderness. Others have found them embedded in the Anglo-Saxon institutions which the Puritans carried with them as incidental baggage; and still others have traced them to the enemies of Puritanism who survived quietly until the fires of bigotry burned out. None of these explanations by itself is quite convincing: it is difficult to see how liberty could have achieved so strong a growth in New England if Puritanism was as hostile to it as at first appears. The fact must be that there were in Puritanism itself strong elements of liberty, elements which spelled death to at least one tyrant, and which inspired not only the defiance of a Roger Williams but also the determination of a John Winthrop.[35]

Ezra Stiles saw these elements and isolated them from the unfortunate tendencies toward tyranny and persecution that had accompanied them in the seventeenth century. His ancestors might have regarded his selection as arbitrary, but they would have had no more difficulty in recognizing him as their grandson than a nineteenth-century American, say a Justice Holmes, would have found in recognizing him as a grandfather.[36]

From the standpoint of the descendants, perhaps the happiest aspect of Stiles's enlightened view of the Puritans was the way he transformed their reverence for Scripture into a platform for liberty of thought. The return to Scripture as the sole authority in matters of religion and indeed in all matters had been a moving principle of the Reformation, and a strict adherence to this principle had differentiated the Puritans from their Anglican countrymen. Unfortunately the Puritans, in their certainty that the Scriptures had an answer for every question, insisted that the answers they found there were the only possible answers; and anyone who disagreed must be either a fool or a knave. This overweening dogmatism, which produced the most unhappy episodes in New England history, was missing in Ezra Stiles. His own reverence for Scripture, though he attributed it to his Puritan heritage, had been acquired, initially at least, in the course of his battle with skepticism; and from that battle he emerged, as we

35. Cf. my *The Puritan Dilemma: The Story of John Winthrop* (Boston, 1958).

36. Justice Holmes did in fact come close—if such a conception is possible—to being a great grandson of Ezra Stiles. Stiles's daughter Mary married Abiel Holmes but died without issue. Abiel Holmes's second wife was the mother of Oliver Wendell Holmes.

have seen, not only with a Puritan reverence for Scripture but with a profound conviction of the fallibility of human knowledge. When he moved from a religion of morality toward a more evangelical Christianity, this conviction deepened, for the more he magnified the omnipotence of God and the corruption of man, the more presumptuous it seemed to him for human beings to judge the hearts and minds of their fellows or to claim positive knowledge of the mind of their Maker. Scripture, not its exegesis, was sacred, and Scripture alone was a sufficient foundation for the Christian church. The erection of creeds and tests, whether of orthodoxy or piety, was an infringement of the divine prerogative. God, not man, must be the judge of heresy, as God, not man, would forgive or condemn the sinner at the last day.[37]

Curiously enough, in spite of his depreciation of human reason, Stiles retained a supreme confidence in the methods of reason. Though human reason might be a dim light, it was the only light that men had in the search for truth. God had given it to them, so that they might apply it to Scripture and to the world around them. Thus far Stiles and his Puritan ancestors agreed. But his confidence in reason differed from theirs. They thought that God had already led them through reason and Scripture to the truth. They therefore undertook with force and arms to establish the truth and to suppress the errors that fallible human reason was always spawning. Stiles thought truth was more elusive and that God guided human reason to it in a more devious manner. Reason, Stiles believed, must be allowed free play to propagate both truth and error. In the competition of the open market, the one would then be distinguished from the other, and truth in its greatness would prevail. Liberty of thought was the means provided by God to overcome the fallibility of fallen man.

Since God had appointed liberty of thought, it was not for man to establish standards of truth by force and compulsion. That was the trouble with creeds and platforms of orthodoxy—not the fact that they interpreted Scripture but that their establishment prevented other interpretations and compelled the acceptance as truth of what was quite possibly only the erroneous opinion of man. Truth needed no creeds or tests, no compulsion or force to support it. If allowed to make its

37. For a good example of Stiles's expression of these views see his *Discourse on the Christian Union*, pp. 34–36, 119–22, 152. For other expressions see *Lit. Diary, 1,* 556–58; Stiles to Philip Furneaux, May 20, 1772; to Thomas Wright, Apr. 10, 1775; "Sermons on Public Fasts and Thanksgivings," Nov. 22, 1759.

way through free inquiry, people would embrace it because of its self-evident excellence and superiority.

Stiles was so persuaded of the power of truth that he avoided even the mild weapons of theological controversy, preferring to state his own views without attacking opposing ones. In 1760 when he had opportunity to address a meeting of Congregational ministers, he told them to shun all tests of orthodoxy, to overlook their differences of belief, to be content with the all-sufficiency of Scripture. And again and again both here and in the years to follow he reiterated this fundamental axiom: "Many considerable errors, if let alone, will correct themselves in time on free inquiry, deliberate and unheated disquisitions." The Congregationalists had not yet reached the degree of perfection which he wished to see, but improvements and purifications would "take place in process of time on free inquiry and universal liberty." [38]

Though Stiles had himself arrived at a religious belief that went beyond logical demonstration, he thus retained that greatest gift of the new philosophy, a faith in the unrestricted use of reason, a faith that he blended with his faith in God. It gratified him to think that free inquiry had led him from skepticism to a closer approximation of God's truth, to that Puritanism which his ancestors had mistakenly attempted to establish by force. And it gratified him even more to think that his new understanding might enable him to present the truth to the men and women he had come to love in Newport. He had chosen, before he fully understood what it meant, to be a minister of God; and it gave him pain to think that some souls might have been lost because the first years of his ministry "were not so evangelical as I could wish them to have been." [39] In later years he labored to make up the deficit; for, keeping pace with his spiritual growth, was a deepening joy and dedication in the way he answered to his vocation.

38. *Discourse on the Christian Union*, pp. 120–21.

39. "Dr. Stiles's Resignation of the Ministry . . . Mar. 19, 1778." This MS in the Stiles Papers at Yale is not in Stiles's hand. There is an extract from it (in the hand of Samuel Hopkins, of the Newport First Church), including the passage quoted, in Bellamy Papers, Archives of the Hartford Seminary Foundation, Hartford, Conn. Cf. *Lit. Diary*, *1*, 295–96.

12

The Ministry

For Ezra Stiles the most sacred thing about the Christian ministry was its origin. Every true minister, he believed, every priest or presbyter or pastor of whatever denomination, could trace his appointment back to the original apostles through an unbroken succession. It was wrong to raise one minister above another, to distinguish some as bishops or archbishops or cardinals (the word "bishop" was simply another word for priest or presbyter, and he and his associates sometimes playfully addressed one another as bishop). But the fact that such corruptions had taken place did not destroy the priestly character of the men who participated in them. A cardinal was still a minister, and so was an Anglican bishop, so long as he had been inducted into the priestly office by other ministers who had in turn been thus inducted, and so on back to the apostles.

Some extreme Protestants, in their disgust with the corruptions of the Catholic church or of other Protestant churches, made no effort to maintain the succession. They practiced "lay ordination," in which the minister was installed with no other minister present to accept him into office and charge him with his duties. Such practices Stiles abhorred. The proper way was to invite several ministers from neighboring churches. They would examine the candidate to determine his fitness and then, if satisfied, proceed with a ceremony that might last three hours. One of the ministers would open with prayer, another preach a sermon, a third make the ordaining prayer, a fourth charge the candidate with his duties, a fifth give him the right hand of fellowship, and a sixth offer a final blessing. In conjunction with the ordaining prayer, all the ministers would lay hands on the candidate and thus impose on him the sacred office. If necessary, one minister could perform all these functions, but there ought to be at least one to carry on the succession.

As his appreciation and understanding of Christianity grew, Stiles came more and more to value the derivation of the office he held. Although the Puritan founders of New England had been less concerned with this matter than he, their ministers had in fact been originally ordained by English bishops, so that they carried the succession with them to New England.

Stiles liked to trace his own ordination back to England. There had been three ministers present at it: his father, the Reverend John Burt of Bristol, and the Reverend Joseph Torrey of South Kingstown (Jared Eliot, though invited, had been unable to attend). Isaac Stiles had been ordained by, among others, Samuel Whittelsey, Whittelsey by Samuel Street, Street by Nicolas Street (his father), Nicolas Street by John Davenport, and Davenport by an English bishop. Through Burt a line went back to John Cotton and through Torry to Bishop Morton of Chester. Since there were usually several ministers at each ordination, the lines of ascent fanned out rapidly as one went back in time.[1]

Stiles gained an antiquarian satisfaction from this game of sacred genealogy. It pleased his vanity—which always sought new outlets as he closed old ones—and it impressed him with the special responsibilities of the office he had undertaken. But he did not allow himself to be carried into inflated opinions of the rights and honors belonging to the clergy, an excess which he deplored in Catholics, Anglicans, and even, to a degree, Presbyterians. His fascination with the derivation of his calling may, in fact, have been partly a compensation for the relatively humble view he took of it; for in keeping with his ideas about creeds, tests, and religious quarrels he regarded all ecclesiastical offices and organizations as purely human arrangements.

God, he believed, had left Christianity to make its way among men in the same manner as any other truth. Men, rightly considering the truth about salvation to be important, had established organizations to spread and perpetuate it from generation to generation. The apostles

1. *Lit. Diary, 1*, 126–27, 190–91, 334. MS notes dated Nov. 25, 1768; Stiles to James Davidson, July 16, 1772. Cf. *The United States Elevated to Glory and Honor* (New Haven, 1783), pp. 59–64.

had led the way, and it was wise to imitate their arrangements. But it must be remembered that God did not require any particular arrangement. The form of the church, the manner of communicating His truth, of nourishing the faith—these were left to men, with the example of the scriptural churches to guide but not compel them.[2]

From such premises it might still have been possible to argue that ministers, who had studied the Scriptures and carried on the work of the apostles, would know best how to organize and conduct a church. But experience had demonstrated that ministers were not to be trusted in this matter. Human ambition had led them in the past to pretentious claims of divine right. The only safe repository of ecclesiastical power was the congregation. And so, while he thought that a congregation ought not by itself to induct a minister into office, that was about the only thing Stiles thought it could not do. A minister could not be a minister unless some congregation asked him to be. Even after proper installation he could not determine how his church should be run or exercise a veto power (as some ministers claimed) if his wishes ran counter to the congregation's. If seriously displeased, they could dismiss him and thus strip him of his priesthood, while he could not, except in unusual circumstances, leave them without their consent.[3]

Although Congregationalists acknowledged more common ground with Presbyterians than with any other denomination, Stiles had no use for the Presbyterian practice of creating ministers in general—unattached to a particular congregation. One of the things he distrusted about the New Divinity was that its adherents tended in this direction. He was shocked when Samuel Hopkins, after dismissal from the church at Great Barrington, administered communion in the First Church at Newport before his ordination there. It was proper for a man to preach before ordination; but only a minister could offer the sacraments, and in Stiles's view Hopkins was not at that time a minister. There was even some doubt in Stiles's mind whether a regularly constituted minister ought to give the sacraments in any church but his own. It had become the practice, in which he joined, for ministers

2. "Reflexions: I. on the present State of the Protestant Religion in British America. II. On the policy of introducing the English Episcopacy and Hierarchy. III. On politically constituting the British Provinces, particularly with respect to Religion. Dec. 12, 1759." This is the draft of a manuscript probably intended for publication as a pamphlet. Cited hereafter as "Reflexions," Dec. 12, 1759.

3. Ibid.; Stiles to Nathan Stone, Apr. 25, 1768.

visiting another church to do so if the occasion arose, but Stiles thought that the founding fathers of New England had tied their ministers more closely to a single congregation.[4]

Stiles liked to follow the founding fathers wherever possible, but in thinking through the responsibilities of his office, he had to adjust his views to situations that they had not faced. As they conceived it, Congregationalism not only tied a minister to his congregation but directed most of his attention to a select group within the congregation, namely to the "visible saints," who could demonstrate to his and one another's satisfaction that they were among the elect of God. A Congregational church, as distinct from a congregation, consisted of such persons joined together by an explicit covenant in which they agreed to "walk together" in the worship of God.[5]

Walking together, as practiced in the apostolic churches that they sought to imitate, required that they select a minister to preach the word and administer the sacraments to them. (They might also choose a second minister, known as a teacher, and several minor officers, such as deacons and ruling elders, but these were not essential.) The minister, therefore, was an officer of the church, and his responsibilities lay entirely within the church. The Puritans thought that he fulfilled his obligations to the rest of the congregation, indeed to the rest of mankind, simply by preaching the word. The unregenerate might listen—the government originally required them to—but they were no part of the church.

So narrow a conception of church and ministry could scarcely have satisfied Ezra Stiles. He saved his admiration for the old Puritans by telling himself that among the first generation of New Englanders the majority had been accounted saints and so had been members of a church.[6] But he knew that this had not been the case ever since.

4. *Lit. Diary*, *1*, 37–38. Stiles later changed his views on this matter. See below, chap. 27, and *Lit. Diary*, *2*, 218–19, 316.

5. The literature on New England Congregationalism is too voluminous to cite here, but see esp. Perry Miller, *Orthodoxy in Massachusetts* (Cambridge, Mass., 1933).

6. Stiles made this statement (like many others referred to in this chapter) in a "Memoir of Transactions in procuring the Charter [incorporating the Newport Second Church] from the General Assembly 1771," hereafter cited as Memoir of procuring the Charter. The memoir is written in the blank pages of an old record book of the Second Church, labeled "Deacon Pitman's Book 1741–1755," now deposited in the library of the Newport Historical Society. The statement here cited may represent

Moreover, the distinction between visible saints and unregenerate sinners had become less clear in subsequent generations than it had been to the founders. Some persons now doubted that saints were visible at all—that you could tell in this world who was to be saved in the next. New Lights and New Divinity preachers thought you could; Stiles and his friends were not so sure. But more perplexing than the problem of identifying saints was the anomalous status of the children of saints. Were they in the church or not?

This problem had vexed New England for a hundred years. The Bible, as Congregationalists read it, required that the children of saints be baptized, and a baptized child was in some implied and undefined manner a member of the church. He did not vote or take communion, but he had been given a "promise" of membership, which would be fulfilled whenever he enjoyed the crucial experience of conversion. But if he grew to maturity without having the experience, was he in the church or out of it? When he had children of his own, were they to be baptized or not? By Ezra Stiles's time opinion on this subject and on the status of the unconverted in general ranged in a spectrum from strict to free. Stiles had to find his own place as a minister within that spectrum and also to carry out his responsibilities to men and women who took different positions than he.

At one extreme, just outside the range of Congregationalism, was the Baptist position: keep the church pure by eliminating children from it altogether; baptize only converted adults. This way the line between the church and the world could be kept clear. To those who felt most assured of the visibility of saints, to the New Lights for example, this position had a strong appeal, and many New Lights wound up as Baptists.[7]

Just short of the Baptist position was one held by Jonathan Edwards and his followers of the New Divinity. Edwards would never have condoned the abolition of infant baptism, but he became more and more concerned with maintaining a church of regenerate members. His solution and that of the New Divinity was to consider all un-

---

an erroneous opinion on the part of Stiles. On the proportion of church members among the first settlers see James Truslow Adams, *The Founding of New England* (Boston, 1921), p. 121, and Samuel E. Morison, *Builders of the Bay Colony* (Boston, 1930), pp. 339–40.

7. W. W. Sweet, *Religion on the American Frontier: The Baptists* (New York, 1931), pp. 4–6.

converted adults, whether baptized or not, as outside the church and not qualified to have their children baptized.[8]

A third possibility, recommended in 1662 by a convention of ministers (called a "synod" but without the authority of a Presbyterian synod), was known as the half-way covenant. This called for adults who had been baptized in infancy, if they had not experienced grace, to appear before the church and acknowledge—or in the phrase of the time "own"—the covenant undertaken for them by their parents at the time of their baptism—that is, to accept the responsibility of endeavoring to lead godly lives. Such persons, though not full members and not admitted to communion, would be half-way members and could have their children baptized.[9]

A fourth position was to open up this half-way membership to adults who had not been baptized in childhood. They would then be baptized as adults and have their children baptized but would not be admitted to communion. With regard to all half-way members there was a division of opinion as to whether they ought to come under the "discipline" of the church—whether, that is, they were subject to admonition, censure, or excommunication for ill behavior.

A fifth position, at the opposite extreme from that of the Baptists, was taken by Solomon Stoddard, Edwards' grandfather. Stoddard offered full membership on the same terms that other churches offered half-way membership. He transformed communion from an exclusive privilege of proven saints to a means of converting potential saints. All he required for membership was a sincere desire on the part of the individual, whether previously baptized or not. Under this scheme the meaning of conversion gradually underwent the change noted in an earlier chapter: from an ecstatic experience of saving grace it was transformed into not much more than a wish to be saved.[10]

By the time the Great Awakening began, a large proportion of New England churches had adopted the Stoddardean position. Al-

8. Jonathan Edwards, *An Humble Inquiry into the Rules of the Word of God* . . . , *Works, 4,* 281–451; Joseph Haroutunian, *Piety versus Moralism* (New York, 1932), pp. 97–130.

9. Perry Miller, *The New England Mind: From Colony to Province* (Cambridge, Mass., 1953), pp. 82–104.

10. Ibid., pp. 209–47; Perry Miller, "Solomon Stoddard," *Harvard Theological Review, 34* (1941), 277–320.

though it might be supposed that this would have obliterated in these churches any distinction between church and congregation, such does not seem to have been the case. Stoddardeanism may have increased the membership where it was practiced, but not greatly. The majority of eighteenth-century New Englanders were unwilling to join the church even on Stoddard's generous terms.[11] And after the Great Awakening, under the aegis of the New Divinity, there was a movement toward stricter standards.

Ezra Stiles had no difficulty finding his own position on the scale, and he did not alter it as he moved toward a more ardent Calvinism. He was a Stoddardean. He welcomed to full membership in his church at Newport anyone who professed a desire to join and was not visibly sinful.[12] In accordance with his belief that God alone was competent to judge and condemn human hearts, whenever a dubious case came to him for decision he decided in favor of granting church privileges rather than withholding them. In baptizing children his only stipulation was that someone who had himself been baptized be committed to see that the child was brought up as a Christian. He baptized a Negro child whose mother and father were not baptized but whose master was.[13] He baptized a child of former Baptists (who had never been baptized) because its aunt was a member.[14] He baptized the son

11. Stiles was much interested in the proportion of communicants in various churches and noted the numbers throughout his Itineraries. Some but not all are printed in *Itineraries and Miscellanies*. I have sampled church records to check his figures and find them substantially correct: the number of communicants in Congregational churches throughout New England, whether on the Stoddardean plan or not, seldom amounted to one-quarter of the society and usually to much less than that.

12. Stiles's views on church membership and his practice at Newport, as discussed in this chapter, are expressed in Stiles to Chauncy Whittelsey, March 6, 1770, in *Lit. Diary, 1*, passim, in Memoir of procuring the Charter, and in the Records of the Second Congregational Church during his ministry, contained in a volume on the flyleaf of which Stiles has written, "This book was Deacon Bissel's—I asked it of his Son; and it belongs to the second Congregational Church in Newport" (hereafter referred to as Records of the Second Church). The book is now deposited in the library of the Newport Hist. Soc. The most valuable part of it is the detailed record of the year 1770, at the head of which Stiles has written "I propose, if it please God I live, to record all my public actions as a Minister, with the occurrences in this church, at least for one year." Stiles's view that an experience of conversion should not be required as a condition of membership is well expressed in a letter to Francis Alison, Aug. 16, 1761.

13. *Lit. Diary, 1*, 240.

14. Ibid., pp. 252–53.

of an unbaptized friend, whose wife had been baptized in the Church of England.[15] He baptized adults who owned the covenant without joining the church, and he baptized the children (provided they had not reached maturity) of any adult he baptized.[16] Conversely if an adult wished to join the church but (under Baptist influence) refused baptism for his children, Stiles did not hold this as a bar to membership.[17] Although no one ever asked for it, he repeatedly expressed his willingness to baptize by immersion (the Baptist method) if anyone should prefer it to the mode he normally used (sprinkling or washing the face).[18] He would baptize in the church or in the privacy of the home.[19]

In offering communion, Stiles followed the same broad policy. In order to join the church and thus accept the privilege of communion, one must subscribe to the covenant that bound the members together. But the covenant which Stiles drew up for the Second Church was little more than a statement of belief in redemption by Christ and a promise to try to lead a Christian life, with no complicated series of propositions such as the New Divinity preachers were beginning to impose.[20] Stiles held the door open not only to his own congregation but to members of other churches. He was ready to accept sober members of any Protestant church, Congregational or otherwise, at the communion table, either for one occasion or (if regularly dismissed or converted from their old church) as permanent members.[21] When a man had belonged to another church but had not attended for several years, Stiles asked him to renew his covenant with God in a public profession, but otherwise there were no tests or creeds or subscriptions.[22]

15. Nov. 17, 1765, Records of the Second Church.

16. There is no indication of the age at which a child ceased to be eligible for baptism on the basis of one of his parents joining the church. When Stiles admitted Hannah Belcher to membership on Feb. 25, 1770, he baptized her and eight of her children. But when he admitted and baptized Hannah Davenport three weeks earlier, he baptized only two of her children, her two other children "being too old to be baptised on the Parents account, according to usage." Records of the Second Church.

17. Memoir of procuring the Charter.

18. Ibid., and Records of the Second Church, June 10, 1771.

19. Baptisms in the home were usually of sick persons.

20. Wright, *Beginnings of Unitarianism*, p. 232; Records of the Second Church, 1770.

21. *Lit. Diary*, *1*, 39; *3*, 162–63, 286. Records of the Second Church, May 4, 1770.

22. Records of the Second Church, July 8, 1771.

Stiles, in other words, conceived of the church in as broad and inclusive a fashion as a Congregationalist could. If he had had his way, he would have swept virtually his whole congregation into the church.

He did not have his way, any more than other New England ministers did. In the seventeenth century New England Congregationalism used to be described as a speaking aristocracy (the ministers) in the face of a silent democracy (the lay members). If that had ever been an accurate description, it no longer was. Eighteenth-century New Englanders formed their own ideas about what a church should be, and within a single congregation opinion might range over the whole spectrum. What is more remarkable, the majority of New Englanders held stricter opinions than their ministers about the necessity of conversion, opinions by which they excluded themselves from membership even when it was open to them.

This independence of mind was very evident in Stiles's church at Newport. There is no doubt that his people liked him. And they were not indifferent to religion, for though there were no laws in Rhode Island to require church attendance, the congregation grew from 470 persons (not counting Negroes) in 1755 to 608 white persons and about 70 Negroes in 1770. Virtually all these would have been entitled, in Stiles's view, to join the church in full membership, but precious few were persuaded to do so. In 1755 there were 47 full members; in 1770 there were 57. The next year produced an unusual number of admissions, but at the end of it the total membership was still only 76.[23]

Thus the great majority of people under Stiles's pastoral care were not members of his church but only of his congregation, or "society" as it was usually called. They approved of his open-door policy or they would not have elected or kept him as minister, but they had qualms about walking through the door themselves. This situation was characteristic of the Congregational churches throughout New England, and so was the fact that far more women were persuaded to join than men. In Stiles's church at the end of the year 1771 there were 16 men and 56 women members, plus four absentees whose sex he did not indicate.[24]

23. Records of the Second Church, 1770.
24. Ibid. A sampling of eighteenth-century records indicates that the proportion of women to men in New England churches was seldom less than two to one and often, as at Newport, as high as three or four to one.

Not only did most of the congregation refrain from church membership, but about a third of them could not even be prevailed upon to accept baptism. Stiles attributed their reluctance to the influence of Baptist and Quaker ideas, which were stronger in Rhode Island than elsewhere in New England.[25] If his view was correct (and since he talked with all these people on pastoral visits, it probably was), then a substantial portion of his congregation, though not sufficiently convinced by the Baptists to attend a Baptist church, were nevertheless sufficiently impressed by Baptist or Quaker arguments to decline baptism for themselves or their children. This factor operated even more strongly in the congregation of Samuel Hopkins, where two-thirds had not been baptized.[26] Hopkins' views of baptism being closer in the spectrum to those of the Baptists, it was natural that Congregationalists with Baptist leanings should gravitate toward his congregation rather than Stiles's.

That two-thirds of Stiles's society had received baptism, while only a small proportion of them were full members, shows that they or their parents believed in the half-way covenant. Stiles, of course, did not. He would gladly have brought all these people to communion. Since they took a more exclusive view of that ordinance than he and thought themselves unworthy of it, he was willing to offer them as much as they would accept. Like other ministers he kept a record of those who owned the covenant, but he could not refrain from expressing his opinion in the heading he placed on one page of it: "persons professing the Faith and Entring into Covenant with God and his people for the Baptism of themselves and theirs but not seeing their way clear to come to the Lords Table; though they have an equal Right to both Ordinances." [27]

Since he could not make them see the way that was so clear to him, Stiles, like other ministers, was obliged to accept the unhappy fact that the vast majority of the men and women who paid his salary and committed their souls to his care were not members of his church and probably never would be. If the original Puritan practice had prevailed, these people would have had no voice in the management of the church. But although the average New Englander did not think

25. Records of the Second Church, 1770, and Memoir of procuring the Charter.
26. Records of the Second Church, 1770.
27. Records of the Second Church, 1773; see also Stiles to Chauncy Whittelsey, Mar. 6, 1770.

himself worthy of church membership, he felt fully qualified, indeed entitled, to assert himself in all the affairs of his church except those that exclusively concerned the members (their private business was to pass on the admission of new members and to discipline or expel immoral members). In the crucial matter of choosing a minister most Congregational churches in the eighteenth century followed the practice that Stiles found at Newport: both church and society had to agree to the choice. This was not quite a bicameral system, since the church members could also participate in the society's vote, but they were too few to affect any but a close decision (only males voted). The society kept separate records from the church, had its own executive committee (which at Newport included some church members), and took charge, without even consulting the church separately, of paying the minister's salary and maintaining the meetinghouse.[28]

Rhode Island, unlike the other New England colonies, levied no taxes for the support of the ministry. Stiles's salary came from contributions collected at the weekly services. The amount of these contributions, however, was not entirely voluntary. Those who attended regularly "bought" a pew or a seat in a pew (it was probably purchased originally from the society but could be resold to another individual) and were assessed a certain amount for it annually. Each person's weekly offering was credited toward this assessment. The society might also receive bequests and hold income-producing property. There is no indication in the surviving records of what property the Newport society owned, except for a share of land in the township of Danvis, in Colonel Lydius' patent, purchased in 1762. When extraordinary expenses occurred there might be a special subscription, as in July 1772 when the society reshingled the meetinghouse at a cost of £803 in the local currency (then worth about £22 sterling). In this enterprise some gave money, some labor; and the society chipped in £11 worth of rum, £2 (4 lbs.) of sugar, and a barrel of beer to make the shingles go on more easily.

A few leading members of the society belonged to the church, but three of the most influential did not. These were Stiles's good friends William Vernon; William Ellery, Jr.; and Henry Marchant. They, along with two or three others, arranged in 1771 to have the society (including the church) incorporated. The purpose was not only to

28. Society Records, Second Congregational Church, Newport Hist. Soc.

make the society's tenure of property more secure but also to enable it to collect delinquent pew rents by law, a provision about which Stiles had misgivings but was over-ruled. They had him draft the charter, discussed and revised it at several meetings, and only after it was completed asked the church to vote its approval. The church did so and empowered two of its members who were on the society's executive committee to help present it to the Rhode Island legislature. However, when the charter came up for consideration, it was a nonmember, Henry Marchant, who carried it through against strong opposition from Quakers and Baptists.[29]

Stiles was continually saddened by the fact that he could not persuade such men as Vernon, Ellery, and Marchant to join the church. He took consolation in regarding all baptized persons as members, whether they thought themselves so or not. And in every relation with his people other than communion he made no distinction between church and society. The discipline of church members by formal votes of censure and excommunication (in which the church by Congregational custom acted alone) he sought to avoid altogether. By anticipating trouble and personally mediating with the culprit, he was generally able to settle a brewing scandal without recourse to action by the church.[30]

Such personal contacts Stiles considered important. It was a self-imposed duty, in which he took pleasure, to visit every family (130 of them) in both church and society at least four times a year.[31] Every day in the late morning and again in the late afternoon he set out. Sometimes the visit seemed purely social—an exchange of news, compliments for the children or for the artistic arrangement of feathers and butterflies which were fashionable on Newport chimney panels. Sometimes he found opportunity for more serious talk. Stiles had a sensitivity to people that enabled him to detect where help was needed,

29. Memoir of procuring the Charter.

30. There are very few disciplinary cases in the church records. See Holmes, *Life*, p. 247. When he participated in ordinations, and gave the charge to the candidate, Stiles always advised him to avoid church censures so far as possible. See, for example, Levi Hart, *The Resurrection of Jesus Christ Considered and Proved* (Providence, 1786), pp. 24–25; Elizur Goodrich, *A Sermon Delivered at the Ordination of the Reverend Matthew Noyes* (New Haven, 1790), pp. 28–29.

31. Stiles kept a record of the number of pastoral visits he made to each family, *Lit. Diary*, *1*, 82–84, 327–28, 428–30, 504–06.

a human warmth and lack of censoriousness that made the help he brought acceptable. He kept alert for signs that his preaching was taking effect, and those whom he thought were on the verge of seeing the light he visited more often, until he could lead them triumphantly into the church. He also called more often on those who needed moral or spiritual bolstering, those he had to consult on church or society business, and those with whom he simply liked to talk. Through his pastoral visits Stiles's people came to know and love him not simply as a preacher but as a man.

Besides visiting people in their homes, Stiles held special meetings for different groups. Beginning in 1771 he held monthly sessions in the evenings for communicants, at the home of one of them. There were usually forty or fifty present, and he would lead them in singing a hymn, pray, discourse on some text of Scripture, pray again, rise to sing a final hymn, give the blessing, and depart. Except for the fact that it took place in the informality of a private home and that Stiles spoke without notes, it was much like an extra church service. He held similar evening meetings for the young men of the society, the young women, and the Negroes.[32]

There were about 1,200 Negroes in Newport, most of whom were presumably slaves. They were accepted in all the churches and did not necessarily attend the same one as their masters. At one of Stiles's special meetings for them in his own house eighty or ninety were present, but such a number was unusual. Although he included them with the children in monthly catechising (usually at 3 P.M. on a Thursday), normally few of them showed up, perhaps because they were kept at work. Of all the Negroes in Newport, Stiles estimated in 1772 that not more than thirty were full church members—seven of them in his church.[33]

In regular Sunday worship the church was not set apart from the society. Each person sat in whatever pew he had rented. Some pews carried a higher rent than others and were doubtless considered more honorable, whether the occupant was a member or nonmember. Seats in the gallery were cheapest, and some must have been free, for the Negroes could scarcely have paid.

The service itself was like that in other Congregational churches, but here as elsewhere Congregationalism invited variety, and Stiles

32. *Lit. Diary,* 1, passim; Records of the Second Church, esp. 1770.
33. *Lit. Diary,* 1, 213–14; Records of the Second Church, esp. 1770.

took pains to set down in the records the way it was done in Newport.[34] He kept Saturday evening as the beginning of the Sabbath and ended it at sundown the next day (this was the old Puritan practice), but most of his congregation observed Sunday evening. At ten o'clock on Sunday morning he began service with a prayer, to which he usually devoted a quarter of an hour or more, with the congregation standing. They then seated themselves while he, following a custom introduced by the previous pastor, read a chapter from the Old Testament. In his first year he chose chapters at random but thereafter proceeded chapter by chapter from the first of Genesis to the last of Malachi, omitting a few that he considered less "devotional" than the rest, such as some in Leviticus.

After the reading came the singing of a psalm, usually just the first four stanzas in Isaac Watts's version. The manner of singing had long been a subject of controversy in New England. At Newport Second Church it was agreed that the pastor should first read the psalm aloud and then the congregation sing it through, without pausing to have each line read separately. Whether or not they should sit or stand was another question. Until December 3, 1758, they sat. On that date, Stiles wrote in one of his almanacs,[35] they began to stand; but in 1770 he noted that "about a third of the Congregation stand, the rest sit in singing." [36] He did not say what position they took on another controversial question, that of singing in unison or every man to his own tune.

After the psalm Stiles preached a sermon, half to three-quarters of an hour in length, with the congregation seated. The service then concluded with a short prayer and a blessing. Stiles's sermons were "plain and practical." Though he wrote them out or made extensive notes beforehand, he never allowed his erudition to lead him into the metaphysical subtleties that he deplored in the New Divinity, nor did he fall into elaborate or recondite figures of speech. Instead he tried to concentrate upon what he considered the essentials of Christianity. As he summarized them, these were "the doctrines of the Trinity in one Jehovah, the true and real divinity of the Lord Jesus Christ, the mysteries of a bleeding Emmanuel, the illuminating and efficaceous

34. The following account is based primarily on this description, which is at the close of the Records of the Second Church, 1770.

35. Gannett Almanacs.

36. Records of the Second Church.

Energies of the holy Ghost in conversion, Justification by faith, thro'
the imputed righteousness and consummate merit of the Redeemer,
with the necessity of a holy life conformed to the precepts institutions
and example of the great author and finisher of our faith." [37]

A Sunday afternoon sermon was customary in eighteenth-century
New England, and Stiles's congregation returned to the meetinghouse at 2 P.M. in winter, 2:30 P.M. in summer. The service was much
the same as the morning one, except that the scriptural reading was
from the New Testament and after the concluding prayer, the deacons carried around the contribution boxes. With the donation completed, the congregation sang a second psalm before the blessing.

Before beginning worship in the morning Stiles published the banns
(three Sundays in succession) for anyone in his congregation who was
about to be married. The wedding itself never took place in the church
but at the home of the bride or bridegroom, frequently on the Sunday
evening of the day when the banns were published for the last time.
If there were announcements of other sorts, Stiles usually made them
at the conclusion of the afternoon service. That was also the customary
time for baptisms, for admissions to the church, and for owning the
covenant, the last two ceremonies being preceded by an announcement
of intention at least a fortnight earlier.

The church members took communion once every two months after
the morning service. On the preceding Friday afternoon Stiles preached
a sacramental lecture to prepare them. While the sacrament was being
administered, first the bread and then the wine, he stood at the sacramental table and spoke on the sufferings of Christ, in "expressions
tending to raise the the soul to a spiritual communion with Jesus."
Nonmembers were welcome to watch and listen in the gallery, where
Stiles doubtless hoped they might catch the urge to join.

In all these procedures Stiles was guided as much by the wishes
and customs of the congregation as by his own views. He did not
think the frequency of communion or the mode of baptism or
whether one stood or sat in singing made any difference. Even in
things that mattered, such as infant baptism, he was willing to let any
member of church or society differ from him. And though he longed
to see more members in the church, the multiplication of members was

37. Extracts of Farewell Sermon, Stiles Papers and Bellamy Papers, Archives of
the Hartford Seminary Foundation. Cf. the charges given by Stiles at various ordinations, cited above, n. 30.

after all only a human yardstick for measuring the ministry and no positive indication of souls saved. What he cared most deeply about and considered the most important aspect of his job was the opportunity to bring the means of salvation to perishing sinners, whether in the church or out. As long as he had freedom to broadcast God's truth as he saw it he would be a happy man, and happy to allow others the same freedom.

13

Christian Freedom

BECAUSE he thought the church a human institution, Stiles ran his own the way the congregation wanted it. For the same reason he vindicated the right of other Christians, or even of infidels, to construct churches quite different from his, even when they created offices of which he disapproved and endowed them with powers for which he could see no justification. Although no church officer, in his view, enjoyed the sanction of divine right, nothing prevented the members of a church from setting up bishops, archbishops, cardinals, or any other potentates their disordered imaginations might conceive, so long as it was understood that the members, not God, had created these offices and that the incumbents had no authority over anyone who did not consent to it.

Stiles would never consent and would try to persuade others not to. What was good enough for the apostles was good enough for him and ought to be for everyone else. But men had the right to make their own mistakes; God propagated truth not by compulsion but by freedom, allowing every man to seek his own way past error. The sacred thing was not any institution, apostolic or otherwise, but liberty itself, the liberty to submit or defy, to choose freely one's own church or minister.[1]

This was a liberty broad enough to satisfy the most enlightened of eighteenth-century philosophers. Yet even a philosopher might have observed that it offered both too much and too little to any Christian who did not believe in Congregationalism or one of its offshoots. The

1. "Reflexions," Dec. 12, 1759.

liberty advocated by Stiles would in effect have reduced all churches to congregations. He would not have denied the charge. The Congregationalism of the old Puritans was no more than the reassertion of the liberty that God allowed. That was why he rejoiced in the old Puritans. Let all philosophers do likewise.

Stiles's Congregationalism, however, was considerably freer than that of his ancestors. They had proclaimed the principle of congregational independence, but they had also believed in uniformity and compulsion. Through united action of the clergy and even through the civil government they had intervened in the affairs of individual churches, as when they forced the Salem church to give up Roger Williams. In the colony that Williams founded there was perfect congregational independence; and after tasting it, Stiles had known it for God's way. In the rest of New England the principle still lay under the shadow of clerical and governmental supervision. As he found opportunity, therefore, Stiles gave his testimony in favor of freedom.

He did not feel called upon to play the prophet to those who repudiated his views. But there were many Christians—Baptists, Quakers, Congregationalists—who ostensibly believed in congregational freedom and might be reminded of their declared principles. Among Congregationalists those who most needed reminding were in Connecticut.

The Connecticut churches in the eighteenth century were organized by counties in "consociations," an arrangement dating from 1708, when a colony-wide meeting of ministers and lay delegates adopted the so-called Saybrook Platform. A consociation consisted of ministers and "messengers" from the churches of a particular county. For the first thirty years there was not much occasion to determine the extent of consociational authority over member churches, but with the coming of the Great Awakening the Old Light ministers found the consociations a useful harness for holding erring churches in line. On more than one occasion they forced a church to retain an Old Light minister when a majority of both church and society wanted a New Light. By this abuse of authority they helped perpetuate the schisms of the Awakening. The New Lights, like many another religious minority, throve under persecution and grew steadily in numbers.[2]

2. Williston Walker, *The Creeds and Platforms of Congregationalism* (New York, 1893), pp. 502–14; Larned, *History of Windham County*, *1*, 393–485; M. L.

While the Old Lights were sacrificing congregational liberties to a presbyterial type of authority, Ezra Stiles, then a Yale undergraduate, had not been troubled. At that time he had not yet become much concerned with religion, and insofar as he was, had little sympathy with the enthusiastic notions of the New Lights. A dozen years later the shoe was on the other foot. The New Lights had grown so rapidly that they now controlled the very consociations that had formerly been a means of suppressing them, and the Old Lights were crying out for congregational liberties.

One place where the contest between the two groups had grown especially hot was Wallingford, where disagreement prevented the settlement of a minister for six years after the Reverend Samuel Whittelsey's death in 1752. Stiles's friend Chauncy Whittelsey, son of the former minister, was the leading candidate; but when the two factions could not agree, he abandoned the prospect in favor of a joint pastorship with Joseph Noyes at New Haven. Finally, in 1758 on the recommendation of some Boston men who had the confidence of both sides, the Wallingford church tried a Harvard man, James Dana. After listening to his sermons and questioning him, the New Lights smelled an Arminian, but the majority prepared to install him anyhow. The minority appealed to the consociation, which issued an order to desist; but the majority was tired of waiting and selected an ordaining council of Old Lights, including Isaac Stiles, Chauncy Whittelsey, and Joseph Noyes, whom nothing could have pleased more than this double opportunity to affirm congregational liberty and at the same time thwart the New Lights. Isaac Stiles declared that "he never was clearer in the Expediency of any ordination." [3] The consociation thereupon expelled all members of the ordaining council and declared the anti-Dana minority to be the real church of Wallingford.

The situation was complicated by the usual family rivalries: Dana

Greene, *The Development of Religious Liberty in Connecticut* (Boston, 1905), pp. 138–272.

3. Memoir of Isaac Stiles. On the Wallingford controversy see also Chauncy Whittelsey to Stiles, Sept. 25, 1759; James Dana to Andrew Bartholomew, May 3, 1762 (copy in Stiles Papers); Dana to Stiles, Jan. 7, 1768; *Lit. Diary, 1,* 196–98; Charles H. S. Davis, *History of Wallingford* (Meriden, 1870), pp. 164–209. There is a long and lucid argument against the authority of consociation in the Wallingford affair, dated Nov. 28, 1759, in the William Samuel Johnson Papers, Conn. Hist. Soc. See also, in these papers, the letter of Johnson to Jared Ingersoll, Sept. 10, 1759.

was opposed by the Halls in the congregation, because they feared
that he would be too friendly with the Whittelseys (they were right;
he later married a Whittelsey); and though Samuel Hall of Cheshire,
one of the most influential ministers in New Haven County, was himself an Old Light, he supported his Wallingford cousins in their attack on Dana's orthodoxy. The conflict embroiled all Connecticut: a
flurry of pamphlets debated the issues, and the Halls came down to
North Haven and stirred up eight or ten families to register a complaint against Isaac Stiles, so that the old man's last years were embit-
tered by a rift in his church.[4]

Ezra made a visit to Connecticut in the spring of 1759 and spoke
with ministers on both sides of the question in an effort to promote
"mutual Forbearance and Peace," but there was no question in his
mind about which side had the right of it.[5] In spite of partisan complications, and in spite of the fact that some of the members of the ordaining council had formerly been guilty of upholding consociation
power against New Light congregations, he considered the question
at stake a clear one: did the majority of a church and congregation
have the right to choose their pastor themselves or did the consociation have a veto on their choice? Since he had taken no part in
the earlier Old Light maneuvers against congregational independence,
Ezra Stiles could support the cause of liberty now with a good deal
more consistency than some of its other patrons. His efforts at peace
rejected, he enlisted his scholarship in the cause, asking Chauncy
Whittelsey to get information for him about the origins of the Saybrook Platform and its original interpretation.[6] The text of the
Platform was somewhat equivocal in speaking of consociational authority, but Stiles found enough evidence to convince him that the authors
of the document had not intended to give the consociation more than
advisory power. The expansion of advice into authority was the
usurpation of a later generation—of Old Lights, but no need to mention that.

Stiles found opportunity to circulate his views when the Congregational ministers of Rhode Island asked him to preach the sermon
at their semi-annual meeting. Taking as his subject the unity of Christianity, and professing an intention to heal the breaches in Congrega-

4. Memoir of Isaac Stiles.
5. Stiles to Francis Alison, July 3, 1759.
6. Stiles to Chauncy Whittelsey, undated; Whittelsey to Stiles, Mar. 4, 1761.

tionalism, he delivered a lengthy criticism of the consociations. He had nothing against associations of ministers or churches for advisory purposes only, "but the moment jurisdiction enters, like the creating *Caesar* perpetual *Dictator,* the beginning of the absolute loss of liberty commences." [7] When he published the sermon, which was his sole public contribution to the controversy, only two Old Light ministers had the consistency to rebuke him: John Devotion of Saybrook and his Uncle Abel.[8] Abel, who had quarreled with his own church at Woodstock in an attempt to make them submit to consociational authority, intimated that his nephew might change his sentiments as he grew older—an insufferable suggestion to a young man, but Abel was never squeamish about expressing his views. He concluded by heaping scorn on another idea of Ezra's. The latter had evidently expressed his intention of going on with his defense of congregational independence by writing a brief history of ecclesiastical councils in New England; would Uncle Abel kindly furnish him with information about any councils that had been held in Woodstock in the past fifty years? The reply was an explosion: "In the Name of Sixpence, I pray tell me, what sort of Alembick would you make use of in order to produce what you Call a Brief history of N. England Councils? Surely you must have a Chymical Talent to perfection, if you Can make your History less Contracted than the Voluminous Synopsis Criticorum —for should you Confine your history to the Councils In Woodstock aforesaid, they'd furnish and Suggest matter Enough for a Volume Equal to Father Cowpers Anatomy—Ergo what World will you find wide Enough to Contain the Books to be wrote on the remaining Results?" [9]

Ezra must have read this advice a little ruefully, for by the time he received Abel's letter on March 23, 1762, he had made a note, dated March 4: "This day I first conceived the Thoughts of writing the History of the World." [10] The advice seems to have been effective: he never did write the history of church councils or of the world either. But he did continue to speak for congregational independence. Besides encouraging the Connecticut Old Light ministers to form an association with no authoritative or supervisory functions, and to ex-

7. *A Discourse on the Christian Union* (Boston, 1761), p. 114.
8. Abel Stiles to Stiles, Feb. 2, 1762; Devotion to Stiles, May 3, 1762.
9. Abel Stiles to Stiles, Feb. 18, 1762.
10. *Itineraries and Miscellanies,* p. 51.

change pulpits with Dana in recognition of his ministerial standing, he worked with Charles Chauncy in Boston to secure even wider recognition for Dana and for those who had upheld the liberties of the Wallingford church. As early as February 7, 1761, he consulted Chauncy about the possibility of honorary degrees from Scotland for the men who had written the right sort of pamphlets in the controversy. Chauncy thought the only way to get the degrees was to make a present of £25 sterling to the University of Edinburgh for each of them. Neither Chauncy nor Stiles could raise that much; but in 1768, after Franklin had obtained Stiles's degree, Dana received one too. Whether or not Stiles had anything to do with his getting it is not apparent.[11]

By this time another occasion for asserting congregational liberties had arisen in Meriden, the town adjoining Wallingford; and once again a relative of Stiles was involved. The pastor of the Meriden church had been a member of the ordaining council at Wallingford, had exchanged pulpits with Dana, and had thereby alienated a substantial minority of his congregation. When he died, Stiles recommended his own brother-in-law, John Hubbard, Jr., for the job, and the majority group accepted the recommendation. The minority, as might have been expected, found Hubbard unorthodox. After all, he was the son of Colonel John Hubbard, an enemy of President Clap; his sister was married to Ezra Stiles, who still was considered an Arminian; and his former business partner (he had been a merchant for twenty years) was Chauncy Whittelsey, now himself reverend and suspect.[12]

The minority complained to the consociation, which promptly forbade Hubbard to preach; and the ordaining council, which Stiles, though invited, did not attend, thought it unwise to proceed with the ordination until there was greater harmony in the church. They were a little afraid, too, of Hubbard's reputation and adduced "the supposed hazzard to the cause of liberty, shd a reputed heretic be ordain'd by a set of reputed hereticks." To Dana, who had attended the council and spoken for immediate ordination, this seemed like cowardice or desertion; and he wrote to Stiles in some bitterness at the latter's failure to appear: "I am exceeding sorry you cou'd not attend. Tho I

11. Chauncy to Stiles, Feb. 7, 1761; Francis Alison to Stiles, July 10, 1761; Stiles to Dana, Nov. 15, 1768.

12. James Dana to Stiles, Nov. 3, 1767.

don't say I despair of the common cause, yet it appears to be sinking, and deserted by its friends. There has never been, in my opinion, so good an opportunity to support it." [13]

The majority of the church evidently shared Dana's views. After an unsuccessful attempt to appease the opposition, they voted to abandon the Saybrook Platform, thus removing themselves from the consociation instead of waiting to be expelled for their next move, which was to summon another ordaining council for June 1769. This time Ezra Stiles was there, along with Dana and Chauncy Whittelsey. There were six members in all, three of them from outside Connecticut. Robert Breck, the Arminian minister of Springfield, whose settlement Clap had opposed thirty-five years before, served as moderator. The council, in spite of dissident grumbling from the congregation's minority about this invasion of foreigners, proceeded with the ordination.[14]

Stiles, by supporting the Meriden church in defiance of the consociation, had gone out of his way to uphold his principles, and in doing so he had violated his instincts and sacrificed his advantage. For a man who automatically recoiled from controversy, it must have taken an effort to make this stand, and one may guess his probable relief when circumstances prevented his attendance at the first ordaining council. Being now a Rhode Islander, he could reasonably have stayed out of the Connecticut fight altogether, and there was a good reason which might have induced him to do so. Yale at this time was looking for a president, and he was being mentioned as a likely candidate. His reputation for learning, which even the University of Edinburgh had seen fit to acknowledge, could scarcely be ignored; and by inquiry the trustees could have found that in spite of his dubious theological past, his views had grown more orthodox. When he defied the consociation at Meriden, however, he personally affronted all New Light clergy and especially three members of the Yale corporation who had taken a strong stand in favor of consociational authority.[15]

13. John Hubbard, Jr., to Stiles, Dec. 2, 1767; Dana to Stiles, Jan. 7, 1768; Chauncy Whittelsey to Stiles, Feb. 17, 1768, Stiles Papers, New Haven Colony Hist. Soc.

14. John Devotion to Stiles, Apr. 25, 1768; *Itineraries and Miscellanies*, pp. 277–78, 286–90, 474–75.

15. Moses Dickinson, Noah Hobart, and Edward Eells had all written pamphlets against Dana's ordination in the Wallingford controversy. The Yale corporation in 1769 was about evenly divided between Old Lights (George Beckwith, Benjamin

He thereby annihilated his own candidacy. John Devotion wrote him wryly from Saybrook: "Upon the whole Dr. you must not expect your Last Tour thro the Colony, nor your Laying on Hands will seat you in the Presidency at Yale." [16] Not that he wanted the presidency, of course—he had actually discouraged a feeler in his direction three years before [17]—but where is the man valuing honor as Stiles then did who does not like to be asked?

Stiles's support of congregational independence was not his only effort in behalf of religious freedom and tolerance. These blessings he wanted for all Christians, but his deepest concern was for the churches that sprang from the Calvinist Reformation. They were the "Lights, Ornaments, and Honor of Christendom"—in Europe the Scottish Presbyterians, the English and Irish Presbyterians and Independents, the French, Dutch, and Swiss Calvinists; in America the Presbyterians of the middle colonies and the Congregationalists of New England. But however pure in other respects, these churches showed a deplorable proclivity toward disagreements. Wallingford and Meriden were only minor episodes in a record so full of blemishes as to obscure the basic excellence of the whole Calvinist movement. In a world where reason was the way to truth, good men were driven to less pure faiths, or still worse to skepticism or deism, by the intolerance of Calvinists for each other. It was imperative, therefore, Stiles believed, that the Calvinist churches turn from internal quarrels and propagate their different but similar brands of truth in Christian harmony.[18]

As early as 1759 he outlined to Francis Alison of Philadelphia the idea of a confederacy between the New England churches and the

---

Lord, Jonathan Merrick, Thomas Ruggles, and Elnathan Whitman) and New Lights (Moses Dickinson, Edward Eells, Noah Hobart, James Lockwood, and Solomon Williams), with a New Light (Naphtali Daggett) as acting president. Whitman, though an Old Light, had sided with consociation against Dana. In the fall of 1769 Solomon Williams and Jonathan Merrick resigned and were replaced by one Old Light (Eliphalet Williams) and one New Light (Warham Williams, who was Samuel Hall's son-in-law).

16. Devotion to Stiles, July 14, 1769; *Itineraries and Miscellanies*, pp. 477–78.

17. Devotion to Stiles, July 7, 1766; Stiles to Devotion, July 25, 1766; *Itineraries and Miscellanies*, pp. 457, 590–91. See also the notations by Stiles on the back of the letter from Chauncy Whittelsey to Stiles, July 9, 1766.

18. Stiles to Francis Alison, July 3, 1759; Stiles to Thomas Wright, Nov. 18, 1766.

Presbyterian synods of the middle colonies with the possibility of bringing in the British and European churches by correspondence.[19] Such a conjunction might enable the members to see their basic oneness. By sharing in a single great mission they would learn to overlook minor differences and carry on the great work of reformation. At the same time the organization would promote mutual forbearance. Each church would go its own way, but by participation in the union would show its respect for the others, its willingness to allow their independence, its confidence in the ultimate victory of Christian truth. Stiles's ecumenical dream was premature. He failed at this time to persuade others to share his extended vision of union with freedom, but he continued to cherish the idea.[20]

By 1761 he had plans under way for another kind of union. In Rhode Island's religious variety he saw an opportunity to join with Christians of other denominations in a project which would exemplify their common faith in free inquiry. What he had in mind was a college in which the major religious groups of the colony should unite in the pursuit of knowledge.[21] He had drafted a petition to the legislature but had not presented it, when he was impelled to action by the arrival in Newport, in the summer of 1763, of a delegation from the Philadelphia association of Baptists. They were there to propose the founding of a Baptist college in Rhode Island. The events which followed have been the subject of a good deal of controversy and speculation ever since, but from the available evidence the main outlines can be reconstructed.[22]

The Baptist delegation, led by James Manning, a graduate of the College of New Jersey (Princeton), indicated that they would be willing to cooperate with other denominations in the project. Josias

19. Stiles to Francis Alison, July 3, 1759. Cf. Stiles to Peter Timothy, Jan. 15, 1760.

20. When Stiles proposed the scheme to Nathaniel Lardner in 1764, Lardner told him, "The Dissenters here are now too inconsiderable and can be of no great service to you in such a design. Nor are they sufficiently united among themselves." Lardner to Stiles, Aug. 20, 1764.

21. *Itineraries and Miscellanies*, pp. 24–25, 583–84. Cf. Benjamin Stevens to Stiles, Oct. 26, 1763.

22. The ensuing account does not differ materially from that given by Walter C. Bronson in his *History of Brown University* (Providence, 1914), which appears to me to be supported by all the sources, both in the Stiles papers and elsewhere. Cf. Reuben A. Guild, *Early History of Brown University* (Providence, 1897), 510–34.

Lyndon and Job Bennett, two Newport Baptists, were authorized to consult the Congregationalists and to draw up a charter. Probably aware that Ezra Stiles had been planning a college, they conferred with him and his friend Ellery. As a result it was agreed, according to an account by Ellery,

> First, that the Corporation shall consist of two distinct Branches by the name of Trustees and Fellows. 2d. That in the former the Baptists and in the latter, the Congregationalists should forever have the Majority's. . . . 3d That the Election of President should always be in the Trustees and that they should have the Negative and Controul upon all the Nomination of Officers and upon the Laws proposed by the Fellows and in short that they should have a disallowance on every Proposal of every Kind made to them by the other Branch.[23]

Ezra Stiles was given the task of drafting the charter in accordance with these provisions, and he took advantage of the opportunity to insert a strong provision in favor of mutual tolerance and religious liberty, prohibiting all religious tests for either faculty or students and forbidding faculty members to proselyte the students away from their existing religious preferences, "so that neither Denomination shall be alarmed with Jealousies or Apprehensions of any illiberal and disingenuous Attempts upon one another, but on the contrary an open free undesigning and generous Harmony and a mutual honorable Respect shall be recommended and endeavored, in order to exhibit an Example in which Literature may be advanced on protestant Harmony and the most perfect religious Liberty." The agreement with regard to control of the two branches of the corporation was carried out by provisions requiring that eight out of the twelve fellows should be Congregationalists while of the thirty-five trustees, nineteen were to be Baptists, seven Congregationalists or Presbyterians, five Friends, and four Anglicans.[24] Stiles worked hard on the charter, neglecting his precious silkworms at the height of their feeding season in order to perfect it. After presentation to the Baptist committee for approval, it was forwarded to the Rhode Island Assembly with a petition for authorization.

When the Baptists in the Assembly saw the document, they were

23. Bronson, *Brown*, p. 23 n.
24. Ibid., pp. 495–99.

evidently not prepared for the large share of power given the Congregationalists, and, since they controlled a majority, the petition was rejected. As a result amendments were made to give Baptists control of both branches of the corporation and to eliminate the provision forbidding proselyting. In this form the charter passed. Though the Baptists would still have given Stiles a seat on the corporation, he politely declined, explaining to his friend Chauncy that the Baptists had absorbed "the whole Power and Government of the College and thus by the Immutability of the numbers establishing it a Party College." Moreover, by the mutilation of his provisions for religious freedom, the Baptists would be empowered "to practice the Arts of Insinuation and proselyting upon the youth." [25]

Stiles was somewhat bitter about the transformation of his scheme, and he was doubtless even more chagrined by the fact that Congregational representation on the trustees was reduced from seven to four, while the Anglican was raised from four to five. The Anglicans in Rhode Island were always at work on the Baptists, raking up old episodes of Congregational high-handedness and seeking for political purposes to keep enmities alive. Once again, it seemed, they had succeeded, so that the college which should have helped to unite Baptists and Congregationalists only served to widen the gulf and give the Anglicans another opportunity for mischief. Nevertheless, though he would not participate in such a party measure, Stiles wished the Baptists well with their college: it might at least help to give their future ministers a learning that was sadly lacking in the present crop.[26]

Stiles continued to nourish his original notion of a nonpartisan college; and in 1770 after the Baptist college had settled in Providence, he and Ellery presented a petition to the legislature for the establishment of a college in Newport, but the Baptists, fearing competition, were able to get this voted down.[27]

In dealing with his Baptist friends thereafter Stiles had plenty of

25. Ibid. Although the Baptists accused Stiles of attempting to deceive them by giving the Congregationalists a majority of the fellows, Stiles always regarded the change of this provision as a betrayal by the Baptists. In one of his almanacs (Yale Univ. Lib.) he noted against the date Sept. 20, 1763, "The Baptists desert their Junction with the Congregationalists and engross all the Power in the proposed Rh. Isl. College to themselves, after they had agreed to share the Ballances with us." See also Stiles to Samuel Hopkins, June 11, 1764.

26. Stiles to John J. Zubly, Aug. 26, 1768.

27. *Lit. Diary*, *1*, 39, 46; Bronson, *Brown*, p. 50; *Newport Mercury*, Mar. 12, 1770.

occasion to exercise the forbearance which he valued so highly, and there is every indication that he was successful. Though he never ceased to lament the party spirit of the Baptists, he was always able to meet them on friendly terms, just as he met Samuel Hopkins, with whom, in spite of the misgivings of his Connecticut friends, he disagreed profoundly. When Hopkins came to Newport, Stiles actually welcomed the opportunity to demonstrate his catholicity. "I have a mind," he wrote his father-in-law, "that there should be one Instance on the Continent, where two Churches in the same place and of the same Denomination should live in harmony. In most Instances they hate one another most heartily." [28] And Stiles carried out his intention to the full: he and Hopkins visited each other, discussed theology without heat, exchanged pulpits, and cooperated in a missionary project.[29] The two could be seen occasionally after Hopkins' evening lecture, walking home together down High Street, Hopkins' great bulk and frowning face towering over Stiles's slight figure as they felt their way toward common ground. Hopkins was as opinionated as a man can be, but his honesty commanded the respect which Stiles gladly accorded it, and Hopkins, in turn, did not allow his dislike for Stiles's theology to penetrate their friendship. So far as one can tell at this date, neither exercised the slightest influence on the other's beliefs.

Allowing Hopkins to preach in the Second Church was perhaps no severe test of Stiles's devotion to free religious inquiry, for though Hopkins commanded a large following among other ministers, he was not an inspiring preacher. But Stiles opened his pulpit to more dangerous men too: George Whitefield, who was still drawing crowds, even though he had outlived the glory of the Great Awakening, and William Bliss, Newport's Sabbatarian Baptist preacher. Bliss, though without a college education, won Stiles's high esteem "for Knowledge of the Scriptures, Gift of Prayer, and Talent at public Instruction." [30]

The only heretic who caused him trouble was a young man who preached in his church without his invitation. Returning from a month's visit to Connecticut in October 1772, Stiles found that one John Murray had been conducting services in the Second Church during his absence and preaching doctrines that strained Stiles's tolerance to the limit. The substance of Murray's message was universal salva-

28. Stiles to Hubbard, Aug. 26, 1769.
29. *Lit. Diary*, *1*, passim; on the missionary project see pp. 363–65, Stiles to Charles Chauncy, Dec. 8, 1773, and to John Rogers, July 15, 1774.
30. *Lit. Diary*, *1*, 61, 566–67.

tion (he ultimately became the father of the Universalist Church in America). He denied that anyone would be damned, a doctrine that horrified Stiles far more than Hopkins' too narrow view. Murray's theology not only impeached the justice of God but destroyed the very foundation of Christian morality. Murray delivered his insidious doctrines in a winning manner, concealing them in the language of orthodoxy, so that his listeners did not at first perceive the extent of his departure from what they had previously been taught. He had come to America only two years before, and without benefit of theological training had successfully assumed the role of itinerant preacher, much in the manner of those who had delivered a quite different doctrine in the 1740s. Stiles, regarding this usurper of his pulpit almost as a devil incarnate, was quite ready to believe every rumor that friends relayed to him of a scandalous past in London. The trouble was that too many of Stiles's congregation had been taken in and were ready to defend Murray with a zeal that vouched for the appeal which the man and his message undoubtedly possessed.

In this difficult situation Stiles kept his head. When Joseph Fish wrote him in November from Stonington for information about Murray (who was now preaching in Connecticut), Stiles told him all the stories he had heard about Murray's being a profligate and having deserted a wife in London, but warned that it was useless to try to disillusion people with this information. It was all hearsay, and even if it were not, those who were flocking to Murray would refuse to believe it. He had found this out by experience, for many of his own best friends, even his neighbor and staunch supporter, Jonathan Otis, had refused to hear anything against Murray. Stiles's method of restoring peace to his congregation had been to disapprove in silence, going about his ministerial work as usual but taking pains in sermons and conversation to emphasize "2 or 3 capital Truths which some understood him [Murray] to deny; tho' with no Allusion to him, because my Congregation in general never understood him to deny them." As a result, he observed, "it pleased God very soon to restore our Tranquillity and peace. But if I had gon to preaching against him as an Imposter, or bruited about the Evidence and stories against him, it would have been pouring Oyl on the flame and rendering it inextinguishable." [31]

31. Ibid., pp. 289–92; Joseph Fish to Stiles, Nov. 23, Dec. 7, 1772; Stiles to Fish, Dec. 11, 1772; Stiles to ———, Dec. 24, 1777.

Unfortunately the episode did not end here, for the following year, at about the same time, Murray reappeared. This time Stiles thought himself obliged to warn his flock openly against the man. The result was that about a dozen families in the congregation, including four or five of his "principal supports" were deeply offended, and for a time he feared there would be a schism or a total alienation from him. By the end of another year, however, he had won his people back through peaceful methods.[32] Even at the height of his opposition to Murray he never suggested the kind of treatment that Connecticut had given itinerant preachers of the 1740s. Still less did he suggest the measures which the Puritans had taken against Anne Hutchinson and Roger Williams.

John Murray was not the only heretic to try Stiles's tolerance during the 1760s and 1770s. Robert Sandeman, another self-appointed itinerant, shocked the orthodox by preaching that faith was nothing more than intellectual consent. Stiles considered him "a haughty domineering man, who mistakes his natural, national [Scottish] arbitrariness for gospel zeal."[33] Henry Dawson, a London linen draper, founded a Baptist church in Newport, in which he went the New Divinity one better by warning the unregenerate not to attend lest they compound their offenses against God by pretending to worship him.[34]

So far as possible, Stiles avoided verbal combat with these extremists. He was sure they were wrong, and he never ceased to marvel at the human capacity for generating such unscriptural, not to say blasphemous, doctrines. But he viewed them without serious alarm and kept his pulpit free from controversy, secure in his belief that God's truth, preached in simple evangelical fashion, would triumph over every error.

32. "Birthday Reflexions," 1772, 1773, 1774.
33. Stiles to Benjamin Stevens, Mar. 17, 1769. Stiles's correspondence in 1764 and 1765 contains a great many discussions of Sandeman. Stiles wrote a lengthy memoir of him in December, 1764.
34. Stiles to Chauncy Whittelsey, Mar. 6, 1770; *Lit. Diary, 1*, 18–19, 40–41.

14

Anglicophobia

WHILE upholding religious liberty whether outside his church or inside, Stiles was constantly aware that tyranny posed as great a danger in the state as in the church. When he denied the divine right of churches, it was not to magnify the state by comparison. In a public disputation delivered at his graduation from Yale in 1746 he had undertaken to demonstrate the proposition that the hereditary authority of kings is not derived from divine right.[1] Only the title of the disputation survives, but he may already then have reached the conclusion repeatedly emphasized in his later papers, that God leaves men to design and construct their own governmental institutions in state as well as church.

Liberty was God's way of dealing with man, and the way men gave it up in state and church alike was for Stiles the strongest evidence of human frailty. For centuries the Roman church had held Christendom under ecclesiastical tyranny and had even subdued civil governments to its dominion. Human history was one long duel between tyranny and liberty, between human corruption and the spirit of God in man. And where tyranny conquered, corrupt kings were often found hand in glove with corrupt priests.[2]

1. "Jus regum non est jure divino haereditarium." From the broadside of commencement theses: *Praeclarissimo . . . Jonathan Law Armigero* (New Haven, 1746).

2. Stiles's view of history, as discussed in the ensuing paragraphs, is expressed in most detail in his Sermons on Public Fasts and Thanksgivings, a number of which he stitched together and marked with that title. Hereafter referred to as Sermons on Thanksgivings.

Stiles rejoiced to live in an age when tyranny was on the run. When God inspired the Protestant reformers to throw off the yoke of Rome, He inaugurated an epoch of liberty, both civil and religious, that was still sweeping all before it. The free inquiry that began with Luther had not only re-opened the revealed truth of the Scriptures and thus made possible the establishment of simple, independent churches on the apostolic model, but it had destroyed, at least in England, the grip of kings who claimed a divine right over their subjects.

Before the Reformation began, the English had already developed a highly desirable governmental institution in their representative Parliament. After Henry VIII cut the ties with Rome, they improved their government by limiting the king's authority and increasing (or Stiles might have said restoring) that of Parliament. When the Stuarts attempted to reduce the country to tyranny again, the people preserved liberty by forcing James II off the throne in 1688. With that Revolution the British Constitution became nearly perfect, for it provided more effective safeguards to liberty than any other people had developed.

Ezra Stiles was fond of reciting this history and proud of being part of the freest nation in the world, for he regarded the colonists as one nation with Englishmen. Much of his admiration for the old Puritans stemmed from the very active role they had played in the long battle for political liberty, not only in England but in America. The American part of the nation had not merely inherited the constitution that guaranteed freedom; Americans had helped to make it. They as well as Englishmen had suffered under tyranny; and when England rose up against James II, New England rose against his agent, Sir Edmund Andros. There had been a Glorious Revolution in America too.

To be born a descendant of New England Puritans was his special good fortune, Stiles felt, because New England was blessed with an even higher degree of liberty than the rest of the British nation. In New England there was no hereditary aristocracy, no feudal tenure of lands, no vassalage of the kind that had held Europeans in bondage. Though there might be rich men like Abraham Redwood and Godfrey Malbone, they did not ride—not visibly at least—on the backs of others. Americans enjoyed the fruits of their industry in a freedom that went beyond that of most Englishmen and Europeans. Though he was no leveler and never repudiated the doctrines of subordination that his father held so dear, Ezra Stiles thought that the general economic equality prevailing in America was more conducive to liberty than the social hierarchy existing in England.[3]

In religious institutions, too, America was freer than England. In England the Puritans had destroyed the divine right of kings for good, but the restoration of the Stuarts had brought back the divine right of bishops and of all other officers of the Anglican church. In America there was no bishop and no ecclesiastical hierarchy, a condition as conducive to religious freedom as the absence of a social hierarchy was to civil freedom.

As Stiles developed his thoughts about the sanctity of freedom and its exemplification in British institutions, he was aware that the nation's affairs were approaching a crisis, in which civil and religious liberty might both be endangered. Since 1754 England had been engaged in war with France, and the first years of it had brought defeat after defeat until the nation faced disaster. If France should conquer, there was surely an end to all freedom, for France spelled absolute monarchy and the Catholic church. English liberty was besieged also by internal dangers. The corruption and ineffectiveness of the government were noticed by every American who visited England, and many doubted that liberty could survive such prevalent vice. When he preached a thanksgiving sermon in November 1756, Stiles rejoiced that liberty did still survive. "Tho' we strongly fear," he said, "the administration too much under the Influence of Corruption . . . yet —are the Sentiments of british Liberty extinguished? is our good Constitution yet overturned or ruind? . . . no." [4]

It was an appropriate sentiment for a thanksgiving sermon, but ominously phrased. In the next two years the outlook grew worse, until William Pitt, "a man of strict Temperance and Frugality," [5] took charge. Pitt brought not merely effective administration but a whiff of the old Puritan spirit, and Stiles applauded. "It is of great importance," he told his congregation, "that the Administration of Mr. Pitt be successful, since on this Success, depends the breaking up of that system of public Bribery and Corruption, which else must end in the Sale of our Nation to France." [6]

When Pitt not only saved the nation from military defeat but en-

3. See esp. the sermon of Nov. 20, 1760.
4. Sermons on Thanksgivings, Nov. 25, 1756.
5. Stiles to Jared Eliot, Sept. 24, 1759.
6. Sermons on Thanksgivings, Aug. 20, 1758.

tirely destroyed French power in Canada, Stiles's optimism soared in a remarkable vision of what the future might hold for America. In a thanksgiving sermon to celebrate the taking of Montreal, he told the people of Newport that divine providence, by delivering Canada to the British, must be

> making way for the planting and Erection in this land [of] the best policied Empire that has yet appeared in the World. In which Liberty and property will be secured. The Tenure of property in Europe for the last 800 years has been in manner little better than absolute Vassalage. So that a few Barons and feudal Lords have engrossed the Labors of Millions. Whereas every man has a natural Right to the Fruit of his Industry. And so much only ought to be deemed surrendered or to be deforced from him, as shall be necessary for the Expences of the public. And we have opportunity and Advantage of a multitude of States to inspect and compare, to see and estimate what shall be necessary for the public Service with frugality. And may find that a much less sum than is in fact expended would effectually answer all the Expences of Government if frugally and prudently applied. Now this Defalcation of superfluous Expences and Frugality and Economy in the application of Revenues, will leave much more to the subject for the fruit of Industry than is generally allowed in Europe. So that We may possess a greater Landed property and this be secure to us. And being freed of the several feudal Tenures which God forbid should ever be brot hither, We shall have more Liberty, the Liberty of Men and Christians—Liberty civil and religious.

> Again we are planting an Empire of better Laws and Religion. Everyone that has any acquaintance with the Laws must be sensible that so many have been retained at home from the catholic Times, so many of contrary Import and Decision according as they were in the Reigns of Elizabeth, of the Stewarts, or since the Revolution, and lastly so many by no means adapted to the Circumstances of this country, not to observe that many are obsolete, that it is almost infinitely difficult for Lawyers themselves to decide what is true Law. In short the Law is so voluminous and undecisive that it is high Time to throw it up and assume an Institute de novo, more intelligible and adapted to the

state of the British Nation in the present age, which every one knows to be different and to require different legal Regulations from those 3 and 500 years ago. And as for Religion. We hope to have it planted in greater purity even apostolic purity as it is already among our churches.

It is probable that in Time there will be found a provincial Confederacy and a common Council standing on free provincial Election. And this may in Time some hundred years hence terminate in an imperial Diet. When the Imperial Dominion will subsist as it ought in Election. The Roman Empire subsisted in annual Election for 300 years.

This Land may be renowned for Science and Arts. We have already two Colleges in New England in which are constantly resident 350 students at least. These diffuse and propagate Science thro' the Land. And tho' we cant have equal Advantages at present with the European Universities, yet we are in a rising growing Way, and shall probably in Time equal the foreign Establishments especially as we have advantages of Communication with the Europeans who come hither. Not only Science, but the elegant Arts are introducing apace, and in a few years we shall have, tho' not manufactures, yet Painting, Sculpture, Statuary, but first of all the greek Architecture in considerable Perfection among us. And as our churches increase, which is with amazing Rapidity, doubling once in 30 years we hope that the knowlege of the genuine Doctrine of the Gospel and public Virtue will increase and become our distinguishing Glory.[7]

It was all there, a new code of laws, government entirely elective, a continental congress, a society without aristocracy, a church without hierarchy, the arts and sciences flourishing, with a Greek revival in architecture coming first. Stiles foresaw these marvels as the inevitable outcome in America of British liberty flourishing under British control. With men like Pitt at the helm, why not?

The death of George II in 1760 did not affect Stiles's optimism. The new king, he thought, could scarcely be any more prone to corruption than his predecessor, who was "said to have been free from Vices—but it is supposed that his Virtues did not receive any Embellishment

7. Ibid., Nov. 20, 1760.

from his Acquaintance with the Countess of Yarmouth." [8] But when George III dismissed William Pitt, Stiles began again to be uneasy about the future of liberty. And when the royal favorite, the Earl of Bute, negotiated a peace that gave the captured West Indian islands of Guadeloupe and Martinique back to France, Stiles publicly denounced the treaty.[9]

By this time there were other grounds for uneasiness. It was becoming apparent to Stiles that he was not the only one thinking about the future of America. Other men were making plans in which the civil and religious liberty that he cherished had no place. He probably did not know that Governor Bernard in Boston was advocating a sharp reduction in the authority of the colonial representative assemblies, nor did he know of similar schemes that various Englishmen were drawing up.[10] But he did know of the plots and plans of the American Anglicans. In Stiles's eyes the Church of England posed a greater threat to liberty, both in England and in America, than any other single institution. Baptists might refuse to cooperate with Congregationalists, and the Connecticut consociations might try to assume powers they had no right to; but these were trifles compared with the threat posed by the Anglicans. If tyranny were to come again, Stiles was convinced to the point of obsession that the church would be the means of bringing it.[11]

He had first become suspicious of the Church of England when as a promising Yale graduate he was solicited to join it. Then the Anglicans had spared neither flattery nor promises in their efforts to win him. Even after he was settled in the Congregational Church at Newport they courted him, again with no arguments of the mind but with mercenary suggestions about the high ecclesiastical offices which they confidently expected would some day be within their power to bestow.[12]

Time had passed and that day seemed to be drawing near. In

8. Ibid., Jan. 19, 1761.

9. Ibid., Aug. 25, 1763; Stiles to Benjamin Franklin, Dec. 30, 1761. In notes dated May 21, 1763, Stiles calculated the cost of British acquisitions in the war at seventy million pounds, of which thirty-four millions worth were given up at the peace: "Half our Conquests given up for Nothing."

10. See Morgan and Morgan, *The Stamp Act Crisis*, pp. 7–20.

11. See esp. "Reflexions," Dec. 12, 1759.

12. Autobiographical Fragment; *Lit. Diary*, 2, 113. See above, Chap. 7.

every direction the Anglicans were reaching for power. When they had enough, they would use it to accomplish their dearest wish—the establishment of an American episcopal church complete with bishops, archbishops, and all the other officers necessary to duplicate the English hierarchy. It was not something Stiles cared to contemplate, for he considered all ecclesiastical hierarchies dangerous. If the Anglicans established one in America, he anticipated that it would not be long before their bishops would claim superiority by divine right over denominations which had no such pretensions. Furthermore the American hierarchy would expect all the rights and privileges enjoyed by the English one, including state support and temporal powers: bishops' courts exercising jurisdiction over morals and the probate of wills. The thought of temporal power in ecclesiastical hands filled Stiles with horror—his notebooks were crowded with historical examples of the tyranny it had led to. As for state support for the hierarchy, it would be a direct step backward for religious liberty, since the Anglicans, he felt, lagged behind in this great trend of the century. In the southern colonies, where their church was already supported by state taxes, all denominations were required to pay, whereas in Connecticut and Massachusetts, where the Congregational churches received state support, there was under way a gradual extension of privileges and exemptions for other denominations—a perceptible forward movement which might eventuate in the full religious liberty he found so fortunate in Rhode Island.

The most direct way for the American Anglicans to achieve their end would be to enlist the help of the English government. Stiles had long been aware of their intention to do so, and during the interval when Pitt was at the head of government, Stiles prepared an argument —perhaps for his own comfort, perhaps with an intention of publication—to show why those who had charge of imperial affairs should halt the Anglican thrust for power in America.[13] In this treatise he rehearsed his view that "neither Episcopacy nor any species of christian Hierarchy now subsisting in the World or that has subsisted since the Apostolic Age, is Jure Divino." This view, he thought, was already widely accepted, and the further progress of free inquiry would doubtless lead to a general abandonment of the divine right of priests of any kind. The Anglican Church as established in England was in fact already an anachronism and must eventually be reduced to a

13. "Reflexions," Dec. 12, 1759.

level with other churches. (He outlined the steps by which it might be accomplished.) How foolish would it be then if those who directed imperial affairs should "be brot to espouse a System which in all probability must fall a Sacrifice to free Inquiry."

Free inquiry, Stiles was sure, would remove the props from all bishops. But if he was correct, the bishops must know it and would not permit free inquiry to go that far if they could help it. The very fact that their authority was declining in England might lead them to look to America as a likely place in which to rebuild it. With an established church and a bishop in each colony, they would have at their disposal many offices of the kind on which political power is built, and with enough political power they might dry up the freedom that would otherwise engulf them. Already in the southern colonies Anglicans held virtually all political offices, and in the northern colonies they held most of the offices filled by royal appointment.

Perhaps Stiles did nothing with his treatise because at the moment nothing seemed to be called for. The British government was too involved in war to give attention to American Anglicans. He could see, however, that the Anglicans were not idle. When the time was ripe to seek help from the British government, the strength of their cause would depend in some measure on the amount of power they possessed. And so they seemed to be pursuing power in every quarter. In Newport, for instance, they had taken over the Redwood Library, which Abraham Redwood, the Quaker donor, had intended as a nonsectarian organization. Superficially Redwood's purpose had been maintained, but the Anglicans gained effective control. In the beginning they had been eighteen out of a total of forty-six members. Within a few years, as the library expanded, they gained a majority. Most of the other members did not notice that they voted as a bloc, but Abraham Redwood did. He used to complain about it to Stiles, saying it was contrary to his intention, and he finally withdrew from meetings rather than subject himself to the will of the invaders.[14]

Stiles saw Episcopal intrigue wherever he looked. In New Jersey, he heard, the governor had tried to alter the constitution of the College founded by Presbyterians (Princeton) so as to make half the trustees Anglicans. The attempt failed, but it showed what the Anglicans were up to.[15] They were more successful in working through the

14. *Lit. Diary*, *1*, 166 n.
15. Notes dated Dec. 3, 1761.

Free Masons. Episcopal intrigue, Stiles was convinced, "has set up and recommended the Fraternity of free Masons and is pressing them apace into a Subserviency and Subordination to the great End of Encreasing the Church."

> It applies to all persons of Influence and opulence in all the Provinces from Nova Scotia to Georgia, and by artifices proselyte here and there one. The Free Masons have already within about a Dozen Years increased from three to 12 or 14 Lodges. A Scheme originating in one Lodge may thus be circulated and recommended thro all the Provinces. In Jersey and Pennsylvania the Church have applied to the Legislatures for Lotteries last year to build first one Church, then to repair another, afterward to build another etc. and it is likely this Card will be played to raise a Contribution on the public till the Jealousies of other Sects be enkindled into Flame and Opposition. Then they may suspend the Thing in one Province and try it under a little variation in a more distant one—till by this Means they may in Time get a considerable Number of Episcopal Churches in America with honorable Appointments.[16]

By such devious methods the Anglicans were accumulating strength. Their efforts, as in the case of the Masons, were directed mainly at "persons of Influence and opulence," the kind of persons suitable for "honorable Appointments" and high government office. But they were working to gain a rank and file too. Ever since the conversion of Yale's rector Timothy Cutler and his friends, the Anglican Society for Propagation of the Gospel had been proselyting in New England. Wherever New Lights quarreled with Old, an Anglican missionary would appear on the scene, murmuring a plague on both their houses, and welcoming the disgruntled to the bosom of the church. The success of these measures had so far not been great. In 1759 Stiles counted twenty-seven Anglican missions in New England serving about two thousand families. According to his calculations of the geometric progression of New England population, unless the rate of Anglican

16. "Reflexions," Dec. 12, 1759. Stiles was so impressed with the Anglican talent for intrigue that in his plans for a learned society he provided that two-thirds of the members should always be Congregational or Presbyterian. The express purpose was "to defeat episcopal Intrigue by which this institution would be surreptitiously caught into an anti-american Intrerest" (Notes dated Aug. 15, 1765).

conversions rose sharply, there would be an even greater majority of Congregationalists in future generations than in his own.[17]

Theoretically the rate of Anglican conversions should not have mattered to Stiles. In the future he foresaw for America, when religious liberty should have triumphed, the Anglicans would everywhere have their place not below the Congregationalists as in the north, nor above them as in the south, but side by side in equal freedom as in Rhode Island. No denomination would need the strength of numbers for protection. Each would be free to practice and to preach its own version of religious truth without fear of the others. If the Anglicans had been content to further their religion by thus preaching and practicing, there would have been nothing to fear from them. But instead of proselyting by evangelical or rational means, Stiles saw the Anglicans converting by bribery—luring the weak with the prospect of ecclesiastical, political, social, or financial advantage. Instead of converting men for the pure purpose of increasing Christ's kingdom, the Anglicans, in Stiles's view, made converts only in order to increase their own temporal power. He had no doubts about the eventual outcome, but if Anglican schemes succeeded, there might be decades, even centuries, of suppression before God intervened to let American liberty triumph.

Anyone who knew Ezra Stiles at all well knew from what quarter he considered liberty threatened. But when the first blow actually fell, not even Ezra Stiles could at first see Anglican intrigue behind it. In the summer of 1763, while Stiles was denouncing the treaty that ended the war with France, a harassed British minister of finance was looking for ways to meet the enormous expenses that war always leaves in its wake. Upon looking at the Treasury records, George Grenville found that the American customs service was costing more in salaries than it collected in revenue. One reason was that the nominal collectors, who drew the salaries, stayed in England and hired deputies at a lower rate to go to America and do the work. The deputies then privately increased their own incomes by collecting bribes instead of customs duties from the American merchants. The system pleased the collectors, their deputies, and the merchants, but it was not, Grenville decided, the way to run a customs service. He ordered the collectors to their posts and told the navy, which no longer had the French

17. Ibid.; *Discourse on the Christian Union*, pp. 102–23.

to fight, to send some ships to America and lend a hand in catching smugglers.[18]

To Americans it seemed an inglorious role for the British navy, especially in New England where most of the smugglers lived. What they smuggled mostly was molasses from the French West Indies (now returned to France), on which a foolish Parliament had placed a prohibitive duty of 6*d*. a gallon in 1733. From molasses New England made rum, a prime article in her commerce—there were over thirty distilleries in Rhode Island alone—without which her ships would lie idle and her prosperity sink. A venal customs service had hitherto been the means of nullifying a law that should never have been passed.

Rhode Island got its first taste of the new policy in late December 1763, when the Man of War *Cygnet* sailed into Newport harbor and began seizing ships. Ezra Stiles watched the officers march arrogantly to Trinity Church on Sundays, and noted that this was also the destination of the new customs officers. When the *Cygnet* departed in January 1764, Stiles wrote bitterly to his father-in-law, "She is gone to New London to our Joy. Tho we soon expect another to suck the Honey and lash us into Obedience." [19]

George Grenville actually had no desire to stifle American commerce. His purpose was simply to draw a revenue from it. This became clear when he secured the passage of a new revenue law (the Sugar Act) in 1764, reducing the duty on French molasses from 6*d*. to 3*d*. a gallon but adding duties on various other items imported into the colonies and requiring all ships to go through elaborate procedures when clearing and entering an American port, in order to make evasion of duties more difficult. The new measure stated frankly in the preamble that its intention was to raise revenue, and it was preceded by the announcement that it might be followed within a year by a stamp tax on legal forms, newspapers, and other documents.[20]

The new law, in spite of the reduction of the molasses duty, alarmed Americans far more than the old one. England had long levied customs duties to discourage trade that conflicted with imperial interests, but to levy customs duties simply to raise money was an innovation. It was a tax, and taxation has always been a delicate subject among

18. Morgan and Morgan, *Stamp Act Crisis*, p. 23.
19. Stiles to John Hubbard, Jan. 30, 1764; *Newport Mercury*, Jan. 2, 1764.
20. Morgan and Morgan, *Stamp Act Crisis*, pp. 23–26.

people who value liberty. Englishmen in particular had made it a principle of their constitution that a government could not tax without the consent of its subjects, given either in person or through their representatives. When George Grenville undertook to tax Americans through Parliament, in which they were not represented, they lost no time in pointing to the violation of the constitution.[21]

Ezra Stiles suspected from the beginning that customs enforcement and taxation were merely the opening skirmish of a general attack on American liberty, and he was not surprised when the Churchmen and Tories in Newport took the opportunity to strike a blow at Rhode Island liberty from within. A small knot of Anglicans, including some of the local customs officers together with a few renegades from other denominations, drew up a petition to the king to revoke the Rhode Island charter and establish a royal government.[22] A royal government would inevitably be a government run by Anglicans— an intolerable prospect in Rhode Island, where that sect comprised only a small fraction of the population.

It is possible that Ezra Stiles knew of the Newport conspiracy as early as April 14, 1763, long before the petition was actually sent. In preaching the annual spring fast sermon on that day, he introduced a disturbing new note. He generally asked his people to humble themselves before the recurring disasters of sickness, death, drought, depression, and war. Now he told them: "It becomes us to be humbled under any attempts or Designs of deforcing from us our civil and religious Liberty in this Land. Let us as ardently pray for the Continuation of Charter privileges in these Colonies, as Gods people did for the Peace and Prosperity of Jerusalem." [23]

When fast day came round again in April 1764, the petition for royal government was already under way and Stiles could be more explicit about the perils to liberty than he had been the year before. He reminded the congregation of the dangers that New England liberty had survived in the past, in 1635 when Archbishop Laud had headed a commission to recall colonial charters, in 1685 when James II consolidated New England into one dominion under the tyrannical

21. Ibid., pp. 27–39.

22. On the petition against the Rhode Island charter and the group behind it see Morgan and Morgan, *Stamp Act Crisis*, pp. 47–52; and Bridenbaugh, *Peter Harrison*, pp. 124–26.

23. Sermons on Thanksgivings, Apr. 14, 1763.

rule of Sir Edmund Andros. God had ultimately thwarted these efforts, but not before weak and corrupt men had shown themselves ready to sacrifice their country's liberties for royal favors. The same danger had now appeared in Newport, and Stiles warned the congregation of the vipers in their midst:

> Factions may arise in our own Bosoms which from the hopes of plunder as in the Days of Randolph and Sir Edmund Andros may surrender and sacrifice our civil and religious Liberties, especially if our most gracious Sovereign should be surrounded with ungracious Ministers—and then as our Governors and Rulers and Judges will be not of our own Election so they will be not of ourselves and Taxes will be heavily increased without Remedy —and if in some distant future period a succession of princes should arise as unfriendly to America as those in the days of our fathers we shall have those that hate us to rule over us and our posterity be yoked and sold like the Vassals of Poland.[24]

Compared to the rosy American future which Stiles envisaged in 1760, this was a gloomy picture. There was serious cause for gloom. The Rhode Island petition for royal government had been timed to fit an already rising sentiment in England against the New England charters. Stiles's English correspondents informed him that Lord Chief Justice Mansfield was reported to have said in the Privy Council, on the basis of charges made by customs officers, that the colonists had forfeited their charters and should lose them. The colonies under indictment were Massachusetts, Connecticut, and Rhode Island, perhaps especially Rhode Island, where liberty was so consistently practiced that outsiders generally called it license. Stiles, from the inside, knew that civil and religious liberty stood higher in Rhode Island than anywhere else, and he liked it that way. By the terms of the charter which Roger Williams had obtained in 1663 Rhode Island was in effect a republic, virtually free from British supervision. A successful attack on colonial charters would thus be a vital blow against liberty. It was a cue that the enemies of liberty both at home and abroad had not missed.

When Stiles heard of the Mansfield opinion, he wrote out a ringing denunciation of it: "the day that puts an End to our Charters com-

24. Ibid., Apr. 12, 1764.

mences an Aera of Reproach to the Memory of the Minister or Judge of the Law who shall do us such a disagreeable service." On the basis of his own knowledge of the law, he argued that failure of allegiance alone could justly forfeit the charters. Acts of the colonial assemblies contrary to the laws of England might be declared void; but only "in the arbitrary courts of James II" could such acts constitute grounds for revocation. And contrary to the reports received in England, he said, Americans were not disloyal. The worst they could be charged with was breach of the Laws of Trade, particularly evasion of duties on foreign molasses. But why blame the charter governments? The bribe-hungry British customs officials were really responsible. "Who received the Gratuities and Considerations to an immense Amount for *not Entering?* Who, but the very Gentlemen who are said to have been instrumental in representing that the Charter Governments obstruct Acts of Trade," namely the customs officers. These gentlemen were indicting the colonies for their own crime.[25]

The letter in which he set down these views seems to have been intended for Richard Jackson, the Connecticut agent in London, but it was probably never sent. By the time he finished writing it, Stiles had succeeded in getting some of the venom out of his system. Besides, he did not entirely trust Jackson, to whose correspondence Jared Eliot had introduced him, because Jackson, while serving as a colonial agent, was also a member of Parliament and George Grenville's private secretary. Stiles suspected that he was too closely attached to the court interest to serve the colonies properly.[26]

Though Stiles refrained from transmitting his sentiments to official ears in England, he spread them voluminously at home. He rejoiced in the torrent of petitions, remonstrances, pamphlets, and newspaper articles that other Americans were issuing against the new British colonial measures. As he saw opportunity, he spoke up himself. He told Thomas Hutchinson that only a friend to charter liberties (he did not know whether Hutchinson was or not) could write a proper history of New England.[27] And when his father-in-law asked his advice about a protest that he was helping to prepare for the Connecticut

25. Stiles to [Richard Jackson], Mar. 26, 1764.
26. Eliot to Stiles, Aug. 21, 1761; Note by Stiles dated Dec. 26, 1765. Cf. Stiles to John Devotion, May 2, 1767.
27. Stiles to Hutchinson, May 7, 1764.

government, Stiles outlined an argument that all the colonies were to pursue in the next few years. He urged that the Connecticut remonstrance be based

> on the privileges of magna Charta which I mentioned to you have been expressly extended to the Colonies by Act of Parliament. And among other Things it is well known to be a fundamental Principle of the British rather English Constitution that no Body of the Kings Subjects be taxed but by their own Consent —and the same principle [that was] opposed to the illegal Taxations of Charles I and subsequent Reigns by Parliament, may be advanced against the Parliamentary Taxations: for in both Cases the principle remains the same, and Equally [valid] against Parliament and King, that no subjects be taxed but by themselves. Now where a Representation in parliament is impracticable, it should seem that the Taxation must interfere with essential Liberty. . . .
>
> Indeed a parliamentary Taxation of America effectually strikes at the Root of american Liberty and Rights and effectually reduces us to Slavery. We are already equal to one quarter of England and may in Time surpass Britain in Numbers, and it will be hard to subject one half the Kings Subjects to the Taxation of the other half. Britain has expended several Millions in our Defence—which we shall soon Pay in Sale of Lands in Commerce &c. and why should she claim perpetual Subjugation in Return for Defence? Why should we be treated as a conquered Country? What more would France have taken from us than the powers of *Legislation, Taxation* and *Government?* Take these away from any Body of Men and what are they more than slaves? [28]

While other colonists rose to the defense of liberty, the Newport anticharter group continued their attack. During the summer and fall of 1764 they filled the pages of the *Newport Mercury* with articles insinuating the advantages of submission to Parliament and the disadvantages of popular government.[29] The Sugar Act, while taxing molasses, put a bounty on hemp. Why not grow hemp in Rhode Island and be prosperous and dutiful simultaneously? When Governor Stephen Hopkins published a spirited defense of the rights of colo-

28. Hubbard to Stiles, May 23, 1764; Stiles to Hubbard, June 12, 1764.
29. Morgan and Morgan, *Stamp Act Crisis*, pp. 48–51.

nies,[30] they countered with a supercilious argument for Parliamentary supremacy.[31] Meanwhile their agent was in England ready to present their petition for royal government.

Although Stiles sounded the alarm both publicly and privately against the enemies of liberty, he did not directly attack the Anglicans or the other Newport conspirators. In his thanksgiving sermon on November 29, 1764, he made oblique reference to them when he asked for deliverance "from the present secret and open attempts of our Enemies to undermine and dissolve our present political Forms of Government, the happy Basis of civil and religious Liberty." [32] But something held him back from public attack on another religion even in this crisis.

From the first onset of danger he had called on his people merely to stay clear of the charter plot and "each one exert himself for the good of our Israel and so far as providence calls us be engaged in a religious Defence of our Liberties civil and religious." Stiles did not specify what he thought the proper form of exertion might be. What was a "religious defence" of liberty? He knew how to defend liberty inside his church by allowing the members the widest latitude of practice. He knew how to defend liberty against consociational authority by ordaining James Dana in defiance of it. But how did you defend liberty against the lurking dangers of corrupt administration and designing Churchmen? You could warn people of the dangers; you could protest to the administration; but if words failed, what then? Ezra Stiles did not say, and he did not know.

30. *The Rights of Colonies Examined* (Providence, 1764).

31. [Martin Howard, Jr.] *A Letter from a Gentleman at Halifax to His Friend in Rhode Island* (Newport, 1765).

32. Sermons on Thanksgivings, Nov. 29, 1764.

15

The Edge of Civil War

In March 1765 Parliament passed the Stamp Act. The many remonstrances, petitions, pamphlets, and appeals sent to England had been in vain. Parliament had ignored the arguments, refused even to hear the petitions. The colonists were shaken. Many had refused to be alarmed by the Sugar Act because, though admittedly designed to raise a revenue, it had taken the form of a regulation of trade, such as Parliament had enacted in the past. But the Stamp Act was unambiguously a tax, perhaps the first of many. If Parliament succeeded with it, there was no telling where, this side of slavery, taxes would end.

News of the Stamp Act reached Newport in April, in time to provide Rhode Island ministers with a more dramatic theme for their annual fast-day sermons than they could usually produce. Ezra Stiles, profoundly disturbed by the Act, was far from sure what to say about it. His sermon followed well-worn analogies to a conventional moral —the familiar likening of New England to Israel, the tribulations with which God visited both, and the necessity of humiliation and renewal of faith as a means to recovery.[1] God had many ways of trying His people. He might cause them to be attacked by enemies from within—and no one needed to be told who they were—or by enemies from without—"a British parliament stripping us of one of those Immunities which heretofore distinguished an Englishman. Tax without our Consent."

1. The notes for this sermon of Apr. 18, 1765, are in the library of the Mass. Hist. Soc.

Inasmuch as the colonists had done nothing to England to merit such treatment, Stiles thought, the Stamp Act must be punishment for offending God in some way. "God may permit others to execute his Vengeance and Judgment," he pointed out, "one Nation to rise against another, or one part of a nation to oppress another, when Gods people may be innocent as to any Trespass against the Instruments of Chastisement." But there was no reason to think that God approved of the enemies He used to scourge His chosen people, because "it is obvious to remark in the Hebrew History that a fatal Judicial Ruin eventually overtook them at last. Where are the Ammonites, the Philistines, the Chaldeans &c those enemies of Israel?"

The lesson to be drawn from these trials was humiliation: "Let us as a part of the church not be discouraged but trust that God in his Time will work a Deliverance and protection. God has often delivered us in 1635 1664 1688 1720 It is probable we shall have more and more of corruption to struggle with—but this is the Trial of our Faith. Let us profess Truth boldly and render unto God the Things &c."

Though urging submission, Stiles's sermon was not necessarily a counsel of despair, and with a little interpretation it might even become a call to resistance. Stiles was not making that call. But there were people in his congregation who could interpret for themselves. Stiles had cited God's deliverance of New England in 1635, but in 1635 the Puritans had "hastened their fortifications" when they heard of Archbishop Laud's commission to take over their government. Stiles had cited 1688, but in delivering New England from Andros and old England from James II in 1688, God did not hesitate to employ men with arms. One might render unto God and unto Caesar as Stiles advised, but it did not follow that a stamp tax was part of Caesar's due.

From April until November, when collection of the Stamp Tax was to begin, the American colonists waited uneasily. Although there was general agreement that Parliament had no constitutional right to tax them, opinion varied about the best way to make England admit her mistake and repeal the tax. Some people felt that if Americans met this assault on their liberties with nothing but more talk, it would be followed by one encroachment after another.

Stiles was not convinced that the time for words had passed. He had built his life on a faith in reason, and he was loath to admit that reason had failed. It had not failed, he decided. The corrupt politicians in charge of England's government had refused to listen to it, but it would triumph in the end. Although only a few members of Parliament had been sufficiently moved by reason to oppose the Stamp Act, these friends of America might land at the head of some future British ministry and re-establish colonial liberty.

Few Americans had Stiles's confidence in the power of reason. And his own confidence was bolstered by despair of any other method, for he thought the colonists not strong enough to risk a clash of arms. In the event of civil war the British would win and crush American liberty under a military dictatorship. Better to wait peacefully until the day of the oppressor came to an end, through a change in the British ministry, through the increase of American population, or through some unforeseen intervention of God.

In spite of these sentiments Stiles was no pacifist. Just a month later, after reading the first volume of Thomas Hutchinson's history of Massachusetts, he wrote a letter rebuking the author for his treatment of the Andros regime. Andros was a tyrant, and the successful efforts of Massachusetts to oust him were not rash, but glorious.[2] As Stiles saw it, in fact, the deposition of Andros was one of the greatest testimonies to liberty of those old Puritans with whom he had come to identify himself. Again and again in the next ten years he would look back on the days of Andros as a type of the tyranny which he saw growing around him.

His admiration for ancestral defenders of liberty is also recorded in a notebook he was keeping at this time.[3] Here he wrote out a seventeen-page inscription for an imaginary column to commemorate the loss of American liberty. It was a bold, if somewhat turgid, recital of American history, emphasizing former triumphs over tyranny, triumphs achieved for the most part by force of arms, against Charles I ("Whose Memory be it execrated Thro' all american Ages"), Charles II ("of the Contemptible House of Stuart"), Edmund Andros ("marked with the Infamy of being the first tyrannical Governor in the Colonies"). There were also laurels for the deserving: Oliver Cromwell ("the first sovereign of England who was a true friend of America"), and William Pitt ("that illustrious Minister").

Writing this inscription was a harmless private gesture against tyranny, but Stiles was equally vigorous in his public denunciation

2. Stiles to Hutchinson, May 7, 1764.

3. The notebook is devoted entirely to the events of the Stamp Act Crisis. Hereafter referred to as Stamp Act Notebook.

of the measures to which he was urging submission. If he thought it
wrong to resist the Stamp Act, he also thought it wrong to call the
spade by any other name. His friends and parishioners were left in
no doubt about his hatred of this and every other act of tyranny.
They listened respectfully to his paradoxical views and dissolved the
paradox by ignoring the part of it that did not suit them. As the
summer wore on toward November and news arrived from other
colonies of bold resolutions in favor of liberty, they prepared for
tyranny with none of the humility that Stiles had advised. The General
Assembly of Rhode Island ordered that when the time came to use
stamps, the officers of government should continue business as usual
without them; and a number of the leading members of Stiles's congregation, irritated perhaps by the insolence of the "enemies within,"
began to contemplate a chastisement that would impede the operation
of the Stamp Act and at the same time reduce the boldness of the advocates for royal government. It was probably the example of Boston
that touched off the explosions. On the night of August 16 the Bostonians hanged the effigy of Andrew Oliver (the man appointed distributor of stamps there), tore down the building which it was reported he would use for an office, and pillaged his mansion house.
Oliver resigned the next day.

When the news reached Newport, two members of Stiles's congregation, his good friends and neighbors Samuel Vernon (William's
brother) and William Ellery, decided that it was time to give the
friends of tyranny in Newport a taste of their own medicine. They
understood and respected their pastor's feelings, but they were used
to picking things up by the handle, and they did not share his doubts
about the colonists' chances of success. Instead of monuments to dead
liberty they preferred to scare the life out of would-be tyrants. They
accordingly made effigies of Augustus Johnston, the Newport stamp
distributor, and of Martin Howard, Jr., and Dr. Thomas Moffat.
The last two were known to be ringleaders of the royalist group.
Moffat was not an Anglican but a Scotsman with high-flown Stuart
ideas of royal prerogative; he and Howard were thought to be the
authors of the royalist letters that had been appearing in the *Newport
Mercury* and also of the pamphlet in rebuttal to Governor Hopkins'
defense of the colonies.[4]

Stiles woke on August 27 to find a gallows erected on the nearby

4. Morgan and Morgan, *Stamp Act Crisis*, pp. 144–47; Stiles to John Hubbard,
Feb. 22, 1765.

Parade. Three effigies dangled from it, and below them Vernon, Ellery, and Robert Crook, another merchant, walked back and forth decked out in "muffled big coats flapped hats and bludgeons." Johnston, Howard, and Moffat, for the effigies were theirs, got the point and left town. It was the appointed day for the quarterly meeting of Newport freeholders, and many people on their way to the courthouse at the head of the Parade stopped to stare and exchange a word with the pacing guards. In the afternoon refreshments were served and a drummer was sent out to arouse more of a crowd; in the evening the figures were cut down and ceremoniously burnt.

There was no violence, and the gentlemen who had fled felt safe in returning to town the next day. It was their mistake. The directors of the performance had doubtless expected that it would lead Johnston to resign his odious office, and nothing less would satisfy them. That evening, just after Johnston, Moffat, and Howard hurried aboard the Man-of-War *Cygnet* in the harbor, a mob raged through the streets of Newport for six hours, destroying the houses, furnishings, and gardens of the fugitives. Johnston got off the lightest. He had been a popular man before he undertook the stamp office and on the basis of this and of his friends' promise that he would resign the office next day, the mob was persuaded not to destroy his house; they made free, however, with stealing his possessions.[5]

The next day, according to his friends' promise, Johnston appeared to make his resignation, and a good part of Newport was there to see him. The affair took place on the Parade, just a stone's throw from Stiles's house, and Stiles doubtless watched it. He was shocked by the night's violence, as were most people, including some of those who had initiated it, for the mob had got out of hand. But today all was orderly enough; the leaders seemed to have things under control, and nothing waxed hot but tongues.

A good many people must have thought the wording of Johnston's resignation statement inadequate, but according to Johnston it was Ezra Stiles who called it "artful base insufficient" and warned the people that in spite of it Johnston would be able to execute the office.[6] If Stiles said any such thing, he was probably right, for by the same account Johnston himself admitted that he had lulled the people into quiescence "by an ambiguous ineffectual declaration in

5. Ibid.

6. Thomas Moffat to J. Harrison, London, Oct. 16, 1765. Chalmers Papers, New York Public Library.

writing which implyd a resignation of the stamp office but as it had been extorted under the threatnings of ruin and destruction He never intended to observe or regard it." [7]

Johnston's resignation was the intended finale of the plan that Vernon, Ellery, Crook, and whatever other conspirators had arranged. Unfortunately it did not turn out that way. Being gentlemen, they had naturally but unforesightedly turned over the dirty work in their plot to men familiar with brickbats, bludgeons, and street brawling. These had done an alarming and unnecessarily thorough job, and had been so carried away by their enjoyment of power that they were reluctant to relinquish it. They rallied round a demagogue from their ranks and for several days threatened Newport with a reign of terror, until at last the leader and enough of his henchmen were jailed to break the spirit of the rest, and the Sons of Liberty, as the original gentlemen plotters began to call themselves, regained control. It was a nasty experience for Newport, and it disclosed a new danger in resistance to British authority. [8]

Stiles's own fears were compounded because American Anglicans were writing home that the anti-Stamp Act riots from Georgia to Maine were fomented by New England Congregationalists, who, they claimed, wrote inflammatory letters and sent rabble rousers from colony to colony. He had expected something like this from them, but he was not prepared at all for their crowning fabrication: they blamed the Newport riot on him, who sincerely preached and believed that the colonists should not resist the Stamp Act. When Stiles heard the rumor to this effect, he went to Augustus Johnston and his rector the Reverend James Honeyman of Trinity Church to explain the situation and assure them that he had had no hand either in the preparation of the effigies or in the violence that followed. Johnston "frankly told me," Stiles later recorded, "that he never thot I had, nay that he knew I had not, and that he well knew who had." In order to belie the rumor Stiles drew up a statement of his innocence and passed it around among the persons who he thought would carry the most weight. He supposed he had cleared himself, and had barely relaxed, when he heard that an Anglican complaint against him had been sent to England. [9]

A more opportune moment to accuse him of disloyalty the Angli-

7. Ibid.
8. Morgan and Morgan, *Stamp Act Crisis*, pp. 191–94.
9. Stiles to Benjamin Franklin, Oct. 23, 1765.

cans could not have chosen, for just about this time he received the
totally unexpected news that he had been honored by the University
of Edinburgh with the degree of doctor of divinity. The Anglican
smear would discredit Stiles in the eyes both of the University that
had honored him and of his friend Benjamin Franklin who had arranged the degree as a testimony of respect and belief in him.[10]
Incitement to riot was certainly not an appropriate pastime for a
minister of the gospel, let alone a doctor of divinity. In understand-
able anxiety he wrote to Franklin protesting his innocence:

> Before the stamp act past, and when we first received the Resolves
> of the Parliament tho' it appeared to me a heavy Grievance as
> it did to all America and to the London Merchants, yet in Con-
> versation I always declared freely that if it past I would submit.
> After it was past, I frequently talked against the Folly of Re-
> sistance by force and said that however others conducted, I would
> continue loyal and submit. These were my sentiments and pur-
> poses from the beginning. . . . I hesitated not to declare my
> Sentiments freely against all Coercion of the Stamp Officers,
> against a proposed Burning of the Stamp papers, and against all
> violence in resisting the Stamp Act whether in the Colony of
> Rhode Island or the other Colonies: I had particularly in July
> or at least before the Mob at Boston, endeavored to dissuade a
> Connecticut Man then at my house against certain forceable
> Measures which he told me were meditated there. . . . I spake
> so freely at Newport long before the Mobs against opposing
> the Act as gave offense. In short in my little sphere I have uni-
> formly persisted from the beginning to this Time in declaring for
> myself my own Resolutions of not opposing this or any other
> Act of Parliament however grievous—and finally gave my Opin-
> ion that in Case of real and unquestionable Injuries, Resistance
> was unlawful till every other Method had been tried, and not
> even then till the Evil of the Oppression exceded the Evil of
> civil Wars. I have labored to convince my friends by a variety
> of arguments that it was best not to oppose by any Violence, tho'
> I deplore the fate of America.[11]

10. See above, pp. 158–59.

11. Stiles to Franklin, Oct. 23, 1765. It is not clear whether Stiles sent this letter or
a briefer one, dated Nov. 6, 1765, or both. Cf. Stiles to Thomas Hutchinson, Oct. 5,
1765.

While the rest of America was preparing to fight if fighting was needed, Stiles continued to urge submission. On a trip to Connecticut in October he found people even more inflamed than in Rhode Island. The old men were talking about the days of Andros and three out of four, man and boy alike, were ready to take the sword.[12] To most of them Stiles's simultaneous devotion to liberty and to non-resistance was an unfathomable contradiction. He tried to explain his position to Uncle Abel, but with no success. Abel apparently thought all he needed was a little stiffening in his thinking and his backbone. Though gentle with his nephew, Abel did not mince words:

> I also am far from friendly to violence unless when sel defence warrants it—yet I Confess myself so far a Phileleutheran, as to rejoyce in the general opposition made to what I take to be quite unconstitutional—and I really think there have been as few things Exceptionable in the Conduct of the people during this alarming season, as could be expected—if I am not mistaken, the present existence of our English happifying Constitution, is next to providence owing to sundry Spirited, united efforts formerly made against unconstitutional measures. . . . doth not the God of nature, the God of Civil liberty and property, also say Stand fast &c. and Contend Earnestly &c. pray what forbids us to resist even unto blood where that freedom is in question, the death of which is the death of property, as the pregnant Mothers death is fatal to the Infant unborn—if by petition and waiting on providence as you say, you mean no more than the Words seem to Import; I hardly Jump in Judgment with you.[13]

What was motivating his nephew, beyond the actual danger of colonial resistance, Uncle Abel did not see. He believed that righteous submission was a less appropriate reaction to tyranny than righteous resistance. Other Americans agreed: from New England to South Carolina they attacked the stamp distributors and forced the courts and customhouses to do business without stamps. The result was not what Ezra Stiles predicted. American resistance was followed not by civil war but by repeal of the Act. Moreover, nothing further was heard of the movement for revoking the Rhode Island charter.

Actually Parliament may have repealed the Act in spite of, not

12. Stiles to Benjamin Ellery, New Haven, Oct. 23, 1765.
13. Abel Stiles to Stiles, Apr. 18, 1766.

because of, American resistance. There had been vigorous objections in Parliament and in the British press from those who, infuriated by American riots, insisted that the Act be crammed down American throats. The primary motive behind repeal was the economic depression in England, which had been heightened by an American boycott of British goods. Nevertheless the colonists were understandably reluctant to belittle the part their resistance had played. Even Stiles thought it impossible to tell "how much the Tumults, the Loss of affection; and future alienations in America conspired with Commercial Motives, in effecting our Wishes. One thing may be said, the Opposition was *dangerous*, and was *important*."

These words are from the sermon Stiles preached when the colony appointed a day of thanksgiving for their deliverance.[14] He devoted most of it to a history of liberty in America and connected the present deliverance with earlier ones. He acknowledged that the violence he deplored sprang from a spirit of liberty, which "spread and operated and broke forth all along the Continent with great force and inextinguishable Ardor—." He admitted that the efforts of the Sons of Liberty (which had expanded to an intercolonial organization) might have helped in securing relief. But he insisted that true credit be given where due: that colonial resistance had not resulted in the disaster he had predicted was thanks to God and to Jesus Christ "the Head of the Sons of Liberty" who "pays a sacred Attention to the Cause of Liberty in all Empires in the World."

In making these admissions Stiles did not attempt to hide his own inglorious role: "During all the late tumultuous period, you know I have said nothing in my Discourses from this Desk to influence you in the part that was taken in America—you well know that I judged the Case desparate and irretrievable. Influenced by Timidity partly, partly by Judgment I took no part. I observed however with Attention the progress of the important Affair and ceased not day nor night to pray my God for Deliverance."

The candor of this confession should prevent us from reading into it more than it says: "by Timidity partly, partly by Judgment." When repeal put an end to timidity, judgment remained. Though he gave credit to those who had fought for liberty when she was dying, he did not admit that his own judgment even though reinforced by

14. The notes for this sermon, dated June 26, 1766, are not bound with the Sermons on Thanksgivings.

timidity had been wrong. He still believed that a clash of arms would have meant ruin for America, and that, though the immediate crisis had been weathered, the danger to liberty was by no means over, nor would a clash of arms in the near future be any less dangerous. As for his conduct in preaching nonresistance, that too was right for him. Though the conduct of the American colonies in any situation could be determined by expediency, what Ezra Stiles should say and do must be determined by the fact that he was a minister of the gospel.

A minister's job was to preach the Scriptures, and that was all he should preach. Uncle Abel might think that "the God of nature, the God of Civil liberty and property," required him to "Stand fast &c and Contend Earnestly," but the God that Stiles found in Scripture told him to stand fast and contend earnestly only for his faith. If God willed resistance to civil tyranny, He would guide men to it. For a minister to do so was presumption. A minister of the gospel should participate in no political movement, nor use his office or pulpit to further any cause but that of saving souls. This seemed to Stiles to be scriptural advice.

It was also a cardinal principle of the Puritans, but once again his application was different from theirs. In seventeenth-century Massachusetts the clergy were, to be sure, excluded from any share in the civil government, but though without formal power they did not hesitate to give political advice from the pulpit, advice which was rendered the more potent by the fact that only members of churches could vote, and church membership was confined to visible saints. By Stiles's time the doors of most churches were wide open and the religious qualifications for voting, which never existed in Rhode Island anyhow, had been eliminated in the rest of New England. Ministers still refrained for the most part from holding political office—but the extent to which they dispensed political propaganda and wielded their influence in civil affairs verged (it seemed to Stiles) on the sacrilegious.

As he interpreted the Puritan doctrine it meant that ministers and churches should keep out of politics. He had watched President Clap and the New Lights and Old Lights in Connecticut turn religious party lines into political party lines, and the results were proof enough that the Puritan principle needed closer application. He had been trying to live according to this principle, but the going had been hard. Where did politics begin and religion end? As practiced by the Anglicans in the past crisis, the two were certainly inseparable. God had smiled on the Americans; was it a sign that He approved and was ready to support them; would He want His ministers to join in the fight?

Stiles was troubled about it. He knew that civil and religious liberty went together, and civil and religious tyranny. Would not fighting for civil liberty, then, be a way of "contending earnestly" for religion? Should he not contend against the intrigues of the Anglicans and against any future assaults by Parliament? As he set candles in his windows to celebrate repeal, and strolled out into the streets with the rest of the crowd, through the Parade, past the ruined shell of Martin Howard's house, he could not have failed to think about it. The whole town was lit up (but not, he noticed, the house of the Anglican minister, James Honeyman), the candles shining on the water when you walked out Long Wharf and looked back. There, silhouetted against the sky, topped appropriately by a bishop's mitre, the steeple of Trinity Church menaced all beneath it with naked power from abroad. Not far away, but a little lower, the steeple of his own church defied the menace. The people of his church had taken the lead in attacking tyranny with more than words, but their minister, who hated tyranny as much as any man, still wondered whether they had been right.

16

Christian Union and Disunion

THE CRISIS WAS OVER. Stiles tried to put behind him the fretful problems of action, hoping to return to the happy combat of reason against reason. He had all along comforted himself with the thought that posterity, after reason had triumphed, would do ample justice ("Justice which a man of Wisdom will dread") to the local Americans who had betrayed their country in petitions for royal government.[1] He was content now to leave vengeance to posterity and recommended to his congregation "an Amnesty Forgiveness and Oblivion of all that unhappy Treatment which we of this Congregation have received from some of our American Fellow Subjects." But in case posterity, reading the notes for this sermon, should not know whom he meant, he helpfully inserted an asterisk and the words "the Episcopalians." [2]

If the Episcopalians had been willing to give up their scheme of dominion, Stiles would have found it easier to forgive and forget. He would have nothing against them, he kept telling himself, nothing important at least, if only they would abandon their claim of divine right. That, he thought, was the probable source of their drive for power. Yet it did not seem to unbalance all Episcopalians. He had been amazed and gratified that in the southern colonies, where the main body of the people were Anglicans, there had been just as vigorous opposition to the Stamp Act as in the north, and he

1. Sermons on Thanksgivings, Apr. 12, 1764.
2. Sermon on Repeal of the Stamp Act, June 26, 1766.

welcomed the southern Anglicans as fellow defenders of liberty.[3]

Even while Stiles was preaching amnesty and forgiveness for the Anglicans of the north, he knew that they had not given up; and shortly after his sermon, news arrived of a petition which a group of New York and New Jersey Anglican clergy had sent to the king a year or two before, asking for the appointment of an American bishop.[4] The petition, which was still pending, was said to have argued that monarchy in the state and independency (i.e. Congregationalism) in the church were incompatible, a statement which could be considered correct only by a monarch who pretended to divine right. According to one story the bishop asked for was to be a purely spiritual creature, with none of the political or juridical powers possessed by bishops in England. This was presumably to make the appointment appear harmless to other denominations; but Stiles and his friends had had a look at the Stamp Act and thought they knew the camel's nose when they saw it. They knew that the Stamp Act was only a beginning. If it had succeeded, it would have been followed by other acts of taxation without limit. A purely spiritual bishop was the same sort of trap: once established he would not be long in acquiring secular powers, and then good-by religious liberty. In fact, the Stamp Act and the establishment of episcopacy might have been planned together. The act had provided for taxation of documents used in ecclesiastical courts, thus suggesting the possibility of a British intention to establish such courts throughout America with bishops to preside over them.

About this time, while riding in the country on one of his journeys to Connecticut or Massachusetts, Stiles fell in with an Anglican gentleman from Massachusetts, a man whose name he was careful not to record but one who claimed to be close to the inner circles of government. This gentleman may have been one of those people who take pleasure in purveying supposedly "inside" information, or he may simply have been pulling a gullible minister's leg; but whether the story he told, with the Anglicans' customary air of assurance, was

3. Stiles to Francis Alison, Sept. 5, 1766; to William Hart, Feb. 2, 1767; to Charles Chauncy, Mar. 19, 1770.

4. Francis Alison to Stiles, Aug. 7, 1766; Stiles to Samuel Langdon, May 24, 1766; to Charles Chauncy, Aug. 26, 1766, Mar. 3, 1768. Stiles made a copy of one of the petitions on July 9, 1766, from one shown him by Patrick Alison and John Ewing, who were visiting him on this date (see below).

genuine or spurious, it fitted all too well with other evidence that Stiles had obtained, and was still obtaining, from other sources. The gentleman affected to be perturbed by the opposition which the Stamp Act had created in New England, because he feared it might delay the carrying out of a larger plan to remodel the colonial governments by reducing the power of the assemblies, increasing that of the royal governors, and establishing the Anglican church everywhere. The details he confided to Stiles were alarming:

> That the Charters would be revoked was certain—then they intended to procede very moderately and win us over by degrees, and give us Time to feel where all power lies and comply. He said Two Branches of Legislation for Massachusetts as well as others would be Episcopal, and all offices in the Governor alone, and the lower house be reduced to a few perhaps 20 or 30 at most, which would be septennial at least and a Majority easily gained and secured in the Episcopal Influence. But the secret he seemed much pleased with, was that upon Revocation of Charter, it would be necessary to re-enact the whole Body of Laws or Statutes; in doing which it was intended to drop all the Laws for Support and Maintenance of the Congregational Ministers—or if a few of them should pass here, yet the Royal Assent would be withheld. That our Ministers or their Successors finding their Strength and support gone from under them, would in Time come over to the Church. . . . He tho't upon the Resumption of Charter, the Ministers might be made sensible of their irrecoverable Loss, as to be ready to listen to the plan of erecting Bishopricks, in New England and all America; . . . for a few rich Livings and a few splendid Titles held up within the reach of any Individuals, would wonderfully influence Multitudes. That upon Reordination some of our most eminent Ministers would be made Bishops, Deans, Prebends . . . that it was not necessary to have Bishopricks as large as in England. . . . I understood him that if we would all come into the Scheme we might have a Bishop &c to every 20 or 30 Ministers and Parishes, or at least we might several Deanics and Archdeacons &c. . . . Now in addition to this, the Presentation to Livings being to be taken out of the hands of the people and put into the hands of Governors Bishops or Patrons would not necessitate Ministers

to court and be so dependent on the Will and humour of the populace, they need only secure the Interest of some one great man, and be easy for Life. On the whole they had such Confidence in this Scheme that they doubted not to predict that it would carry all before it. Much more of this kind he unbosomed to me in Conversation, with a frankness and plenitude of Discovery or Avowment (if I may coin the Word) that I had not perceived before from the Episcopalians. It was distant in the Country, when we rode alone by ourselves, for shady miles.[5]

Stiles was perhaps too credulous in accepting everything that this rumor-monger confided in him, yet he had heard most of the details at one time or another from the Newport Episcopalians, especially during the period before they gave up trying to win him over. They were, for the moment, feeling whipped. Their petition for royal government and their support of Parliamentary authority during the Stamp Act had discredited them with the rest of the population in Rhode Island, but elsewhere the Stamp Act crisis had muddied the waters of local politics so thoroughly that the Anglicans were finding new opportunities for intrigue.

In Pennsylvania, Stiles heard, they had schemed themselves into control of the college in Philadelphia, and they were looking forward to new power in the legislature. A leading Presbyterian told him how "they rejoyce at the Quarrel between us and the Qu—rs and no doubt expect that in the midst of our Contests theyll one day or other get the upper hand of us both; they are certainly more jealous of us as a growing Body than of the Qu—rs and well know our Spirit to oppose them, for which Reason they throw their Weight into tother Scale against us; and besides all this we have strong Reason to suspect the Episcopals want to engage the Qu—rs to a Neutrality about their present favourite Object a Bishop and have gone into their Alliance on that Condition." [6]

In Connecticut the Anglicans were just as busy. The Old Lights there were in disgrace, because Jared Ingersoll, the appointed Stamp Master for the colony, and Governor Thomas Fitch, who had taken the oath to enforce the act, were both Old Lights. The oath was

5. Stiles to Charles Chauncy, Mar. 3, 1768.
6. Samuel Purviance, Jr., to Stiles, Nov. 1, 1766; *Itineraries and Miscellanies,* pp. 554–58.

required of governors by the terms of the act, and Fitch had taken it for fear that a refusal might endanger the charter. Nevertheless the New Lights had seized the opportunity to fasten all the odium of the Stamp Act on their opponents, and the Episcopalians were quick to get in on the game. As it happened, William Samuel Johnson, a prominent Churchman, had taken a strong stand against the Stamp Act. Though Johnson was not expressing Episcopalian views in this matter, his fellow churchmen joined with the New Lights to elect him to the Council. This was the first time an Episcopalian had landed a seat on the Connecticut Council. It was a notable achievement.[7]

From Pennsylvania to New England, then, Presbyterians and Congregationalists, with good reason, continued to fear the Anglican menace. Stiles saw the dangers, talked about them, wrote letters about them, perhaps magnified them out of all proportion to the actuality. And while he talked, others, as in the time of the Stamp Act, prepared to act. This time they surprised him by proposing something that he had privately advocated for years: a union of Calvinist Protestants. In spite of rebuff after rebuff he had never stopped pushing this idea. In the midst of the past crisis he had brought it up again when writing the University of Edinburgh a letter of thanks for his doctorate.[8] Again nothing had come of it. Now, he heard, the Presbyterians of New York and Pennsylvania, moved perhaps by his correspondent, Francis Alison, had begun to take steps.

Meeting in the United Synod of New York and Philadelphia in May 1766, they voted to approach the consociated churches of Connecticut.[9] The Connecticut churches already had a semi-Presbyterian organization and might be expected to receive the motion more hospitably than the other Congregational churches of New England. Accordingly at the next general meeting of the Association of Connecticut pastors in June, two Presbyterian ambassadors were on hand to open negotiations. They were John Ewing and Patrick Alison, both young men of considerable ability. Ewing was minister of the Presbyterian church in Philadelphia, an open, affable man with wide scholarly tastes somewhat resembling Stiles's, so deft in conversation that a few years later, on a trip to England, he succeeded in turning one

7. Morgan and Morgan, *Stamp Act Crisis*, pp. 234–37.
8. Stiles to William Robertson, Nov. 26, 1765.
9. William M. Engles, ed., *Records of the Presbyterian Church* (Philadelphia, 1841), pp. 363–64; Chauncy Whittelsey to Stiles, June 12, 1766.

of Dr. Johnson's outbursts of invective into amiability. Alison (no relation to Francis Alison) was minister of a log church in Baltimore, Maryland, a town which had just sprung into existence and was growing with almost frantic speed. Alison, only twenty-six in 1766, was to grow with the town and remain its foremost advocate of religious liberty.[10]

The two men had somehow managed to obtain and now carried with them what were said to be authentic copies of the Anglican petition for a bishop. Holding up this fearful document, they proposed a union not merely with the Connecticut clergy but with those of the rest of New England as well, in fact with all dissenters in America. The chief purpose would be to counteract the efforts of the Episcopalians to discredit American dissenters in the eyes of the British ministry, for a less hostile ministry would presumably be less inclined to grant the Anglican petition. In order to effect the union a joint conference was arranged for the following November in New York.[11] This settled, Alison and Ewing headed east to consult Dr. Stiles.

Stiles heard of the plan from his Connecticut friends before Alison and Ewing appeared on his doorstep in July. "I send the young Infant to you Reverend Doctor," wrote his cousin and former student, John Devotion of Saybrook, "to view its Physiognomy and prescribe such Potions as your Wisdom may thinke meet." [12] In spite of his long-standing interest in such a scheme, the Doctor's first reaction was cautious. "I chuse to think more before I say much," he wrote to Devotion, and then went on to say a great deal. The scheme was good, he said, if it could be accomplished without impairing the rights of the member churches. There must be no jurisdiction or authority involved; rather it must be in the nature of an alliance. If the Scottish church would join, this form would be better ensured, for the Scots would certainly remain a "Noun Substantive" and not allow themselves to be absorbed in any new polity. The American churches would make another noun substantive with respect to the Europeans. There was some danger that the New England Congregational churches would become ensnared in the folds of Presbyterianism, and though he respected and honored the Presbyterians, he was "more and more

10. William B. Sprague, *Annals of the American Pulpit* (New York, 1859–69), 3 216–19, 257–62; Francis Alison to Stiles, May 29, 1766.
11. John Devotion to Stiles, June 19, 1766.
12. Ibid. See also Chauncy Whittelsey to Stiles, June 12, 1766.

persuaded the New England Churches are apostolical rather than the Presbyterian." Even such a powerless social organization as he envisaged held some risk, for these harmless little embryos might turn out to be lions when they grew up.[13]

While Devotion circulated Stiles's initial communication on the subject among other Connecticut ministers, Stiles continued to ruminate on the advantages and dangers of union. The more he considered it, the better he liked it. It was, after all, what he had been advocating for seven years, as many of his friends knew. Devotion urged him to draw up for the coming meeting "an Original, generous, Catholick Plan, such as you would be willing should take place." [14] Accordingly, by the time Alison and Ewing walked up his garden path to lay their proposal officially before him, they found him with a tentative constitution for the organization already in mind. As he gathered mulberry leaves and fed his voracious silkworms, the three men discussed the details and the benefits of the plan in great harmony, and the visitors departed highly encouraged.[15] A few weeks later Francis Alison sent him another Philadelphian, a young merchant by the name of Samuel Purviance, Jr., who, Stiles reported, was "a feast of intelligence." [16] Alison communicated his own approval of the scheme and the urgency of its adoption.[17]

Stiles, in fact, became a kind of clearing house for advance discussion of the plan. On July 14, four days after Patrick Alison and Ewing left, he rode to Cambridge for the Harvard commencement (it was probably at this time that he met the mysterious gentleman who told him of the grand plan of the Anglicans) and sounded out the Massachusetts ministers who annually assembled for that event. Their reaction appears to have been friendly but cautious. Unless the plan was "very acceptable indeed," they thought that a correspondence between the Boston convention of ministers and the united synods was the most that could be expected for the present.[18] Unfortunately Charles Chauncy, the giant of the region, was not at hand, but Stiles

13. Stiles to Devotion, June 27, 1766.

14. Devotion to Stiles, July 7, 1766.

15. Patrick Alison to Stiles, July 30, 1766; John Ewing to Stiles, Aug. 6, 1766. Alison and Ewing left on July 10, 1766 (Gannett Almanacs)

16. Stiles to Francis Alison, Aug. 26, 1766.

17. Francis Alison to Stiles, Aug. 7, 20, 1766.

18. Stiles to Francis Alison, Aug. 26, 1766; to Patrick Alison, Aug. 26, 1766; to John Ewing, Aug. 26, 1766.

left a note at his house and sent him more letters after returning to Newport.[19] When Chauncy answered, he seemed to be more enthusiastic than the other Massachusetts ministers, proposing that the organization begin on a small scale with a committee of Congregational and Presbyterian delegates to correspond with the dissenters in England. He even thought that the Quakers and Baptists might be persuaded to join—but nothing came of this because, as Stiles saw it, they were too wrapped up in their old grudges to recognize the Anglican menace.[20]

Stiles was unable to get to the Yale commencement in September, but his friends reported to him that the union had been the main topic of conversation. Most people seemed to be as wary as he of entering a union unless there were some guarantee that the united assembly should have no authority. At least that was the way his friends, most of whom were Old Lights, felt about it. Not only did they fear the erection of an authority superior to the individual congregation, but they feared particularly the authority of a body in which New Lights might be expected to have a majority. They had had enough bitter experience with New Light dominance of the consociations.[21] As Stiles had expressed their problem earlier to Alison, "It is easy to foresee what Cast the plurality will be of, which if armed with power will play the sacred Artillery on the innocent as well as the guilty." [22]

There were other objections: Chauncy Whittelsey thought it would be wrong for Connecticut to join with the Presbyterians unless the rest of New England did. To do so would accelerate the tendency toward Presbyterianism which already existed there and thus widen instead of narrow the gulf between the consociated churches of Connecticut and the more strictly Congregational churches of the other New England colonies.[23] Others feared the union would defeat its own purpose by alarming rather than mollifying the anti-American party in England. It would be looked upon as a "Twin Brother" of the Stamp Act Congress, an intercolonial meeting which had met at New York in 1765 to draft a protest against parliamentary taxation

19. Stiles to Chauncy, Aug. 26, 1766; Chauncy to Stiles, Sept. 29, 1766.

20. Chauncy to Stiles, Sept. 29, 1766.

21. Chauncy Whittelsey to Stiles, Sept. 17, 1766; Stiles to John Ewing, Sept. 26, 1766.

22. Stiles to Francis Alison, Aug. 26, 1766.

23. Whittelsey to Stiles, Sept. 17, 1766.

and which had been roundly condemned in England. An intercolonial congress of dissenters might be similarly condemned and construed as a devious method of promoting American independence.[24]

Stiles thought the various objections might be resolved. He had begun drafting articles of union when Alison and Ewing visited him early in July.[25] On September 2, 1766, on the back of a letter from Francis Alison, he drew up another set [26] and sent it along to Chauncy Whittelsey for comment. Though he had originally favored an occasional rather than an annual congress, with a preliminary consolidation of all the New England Congregational churches, he now called for an annual general assembly of two delgates from each Congregational association and each presbytery, the place of meeting to circulate. The most important articles were the third and fourth:

> III. That this General Assembly shall not be vested, nor in any Time to come be permitted to assume any Power, Dominion, Jurisdiction or Authority over the Churches or Pastors. And particularly the Congregational Consociated and presbyterian Churches shall subsist intire distinct and independent Bodies. These Ministers and Churches may be left to their Option to follow Advice &c without incurring Censure or Ejection.

> IV. That the general Design and Use of this Assembly be to Inspect the public State of this united Cause and Interest; to circulate and diffuse Union and Harmony among the Churches; to recommend Loyalty and Allegiance to the Kings Majesty and a peaceable Submission to the public Laws and Government; and also to address his Majesty or the Kings Ministers from Time to Time with Assurances of the public Loyalty of the Churches comprehended in this Union—or with Vindications of the united Denominations as a religious Body from the Aspersions with which they have been or shall be Vilified by their Episcopal Fellow Protestants, who cease not to represent us as disaffected and Enemies to the Kings Person and Government.[27]

When Whittelsey saw this, he thought the third article should be made more explicit, because the power of any large body of clergy

24. John Devotion to Stiles, July 7, 1766.
25. The first draft among his papers is dated July 10, 1766.
26. Alison to Stiles, Aug. 7, 1766.
27. Stiles to Whittelsey, begun Aug. 14, 1766, completed Sept. 2, 1766.

would inevitably grow unless hemmed in by very specific limitations. On the other hand the fourth article should be less explicit: there was no use mentioning the Episcopalians by name and thus starting unnecessary trouble.[28] Stiles amended his draft along these lines, phrasing the fourth article in more general terms and inserting in the third a provision that the three types of church, Congregational, consociated, and Presbyterian, should always retain "their respective Usages and peculiar forms of church Government and ecclesiastical Polity and that no Endeavors be attempted to change or assimilate the Same." In this form he sent the draft to other New England ministers and to Francis Alison.[29]

When the congress met on November 6 (at Elizabethtown, New Jersey, instead of New York), Stiles himself was not there. None of the New England associations outside Connecticut had been willing to send representatives, and two of the Connecticut associations likewise failed. But thirty delegates assembled, from the Presbyterian and consociated churches, and to them Francis Alison presented a plan of union based on the draft which Stiles had sent him. The delegates readily agreed to it, though only provisionally, since those from Connecticut were not empowered to accept anything until their constituents should review it. Invitations were sent to the missing New England churches to join in another meeting at New Haven in September on the day after the Yale commencement, and then the congress broke up.[30]

When the articles of union were made known in Connecticut, some of the Old Lights thought the restrictions on the assembly's powers were still not strong enough. William Hart, one of the champions of Congregational independence in the Wallingford controversy, told Stiles it was nonsense to talk about accepting or rejecting the advice of the congress when it was offered. This was like saying "I will have a right to throw mount Atlas on your shoulders when I think proper. But you shall have liberty to bear it, or throw it off, and kick it before you as a football, as you judge best. If we constitute them our *advisers general*, they will soon become our *masters sovereign*."[31] Stiles reported the objection to Francis Alison, and between

28. Whittelsey to Stiles, Sept. 17, 1766.
29. Stiles to Francis Alison, Oct. 8, 1766.
30. Francis Alison to Stiles, Dec. 4, 1766; John Rodgers to Stiles, Dec. 22, 1766.
31. Hart to Stiles, Nov. 6, 1766.

them they worked up an amendment to the third article, which prevented any member of the assembly from giving or asking advice on internal affairs. Stiles thought this amendment should remove all fears that the assembly would grow into a Presbyterian synod.[32]

In spite of all revisions, however, the Connecticut Old Lights continued skeptical. A union dominated, as this one would be, by Presbyterians and by Connecticut New Lights with Presbyterian leanings simply looked too dangerous. They continued also to fear that the union would spur the Anglicans to new efforts. The Anglican hierarchy in England had so far been cool to their American brothers' plea for a bishop. A union of American dissenters might be just the argument needed to swing the weight of the hierarchy behind the pending petition.[33]

In Massachusetts and Rhode Island the scheme for union had never aroused much enthusiasm except in Ezra Stiles and Charles Chauncy. The churches there too feared that the organization would eventually assume authority over its members and would arouse needless opposition in England. Chauncy himself finally swung against it for these reasons. In the end no church or association from Rhode Island or Massachusetts would have anything to do with it; and it remained, as it had begun, a union of Presbyterians from the middle colonies and Connecticut New Light consociations.[34]

Stiles was not particularly saddened by these developments. One of his principal purposes in backing a joint religious body had been to "diffuse Union and Harmony among the Churches," but had this one materialized it promised to have been a source of friction and discord. Besides, union was still possible in the future. He recalled that the American colonists had declined a political alliance proposed at Albany in 1754, yet within eleven years they had cooperated in the Stamp Act Congress. Similarly, the refusal of Congregationalists to join Presbyterians at this time did not mean that there was no real union of ideas and sentiment between them.[35]

32. Stiles to Francis Alison, Mar. 11, 1767; Francis Alison to Stiles, June 19, 1767; Stiles to Francis Alison, Aug. 27, 1767.

33. John Devotion to Stiles, Aug. 12, 1767; William Hart to Stiles, Aug. 20, 1767.

34. Charles Chauncy to Stiles, Mar. 30, June 29, 1767; Stiles to Noah Welles, Aug. 12, 1767; to Chauncy Whittelsey, June 11, 1767. The transactions of the Rhode Island Association of ministers with regard to the union are in Vol. 16, pp. 86–95, of the MS collections of the R.I. Hist. Soc., Providence, R.I.

35. Stiles to Chauncy Whittelsey, July 31, 1767; to Francis Alison, Aug. 27, 1767.

Since the Rhode Island churches had not joined the union, Stiles was not obliged to play any public role in it, but if he had been asked to, it seems likely that in the end he too would have declined, though for reasons different from those that moved the other abstainers. For all his excitement and delight in drawing up and revising articles —it was something like the family constitutions or the plan for a learned society—he began to have his own special doubts about the project as soon as the first meeting took place. By the time the organization was complete, he had thought further about the role of churches and ministers in the world, and his conclusions left little room for such an organization as he saw taking shape.

It is evident from all his correspondence on the subject that Stiles originally conceived the union partly as a means of protecting the apostolic Calvinist churches from attacks by the Anglicans. In a letter to Alison proposing union in 1759, he had spoken of their common danger from "a Church which I wish did more Honor to the Cause of Jesus." [36] In drafting the articles of union Stiles had specifically mentioned the Anglicans and only deleted the reference at the suggestion of Chauncy Whittelsey. As union proceeded, he continued to think of it in these terms, but gradually it dawned on him that he did not want the union to take the kind of stand against Anglicanism that his own words seemed to suggest. He wanted the apostolic churches to defend themselves without attacking their enemies. Perhaps he would not have made such a distinction before the Stamp Act troubles, but in that crisis he had learned to speak out for the right while urging submission to wrong. Now, even as he asked his friends to unite against the Anglican menace, he told them to avoid attacking it. "Let us not," he wrote to Francis Alison in August 1766, "be caught with the spirit of Intrigue and political cunning." [37]

What he meant by intrigue and political cunning may not have been entirely clear in August either to Alison or to himself. By the end of the year, however, he included far more under that heading than most other Congregationalists or Presbyterians would have. The difference between his views and those of the men he was urging to unite had become apparent at the Elizabethtown organizational meeting in November 1766.

The meeting, after adopting the articles Stiles drafted, had con-

36. Stiles to Francis Alison, July 3, 1759.
37. Ibid., Aug. 26, 1766.

sidered the question of implementing his Article IV, by addressing the king or the ministry against the proposed American bishop. Because this was simply a meeting for organization, with union not yet properly in existence, the delegates had decided not to send any address as a group, but as individuals they agreed to bombard all the influential Englishmen they knew with letters on the subject. Then at the next meeting they could draft a joint protest. To the delegates present this seemed a proper way to defend the apostolic churches against Episcopal encroachment.[38]

Stiles was not there to explain his views, but when he heard what the meeting had proposed, he was upset. This was not at all his idea of defense. He sat down on the day before Christmas 1766, and wrote out a long letter to explain why. Like many of his best letters, it was never sent: though he addressed it to the "moderator and members of the convention," he was writing as much to himself as anyone, thinking with pen and ink.[39]

The union, he insisted, should not be "an offensive Measure to oppugnate Episcopacy." Rather, the purpose should be to perpetuate the pure religion of Christ "unsowered with polemical Divinity and Controversy." Never should the members devote themselves to opposing other sects, Anglican or otherwise. Never should they throw their united weight "into any political scale whatever."

Should nothing then be done against the scheme of episcopizing America? No, nothing but preaching the good old Puritan doctrines. "It will be our duty indeed to represent the Truth to our people, and write on the Episcopal Controversy. Let us do it with Candor, as we have without all Question Justice Truth Scripture and primitive Antiquity on our side. But let us not be wro't upon by political Enemies to espouse any political Measures as a Body."

On these principles Stiles opposed any formal action by the churches against the current movement for an American bishop. He did not doubt that a petition had been sent, in which the Anglicans slandered the Presbyterians and Congregationalists and asked for a bishop as a means of keeping the colonies dependent on England. He did not doubt that many of his colleagues would favor an address to the king, refuting the slanders and emphasizing the alarm and disgust that a

38. Noah Welles to Stiles, Nov. 21, 1766.

39. Stiles "to the moderator and members of the convention to assemble on Sept. 10, 1767," Dec. 24, 1766. Cf. Stiles to Charles Chauncy, Mar. 3, 1768.

bishop would excite among a million of the king's loyal subjects in America. But as he had preached nonresistance to the Stamp Act, so now he disapproved the union's sending any petition or declaration to resist the appointment of an American bishop. He did not even wish to see the people of America aroused to indignation against bishops. For ministers to excite such a spirit was "inconsistent with the mild and peaceable Religion of the great Lover of Souls." Rather than be concerned in any such measures he would prefer to suffer persecution.

Stiles's stand on the American bishop marked his emergence from a period of confusion. He now believed, without doubts, that politics and religion did not mix at all. Any kind of political activity was wrong for a church or for its ministers. The Stamp Act had started his thinking in this direction. He was pushed the rest of the way, through confusion to conviction, by the problems of union and by certain events that had been taking place simultaneously in Connecticut.

It was bad enough that the New Lights there had politicked their way into control of the government by fastening the odium of the Stamp Act on the Old Lights and by an alliance with the Anglicans. This in itself demonstrated the corrupting influence of politics on religion. But the blind reaction of the Old Lights was still more instructive. They were so outraged by the tactics of their opponents that they considered going the New Lights one worse. Benjamin Gale wrote to Stiles in August 1766, evidently hoping to get his blessing for a scheme to reinterpret the Connecticut charter so as to take the election of the governor away from the people at large and assign it to the assembly.[40] Stiles was horrified. After warning Gale that the "Antiamerican interest" was still plotting the revocation of colonial charters, he affirmed his faith in popular elections in words that anticipated Jefferson:

> I am of Opinion that Liberty is much surer in popular Elections than if 130 persons only had the Election in their own hands. Not to observe the Allotment of Officers etc. among 130 would corrupt them easily into any Measure, at least it would be easier to corrupt 70 out of 130 than the whole Body of People—it may be remembered that New Light Politics would more surely prevail in the assembly on your plan than on the former practice.

40. Gale to Stiles, Aug. 23, 1766.

I have not Time to add—but give my opinion frankly and fully for the most popular Elections—I could wish the house of Deputies consisted of 300 instead of 130, and that the Conditions of Freedom were so lowered as to comprehend three Quarters of the people instead of a Ninth only. The Security of American Liberty lies in the Houses of Representatives.[41]

When Gale was unconvinced by these observations and proposed to open his plan to William Samuel Johnson (Gale was ready to court the Anglicans too), Stiles wrote again, not only to Gale but to John Devotion, who seemed to be showing sympathy with Gale and even talked of giving up the charter. Stiles begged his friends to show some sense of proportion. Which was better, he asked, "Governor, Lt. Governor and Council Episcopalians or Majority so, and an awd lower house, with £15 or £20,000 sterling Tax for Support of Government, which said Governor etc. hate Dissenters more than New Lights can— or—New Light Administration with the Retention of Charter Liberty and Religion, and only 3 or £4,000 sterling Expenses of Government?" The New Lights might be guilty of underhanded politics, but at least they were sound on the fundamental question of charter liberties. "I shall never be a New Light," said Stiles, "but I hope I shall never be bro't to make a Transition from hatred of New Light to wish the Loss of the Charters." [42]

Stiles had obviously not relaxed his love of civil liberty, but he had revised his views of the relation between civil liberty and religious. He still believed that they went hand in hand, that the loss of one meant the loss of the other, but he had decided that each must be defended by its own proper methods. When religious and political tyranny threatened, the church and her ministers must not follow the methods of the world to attack—nor yet to condone—either one. But what about laymen—the ordinary citizens who made up the body of the church? In a free state they would participate in the choice of their governors, and some might be among those chosen to govern. Should they not unite in politics to protect their church?

With one eye on what had been happening in Connecticut and the other on the future of the dissenters' union, Stiles decided not. He

41. Stiles to Gale, Oct. 1, 1766. Cf. Stiles to Charles Chauncy, Mar. 3, 1768.

42. Gale to Stiles, Apr. 17, 1767; Stiles to Gale, Apr. 30, May 1, 1767; to John Devotion, May 2, 1767.

worked out his thoughts in a letter to William Hart, the Old Light
minister of Saybrook, who was one of those most fearful of the union
as a step toward New Light and Presbyterian control. Stiles was so
confident of his views by this time that he sent the letter, all eighteen
pages of it.[43]

Anyone who looked at history, Stiles wrote, would find support
for his position that religion and politics should not be mixed. After
centuries of fighting to further their churches by political action, and
by holding the stirrup for one rising politician after another, the dissenters of England had gained nothing for all their efforts but the
barest toleration. The Episcopalians at the moment seemed successful
in advancing themselves by means of intrigue and politics. But this
very practice would in the end bring about their ruin, just as surely
as the blending of religion with politics, the acquisition of immense
temporal powers, had throughout history been the ruin of other religions. For these reasons alone it would be wisdom for American dissenters to keep their religion and politics separate. But all question
of expediency aside, the decisive argument for the case was that the
spirit of the gospel was not the spirit of intrigue. And for Stiles intrigue
and politics had become virtually synonymous.

Included in his letter to Hart were some specific recommendations
about how Americans should keep their religion and politics separate.
They should put their trust in "public religious liberty." Where complete religious liberty was allowed—as in Rhode Island—it would
inevitably result in a variety of religious sects, the existence of which
would automatically perpetuate religious liberty without the need of
any sect resorting to politics to protect itself. "Our grand security,"
he said, "is in the multitude of sects and the public Liberty necessary
for them to cohabit together. In consequence of which the aggrieved
of any Communion will either pass over to another, or rise into new
Sects and spontaneous Societies. This and this only will learn us wisdom *not to persecute one another.*"

Inasmuch as power provokes jealousy and attack, religion could
best prevent attack upon itself by eschewing power and by "inculcating
Piety towards God, unblemished Morals, loyalty to our King, and a
peaceable Submission to civil Government tho' (which we are by no
means to expect) as tyrannical as that of the Caesars." The same behavior was also the best defense for religion if attack or even conquest

43. Stiles to William Hart, Feb. 27, 1767.

actually came. Resistance would simply demonstrate power and confirm the attackers in their course.

Stiles considered it the layman's responsibility to guard his church from the acquisition of power or even the appearance of hungering for power. Laymen should not take sides as a religious group on any political issue, not vote in a block as the Anglicans and the Old Lights and New Lights did. They should vote as individuals, dividing some on one side of every political question, some on another. Not of course that he wanted to see any Presbyterian or Congregationalist give aid and comfort to tyranny, if that were the issue at stake.

Stiles's plea for the complete separation of politics and religion was baffling to his reverend Connecticut friends. William Hart answered him at once with a letter that made Stiles's reasoning seem as remote from reality as the subtleties of the New Divinity. Did Stiles think it possible to keep men from uniting in political schemes for defense of their rights? "Why should we wish them divided? If they are vigorously attacked . . . they ought to unite, and they will unite." The dissenters in England may have gained no more than toleration by their political efforts, but they had at least gained that—which they would not have done "if they had not convinced their opponents that they were to be feared, that it was dangerous to oppress them." Hart was a political realist, and he saw no virtue in humble submission to tyranny. "The spirit of manly and vigorous resentment of wrongs," he told Stiles, "is the guardian of the peace and liberties and rights of the world. Where this is subdued in a people, Tyranny rides in triumph and reigns secure til the broken spirit recovers its spring." [44]

It was an argument that Stiles might have made himself before the Stamp Act troubles. Now he remained unmoved by it. He had a set of principles that satisfied his inmost desires and that could not, he thought, be shaken by Hart or anyone else. Reason, liberty, and truth would triumph in the end without political maneuvering by him or other men of God, better indeed without such help than with it. He would continue to preach the truths of the gospel as he found them in Scripture, the good old Puritan doctrines; he would support the widest latitude of practice within his own church; he would insist on the autonomy of the individual congregation, whether that congregation exercised its autonomy to his liking or not, whether it chose a John Hubbard or a Samuel Hopkins; and finally he would keep free

44. Hart to Stiles, Mar. 4, 1767.

of politics. These principles were as much the expression of his personality as they were of a rational faith. Under most circumstances they would make him a spectator, rather than an active participant in the world around him. He could take as much interest in politics as he chose, but he must not influence them in any way. Occasionally he might be called upon to stand up for congregational independence, as he did by helping to ordain John Hubbard, but he need not engage in controversy, theological or political. He could believe in liberty, but he need not fight for it, just as he could read books indefatigably without feeling the need to write them.

It was not a position that would have appealed to most men, and the friends of liberty who heard Stiles sing praises of freedom and urge submission all in the same breath, were sometimes impatient with him. But no one doubted the sincerity of his conviction, and no one blamed him for it. Other honest men up and down the colonies, who sincerely believed in liberty but urged the inexpediency of resistance to the Stamp Act, had lost their popularity and been branded for posterity as enemies of their country. But not Ezra Stiles. There was an innocence and integrity in the man, which gave his character the simplicity that people love. Despite the apparent tortuousness of his reasoning, despite his acknowledged timidity, despite his reluctance to do anything, people knew that he was on the side of the angels—their side.

Though Stiles had relegated himself to the sidelines, he could still watch, with growing excitement, the defense of reason, truth, and liberty by men of the world who used the methods of the world. Though the union of churches had failed—and happily, since it would have been tainted with politics—another kind of union was growing in America, a union in which the churches would have no part but which was nevertheless a noble work of Providence, a union by which God would ultimately make America safe for both Christ and reason.

17

The Making of an American

ONCE he decided to be a spectator and not an actor, Ezra Stiles was a happier man. He could watch what was going on around him with a lively partisan interest but without the agonizing concern he had felt over his involvement in the Stamp Act troubles or in the projected ecclesiastical union. Withdrawn in the study on Clarke Street, he could look out over the Parade and see the drama of American liberty enacted before him. Though his church across the street blocked his view of the harbor, it did not cut him off from the world of which that harbor was a symbol, the world he had renounced for his hands but not for his eyes and ears. Every ship that came in from Connecticut or Boston or Philadelphia or London would have a number of letters addressed to Doctor Stiles, letters on comets and asbestos and biblical chronology and church history, and letters also on the latest Anglican intrigue, the latest upset in provincial politics, the latest outrage committed by the administration in England. He kept up all the studies which his thirst for knowledge continued to demand, but he often looked up from his books to examine with equal interest the world which lay through the windows.

What was happening out there continued to be alarming. Though he constantly told himself that Providence would secure the triumph of liberty in the end, it was becoming increasingly clear that the British government, playing the role of Satan, would do everything possible to frustrate Providence. The scheme of an American bishop seemed to be thwarted in 1767, when one of the secretaries of state made known that he would oppose it. But the threat revived in 1768, and by 1772

Stiles was convinced that the appointment was only a matter of time.[1] Meanwhile, the British showed the cloven hoof in another attempt to tax the colonies. In 1767 Parliament levied duties on American imports of lead, glass, tea, paper, and painter's colors. At the same time a Board of Commissioners of the Customs had been appointed to reside in America with headquarters at Boston.[2] This would mean a new swarm of royal officials to be supported out of the pockets of Americans.

The only encouraging thing was the way Americans reacted. They agreed in town meetings not to buy British goods; they petitioned the king and Parliament, declaring the new acts to be unconstitutional; they defied the customs officers, both secretly and openly; and they set about manufacturing for themselves the things they had previously imported from the mother country. The evidence of American determination poured in from all sides. Down on Thames Street the wheelwrights were doing a rush business in spinning wheels: orders for them had increased tenfold.[3] At college commencements, whether in Cambridge or New Haven or Providence, the students were dressed in homespun or other American cloth.[4] At home the click of knitting needles and the whirr of the spinning wheel became the most familiar sound. Occasionally the Clarke Street house would fairly roar when the ladies of his congregation came to spend the day in a spinning match, each bringing her own wheel. There might be as many as seventy wheels going at once, and at the end of the day Mrs. Stiles would have a couple of hundred skeins of wool presented to her.[5]

From Connecticut Benjamin Gale wrote him about another form of American enterprise: Abel Buell of Killingworth had designed and cut punches for casting printers' type. Without previous training Buell

1. John Rodgers to Stiles, May 13, 1767; Francis Alison to Stiles, June 19, 1767; Charles Chauncy to Stiles, June 29, 1767; Stiles to Chauncy, May 28, 1772. A. L. Cross, *The Anglican Episcopate and the American Colonies* (New York, 1902), pp. 161–225.

2. On the activities of the Customs Commissioners see O. M. Dickerson, *The Navigation Acts and the American Revolution* (Philadelphia, 1951); D. M. Clark, *The Rise of the British Treasury* (New Haven, 1960), pp. 181–84.

3. *Newport Mercury*, June 19, 1769.

4. Dexter, *Biographical Sketches*, *3*, 303; Josiah Quincy, *The History of Harvard University* (Cambridge, 1840), *2*, 163; *Newport Mercury*, Sept. 11, 1769; *Massachusetts Gazette*, July 19, 1770; *Connecticut Journal*, Jan. 6, 1769.

5. *Newport Mercury*, Feb. 13, May 1, 1769, June 24, 1770; *Lit. Diary*, *1*, 53, 237, 376.

thus became the first American type designer and type founder, and demonstrated that America need not depend on England for this vital weapon of liberty. Gale hoped it would alarm the English type founders and make them "more Careful of Acts of Parliament in Future." [6] At the same time Isaac Doolittle, a New Haven watchmaker, constructed a printing press for William Goddard of Philadelphia, and some enterprising Rhode Island craftsman, probably Stiles's friend and parishioner Benjamin King, did the same for Solomon Southwick, who printed the *Newport Mercury*. There were paper mills in several colonies, including Rhode Island, so that when Southwick published the sermon which Stiles preached at Hopkins' ordination, he could advertise that "The Press in which this Sermon was printed, and the Paper, were made in this Colony, and some of the Types were manufactured in Connecticut." [7]

In most towns the merchants showed their attachment to the cause of liberty by agreeing not to import British goods. Unfortunately Newport's merchants lagged behind those of Boston, New York, and Philadelphia in these measures. Instead of striking at the root of the trouble by boycott, they expended their energy in protesting the high fees (not duties) charged by the customs officers for entering and clearing vessels. [8] They came to their senses only after the merchants of other colonies threatened to cut off all trade with Newport (like most American ports Newport depended heavily on coastwise trade with other colonies). Stiles was mortified at the shame which the merchants had brought upon the town, particularly since the trouble sprang from a few individuals like Aaron Lopez, whom otherwise Stiles loved and honored. [9]

The fact that Newport as a whole had no love for the new measures could be seen not only by the zeal for home manufactures but also by the daring way in which the people resisted enforcement. When the armed sloop *Liberty* came into port with two Connecticut vessels seized for smuggling, the Newporters forced the crew to leave the

6. Gale to Stiles, Apr. 1, 12, May 9, 1769; Charles Chauncy to Stiles, May 8, 1769; *Newport Mercury*, Aug. 21, 1769. On Abel Buell see Lawrence C. Wroth, *Abel Buell of Connecticut* (Middletown, 1958).

7. *Newport Mercury*, July 23, 1770.

8. Ibid., Sept. 25, Oct. 9, 1769.

9. *Lit. Diary*, 1, 53-54, 270-71; 3, 24-25; A. M. Schlesinger, *Colonial Merchants and the American Revolution* (New York, 1918), pp. 153-55, 195-96; and *Newport Mercury* for 1769 and 1770, passim.

Liberty and scuttled her off Goat Island in the harbor. Two weeks
later, while Stiles was entertaining his friend James Dana on a visit
from Wallingford—they were doubtless congratulating each other
on the successful ordination of John Hubbard at Meriden the preceding month—the sky behind the Second Congregational Church
was lit up in a wild glare: the navy had not yet raised the *Liberty*,
and now she burned to the water's edge. Stiles, who had begun to
keep a diary that year, recorded the episode without comment under July 31, 1769: "Sloop Liberty burnt." [10]

The Rhode Islanders escaped punishment for their daring. But in
Boston, when another sloop named *Liberty*, this one belonging to
John Hancock, was seized by revenue officers, the town mob broke
out in a riot that brought British troops to Massachusetts a few
months later. Now the army as well as the navy was engaged against
the colonies. "Military government," Stiles called it; and he saw it as
part of a total scheme that included Anglican bishops, revocation of
charters, dissolution of assemblies, and proliferation of royal officials—
in a word, tyranny.[11] When a Boston boy was shot in a fracas that
followed a hanging of effigies, Stiles hailed him as "the first Victim
or Martyr of American Liberty." [12] The Boston Massacre, coming
hard after, he saw as another of "the fruits of military government." [13]

In the next five years the pace of British tyranny and American
resistance accelerated. In 1771 word came that troops were destined
for Rhode Island as well as Massachusetts. Stiles expected the Rhode
Island Assembly to resist this violation of their charter rights. When
the Assembly voted not to do so if the troops came "only as marching
Troops and not to make any Stay," he observed: "This Concession
seals the Death of American Liberty. May God humble us for those
sins which have brot down these heavy Judgments and Calamities
upon us." [14] Fortunately the troops did not come, but the papers soon
brought news of British misbehavior in another colony. In North
Carolina, it was said, the governor had led an army against a group
of "obstinate and infatuated Rebels" (they called themselves "Regulators") at Alamance; he had captured the ringleaders, who were

10. *Lit. Diary, 1,* 19; *Newport Mercury,* July 24, 1769.
11. Stiles to William Hart, Feb. 27, 1767; to John Hubbard, Apr. 4, 1769.
12. *Lit. Diary, 1,* 40.
13. Stiles to John Hubbard, Mar. 9, 1770.
14. *Lit. Diary, 1,* 103.

promptly tried by the chief justice of the colony and hanged. Without knowing much about the local issues involved, Stiles could discern the pattern of tyranny. He knew the chief justice, and so did everyone else in Newport. It was Martin Howard, Jr., the Newporter who at the time of the Stamp Act had written in favor of Parliament's authority to tax the colonies.[15] They had driven Howard from Newport and he had fled to England, where the ministry rewarded him for his devotion to tyranny by making him chief justice of North Carolina. Now, it appeared, he was taking revenge on the people of North Carolina for the insults he had suffered in Newport. Stiles suspected that it was he who had written the newspaper accounts describing the governor's glorious victory. Though the governor's forces had been American, not British, Stiles believed (incorrectly) that "in Truth all the Province except the Crown Officers And Connexions are in heart Regulators," and he was certain that the rebellion was justified. "What shall an injured and oppressed people do," he asked, "when their Petitions, Remonstrances and Supplications are unheard and rejected, and they insulted by the Crown Officers, and Oppression and Tyranny (under the name of Government) continued with Rigour and Egyptian Austerity?" [16]

These sentiments did not mean that he had altered his own position with regard to the world. When William Tryon came to New York as governor, fresh from his triumphs in North Carolina, Stiles was shocked to find that the Presbyterian ministers had joined in an address of welcome. To one of them, John Rodgers, who had been a particularly strong advocate of Congregational-Presbyterian union, Stiles wrote an admonishing letter pointing out that all crown officers hated Presbyterianism and would rejoice in its destruction; he reaffirmed his belief that ministers must suffer these officers as lawful authority, but suffering them did not mean thanking them for their tyranny. The New York ministers had greeted the new governor as though he were Abraham returning from the defeat of Chedorlaomer whereas in fact Tryon had come fresh "from the slaughter of our Brethren." [17]

In Newport itself the face of tyranny grew uglier as the revenue officers, with the aid of the navy, continued their campaign against

15. Ibid., pp. 111–14, 124, 136–37, 149.
16. Ibid.
17. Stiles to Rodgers, July 29, 1771; *Lit. Diary*, 1, 124.

smuggling, singling out the Sons of Liberty for their special attention. Aaron Lopez and others who had kept out of the nonimportation agreements might run cargoes as they pleased, Stiles noticed, but let a patriotic merchant bring a ship into port, and the officers would descend on her like hungry spiders and generally manage to snare the victim somewhere in their tangled web of regulations. The owner would then have to bribe his way out or suffer seizure. For example, on one of Christopher Ellery's vessels they found that a sailor had a small bag of tea. On this pretext they seized the ship, and it cost Ellery a trip to Boston and sixty or eighty dollars to get her back. The customs officers were all parasites who had obtained their jobs by knowing the right people in England. Stiles considered Charles Dudley, the collector at Newport, typical. The man's father was an Anglican clergyman in a rotton borough, the "omnis Homo of the Parish," who obtained the collectorship for his son as the price of supporting the right candidate in a Parliamentary election. And now the son grew fat on the bribes he extracted from American merchants.[18]

The naval officers who assisted the revenue men were not much better. There were occasional exceptions, like Sir Thomas Rich, commander of the Sloop *Senegal,* "whose Civility, and Politeness of Behaviour," the *Newport Mercury* said, "merited the Esteem and good Wishes of this Town, which he possessed in a high Degree." [19] Unfortunately the general run of naval officers was far different. As they cruised up and down Narragansett Bay, they sometimes behaved like an army living off the country, stealing sheep, cutting down fruit trees for firewood, and detaining every craft they could find for the most trivial offenses, even the small boats that brought wood for Newport's fireplaces. The inhabitants did not suffer these affronts patiently. In the newspapers they complained openly of the "parcel of dependant tools of arbitrary power, sent hither to enrich themselves and their MASTERS, on the *Spoil* of the honest and industrious of these colonies; whom Satan envies as he did Adam and Eve in paradise; and therefore has let loose *his* Legions to work their final overthrow." [20]

As the numbers of the revenue and naval officers multiplied, it was inevitable sooner or later that the incident of the Sloop *Liberty* should

18. *Lit. Diary,* 1, 270–71.
19. *Newport Mercury,* Mar. 19, 1770.
20. Ibid., July 13, 1772.

be repeated. It happened in June 1772, when His Majesty's Schooner *Gaspée* drove aground in Narragansett Bay while trying to overtake an American ship. As before, Stiles recorded the incident without comment. "The Gaspee Skooner was burnt off against Warwick yesterday Morning about IIh and the Captain wounded." [21] This time the British government decided to make an example of the case and appointed a commission to investigate the crime and apprehend the offenders. Though the powers of the commission were somewhat vaguely expressed, one thing was clear: the persons whom they indicted were to be tried not in America but in England. This would be a direct and indubitable violation of a right that had been sacred to Englishmen for centuries, the right to trial by a jury of one's peers in the place of the crime. Since the commission was to sit in Newport, in the courthouse that was only a stone's throw from his front door, Stiles would have plenty of opportunity to observe this latest step in the progress of British tyranny.

It was the warmest January Newporters could remember when the commissioners arrived and in solemn procession marched up the Parade—perhaps the warmest New England January on record. Stiles was picking fresh lettuce leaves from his garden; the new shoots on the roses were four inches long. Pansies, marigolds, and dandelions were in bloom. [22] But the smiling appearance of the town was belied in the eyes that followed the members of the "Court of Inquisition" as they passed through the heavy courthouse door. Doubtless there were some who welcomed them, but most people remembered the words they had just read in the *Mercury*:

> Ten thousand deaths, by the *haltar* or the *ax*, are infinitely preferable to a miserable life of slavery, in chains, under a pack of worse than Egyptian tyrants, whose avarice nothing less than your whole substance and income will satisfy; and who, if they can't extort that, will glory in making a sacrifice of you and your posterity, to gratify their master, the d—l, who is a tyrant, and the father of tyrants and of *liars*. [23]

Within the week it began to snow. [24]

21. *Lit. Diary, 1,* 242.
22. Ibid., p. 332; *Newport Mercury,* Jan. 11, 1773.
23. *Newport Mercury,* Dec. 21, 1772.
24. *Lit. Diary, 1,* 332.

The members of the commission, though tinged with Toryism, were almost without exception honorable men, whose worst offense was accepting the task that the ministry had thrust upon them. One of them, Peter Oliver, was a Congregationalist and while in Newport attended Stiles's church and dined with him; together they talked amiably about the common law and the Baptists and Negro slavery and cures for cancer.[25] Stiles carefully avoided any mention of the business which was keeping Oliver in Newport, but he watched the proceedings intently and received reports from various people whom the commissioners questioned. After a couple of weeks the hearings were adjourned to the following May and then in June concluded without finding anyone to indict. Before leaving in June, Oliver voluntarily broached the subject of his commission and explained to Stiles that there had been no powers involved beyond those of inquiry for the sake of collecting evidence. Moreover, the commissioners were empowered to examine the misdeeds of the navy and the revenue officers as well as those of the colonists. Stiles, however, was not reassured. "Notwithstanding all Palliatives and Softenings, the Commission was justly obnoxious alarming and arbitrary—it not only meditated but directly provided for seizing and sending home persons to London—nothing looks like bringing the *Trial* of offenders before our Superior Court; the Trial was to have been in England." [26]

Stiles did not make these objections to Commissioner Oliver. He was adhering closely to his decision that ministers must stand aloof from the tumults of politics. But to his diary and his friends he spoke freely, and when asked about the doings of the commission he wrote a letter of 3,000 words, describing minutely the proceedings of their first sitting. In closing he achieved an admirably clear formulation of his own position:

> I am a Friend to American Liberty; of the final prevalence of which I have not the least doubt, though by what means and in what ways God only knows. But I have perfect Confidence that the future Millions of America will emancipate themselves from all foreign Oppression. I am a Spectator indeed of Events, but intermeddle not with Politics. We [ministers] have another Department, being called to an Office and Work, which may be

25. Ibid., pp. 332–33.
26. Ibid., pp. 382–85.

successfully pursued (for it has been pursued) under every species of *Civil Tyranny* or *Liberty*. We cannot become the Dupes of Politicians without Alliances, Concessions and Connexions dangerous to evangelical Truth and spiritual Liberty.[27]

The *Gaspée* Commission was followed by the Tea Act, the Tea Act by the Boston Tea Party, and the Boston Tea Party by the Coercive Acts. As Stiles watched the tragedy unroll, he saw that he must revise some of the views he had kept alive through the worst of the Stamp Act troubles and for a good while thereafter. Then he had looked upon the British Constitution as the strongest bulwark of liberty. But the events he had been watching from his spectator's seat demonstrated that something had gone awry. George III had repeatedly disappointed his expectations. Stiles clung to his confidence in the king as long as he could, blaming America's troubles on wicked officials who hid from their royal master the expressions of loyalty which his American subjects repeatedly offered him. But by the 1770s it had become difficult to believe that the king was wholly guiltless, or if he was that the British Constitution offered Americans sufficient protection against tyranny.

Stiles's disillusionment was accentuated by the letters that came to him from the mother country. Henry Marchant, his young lawyer friend, went there as the agent of the Rhode Island government in 1771, armed with a host of letters and a kind of pocket Baedecker which Stiles had written for him.[28] Without having set foot in England, Stiles probably knew more people there by correspondence than any other man in Newport. Upon his arrival, Marchant became another of Stiles's listening posts and reported to his pastor in vivid terms the hopeless corruption that was grasping England. It was impossible, he said, for a state to be ruled under baser principles than Britain today. Wise men agreed that destruction could not be far off and looked to America as a refuge for themselves and their children. Catharine Macaulay, the celebrated woman historian, talked to him with pleasure of "the two Common Wealths of Rhode Island and Connecticut, and was surprized that amidst such Havock and Slaughter of Liberties and Privileges, there should at this Day exist two such

---

27. Ibid., pp. 345–51.
28. Ibid., p. 117; The Stiles Papers contain drafts of letters recommending Marchant to Franklin, William Samuel Johnson, Joseph Jennings, Thomas Wright, and Philip Furneaux.

free States. She earnestly hopes we shall preserve Them to the latest Times." [29] Marchant presented Mrs. Macaulay with a copy of Stiles's *Discourse on the Christian Union,* and added her to his pastor's list of correspondents. Neither she nor anyone else who wrote to Stiles from England altered the picture that Marchant gave him of corruption and decay.[30]

It was apparent, then, if he read the signs correctly, that the cause of liberty was all but lost in England; the British Constitution had proved vulnerable. Hitherto Stiles had continued to hope that the Constitution would withstand the attack, but he saw his mistake now and confessed it in a letter to Catharine Macaulay: "My Ideas of the English Constitution have much diminished. It seems to have become or arisen into a kind of fortuitous Consolidation of Powers now in opposition to the true Interest of the people." [31] As Stiles saw it, there was only one step left for the completion of the tyrannical system: the ministry had succeeded in establishing a "particular Mode of Absoluteness," but they had not yet succeeded in persuading the mass of the people to accept it.

> And now they have a Work peculiar to the present Age of reconciling and tameing the body of the people to it. Thus when the Prerogative in Spain and France had gained the absolute Dominion out of the hands of the *Cortes* of the one and *Parliaments* of the other, it required Management to compleat the subjugation on the popular spirit. The British Empire is sustaining a like Mutation of Polity and Laws—into a System almost as new and aliene as that brot by the Roman Senate over the conquered Kingdoms of Spain, Gaul, the East—or by the Mahometans over the Oriental Empires. Old Laws Politics and Dominion must give way to the new.[32]

In the process of taming the people, the ministry had already achieved a good deal of success in Great Britain; but thus far at least the Americans had proved more difficult, and Stiles knew why: the Americans, and especially the New Englanders, had inherited from

29. Marchant to Stiles, May 14, 1772; *Lit. Diary, 1,* 251.

30. Cf. Stephen Sayre to Stiles, July 20, 1772; James Sterling to Stiles, May 9, 1759; Stiles to Jared Eliot, Sept. 24, 1759.

31. Dec. 6, 1773.

32. *Lit. Diary, 1,* 381–82.

the old Puritans a way of life which would not collapse before the first blast of corruption. The British knew this as well as he did, according to Henry Marchant's letters from England. "You will often," Marchant wrote, "hear the following Language—Damn those Fellows we shall never do any Thing with Them till we root out that cursed puritanick Spirit—How is this to be done?—keep Soldiers amongst Them, not so much to awe Them, as to debauch their Morals—Toss off to them all the Toies and Baubles that genius can invent to weaken their Minds, fill Them with Pride and Vanity, and beget in them all possible Extravagance in Dress and Living, that They may be kept poor and made wretched—" [33]

The British might not see what Stiles did, that the strength of liberty in America lay not simply in Puritan morality but also in Puritan reverence for Scripture, in Congregational independence, and in separation of church and state; but the British evidently did perceive that liberty and Puritanism, or more specifically Congregationalism, were inseparable and that they could never kill one as long as the other survived. For that reason, Stiles believed, they concentrated their main attack on New England. For that reason the Anglican Church did likewise.[34] Although the Anglicans had got no further with their plans for a bishop, they were scoring notable successes in their attempt to undermine Puritan unity by antagonizing the other dissenting churches against the New England Congregationalists. The Baptists and Quakers in Massachusetts were raising a furor over taxes for the support of the church. Theirs was a legitimate grievance, but the timing and direction of their attack, in Stiles's view, argued a real indifference to their avowed principle of religious liberty. The taxes were trivial in amount and in most cases could be avoided simply by filling out an affidavit of membership in a Baptist or Quaker church. If they really cared for religious liberty, they would aim their fire at the Anglican establishment in the other colonies, where there was no escaping taxes in support of the Anglican Church, instead of taking pot shots at the Congregationalists of Massachusetts, who were even then (under military occupation) bearing the brunt of British tyranny. The Baptists and Quakers showed so little concern about British tyranny that if all America were "of their Temper or Coolness in the Cause the Parliament would easily carry their Points and

33. Marchant to Stiles, Mar. 17, 1772.
34. Cf. *Lit. Diary*, *1*, 344–45.

triumph over American Liberty." [35] Stiles saw Anglican influence behind it all, and doubtless found his prejudice justified when the Baptist-dominated college in Providence elected to the corporation three Anglicans, all known for their Tory sentiments. [36]

While they split the Puritan colonies by internal disputes, the Anglicans were also preparing an encircling attack from without. Since the capture of Canada, they had been attempting to win over the Catholics there. The bishops in England had raised no objection to the establishment of the Catholic Bishop Briand in Quebec in 1766. At the time Stiles surmised that they hoped thereby to set a precedent for sending a bishop of their own to the other colonies. In 1773 he heard from a visiting Lutheran minister that the plan was far more clever:

> that the Successor to Bishop Briand should be an English Protestant Bishop—that the present romish Clergy were to die out— that when any parish became one Quarter of them protestants the Minister should be of the Church of England and then the Inhabitants should pay but one Thirtieth of their Produce to him instead of one twelfth which they now paid to the romish Clergy—that the Churchmen at New York &c did not doubt that this would be such an Easment to them as to Ecclesiastical Taxes that the Romish Laity would be pleased with it and turn to the Church of England. This matter is all secret as yet and is only circulating among the Episcopalians and so preparing to be passed into an Act of Parliament. [37]

The reality proved worse than the rumor when Parliament in 1774 passed the Quebec Act, continuing the right of the Catholic church to collect tithes in the province of Quebec and expanding that province to include all the new British territory in the Mississippi Valley north of the Ohio. The prospect of English bishops voting in Parliament for such a measure, Stiles assured Richard Price, must have caused "a Jubilee in Hell and Thanksgivings throughout the Pontificate." [38]

35. Ibid., pp. 78, 491; cf. Stiles to Philip Furneaux, Nov. 20, 1772.

36. Joseph Galloway of Pennsylvania, and the Rev. George Bisset and Simon Pease of Newport. *Newport Mercury*, Sept. 16, 1771. Cf. Stiles to John Devotion, May 2, 1767.

37. *Lit. Diary*, *1*, 427.

38. Stiles to Price, April 10, 1775.

Puritanism and liberty were now assailed from within and without. Stiles had never faltered in his belief that the two would triumph together, that "the present Endeavors of Episcopalian and deistical Crown Officers to break up the present Policies and to plague and become a scourge to the New England Puritans . . . will be defeated by the irresistible and overruling Providence of the Most High." [39] But the question was rising in his mind whether Providence in carrying out this design intended the New England Puritans and other free Americans to triumph within the British Empire or without it.

Stiles had long been convinced that English America, and particularly New England, would eventually become an independent state, with the great majority of its population Presbyterian or Congregational.[40] When he first reached this conclusion, it was a long-range prediction based simply on the laws of population growth, as he had induced them from his many observations. The Congregationalists and the Presbyterians, with a head start, would expand most rapidly and fill in the empty spaces of America, and this space, once filled in, would contain a population far larger than that of Great Britain. It was unthinkable that the larger country should forever remain dependent on the smaller.

Stiles was not the first person to surmise that America would one day be independent, but he at first assumed, as did others who ventured such a prediction, that the mutual interests of England and America would dictate a preservation of their attachment for several generations to come. As early as 1762, however, after surveying the history of English land grants in America, he concluded that the mother country had "a separate Interest from the provinces . . . tho' good policy would make them joynt." And he deplored the manner in which English politicians viewed the colonies "in no other Light than as they subserve *Commerce* and *Dominion* and make Livings for hungry and avaricious Dependents and discontented Highlanders." [41] When the Stamp Act revealed a determination on the part of Great Britain to reduce the colonists below the level of Englishmen, he was quick to see that American and British interests were becoming incompatible. In the summer of 1765 he concluded

39. *Lit. Diary, 1,* 345.
40. Ibid.
41. "The Right of the Crown of Great Britain to lands in America and the Assignments thereof." MS dated March 31, 1762.

his columnar inscription on the death of liberty with a statement that the Stamp Act had "Diffused a Disgust thro the Colonies And laid the Basis of an Alienation Which will never be healed. Henceforth the *European* and *American* Interests Are Separated Never More to be joyned." [42]

Although the repeal of the Stamp Act probably caused him to suppress this opinion for a time, the succession of events that followed made its correctness more and more obvious. When he heard of the Boston massacre in 1770, he was ready to predict a colonial revolution against England within two generations. From this time on, as the pace of tyranny quickened and he saw the British constitution crumbling and corruption eating out the heart of all that was good in the mother country, it became ever more obvious to him that as long as the Americans remained within the empire, their liberties and their virtue would be much more vulnerable than if the ties with Great Britain were cut.

At the time of the Stamp Act, Stiles had not considered a break with England feasible. He had stated, to himself at least, that forcible resistance was not justified, "even in real and undoubted violations of Right, till a Body of People are capable of Self Defense." [43] And America in 1765 had not yet become capable of self-defense against the most powerful army and navy in the world. Ten years later the Americans, though growing rapidly by immigration as well as natural increase, still looked small beside the mother country. But there was another factor that altered the picture, a factor Stiles had hitherto overlooked, perhaps because he had not previously wanted to face it. This was the growth of a feeling of pride and confidence in America, a feeling that helped to fill the anxious vacuum a man discovered in himself when he contemplated shedding his loyalty to the king.

It was a feeling that grew surreptitiously, almost without one's being aware of it. Stiles had known it at least as early as the French and Indian War, when he contrasted the sturdy Puritanic virtue of the American soldiers with the debauchery and corruption of the British troops, and feared that the British corruption would prove contagious. [44] He had felt it when he predicted the future glory of the

42. Stamp Act Notebook.
43. Stiles to Thomas Hutchinson, Oct. 5, 1765 (not sent).
44. Stiles to Jared Eliot, Sept. 24, 1759.

American Empire after the conquest of Canada.[45] He had felt it when he compared the simplicity of American government to the top-heavy bureaucracy of England, riddled with sinecures and pensions. He had felt it when he sensed how little European scholars thought of American culture. It was this, in part at least, that made him dream of an American learned society, "for the Honor of American Literature, contemned by Europeans." In one of his plans he had specifically provided that "the Associates be all Americans and if born in America of the 2d Generation it shall be indifferent whether of English, Scotch, Irish, French or German Blood all these distinctions being lost in American Birth." [46]

For Stiles the feeling was associated mainly with New England, but in the late sixties and seventies he sensed it expanding to take in the other colonies, as they lined up with New England in defense of liberty. New England, of course, with its inheritance of Puritanism, must be the mainstay of liberty, but the Presbyterians of the middle colonies, who also inherited a Puritan tradition, were living up to it. Most encouraging, however, was the fact that the Anglicans of the southern colonies had proved quite unlike their ambitious, intriguing brethren of the north. From a correspondent in South Carolina Stiles heard that the southerners were enraged at the Tory clergymen in the north; many declared they would turn dissenters in a body if bishops were sent to America.[47] When Stiles considered the devotion of all these people to the cause of liberty, he found that his attachment to New England, though not diminished in any way, had been joined by an exultant pride in America.

When Stiles found that his fellow Americans shared his sentiments and were prepared to exercise them in a political union, he openly rejoiced. He had drawn back from the proposed ecclesiastical union because he feared it might involve the churches in politics. But a purely political union was something he could welcome without a scruple. He even anticipated one in 1760 and again at the time of the *Gaspée* Commission; if the commission had sent anyone to England for trial, he was certain an intercolonial congress would have followed.[48]

45. See above, Chap. 14.
46. American Academy of Sciences, notes dated Aug. 15, 1765.
47. William Tennant to Stiles, Charleston, Aug. 18, 1774.
48. *Lit. Diary, 1,* 385.

When the first Continental Congress was called in 1774 to support Massachusetts against Lord North's repressive measures, he did not think it inconsistent with his principles to give the Rhode Island delegates, Stephen Hopkins and Samuel Ward, his encouragement. He had great admiration for both these men, who had for many years been political rivals and were now the elder statesmen of Rhode Island. Stiles spent an evening with Governor Hopkins before he left for the Congress—a shrewd penetrating man, a deist, Stiles suspected, but nevertheless a steadfast defender of liberty. Governor Ward, though a Baptist, was as strong for liberty as Hopkins, and of the two Stiles considered him the abler man. Stiles gave him letters of recommendation to friends in Philadelphia, and Ward on his return, gave Stiles a full report of the proceedings, as did Robert Treat Paine, a Massachusetts delegate who stopped in Newport on his way home.[49]

Stiles consumed every piece of information about the Congress with the exuberant excitement of his growing American patriotism. The Congress, of course, was not aiming at independence, nor did Stiles's patriotism reach that far as yet, but there was something glorious about this united defense of liberty that far outshone the efforts of individual colonies. Stiles had feared that British ministerial spies would infiltrate the Congress and by the free use of silver procure the adoption of "such a faint selfcontradictory and indeterminate decision respecting a Cessation of Commerce as would prove an abortion of the only means of Redress short of the last Appeal."[50]

When the Congress proved firm as he could have hoped, Stiles was exultant. The devotion to liberty had been not that of New England or Virginia or Pennsylvania, but that of America. In this exciting harmony the only sour notes came from the quarters where Stiles already expected them: from the Episcopalians in the north and from the Baptists and Quakers who had been duped by them. The Baptists had taken advantage of the Congress and the desperate situation of Massachusetts to try to wring concessions for themselves. What they wanted was a total exemption from taxes in support of the church, and they persuaded the Philadelphia Quakers to join them in a conference with the Massachusetts delegates to the Congress. The purpose was to embarrass Massachusetts by alleging that she denied to others the

49. Ibid., pp. 231, 455, 457–59, 470–72, 475; 3, 172; Stiles to ——, Aug. 29, 1774.

50. Stiles to ——, Aug. 29, 1774.

liberties she claimed for herself. This was good politics, but Stiles had no use for a church that sought religious ends by political means. Though he might approve the end the Baptists sought, the means they were using verged on blackmail. By their willingness to employ it they showed that they had no true religion, no devotion to liberty, no patriotism. "In truth," he concluded, "the Baptists intend to avail themselves of this opportunity to complain to England of Persecution—because they hate Congregationalists who they know are hated by the King Ministry and Parliament. They will leave the general Defence of American Liberty to the Congregationalists to the Northward and Episcopalians to the Southward:—and make Merit themselves with the Ministry, who are glad to play them off against us, and for this End promise them Relief. . . . we shall not forget this Work of our Brother Esau." [51]

The Quakers were as bad as the Baptists. While the Congress was sitting, they sent out a circular letter, which Stiles supposed must have been prompted by the British ministry. It was "conceived in a certain subtil and artful phraseology, seemingly very innocent and harmless —but the true Design of it, as they freely own, is to recommend to the whole Quaker Interest not to joyn the Colonies in their present Opposition to the Ministry and Parliament—and so in effect to contravene and nullify the Letter of the Congress with respect to the Friends—and so to conform to the Wishes of the Ministry to divide us." [52]

When John Pemberton, a leading Philadelphia Quaker, appeared in Newport in December, Stiles guessed that he was on a mission following up the circular letter to consolidate the Quakers against the rest of America. The sight of a religious sect organizing its adherents to serve such base political ends was enough to bring Stiles off his spectator's seat. He could not sit by and watch this sly Quaker subvert American unity unopposed. With an anger that he seldom permitted himself, he flew at the astonished Pemberton, asking him whether the circular letter was designed "to detach the whole Quaker Interest from the rest of America." Pemberton answered evasively, "saying he was little, and no polititian, and that Friends were a humble inoffensive peaceable people, and that there was much of a worldly spirit in the Times." This pious condescension infuriated Stiles the more.

51. *Lit. Diary*, *1*, 472–75.
52. Ibid., p. 493.

He accused the Quakers of duplicity and asked Pemberton "to consider how it would be remembered in History two hundred years
hence, that in the important grand and hopefully decisive Conflict
of the present Day, when the American Colonies united in a bold and
firm stand against Parliamentary Taxation and oppression—in that
critical Time, the *Body of the Quakers* in America *took in with the
Ministry* and Parliament against their Countrymen and *deserted the
Cause of American liberty.*" The altercation went on for some time,
Pemberton protesting that the Quakers were innocent and holding his
temper better than Stiles, who finally excused himself (somewhat
half-heartedly) for his "warmth" and concluded by saying to Pemberton "it is necessary *that you should be told these Truths,* that you
may not carry home the report that that Letter gave universal Satisfaction—and that *Friends may know in what Light that Letter and
their Conduct are viewed by other Sects.*" As he finished recording
the incident in his diary, Stiles observed without remorse, "I believe
he will never forgive me." [53]

The warmth with which Stiles assailed Pemberton, almost without
precedent in the earlier pages of his diary and correspondence, was
generated by the Quaker's desertion not merely of the dissenting interest but of the American interest. The unity which prevailed in the
Continental Congress had become for Stiles and for many other
Americans a sacred thing, something more than an instrument for
bringing the ministry to terms, something, rather, that was good in
itself. Whenever it was attacked or threatened, by Baptists, Quakers,
Episcopalians—or even by the ministry itself—Stiles was moved to
a resentment that could not be measured in rational terms. When royal
governors suggested to their assemblies that they petition the king and
Parliament separately instead of standing by the resolves of the Congress, Stiles was ready to defend the legality of the Congress in words
that conveyed far more than a concern with legality or illegality.

> Is it not an Insult, implying that America had not used this regu-
> lar Mode for Redress?—when in Fact the Assemblies have been
> *petitioning,* and *petitioning* and *petitioning* again and again for
> nine years past; and their Petitions been treated even by the
> Sovereign, not merely with *Neglect,* but with Marks of Royal

53. Ibid., pp. 493–96.

Aversion, Despication and Contempt. And yet now the *Ministry* and their *Hirelings* and *Banditti* ask us, forsooth, why the Assemblies dont petition; that it cannot be expected that the King will hear the Petitions of *Mobs* and *Congresses* illegal and irregular Assemblies; but ask in a legal manner *by the Assemblies*, and you shall assuredly be heard. But the King must know, the British Parliament must know, for the World will know it, that the American Continental Congress of September last was a regular legal patriotic Body, wherein Two millions were as justly and truly Represented as ever any Body of Mankind were before—and that the *Mode of their Election* by a patriotic spontaneous selforigination from the People is defencible on the first Principles of Society and the English Constitution, and justifiable and glorious on the principles of the Law of Nature and Nations and the finest Reasonings of the Jus civile. It is more over exemplary. It holds up Light to Engld, to Europe, to the World, to shew to all the enslaved Empires around the Globe, How they may put their lives in their Hands, and from orderly and regular Congresses for Petitions to Tyrants the Higher Powers, rise into a System of irresistable Vindication and Liberty.[54]

As his pride in America grew, Stiles altered his opinion about the ability of Americans to fight the British army. He had watched the New England provinces gather ammunition and supplies. He had watched the militia train in preparation for combat, when no Frenchman or Indian threatened them. He had watched them spring to arms the preceding September when a false rumor was spread that General Gage had sent a force from Boston to seize the store of gunpowder at Cambridge. The false alarm spread as far as Virginia before it was overtaken. Thousands of men took arms and marched for Cambridge. Stiles collected all the reports he could get about it, fascinated by this exhibition of American determination. Women everywhere had been making cartridges, sending their sons and husbands off to battle, bidding them "fight courageously and manfully and behave themselves bravely for Liberty—commanding them to behave like men and not like Cowards—to be of good Courage and play the

54. Ibid., p. 521.

men for our people and for the Cities of our God—and the Lord do as seemeth him good. They expected a bloody Scene, but they doubted not Success and Victory." [55]

When Stiles saw their determination, he could not doubt victory either. His mind was not changed just by the evidence that his countrymen could put a respectable force into the field against British regulars. It was their patriotism that moved him and made it almost sacrilegious to doubt their success. And though neither he nor they had wanted independence, there was now little doubt in Stiles's mind that independence would be the outcome. On April 10, 1775, he wrote to Richard Price in London that the die was cast: "a Ministry devoid of Policy with a controll'd Parliament have precipitated the Decision of Points (which of how much Importance soever for us to have defined and ascertained yet) it would have shewn the sagacity and Wisdom of an English Minister long to have kept out of sight, and as untoutched as many important Exercises of the royal Prerogative which would suffer by Discussion." America had not pushed these points to decision, but since she was obliged to, America was ready to decide them and did not fear "to meet her Brethren in Bello sociali." Already a new system of American government was forming, as irregular provincial congresses gained authority and royal governors and their councils lost it. The system would probably terminate in the congresses becoming legislatures, with an annual continental congress for matters of common concern. "If there be no Relaxation speedily," Stiles predicted, "a Continental Army will soon be raised, and under repeated supposed Defeats will survive and perpatuate itself till such a System of Policy shall be eventually established." [56] Nine days later was Lexington, and Stiles looked out from his study windows on a people ready to fight and win through many supposed defeats.

55. Ibid., pp. 476–85.
56. Stiles to Richard Price, Apr. 10, 1775.

18

Uprooted

As THE MILITIA of the other colonies hurried toward Boston, the warships in Newport harbor trained their guns on the town and threatened bombardment if the citizens should aid their rebellious countrymen. When patriots marched from the island, the guns remained silent, but there were anxious days in the summer and fall of 1775 as the navy again and again renewed the threat. Stiles was told that whenever the bombardment should start, his church would be one of the first targets.[1]

The years that followed Lexington were not easy for anyone, but they presented special difficulties for a man who had committed himself to live close to his fellow men without participating in their worldly affairs. The Episcopalians and other Tories, of course, had never accepted his unpolitical self-portrait as genuine, and continued to attack him. Only three weeks before Lexington a New York Tory newspaper satirized his widely known views on the future growth of Congregationalism; and in Newport, eleven days after Lexington, he heard that the officers of the men-of-war had his name on a list of rebels whom they intended to seize.[2] But regardless of what his enemies chose to think, Stiles's course was set and his conscience clear. He intended, as long as God left it possible, to go about his regular daily routine: up at dawn to begin the day with private prayer, then family prayers and a chapter of the Bible read aloud. After breakfast he retired to his study to read three or four more chapters of the Bible,

1. *Lit. Diary*, 1, 589.
2. Ibid., pp. 531–33, 543.

with frequent references to the original Hebrew and Greek texts and the various commentaries, both ancient and modern. Recently he had also been giving a good deal of time to the Zohar. About 10 or 11 o'clock he would stop and go out to visit among his people. After dinner at noon he read for an hour or two and then visited again. In the evening more reading, family prayers again, and a final period of private prayer before going to bed. In his visits he heard of everything that was going on in town, and in the afternoon or evening he found out from his newspapers and letters what had been happening in the rest of the world. It was a way of life perfectly tailored for a man who lacked the thirst for action, and he would gladly have kept on with it indefinitely.[3]

Unfortunately the world now bore in on him from an unguarded quarter. In all his life hitherto the house on Clarke Street had been a kind of ivory tower in which he could be alone with truth. While the walls rang with the hum of spinning wheels or the rattle of pots and pans, he could sit in his study and live in the greater world that extended from Newport harbor around the globe and outward into the wider spheres of the "intellectual and moral world." In all his correspondence and notes and diaries he scarcely seemed to be aware of the other occupants of the house, of his wife or the seven children she had borne him. Though he loved them all, they moved in a realm of his consciousness that lay far below the surface, a natural, taken-for-granted realm. When he stepped outside his study, the gentle nature, lively human interest, and warm common touch that captivated most people who met him seems to have generated in his family too—especially in the girls—a real affection for "dear papa." They knew the kind of man he was and shared his life as far as it came their way. His wife gladly helped with the silkworms when they needed feeding or cleaning, watched the clock for his astronomical observations, never complained when he rose from his bed to peer through a telescope at some new comet. But she did not follow him in most of his interests. Indeed she could not have done so if she would, for she made them possible by not partaking of them. She made it her business to protect him from the petty problems of running a household, and did the job to perfection.

Now he lost her. In May of 1775 she died, and the aching emptiness of the house without her presence told him how much he had loved

3. Ibid., pp. 555–56.

and depended on her.[4] As best he could, Stiles rearranged the life of his family. Betsy, the oldest child, was seventeen, and she assumed the running of the household. Ezra, Jr., was away at Yale, which he had entered the previous fall (prepared by his father to read Latin, Greek, and Hebrew). Kezia, the next child, was fourteen, and Stiles thought she needed closer direction than he or Betsy could give her. She went in June to live with her uncle John Hubbard at Meriden, where Stiles asked that she be "kept to Business, Spinning, Milking, Dairy &c. so as to lay a foundation of a notable woman." [5] He considered sending Emilia, aged thirteen, to live with Benjamin Gale at Killingworth but does not seem to have done so. She and the rest of the children, Isaac, Ruth, and Polly, stayed with him.

With their help and that of the slave Newport, Betsy did the housework, but she could not protect her father from the infringement of the world as her mother had. The decisions that Elizabeth had made, the responsibilities she had shouldered, now fell to him; and instead of deciding on the proper translation of a Hebrew text, he must decide whether to see the doctor about Isaac's cough, whether to buy a barrel of sugar while it was available or wait to see if the price would go down a little, whether to get in wood for next winter's fuel —would they be here next winter anyhow, and if he decided to get it, who would sell it with the warships stopping all the woodboats? The slave boy worried him too. Now that Elizabeth was gone, he needed the boy more than ever. But was it right to keep him? If the British were wrong in seeking to enslave the Americans, what about the Americans who enslaved the Africans, or at least kept them in slavery? The question gnawed for attention, along with the dozens of other questions that his restless mind generated. Inevitably he found some time for study, because a curiosity like his cannot be put off, but for the most part he must stir himself to keep the family going properly, do Elizabeth's job and his own too.

Somehow he managed it, managed to supervise his family, write his sermons (he did not write them out fully now as he had when he began preaching, but only jotted down brief outlines), visit his congregation, and yet keep an eye on the war. It was an exciting time to be alive, a time of great hopes and great fears, when the workings of God's providence were wonderful to watch. In Newport you could see the

4. Ibid., pp. 563–66.
5. Stiles to John Hubbard, Jr., June 28, 1775.

enemy every day, not merely in the Tories, who were more numerous than in most other towns, but in the British warships which lay anchored in the harbor. You heard the war, too, when the warships went cruising and tangled with some Yankee privateer or when the sailors sent an occasional ball or two into the town. The ships were close enough so that a man could hail them from the wharves, and from the end of Long Wharf they were only a few rods away. When some patriot in his cups felt called upon to stand up and curse the navy to their faces, he was apt to be greeted by cannon balls, which would plow through the houses and shops behind him. Once while walking abroad on his after-dinner visits, Stiles wandered out on one of the wharves off Thames Street. A small open boat was heading in and refused to come to, when hailed by the *Glasgow,* a ship of twenty guns. The *Glasgow* opened fire, and since the boat was proceeding toward the town, cannon balls were soon flying into the busy wharves. As Stiles turned to flee, one splintered the planks a few feet from him, and another tore through the adjacent shops.[6]

Repeated threats of destruction and incidents such as this started Newport packing. When the fleet sailed out one day and bombarded Stonington, Connecticut—the firing could be heard in Newport—people began to leave. Newport would surely be next. The following Sunday Stiles preached to a congregation shrunk to about half its usual size, and during the ensuing weeks the exodus continued. Carts and wagons rolled up the Parade and out Broad Street, heaped high with furniture and sad-eyed refugees. In their place 500 American soldiers marched in, commanded by Esek Hopkins, to prevent the navy from taking sheep and cattle off Rhode Island for the besieged British army in Boston. The presence of the soldiers provoked more threats of bombardment from the warships, as the two forces eyed each other across the narrow gap of water and occasionally grappled over a herd of cattle.[7]

Stiles did not share the panic that had already driven so many out of town. He sent one load of his most valuable furniture and books away but stayed on himself with 30 of the 130 families of his congregation. They urged him to go to Bristol for safety, but surmising, and correctly, that Bristol was as likely to be attacked as Newport, he decided to stick it out where he was. He doubted that the ships would

6. *Lit. Diary, 1,* 641–42.

7. Ibid., pp. 610–11, 620–21, 625; *Newport Mercury,* Oct. 9, 1775.

cannonade the town. The real danger, as he saw it, was from a famine of wood and provisions. Newport was all but blockaded on the waterside, with the warships daily seizing provisions meant for the town. Captain Wallace, the commander of the naval forces, was again threatening bombardment if the town did not supply him, but the town had little to give. Only a trickle of goods came overland, for the mainland towns were reluctant to send to a place that housed so many Tories, through whose hands supplies would leak to the enemy; nor had they forgiven Newport's poor showing in the early days of the nonimportation agreements.[8]

As the exodus of refugees continued, supply ceased for a while to be a crucial problem, but Stiles knew the improvement would be only temporary. As the weeks went by, his position in Newport became less and less tenable. The people who had fled were mostly those who sympathized with the American cause. Their departure left the town meeting in the hands of the Tories.[9] There were few families for him to visit now, and on the streets he faced the bold stares of men who hated him for a rebel and whom he despised as traitors to their country. It became increasingly unpleasant to go on living in a town that no longer held his dearest friends, though its ground now held the one dearest. Furthermore, his diminished congregation was no longer adequate to support him. By the opening of 1776 he was ready to join the exodus.

He thought of starting a school in some interior town, say Worcester, Hartford, Northampton, Windham, or Norwich. Perhaps he could read public lectures in one of the colleges on oriental languages and ecclesiastical history. The difficulty was that American colleges had not reached university status and did not go in for lectures of this kind the way European universities did. If God should see fit to offer another opportunity in the ministry, that would, of course, be the best thing for him.[10] But a chaplaincy in Washington's army was out of the question because of his family responsibilities—he was probably not sorry. In the end he decided to move to Dighton, a sleepy little Massachusetts town on the Taunton River off Narragansett Bay. In the south part of the town a Congregational society, not yet formally gathered as a church but with a good meetinghouse already built, wanted him

8. *Lit. Diary, 1,* 611; *Newport Mercury,* May–Oct. 1775, passim.
9. *Lit. Diary, 1,* 631, 643; *Newport Mercury,* Apr. 8, 1776.
10. Stiles to John Lewis, Jan. 21, 1776; *Lit. Diary, 1,* 659.

to preach occasional sermons to them.[11] Here he would be remote from
the alarms of war; his family would be safe from naval attacks; and
he would be within range of a large number of churches which were
familiar with his talents and which might invite him to give occasional
sermons. He would even be near enough to Newport so that he could
preach there regularly once or twice a month to the remnant of his
beloved congregation.

On the evening of March 13, 1776, Stiles loaded his family and
possessions into a sloop at Fogland Ferry and shoved off into the
darkness to join the growing band of American exiles. All night, alert
for enemy patrol boats, they cut through the cold, choppy waters of
Mt. Hope Bay and up the Taunton River, while their home, their
church, and their town receded into the distance and the past. In the
grey light of a March morning they stepped ashore at Dighton and
headed for their hired half house, lucky to be together under one roof,
when so many other families were split and scattered wherever a
relative or friend offered a bed. Ezra, Jr., was still at Yale and Kezia
at Meriden, but the rest were all there.

Stiles had inadvertently moved his family just in time to escape
a three-weeks' nightmare in Newport. The Sunday after arriving in
Dighton he had to compete with the throb of distant cannon for the
attention of his congregation. The sound certainly came from Boston
way and as certainly indicated some major action. The astonishing and
agreeable news arrived Monday morning: the king's troops had evacuated Boston. The evacuation, though a blessing for Boston, brought
new problems to the continental army and new fears to all American
coastal towns. While the British remained at Boston, there they were;
but now where were they?

For three weeks the nervous inhabitants of the Narragansett Bay
area seized every fresh rumor as fact and exhausted themselves with
rapidly alternating alarm and relief: the fleet was headed for Newport; no, the troops were embarked but the fleet not yet sailed. Yes,
they had sailed but were heading for Halifax. No, the cannon were
heard today, and again the next day, so the ships must be still near.
Wallace and his ships had left Newport, to join the Boston fleet. No,
they were back again. Days of thick fog and a heavy snowstorm, eyes
straining seaward to penetrate the swirling wall, a glimpse of twenty
ships. The alarm is raised, the beacon at Providence fired to warn the

11. *Lit. Diary*, 2, 1.

countryside, an express sent to General Washington, fifteen thousand men said to be marching for the island. It is a false alarm: no fleet has passed Nantucket, so they must be heading for Halifax. Wallace with his fifteen sail is here again, gone again, here again.[12]

Stiles was on hand for all the excitement; he had returned on March 29 to preach in his own pulpit for two weeks—was preaching in fact on that fearful Sunday morning when the enemy ships were reported in the fog. Again and again during these tense days the early morning silence or the mid-day bustle was rent by the roar of cannon. There was a great naval encounter off Block Island when one of the ships left the battle and stood in from sea firing every ten minutes as she came. The alarm was sounded and on the hills people gathered to scan the horizon until at last the outlines of the *Glasgow* became apparent, limping back to port to lick her wounds but barking and snarling all the way.[13]

The American forces on the island grew bold: they dug trenches on the point, though Wallance warned that such preparations would necessitate his burning and bombarding the town; they snatched back American ships under seizure; they moved cannon to the shore under cover of night and fired at Wallace's anchored fleet. Once the fog was so thick that the targets were scarcely discernible, but Stiles "could hear the shrieks and distress and Confusion or noise of Tumult on board," as the cables were cut and the vessels slowly got off and out of range.[14] This action took place at five in the morning off Brenton's Point, and to be on the spot Stiles must have started long before dawn with knowledge of what was about to take place. Whatever went on in Newport, he was apt to be there or to have, almost immediately, an authoritative report from someone who had been there. Many of his parishioners were active patriots, and the new island commander, Colonel Henry Babcock (Hopkins took command of the American naval forces), had been his student at Yale.

Stiles had to return to Dighton for a promised Sunday sermon before the excitement was over. After one false start and return to investigate cannon fire, he left the island still wondering whether a British invasion fleet had arrived.[15] It had not, and within a week

12. Ibid., pp. 1–5.
13. Ibid., p. 5.
14. Ibid.
15. Ibid., p. 8.

Wallace and his fleet sailed away to other tasks, leaving Narragansett Bay temporarily unpatrolled. General Washington left New England for New York. Apparently the present danger was over; Rhode Island could relax.

Even so, it was a bleak time, with cold, hunger, and homeless refugees everywhere. In these trials of the flesh Stiles was better off than most men, but in heartaches he had his own share: his wife dead, his church broken, his friends scattered, himself and family exiled from all they held dear.

While he wandered about on his horse, trading sermons for the money to keep his family fed and clothed and sheltered, he could take comfort in the magnificent response of his fellow Americans to the challenge of tyranny. Probably no one in the country apart from the generals of the armies took so comprehensive an interest as Ezra Stiles did in the progress of American arms. Twice he visited the American encampment outside Boston. From newspapers, letters, and the conversations he held as he rode from town to town in Massachusetts, Rhode Island, and Connecticut, he gathered and filed away every scrap of information he could get about every engagement of the war. He knew that one report might not be as reliable as another, but he set them all down and then tried to sift the true from the false, the good guesses from the bad, seeking to establish the numbers engaged on each side, and the course of the action, until his diary came to read like nothing so much as an intelligence report. Even today, when the official reports are available, the accounts which Stiles gathered provide unique information about such important battles as Lexington and Bunker Hill. Here was another book he could have written: a military history of the Revolution. In spite of the fact that he never observed an important action and did not have access to official information, his comments show that he had a keen understanding of how the war was being fought and how it must be fought. Even before the defeat of Burgoyne, he discerned what the British army was learning more slowly, "that whenever and as often as they shall be inclined to make a Marchment into the Country, they must count upon two things (1) that considerable Numbers will soon gather and attend them in their March. (2) that they must expect to be harassed either from behind stone walls or in open field, with a Loss equal to a pitcht Battle." [16]

16. Ibid., p. 164. Stiles used his diary to record accounts of military events. Many of these are omitted in the printed edition.

Stiles's fund of information about population enabled him to assess the strength of the opposing forces far better than another man might have. He was used to interpolating numbers in statistical series, and learned quickly to estimate the relative numbers of dead, wounded, and missing in an engagement. He could detect extravagant claims by either side. He could discount the support the enemy might gain from the Indians, because he knew the Indian population was small. And while others wondered about the capacity of the American economy to sustain the war, he demonstrated, to himself if to no one else, that America could sustain a national debt of forty million pounds sterling as easily as Great Britain could the debt of 150 million which she already owed. And American population and property were growing so rapidly (while Great Britain stood still) that in another twenty years an American debt of eighty million would be feasible: "So that if the War for Independence generate a Debt of 20 Million Sterling (and hitherto it is not, say, three Million Sterling) yet the Prize of Liberty will be well purchased." [17]

From such considerations Stiles drew confidence in American success, but his mind did not rest in these mechanisms nor in the patriotism which could put them to use. Behind and beyond the men who snatched their rifles to harass the British armies, he saw the hand of an overruling Providence, a God who had willed American independence in order to preserve the free play of reason and evangelical truth. "Who gave the Americans one heart?" he asked himself:

Who poured down Wisdom into the General Congress and Colonial Conventions and Assemblies? Who has in this very short Space of one year sprung into Existence and aroused into the field Armies and Forces, say, to the amount of 70 to 90 Thousand? While Great Britain has brought against us a combined Armament of say 40 to 50 Thousand, with the Thunder of the Navy—an Armament and Force which, had it been bro't against any Kingdom or Empire in Europe, would have spread Terror and Dismay to the most intrepid Power on the other side of the Atlantic—yet while this combined force is brot against us, and now in actual Vengeance, we receive the Lash without Flinching, without a Shudder—we sustain the Vengeance without Terror—and instead of spreading Terror and Dismay thro' the Continent, it excites Heroism and an unparalleled Intrepidity thro'

17. Ibid., p. 74.

the Millions of America! It is given to all to rush to Arms with amazing Avidity! For what great Work is this Spirit permitted or excited by a holy Providence? Zion's King will get Honor and Glory to himself among the Tumults and Revolutions of Empires.[18]

In giving God the credit for American patriotism and American success, Ezra Stiles did not fail to learn the lesson which a good Puritan must always learn from the tribulations of this world. When the Indians fell on New England in 1676, there was rejoicing in the success with which the people withstood the onslaught, but there was also mourning for the sins which had induced God to permit the attack in the first place. Ezra Stiles did not forget that if God was the author of American independence, he was also author of the suffering which Americans were undergoing, and undergoing justly, for the sins by which they had offended God. On the Sunday after the Battle of Lexington he reminded himself and his congregation "that Sin is the procuring Cause of all Calamities—that Humiliation Repentance and turning to the Lord is our Duty peculiarly when his Judgments are abroad in the Earth." [19] When the British navy ravaged the coastal towns, he called the naval commander an "inhuman Wretch," but also observed: "It is a righteous and holy thing with God to bring the Severest Calamities of this civil War upon the maritime Towns, because most abounding with Vice and Wickedness." [20]

This larger providential perspective nourished Stiles's zealous interest in the progress of the war and also his unflagging confidence in ultimate victory for America. During the year after he left the island, away from his family as often as not, preaching alternately in Newport and Dighton, occasionally in Providence, Bristol, Taunton, and other towns in the area, he doggedly looked forward to the reassembling of his congregation. Churches in Providence and Taunton, not sharing his confidence in the future, begged him to settle with them, but he refused.[21] His years in Newport had been immensely happy ones, and as long as he could be of any use there he would not commit

18. Ibid., p. 48.
19. Ibid., 1, 538.
20. Ibid., pp. 623–24.
21. Ibid., 2, 15, 58–59.

himself to serve elsewhere. As long as there was a ray of hope he would keep himself free to return.

Suddenly hope was extinguished. On December 6, 1776, Stiles entered in his diary the latest evidence that the British fleet, rumored to be enroute from New York to Newport, was instead headed for England. The ink was hardly dry on the paper when cannon were heard, and as the day went on, refugees began arriving. Stiles took up his pen again:

> I expect tomorrow Newport will be in the hands of Enemy, who doubtless intend to winter there. . . . May God deliver us in his own Time out of all our Destresses. I hope God will uphold the Spirits of the people and prevent a spirit of Intimidation and Dispair spreading thro' the Land. The Conflict is severe, but it is glorious. A Shudder went thro' the Continent in Oct. and November—but we had nearly recovered our former Firmness. This new aspect will I expect excite a considerable Shudder, especially in these parts—but after the first shock we shall resume Courage, and I trust heroically go thro' the trying Conflict, which I doubt not in gods holy providence will be eventually crownd with Victory and Honor.

But victory, though sure, might be a long way off. As he sifted reports about the invading force, Stiles concluded that the number was much smaller than most people claimed, but still sufficient to hold the town. His trips back to his people must cease now. He heard the enemy were going to tear the pews from his church and use it for a ballroom; later rumors said a stable.[22]

With the occupation of Newport there was no longer any point in keeping up his peripatetic existence. For a man of frail constitution, it was a strain to be so constantly on the road, and it was, besides, too precarious for a man with seven children to be living on a hand-to-mouth basis. When the Dighton people, to whom he had been preaching twice a month, asked him to preach regularly, in return for firewood, a house, and £60 a year, he gratefully agreed to do so, at least until spring.[23]

It might have been a permanent position for Stiles, but he regarded it as only temporary. Though his spirit longed for permanence and

22. Ibid., pp. 93–104.
23. Ibid., pp. 113 n., 122, 145.

stability, he must be ready to return to Newport when God willed to set her free. Furthermore, were not all human arrangements temporary? There was no stability on earth, only the illusion of it. He was becoming more and more what he felt a Christian should be, a pilgrim passing briefly through the world with heart fixed firmly on what lay beyond. He was, to be sure, a paradoxical sort of pilgrim, one who followed the tumults and revolutions of the time with a consuming and partisan interest; yet even as he piled up reports of troop numbers in Newport and accounts of the battles at Long Island and Quebec, he gave his deepest attention to reading the New Testament (in Syriac) and to the Jerusalem Targum.

Looking back on his career—as he was bound to do, now that one stage of it had so clearly terminated—he saw that it had all along been moving in a uniform direction. Though this had not always been clear to him at the time, he saw now that he had regularly avoided the groupings and associations of men in this world. In the beginning, when the Christian doctrines of grace were first mingling with the rational humanism he had learned in the Yale library, he had looked on all men with admiring charity, and supposed their religious divisions, at least among the Protestants, to be founded on conscientious differences of judgment. All churches, he supposed, were sincerely devoted to Christianity in their different ways. Experience had taught him otherwise. Stockbridge was the first lesson, the Newport Anglicans another. Gradually he had bowed to the realization that human corruption poisoned everything that man touched, even his churches. The Anglicans especially, but all churches in some measure, were enmeshed in the lusts and hopes and hates of men who looked no farther than earthly gain or glory, all zealous "to build up Sects rather than make Christians." [24]

As the New Year of 1777 opened and he sat in his hired house at Dighton summing up what life had taught him, he determined that whatever happened, he would continue to devote himself to God and not to men or the affairs of men. With his wife gone, his house and church in the hands of the enemy, his children growing up, he felt more alone than ever, and the feeling seemed to be a fulfillment of everything that had gone before. The openness and affability that had won him so many friends and endeared him to his congregation and family were still there, but subdued now, reduced to their proper sub-

24. Ibid., pp. 113–15.

ordination; and the instinct that had made him draw back from Stock-bridge, from the Stamp Act controversy, from the union with the Presbyterians had grown into a wisdom that set the triumphs of the world, even the triumph of American independence, into insignificance. "I have neglected," he thought to himself, and wrote in his diary, "several opportunities of forming or at least taking part and figuring in several respectable Coalescences."

> But foreseeing the Lengths their Systems would carry me, I stopped—and am, perhaps more than any man of my extensive Acquaintance and Correspondence—ALONE—and unconnected in the World: while I have the pure and daily pleasure of an inward conscious and cordial Union with all the *good*, with those who love and those who hate me, with the numerous Millions who know me not, with the whole Collection of Characters in all Nations of every kind and degree of Excellence, literary or moral Worth; above all, my soul unites most sincerely with the whole Body of the Mystical Church, with all that in every Nation fear GOD and love our Lord Jesus Christ. These, stript of all the peculiarities which externally separate them from one another and from me, I embrace with a true spirit of universal Love. But to love a whole Character, or a whole Church, or any whole Fraternity whether literary, religious or politic, I do not find within me. Entering into whatever scene, I meet with many Inconcinnities and am disgusted too much for Acquiescence in any here below. I never shall cordially and externally unite with Mankind in any of their Affairs, Enterprizes and Revolutions. There is a preference of Systems, but no perfect one on Earth. I expect no great Felicity from fellowship and open Communication with Mankind. But intend to become more and more the recluse—waiting for the REST of Paradise, where I foresee my soul will unite with perfection and acquiesce in eternal universal Harmony.[25]

Ezra Stiles was an honest man, and he made this reflection honestly. But he knew that he could not carry it to its logical conclusion: he had no wish to become a hermit, living on bread and water which someone else might perhaps provide for him. God did not put men in the world without reason, and when He saw fit to take them out He

25. Ibid.

did so. Meanwhile each one must find his own way to live in the world without forgetting God. The ministry had been Ezra Stiles's way and Elizabeth Hubbard had been his way too. Perhaps his determination to withdraw himself more from the world was partly a revulsion from the thousand pricks of irritation he had suffered since he lost her protection. At any rate the ministry was still his way.

Dighton was a good enough place in which to follow it, but had one disadvantage: now that the British had occupied Newport and the rest of Aquidneck Island, Dighton was close enough by to invite marauding attacks. He was thinking that he should take his family to some equally quiet interior town, when a messenger arrived from Portsmouth, New Hampshire, with an invitation to take the ministry of the First Congregational Church there.[26]

It was not an offer that he could ignore. The Portsmouth church was one of the largest in New England. It had formerly been under the ministry of Samuel Langdon, who had just left it to become president of Harvard College. The messenger of the church carried letters from both Langdon and Samuel Haven, the other Congregational minister of Portsmouth, urging Stiles to take this wider avenue of usefulness in the service of Christ. The salary, though no sum was mentioned, would doubtless be far larger than what he was getting at Dighton. With Ezra, Jr., in college and no Elizabeth to manage the family budget, his expenses were getting ahead of him. Furthermore there was nothing to keep him in Dighton: by March he would have preached off the 550 pounds of beef, 320 pounds of pork, 2 bushels of corn, 3 bushels of potatoes, and 20 pounds of tallow which had been advanced on his salary; and with the enemy cutting him off from his own congregation, there was no need on their account to stay nearby. There was one difficulty: the Portsmouth church wanted a pastor to settle permanently with them. Though Stiles was free to leave and eager to do so, still, with American victory in mind and the eventual regathering of his Newport church, he could not agree to take permanently the ministry of another: he would engage for a year or until the end of the war.[27]

When he received no further communication from the Portsmouth church, he assumed that his proposals had been unacceptable, but in the middle of March came a letter, delayed in the post, stating that

26. Ibid., p. 121 (Feb. 6, 1777).
27. Ibid., pp. 113, 121–23.

the church would expect him the first of March. The same post brought a letter from Dr. Chauncy in Boston, inviting him to share the pulpit and the weekly contributions of the First Church there. He could easily make additional money by supplying vacant pulpits in and around Boston, which, Chauncy assured him, was now the safest town in America.[28]

Stiles wrote back to Chauncy that he had been wishing for "a more retired and less conspicuous Situation than either Boston or Portsmouth"; nevertheless, he agreed to visit Portsmouth in April and to stop in Boston on the way.[29] Boston was an inviting prospect, the intellectual capital of New England, but Stiles stayed only to give a morning and afternoon service in the First Church and hurried on to Portsmouth.

It was a somewhat harrowing journey for him, because he broke out in a rash of pimples, with large pustules on his wrist. He thought it might be the smallpox and, after recovering, hoped fervently that it had given him immunity. Meanwhile, though he did not take to bed, he was acutely uncomfortable and distressed.[30] He nevertheless preached for three Sundays so effectively that the church unanimously voted to offer him a house, firewood, moving expenses, and £110 for one year. Stiles was overcome:

> Wonderfully providential! Acceptableness of my poor Labors! Opening for some little Usefulness! and liberal Provision for my family! in this Time of public Calamity. It demands my Gratitude to Heaven! Let me never distrust a gracious Providence. It is a Seaport and exposed to the Enemy: but Dangers and Troubles and Streights await us every where. In Gods holy Protection only is Security. I have taken the matter into a little time of Consideration, and desire to carry it to Jesus for his Light and Blessing. For tho' the Case appears comfortably clear at first View, yet our best Prospects are so easily disajusted and broken up and disappointed, that I desire first to ask Counsel of Heaven. If God has a Work for me anywhere, he will manifest it. If Gods Glory, his Presence and Blessing is not to go with me, I would not be carried up hence by the most flattering Prospects.

28. Ibid., p. 143. Chauncy to Stiles, Feb. 18, 1777; Samuel Penhallow to Stiles, Feb. 14, 1777.
29. *Lit. Diary*, 2, 144–45.
30. Itineraries, 5, 87–106.

In short I have found by sufficient Experience that without Gods Guidance and Blessing we are Nothing—and with it we are smiled upon and happy. I desire to refer this and all my Concerns to God.[31]

The next day he accepted the offer, and returned to Dighton only to gather up his family and furniture. On May 22 they set off in three carriages—nine people, the father, seven children ranging from ten to twenty, and the slave, Newport. By the first week in June they were settled in the house the church had provided. Although Portsmouth was not as large as Newport, nor as handsome, it was an attractive town, with chaste Georgian houses, a noble river, and elm-lined streets, where well-dressed ladies and gentlemen paraded of a summer evening. It was the world again, where Stiles would find men of affairs and men of learning to keep him in touch with what was going on. Here he would sit at breakfast with General Stark, who fought at Bennington. Baron Steuben would talk to him about Prussia. John Adams, up from Boston to try a lawsuit, would give him the latest developments in Congress, and the two would remind each other of the high daring with which their Puritan ancestors had stood fast for liberty. President Langdon would often come up from Harvard to visit his old congregation, and he and Stiles could mull over their theological differences. Privateers would hand him the mail bags taken from English ships and the Reverend David McClure, who had once spent half a year among the Indians near Lake Ontario, would ride up from North Hill parish in nearby Hampton to woo his daughter Betsy and bring him a large tooth found near the Ohio River, "a Grinder Tooth of some great Animal, but whether an Elephant or Gyant, is a Question." [32]

Stiles could not deny that he loved it all, distracting as it might be, and the people, as always, loved him. The Portsmouth church, after Dr. Langdon's departure, had been divided in their search for a successor: The well-to-do portion of the congregation wanted a man of learning, the rank and file an evangelical preacher, whether learned or not. They had tried several candidates, but those who pleased one group invariably displeased the other. In Stiles they discovered what

31. *Lit. Diary*, 2, 156.
32. Ibid., p. 201

they had all but ceased to hope for, a man who united erudition with
evangelical piety.[33]

The labor of serving a congregation of 230 families was a good
deal heavier than Stiles was used to. This and the many distractions
of life in Portsmouth cut sharply into the time that he liked to reserve
for contemplation and study. By leaving Dighton he had certainly
entered a more exciting scene, but he had also made it far more difficult to follow his resolution of withdrawing from the world. Before
he had time to assess the pattern of his new life, before he could attempt to recover his private world of communion and contemplation,
he found the whole direction of his life challenged by a new proposal.
The corporation of Yale College wanted him to be president.

33. Ibid., p. 260.

19

Parson or President

Yale College in New Haven
Sept. 10, 1777

Reverend Sir

These are to inform you that the Fellows of Yale College at their present meeting have made choice of you as PRESIDENT, and appointed the Reverend Mr. Johnson one of their members, to wait upon you with their choice, and solicit your acceptance.[1]

Mr. Johnson presented himself in Portsmouth on September 27.[2] Would Dr. Stiles accept? Dr. Stiles did not know. News that the offer was coming had reached him ten days earlier in letters from James Dana and Chauncy Whittelsey,[3] but two weeks of floundering in cross-currents of thought and emotion had brought him no closer to a decision, though even if he had reached one, ceremony would have demanded that his answer be deferred.

Actually he had had not two weeks but more than ten years in which to make up his mind. Old President Holyoke of Harvard had once told him that he was the intended heir of President Clap,[4] and when Clap resigned in 1766, Stiles's friends, including a few on the corporation, favored him for the job. When they sent him the customary indirect inquiry about his availability,[5] he had considered the whole

1. *Lit. Diary*, 2, 213.
2. Ibid.
3. Ibid., pp. 208, 211.
4. Ibid., p. 265.
5. John Devotion to Stiles, July 7, 1766, *Itineraries and Miscellanies*, p. 457; Ben-

question and made up his mind, he thought, for good. It was just after the Stamp Act crisis, when he was feeling his way toward a spectator's position in the world, and he saw that the presidency of Yale would inevitably plunge him into the thick of things.

In 1766 he therefore answered no.[6] But like most unwilling candidates for high office, he was not quite unequivocal. The reason he offered was not merely his own distaste for the burdens of the office but the fact that his election would inevitably be the product of party maneuvering. He still had a reputation for Arminianism; he was still the son of Isaac Stiles; New Lights still distrusted him. If he were chosen, they would form a strong minority against him and therefore against Yale under his guidance. Yale had suffered enough as a party football in the Connecticut melee of religiopolitical alliances and schisms. He would not be the occasion for more of it. The only condition that would make him consider acceptance was a unanimous choice by the corporation and wide public approval. This was his way of closing the question in 1766. Only a miracle could fulfill his condition, and it did not occur to him to think of himself as a fit subject for a miracle.

Probably the corporation could not have reached even a majority vote for him in 1766 anyhow. They did reach one for James Lockwood, one of their number, but Lockwood also said no. Thereupon they made Naphtali Daggett (Yale 1748) acting president. Daggett had become Yale's first professor of divinity in 1756 and pastor of the college church in 1757. As president he retained these offices. But in 1777, faced with a student rebellion, he decided that three jobs were too many and resigned the presidency.[7] Daggett's resignation set in train the events that brought Johnson, without preliminary feelers, to Stiles's doorstep in Portsmouth.

As Stiles considered Johnson's proposal, the wisdom of his earlier decision seemed greater than ever, and his hesitation in giving an immediate refusal did not arise from any conscious intention of reversing it. He was no longer interested, he told himself, in the honor and acclaim attached to the office. His vanity, he hoped, was dead. Teaching he would enjoy again, but student discipline, never easy to

jamin Gale to Stiles, Aug. 23, 1766. See also Stiles's notations on the back of the letter from Chauncy Whittelsey to Stiles, July 9, 1766.

6. Stiles to John Devotion, July 25, 1766.

7. Dexter, *Biographical Sketches*, 3, 641–42.

him, now seemed formidable, and he told himself, "An hundred and fifty or 180 Young Gentlemen Students, is a Bundle of Wild Fire not easily controlled and governed—and at best the Diadem of a President is a Crown of Thorns." [8] It was the reaction expected from desirable candidates for college presidencies—the preference for teaching, the dislike of administration—but it was also the reaction of a tired, aging man, who yearned for a life of retirement, study, and contemplation. In two months Stiles would be fifty, and he felt it. Had he not deliberately turned his back on the world, intending "to become more and more the recluse—waiting for the Rest of Paradise?" [9] If the world impinged on him more than he liked as a minister, how would he endure the life of a college president?

There were practical reasons for refusing too. For years Yale had been struggling to make ends meet and had often failed. This had been a principal reason why Lockwood refused the presidency in 1767 and why there had been no permanent appointment since.[10] After Clap's resignation and death the Connecticut Assembly had from time to time made a grant to cover the college deficit, but since 1774 they had granted nothing.[11] How, in the midst of a revolutionary war, could Yale afford to pay both a professor of divinity and a president— Stiles had no intention of doing both jobs—when in peacetime she had been unable to manage an adequate salary for one man? The job would be a poor financial risk.

Suppose there was universal approval of his election—how long would it last? Stiles knew, from the experience of past presidents, the impossibility of giving continuing satisfaction to the public. One student riot and tongues would start wagging. And student riots there would be. It was the nature of college governments to be "subject to frequent and unavoidable convulsions," as it still is.[12] Why tax his feeble health, why exchange a position he enjoyed, a tranquil position as the respected and loved leader of a harmonious congregation, for a life of inescapable conflicts and certain opprobrium?

These were important considerations, all pointing toward refusal, but they had to be weighed in another scale than that of personal

8. *Lit. Diary*, 2, 209.
9. Ibid., p. 115.
10. John Devotion to Stiles, Nov. 1, 1766, *Itineraries and Miscellanies*, p. 458.
11. Dexter, *Biographical Sketches*, 3, 207–08, 263, 302, 365, 399, 466, 513.
12. *Lit. Diary*, 2, 267.

comfort and convenience. Stiles was a religious man, in the Puritan tradition. It was incumbent on him to examine the path of duty, the will of God. For those not equipped with a mystical access to divinity (no Puritan thought he was) the process of discovering the will of God has always been a difficult matter. But Puritans, old and new, had generally gained a good deal of experience at it by the time they reached Stiles's age. Stiles knew that God gave signs to indicate His will: positive signs making one course clearly preferable to another, or negative signs to make one course less desirable. To read the signs was the problem, because obstacles might be sent merely as a test— perhaps God wished to see if one could triumph over them. And good signs might be meant as temptations—perhaps God wished to see if one could withstand them. One observed all the signs, weighed them for validity, prayed, searched one's soul, consulted one's friends, and then made the decision.

In the absence of other signs to the contrary, his own distaste for the office of president, together with the shaky condition of Yale's finances, would be governing considerations. His friends Whittelsey and Dana had urged him to accept on the ground that he would be more eminently useful as president than as the pastor of any particular church, and would thus "do more towards advancing the glorious Cause of the blessed Jesus." [13] But Stiles was not convinced that the presidency was so important, and he did not quite trust the judgment of friends who were prejudiced in his behalf and eager to have him in New Haven.

Nevertheless, he did not wish to make a snap judgment. He must consult more friends, get the reaction of his Newport church (to which, in spite of its dispersed condition, he still felt bound), and above all he must assess more carefully the demand, the need for him in Connecticut. When Johnson departed, after a week of talk, he carried a letter to the corporation, deferring Stiles's decision. "It is of great importance," Stiles wrote, "that the Head of the College should be acceptable to the Fellows, to the Body of the Churches and Pastors, to the General Assembly and the People at large." [14] Johnson had admitted that the vote was not unanimous but insisted that the four votes for Elizur Goodrich were simply an expression of preference for Goodrich, not of opposition to Stiles. Stiles was

13. Ibid., p. 214.
14. Ibid., p. 215.

doubtful. But he agreed to go and see for himself: at the end of the month he would leave for Connecticut and interview the corporation at their November meeting. To his diary he confided: "nothing short of Unanimity shall induce my Acceptance." [15]

Even unanimity would not be enough if his Newport church refused to let him go. In fact, a fair prospect of returning to Newport in the foreseeable future might be sufficient to determine him. He sent letters to arrange a meeting of as many of his Newport congregation as could assemble at Dighton on October 28, so that he could consult them on the way to Connecticut.[16]

On October 20 he set off and on his way met joyful news. The tides of war had changed. The sound of Salem and Boston guns, roaring approval of Burgoyne's surrender, accompanied him to Cambridge, where on the evening of the twenty-third elated crowds celebrated around a bonfire, and victory candles beamed from every window. Two days later at Taunton he heard that an army of several thousand stood ready at Howland's Ferry to launch an attack on Aquidneck Island. It began to look as though he might indeed be going back to Newport.[17]

The attack was never made. The commanding general's poor judgment, bad weather, and the impatience of the militia (who departed as their short-term enlistments expired) all combined to defeat the high hopes of hundreds of exiled and impounded islanders. Everyone knew that with winter so close another attempt to free Newport would not be made for a long time. With heavy heart Stiles rode into Dighton to find that the confusion of the times and the expense of traveling had made impossible the meeting he had asked for. Disappointed, he sailed to Providence, listening en route to the excuses of the unsuccessful General Spencer; and there he took the road for Connecticut, stopping to visit and consult wherever a friend or member of his dispersed church lived not too far out of the way.[18]

On November 5 he met the Yale corporation, and for two days they conferred on finances, the present state of the college, future plans, and public opinion. Finally they considered each other. Of this Stiles wrote:

15. Ibid., p. 214.
16. Ibid., pp. 216, 242.
17. Ibid., pp. 220–21.
18. Ibid., pp. 221–23.

In the Course of our Interview, I very fully laid before them all my own Deficiencies, and what they must not expect from me; particularly my infirm Health, want of Talents for Government, doubts of becoming acceptable to the Pastors, the Assembly, the public, and many other Things. I also communicated to them my sentiments in Religion, both with respect to the *System of Theology*, and *Ecclesiastical Polity*, and desired them particularly to consider wherein I coincided with and differed from others. I did this with all Sincerity as in the presence of God. I requested them to take full Knowledge of me on these and all other accounts, and wished them to interrogate me to their intire Satisfaction. They heard me till they said they were satisfied.

It was then his turn to interrogate:

I at length observed that as they were divided between Mr. Goodrich and myself as to the Presidency at their Choice in September I desired to know whether they were all so satisfied that I might not only relye upon their unanimous Acquiescence which they had repeatedly expressed, but whether I might depend on their Cordiality if I came into that venerable Body? Their answer was not only Nem. Con. but in general they spoke out and I think one and all the most express approbation.[19]

The fellows wished an answer at once, but Stiles was far from ready to commit himself. He persuaded them to wait until early spring and rode off on a tour of the state, sounding out the governor, councilors, assemblymen, clergymen, professors, and tutors. Homeward bound, he stopped overnight in Woodstock with Uncle Abel, now in his sixty-ninth year and as opinionated as ever, not the man to guide him in this delicate decision. At last, after five weeks' travel, he reached Portsmouth again on November 26.[20]

The trip had been an exhausting experience emotionally and physically, and the results had not been what he expected. The signs had all indicated that God willed him to go to Yale. His interview with the corporation had erased most of his doubts about their unanimity, though two members had been absent. He visited one of them and received his approval too.[21] The other, Nathaniel Taylor of New

19. *Ibid.*, p. 225.
20. *Ibid.*, pp. 225–32.
21. *Ibid.*, p. 228.

Milford, was the only one about whom he still could doubt, and Taylor was an Old Light, not likely to oppose him.

The cordiality of the fellows had been apparent when they acceded to Stiles's request that he be appointed professor of ecclesiastical history as well as president. This would enable him to teach the subject that most interested him. The question of finances had been settled too. Yale's incomes had been thoroughly explained to him; and whether by wizardry or gullibility, he was persuaded he would get his salary, £160 Lawful Money (£120 Sterling), plus the fees paid by seniors and masters for their degrees, the use of the president's house and lot, and ten acres of land that rented currently for £9—the whole estimated at £220 Lawful Money annually. It was no inducement, for his ministerial income had been equivalent, but neither was it any longer an obstacle.[22]

His Newport congregation would probably not oppose his acceptance, though many members were yet to be heard from, and he could not be sure until advised by a general meeting, which was to be attempted again in December at Providence. The question of greater usefulness seemed to be resolving itself in favor of Yale too. Not one of the ministers he consulted in New Hampshire, Massachusetts, Rhode Island, or Connecticut had thought there could be any question that the presidency should take priority. But Stiles, finding the individual opinions unwelcome, submitted the question formally to the ministers' associations in Boston and Rhode Island.[23]

It would take time to get their answers, but meanwhile all signs pointed toward Yale, and so, even more unequivocally, did another: there was wide public approval of his election. Of approximately one hundred leading men in Connecticut whom he visited, each encouraged him to accept. If there was any opposition (and he was sure there must be) it was small enough to be of little weight, and it was keeping quiet. No one he spoke to knew of any, with the single exception of Colonel Abraham Davenport, a council member, who thought the corporation should have chosen his nephew, Timothy Dwight. The suggestion was not to be taken seriously, for though a popular and highly successful tutor of recognized promise, Dwight was only twenty-six years old, with neither the experience nor the reputation to grace the president's chair. A few ministers openly

22. Ibid., pp. 224–25.
23. Ibid., pp. 223, 244.

wondered if Stiles might not too much favor James Dana, but this was probably only a warning to guide the future conduct of the president, and Stiles counted on his friends to let him know if any antagonism developed in this or any other quarter. He was satisfied that there was no real opposition to him.[24]

Moreover, it seemed apparent that Ezra Stiles was the only man on whom all parties could agree; and for the future of Yale College it was vital that all parties should agree. At this juncture any Connecticut clergyman qualified for the presidency would have been automatically rejected by a part of the population simply because of his religious party attachments. Stiles, steering his solitary course in Newport, proclaiming Christian charity to all believers in Christ of whatever sect, had earlier reaped the disapproval of both parties. He was nevertheless still acceptable to the Old Lights and had now become acceptable enough to the New Lights. The Yale corporation, New Lights and all, were for him; and so was the rest of Connecticut.

In fact, the most compelling thing about his election was that it had arisen from an attempt to halt the feud which President Clap had started between Yale and the people of Connecticut. After Dagget resigned in April 1777, the Corporation addressed a memorial to the state Assembly, asking that a committee be appointed to confer with them on the state of the college. Yale had been financially staggering for years, and the war was proving too much for her. Now, without a president and with her finances disrupted by the fluctuating currency and soaring price of provisions, Yale had closed her doors and sent the students home until arrangements could be made to set up instruction in a safer and cheaper inland location. Yale had her back to the wall and was asking the state for help.

At the conference, which was held in July, the corporation presented Yale's need for money, and it was the committee's encouraging opinion that the Assembly might grant funds to increase the library and philosophical apparatus and to support several new professorships, provided "only that they should have a voice in concurrence with the Fellows in appointing professors supported by the State." The committee also volunteered some advice: they knew the corporation had the Reverend Elizur Goodrich in mind for the presidency; but, in their opinion, the right man for the job was Ezra Stiles. The presidency of Yale, as well as its deplorable condition, had been widely

24. Ibid., pp. 229-31.

discussed; and they were willing to say, almost with certainty, that the Assembly unanimously approved Dr. Stiles, as did gentlemen of character, both civil and ecclesiastical, in all their various counties. They were willing to say, in fact, that if the corporation took their advice on these things, "the Assembly would do every Thing for the aggrandizement of Yale College otherwise they should not." The meeting concluded with the agreement that if the committee's proposals were acceptable, the corporation should signify its desire for a further conference.[25]

The corporation was, of course, quite free to disregard the advice of the Assembly. There was nothing in the charter that required them, in their choice of president, to please anyone but themselves, and for the past quarter-century they had pleased hardly anyone else. But in 1777 they were ready for conciliation. If a plan could be devised by which the Assembly could have a hand in running Yale without violating the charter, it was all right with them. The proposals of the committee sounded too good to be true, but the corporation hastened to signify their desire for a further conference, and in September they showed their good will by electing Ezra Stiles president.

When Stiles learned that the Assembly had proposed his election, he was not pleased. James Dana had written that if the corporation did not choose him, "Another College will be immediately set up, over which you will be invited to preside." [26] With this in mind, Stiles at first regarded his election as the result of pressure: "The Assembly have caused this change, and the Fellows have elected me to prevent the Assembly's building another College. Will it have this Effect? doubtful." [27] Dana had intended his remark to persuade Stiles, but its effect had been the opposite. The suspicion and distrust in Stiles's mind were not dispelled until his trip through Connecticut convinced him that collusion and intrigue had played no part in the choice, and that his particular friends had had no hand in it. Everyone was sure that he was the man for the job. From conversation and from letters, from fellows, legislators, clergy and laymen, over and over again he heard the same story: he might be "the happy means of removing *intirely* all that Alienation or Jealousy, which seems to have subsisted in times past between the State and the College, and thus

25. Ibid., pp. 207–08, 214.
26. Ibid., pp. 207–08.
27. Ibid., p. 209.

of promoting the Interest both of the College and the State, to which he once belonged"; [28] "that the Expectation of Harmonizing all Parties, and taking off that Coolness which has heretofore too much taken place between the Legislature and that Corporation, was now great and very pleasing: that they had the greatest hopes of your acceptance." [29] It was an appealing thought—even to a man who hoped his vanity was dead: that he, Ezra Stiles, might become the means of erecting upon the old foundation a greater Yale with more buildings, more professors, more books, and more students.

Returning from Connecticut, then, Stiles was much closer to decision. Though still unwilling to say yes—his church had not yet consented—he admitted the possibility to himself by engaging (but only conditionally) some beds and other furniture at New Haven.[30] And back in Portsmouth he set himself to studying the administration of colleges. He consulted John Adams about law lectures,[31] and Professor Wigglesworth of Harvard about a medical professorship and about the statutes of his university's Hollis professorships of divinity and of mathematics and natural philosophy.[32]

During the first two weeks in December President Langdon was in Portsmouth, and Stiles learned from him, what indeed he already knew, that a president's life is not a happy one. At this and other times Langdon was very cooperative in giving information: he spoke of Harvard's incomes, salaries, and the proportions of them paid by the Massachusetts Assembly; he even communicated the salary of President Witherspoon of New Jersey College.[33] A comparison with Yale's figures was discouraging; but the great difference (in spite of Harvard's larger endowment) was accountable to the generosity of the Massachusetts Assembly. Stiles was again impressed with the necessity of harmony between Yale and the public. He would know more about that when the results of the next conference between Assembly and corporation (scheduled for December 18) reached him. By that time he should also be getting the results of the December 16 meeting of his Newport congregation.

28. Ibid., p. 214.
29. Ibid., p. 251.
30. Ibid., p. 228.
31. Ibid., p. 238, and note dated Dec. 18, 1777, on back of Hebrew oration written 1778 and delivered 1781.
32. Stiles to Wigglesworth, Dec. 8, 1777.
33. *Itineraries and Miscellanies*, pp. 382–83.

Unfortunately neither meeting took place, the congregation prevented by the same reasons that prevented their meeting at Dighton, the Connecticut conference postponed by a national thanksgiving being set on the appointed day.[34] And so Stiles waited longer, but not idly. The rapidly plunging currency and skyrocketing prices required him repeatedly to recalculate the value of the salary he had been offered, to see if it remained a living wage. Fretting about the unknown sentiments of the tenth Yale fellow, he investigated the elections of other college presidents and found that unanimity was not the rule. Even the excellent President Holyoke of Harvard had been elected only after a three-way fight and a bit of undercover politicking. Stiles had it straight from the Reverend Daniel Rogers, who had participated in the election; but he took no comfort in the knowledge—the election of Stiles must be unanimous.[35]

In early January the vanity that he had once so deliberately buried rose from its grave to worry him. He felt its presence and conscientiously searched his soul to find it, but he never did recognize it guiding a work of his own hand, a sermon about his biblical namesake, Ezra the Scribe. According to Stiles: "There was a Restoration of the School of the prophets, and Ezra became the first President or Head of the College at Jerusalem, after the return from Babylon"; Ezra responsible for a new and more glorious college rising from the ruins of the old. Furthermore the learning of Ezra was the pure uncorrupted learning of the ancient Hebrews, which told of a suffering Messiah. Modern Jewish learning did not teach a suffering Messiah, an omission which Stiles believed to have originated from the corruptions of Ezra's rival, the scholar Hillel. In this wistful double analogy the wraith of vanity disguised itself as history and hid from the eyes of the author—Stiles of the pure old religion—Stiles, builder of the great Yale-to-be.[36]

Although discerning God's will about Yale was uppermost in his mind during these months, he was of necessity mostly occupied in other pursuits, the usual ones of ministering to his large congregation and keeping track of the war. And then there were always letters

34. *Lit. Diary,* 2, 241, 251; Chauncy Whittelsey to Stiles, Jan. 28, 1778.

35. *Itineraries and Miscellanies,* p. 383.

36. *Lit. Diary,* 2, 243; Stiles delivered the sermon as a Hebrew oration at Yale commencement, Sept. 12, 1781. His papers contain copies of it in both Hebrew and English.

to write. The old Murray-Stiles feud had opened up again. Yes, he had said everything he was supposed to have said about Murray, and he would say it here again in black and white so it would not be hearsay.[37]

During January letters began arriving from his Newport congregation. Though a church meeting and vote were impossible, they would give him their individual sentiments. Stiles methodically tabulated the results: members he had seen or had a letter from, members consenting directly or by certain information, members not consenting. He listed, too, the names of those locked up in Newport and his judgment of whether or not they would consent. And finally he added symbols indicating who would be most grieved if he left and who cordially wished him to stay, the last including everyone but Captain Newton, that unconverted Murray man.[38] There were a very few who absolutely refused to let him go, but the great majority, doubtful that they could ever reassemble or support him, reluctantly gave him permission to do whatever, with God's guidance, appeared his duty. The letters were poignant reminders of the happy past that he was about to turn his back on: "My Wife says (and I am the same way of thinking, as well as others of your Congregation) if we live to go home and Dr. Stiles is not there, it will not be like Newport." [39] One man had a practical suggestion to offer: "that if you could take a rich Wife at Portsmouth and could make it in your Bargain that she should go with you to Newport, when Peace and Independency shall be Established, it might settle this knotty Business." [40]

The letters from Newport pulled hard at him, and the balance swung again in favor of the ministry when, on January 27, the Portsmouth congregation unanimously called him to settle with them for life. He had come to New Hampshire with the agreement (at his own request) that he should not be asked to settle; but that was because of his ties to Newport. If he considered breaking these, the Portsmouth congregation thought they had as good a right to bid for him as Yale did. Stiles was once again in a complete quandary, and dashed off more letters to friends, to the corporation, and to the

37. John Murray to Stiles, Jan. 19, 1778; Stiles to Murray, Jan. 20, 1778; Jonathan Sewall to Stiles, Jan. 23, 1778; *Lit. Diary*, 2, 244.
38. Notes, dated Jan. 1, 1778.
39. *Lit. Diary*, 2, 251.
40. Ibid., p. 250.

Boston ministers' association, asking for advice. How could he trust his own judgment in weighing a sign that so heavily reinforced his own inclination? The congregation pushed their advantage: he could even have the option of returning to Newport after the war if that became possible and he still wished to. They pleaded that his great success with them was a sign that he should stay: not only had he reunited a split congregation, but he had achieved a minor awakening. Many people were still "under serious impressions" and ripe for the plucking. Could he in conscience "resign the Ministry and retire from the Vineyard in the midst of a Vintage?" [41]

On February 12 came still another sign pointing against Yale: a letter describing the second conference between corporation and Assembly, which had finally taken place on January 14–15. The demands of the Assembly were higher than first stated, and though the corporation would make some concessions, the Assembly appeared indisposed to make any. They wished to give the state an equal share in the election of president, tutors, and all professors except the professor of divinity. What Yale would gain by this merger was not apparent. It was suggested that the college ought to have new buildings, new philosophical apparatus, more books, and two or more new professorships, but the committee of the Assembly did not say how much if anything the state would contribute toward these objectives. To allow the corporation time to deliberate, the conference adjourned to February 10. Elizur Goodrich, who reported the developments to Stiles, could see little or no advantage for Yale in the Assembly's proposal, and Stiles himself was inclined to agree that "the Assembly hold their Favor at a very high price." It seemed likely, therefore, that nothing would come of the negotiations.[42]

Meanwhile, Goodrich was obliged to confess, Yale's finances were getting rapidly worse: "embarrassed on the one hand by a sinking medium, and on the other by the *dubious event of this difficult negotiation,* during which we cannot with decency, exert ourselves even for private benefactions, we must leave it with you, as a matter to be determined by your own prudence, whether to give your answer, which we hope will be favorable to our wishes, before it be known what may be effected at our next interview with the Committee." The letter concluded with a suggestion of strategy: the Assembly

41. Ibid., pp. 244–67; Birthday Reflexions, 1778.
42. Elizur Goodrich to Stiles, Jan. 20, 1778; *Lit. Diary,* 2, 253–54, 257–58.

might be moved to favorable action if it were known that the president-elect was suspending his answer because of their dalliance. Whether as an accommodating strategy or as a welcome reprieve, Stiles wrote notes deferring answers to both the Yale and the Portsmouth calls.[43]

There followed weeks of great anxiety—of fasting, prayer, and introspection, to identify which signs were self-deception, which ones sent to try or to tempt him, and which were the true ones to be heeded. The call at Portsmouth, for instance, was it meant to encourage his going to Yale? Had it been sent in the crucial moment of the college-state negotiations to sway the Assembly, or to excite a grateful reception in Connecticut if he chose to go there when a pleasanter easier job was open to him? Or had God given the call to try or to tempt him: "I might perhaps have thot and said, I should not have accepted the Presidency had an effectual door opened for the Ministry. I am now cut off of this self-deception." Or was it the real will of heaven that he should abide in the ministry—had Providence brought about his election at Yale simply to stimulate the Portsmouth congregation to call him? [44]

The complications and inversions in reading the signs were endless. He thought his mental inabilities and infirm health weighed against his undertaking the presidency, but others brushed these aside and sternly referred him "to the Grace of God and the strength of Jesus to be perfected in my Weakness." [45] He was convinced that he was not properly qualified for the job; but everyone overrode this objection and from several sources he even heard that many people in Massachusetts would like to see him at the head of Harvard; Charles Chauncy had gone so far as to say that he would have succeeded President Holyoke had he been educated at Harvard. From all this he wondered if he might infer "that the public discern some qualifications in me, which I have never seen in myself? But alas, the few Qualifications I may be supposed to have are overballanced by numerous Disqualifications." [46]

Finally another letter from the corporation cut short his deliberations: the committee had not showed up for the February 10 meeting, and only six of the corporation, but these had drawn up a statement

43. Goodrich to Stiles, Jan. 20, 1778; *Lit. Diary*, 2, 256–58.
44. *Lit. Diary*, 2, 259–60.
45. Ibid., p. 256.
46. Ibid., pp. 227, 265.

from which they could not retreat. In their opinion the committee's plan would be "not an Addition and Enlargement but Abolition of the original Constitution of the College which they hold sacred." As nothing more was to be expected from the Assembly it was the "unanimous opinion" of the Fellows present that Dr. Stiles's answer should be delayed no longer. The letter assured him *"that it will be the Endeavour of* ALL *the Members of the Corporation to support you in the Office,* to which they have invited you, and as far as possible to bear every Burden with you, and render your situation easy and comfortable." Stiles looked down the list of members present at the meeting: there was the name of Nathaniel Taylor! With satisfaction he noted in his diary: "I now have the Unanimous Voice of the whole Corporation"—and they still wanted him even though his original sponsors had reneged on their initial proposition to the college.[47]

Stiles now had in hand all the signs he was going to get, but he was almost another month in making up his mind. The unanimity of the corporation was a great personal satisfaction and triumph for him, as was also the unshaken public approval of Connecticut; but the presidency continued to repel him. The opportunity to teach was a mitigating rather than inducing aspect of the job, and his vision of building a greater, more glorious Yale had shattered against the unyielding wall of the Assembly. There might not be a salary for him, there might not even be a Yale. His popularity of today would be gone with tomorrow. He could think of too, too many objections to Yale— and yet, he could not choose Portsmouth. He had asked for advice and it had been given: the united opinion of the ministers of New England expressed in their associations was that the path of duty for Ezra Stiles lay at Yale, that this was God's will.[48]

The ministers based their opinion on their belief that the presidency was a position of greater usefulness to God than the ministry. Only one clergyman, Samuel West of Dartmouth, had ventured a doubt, and he had offered no reasons. The others all agreed that the presidency was the more useful position, because the college prepared youth for the ministry, and because many men were qualified to serve God as pastors, and but few as presidents. Every man, however humble his position, was of course useful to God if he served according to his ability; but to serve in a position below one's ability because one

47. Elizur Goodrich to Stiles, Feb. 12, 1778; *Lit. Diary,* 2, 260–61.

48. *Lit. Diary,* 2, 249, 252, 257, 264, 267–69; Stiles to the Second Congregational Church in Newport, Mar. 19, 1778, Charles Chauncy to Stiles, Feb. 8, 17, 1778.

disliked the burdens of a higher office was undeniably to shirk one's duty. Regardless of what Ezra Stiles thought of himself, all New England considered him abundantly qualified for the higher office. Naturally there were obstacles to Yale—every minister and friend admitted he would have a less happy life as president—but he must shoulder the burden and trust in God to help him bear it.

Stiles had not needed the ministers of New England to tell him all this. It was basic in God's arrangement of the social order. His unwillingness to see it without being told was a confession of modesty and self-distrust rather than of ignorance. What he really wanted was their opinion of the usefulness not of the jobs but of Ezra Stiles. It would be a disservice to God to accept an office he was not fitted for. As for refusing the presidency because of the burdens, he had already taken himself to task for his inclination to do just that. The previous August he had gone through a period of great discontent because the oversight of his large congregation kept him so incessantly busy. This unworthy mood had been checked by a sudden suffusive sentiment: "Why should I repine at a short Life of the most laborious Activity for the Glory of Jesus and the Salvation of precious and immortal Souls. It will soon be over and I shall be at rest—is there not a whole Eternity to rest in? . . . Let me gird up my Loins and devote myself with Zeal chearfulness and Activity to my dear Lords Work." This had taken place before his election to Yale but it occurred to him every time he thought of the laborious office of the presidency. It seemed to him a providential preparation of his mind.[49]

For a man who had avowedly dedicated his life to the service of God, there was really no choice left. In these last few weeks Ezra Stiles was not so much making up his mind as gathering his courage to do what clearly had to be done. Reluctantly, and still wondering whether his own judgment of Ezra Stiles was not better than New England's, still wishing that he could have kept his resolve to become a recluse, he resigned himself to wearing Yale's "crown of thorns." On March 20, after a day of fasting and prayer, in which he again rehearsed all the arguments on both sides, he wrote to the Rev. Eliphalet Williams, the senior fellow: "I do now hereby signify to the Reverend Corporation *My Acceptance of the Presidency of Yale College.*"[50]

49. Birthday Reflexions, 1777.
50. See the manuscript Literary Diary, under March 20, 1778. Dexter, in printing the Diary, omitted five pages in which Stiles recapitulated the arguments.

20

New Haven Again

THE CARRIAGES came for him on the fifth of June. The corporation was anxious to have the new president in New Haven as soon as possible.[1]

Stiles was ready. For the past two months he had been tying up loose ends, the most important being a matter of health insurance. Three days after deciding for Yale, he sent Betsy to Boston to be inoculated against smallpox; and on April 18 for the same purpose he took Isaac, Kezia, Polly, and himself to the hospital on Henzels Island, just out of Portsmouth.[2] He had been hoping that his outbreak of boils, the year before, was smallpox. It was not, for the inoculation took.

Smallpox inoculation was not the simple matter that vaccination is. It involved the injection of live germs into the patient, and the result was a mild case of the disease. No one understood why it was mild when taken in this deliberate manner, but the statistics showed conclusively that it was. Not one in fifty died, as against one in six among those who caught it naturally.[3] (The statistics for newly elected college presidents were not as good: Jonathan Edwards, when elected president of Princeton in 1757 had, like Stiles, been inoculated, and had died of it.)

Stiles broke out in pustules twelve days from the injection, but in

1. *Lit. Diary*, 2, 270–71.
2. Ibid., pp. 265–69.
3. Otho T. Beall, Jr., and Richard H. Shryock, "Cotton Mather: First Significant Figure in American Medicine," Amer. Antiq. Soc., *Proceedings, 63* (1953), 148, 159.

thirteen more days he was well again. During the entire twenty-five days he and the three children had to stay at the hospital, lest they give the disease to others (hence the island location for the hospital, which was used exclusively for smallpox inoculation). When they were ready to leave, Emilia, Ruth, and Newport the slave entered.[4] All came through it successfully, as did Betsy in Boston. Since Ezra, Jr., had been inoculated six years before (on an island off Stonington, Connecticut),[5] the whole family were now immune from the century's most dreaded disease.

The slave was another piece of unfinished business. In the years since Stiles acquired him, ideas about slavery had been changing in America. The colonists, complaining that British taxation would make slaves of them, were embarrassed to find that they themselves had made slaves of other men, and they began to take steps against both slavery and the slave trade.[6] Stiles had bought his own slave without pangs of conscience, seeing no contradiction between his religion and slavery. Indeed one of the pillars of his Newport church, one of the few men who would join in communion, was a "Guinea Captain," Pollipus Hammond. Captain Hammond, who lived an austere, sober life, was noted in Newport for his charity to the poor. He had given up the slave trade some years before his death in 1773, and the new feeling of the times is suggested in Stiles's conjecture that if Hammond "had his Life to live over again, he would not chuse to spend it in buying and selling the human species." [7]

The astonishing thing is that such a man should have been in such a business at all, and it is equally astonishing that Stiles himself still owned a member of the human species in 1778. No doubt Stiles was a good master. No doubt he was much concerned about Newport's soul—Newport was admitted to full communion in 1775.[8] But on Stiles's last Sunday in Portsmouth, when he concluded his pastorship by adding seven new members (all women) to the church, Newport, now about thirty years old, was still a slave. Two days later, on June 9, before climbing into the carriage for New Haven, Stiles liberated

4. *Lit. Diary,* 2, 269.

5. Ibid., *1,* 297, 299, 303–04. He was shipwrecked on the way back.

6. J. Franklin Jameson, *The American Revolution Considered as a Social Movement* (Princeton, 1926), pp. 30–39.

7. *Lit. Diary, 1,* 340–41.

8. Ibid., pp. 521, 525.

him.[9] Thus, as he left his spectator's seat and entered the turbulent secular world, he was unencumbered by a moral burden that had begun to weigh upon him perhaps a little more lightly than it should have.

The journey to New Haven, except for the June heat, was comfortable. The corporation had sent two carriages. One, a covered wagon with four beds, headed south from Portsmouth with four of the children at 10:30 in the morning. The other, "a neat genteel Caravan," suspended on steel springs, followed after with the president and the other three children, Newport staying behind to taste his new freedom. They went first to Boston and Cambridge, where Stiles lodged with Stephen Sewall, the professor of oriental languages, and then headed west by way of Worcester, over roads deeply rutted by the heavy wartime traffic.[10]

It was a leisurely procession, twenty-five or thirty miles a day, cheered by bowls of toddy, milk punch, and flip at taverns along the way, and interrupted by good talk with old friends they happened to pass. At Leicester they saw Jacob Rodriguez Rivera, a merchant from Newport, who sent them on their way with half a dozen bottles of wine; and at East Hartford Stiles discussed Yale with Eliphalet Williams, senior fellow of the corporation.[11] From Hartford to New Haven the scene was familiar: wheat, flax, tobacco, onions (in Wethersfield, it seemed, they grew nothing else), oak trees, mountain laurel, worm fences, black cattle, red earth, red road, red brooks, red dust.[12]

New Haven was familiar too, even to the children, who had often visited there, but it was not the town that Stiles had known before. When he first went to live there in 1742, there had been only one meetinghouse on the green. Now five steeples stood against the sky, one of them rising from Yale's brick chapel (built 1761–63) behind the old wooden "college." This long, barracks-like structure had been all there was of Yale when Stiles was a student. Now its faded blue paint and falling clapboards showed it to be in the last stages of disrepair, and one end of it had in fact been demolished in

9. Ibid., 2, 271–72; Birthday Reflexions, 1778.

10. *Lit. Diary*, 2, 272.

11. Ibid., p. 273.

12. On the scenery between Hartford and New Haven see Samuel Davis, "Journal of a Tour to Connecticut," Mass. Hist. Soc., *Proceedings, 11* (1869–70), 9–32; John Pierce, "Journey to Providence and New Haven, 1795," ibid., 2d ser., *3* (1866–67), 41–52.

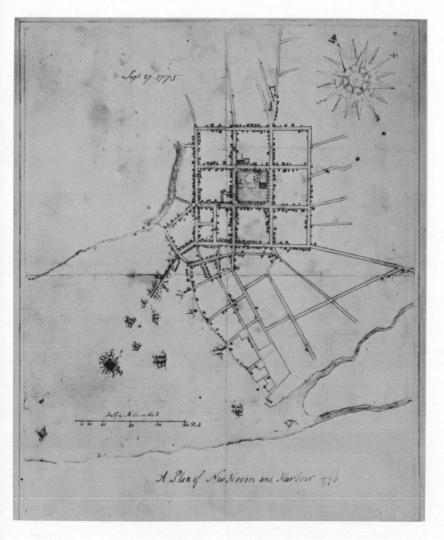

3. New Haven, 1775, by Ezra Stiles.

4. Yale College, 1786, woodcut printed by Daniel Bowen.

1775. Back of it and to the north, next to the chapel, stood a more dignified brick college, built while Stiles was a tutor. The brick college, the chapel, and the shabby remnant of the old college were the Yale of which Stiles was now to take charge.

The public green, on which these buildings fronted, had been transformed from a rough field into a park by 250 buttonwood trees that public-spirited citizens planted round it in 1759.[13] They had placed trees along the streets too, a practice that other towns had not yet taken up, so that New Haven seemed to strangers to have a rural appearance.[14] The impression might have been confirmed by the swine and geese wandering through the streets and by the fact that its merchants still traded in furs and put advertisements in the papers instructing prospective sellers in the proper way to skin fox, mink, otter, bear, and wildcat.[15]

Actually Connecticut was one of the most thickly settled states in the new union, boasting ten towns with a population approaching 5,000 or more.[16] New Haven had over 8,000 in 1778 and was growing fast.[17] It had begun to grow just before Stiles left, and on periodic visits he had recorded the spectacular increase in dwelling houses from 150 in 1750 to 200 in 1758, 328 in 1772, and 370 in 1775.[18] The rapid growth had been accompanied, or perhaps caused, by a revival of commerce. The inhabitants had overcome some of the disadvantages of their shallow harbor by building a wharf at the edge of the deep water and a pier a third of a mile long to reach it.[19] Before the war cut off trade in 1776, they were putting thirty or forty vessels to sea, mostly brigantines and sloops of about ninety tons. Designed for the cattle trade, these ships carried a thousand horses and almost

13. *Itineraries*, *1*, 514; *Itineraries and Miscellanies*, p. 157.

14. Davis, "Journal of a Tour," p. 14; *New Haven Gazette* (Meigs, Bowen, and Dana), Aug. 25, 1785.

15. *Connecticut Journal*, Mar. 3, 1784; *New Haven Gazette* (Meigs, Bowen, and Dana), Jan. 13, 1785. On New Haven at the time of Stiles's return see in general Rollin G. Osterweis, *Three Centuries of New Haven 1638–1938* (New Haven, 1953), pp. 110–13, 157–62.

16. Evarts B. Greene and Virginia D. Harrington, *American Population before the Federal Census of 1790* (New York, 1932), pp. 58–61.

17. Ibid.

18. *Itineraries*, *2*, 414; *3*, 230; *Itineraries and Miscellanies*, pp. 2, 104, 265, 355; *Lit. Diary*, *3*, 15–17.

19. Thomas R. Trowbridge, "The History of Long Wharf in New Haven," New Haven Colony Hist. Soc., *Papers*, *1* (1865), 83–103.

as many oxen annually to the West Indies, usually to St. Christopher, whence the sugar planters from other islands fetched them home to turn the heavy mills that squeezed the juice from their sugar cane.[20] After the juice was boiled down, other vessels carried the molasses back to New England to be turned into rum.

Connecticut was not as heavily engaged in the rum business as the rest of New England, but there were a few distilleries in New Haven now and a brewery, a paper mill, a newspaper (the first was issued in 1755), and shops full of books, textiles, and hardware imported from Europe.[21] The merchants did not trade directly with Europe even before the war, but got their imported goods by way of Boston or New York.[22] Though war had cut off the supply of English goods, full prewar inventories and trade with other parts of Europe enabled the shops still to offer a wide assortment.

New Haven, in short, had grown up and now furnished a more congenial setting for a man of Stiles's tastes than it could have twenty years before. But while the town was growing, a larger transformation had been taking place, not simply in New Haven but in Connecticut and to some degree in the rest of New England. Stiles had seen it from Newport and Portsmouth, but as he settled into the President's house on College Street, he had to confront it as he never had before: as New England grew, it was growing away from the faith of its fathers, from the old Puritanism that he loved, indeed from anything properly called religion at all.

Stiles blamed the ministers. They were not, to be sure, guilty of the grosser forms of clerical negligence. They did not desert their congregations for the bottle or the gaming table or even for the counting-house, but for the study. It was a failing that Stiles could easily understand, but one he had always withstood. He had never allowed the study door to come between him and his people. He might long for the life of a recluse and busy himself with recondite problems that meant nothing to his congregation, but he did not turn his pulpit into a sounding board for his own intellectual idiosyncrasies.

20. Thomas R. Trowbridge, "History of the Ancient Maritime Interests of New Haven," ibid., 3 (1882), 85–204; William Gregory, "Journal," *New England Magazine*, 13 (1895), 343–52; *Connecticut Journal and New Haven Post Boy*, passim, see esp. advertisements in issues of Aug. 5, 1768, Dec. 10, 1773.

21. *Connecticut Journal and New Haven Post Boy*, passim.

22. *Connecticut Courant*, Sept. 10, 1770.

The Connecticut ministers, particularly those attached to the New Divinity, had somehow lost contact with their people.

During the excitement of the Great Awakening the New Light ministers had been able to carry masses with them into new theological territory. The schisms of the 1740s were the result of theological differences, heavily charged with emotion, among the rank and file of the churches. The Second Church of New Haven (known as the White Haven) had split from the First, because of popular dissatisfaction with the easygoing Old Light theology and preaching of Joseph Noyes. When the Third Church split from the Second in 1767, the circumstances were reversed. The Third Church (known as the Fair Haven) was formed of persons who could not stomach the strict New Divinity of a new minister, Jonathan Edwards the younger. While the Second Church had been formed by persons swept up in the enthusiasm of a great religious revival, the Third Church expressed the subsidence of that revival among the people at large and its simultaneous intensification among the clergy.[23] The New Lights had been a God-intoxicated host of enthusiasts, led by ministers who shared and molded their opinions. The New Divinity, on the other hand, as the name suggested, was not a popular movement but a school of thought, a clerical continuation and refinement of the religious impulse that had produced the Awakening, but without any awakening to go with it.

No one can say for sure why the New Divinity failed to win a popular following. Earlier generations of New Englanders had relished the fine points of theological controversy when John Cotton fought with Roger Williams or Increase Mather with Solomon Stoddard. In the 1760s and 1770s when Hopkins and Bellamy and the younger Edwards and dozens of bright young men trumpeted forth their fearless, intransigent, ridiculous brand of Calvinism, the only people who would listen were other bright young men. The New Divinity required a subtle mind and deep religious motivation. Whether because they had spun the thread too fine or because New England had grown dull and secular, these new Savonarolas found themselves in the unhappy position of talking mainly to one another. The New Divinity swept up some of the best students in the colleges, especially at Yale, but it left almost everyone else cold.

The resulting situation was the worst possible one for the survival

23. *Itineraries and Miscellanies,* pp. 276, 311–18; *Lit. Diary, 1,* 117–20.

of Christianity. With a rapidly expanding population and a rising demand for ministers, the total number of students preparing for the ministry had declined; and of those who did prepare, the vast majority, in Connecticut at least, were attached to the New Divinity. (Students who clung to the old ideas tended to enter secular vocations.) When a minister died and his congregation sought to replace him, they often found that they had the choice of a New Divinity man or none. In New Haven County alone by 1786 there were more than a dozen churches with New Divinity pastors, although the congregations, according to Stiles, were "so generally old Divinity that probably not so much as two or 3 persons or Individuals can be found to a Parish who are in the New Theology." [24] In New Haven itself the Second Church grew so sick of the doctrines of Jonathan Edwards the younger that the members gradually drifted away into other churches, until the remaining handful finally voted to dismiss him.[25]

The progressive alienation of pastors from their congregations, of which this was not an isolated example, had no visible effect on the principles of the New Divinity. Its exponents were unwilling to dilute their doctrine for the sake of appeasing the wicked world. They were men of considerable courage and not often gifted with humility. Joseph Bellamy was a good example—brilliant, dogmatic, overbearing, impatient. From his pulpit in the small parish of Bethlehem, he managed to dominate the rest of the clergy in Litchfield County. Stiles observed "his pious, ardent, turbulent and well meant Zeal," and thought that a man of such "Borgian Complexion" would disturb the peace and tranquillity of churches in any age.[26] In North Haven Benjamin Trumbull (who succeeded Isaac Stiles) was of the same temper. In fact, Stiles thought that he even surpassed Bellamy in fieriness.[27] In Hartford similarly no one liked to cross Nathan Strong, a man of rough manners, sloppy dress, quick mind, and sharp tongue.[28] Within their congregations such men often assumed

24. *Lit. Diary*, 3, 247; cf. Stiles to William Williams, Aug. 15, 1793: "none of the Churches in New England are new Divinity, this commodity being monopolized by a Selection but increasing Body of the Clergy."

25. *Lit. Diary*, 3, 344, 438, 562.

26. William B. Sprague, *Annals of the American Pulpit* (New York, 1857–69), *1*, 404–12; *Lit. Diary*, 3, 384–85.

27. *Lit. Diary*, 2, 496 n. The characterization of Trumbull is on one of the pages here noted as missing, since restored through the generosity of Lewis S. Gannett.

28. Sprague, *Annals*, 2, 34–41.

powers to which Stiles thought they had no scriptural claim. Sometimes they exercised the sole determination of a man's qualifications
for membership. Universally they despised the half-way covenant
and would baptize none but converts and their children. Members
of the congregation who did not join in these sentiments were consequently driven to other churches or to the Church of England or still
more likely to no church at all. Even full members sometimes dropped
out, muttering that they would "as soon join with the church of
Rome." [29]

Wherever they went, the disgruntled carried a resentment against
the men who intoned damnation with such assurance, and this feeling
gradually developed into a general resentment against clergymen.
In the late sixties and seventies, for the first time in the history of
Connecticut, anticlericalism became a common and accepted attitude
among a substantial part of the population.

The new feeling found expression first in general impatience with
theological controversy. Connecticut newspapers received letters complaining of the neglect of "practical" divinity and reciting the old
aphorism that "where there is much dispute about *religion*, there is
commonly but a little of the power of it." [30] One critic protested in
verse:

> Would God that all Christ's ministers would cease
> Their paper war, follow the prince of peace,
> Forebear to wrangle with their scribling pens,
> And show the world that christians can be friends.[31]

From here it was a short step to complaints against the clergy on
other grounds. In a dialogue printed in the *Connecticut Courant* in
1773 one of the speakers asks why the clergy have always been so
successful in obtaining power. The answer discloses an attitude that
would have shocked Connecticut a generation earlier: the clergy were
powerful because "they have what Archimedes (the famous Mathematician) desired, which was another world, whereon he might fix
his Machine, and then he said he could do what he pleased with this:

29. The remark was made by Christopher Todd, a departing member of Benjamin
Trumbull's church in 1772. North Haven Manuscripts (Rare Book Room, Yale Univ.
Lib.).
30. *Connecticut Courant*, Oct. 9, 1769, Feb. 11, 1772.
31. Ibid., July 16, 1771.

they take advantage of the Ignorance and Superstition of the People, those two efficaceous and sure Engines of despotic Sway— From which may the good Lord deliver us." [32]

Anticlericalism did not necessarily lead to deism, but it furnished an atmosphere in which deism could grow as it never had before. After Ezra Stiles recovered from his own early bout with infidelity, he mistakenly supposed that his discovery of faith was in the pattern of the time. The age of deism, he concluded, was nearly at an end.[33] By the time he reached Yale again, he knew he was wrong. Deism, in the company of anticlericalism, had grown bolder. Whereas in the 1750s he had felt obliged to hide his mild skepticism, outright deists now spoke their minds publicly and laughed at theological controversy and practical piety alike. In 1773, for example, in the town of Salisbury, Nathaniel Buell, the constable, jailed two strangers for blasphemy when he heard them speaking facetiously about some of the principal doctrines of Christianity. They broke out of Buell's jail, and when he offered a reward for their arrest, publicly thumbed their noses at him by advertising in the newspapers that they did not believe in the divinity of Christ, being anti-Trinitarians, that they considered themselves less blasphemous than many of the Connecticut "pulpit thumpers," and that Buell was "sparingly stocked with intelligence and largely stocked with zeal and superstition" which he had imbibed from his "nurses and ghostly teachers." [34]

It would be wrong to suppose that such extreme sentiments were common in Connecticut at the time when Stiles returned there; but deism was in the ascendant, and the anticlericalism which attended it was rampant. Still worse, because of the part played by Yale in the religious quarrels of the preceding decades, the principal target of both deistic and anticlerical feeling was Yale itself.

At the time Stiles left Yale in 1755, President Clap had already succeeded in antagonizing the most influential men of moderate religious views in Connecticut. While Stiles ministered to the Newport church and fought his way toward religious faith, he had kept in touch with developments at Yale, and watched with horror as Clap drove the college into the ground. By sheer strength of will Clap could dominate those around him, the members of the corporation

32. Apr. 13, 1773.
33. Stiles to Thomas Wright, Dec. 22, 1767.
34. *Connecticut Courant*, Apr. 27, 1773.

for example, and since the corporation filled its own vacancies, he soon had a body of hand-picked yes-men to support him in his folly. Stiles had a taste of his old benefactor's new madness when a Newport Baptist, Henry Collins, offered through Stiles to donate a number of books to the Yale Library. The only condition which Collins imposed was one that no library should be without: all the books, heretical or orthodox, should be available to students. Clap, bent on maintaining orthodoxy by fair means or foul, refused the bequest, and Stiles was left to reflect on the kind of education he would have received at Yale if he had gone there ten years later than he did.[35]

Clap compounded bigotry with needless offensiveness. In 1760 he attempted to deny most of the senior class their degrees because they laid in the traditional supply of rum for commencement.[36] In 1762 he advanced commencement on three weeks' notice, from September to July.[37] Some of the public were sufficiently annoyed by the president and corporation to present a memorial to the Assembly in 1763, demanding that the government supervise the running of the college. Though the memorial was ably argued by two lawyers, Jared Ingersoll and William Samuel Johnson, Clap went to the Assembly and with his usual forcefulness talked his opponents out of court.[38] It was another of the pyrrhic victories he had been winning ever since he took the president's chair. By 1766 he had lost all his tutors and most of his students, and those who were left petitioned the corporation for his removal. Because he was a tired and dying man and not because he thought he had been wrong, he let them have their way and resigned.

It was at this time that Stiles was first asked to consider the presidency and refused.[39] Though he did not then wish to take charge of the college, he remained fiercely loyal to it and in some measure to the memory of Clap, who had befriended him as a young man and kept him as tutor in spite of his flirtation with deism. For all his faults Clap had been a man to reckon with. He had kept the college going and had even built a college chapel, in spite of the Assembly's with-

35. Dexter, *Biographical Sketches*, 2, 565–66; Stiles to Clap, Aug. 6, 1759, Apr. 16, 1760; Stiles to Jared Eliot, Sept. 24, 1759.
36. Chauncy Whittelsey to Stiles, Sept. 15, 1760.
37. Ibid., July 23, 1762; note dated July 21, 1762.
38. Morgan and Morgan, *Stamp Act Crisis*, pp. 227–28.
39. John Devotion to Stiles, July 7, 1766.

drawal of funds. When he died shortly after his resignation, Stiles composed an obituary, which he called "The Literary Character of President Clap," dealing only with his erudition, because, Stiles said privately, "I have not the same idea and opinion of the wisdom of his *Conduct,* as I have of his *Learning*." When his New Haven friends, who had been obliged to live with Clap for twenty-five years, demurred from his charitable reflections, Stiles replied, "I thank God, I can honor merit, when I can distinguish it even amidst Demerit, whether in a political or real New Light, an Episcopalian, or a Roman catholic." [40]

Stiles's defense of Clap was partly loyalty to a former friend, partly tolerance, but more than either of these it was loyalty to Yale. Every blow at Clap was a blow at Yale, and Yale needed the support of all her friends. By the spring of 1767 there were only fifty students left, and the reputation of the college outside Connecticut as well as inside had reached a new low. Stiles thought the blame did not lie entirely with the administration and wrote bitterly to his wife's nephew, Stephen Hubbard:

> Formerly the Complaint was on the subject of its orthodoxy. Those who 15 years ago were for building up Jersey College alledged that Yale College was *not orthodox:*—but now that she is orthodox, it is by the Western Gentlemen and their New England Connexions asserted that she is contemptible as to *Learning*. And if she was to become as eminent for Learning, as she is for soundness in the Faith, she might be found to fail as to *Government* or something else;—till she should be transferred into certain European Hands, when she would instantly be pronounced a College of the first Eminence for *Religion* and *Learning* in America.[41]

The last clause was a reference to the sudden boost in reputation which the college of New Jersey had just achieved by calling a Scot, John Witherspoon, to the presidency.

With Naphtali Daggett's assumption of the presidential duties, Yale's reputation began slowly to recover. Lacking Clap's proclivity

40. Stiles to Chauncy Whittelsey, Jan. 20, 1767, July 28, 1767; to Naphtali Daggett, July 28, 1767; from John Hubbard, Mar. 21, 1767.
41. Stiles to Stephen Hubbard, June 15, 1767.

for making enemies, he managed during his first years in office to win the support not only of the students but also of the Assembly, which contributed regularly though not largely to the college from 1767 to 1774.[42] By this time, however, the tide of anticlericalism had set in, and Yale with a corporation composed entirely of clergymen stood obviously in its path. Furthermore, in spite of Daggett's own comparative moderation and the election to the corporation of a number of other moderates, the young ministers turned out by the college almost all embraced the New Divinity. As these young pundits elevated themselves into the rarefied air of theological controversy, they earned for Yale as well as for themselves a widespread popular dissatisfaction. This combined with the heritage of disgust that Clap had bequeathed resulted in a revival, with variations, of the old demand that something be done about the college. Though only a minority of its graduates entered the ministry, it was said that Yale was oriented too exclusively toward that profession. Consequently, many of the boys who went there returned "rather unfitted than fitted for business." Yale should be shaken up and reconstituted to meet the new demands of the age.[43]

A promising step was taken in this direction in 1770 when the corporation, with the financial help of the Assembly, instituted a professorship of mathematics and natural philosophy. A contributor to the *Connecticut Courant* hailed the change, because a knowledge of these subjects would help "dissipate superstitions, chimeras, and old women's fables, which are the natural attendants of ignorance, and the offspring of overheated imaginations." [44] And to combat the plague of quack doctors and the want of trained physicians in Connecticut the writer urged the appointment of "a professor of physic, who should reside at our college, and read daily lectures upon chymistry, botany, etc." [45]

With the continued assistance of the Assembly this innovation might have been achieved, but the anticlerical element was strong enough to prevent the Assembly from sinking more money in an institution run by clergymen. The newspapers revived the old campaign to give

---

42. Dexter, *Biographical Sketches*, 3, 207–08, 263, 302, 365, 399, 466, 513.
43. *Connecticut Courant*, Sept. 3, 1771.
44. Ibid. Apr. 16, 1771.
45. Ibid.

the Assembly a hand in the government of the college. Once again Yale was attacked on all fronts: the food was bad, the discipline too severe, the finances mismanaged.[46]

While belaboring clerical control, the critics of the college discovered a new grievance. The instructors, it seemed, were making reforms in the curriculum but of the wrong kind. As early as 1767 several of the tutors began to introduce students to English grammar and English oratory, not in place of Latin but in addition to it. In 1771 two aspiring poets, Timothy Dwight and John Trumbull, were made tutors, and a lively interest in belles lettres developed in the college. Student societies began to produce plays, both comedies and tragedies, and the impression arose that the students were neglecting solid learning for these frivolous diversions, and had "turn'd College . . . into Drury Lane." [47]

This was not at all the sort of thing that the critics had wished for when they attacked the narrowness of the curriculum, and the development strengthened their conviction that the college needed "regulating." What they wanted was what the public has always wanted from the liberal arts college, something more practical. Though they did not wish their sons trained as ministers, neither did they want them turned into fops. Not belles lettres but something like medicine or law was what the boys needed. It was the old demand, though newer then, that the college be a vocational school. In a way the corporation had brought the demand on itself by its insistence, especially under Clap, that the object of Yale was to supply the churches with ministers.[48] As the ministry ceased to be the only learned profession in New England, it was natural that law and medicine should demand a place in Yale. But the proper function of the college was not to produce ministers or doctors or lawyers, but educated men. The clergymen who made up the corporation had some sense of this, more than President Clap had had, in his later years at least, and far more than the public at large would ever have. Even by their own standards the Yale curriculum needed broadening, but they felt that the broadening should come under their direction, for

46. Ibid., June 4, 18, Aug. 13, 1771.

47. *Lit. Diary*, 2, 230.

48. Thomas Clap, *The Religious Constitution of Colleges* (New London, 1754), pp. 1, 7–8; Clap, *Annals or History of Yale*, pp. 1–3, 84; Shipton, *Harvard Graduates*, 7, 33.

they believed, and not without reason, that they had a purer devotion to truth for its own sake than any group of politicians could claim.

The corporation therefore resisted the pressure to give the Assembly an equal share in the government of the college, and in the absence of funds did nothing to expand the curriculum. But they did bow to the suggestion that Ezra Stiles be made president, and under the circumstances Stiles was a peculiarly happy choice, not merely because he commanded the respect of both public and clergy but also because the problems of Yale in Connecticut paralleled the problem he had wrestled with for many years: to live the life of the mind and the spirit in a political and pragmatic world. Actually the problem had larger dimensions than anyone could have realized at the time. Connecticut was witnessing, somewhat earlier than the rest of America, the opening of a breach that has troubled American civilization ever since, the alienation of the intellectual from the community. The anticlericalism of the 1770s was an early brand of American anti-intellectualism, and the New Divinity preachers were forerunners of later American intellectuals who ignored or defied their countrymen from an ivied tower, a woodland shack, or the left bank of the Seine.

Ezra Stiles knew as well as anyone that the intellectual in any country must keep much to himself, for thought shrivels in public. But he also knew that the intellectual owes responsibilities to the world. He had tried to ignore the fact, but when asked to run Yale College, he had not been able to refuse. No more could Yale turn her back on the needs of Connecticut. The breach that had grown between Yale and the people of Connecticut troubled him. He thought that the fault did not lie entirely with the college, and he was sure that the answer did not lie in capitulating to every demand of the public. The intellectual could not fulfill his responsibilities by ceasing to be intellectual, nor the college by becoming a trade school. Yet the needs of the world could not be ignored, and before he admitted that he was going to accept the presidency, he wrote out his plans for making Yale into a university that the people of Connecticut would cherish.[49]

He was at his best in making plans. He never enjoyed himself more than when he was drafting the family constitutions or the by-laws of his projected learned societies. But the plans he made now were

49. Stiles to Eliphalet Williams, Dec. 3, 1777. Quotations in the paragraphs following, except where noted, are from this letter.

not for an ideal university in an arcadian future. He planned for Yale in the state of Connecticut in the year 1777.

Connecticut needed doctors. Everyone said so, and Stiles agreed. Let there be a professor of physic at Yale and let him offer three series of lectures (one series per year), on anatomy, on the materia medica, and on what would now be called pathology. In addition to his regular undergraduate work a student would follow these lectures and emerge with a bachelor's degree in physic. In order to qualify as a doctor he would attach himself to a physician for further instruction, attend another course of clinical lectures, and by observation and study earn a graduate degree. If Yale could furnish candidates with this kind of training, they would quickly run the quacks out of business and win the gratitude of the public.

Connecticut needed good lawyers as much as it needed good doctors. This was plain to the lawyers and statesmen, who knew what legal training meant, but less so to the public, which always tends to look on lawyers as the authors of the misfortunes they attend. Stiles therefore took pains to explain why Yale should have a professor of law, not to make lawyers but to make good citizens—"civilians" he called them—who could guide the state in the stormy years ahead.

Most graduates of Yale, Stiles explained, did not enter any profession but returned home to "mix in with the Body of the public, and enter upon *Commerce,* or the *Cultivation of their Estates.*" These men, in Stiles's plan, held the key to the public welfare. For most of them, in the course of their lives, were summoned to public office as selectmen, justices of the peace, members of the legislature, judges of courts, and delegates to Congress. A professor of law at Yale should offer instruction with such men in view, and Stiles described a course designed to make civilians of maximum usefulness to the state. They should study the elements of civil and common law, parts of which would undoubtedly continue to operate in independent America, but they should also study the laws and governments of the thirteen states, especially Connecticut, and of the various states of Europe and Asia, including China.

The advantage of public leaders instructed in these matters was obvious, but Stiles emphasized that the advantage would go far beyond the individuals concerned. "This Knowledge," he argued, "is catching, propagates to all around and transfuses itself thro' the public." The thought had appealed to him ever since he became enamored of learning. While a tutor at Yale he had conceived a scheme of adult education, in which college graduates would direct little cells of earnest workingmen in the study of natural philosophy. Not everyone could afford a college education, nor was everyone capable of profiting from one. Most men, inevitably, had to do the work of the world with their hands, but there was plenty of time, especially in the long winter evenings, when they would not be working anyhow. Instead of diverting themselves in the dubious joys of the local tavern, they might gather in groups of a dozen or more under the direction of a local Yale man and pass the time "in the most agreeable Philosophic Discourses, Lectures, Conversations and Amusement." [50] If the proposal exhibited a young tutor's naive conception of the tastes of workingmen, it also represented an early concern for bridging the gap between college and community, the problem still before him.

In 1777 Stiles believed that even without formal organization the diffusion of knowledge took place. Many Americans in Connecticut and elsewhere had successfully educated themselves "without the usual helps and while immersed in laborious secular Employments." Stiles thought, perhaps gratuitously, that the abundance of such men was owing to the intellectual contagion of college educated men. The colleges, he said, had spread the seeds of knowledge that made possible the conduct of American affairs "with that Wisdom Magnanimity and Glory, which already astonishes Europe, and will honor us to the whole World and to the latest Posterity." But the process had only begun. The future, he hoped, would see "the Wisdom of all Countries and Ages" transplanted to America with the colleges playing an even larger role in the independent nation than they had in the colonies. This might be possible if "the several States may perhaps see the Expediency of establishing and endowing Professorships of Law in the american Universities. . . . Remembering that it is scarcely possible to enslave a Republic where the Body of the People are Civilians, well instructed in their Laws, Rights and Liberties."

It was a noble appeal, transforming a public demand for vocational training into a program of liberal education for free men. And it did not stop there. Stiles planned mainly with an eye to the needs of the state, but he did not forget the needs of the college. Yale needed more than a professor of law and a professor of physic. In order to make the college into a university, Stiles proposed a total of eight professor-

50. Notes dated May 25, 1750, Stiles Papers, Mass. Hist. Soc.

ships. Besides those already established in divinity and natural philos-ophy and the new ones in law and physic, there should be chairs in ecclesiastical history (which he would fill himself), civil history (he hoped Catharine Macaulay would contribute funds), Hebrew and oriental languages, and oratory and belles lettres.

Stiles was content that law and physic should come first because most needed by Connecticut; and he was eager that the endowment for them, or at least part of it, should come from the state, not simply because the state was the most likely source of the large sums necessary, but in order to give the public once more a sense of participation in the college. "It is much to be desired," he wrote, "in order to cement a Seat of Learning with the public, that some at least of the principal Foundations should be instituted by the *State*, tho' not to the Exclusion of *personal Foundations* and Endowments by those whom God may have blessed with Riches and a Heart to dispose thereof for the good of Mankind."

Stiles carefully skirted the vexed question of clerical control, but he clearly did not want the college to become the creature of the state. Though he probably would have been pleased to see the state share in the appointments to any professorships it helped to endow, he thought it would be disastrous for the existing corporation to abdicate exclusive control in appointing tutors and the professor of divinity. What he wanted, in short, was a private or semiprivate university that recognized its public responsibilities. Once Yale met its responsibilities, the outcry against clerical control would cease. He sent his plan to Eliphalet Williams on December 3, 1777, and hoped for the best.

Before he accepted the presidency he knew the worst: the rift be-tween Assembly and corporation had proved too wide to bridge, even though both professed admiration for his scheme. He arrived in New Haven, therefore, knowing that he would have to serve Yale and serve Connecticut without the cooperation he had hoped for. His plan would have to be shelved, temporarily he hoped, but the aims that directed it would still guide him.

2 I

Wartime President

YALE was founded as a rival to Harvard and has played the role in one way or another ever since. It has always had to do so on a comparatively small budget, but when Stiles took charge in 1778, Yale's financial resources were so much smaller than Harvard's that he sometimes looked wistfully, though with a kind of poor man's pride, at the difference. Yale's income from sources other than charges to the students in 1778 amounted to roughly £236 Lawful Money. Of this sum, £160 came from the rent of lands owned by the college and £76 from the interest on £1,230 (obtained from the sale of lands and from legacies left to the college) which had been invested in 1777 in a loan to the United States government.[1]

Harvard, when Stiles consulted the librarian about it in 1774, could count on £900 a year from the interest on £15,000 worth of bonds, £100 from the Charlestown Ferry, to which Harvard held the charter, perhaps another £100 from rent of lands and other miscellaneous funds, plus an annual grant of £450 from the Massachusetts legislature. Thus in the years just prior to the Revolutionary War Harvard's annual income, exclusive of charges to students, was about £1,550 Lawful Money, more than six times that of Yale.[2] By 1778 Harvard's income had been sharply reduced by depreciation of the Continental securities in which most of the capital was invested.[3] But the Harvard

1. Itineraries, 5, 108–09; *Lit. Diary*, 2, 232; 3, 426–27.
2. *Lit. Diary*, 1, 468; cf. *Itineraries and Miscellanies*, pp. 382–83.
3. Quincy, *History of Harvard*, 2, 238–40.

salary scale remained much higher than Yale's. Yale tutors got £70 as against £100 at Harvard; the Yale professor of divinity got £90, Harvard's £150; the Yale professor of mathematics and natural philosophy £70, Harvard's £200; Yale's president £160, Harvard's £260. Yale needed £530 a year for salaries and something for the maintenance of its dilapidated old buildings. With the Assembly unwilling to contribute (unless granted an equal share in management of the college), Yale could balance her budget only by charges to students.[4]

This dependence on student fees was nothing new, and it offered a healthy challenge to the administration. It should, in fact, have helped to keep Yale in touch with the needs and demands of the community. In the past, however, it had not done so. President Clap, quite apart from his religious and political offenses, had antagonized parents by obtaining a substantial revenue through fines levied on the students. Though he kept tuition charges low, he fined the students for every infringement of college regulations, and the parents had to foot the bills, which varied according to their son's behavior and the president's temper.[5]

Daggett abandoned this practice. Though the college laws continued to prescribe fines as punishments, the accounts for Daggett's administration show that he collected only trifling amounts in fines and thus removed the grounds for this grievance.

4. *Lit. Diary*, 2, 232; *Itineraries and Miscellanies*, pp. 382–83.
5. The records of quarter bills (Yale Univ. Lib.) show that tuition was 8s. 8d. from 1759 to 1762, 10s. from 1762 to 1764, and 12s. from 1764 to 1777, when it became 20s. The income of the college from fines imposed as punishments and collected in the regular quarter bills was as follows during the last ten years of Clap's administration:

	£	s.	d.		£	s.	d.
1756–57:	73	17	7	1762–63:	20	12	8
1757–58:	53	3	1	1763–64:	27	14	0
1758–59:	34	1	8	1764–65:	17	17	7
1759–60:	35	15	4	1765–66			
1760–61:	31	12	1	(through			
1761–62:	31	11	6	June):	8	15	8

In 1766 the Assembly made a grant of £160 to the college, accompanied with a recommendation that the number of fines be reduced. After 1766 scarcely any income from fines was recorded.

The fact remained, however, that the college could not operate without a substantial revenue from the students, and any manner of extracting it was likely to prove painful. The cost of going to college at this time probably amounted for most students to between £25 and £35 Lawful Money a year,[6] a sum equal to about one-third of the salary Stiles had earned at Newport and a fifth or a sixth of his salary as president. Though Stiles noted that it was no more than the price of a yoke of oxen,[7] few men had that price to offer every year for four years running; for Yale was not only poor itself, it was a poor man's college. Student letters to parents in any century have consisted usually of appeals for money, but the letters of Yale students in the eighteenth century plead desperately for small amounts to buy basic necessities, as when a boy is afraid his breeches will wear through before vacation.[8]

The chief expense of four years at college was not tuition but the cost of living. Insofar as there was room, students were expected to eat and sleep in college. They were charged only six shillings a year for their rooms, but board usually ranged from six to eight shillings a week, depending on the price of commodities. The college did everything possible to keep these charges low. The corporation appointed a steward, whose job was to furnish food in "commons," and collect the bills for this and other college charges. His only compensation was what he made on the meals, but the corporation fixed the amount he was allowed to ask, and the rate was usually below that charged by private families in town.

Even so, board was the principal item, usually about three-fourths of the total, in the bills a student had to pay. Tuition had been set at £1 a quarter (£4 a year) in 1777, but board might cost anywhere from £12 to £20 a year. In order to save money, students would frequently linger at home for a week or two after vacations—they were not charged for the period of their absence—and they were always seeking permission to board in town, with the hope that they could somehow eat cheaper and better than in commons.[9]

6. Stiles to Peter Thacher, Feb. 26, 1785; cf. account book of John May (Yale Univ. Lib.), whose expenses at college 1773–77 totaled £112 13s. 4d.

7. Lit. Diary, 2, 411.

8. Jedidiah Morse to his father, Mar. 9, 1781, Morse Papers, Yale Univ. Lib.

9. It was not unusual for 20 per cent of the student body to be absent for one reason or another. Usually the number present reached a maximum in December. In

Fortunately for Yale it cost as much to live in Cambridge as in New Haven, and in spite of her wealth Harvard collected as much from her students in other charges as Yale did, sometimes more.[10] Since Harvard offered no financial advantage to students, and since, moreover, it was known to be a hot-bed of Arminian and other iniquities, most Connecticut boys who went to college at all went to Yale. For seventy-seven years Connecticut farmers, lawyers, merchants, and ministers had sent enough of their sons there to support the college.

When Stiles arrived, 132 were enrolled,[11] enough in normal times to make Yale a going concern, with or without help from the Assembly. But Stiles was not faced with normal times: no previous president, with the exception of Daggett in the preceding two years, had been obliged to run the institution during a revolutionary war.

Stiles had long ago identified the Revolution as the great event of his century. It would change everything—for the better he thought —but he could not foresee exactly how it would affect either himself or Yale. Other things being equal, one might expect it to reduce enrollment: men would be off fighting the British instead of studying Latin and logic. But the Revolution occupied a smaller proportion of the country's manpower than any other major war in our history; and the Connecticut Assembly, for all its hostility to Yale, recognized the need for educated men and exempted all students in college from militia duty. Even graduates who had not yet taken their master's degrees regarded themselves as students and claimed exemption.[12] At the same time the Continental armies, like all armies, consumed enormous quantities of provisions and sent prices of foodstuffs soaring. The farmers who grew the food found themselves suddenly prosperous and better able to send their sons to college. As a result, Stiles never needed to worry about enrollments, which held up and even increased during the war.

1781–82, for example, when 223 students were enrolled, the maximum number present at one time was 207 on December 1. Thereafter the maximum was 194 on March 5.

10. *Itineraries and Miscellanies*, pp. 384–85; *Lit. Diary*, 3, 283.

11. Stiles recorded the numbers, along with other statistics and events, in a separate journal, which he entitled "Memoranda: Yale College."

12. Charles J. Hoadly, ed., *The Public Records of the State of Connecticut from October, 1776, to February, 1778* (Hartford, 1894), p. 92; Wetmore and Meigs to Noah Webster, Aug. 20, 1779, Webster Correspondence, N.Y. Public Lib.; *Itineraries and Miscellanies*, pp. 485–86; *Lit. Diary*, 2, 458, 564.

Not all the effects of war were so beneficial to the college. There was, after all, an enemy, and New Haven was invitingly close to his New York headquarters. The students had been dispersed to inland towns in 1777, partly for fear that the British might think it worth while to raid New Haven and capture such a conveniently assembled group of the state's future leaders. The freshmen went to Farmington under Tutor John Lewis, the sophomores and juniors to Glastonbury under Professor Nehemiah Strong, and the seniors to Wethersfield under Tutor Timothy Dwight. But it seemed unhealthy for the institution and disrespectful to a new president to keep it long in this scattered condition, and so the students reassembled in the summer of 1778. The danger had not diminished, however, and everyone was nervous about a possible British raid.

Another reason for dispersing the college in 1777 had been a food shortage in New Haven. After the corporation decided to summon the students back, it advertised in the newspapers urging parents and other friends of the college to sell provisions for commons to the steward, Jeremiah Atwater.[13] But the scarcity continued during the next two years and posed a more immediate threat to the college than the British armies did.

Still another difficulty arose from the wild fluctuation of American currency. The state of Connecticut could not pay for its share of the war out of current taxes, and the Continental Congress had no power to tax at all. Both paid their creditors with paper money, which rapidly depreciated in value. Prices, which were rising even in terms of hard money, ascended fantastically in paper. In September 1778 Continental money was accepted in New Haven at about ¼ of its face value; in April 1779, at ½₂; in June, ½₅; July, ½₈; December, ½₀. It held briefly in January 1780, as a result of a foreign loan to the United States, but by May 1781 it was offered at the rate of a hundred to one.[14]

Conducting business with so variable a means of exchange was difficult, but Americans had had experience in dealing with the problem before. Stiles had his Newport salary stated in silver so as to avoid the effects of inflation. In his agreement with the Yale corporation he devised a formula that insured him against both the rise in prices induced by scarcity and that resulting from the flood of paper money.

13. *Connecticut Journal*, May 13, 27, 1778; *Connecticut Courant*, June 2, 1778.
14. *Lit. Diary*, 2, 301, 328, 346, 350, 396, 401, 532.

His salary of £160 was to be reckoned, one quarter "in wheat at four Shillings and six Pence per Bushell, one quarter in Indian Corn at two Shillings and three Pence per Bushell, one quarter in Pork at twenty four Shillings per Hundred weight, and the other Quarter in Beef at eighteen Shillings per Hundred Weight, or an Equivalent in Money, to be determined annually by the President and Fellows according to the current Prices in New Haven, viz. of Pork and Beef in December, and of Wheat and Indian corn in January." [15]

This formula did not mean that Stiles was actually paid in commodities but that he was paid a sum sufficient to buy the commodities at the prices named. If he were paid in silver, and the market price of the commodities in silver were twice the price named, he would get £320 instead of £160. If paid in Continental money, and the price in Continental money were a hundred times the prices named, he would get £16,000 in Continental money. Although his salary was paid from time to time during the year, as funds became available, the account was not settled nor the exact amount determined until after each year was up. Stiles thus avoided any loss either from the depreciation of paper money or from an actual rise in commodity prices as stated in silver.

The corporation at first did not attempt to apply this formula to their other transactions. They tried, for example, to state tuition in terms of Continental money, setting it as £3 12s. per quarter in September 1778, at £6 in December, and at £10 10s. in March 1779.[16] But depreciation was so rapid that this method produced huge losses. Harvard had the same difficulties. President Langdon complained to Stiles that his and the professors' salaries were paid "at much less than their proper value." The Harvard steward, who, unlike the Yale one, was paid a fixed salary and furnished meals at cost, found that the amount received in one quarter was not enough to buy half the provisions needed for the next.[17] At Yale, Stiles finally overcame the money problem by having tuition set in terms of silver at one pound a quarter (where it remained throughout his presidency) and by having a committee of the corporation fix the price of commons every month in accordance with the formula established for his salary. This

15. Corporation Records, Nov. 4, 1777.

16. Records of Quarter Bills.

17. Samuel Langdon to Stiles, June 8, 1779, June 26, 1780; Quincy, *History of Harvard*, 2, 243.

took care of the real rise in prices; the rise resulting from paper money was met by requiring payment of quarter bills either in hard money or in provisions.[18]

These measures ultimately subdued most of Yale's wartime financial problems. But there were times when provisions were unavailable at any price. During the summer of 1778, partly as a result of the appeal to farming parents, partly perhaps because of a state embargo, the steward was able to keep commons going. In September, Atwater made another appeal to parents, but by December 28 the cupboard was bare, and Stiles had to send the students home more than two weeks before the winter vacation was supposed to begin.[19]

Five days before vacation was to end, bread and flour were still so scarce that the holiday had to be prolonged for another two weeks. Stiles notified the students in a public advertisement, in which he also read a testy little lecture to their parents, pointing out to them that they were probably better able to afford a college education at this than at any other time, that "it is only a delusion that scholars can study nearly as well at home as at college," that the boys would not get their degrees without spending their full time at college, and unless the parents furnished provisions, it would be impossible to keep the place open.[20] This apparently had the desired effect: provisions appeared, the boys returned, commons opened, and college was going full blast the following July when the war finally reached New Haven.

July 4, 1779, was Sunday. In the college church Professor Daggett admitted a new member and administered communion while the president and students sweltered in the summer heat (Stiles's thermometer registered 84). Stiles gave the prayer and the blessing, and the boys trooped out to await the conclusion of the New England Sabbath before beginning the celebration of American independence. At ten o'clock that evening word reached New Haven that a large British fleet had been sighted off Westfield (Bridgeport), fifteen miles away. Stiles urged the militia officers to call out their men. Cooler heads said wait.[21]

18. *Lit. Diary*, 2, 332; *Connecticut Journal*, May 11, 1779; Lynde Lord to Stiles, Dec. 18, 1780; Stiles to Lynde Lord, Dec. 22, 1780; Corporation Records, Sept. 13, 1780.

19. *Connecticut Journal*, Sept. 30, 1778; *Lit. Diary*, 2, 315–16.

20. *Connecticut Journal*, Feb. 3, 1779; *Connecticut Courant*, Feb. 9, 1779.

21. The following account is based on *Lit. Diary*, 2, 351–62; Chauncey Goodrich,

At two o'clock in the morning the alarm guns were heard. A watchman had discovered the fleet, some forty vessels, the largest ever seen in Long Island Sound, anchored off West Haven. This time bells rang and drums beat as sleepy militiamen poured from their houses. But most of the women and older men, consulting with one another in the dark streets, concluded that so large a force could not be intended for New Haven—what would be the point? Only a few prepared for the worst. Stiles, who could not afford to take chances, assembled the students and told them college was dismissed until further notice. He then packed up the college records and his own valuable manuscripts, including his precious diary, ready to take flight if necessary.

Dawn found him at the top of the college steeple, his eye to a telescope. As the light came up, he could make out twenty square-rigged ships and about the same number of smaller vessels. It was high tide, and they would have no trouble sending men ashore if they chose to. As the sun began to hit the rigging, Stiles saw boats push off for the beach at Savin Rock.

As the word went round, the streets filled with men running to meet the enemy or to get away from him. Housewives hid silver and jewels up the chimney, buried them in the garden, thrust them into the cracks of stone walls. Anyone who owned a wagon loaded it with furniture and headed northward. Stiles sent his daughters off on foot in the direction of Mt. Carmel and gave his records and papers to Isaac, about to turn sixteen, who carried them to some unnamed place of safekeeping three miles out of town. Stiles sent a horseload of clothes in another direction, and when Isaac returned told him to overtake the girls with a carriage. Before he succeeded in doing so, according to one story, two of them had been given rides behind the saddles of friends who picked them up, dusty and footsore, on the road to Cheshire. As the sun rose higher, Ezra Jr. rode off to the west, in command of a group of mounted students and volunteers, to meet the enemy. Stiles himself followed Isaac and the girls out of town. Professor Daggett, on the other hand, seized a long fowling piece, mounted his old black mare, and galloped off after the volunteers.

Besides about 2,000 sailors, the British troops were estimated at

"Invasion of New Haven by the British Troops, July 5, 1779," New Haven Colony Hist. Soc., *Papers*, 2 (1877), 31–92; and Charles H. Townshend, *The British Invasion of New Haven, Connecticut* (New Haven, 1879).

2,500 or 3,000 men, though Stiles thought that 2,000 might be closer. Even 2,000 was a large number, greater than the total of able-bodied men in New Haven and its suburbs. About a thousand landed at Savin Rock on the west side of the harbor, and a few hours later another thousand came ashore at Five Mile Point on the east side.

On the west side militia and volunteers to the number of three or four hundred, including many students, prevented the enemy from crossing West River by the West Bridge, forcing him to detour to the north by way of the Derby Bridge and thus gaining a little time for the women and older inhabitants of the town to get themselves and their possessions out of the way. Though there was a great deal of firing from the time the boats approached the beach until the troops reached New Haven, the outnumbered militia could not hope for more than a delaying action. The most spectacular role was that played by Professor Daggett. He took up a position on the far side of West Bridge, and neglecting to retreat when the others did, found himself face-to-face with the main body of British troops. He blazed away at them from the bushes, until a detachment was sent to take the "damned old rebel." Asked why he fired on the king's troops, Daggett replied, "Because it is the exercise of war." At this, one of the soldiers thrust at him with a bayonet. Daggett sprang in close and pushed the weapon aside, but the soldiers gave him several blows on the skull and body with bayonets and musket barrels. Worse than this, they made him march in front of the column barefooted and bareheaded into New Haven. Daggett was fifty-one years old, and it was the hottest day anyone in New Haven could remember. Whenever he paused they kicked him and pricked him. By the time they reached the green a little before one o'clock he was nearly dead. He never fully recovered.

The troops approaching from the other side met with stiffer resistance, and the main body of the eastern column did not get beyond East Haven, though the commander, General William Tryon, crossed over to town and held a council of war with the other officers.

From the time the troops reached New Haven until about eight in the evening the soldiers indulged in "Plunder, Rape, Murder, Bayoneting, Indelicacies toward the Sex, Insolence and Abuse and Insult towards the Inhabitants in general." Apparently a substantial number of the inhabitants had remained in the town, most of whom lived to tell their grandchildren of necklaces ripped off, furniture smashed, and drunken soldiers who would as soon kill you as not. Fortunately, when thirty-eight boats appeared on the shore, loaded with sailors to join the orgy, the generals ordered them back, lest they be caught on the flats at low tide. At night the troops camped on the green, many of them too drunk to stir. They left the next day, some by way of East Haven, others directly from Long Wharf, harassed again by militia and volunteers.

Ezra Jr. fought them on both days. On Monday afternoon, after the group proceeding by the western route had entered town, he evidently took his volunteers to the east. Here he got himself ambushed and narrowly escaped. As he told it later to David McClure, "a number of students under my command fought with intrepidity that reflects the immortal honor upon them and eternal disgrace to near 300 Militia who remained idle tho terrified spectators at some distance from us affording us no assistance, tho we engaged four times our number and took as many Prisoners as there were collegians with me tho' I had a considerable party of young lads of the Town Volunteers under me." [22]

By Tuesday evening the whole thing was over. The shops and vessels at Long Wharf had been burnt and so had several houses on the east side of the harbor. A great deal of furniture had been destroyed. But the total casualties were not large: 27 Americans dead and 19 wounded, and (according to Tryon's official report) 10 British dead and 49 wounded. The British did not burn the town, as at one point they seem to have intended, nor were the atrocities as great as they might have been. When Stiles rode in on the heels of the British departure, he found the college buildings, including his own house, intact except for one mirror. They had perhaps been spared by the intercession of Tories loyal to Yale as well as to the king (Tryon's son-in-law, Edmund Fanning, who commanded one British regiment, was Yale 1757).

It is difficult to see precisely what the British hoped to accomplish by the raid. Their orders suggest that it was part of a larger plan, possibly a diversionary action. They may have hoped to capture provisions, but if so they came to the wrong place. There certainly was no intention of holding the town, nor does there seem to have been any idea of debilitating future New England leadership by capturing a crop of Yale men. Though the British carried away a few prisoners,

22. Ezra Stiles, Jr., to David McClure, Aug. 24, 1779.

none held high rank either civil or military, and no Yale students were among them. Professor Daggett they evidently considered not worth taking with them. But someone did take, from Mrs. David Wooster's house, a trunkful of papers written by her father, President Clap. When Stiles tried to get them back, Tryon professed ignorance, and Stiles discovered that a few of the papers had been picked up in Long Island Sound.[23] Whoever took them evidently concluded that they were valueless and dumped them overboard, thus creating serious problems for future historians of the college but for no one else. Many Yale men doubtless wished that everything Clap had done could be as easily jettisoned.

But if the raid served no important military purpose, it did complicate the job of a rebel college president. After they left New Haven, the British continued to jab at other Connecticut towns, and no one knew when they might return. On the Sunday following the raid, before most of the inhabitants had yet returned to town, Stiles was preaching to a small combined congregation of the First and Second Churches when news of a landing at Norwalk emptied the meetinghouse and sent people packing for the interior again. Stiles did not think it safe to bring back his papers until August 10, and did not call his children home or reassemble the college until October, though he held a private commencement to give the seniors their degrees on September 8. The children meanwhile lived with friends and relatives at Hartford, Cheshire, Meriden, and North Haven. Stiles boarded with his neighbor Isaac Beers and also visited Rhode Island.[24]

When college reopened in October, the same old problem of provisions continued, and on December 16 Stiles had to dismiss the students once again, though he continued until the regular beginning of winter vacation (on January 10, 1780) to hold classes for about forty boys who succeeded in finding board in the town. That winter was the worst since 1740–41. In January temperatures dove below zero and the snow lay four and a half feet deep on a level, with drifts ten feet high and roads often impassable. By the end of the month there was no prospect of supplying commons; and rather than keep college closed, Stiles advertised that classes would be held starting February 1 for students who could find board in town. About fifty showed up and kept the college going until the steward was able to reopen com-

23. *Lit. Diary*, 2, 362, 366, 398–99.
24. Ibid., pp. 361–62, 383; *Itineraries*, 3, 403–10.

mons on May 27.[25] The war and the armies had moved south now; and as shortages disappeared, Stiles no longer had to worry about the elementary problem of keeping the students fed. Meanwhile he had been confronting problems unrelated to the war and in the long run more serious for Yale.

According to the charter procured by President Clap in 1745, the government of Yale was vested in a self-perpetuating corporation of ten fellows, sitting with the president as presiding officer. This group, so much criticized by the public, controlled all the resources of the college. It appointed the officers and paid their salaries. It granted degrees. It fixed the fees paid by students, the times of their vacations, even the number who were to live in a room. Though it delegated to the president and tutors the authority to admit, dismiss, discipline, and test students, it might resume these powers and restore a student whom the faculty had expelled. In other words, it had (and still does have) complete authority. The president, of course, had a voice in its decisions, but he did not have a veto power. Hence the importance of a genuine rapport between corporation and president and hence Stiles's concern that his election be unanimous. There would be enough occasion later for disagreement about college measures without any initial opposition to him as a man.

He had been right in thinking that there was no such initial opposition. The corporation had completely altered in the preceding ten years, and not a single member survived from the Clap administration. Eliphalet Williams, the senior member, had been elected only in 1769. Those who had supported consociation power most actively in the Wallingford and Meriden controversies had died or resigned. The majority now, by six to four, were Old Lights, and the four members who favored the New Divinity were moderates with whom Stiles thought he could get along.

Probably the most influential member was a new one, Elizur Goodrich (elected in 1776) pastor of Durham, whom several members had originally favored for the presidency. Stiles had first known Goodrich when the latter came under his tutorial instruction in the junior class in 1750–51. Goodrich had shown a remarkable talent for mathematics, and Stiles regarded him now as "an excellent and great Scholar,

25. *Connecticut Courant* and *Connecticut Journal* for January, passim; Stiles, Memoranda: Yale College; *Lit. Diary*, 2, 427.

one of the greatest of the American Literati." In theology Goodrich classed as an Old Light, but he had supported consociation power in the Wallingford affair and was therefore friendly with the New Lights who controlled the consociations.[26]

The member who most nearly matched Goodrich in influence was the pastor of Northford, Warham Williams. Williams had graduated in the class ahead of Stiles and was senior tutor when Stiles began tutoring. At that time Stiles thought him "rather fixt and rigid" in his New Light sympathies. Although he adhered to the New Divinity, he had now become "mild and condescending but always steady and uniform." Stiles thought him "a worthy Example . . . among the superior and most weighty Characters in the Ministry."[27]

The other members, if less distinguished, were able men, and Stiles found none of them obnoxious or disagreeable. He saw more of Williams and Goodrich than he did of the others, because these two were usually assigned to the prudential committee, which conferred with the president about any business that came up between the regular meetings of the corporation in September. But however agreeable Williams and Goodrich and the other members may have been as individuals, when they came together as the almighty members of the Yale corporation, their actions sometimes seemed to justify the outcries of the public.

When Stiles was elected in 1777, instruction in the college was in the hands of four tutors and two professors. Of the latter, only Nehemiah Strong, the professor of mathematics and natural philosophy, actually gave lectures. Daggett, the professor of divinity, served as pastor of the college church and informal mentor of graduate students preparing for the ministry. For the four tutors Stiles had great respect: Abraham Baldwin, Timothy Dwight, John Lewis, and Joseph Buckminster were young men of exceptional promise. Lewis he knew from Ezra Jr.'s days at Yale, when Lewis had been Ezra's tutor. At that time Stiles had carried on a friendly correspondence with the young man on educational subjects.[28] Buckminster had preached in the Portsmouth church before Stiles's departure. Stiles formed a very favorable opinion of him, and Buckminster, who

26. *Lit. Diary*, 2, 500–01.
27. Ibid., 3, 313–14.
28. Letters dated Jan. 16, Feb. 15, Mar. 16, and Aug. 3, 1775; *Lit. Diary*, 1, 517–18, 600.

thought Stiles "an honor to mankind," succeeded him at Portsmouth.[29] Timothy Dwight, though Stiles later found plenty of reason to dislike him, at this time probably retained the esteem Stiles felt in 1773 when he called Dwight an honor to Yale.[30]

Unfortunately, before Stiles's arrival in New Haven in 1778, these three men had resigned, and the word was that the corporation had forced them out in a most unseemly way.[31] Stiles swallowed whatever chagrin he may have felt at the loss and set to work with the remaining tutor, Abraham Baldwin, and the two new ones with whom the corporation replaced the three who had left. The survival of Baldwin at least was a comfort to him, for he rated Baldwin even above his departed colleagues.[32] In August he was cheered by a letter from Silas Deane, a Connecticut man who was serving the Continental Congress in France. Deane offered to solicit funds from "his very noble and opulent Friends" there toward the establishment of a professor of French at Yale. Deane realized that in spite of the current enthusiasm for France engendered by her assistance to America in the war, the prospect of a French Catholic teaching at Yale might be hard for the corporation to accept. Accordingly he suggested that in Protestant Switzerland, say Geneva, they might obtain a professor "whose principles as well as manners could not fail of being agreeable." [33]

Stiles was enthusiastic. He had not included a professorship of modern languages in his plan for expanding the Yale curriculum, but he was not disposed to look this gift horse in the mouth. In the midst of a war, with England the enemy and France the ally, it appeared that the future commercial and diplomatic orientation of the nation might well be toward France, in which case it would be advantageous for Americans to learn French. A French professorship would strengthen Yale and serve the public. Moreover, Deane himself, though currently under fire in Congress, was still popular in Connecticut.

During the next few days Stiles sounded out various people on the

29. *Lit. Diary*, 2, 270, 496; Buckminster to Joel Barlow, Oct. 5, 1778, Jan. 17, 1779, Pequot Collection, Yale Univ. Lib.

30. *Lit. Diary*, 1, 369.

31. See below, Chap. 22.

32. *Lit. Diary*, 2, 291, 347, and the passage dated Jan. 11, 1781, at 2, 496, missing from the manuscript diary at time of publication but restored in 1958.

33. Ibid., 2, 296–97.

subject. First reactions were cautious, but when he read Deane's letter to the judges of the Superior Court, they all were strong for accepting, "think no danger of popery." Even straight-laced Roger Sherman was for it, and so were most of the ministers Stiles talked with, except Chauncy Whittelsey. Governor Trumbull discussed it with the Council, and Stiles heard that they all approved without hesitation. His own enthusiasm grew.[34] But he had reckoned without the corporation.

When they met just before commencement in September and he laid Deane's proposal before them, he was obliged at their behest to write a pussyfooting letter declining the offer until they were sure that public opinion would endorse such a radical step. "You are sensible, Sir," the words must have come reluctantly, "that great Delicacy is requisite in conducting any public Matters, that require a Reconciliation of the minds of the People at large to new proposals which however safe and salutary, may yet be apprehended to involve the most distant Idea of a tendency to bring them under a foreign Influence, to to affect their internal state as to Policy or Religion. This prudence appears to the corporation necessary in the case of your kind and honourable proposal." [35] Stiles knew perfectly well that the corporation's new-found concern for public opinion was the sheerest hypocrisy. The public would approve of Deane's offer, as the enthusiasm of the governor, the Council, and the Superior Court plainly showed. Even the ministers of the New Haven County Association thought it should be accepted when he told them of it at their meeting in September.[36] What stood in the way was not the people of Connecticut or even the ministers of Connecticut, but the provincialism of the Yale corporation. It was they, not the public, who apprehended "a foreign Influence" on their religion.

The corporation's next move was to ease the professor of mathematics and natural philosophy out of office. Nehemiah Strong was probably not an easy person to get along with. It was not his fault that he had his wife plucked away from him in 1761, when a court reversed her divorce decree and gave her back to her former husband, Andrew Burr. But Strong showed a certain ungenerousness of spirit when he turned around and sued Burr for the cost of the lady's

34. Ibid., pp. 297–98. Cf. "Parnassus" in *Connecticut Courant*, Mar. 11, 1783.
35. Stiles to Deane, Sept. 9, 1778.
36. *Lit. Diary*, 2, 304.

maintenance during the time he had mistakenly kept her as Mrs. Strong.[37] He also had troubles in his preprofessorial career as minister at Turkey Hills (East Granby). The congregation finally charged him with immorality and fraudulent dealing, and though he was exonerated by the consociation, the church dismissed him in 1767.[38] One gets the impression that Strong had a somewhat prickly character, and by his own admission his lectures were not popular with the students.[39]

Nevertheless there would seem to have been no justification for the way in which the corporation treated him. He had taken the professorship, which paid no more (£70 a year) than he was earning as a schoolmaster, on the expectation of lifetime tenure. But after 1779 the corporation first reduced his salary, then refused to pay him regularly at all, forbade him to give any lectures except when specifically invited, and finally goaded him into resigning in 1781 by requiring him to take the oath of allegiance—a suggestion that he was a Tory.[40]

The members of the corporation were not motivated by the desire to get a better man, for they made no move to replace Strong for thirteen years; and it seems doubtful that they were justified by financial necessity. Though there may have been difficulty in collecting sums due the college,[41] Yale's total income at this time was well above its liabilities.[42]

There is no indication that Stiles shared the corporation's animus against Strong, and Strong evidently admired Stiles. In his letter of resignation, after castigating the corporation, Strong devoted several

37. Nehemiah Strong Papers, Yale Univ. Lib.

38. *Connecticut Courant*, May 26, 1766, May 30, 1768.

39. Nehemiah Strong, Address to the Corporation, Sept. 10, 1781, Yale Univ. Lib.

40. Ibid., Sept. 10, Dec. 14, 1781, Yale Univ. Lib.; *Lit. Diary*, 2, 564, 572–73; Corporation Records, Sept. 8, 1779, Sept. 13, 1780, Sept. 12, Dec. 18, 1781; *Connecticut Courant*, Apr. 1, 8, June 10, 1783.

41. See the advertisement by Jeremiah Atwater, *Connecticut Journal*, Nov. 29, 1781.

42. In 1780–81 the income from quarter bills was £824 2s. 4d. and in 1781–82 was £1114 2s. 8d. During these years the value of the interest on £1230 invested in the Continental Loan Office was probably negligible, but the rents from the college farms, stated in silver, probably amounted to at least £160 a year. In April 1781 five years' back rent was paid on Whitehall Farm, in Middletown, R.I., amounting to $500 (£166) in silver. Salaries and other expenses authorized by the corporation in 1780–81 amounted to about £615 and in 1781–82 to £833 (from Daggett's death in November 1780 to Wales's inauguration in June 1782 there was no professor of divinity to pay).

paragraphs of praise to the president [43] and in 1784 dedicated a volume of astronomical lectures to him.[44] Though Stiles did not record his own sentiments even in the Diary, there is no reason to think that the two men did not get along or that he favored a resignation which would reduce his college to a still narrower compass.

Perhaps the corporation acted as it did because of financial timidity, for when Stiles found his own pay inadequate they did nothing about that either. He had left Portsmouth free of debts, but on December 10, 1779, his fifty-second birthday, he noted that he was reduced "to greater worldly Straits this year than ever," and in November, 1780 he wrote: "the Corporation keep me in so poor and parsimonious a manner, that domestic Cares and the RES ANGUSTAE DOMI are a heavier Anxiety to me than all my College Cares"—an amazing comparison in view of all the college cares which, at this time, he was gratuitously taking upon himself.[45]

Professor Daggett had died in November. Strong was giving only an occasional lecture. And there were only three tutors. Instead of expanding into a university, Yale was in danger of contracting into a grammar school. And when the corporation prepared to replace Daggett, they discovered that their high-handed actions with the tutors in 1777 and their current unpleasant relations with Strong made men wary of serving Yale.

Their first choice and the man who would most have pleased the students was Abraham Baldwin—"the Genius, the fine classical belles Lettres and philosophical Scholar, the Historian, the Divine, the Orator, the every Thing excellent!" [46] Baldwin had survived the tutorial purge of 1777–78 but had gone off a year later to become chaplain in the Continental Army. Though he was only twenty-six years old and sufficiently tempted by the offer of a professorship to preach a number of times in the college chapel, he finally declined, ostensibly on the grounds that the salary offered (first £130, and when he refused that, £150) was inadequate, but secretly, Stiles suspected, for

43. Strong, Address to the Corporation, Dec. 14, 1781; *Connecticut Courant*, Apr. 8, 1783.

44. *Astronomy Improved* (New Haven, 1784). The dedication is dated Nov. 1, 1781.

45. *Lit. Diary*, 2, 396, 484.

46. Ibid., pp. 496 (and missing pages in manuscript), 499–501.

another reason: "He did not chuse to trust himself with our Corporation." Three months later, riding with him along the road to Milford, Stiles asked point-blank whether any salary, say £200, would induce him to accept, and he said flatly no.[47]

Unfortunately Baldwin was not the only man in Connecticut who distrusted the Yale corporation.

47. Ibid., p. 556; 3, 8–9.

22

Peacetime Battles

As PRESIDENT OF YALE, Ezra Stiles was very much the citizen of Connecticut, riding out to talk with this minister or preach a sermon for that one, hungrily gathering news, gossip, advice, and criticism wherever he went. Everyone knew President Stiles; most people found him good company and opened up to him. He must therefore have heard only too often what people thought of his masters, the Yale corporation.

During the height of the war there was only one public attack on the corporation—in the *Connecticut Courant* of July 28, 1778. The author, said to be the Reverend Allyn Mather of New Haven's Third Church,[1] complained that the experience of clergymen was too narrow to qualify them for sole control of the college. This was old stuff, and Mather offered no specific evidence to refurbish the argument. But Stiles knew that the evidence was there and that the public, if not hostile, were at best indifferent to the college. Before Cornwallis surrendered, they simply had more important matters than Yale to occupy them.

As the war drew to a close, however, the people of Connecticut entered a new, expansive mood in which no one could predict what they might do. They were poor, debt-ridden, but proud and excited. They had whipped the British; they were going to show the world a thing or two, and one of the things was how to run a republic. Even before the war they had begun talking about equality and took the idea

1. Eliphalet Williams to Stiles, Aug. 14, 1778.

pretty literally.[2] A perfect equality of property, they admitted, was impossible but not therefore undesirable, and a near equality they considered essential to republican government. In the Connecticut Assembly in the 1780s measures were both attacked and defended on this premise. "We may as well think," one assemblyman proclaimed, "to repeal the great laws of attraction and gravitation, as to think of continuing a popular government without a good degree of equality among the people as to their property." He therefore favored a bill in relief of debtors. His opponent argued, not that an equal division of property was wrong, but that Connecticut already came "as near to it as can be expected." [3]

In this egalitarian mood people scanned every public measure for signs of special privilege. When Congress proposed to reward the ill-paid officers of the Revolutionary Army with five years' extra pay, Connecticut sent up a howl of protest: this would establish aristocracy. The Society of the Cincinnati founded by the officers was thought insidious for the same reason.[4] When doctors in the state proposed to raise standards by forming a society to license medical practitioners, they were denounced for endangering liberty: the members of any medical society ought to be annually elected.[5]

Though quick to cry out against any hint of aristocracy, people were also in a highly experimental temper, ready to try new ideas, new books, new styles, new wives—the divorce rate was way up [6]—and new schools. The 1780s saw a rash of academies, designed either to prepare for college or to take the place of it. Connecticut gained at least a dozen, many of them coeducational.[7] Before long, surely, someone moving in these egalitarian, experimental currents, would revive the project of overhauling Yale or advance a scheme for a new college.

2. See, for example, Benjamin Trumbull, *A Discourse, Delivered at the Anniversary Meeting Of the Freemen* (New Haven, 1773), pp. 30–31.

3. *New Haven Gazette and Connecticut Magazine*, June 21, 28, 1787; cf. *New Haven Gazette* (Meigs, Bowen, and Dana), Sept. 1, 1785; *American Mercury*, Apr. 26, 1787.

4. *Connecticut Courant*, 1783–84, passim.

5. *New Haven Gazette and Connecticut Magazine*, June 21, 1787.

6. In New Haven County, for example, divorces averaged fewer than one a year between 1741 and 1766. From 1767 to 1776 they averaged 2.7 a year and from 1777 to 1793, when they began to go down again, there were 5.4 a year. (Compiled from Records of the Superior Court, Conn. State Lib.)

7. *Lit. Diary*, 2, 451; 3, 247–48.

While waiting for such a frontal assault, Stiles had to deal with a flanking attack, led by one of the most able Yale graduates of the preceding generation. The details of Timothy Dwight's feud with Yale will probably never be known. His own papers have mostly disappeared, and parts of Stiles's Diary that apparently dealt with it have been destroyed since Stiles's death by well or ill-meaning survivors.[8] From what remains it is possible to recover only the bare outlines of the story.

Timothy Dwight, who graduated in 1769, became a tutor at Yale in 1771. Naphtali Daggett was at this time beginning to bring the college out of the doldrums in which President Clap had left it, and the students, to judge by a few surviving letters, seem to have formed a high opinion of him.[9] By 1776 their opinion had fallen so low that they petitioned the corporation for his removal.[10] The immediate source of discontent is not easy to determine. There were the usual complaints about bad food and arbitrary discipline; and the hostile feeling against Yale in the community at large must have been communicated in some measure to the students. The seniors in particular were dissatisfied, because the president, who traditionally taught their class, gave no instruction in belles lettres, the fashionable new subject which Tutor Dwight had taught them to admire and which Tutor Dwight, they were sure, would gladly teach them now.[11] Many years later one of Dwight's critics wrote in the back leaves of a pamphlet the charge that Dwight had deliberately undermined Daggett's reputation, "by Wantonly displaying his Foibles." [12] But such a strategy was quite unnecessary. The brilliance, elegance, and good looks of the young tutor were enough to inspire cruel comparisons with the plodding speech and careless manners of the president. The boys nicknamed Daggett "Tunker" and scribbled uncomplimentary comments

8. See below, A Note on the Stiles Papers.

9. See, for example, the letters quoted in E. H. Gillette, "Yale One Hundred Years Ago," *Hours at home, 10* (1870), 335. Enrollment rose under Daggett and continued high (above that of Harvard) until the onset of war.

10. *Lit. Diary, 2,* 12.

11. The corporation, on petition of the seniors, allowed Dwight to give them special instruction in "Rhetorick, History and Belles Lettres." Corporation Records, Oct. 23, 1776.

12. In the Yale copy of John Cosens Ogden, *Friendly Remarks to the People of Connecticut* (n.p. 1799). The note, in a contemporaneous hand, states that Dwight was irked "because the Corporation would not remove him [Daggett] and give the Presidency to Dwight." Cf. Sprague, *Annals of the American Pulpit, 1,* 483.

on his crude eating and drinking habits in the margins of library books.[13]

When Daggett actually did resign, the students' reaction suggests that their discontent had been not much more than the normal griping of undergraduates against their academic overlords. According to Elijah Backus, a senior at the time, the students abruptly changed their tune, "for it used to be *old damned Tunker* but now *Bona Prefex.*" [14]

With the resignation of Daggett the future of the college became uncertain. Timothy Dwight was frankly pessimistic about it. Elijah Backus recorded on March 29: "Mr. Dwight thinks that College wont be called together again in this Town and that our class wont be Called Together at all. . . . Mr Dwight has been talking with several of our Class to know their minds whether if he should Call them together in his own name they would be willing to meet at any place he should appoint." [15]

Evidently Dwight had already thought of starting a school of his own, but a few weeks later the corporation arranged that the senior class should finish their studies with him at whatever place he found most convenient. The corporation also ordered that when the seniors were dismissed in July, the customary public examinations and oratorical exercises should be omitted.[16] Dwight's failure to observe this ruling (by presiding over the traditional program of speeches) may have given the impression that he was gratuitously assuming the role of president.[17] Perhaps too the corporation saw a hidden challenge in the text of two sermons which he preached to his graduating class: "I love them that love me, and those who seek me early shall find me!" [18] Was he inviting them or their friends to a new school, or suggesting his availability for the presidency of Yale?

When Daggett resigned, Dwight was only twenty-five years old,

13. See, for example, the marginal comments in the Yale copy of *The Works of the Famous Nicolas Machiavel* (London, 1720).

14. Elijah Backus, Diary, Mar. 22, 1777, photostat in Yale Univ. Lib.

15. Backus, Diary, Mar. 29, 1777.

16. Corporation Records, Apr. 30, May 27, 1777.

17. It was later asserted (see below, p. 350) that Dwight's violation of the corporation order was the pretext for his dismissal. Another possible source of the corporation's disapproval of Dwight and the other tutors was the memorial signed by "officers" of the college (see below, p. 353).

18. Charles E. Cuningham, *Timothy Dwight 1752–1817* (New York, 1942), p. 56; Calvin Durfee, *Sketch of the Late Rev. Ebenezer Fitch* (Boston, 1865), p. 32.

but according to a memoir prefixed to the first volume of his *Theology Defended* (1818), the students drew up a petition asking the corporation to make him president. Dwight, the story goes, persuaded them not to present it.[19] Whether the story is authentic or not, at least one influential Connecticut politician and landholder, Abraham Davenport of Stamford, favored Dwight's election.[20] But the corporation had had its fill of Dwight, and forced his resignation. Davenport, not being a member, had no say in the matter. Davenport was, however, on the committee of the Assembly that a few months later negotiated for union with the college. His presence may not be irrelevant to the failure of the negotiations.[21]

Whatever the faults of the corporation, and whatever the merits of Timothy Dwight, Stiles blamed him for what followed. This gifted young man, Stiles was convinced, would sacrifice anything, including Yale, in order to gratify his ambition to be a college president. It is not strange that Stiles, though usually charitable, should have judged Timothy Dwight harshly, for Dwight was the one type of man that Stiles most disliked: a minister of the gospel who meddled in politics. Nor did events disprove Stiles's estimate of the young man's aim in life.

On November 30, 1779, Dwight publicly issued the challenge which the Yale corporation may have sensed during his last year as

19. Timothy Dwight, *Theology Explained and Defended* (5 vols. Middletown, 1818), *1*, xv. The memoir is by Sereno Dwight. I have found no contemporary evidence of such a petition.

20. *Lit. Diary, 2,* 231.

21. Davenport (whose wife was a cousin of Timothy Dwight's mother and whose son had been a student of Dwight's at Yale) was a man of strong opinions. Dwight, who admired him, spoke of him as a rough diamond, whose virtues were "all of the masculine kind; less soft, graceful, and alluring than his friends wished." He had an "invincible firmness of mind" and a "weight of character which for many years decided in this County [Fairfield] almost every question, to which it was lent" (*Travels in New England and New York*, New Haven, 1821–22, *3*, 497–99). The negotiations between the corporation and the committee of the Assembly had opened in a promising manner in the summer of 1777. They broke down in the following January after a new committee had been appointed with Davenport as a member. Davenport opposed the Assembly's spending any money on Yale "judging that smaller Colleges are more advantageous for Education than larger Seats of Learning" (*Lit. Diary, 2,* 231). He may have had in mind the possibility of providing another academic berth for his protégé, Dwight, who had been eased out of Yale between the sittings of the first and second committees.

a tutor. On that day, in the *Connecticut Courant* he announced a school in Northampton, Massachusetts, to teach "elegant Reading and Writing, Arithmetic, Eloquence, English Grammar, Geography and the Latin and Greek Languages." It was not a college but an academy, yet several of the subjects proposed were taught at Yale. It could easily become the nucleus of a rival institution, for Northampton was in the Connecticut Valley and had its cultural affiliations with Yale rather than Harvard. Dwight's name was still popular among the students at Yale, and he also had something to offer that New Haven with its scarce provisions and raids by the enemy could not match; in Northampton, the advertisement boasted, "Board may be obtained, in a secure situation, upon easy terms." Furthermore, it had an attraction that Yale still lacks: it was coeducational.

The threat posed by Northampton materialized on April 28, 1780, when a sophomore came to Stiles and asked to be dismissed to go and study with Dwight.[22] On May 4 another applied, and Stiles heard that Dwight was expecting to draw thirty students from the sophomore and junior classes.[23] He was pleased to note, six weeks later, that only seven had been decoyed, and the next fall three of these applied for readmission.[24]

Though no mass exodus to Northampton occurred, Stiles received periodic reminders that Dwight wanted a university of his own: there was talk of starting one at Bennington for him and then at Fairfield.[25] Stiles was convinced that Dwight and his friends were determined to supplant Yale, and that Dwight with this in mind had influenced Abraham Baldwin not to accept Yale's professorship of divinity, by holding out to him instead "the Prospect of being called, together with a Group or Cluster of Geniuses into a Literary Institution hereafter."[26]

Meanwhile, Stiles heard, Dwight's friends were also talking about raising a subscription to endow a professorship for him at Yale. Stiles would have been happy to have another professorship for Yale, even with Dwight in the chair. Yale would be safer with the dynamic young man in her service instead of working against her. But Stiles

22. *Lit. Diary*, 2, 422.
23. Ibid., p. 423.
24. Ibid., pp. 438, 470.
25. Ibid., pp. 449–50, 512, 531, 557.
26. Ibid., p. 556; 3, 9.

doubted that he would accept so modest a post. "He is waiting for the meditated stroke upon Yale college," Stiles wrote in one of the few passages of his Diary concerning Dwight that have escaped destruction, ". . . He meditates great Things and nothing but great Things will serve him—and every Thing that comes in the Way of his preferment must fall before him. Aut Caesar, aut nullus." [27]

The meditated stroke, the frontal assault, finally began with an article signed Parnassus, in the Hartford paper on February 4, 1783.[28] Letters attacking the college continued to appear over this signature for the next three months. It has proved impossible to discover who Parnassus was. Stiles said the name was used by four or five persons working together,[29] but if he knew their identities he did not record them in any surviving document, and a search of the correspondence of other Connecticut figures has failed to turn up any clues. The letters themselves reveal only that the authors were able polemicists, far abler than any who had previously written against Yale, and that Parnassus, whoever he or they may have been, knew a great deal about the inner history of Yale over the preceding ten or fifteen years, far more than was contained in the official records of the institution. Nehemiah Strong publicly denied the authorship.[30] Timothy Dwight did not, and though no evidence connects him with the letters, he had the ability, the access to inside information, and, if Stiles's estimate of him was correct, the inclination.

Parnassus began with the usual remarks about the limited experience of clergymen. While taking advantage of the prevailing anticlericalism, he was careful not to offend good church-goers. The clergy, he said, were underpaid and overworked; they had another job to do and no time to become familiar with the complicated secular matters that must be understood by men properly equipped to run a college. The members of the corporation were, besides, rather old; perhaps some of their mistakes might be attributed to a fear of being eclipsed by the young. In short they were back numbers, lovable perhaps but bungling, in a job that was too big for them.

From this condescending start, calculated to flatter the lay reader (wiser in the ways of the world than any clergyman), Parnassus went

27. Ibid., 2, 531.
28. *Connecticut Courant*, Feb. 4, 1783.
29. *Lit. Diary*, 3, 59.
30. *Connecticut Courant*, Apr. 15, 1783.

on week after week to cite chapter and verse of the corporation's insufferable stupidity. The facts suggested not merely incompetence but blind arrogance.

Perhaps the most damaging revelation concerned the treatment of the three tutors who had resigned just before Stiles was installed. Though none of them was mentioned by name, no one familiar with Yale could have had any difficulty identifying them. Timothy Dwight it now appeared, had been called on the carpet and forced to resign, ostensibly for presiding over the forbidden July exercises of his class, but in fact because the corporation wished, as one member of it allegedly said, "to be well rid of them all." The tutors, it seemed "had become too big for the corporation." They had, besides, "turned all solid learning into show; for they taught the students Lowth's Grammar." This accusation was evidently made to Joseph Buckminster, who took the hint and resigned.[31]

John Lewis, the last to go, had been forced out in a more unseemly manner. Lewis, a married man, had resettled his family at Farmington, where he instructed the freshman class, as ordered by the corporation at the dispersal of the college in March 1777. He made the move at considerable expense, doubtless expecting to remain in Farmington for the rest of the war. But in May 1778 the corporation summoned him to New Haven and told him that college would reassemble there in June. According to Parnassus, there then occurred the following interchange:

> "Well, we have determined to call College to New-Haven. Will you come with your class?"
>
> Answer, "On the earnest request of my class, and from my very great respect to the President elect, I have determined to come. But, gentlemen, I hope you do not want an immediate, decisive answer. I have a family, am not, at this moment, certain of an house to accomodate them, and cannot resolve to remove them into the street."
>
> "We must have an *immediate* answer!"
>
> "Then, gentlemen, I must resign."
>
> "We must have an *immediate* answer!"
>
> The gentleman thought of his promise to his class, and, though

31. Ibid., Mar. 18, 1783.

chagrined, being desirous of tarrying at college, replied, "Gentlemen can you give me no time?"

"We give you half an hour!"

He waited on his father in law, a respectable inhabitant of New Haven, returned within the time, and told the corporation that he resigned.[32]

The dismissal of the tutors demonstrated not merely bad manners but a smallness of mind that substantiated the growing popular prejudice against clergymen. The reference to Lowth's grammar showed that the corporation had no understanding or appreciation of student interest in poetry and belles lettres. Lowth's grammar was an English grammar, suited to living men writing English.[33] The corporation, obviously, wanted only the dead languages.

Having spoken to the literary avant-garde by condemning the treatment of Dwight, Lewis, and Buckminster, Parnassus appealed to the practical and old-fashioned by exposing the treatment of Professor Strong. Strong, it was said, had accepted his appointment at some financial sacrifice, with the understanding that it would last for life. When the corporation reduced his salary because of wartime exigencies, he cheerfully accepted the sacrifice from a willingness, as he said, to share in the common adversity of the times. But the corporation, having raised tuition, proceeded to reduce his salary again until it reached the vanishing point, and then forbade him to offer more than occasional lectures. They thus closed down instruction in mathematics and natural philosophy, the more solid branches of learning, while the students diverted themselves with the foppish trivialities of the drama.

Though Strong denied that he had written the account of his treatment or that he had even furnished the author with information, Parnassus was able to print in full two letters of Strong to the corporation.[34] No one denied their authenticity nor did anyone attempt to demonstrate that the account of the dismissal of the tutors was wrong.

Parnassus had something to offer everyone. He knew about the

32. Ibid.

33. Robert Lowth, *A Short Introduction to English Grammar* (London, 1762; Hartford, 1780).

34. *Connecticut Courant*, Apr. 1, 8, 1783.

Collins bequest of books that Clap had refused and cited it as an example of the losses the college had suffered through clerical narrow-mindedness. He knew about Silas Deane's offer to solicit funds for a French professorship and used it to the same effect. He knew also about something of which no other record survives, that the three discharged tutors had collected £200 worth of subscriptions for an orrery, all of which were withdrawn when they left. And while the corporation was recklessly throwing away offers of this kind, it raised tuition in order to sustain its freedom from the state control which it badly needed and which might have brought it financial assistance.

The appointment of a new professor of divinity was another cause for complaint. After Abraham Baldwin refused the job, the corporation offered it to Samuel Wales, pastor of Milford. Milford was unwilling to release Wales, but he got a council of ministers to declare him free on the grounds that the professorship was a position of greater usefulness. The council, Parnassus said, was irregularly constituted and had violated the rights of the Milford church, another example of the corporation's high-handedness.

Throughout the articles Parnassus sought to deprive the corporation of any benefit it might gain from association with a popular president. In fact one of the charges against it was that the members did not pay a proper deference to the president. Stiles, Parnassus said, "has not that ascendency nor influence in the corporation to which his rank and merit entitle him." [35] And again Parnassus was able to cite chapter and verse: the corporation had violated Stiles's wishes not only in rejecting Silas Deane's offer but also in their treatment of Professor Strong.

Parnassus had written the most powerful indictment ever drawn against the Yale corporation, and its effectiveness was heightened by feeble attempts to answer it. Stiles, with his distaste for controversy, kept silent, and so, presumably did the other members of the corporation. It is to be hoped, at least, that the letters written over the signature of "An Aged Layman" were not written by a corporation member, for these were so weak as to suggest not only age but senility. The Parnassus papers, the Aged Layman said, were the work of Arminians. This accusation might once have been effective as a red herring but was now so outworn that no one abreast of the times would have ventured to use it. The Aged Layman went on to exemplify the

35. Ibid., Feb. 18, 1783.

provincial incompetence that Parnassus had cited against the corporation by arguing that it had been wise to refuse the French professorship because French was not a proper subject for young gentlemen
training to be ministers; and as for the Collins bequest, it was all to
the good that erroneous books should be kept out of the library.[36]

A somewhat more effective answer quoted a passage from a letter
by Stiles, stating that the corporation had always treated him with the
greatest respect. But the passage was printed without his permission,
and he never acknowledged or denied, either publicly or in his diary,
its authenticity.[37]

The Parnassus charges were echoed during 1784 in another series
of letters, over the signature "Complures," [38] and in a pamphlet entitled *Yale College Subject to the General Assembly*.[39] The title
indicates the purpose of the attacks. What the critics all proposed was
what the committee of the Assembly had asked in the negotiations of
1777–78, that the Assembly be given a share, in fact an equal share,
in the management of the college. The pamphlet even quoted a
memorial (otherwise unknown) prepared by the officers of the college but not presented because of the onset of the war. The memorial,
while showing Yale's need for state support, admitted that "there are
parts to be performed in the regulations of such a seminary, which require other qualifications than those commonly found in the ministerial character." [40]

The culminating attack on the college began on March 11, 1784,
when the students presented a petition to the corporation asking for a
public accounting of the tuition money they had paid.[41] Newspaper
letters suggested that part of this was being used for purposes other
than tuition; [42] and indeed it must have been, for it amounted to more

36. Ibid., Apr. 22, 29, May 20, June 3, 1783.

37. Ibid., May 20, 1783.

38. Ibid., Apr. 20, 27, June 1, 1784; *Connecticut Journal*, Apr. 14, 21, May 12,
June 16, 1784.

39. New Haven, 1784. The author is said to have been Samuel Whittelsey Dana
(Yale 1775).

40. Page 27. The officers of the college at the outbreak of the Revolutionary War in
April 1775 were Naphtali Daggett, professor of divinity and acting president; Ne-
hemiah Strong, professor of mathematics and natural philosophy; and Timothy
Dwight, John Lewis, Solomon Williams, and Joseph Buckminster, tutors.

41. *Lit. Diary*, 3, 116. The petition, which is couched in respectful language, is
in the Yale Univ. Lib.

42. *Connecticut Courant*, Mar. 11, 1783, Apr. 20, 27, 1784.

354 CHAPTER 22

than the total salaries of the college officers.[43] But that the term "tuition" was used with intent to deceive, as the critics implied, is doubtful. In the absence of further endowment or aid from the state, the college had to pay virtually all its operating expenses from charges to the students. Whether these were labeled "tuition" or something else was scarcely worth a public argument. Although the corporation did not formally answer the petition, Stiles explained matters to the students privately. But even as he did so, another petition against the college, directed not to the corporation but to the Assembly, was set in motion. Timothy Dwight was said to have been the author of both.[44]

Precisely what the petition to the Assembly said will probably never be known. Stiles noted on March 19, 1784, that he was "Reading Dwight's Memorial &c." On May 10 he reported "Much Conversation respecting the Memorial to the Assembly against College, for altering its Constitution, and joyning Civilians in the Corporation." By the time the Assembly met, three more memorials or petitions had appeared, all to the same effect and signed by persons from every county in the state. Stiles, who attended the opening of the Assembly, observed that the petition by Dwight "praying for a Board of Civilians to correct etc and otherwise to build a new College," was "generally rejected as abounding with Accusations and Aspersions and injurious Reflexions on the College." Another prepared by the Reverend Robert Ross, a Princeton graduate and pastor in what is now Bridgeport, was equally obnoxious. Stiles made no comment on the third one, by Nehemiah Strong, but he said that the fourth, by Colonel Jesse Root (a Princeton graduate and Hartford lawyer), was "decent and well, excepting one sentence." This one had received the most signatures.[45]

The petitions were the climactic effort of Yale's critics, and one would give much to know more about them. If Stiles left an account in his diary, the passage was destroyed after his death (see below, pages 470–71). His surviving papers contain only a few cryptic clues.

43. Income from tuition charges in 1783–84 was £1044; other charges to students amounted to £192 14s. 9d. more. Salaries of officers in that year amounted to £899 19s. 5d.

44. Lit. Diary, 3, 116–17.

45. Ibid., pp. 117, 120–21.

On the last leaf of his "Memoranda: Yale College" for 1783–84, he wrote as follows:

> Feb. 24 to Mar. 2. 1784
> Judge Dyer
> Judge Huntington
> Rev Mr Whittelsey
>   Mr Dwight
>   Dr Dana
> Mr Sturges
> Mr Edwards
> Mr Chauncy   not
> 1. Petition to Assembly signed in
>   every Co. by Mr Dwight
> 2. And Do at Coll. among Undergr.
>   to Corporation
> 3. Do Undergr. to Assembly for
>   deficiency of Instructors
> 4. Tare up Coll if no otherwise &c
>   Above sd to be minutes and proposals
>   in a Conference at ——— in N. Haven.

The only other reference to this meeting is in Stiles's Diary for March 29: "Find party vigorous. There was a Conference during session Superior Court Judges Dyre and Huntington, Mr. Whittelsey Dr. Dana and Mr. Dwight &c." [46] The minutes of the conference suggest that all the petitions against Yale (including one from the students, of which there is no other evidence) were the result of a concerted drive by opponents of the corporation. Several of them, despite their hostility to the corporation, were close friends of Stiles and probably kept him informed.[47] The text of only one petition to the Assembly has survived, in a printed broadside without signatures.[48] Probably

46. Ibid., 2, 117.

47. It is possible that some of the members of the conference were looking for an election issue. The contest that spring was a close one. With the retirement of Governor Trumbull, no candidate for the governorship received a majority, and three councilors failed of re-election. Among the three was Colonel Eliphalet Dyer. Samuel Huntington, running for governor, achieved only the lieutenant-governorship. *Lit. Diary*, 3, 120.

48. In the Trumbull Papers, Conn. State Lib. I have searched in every repository of Connecticut manuscripts known to me without discovering another copy.

the one by Colonel Root, it asks that the Assembly, in view of the unfortunate and impecunious condition of Yale College,

> confer and advise with the Rev. President and Fellows, on the subject, that the united wisdom and abilities of all, may be engaged to raise that seminary from its present depressed unpopular situation, to a state of the greatest eminence, respectability and usefulness, and to place it in future on a more liberal foundation under the superintendence and direction of a suitable number of the clergy and of learned civilians: or that your honours would in some other way promote the interest of learning in this state, as in your great wisdom and goodness you shall see most fit and proper.

The last suggestion was, of course, a thinly veiled proposal for another college.

There was plenty of reason to expect that the Assembly would act favorably on one of the petitions. Impatience with special privilege was at its height in Connecticut at this time. The most ardent levelers had just held a convention at Middletown, where they protested against the Congressional grant of five years' extra pay to officers of the Continental Army and organized for control of the state's politics.[49] Yale would be an appropriate target for such a group, and perhaps an easy victim at a time when so many of the intellectuals who might otherwise have defended her were aligned behind the petitions.

All the critics had taken pains to dissociate Stiles from the Yale corporation. Parnassus suggested that if the corporation refused to give way, Stiles be asked to preside over a new college. This was not the first time the suggestion had been made.[50] Whatever was wrong with Yale, no one thought it was the president's fault. Stiles was undoubtedly flattered but embarrassed by these references to his merits, and there may have been some intention to embarrass him. It would have been undignified at the least for him to desert the corporation

49. The Middletown Convention was the high point of Connecticut opposition to the Cincinnati, to the grant of extra pay to officers, and to the authority of the Continental Congress. There is no good treatment of it by a historian, and the records of its proceedings, if any were kept, do not appear to have survived. There are numerous references to it in Connecticut newspapers of the 1780s.

50. *Connecticut Courant*, Feb. 18, 1783; *Lit. Diary*, 2, 207–08; 3, 9.

when it was under fire, and in any case he had no wish to desert either it or Yale.

Another kind of man in his position, a Clap or a Dwight, would probably have met the attack head on and fought the petitions in the Assembly and in the press. Stiles watched the events closely, as always, but he kept out of it. In spite of the circumstances favoring the petitioners, he had reason to doubt their success. After the May legislative session closed, he noted in his Diary, "The Assembly have rather declined intermeddling in College Affairs." This did not mean that they had actually rejected all the petitions, but they had deferred further action until the next session, in October. Shortly afterward he received a reassuring letter from one of the Assembly, stating that "the Memorial of the Enemies of the University sleeps till October, the then situation etc. of the Assembly will be more favorable than the present I trust." [51]

The author, William Williams, was one of the most successful politicians of the 1780s. His father, the deceased Reverend Solomon Williams, had been the highly esteemed minister of Lebanon, a fellow of the Yale corporation, and Yale's first professor-elect of divinity. William Williams was an influential man. As the outspoken enemy of special privilege, he had earned the reputation of a demagogue and later became the butt of satirical verse by incipient Federalist poets (which had no apparent effect on his electoral majorities).[52] Whenever the showdown came in the Assembly, he would be able to deliver a good many votes, and Stiles could now be sure that they would be cast against "the Enemies of the University."

The showdown never came. In the fall session consideration of "the Memorial De Yale College and Litterature" (evidently only one memorial had survived) was referred to the next Assembly, which in turn referred it to the next,[53] with the stipulation that the Secretary

51. *Lit. Diary*, *3*, 124; William Williams to Stiles, June 8, 1784, New Haven Colony Hist. Soc. Williams may have been referring to a hoped-for change in composition of the Assembly or he may have referred to the fact that the October meeting was held in New Haven rather than Hartford.

52. The verses, entitled "The Anarchiad," appeared in the *New Haven Gazette and Connecticut Magazine* in 1786–87 and were widely reprinted. They were published in book form at New Haven in 1862, edited by Luther G. Riggs.

53. Journal of the House of Representatives, May 1783 to May 1785, pp. 137, 196, 216, Conn. State Lib.

"furnish the Reverend President and Fellows of said College with a Copy of the same." No copy is in the Yale records, and no further mention of the memorial is found in the records of the Assembly. It was simply allowed to die.

For an attack so vigorously and skillfully inaugurated, this was a surprisingly feeble ending. Concurrent with the gradual demise of the petitions, public criticism of the college also declined. The energetic campaign in the press had been handled by men shrewd enough to recognize defeat and to avoid risking their own popularity in a lost cause. They had done their best to enlist the public against Yale, but the public refused to be drawn into a feud between intellectuals. Perhaps the ordinary man was put off by the evident diversity of motives among the critics. Some told him that too much attention was given to belles lettres, others not enough. Some derided philosophy (speculative), others praised philosophy (natural); but what the difference was he knew not. His Anglican neighbor might object to the college because it was a Congregational institution, his New Light neighbor because it had an Old Light corporation, his Old Light minister because it turned young men into New Light ministers. The only concrete proposal the critics of the college had to offer was that civilians be admitted to the corporation as a prelude to a new grant of funds from the Assembly. But why give money to the college when the local secondary schools needed it more? As early as 1782 Abraham Baldwin had told Stiles that, in his opinion, most members of the Lower House thought that people who sent their children to college should pay for it and not try to thrust the burden on the state. For this reason, Baldwin believed, even if the corporation were altered as the critics demanded, the Assembly would do little for Yale.[54]

The force of the arguments Baldwin described must have been even greater when the petitions were presented, for by then Connecticut was entering a postwar depression. Money was scarce, taxes high, and the state (and nearly everyone in it) in debt.[55] Under these circumstances, whatever the reasons in its favor, a proposal that

---

54. *Lit. Diary*, 3, 8–9.

55. The postwar depression that affected all the American states seems to have lasted longer in Connecticut than elsewhere. See L. W. Labaree, *Public Records of the State of Connecticut from May 1789 through October 1792* (Hartford, 1948), pp. xv–xvi. An excellent, though brief, account of Connecticut's economic situation in the 1780s is Forrest McDonald, *We the People* (Chicago, 1958), pp. 136–48.

would take money out of the state treasury was likely to be coolly received.

Nevertheless, the Assembly could have given the Yale corporation a trimming if it had wished to, even without making a grant. In the last analysis, the attack on Yale failed because Yale succeeded. In spite of shutdowns for lack of food, in spite of raids and fear of raids, in spite of a corporation that excelled in making enemies, Ezra Stiles by 1784 had made Yale the most popular and flourishing college in the United States. The surviving memorial speaks of Yale's "present depressed unpopular situation." But at the time the words were written, Yale had some 270 students, the largest enrollment there had ever been at one time in an American college, over a hundred more than the current number at Harvard. The large student body gave Yale an income (apart from charges for food) of £1,236 14*s.* 9*d.*, a sum well above its annual liabilities.

In the face of such figures, it was no use talking about the depressed unpopular situation of the college. Stiles had made Yale a crashing success and everybody knew it.

23

The Collegiate Life

EZRA STILES succeeded as a college president partly because the job brought out the worst in him. All his life he had fought against vanity and had it well in hand by the time Yale called him. In New Haven it revived and proved an asset. The inhabitants of universities have always fostered the ceremonies and trappings by which men assure themselves of their own importance: robes, rituals, secret societies, hierarchies, titles of honor. Stiles loved the whole business. At Yale, in line of duty, he could give his vanity free rein to magnify the traditions and rituals of which he was now the guardian.

Happily this was just what the college needed. Academic formalities have persisted over the centuries not simply because they flatter but because they help to bind a highly transient population into a single community. When Stiles took charge, Yale scarcely existed as an institution; for more than a year, with the classes dispersed to various inland towns and the students scattered in private lodgings, there had been no Yale community. And during his first two years as president, the scarcity of provisions and the danger of enemy attack sent the boys home again and again in term time. Under these disruptive circumstances the common life of the college hung precariously from the few customs and traditions that could be maintained.

Stiles did not deceive himself into thinking that ceremony was a substitute for teaching and scholarship, but he did recognize its importance and took undisguised delight in the solemnities that punctuated the academic calendar. The first was his own formal inauguration on July 8, 1778, when the student body, corporation, professors, tutors, and various public dignitaries marched in procession to his house and escorted him to the chapel. There followed prayers, oaths of office, and Latin orations in quantity, including one of thirty-four minutes duration by the new president.[1]

Stiles's favorite ceremony was the annual commencement, held on the second Wednesday in September. During most of the eighteenth century this was the closest thing to a theatrical performance that Connecticut permitted itself, and everyone wanted to see the show and be seen there. The governor of the state, owing perhaps to the estrangement between Yale and the Assembly, had not regularly attended, but nearly everyone else of consequence did. Councilors, merchants, lawyers, doctors, ministers from all over Connecticut and even from adjoining states—everyone who thought of himself as belonging to the learned elite—mounted a horse and descended on New Haven to enjoy the festivities.

From 1774 until 1781 graduating seniors received their diplomas in a simple private ceremony: it would have been unseemly in wartime to indulge in the new coats and gowns, the extravagant coiffures, the elegant wining and dining that the occasion demanded, not to mention the temptation it would offer British headquarters in New York to crash the party with a raid. But in 1781 when the enemy's main force was engaged farther south, Stiles and the corporation screwed up their courage to announce the restoration of public commencement for September 12. The royal navy almost spoiled the show by renewing their attacks on Connecticut coastal towns shortly before the great day. They raided West Haven, burned Groton and New London. New Haveners snatched up their possessions and started inland; militia poured into the area. But in spite of the risk, and much to Stiles's delight, a remarkable number of ladies and gentlemen showed up at the college on September 12. Then and every September thereafter Stiles directed an extravaganza of oratory, anthems, and formal disputations, in English, Latin, and sometimes Greek or even Hebrew.[2]

The celebration traditionally got off to a noisy start the night before, when the undergraduates "illuminated" the college by placing candles in all the windows—standard procedure for great occasions in the eighteenth century. By candlelight the students marched in

1. *Lit. Diary*, 2, 278–82.
2. Ibid., pp. 552–56.

procession around the college yard and sometimes wound up with a display of fireworks. Unfortunately the candles in the windows and the young gentlemen in academic gowns offered targets too inviting for the town boys to resist. The commencement bills for broken panes were always large, and too often the whole affair turned into a town-and-gown riot. In 1762 and 1765 the corporation had forbidden the proceedings because of their tendency "to call together a great number of Spectators and disorderly Persons; and very much prepare the way for those Riots and violent actions, which oftentimes ensue." [3] When Stiles resumed public commencements in 1781, he expressly sanctioned the processions, and thereafter on commencement eve the students usually lit candles not only in the windows of the college and the chapel but also in the president's house, which stood on College Street just outside the yard. [4]

The next morning everyone gathered in front of the college, treading carefully to avoid broken glass. [5] At ten o'clock, with less than military precision but with full attention to rank, they formed a procession and moved toward the green, the students in the lead, arranged by classes "in the reverse order of their standing." Evidently the idea was to build to an academic peak at the middle of the procession, for after the seniors came the candidates for masters' degrees, and after them, preceded by the "bedellus" with a white wand, in lordly dignity walked the president. In his wake the corporation, professors, tutors, ministers and "other respectable gentlemen" formed a genteel anticlimax. When visiting dignitaries were present, like the president of another college or the governor of the state, they might march with the president or between him and the corporation.

The goal of the procession was the Brick Meetinghouse of the First Church. Here a special platform, eighteen feet square and covered with a Turkey carpet, was laid across the tops of the first pews, with

3. Corporation Records, July 21, 1762, Sept. 12, 1765.

4. *Lit. Diary*, 2, 553; 3, 92, 135, 184, 238, 328, 365; Stiles, Memoranda: Yale College, passim; Walter Bradley to Henry P. Dering, Sept. 1781, Yale Univ. Lib.; Diary of Dyar Throop Hinckley, Sept. 7, 1784, Conn. Hist. Soc.

5. In 1783 Stiles counted 74 broken panes, *Lit. Diary*, 3, 94. Stiles generally recorded the events of commencement day in his diary in some detail, but the fullest account is that of the commencement of 1782 in *Lit. Diary*, 3, 37–42. In the manuscript Stiles drew a diagram of the seating arrangements, which is not reproduced in the printed edition. For a satirical description of Yale commencements see *Connecticut Courant*, Sept. 26, 1791.

stairs mounting to it from the central aisle. The president and the two senior fellows of the corporation ascended to the places of highest dignity, in the pulpit. The other fellows sat at the back of the platform on Windsor chairs, while the tutors climbed to green draped desks in the side galleries, and the candidates for degrees, both bachelors and masters, settled in the gallery "Foreseat."

At about 10:30 the ceremony began with a prayer by the president and an anthem by the whole assemblage. Stiles often kept track of the time required by each event and in 1782, for example, found that his prayer lasted eight minutes and the anthem six. A salutatory oration in Latin by John Lovett went on for thirty-six minutes. At this point the printed broadsides of commencement theses were distributed, displaying a hundred or more propositions (in Latin) that the graduating class were prepared to defend or attack before the learned world. To give a sample of how they could do it several of them debated one or two propositions, either forensically (in English) or syllogistically (in Latin and by formal logic). In 1782 the forensic disputation took forty-five minutes, the syllogistic seven minutes. These were followed by a dialogue, resembling a one-act play (twenty-two minutes) and an English oration (fifteen minutes). All the performers were members of the graduating class.

After the morning exercises ended, usually around 12:30 or 1:00, the college hall was thrown open for a public dinner. Everyone reassembled around 4 o'clock and once more marched to the meetinghouse for orations and disputations by the candidates for masters' degrees. In between a forensic disputation and a valedictory oration the president, making as much as possible of this part of the program, conferred the degrees—bachelors, masters, honorary, and *ad eundem.* Stiles was the first in America to confer honorary degrees with full academic ceremony; and like all wise college presidents he conferred them on illustrious public figures, such as George Washington, John Adams, and Thomas Jefferson, as well as on eminent ministers and laymen of Connecticut—men who generally had a full share of honor already, some of which might hopefully rub off on the institution.

The proceedings were sometimes enlivened by music. In 1785 the morning session was closed by the performance of Handel's Water Music on a flute, and in 1792 a six-man German band was imported from New York to accompany the procession.[6] But the important

6. *Lit. Diary,* 3, 184, 474; *Connecticut Journal,* Sept. 5, 12, 1792.

music came in the evening. By the time the afternoon formalities concluded it was close to sunset; and the newly dignified graduates together with the ladies and gentlemen who had been watching them from the pews of the Brick Meetinghouse, retired to prepare for the commencement ball at the state house. For Betsy, Kezia, Amelia, Ruth, and Polly Stiles this was doubtless the high point of the whole affair, but their father seems to have taken little interest in it. He did not at any rate stand by to time it and left no account of how it was conducted, except to record the indignation of the seniors in 1782 when a group of New Haven gentlemen, mostly alumni, attempted to commandeer the state house for a "politer Ball," where the hayseed friends and relatives of the students would not clutter up the floor. One of the city gentlemen, a recent graduate, "spake with less Delicacy than was prudent upon the Candidates and their Company," whereupon the undergraduates gave him a bath under the college pump. Stiles thought this "an high Indignity to any and especially towards a Graduate." But the victim's dignity scarcely seemed worth the £1,000 that he immediately sued for. The suit was withdrawn, but Stiles did not say who got the state house.[7] In later years the problem was solved by a second, more exclusive ball on the evening of the day after commencement.

Commencement, coming at the end of the final term in the academic year, was the most imposing but by no means the only occasion when the college displayed itself in public exercises. Each of the other three terms or "quarters" was dignified by a Quarter Day, a miniature commencement, with public "exhibitions" performed in the chapel, in December by the seniors, in March by the juniors, and in June by the sophomores. The exhibitions generally included orations in Latin and English, and a dialogue designed to show off the students' conversational polish and sophistication. Sometimes there was instrumental music, and sometimes the dialogue became a "dramatic representation," resembling a modern pageant. The one in March 1779 depicted the Wyoming Massacre ("in which Pixley acted the Indian Warrior inimitably"); that in December 1781 represented the capture of Cornwallis at Yorktown.[8] The performances lasted an hour or two in all; and while they were not as heavily attended as commencement, the best people of New Haven normally turned out for them. They

7. *Lit. Diary*, 3, 36–37.
8. Ibid., 2, 325, 572.

were followed in the evening by a ball. To be selected by the president for a role in the exhibitions was every student's ambition, and when the appointments were announced, about a month beforehand, the college talked of nothing else, sometimes with heated arguments over the merits or demerits of the lucky few.[9]

Examinations offered another opportunity for scholarly display. Twice a year, May and September, each class demonstrated its academic progress, partly by answering questions (always put orally) and partly in Latin and English orations and dialogues performed by selected members. In July, when the seniors faced their final examination for the bachelor's degree, Stiles continued the procedure he had instituted while senior tutor under Clap.[10] This involved a great deal of ceremonial going and coming between the examiners and students in the chapel and Stiles in the library, concluding with a flurry of Latin speeches on both sides. The dinner which followed was a gala farewell to the seniors, who would leave college the next day and reappear only to collect their degrees at commencement. During the course of the meal Stiles rose and in a toast to the outstanding member of the graduating class, explained that his drinking would be the signal for the "transition of the classes." When his lips touched the glass, freshmen would become sophomores, sophomores juniors, juniors seniors, and the seniors "sirs," the title accorded to a graduate, before the master's degree entitled him to the greater dignity of Mister. After dinner the farewell was prolonged by the inevitable orations, disputations, and dialogues.[11]

The students liked it all as much as Stiles did. They could never get enough of the interminable ceremonial talking. Not content with speeches on Quarter Days, examination days, and commencement, they made their undergraduate societies the vehicle for more of the same. Yale clubs have always had a remarkably intellectual flavor, and the two which predominated in the late eighteenth century— Linonia, and Brothers in Unity—seem to have devoted themselves

9. See Jeremiah Day to Mills Day, Mar. 10, 1802, Yale Univ. Lib. Cf. Thomas Robbins, Diary, Conn. Hist. Soc., 1795. "In January appointments were made in my class for March quarter day. I had none; this was one of the greatest mortifications I have ever had."

10. See above, Chap. 4.

11. Stiles, "Memoranda: Yale College"; *Lit. Diary*, 2, 287–88; 3, 31–32, 79. After 1787 the after-dinner exercises were abandoned.

to reproducing the college exercises on a smaller scale. For their regular meetings the members (who could join immediately upon admission to college) prepared disputations of the kind that they did for their tutors, and four times a year they performed exhibitions like those of Quarter Day.[12]

Stiles smiled on these activities, though he drew the line at public performances of regular stage plays, which the societies attempted in the early 1780s, and which he knew would bring criticism. Some of the boys, including apparently his son Isaac, raised a small tempest within the clubs by trying to turn them wholly to the drama. Stiles was not supposed to know about the dispute and kept his hands off, but he was pleased when the extremists withdrew (or like Isaac were expelled "for insolent and dishonorable language") to form a society of their own. With all the "Wild Characters" of the college in one society, they would either go too far, so that he could fairly suppress them, or else they would behave themselves for fear of angering the corporation, which they knew would be more severe than he. Meanwhile the older societies, purged of their "gay jovial tumultuous Members," could continue their traditional programs. No matter if they sometimes acted plays for their own amusement.[13]

Stiles never questioned the place of the clubs at Yale, because in his time they were a useful part of college life and never threatened to displace it. The story would have been different had the members been disposed to break up into groups to live together outside college. Yale did not have what it desperately needed, enough space to feed or house all its students. But no one considered having the clubs assume these functions. Eating and living together was part of the ritual which made the college community, and Stiles insisted on the right to decide which boys needed it and which did not. Economy-minded parents (under the mistaken impression that private board and room were cheaper) frequently tried to bypass the president through friends on the corporation. On at least one occasion, when Stiles dismissed a student for refusing to live in college, the corporation restored him. Normally, however, the president had his way, as in the following

12. The records of the societies are in the Yale Univ. Lib. See also Thomas Robbins' Diary and Liber Compositionum, 1793, Robbins Papers, Conn. Hist. Soc., in which some compositions are addressed "ad Tutorem et Classem meam" and some "ad Societatem Fratrum in Unitate."

13. Records of the Linonian Society, Apr. 5, 1782; Lit. Diary, 3, 14–15.

notation in his record of college affairs: "February 4, 1790 Mather and Brewer come and tell me that their friends [i.e. parents or guardians] say they shall leave college if they may not live out. Accordingly I tell them peremptorily they shall live in. And so they leave College." [14]

Stiles never wept over the loss of a student who persistently refused to abide by the laws and customs of the college. But occasional misdemeanors were a standard part of collegiate life. Entering freshmen heard the president read the college customs at the beginning of the fall term, and each one received a printed copy of the laws. From these he learned some of the traditional pranks that the authorities had found it necessary to honor with specific prohibitions. The books in the library, for example, constituted a perpetual challenge. Since it was strictly forbidden to mutilate or mark them in any way, there was a real thrill to be had by writing in the margins such comments as "Calvin chapin an old Hypocrite and a whore master and tutor of Yale College 1792," or, next to a gap where several pages are missing "I cut 15 Pictures out of this Book by god and hant got found out yet By god old Ezra dam your ies." [15]

Certain outrages were repeated regularly—Stiles doubtless remembered them from his own days as student and tutor—burning the college privy, rioting in commons against the bad food, fighting with the sailors from the harbor. After one such battle in 1793 the students tore down the college fence and blamed it on their opponents.[16] In 1782, they wrecked the old college building (slated for destruction anyhow) in protest against a punishment for damaging the Hall and Buttery earlier.[17]

Pranks that upset college routine were, of course, particularly delightful. Students lived by the bell, which awoke them in the morning, called them to prayers, meals, recitations, study, and play. They never tired of ringing the bell in the dead of night or cutting the rope so that it could not be rung at all. The more ingenious boys devised novel methods of interrupting chapel: sheep were shut in the pulpit, dead

14. Stiles, "Memoranda: Yale College," Feb. 4, 1790.

15. See the Yale copy of Sir Hans Sloane, *A Voyage to the Islands* (London, 1707–25).

16. Oliver Wolcott, autobiographical fragment, Conn. Hist. Soc.; Daniel Parker to Thomas Day, Dec. 25, 1793, Thomas Mills Day Collection, Yale Univ. Lib.

17. *Lit. Diary,* 3, 12–13; Jedediah Morse to his father, Apr. 3, 1782, Morse Papers.

ducks placed under the cushion, the great Bible hidden, rocks thrown through the windows, fuses imbedded in the candles, so that they would explode in the midst of evening prayers. At a given signal all the students might shuffle their feet on the floor. Once, while a disputation was in progress, a sophomore broke up the ceremonies by pouring a torrent of water on the performers through a crack in the ceiling.[18]

Stiles did not spoil the fun by a permissive attitude but assumed an air of high displeasure at every infraction of the rules. For the rest of their lives students remembered his penetrating eye, his "air of authority and even majesty." [19] Though he was only fifty when he became president and only five feet four inches tall, he seemed older and larger than life to the undergraduates—an impression that he cultivated by wearing a wig and academic robes whenever he appeared before them. And of course he exacted the full measure of respect that the college laws and customs prescribed. "Him to honor," one freshman wrote, "(raining or not) we must never approach nearer than ten rods without pulling off our hats; and five rods for a tutor." [20]

To punish violations of the college laws and customs without raising a storm of protest from parents was not easy. The laws provided fines, admonition, rustication, and expulsion (in that order) as the weapons of academic authority, but Stiles, like any intelligent autocrat, dealt with many offenders privately. This was the "parental" mode of discipline, widely advocated in Connecticut after President Clap's too rigorous application of fines and penalties. It was also the method Stiles had followed as a minister in church discipline. When an offense was public and required serious rebuke Stiles avoided fines—which bore more heavily on the parents than on the actual culprit—and relied on admonitions (before the rest of the college), rustication (exiling a boy from the college community to study alone for a period of weeks under the direction of a minister at some distance from New Haven), and expulsion.[21]

18. Stiles, "Memoranda: Yale College," passim; Diary of John Cotton Smith, Feb. 21, 1783, Conn. Hist. Soc.

19. William B. Sprague, *Annals of the American Pulpit* (New York, 1859–69), *1*, 476–77.

20. From the journal of William Wheeler (Yale 1785), in Cornelia P. Lathrop, *Black Rock, Seaport of Old Fairfield* (New Haven, 1930), p. 38.

21. See above, p. 326, n. 5. Stiles recorded his punishments in his "Memoranda: Yale College," and there are a number of loose records of punishments preserved in the Yale Univ. Lib.

Expulsion was only for extreme cases. So far as possible Stiles avoided it by urging parents to withdraw boys who seemed to be headed for it. If a boy did have to be expelled, he might be readmitted (like a member excommunicated from a church) after prope repentance. The parental mode of discipline required mitigation of punishment in return for repentance. Stiles insisted only that the student demonstrate the authenticity of his remorse before the rest of the college in a solemn confession—another ceremony to bind the group together.[22]

Discipline was supposedly facilitated by the collegiate hierarchy. Each class had its own prerogatives, the most valued of which was keeping the classes below it in line. At the bottom, the mud sill of the college community, stood the freshmen. In the presence of upperclassmen or faculty, they could not wear that symbol of male dignity, a hat, nor could they wear one in the college yard during their first two quarters. They must not speak unless spoken to and must rise when upperclassmen entered a room. In chapel they must rise at the entrance of a tutor. They must not run in the college yard or up or down stairs or call to anyone out a college window. They must not whistle, eat, kick, jump, hop, dance, or sing in the streets of New Haven. And they must run errands for their superiors.[23]

To teach freshmen these respectful and decorous manners was the special responsibility of the seniors, but every upperclassmen could demand the prescribed deference and call offenders to account. The sophomores, who could not lord it over anyone else, were particularly keen about "trimming" the freshmen. William Wheeler (Yale 1785) described the rite:

> At the first entrance of a Freshman into this College, he is sure to be ordered up and disciplin'd or as the Sophimores term it Trimming
> They endeavour to find some occasion of animadversion against them which they are not long in quest of as he is generally too free with his Superiors—runs in at the Gate before them—sets without leave—or something—

22. Holmes, *Life*, pp. 364–65; *Lit. Diary*, 3, 78; Corporation Records, May 13, 1791.

23. *The Laws of Yale-College* (New Haven, 1774), pp. 14–15. The *Laws* of 1787, p. 19, do not impose these detailed restrictions, which were evidently customary. See *Lit. Diary*, 3, 244 n., 299. Lathrop, *Black Rock*, pp. 40–41; Judd Manuscripts, 9, 93, Forbes Library, Northampton, Mass.

After he has committed the Crime they assemble a dozen good
Voices and summon him with a stamp and a step up to my Room—

He entering trembles and is discomposd and 'tis ten to one
commits a greater offence than the other.—perhaps he forgets to
make a bow, then they all fetch a stamp, asking him what he
meant to enter so without bowing,—if he bows to one, the rest
are affronted and ask him if he likes that one better than all the
rest—if he bows in an awkward manner they take great pains to
shew him—keeping him bowing for half an hour almost to the
floor.

They ask him what he was ordered up for, "for insulting the
Sophs"—Well what did you insult them for"—

I say you did, don't contradict me, tell me now whether you
did or not.—I don't think I did—That is not my question you
are obliged to answer all questions, answer me immediately—I
didn't mean to—Did you ever do anything without a meaning—

If he confesses they tell him there is 4 parts to a confession—
1st to confess the Crime—2nd to be sorry for it—3d to ask forgiveness and 4th to promise Reformation—

Sometimes a verbal, sometimes a written confession answers.

If he is obstinate they put the fists in his face, keep him constantly turning around to see those that are behind him—blow
tobacco smoke in his face, make him hold a candle, toe a crack,
bow to his shadow and when his back is turnd they are continually
going in and out to trim him for not bowing,—two or three talking to him at once while he all passive obedience and non-
resistance is obliged to stand mute and answer only to the questions they ask him—

In short a Soph is absolute and despotic as the great Mogul— [24]

The Sophs could not go much beyond the not very grave terrors
that Wheeler described, because the seniors were supposed to keep
an eye on them. Jonathan Walter Edwards (Yale 1789) found freshman fagging "not half as bad as I expected we are obliged to go any
reasonable errand. The sophimores cannot trim us or as it is called
discipline us without special leave from the seniors and then they
cannot detain us more than 15 minutes at the farthest. And the seniors
scarce ever give them leave to discipline us unless in case of a very

24. Lathrop, *Black Rock*, pp. 39–40.

high insult." [25] Samuel Goodrich (Yale 1783) wrote to a friend at the beginning of his freshman year, "you know that freshmen are perticuler under the care of the Senior Class, they use us all like Gentlemen." [26]

Although the sophomores undoubtedly made the most of their rank, the freshmen enjoyed defying them. Freshmen could avoid errands by claiming a prior one, or by dawdling indefinitely. In 1793 one gleefully described to a friend his daring insolence when a group of sophomores attempted to trim him. They took him in high indignation to the president, who told them to consult the tutors. "But on the way," as the freshman told it, "they happened to Sware which happened well for me." He complained to the tutors of their profanity and turned the whole affair against them. "Thus," he exulted, "the Freshmen for the most part come off victorious, and greatly perplex the Sophamores." [27]

When the first snow fell, the freshmen had another chance to perplex their masters, by challenging them to a snowball fight in the college yard. These traditional brawls became so bloody that Stiles had to end them in 1786.[28] Perhaps as compensation he also abolished the practice of freshmen rising when tutors entered chapel at prayer time. Later he reduced the period when freshmen went hatless from two quarters to one.[29] And in the last years of his administration he and a committee of the corporation were working on a revision of the college laws, in which freshmen were probably freed from running errands.[30]

25. Jonathan Walter Edwards to Benjamin Trumbull, Jr., Nov. 30, 1785, Yale Univ. Lib. Though the senior class was by law charged only with supervision of the freshmen (Corporation Records, July 21, 1762), it seems to have acted as a general student government body, not only by controlling fagging but by punishing upper-class misdemeanors. John Cotton Smith Diary, Feb. 21, 1783. In 1795 the new laws incorporated this practice. *The Laws of Yale College* (New Haven, 1795), p. 11.

26. To Henry P. Dering, Nov. 17, 1779, Yale Univ. Lib.

27. Daniel Parker to Thomas Day, Dec. 9, 1793, Thomas Mills Day Papers, Yale Univ. Lib.

28. James Wadsworth to his brothers, Dec. 2, 1783, Yale Univ. Lib.; Diary of Dyar Throop Hinckley, Dec. 12, 1784, Conn. Hist. Soc.; *Lit. Diary*, 3, 247 n.

29. *Lit. Diary*, 3, 244 n., 299.

30. Corporation Records, Sept. 11, 1793; *Lit. Diary*, 3, 512, 514, 524, 555, 560; "Memoranda: Yale College," Feb. 13, 15, 1794. Because the laws underwent further revision after Stiles died and before they were printed, it is not certain how they stood at his death. The committee of revision had held several meetings and had already

While he mitigated the rigors undergone by freshmen, Stiles retained enough difference in class prerogatives to give the students an interest in climbing the ladder of collegiate privileges. Freshmen began the ascent with the transition of classes at the July examination dinner.[31] From then until September they planned for the exercise of their first class prerogative, supervision of the events and illuminations in the yard on commencement eve. Walter Bradley, an absentee, in 1781 shared his class's triumph in regaining this traditional privilege at the first public commencement after the war:

> I received your Letter and am very happy to be informed that after so many and frequent petitions have been made to the President by the Class have at last obtained liberty to walk the yard and to perform the other sports and amusements which we made application for, and am very happy to hear that the class seem to be spirited about the affair and hope you will persue the matter with the greatest Vigour and energy and make every thing appear respectfull. I think it stands us in hand to make as splendid a Commencement as we possible can as it will be expected . . . that we shall have all things prepared and go on with the greatest decency and regularity.[32]

The festivities that year were as decent and regular as anyone could wish. And each year thereafter the class looked forward to greater dignity and new privileges: six weeks after commencement they would return to college as sophomores to wield authority over the new fresh-

---

ordered a fair copy made, but on June 25, 1795, at the corporation meeting which elected Timothy Dwight president, the committee was instructed to consult with him about further revision. On August 17 Dwight wrote his letter accepting the presidency. On August 18 Josiah Meigs and the three tutors signed a petition to the corporation, defending fagging as a means of taming the tough country boys who entered college each fall. Its abolition, they said, would result in insufferable haughtiness among the freshmen and "subject the higher classes to constant scurrility . . . lessen their manhood and dignity, reduce all to an equal rudeness, render College a meer great common school" (Yale Univ. Lib.). On September 23 the prudential committee "proceeded to a further revision of the laws," and on October 5 a meeting of the corporation completed discussion and revision of them and ordered 300 copies printed. The laws as printed (1795, p. 10) allowed juniors and seniors but not sophomores the traditional privilege of sending freshmen on errands.

31. In 1793 the freshmen gave a special fillip to the transition: before moving into the seats in chapel formerly occupied by the sophomores, they hired a Negro to wash them. Thomas Robbins, Diary, Conn. Hist. Soc.

32. Walter Bradley to Henry P. Dering, Sept. 1781, Yale Univ. Lib.

men; as juniors in charge of college singing they would elect six of their members to lead the anthems in chapel; as seniors they would supervise the other classes, prepare the commencement theses, manage the commencement ball. Each year they would conduct a Quarter Day exhibition of their own and seek to outdo the other classes in the splendor of their performance. Regardless of its faults the system of subordination contained aspects that were gratifying to the students and useful to the administration.

The desire to take advantage of every channel in which Yale's community life could flow probably prevented Stiles from tampering with one institution which he would never have taken a hand in starting. The college church had been established by Clap in order to take the students away from the preaching of Stiles's good friend Joseph Noyes. To form a church of college boys was at best a very dubious enterprise, for it was not common for New England children to enter into full church membership during their teens. Whether a church followed the practice of closed communion favored by the New Divinity, in which a definite experience of conversion was requisite to membership, or whether it followed the open communion originated by Solomon Stoddard, in which the only condition of membership was a decent life and an open profession of Christianity—whichever practice it followed, the time for joining was normally later in life than the age at which most boys attended college.[33] Stiles himself did not join his father's church until after graduation, and Yale records indicate that many tutors were even later. If a boy did wish to join a church, it was likely to be the one in his home town instead of the college church.[34] Moreover, the largest category of joiners—the women —were out of Yale's reach.[35] As a result the college church, though it seems to have been liberal in its admission policy, had never contained more than a small fraction of the student body as full members; and it was always on the point of expiring as its communicants graduated.[36]

33. A sampling of New England church records shows that eighteenth-century New Englanders, when they joined a church at all, generally did so between the ages of twenty-two and forty.

34. But Stiles did record two instances in which the college church admitted to membership students who already belonged to local churches: Lit. Diary, 3, 211, 549.

35. See above, Chap. 12. Women outnumbered men by more than two to one in most New England churches in the eighteenth century.

36. See my article "Ezra Stiles and Timothy Dwight," in the forthcoming Mass. Hist. Soc., Proceedings, Vol. 72.

Stiles evidently considered dissolving the church, but as long as Professor Daggett lived, it would have done more harm than good to raise the question. After Daggett died in 1780, Stiles sought the advice of Charles Chauncy, and Chauncy urged disbanding the church, which he said had been founded from sinister motives anyhow.[37]

Stiles did not take the advice. Probably the corporation would not have consented even if he had wished to. Whatever its origins and however difficult to maintain, the church did furnish a medium of college life. Though only a handful became members, Stiles made every student show up at chapel every Sunday and in spite of protests from Anglican parents, allowed cuts for the purpose of attending other churches only once a term.[38]

Within the church the college ranks were maintained as strictly as outside. The president and his family occupied the place of highest honor. Next came the other faculty members, though there was once a dispute as to whether the daughters of the president outranked the wife of a tutor. After faculty came the sirs, and finally the under-graduates in the usual order. One of the gratifying signs of growing academic dignity during four years at college was to watch one's place in chapel improve.[39]

Under Stiles's presidency the college church prospered as never before. After Daggett's death, while he looked for a new professor of divinity, Stiles undertook to preach himself and was soon rewarded by a number of conversions. When Professor Wales took over in 1782 Stiles rejoiced to see the revival take hold in earnest. Wales, whose preaching Stiles greatly admired, brought twenty-four students to full communion in a single year. This was more than the church had contained at any time in its history and was not surpassed until 1802, when a later president reaped the benefits of a state-wide revival.[40]

Unfortunately Wales's successful career slowly disintegrated. Beginning in 1783 attacks of the "falling sickness" (epilepsy) incapacitated him more and more often. Wales was a favorite with the students

37. Chauncy to Stiles, Jan. 17, 1781. Stiles's letter to Chauncy has not been pre-served.

38. *Lit. Diary*, 2, 521.

39. Ibid., *3*, 46; Elizur Goodrich to Simeon Baldwin, Dec. 28, 1782, Baldwin Papers, Yale Univ. Lib.

40. Records of the College Church, Yale Univ. Lib.; E. S. Morgan, "Ezra Stiles and Timothy Dwight," Mass. Hist. Soc., *Proceedings, 72.*

and Stiles was so fond of the man and so impressed with his abilities
that he did not relieve him of office until 1793, after his condition
became hopeless. An earlier dismissal of the ailing professor could
have brought severe public criticism, which might have occurred even
in 1793 had Wales not placed a letter in the newspapers vouching for
his incapacity and lauding the college for its past indulgence to him.
Within five months he was dead.[41]

In spite of contemporary sympathy Stiles was undoubtedly delinquent in not removing Wales sooner. When Wales was normal, his
preaching was excellent, but no church could sustain a healthy religious life where the congregation sat nervously at every meeting,
waiting for the preacher to have a fit. On the other hand, it is ques-
tionable that the college, even with another professor, could have
sustained the religious pitch that marked the height of Wales's career.
Fervor in New England was notoriously cyclical, and outside Yale
the 1780s and 90s were a time of declension.

Fervid or not, the students shared in the college church, an experience that helped to cement them together and to the college. Through
church ceremonies and through the other rituals which Stiles conducted with such loving care at commencement and Quarter Days,
and through the fagging and the snowball fights and the taking off
of hats to the president, Yale preserved her identity. It was these
things, absurd as they might seem, that endeared the place to those
who spent four years there, so that one could write in 1782, using the
stilted language of the undergraduate: "Leaving College is like kissing
a dear Girl for the last time. The remembrance is sweet continually
exciting a wish to renew the enjoyment. Almost four years have
expired since I began courtship with the lovely maiden. At first only
tolerable she grew finally the object of rapturous love." [42]

If Stiles had done no more than this, if he had merely perpetuated
traditions and nurtured in students that irrational fondness for collegiate rigmarole that still constitutes so large a part of college life,
he would have earned credit only for keeping Yale alive when war,
depression, and public hostility threatened to leave her dead. But Stiles
was not content that Yale should merely live, or even thrive on a diet
of ceremony and tradition. Much as he loved these things, he knew
them to be vanity. The business of a university was learning, and he
wanted Yale to be a university in every sense of the word.

41. Corporation Records, Sept. 11, 1793; *Connecticut Journal*, Oct. 2, 1793.
42. Asher Robbins to Henry P. Dering, Aug. 1, 1782, Yale Univ. Lib.

24

The Academic Life

STILES had made known his ambitions for Yale before accepting the presidency. When the anticipated state subsidy failed to materialize, he had to drop the main features of his program, the new professorships in law and physic. He determined, nevertheless, to expand the curriculum wherever his own knowledge and energies would allow. In medicine and law (despite his early training) he did not feel competent to offer more than an occasional lecture. But there were other subjects that he knew as well as anyone in America, and he wanted his students to know them too.

At the time of his appointment it was arranged that he should be professor of ecclesiastical history as well as president.[1] On Thursday, August 6, 1778, at five in the afternoon, he delivered his first lecture. Thereafter on Thursday afternoons in term time Yale assembled in the chapel to hear a course of lectures which took until the end of the summer term in 1781 to complete and which started again in the fall of that year. The first year he dealt with biblical chronology and the church fathers, the second with the Reformation, the third with the American churches. He gave the series in continuous succession throughout his career as president, generally requiring four years rather than three to complete it, because of interruptions from other presidential duties or from sickness.[2]

1. *Lit. Diary*, 2, 225.
2. Ibid., pp. 293, 392, 479, 563, 565; 3, 510. Some of the manuscript notes for the lectures (or for Stiles's proposed book on the subject) are in the Mass. Hist. Soc.

At a time of religious decline, with the college under attack for clerical domination, Stiles may have seen ecclesiastical history, in part at least, as a way of resuscitating interest in religion. In the lectures on American churches he could link the lives and struggles of the early ministers to the ascendant mood of patriotism. In speaking on the history of the Catholic Church he presented the students with a list of errors that New Englanders, whatever their differences, could join in abhorring: "the supremacy of the Pope—his Infallibility—his Vicarship—Transubstantiation—Worship of the host—Supererrogation, or, the power of pardoning other men's Sins—Refusing the Cup to the Laity—Liberation from Purgatory—Doctrine of Penances—Flagellants—Celibacy of the Priests—Monasteries—Keeping the Scriptures from the Laity—Worship of Images in the forms of Saints and Angels." [3] From such horrors, it might be hoped, the students would recoil toward the faith of their fathers.

In order to strengthen the regular religious instruction offered in Sunday sermons by the professor of divinity, and perhaps to give the students a taste of doctrine that was a little more remote from the New Divinity than Daggett's or Wales's preaching, Stiles every Saturday at evening prayers delivered a lecture on some part of the Westminster Confession or the Savoy Declaration (the standard English formulations of Calvinist doctrine). The series lasted six or seven quarters and ran continuously, like the lectures on ecclesiastical history.[4]

Beginning July 29, 1780, he also carried on what he called "a Chamber Theological Lecture" on Saturday afternoons, for any pious graduates or undergraduates who wished thus to prepare for the Sabbath. The students first delivered compositions of their own on an announced topic (say, the evidence and proofs of the being of God, or the divinity of Christ), and then Stiles lectured on the subject himself. When Daggett died a few months later, and Stiles assumed his preaching duties, he continued these Saturday afternoon sessions, which probably contributed to the ensuing growth of the college church. He seems to have stopped them after Wales's inauguration in the professorship.[5]

Before Stiles became president, Hebrew was taught only sporadi-

3. Diary of Dyar Throop Hinckley, June 10, 1785, Conn. Hist. Soc.
4. *Lit. Diary*, 2, 277, 430; 3, 104, 145.
5. Ibid., 2, 453–54, 481, 512.

cally.[6] He determined that no future graduate should leave Yale as ignorant of this important subject as he had been. During the summer quarter, when the departure of the seniors eased his academic load, Stiles gave the freshmen a concentrated Hebrew course. "This is not required of a President," he noted in his Diary, "but I wish to benefit the College to the utmost of my Power."[7] Some of the freshmen became so interested that they wanted more; and so throughout each academic year he also taught advanced groups, occasionally hearing as many as five recitations a day from upperclassmen, graduates, and even tutors and local ministers who had had no previous opportunity to learn. Stiles wanted his students to know Hebrew, he explained in a flash of humor, because it was the language in which they would hear psalms sung in heaven.[8] In 1789, out of deference to public opinion and the protests from a softer generation of students, many of whom were headed for secular careers, Stiles offered to excuse from recitations any freshman who did not care to learn the language. Five excused themselves.[9] Hebrew was never again compulsory at Yale, but Stiles continued to teach it to volunteers from each class until the end of his career.

At Stiles's inauguration the college had a professor of mathematics and natural philosophy (which included most of what we now call science), who lectured every Wednesday. In 1781, after Nehemiah Strong resigned the chair and the corporation failed to refill it, Stiles undertook the responsibilities of that job too.[10] During the period when the corporation was reducing Strong's teaching, he had already tried to fill the gap with occasional lectures of his own. It was impossible, in the midst of his other duties, to give a weekly lecture on natural philosophy, but he slipped one in whenever he could find time, on Wednesday afternoons or after evening prayers or in place of ecclesiastical history. If a sudden thunderstorm, ascending comet, or other striking natural phenomenon appeared when he had the students before him for another purpose, he shifted to an impromptu talk on science instead. And when a book or correspondent informed him of

6. Tutor John Lewis taught it in 1775: Corporation Records, Sept. 13, 1775.
7. *Lit. Diary*, 2, 291.
8. Ibid., 3, 306 n.
9. "Memoranda: Yale College," July 14, 1789, June 28, 1790; *Lit. Diary*, 3, 397.
10. He received occasional assistance from Tutor Josiah Meigs (Yale, 1778, tutor 1781–84): Corporation Records, Sept. 10, 1783.

some new discovery, his excitement was sure to break out in a lecture on the subject.

A hint of scientific curiosity or deficiency might bring the president's personal instruction to the students. He once spent five continuous hours teaching a group "Astronomy, the Calculus and Delineation of a solar Eclipse; calculating the Eclipses of Jupiters Eclipses [i.e. Jupiter's satellites], the Place of Saturn and the other planets, and the Trajectory and places of Comets both heliocentric and geocentric." [11] Stiles also managed to get in some scientific instruction during vacations, if he was not leaving town and if any boys wanted to stay for it. Sometimes he allowed the students to share his own researches, counting noses and houses and measuring about New Haven, but whether as volunteers or as impressed labor his Diary does not tell.

In order to teach natural philosophy effectively it was necessary to have "philosophical apparatus," what we would call laboratory equipment: air pumps (to demonstrate the weight of the atmosphere), orreries (to demonstrate the movements of the solar system), telescopes, microscopes, electrical machines (for generating static electricity by friction). When Stiles became president, he hired Isaac Doolittle, a New Haven mechanic, to put the existing apparatus in repair and keep it there, but during the raid on New Haven much of it was injured in removal to a safer location. [12] New apparatus was badly needed, but the best, obtainable only in Europe, was beyond Yale's budget. Stiles, taking advantage of the mechanical genius which Connecticut produced in abundance, in 1784 got a talented junior, Joseph Badger, to construct some of the essential pieces. The most elaborate was an orrery, six feet in diameter, with internal gearing, showing the places of all the planets, including the newly discovered Uranus (then called Herschel after its discoverer) and three comets of known revolutions. Badger made the whole thing in a little over two months and used only thirty-six dollars worth of materials. [13]

Even with this addition the Yale philosophical apparatus was sadly

11. *Lit. Diary*, *3*, 35.

12. On the existing apparatus see *Lit. Diary*, *2*, 348–49; "Memoranda: Yale College," 1786, and Henry M. Fuller, "The Philosophical Apparatus of Yale College," in *Papers in Honor of Andrew Keogh* (New Haven, 1939), pp. 163–80. Doolittle's bills for repairs are in Yale Univ. Lib.

13. "Memoranda: Yale College," Mar. 16, 23, 1784; Corporation Records, Sept. 9, 1784.

deficient. Two years later, Manasseh Cutler (Yale 1765) on a visit
to the college found it contemptible: "an air-pump, tolerably good;
a reflecting telescope, wholly useless, for the large and small mirrors
are covered with rust, occasioned by poking in greasy fingers; a microscope of the compound kind, but very ancient; a miserable electrical
machine, a large, homely orrery, made by one of the students; a hydro-
static balance, and a few other articles not worth naming." Cutler
added, however, what was in fact true, that "a handsome sum . . .
is now being collected for purchasing a complete Philosophical apparatus." [14]

Beginning in September 1786, subscriptions were solicited throughout Connecticut and even as far as Boston, where Charles Chauncy
signed up for four guineas. In Connecticut people of all religious
and political complexions subscribed. Governor Huntington gave ten
pounds, Jeremiah Wadsworth (who might have afforded more) seven.
Stiles himself gave six, Isaac Beers, New Haven's leading merchant,
ten. The largest donation was £100 from Samuel Lockwood, a member
of the corporation and minister of Andover, Connecticut. All subscriptions were contingent on a total contribution of £300. By May
1787 £275 Lawful Money had been pledged, and in September the
corporation decided to proceed. Cash, however, proved more difficult
to collect than promises, and it was not until April 13, 1789, that Stiles
had enough money in hand to write his friend Richard Price in London, asking him to supervise the purchase of about £200 sterling worth
of equipment. Price himself contributed £6 6s. 3d. more.[15]

Stiles sent a list of the items the corporation hoped to get, leaving
it to Price to omit what could best be spared, if the sum would not
cover the whole. He emphasized, however, "that Utility and not
Ornament must be studied, that we wish for great plainess and that
the expenses of decoration may be laid out in more instruments."

The first shipment arrived in eight boxes on the day before Christmas 1789. When Stiles and the tutors opened the boxes, they found

---

14. Dexter, *Biographical Sketches*, *4*, 521–22.

15. The letter was not sent until Apr. 23. Information about the purchase is derived
from the *Lit. Diary*; College Treasury Book, pp. 133–34; the Simeon Baldwin Papers
(Baldwin was in charge of subscriptions in the New Haven area); an account of the
purchase by Stiles in a manuscript volume recording donations to Yale; and a collection of loose papers relating to the purchase, including invoices and correspondence—
all in Yale Univ. Lib.

a machine for demonstrating mechanical powers by pulleys and levers, a whirling table for showing centrifugal force and "the laws of accelerated, retarded, and rotatory motions," an air pump, glass tubes and vases for experiments in hydraulics and hydrostatics, an astronomical clock, an electrical machine, a pair of globes eighteen inches in diameter and "with all the latest discoveries," a solar microscope, a magic lantern, and various smaller items. The two largest and most expensive pieces that had been ordered, a three-foot reflecting telescope and an orrery ("to move with a Winch and Clockwork, to shew the Ptolomaic and Copernican System with a Tellurian and Lunarium pack'd in a Neat Mahogany Case") arrived a few months later.

They were all carried up to the "apparatus chamber" above the library in the northeast corner of the college. Benjamin Silliman, who entered Yale in 1792, recalled the room in his old age: "It was papered on the walls—the floor was sanded and the window shutters always kept closed except when visitors or students were introduced. There was an air of mystery about the room, and we entered it with awe, increasing to admiration, after we had seen something of the apparatus and the experiments." [16] A somewhat less imposing aid to science, probably housed in the library, was the college museum. It consisted of various skeletons, bones, horns, shells, fossils, minerals, stuffed animals, and Indian curiosities, plus a variety of miscellaneous junk which misguided donors had thrust upon the college. [17]

Besides supplying the Yale curriculum with ecclesiastical history, divinity, Hebrew, and natural philosophy, Stiles each year undertook to give coherence to the whole undergraduate program in a series of lectures which he called variously the Cyclopaedia (or Encyclopaedia) of Literature, the Cyclopaedia of Science, or the Circle of the Sciences. The words "literature" and "science" in the eighteenth century lacked the special meaning we have given them and were used interchangeably to signify formal knowledge. Stiles's lectures ranged widely over the fields of learning, covering language, geography, mathematics, natural philosophy, and astronomy in that order. [18] It seems probable

16. Silliman, "Origin and Progress of Chemistry, Mineralogy, and Geology in Yale College, with reminiscences of Personal History," Yale Univ. Lib.

17. Josiah Meigs, "Catalogue of Articles in the Museum of Yale College," Aug. 1796, Yale Univ. Lib.; *Connecticut Journal*, Feb. 25, 1774.

18. Diary of Dyar Throop Hinckley, Nov. 10, 22, Dec. 21, 27, 1784; *Lit. Diary*, 2, 308; 3, 436–39, 479–83.

that they were designed to give the students an over-all perspective of human learning, to furnish a framework that would comprehend all the subjects they studied. The effort was reminiscent of the seventeenth-century Technologia. Propositions under this heading, devoted to general statements about learning, continued to appear on Yale commencement broadsides throughout the eighteenth century. Stiles was probably seeking to give them meaning. Unfortunately there is no way of telling how he did it. He continued to believe in the picture of the "Moral and Intellectual World" he had constructed in his days as a tutor, but whether he attempted to convey this to his students is not apparent.[19]

In Stiles's view a college differed from a grammar school, and a university from a college, not merely in the level of instruction but in the abundance and variety of subjects taught. In seeking to furnish lectures in so many fields Stiles was trying to raise Yale toward the stature of a university.[20] In addition to those already mentioned, he prepared lectures on the oriental languages, on moral philosophy, and on the structure of the eye and nature of vision. These he gave irregularly but often enough so that each college generation had a chance to hear them. On the same basis he gave a series of three lectures on the learned professions: law, medicine, and the ministry. These were a form of vocational guidance, to give students a quick view of everything they would have to study in preparation for each of these careers.[21]

In spite of his desire that Yale be well supplied with lectures, Stiles did not suppose any more than his contemporaries, that lectures should take the place of other types of instruction. In each assigned subject a college or university student was expected to study a designated book and "recite" it in class to a tutor. Professors, or in their absence the president, gave lectures; tutors guided the students' absorption of books. At Harvard, after 1766, tutors taught a particular subject to all classes that studied it; [22] at Yale a tutor taught all subjects to a single class. Moreover, a Yale tutor normally accompanied the same

19. On Mar. 10, 1785, the *New Haven Gazette* (Meigs, Bowen, and Dana) carried an article on the universe, which was almost certainly by Stiles, expounding the views contained in his essay on the subject written while a tutor at Yale. See above, Chap. 4.

20. Stiles to Eliphalet Williams, Dec. 3, 1777.

21. A synopsis of the contents of the lectures on law and medicine will be found in *Lit. Diary, 3*, 444, 486–87.

22. S. E. Morison, *Three Centuries of Harvard* (Cambridge, Mass.., 1937), p. 90.

class up the academic ladder. He would be assigned, in the year of his appointment, to the freshman class. The next year he would take the same students as sophomores and the following year as juniors. By this time he might be ready to resign the tutorship. If not, he would assume charge of another class, for seniors came under the supervision of the president.[23] Under this arrangement the tutor's relationship to his students was close; during the two or three years they were in his charge he was their principal instructor in every subject. It was obviously important to have good tutors.

Yale recruited them from recent graduates. President Clap used to pick out likely candidates while they were still in college and groom them for the job. When Daggett took over, the corporation did not trust his judgment and itself chose a leading scholar from each class two or three years after graduation.[24] Under Stiles, and perhaps before, the existing tutors took a large hand in the choice of new ones. Elizur Goodrich (Yale 1779), who served from 1781 to 1783, in December 1782 told Simeon Baldwin (Yale 1781) that he would be selected at the following commencement: the corporation, of course, would have to confirm the choice, but Goodrich assured his friend that "Tutors are (inter nos) appointed by tutors."[25] Baldwin was chosen.

The position was not lucrative; it paid no more than a man might get from teaching a prosperous secondary school.[26] And though a tutor could count on having his salary supplemented by a substantial yearly gift from his students, the job was sought for prestige rather

23. When a class rose above eighty students, as some did in the early 1780s, it was divided between two tutors. When it reached the senior year, the division was retained, but Stiles taught both sections.

24. *Lit. Diary*, 2, 514.

25. Elizur Goodrich to Simeon Baldwin, Dec. 28, 1782, Baldwin Papers, Yale Univ. Lib.

26. When Stiles became president, the salary of a tutor was £70. In the 1780s it rose to £85, but by 1792 it was back to £70. The senior tutor, serving as librarian, usually got £5 or £10 more than the others, but during Stiles's presidency no tutor received more than £90 a year. Tutors in the early 1780s had charge of 50, 60, or even 70 odd students. After 1785 the classes diminished again, and the corporation may have returned to the old salary for this reason. Occasionally a tutor might supplement his income by holding the Berkeleian fellowship (known as "scholar of the house") for graduates residing at college who had not yet taken the master's degree. Three such fellowships could be awarded each year, each paying an amount that ranged from a low of £11 2s. in 1783 to a high of £14 3s. 4d. in 1793.

than profit. Few men held it more than three or four years, and with none did it become a permanent career.

Superior men were induced to take it, because it advertised their superiority. It meant that in the judgment of the president and corporation the recipient was the ablest recent graduate. To such a person the opportunity of pursuing the academic life for a few years longer was often attractive. Moreover, since only recent graduates were selected, they were still close enough to their college years to value the dignity of standing above everyone else in the college community except the president and professors (if any). It was an established principle at Yale that a tutor, whether or not he had yet received his master's degree, outranked any other recent graduate who was not a tutor. Tutors were so conscious of rank that even gradations within the tutorial body had to be settled. Normally these went by seniority, but the question arose in President Clap's time whether the date of the bachelor's degree or the date of becoming a tutor should govern. Clap ruled in favor of priority of election to the tutorship. Thus Warham Williams (Yale 1745), elected tutor in 1746, outranked Alexander Phelps (Yale 1744), who was not elected until 1747.[27]

In order to avoid injured feelings it became the practice to elect tutors only in the order of their graduation. Stiles thought this a mistake. "The governing principle," he said, "ought to be to elect the best Scholars into the Tutorship. And it is such an Honor as Token of literary Merit, that I should not be ashamed to take the Office tho' elected after a Junior." Most of the tutors elected under Stiles did follow the order of graduation, but he often passed by an entire class to choose several tutors from another, more gifted one. When an exceptionally able man from an older class became available, he did not hesitate to appoint him after his juniors. Thus in 1786 he persuaded Abiel Holmes (Yale 1783), returning from a stay in Georgia, to accept an appointment; in 1789 he did the same with Amos Bassett (Yale 1784), who had been preceptor of an academy in Schenectady.[28]

A total of twenty-seven men served as tutors under Stiles. Most of them achieved eminence in the state and several in the nation.[29]

27. *Lit. Diary*, 2, 513–14.
28. Ibid., pp. 513–15; 3, 244, 356; "Memoranda: Yale College," June 8, 1789.
29. The most distinguished were Abraham Baldwin, member of the Continental Congress, the Constitutional Convention, and the United States Senate; Chauncy

Before Stiles they had generally been selected from graduates who were preparing for the ministry. Stiles seems to have aimed at a balance between men headed for the ministry and men headed for secular careers. From 1779 to 1792 both were always on his staff. In 1792 for the first time all his tutors were ministerial candidates. During the previous two years, when Professor Wales was increasingly unfit to fill the pulpit, the tutors who could do so had been called upon more and more to preach.[30] Probably in order to spread the burden, Stiles filled three successive vacancies with ministerial candidates. But he followed these with several secular appointments when Wales's complete deterioration heralded the election of a new professor of divinity.

In the absence of a professorial staff the tutors were, in effect, the faculty. As Stiles put it, "The Tutors have ever been the efficient Instructors in this University; being of the same weight in this Institution as the Professors in the foreign Universities." [31] The tutors enjoyed complete freedom in conducting their classes and undoubtedly interrupted the routine of recitations to discuss with the students the lectures of the president and professors, or to give their own views on some topic in the textbook that particularly interested them, just as Stiles himself did when hearing the recitations of the seniors. Monday through Friday freshmen and sophomores met their tutors three times a day for recitations, the first coming before breakfast, about seven in the morning, the second at eleven, and the third at five in the afternoon. Upperclassmen were more on their own: juniors recited twice a day (at eleven and five), seniors only once (at eleven).

The subjects recited when Stiles became president were about the same as they had been when he was a student, and many of the same textbooks were still in use.[32] Locke had been assigned to the seniors

---

Goodrich, also a United States senator; Ebenezer Fitch, first president of Williams College; Josiah Meigs, president of the University of Georgia; Jedidiah Morse, geographer; and Abiel Holmes, historian.

30. The usual procedure was for a tutor to preach in a neighboring church while the minister thus relieved would preach in chapel.

31. Stiles, Sermons on Thanksgivings, July 1787.

32. The problem of ascertaining the curriculum followed at any given time is difficult. The Corporation Records say nothing about it, and there are no records of faculty meetings. The college laws, of which there were new editions in 1774, 1787, and 1795, prescribe the subjects to be recited by each class, but they do not prescribe the books. Moreover, it is plain from other evidence that the laws sometimes anticipated

instead of the juniors, and logic to the sophomores. So far as new books had been introduced in Clap's later years and under Daggett, the changes had been of mixed value. Robert Lowth's *Short Introduction to English Grammar*,[33] a brief but adequate survey of the parts of speech, tenses, irregular verbs, construction of sentences, and punctuation was an improvement on Watts's *Art of Reading and Writing English*, but the substitution (about 1760) of Benjamin Martin's *Philosophical Grammar*[34] and three-volume *Philosophia Britannica*[35] for Gravesande's *Natural Philosophy*[36] was the replacement of a professional by an amateur. Martin's works were more comprehensive than Gravesande's. They covered what later became biology, geology, and meteorology as well as Newtonian physics, but they offered breadth at the expense of depth. In addition to these two changes, geography had been added to the curriculum in William Guthrie's *New Geographical, Historical, and Commercial Grammar*.[37] Sophomores must have been amused by some of the English author's statements: he believed, for instance, that New England still banished Quakers on pain of death.

Under Stiles the changes, though not extensive, were larger than in preceding decades. The freshmen still recited Latin (usually Virgil and Cicero),[38] the Greek Testament, and arithmetic. The principal

---

changes that were not actually made until later and sometimes recognized changes made some time before. The only reliable evidence comes from student notebooks, diaries, and letters, and from Stiles's *Lit. Diary* and "Memoranda: Yale College." The following account is pieced together from a variety of such sources. See especially *Lit. Diary*, 2, 387–88; 3, 99 n.; "Memoranda: Yale College," 1793; and Thomas Robbins, Diary 1777–95, Conn. Hist. Soc. The last is not really a diary but an autobiographical account written 1796–98. The author entered Yale in the class of 1796 but transferred to Williams for his senior year.

33. London, 1762; Hartford, 1780. *Lit. Diary*, 2, 388. There were many editions both in England and in the United States.

34. London, 1735; "Memoranda: Yale College," Nov. 22, 1787.

35. Reading, 1747; a compendium and abridgement in 3 vols. of the writings of various scientists.

36. Willem Jacob van's Gravesande, *Mathematical Elements of Natural Philosophy*, trans. J. T. Desaguliers (London, 1720).

37. London, 1770.

38. In 1793 and perhaps regularly the freshmen also recited a Latin grammar: John Clarke's *Introduction to the Making of Latin* (17th ed. London, 1757). "Memoranda: Yale College," 1793.

changes for them were a new recitation subject, English grammar,[39] and a new arithmetic book. The English text in the early years was probably Lowth, but sometime before 1793 Stiles supplemented it with the *Plain and Comprehensive Grammar of the English Language*,[40] by Noah Webster (Yale 1778). Webster presented the subject in simple questions and answers, with examples of correct and incorrect usage, much more easily grasped than the more formal rules offered by Lowth.

The new arithmetic text introduced in 1785 was the *New and Complete System of Arithmetic* [41] composed by Nicholas Pike of Newburyport, Massachusetts "for the use of the Citizens of the United States." It replaced John Ward's *Young Mathematician's Guide*,[42] familiar to the preceding two generations of Yale men. Pike, like Webster, gave attention to making his book intelligible. Since the existing textbooks were "generally deficient in the Illustration and Application of the rules," he demonstrated the rules through problems faced by tradesmen, merchants, surveyors, navigators, or mechanics.

As sophomores, the students continued to study Pike's *Arithmetic* but supplemented his treatment of algebra with a less practical, more advanced work of Nathaniel Hammond.[43] They also recited Latin (usually Horace), the Greek Testament, logic (probably Watts's),[44]

39. "Memoranda: Yale College," 1793.

40. Pt. II of Webster's *Grammatical Institute of the English Language* (Hartford, 1783–85). Webster adopted the latter title at Stiles's suggestion: "Memoranda: Yale College," 1793; Harry R. Warfel, *Letters of Noah Webster* (New York, 1953), pp. 20, 527. In 1790 Webster had donated one per cent of his Connecticut royalties toward a yearly prize for the best student composition on belles lettres, ethics, or moral philosophy. It is not clear whether the donation was made before or after the adoption. *Lit. Diary*, *3*, 382; Stiles to Webster, Mar. 16, 1790, Pierpont Morgan Library.

41. Newburyport, 1788. *Lit. Diary*, *3*, 312.

42. London, 1709. But in 1793–94 Thomas Robbins used Ward in addition to Pike: Diary, Conn. Hist. Soc.

43. Nathaniel Hammond, *The Elements of Algebra* (London, 1742). In 1793 the sophomores were also studying trigonometry and conic sections, both treated more briefly in Pike than Stiles would have wished. The author had consulted him before publication. "Memoranda: Yale College," 1793; Pike to Stiles, Jan. 17, Aug. 21, 1786.

44. Isaac Watts, *Logick: or the Right Use of Reason in the Enquiry after Truth* (London, 1725); Robbins, Diary; Dyar Throop Hinckley, Diary, Dec. 17, 1784; "Memoranda: Yale College," 1793.

geography, English grammar, and rhetoric. In 1789 Stiles introduced the new *American Geography* [45] of Jedidiah Morse (Yale 1783) for study of the western hemisphere, but retained Guthrie for the rest of the world, because Morse's work lacked adequate maps.

In 1785 Stiles brought Yale's English course to maturity by requiring sophomores to recite Hugh Blair's *Lectures on Rhetoric and Belles Lettres*.[46] Published in London in 1783, this work became, in effect, the first textbook on literature and had a long life in American college curricula. It began with a discussion of language and the elements of style and then moved to a critical examination of various types of literature and oratory as exemplified by the classic practitioners of each type. It was in every way more advanced than anything hitherto studied at Yale in the field of belles lettres.

Juniors recited Cicero on oratory and briefly reviewed the Greek Testament. They continued their mathematics with trigonometry, navigation, and surveying,[47] and they plowed through Martin's volumes of natural philosophy. Stiles dropped the *Philosophical Grammar* in 1786 and the *Philosophia Britannica* in 1788, replacing them with William Enfield's *Institutes of Natural Philosophy*.[48] Enfield, like Martin, was a popularizer, not a practicing scientist, but as rector of Warrington Academy in England he had experience in teaching natural philosophy and had written his book when he found that the

45. Elizabethtown, New Jersey, 1789; *Lit. Diary, 3,* 351. After Morse published his 2-volume *American Universal Geography* (Boston, 1793), Stiles seems to have used the first volume (which was confined to the Americas) but not the second: Stiles to Morse, Feb. 18, 1794, Morse Papers, Yale Univ. Lib.

46. London, 1783. There were many English and American editions. Stiles, "Memoranda: Yale College," Nov. 21, 1787. Cf. Robert Aiken to Stiles, March 17, 1784. It seems probable that Stiles, before adopting Blair, abandoned John Holmes, *The Art of Rhetoric Made Easy* (3d impression, London, 1766) which was in use at his accession and still in use in 1781. Elijah Leonard to David Daggett, July 3, 1781, Daggett Papers, Yale Univ. Lib.; *Lit. Diary, 2,* 388. It is also possible that Stiles later supplemented Blair with Noah Webster's *Dissertations on the English Language* (Boston, 1789). Sophomores in 1793 were reciting "Webster Eng. Lang.," which may have been either the *Institutes* or the *Dissertations,* but Thomas Robbins says that he read the *Dissertations:* "Memoranda: Yale College," 1793; Robbins, Diary.

47. In 1794–95 Thomas Robbins used James Atkinson's *Epitome of the Art of Navigation* (London, 1706) and John Love's *Geodaesia; or the Art of surveying and measuring of Land, made easie* (London, 1688); Robbins, Diary.

48. London, 1785. *Lit. Diary, 3,* 272, 312; "Memoranda: Yale College," Feb. 17 1786.

only existing ones were either "deficient in Mathematical Demonstration" or else too abstruse for beginners. He included not only mathematical demonstrations of the different principles of natural philosophy but also descriptions of experiments to be performed on the philosophical apparatus. Enfield was supplemented by recitations in James Ferguson's *Astronomy* [49] (which dealt at length with the transit of Venus) and probably by reading in Joseph Priestley's *History and Present State of Electricity*,[50] a large and handsome volume, containing not only a history of the subject (with appropriate attention to Franklin) but also instructions for building electrical apparatus and conducting experiments.

Enfield, though clear and competent, was only one volume. Its substitution (even with the addition of Ferguson and Priestley) for the three-volume *Philosophia Britannica* and one-volume *Philosophical Grammar*, reduced the time spent by juniors on natural philosophy and made room for a new subject in the junior curriculum. In the summer of 1790 Tutor Barnabas Bidwell started the juniors reciting Joseph Priestley's *Lectures on History and General Policy*.[51] This discussed the various classical historians and the later chroniclers, but the organization was topical rather than chronological. Like many eighteenth-century works on the subject, it used history to teach political and moral philosophy—a use that Stiles himself thought proper, for he considered the study of politics, to be "itself civil History of the best kind." [52] Priestley drew from history precisely the lessons that Stiles himself liked to draw: Priestley found in every age and every nation a justification for the principles of republican liberty.

49. *Astronomy explained upon Sir Isaac Newton's principles, and made easy to those who have not studied mathematics* (London, 1756). Stiles identifies this book simply as "Ferguson," in "Memoranda: Yale College," 1793, and it is possible that he meant Adam Ferguson's *Essay on the History of Civil Society* (Edinburgh, 1767). But Thomas Robbins (Yale 1796) says in his Diary that he recited "Ferguson's Astronomy." Ferguson's *Civil Society*, however, was used in senior recitations by Stiles's successor in 1796. See Charles Dennison to Thomas Robbins, Jan. 4, 1796. Robbins Papers, Conn. Hist. Soc.

50. London, 1767. Stiles noted in "Memoranda: Yale College," 1793, that the juniors were reciting "Priestly" and also that they were reading "Priestly," but he listed no titles. On Feb. 1, 1794 ("Memoranda: Yale College") he noted that they were reading "Electy." but he listed no author. It is clear, however, that the volume recited was the *Lectures on History* (see note 51, below).

51. Dublin, 1788. "Memoranda: Yale College," June 11, 1790.

52. Stiles to Eliphalet Williams, Dec. 3, 1777.

According to the college laws, the studies of the seniors were to center around metaphysics and ethics. Stiles used Lock's *Essay concerning Human Understanding* as the basis of the daily class discussion and probably took the opportunities it offered for excursions into his own views of the universe and the varying capacities of men and angels to perceive it in this world and the next. He ended the year with a whirlwind two-week course on moral philosophy, lecturing on the subject and hearing the students go over President Clap's book on ethics.[53]

When Stiles first became president, the seniors had petitioned him for a second recitation period. They never got it, probably because they already had more work to do than they could creditably perform.[54] But in 1789, when he had improved academic standards sufficiently to warrant expansion of the senior curriculum, he added a new subject, political philosophy, making room for it by shortening the time devoted to Locke. Political philosophy had been one of Stiles's lifelong enthusiasms. In 1775, when listing for his son's tutor the various branches of knowledge he considered important, he had included "a general knowledge of the Nature of Government, and the different *Policies* in all the Kingdoms and Empires on Earth."[55] In 1777 he elaborated the idea to Eliphalet Williams in his plan of a university. Among the lectures Stiles wanted the proposed professor of law to give was a series "exhibiting the Policies and Forms of Government of every and all the Kingdoms Empires and Republics in the World, especially those of Europe and China." Knowledge of this kind, he hoped, would enable Americans "to distinguish and avoid Precedents dangerous to Liberty."[56]

In a revision of the college laws in 1787 the study of "History and civil Policy" was approved for senior recitations,[57] but Stiles did not

53. Thomas Clap, *An Essay on the Nature and Foundation of Moral Virtue and Obligation* (New Haven, 1765). This work, printed just before Clap's retirement and death, had been "sometimes recited" earlier. It was evidently replaced by Jonathan Edwards' *Careful and Strict Enquiry into the Modern Prevailing Notions of . . . Freedom of the Will* (Boston, 1754). But for several years preceding Stiles's accession there had been no recitations in ethics. *Lit. Diary*, 2, 349. Cf. James Dana to Stiles, Dec. 18, 1782; Chauncy Whittelsey to Stiles, June 30, 1768.

54. *Lit. Diary*, 2, 277; in 1793 Stiles thought the seniors "too fully employed": "Memoranda: Yale College," 1793.

55. Stiles to John Lewis, Feb. 15, 1775.

56. Stiles to Eliphalet Williams, Dec. 3, 1777.

57. *The Laws of Yale College* (New Haven, 1787), p. 9.

implement the order until two years later. In 1789 the time was opportune to start Yale students thinking about precedents dangerous to liberty. The new federal Constitution had been adopted after heated controversy over its omission of a bill of rights. Abroad the French Revolution challenged the imagination of everyone who believed in liberty. To cope with a new era, America needed politically sophisticated citizens. That people in Connecticut were saying so undoubtedly encouraged Stiles to admit the study of political philosophy and history into the Yale curriculum. On March 12, 1789, after hurrying through Locke, he began the seniors in Montesquieu's *Spirit of the Laws*,[58] a work that had been often cited in debates on the Constitution. In succeeding years Stiles also squeezed in senior recitations of Emmerich de Vattel's *The Law of Nations*[59] and William Paley's *Principles of Moral and Political Philosophy*.[60] The latter, besides adding to the program in political philosophy, supplemented the work in President Clap's ethics.

Although it was assumed that training for a career would come after graduation rather than before, Stiles directed some of the outside reading of seniors toward their chosen professions. Future lawyers read Pufendorf, Grotius, and Blackstone; future physicians read books on anatomy, natural history, and chemistry. In the absence of professors of law or medicine, the seniors might also seek out local lawyers and physicians "for as much Instruction, as it is best for them to be charged with, during that general Course, which must be the foundation of universal and great Literature."[61]

Seniors headed for the ministry could get advice from the president or the professor of divinity about reading in "the proper initial theological Treatises and ecclesiastical History."[62] But Yale was never a mere theological seminary; and for all undergraduates divinity was a minor subject: freshmen studied it only incidentally in their transla-

58. *De l'Esprit des loix* (Geneva, 1748); *The Spirit of Laws*, trans. from the French (London, 1750); *Lit. Diary*, 3, 346. Although neither history nor political philosophy had hitherto been recited, student notebooks show that they had read books on these subjects (probably assigned by the faculty) even before Stiles became president.

59. London, 1760. trans. from the French. Yale students seem to have used the Dublin, 1787 edition: "Memoranda: Yale College," June 20, 1792.

60. London, 1785. "Memoranda: Yale College," June 17, 1791 (the date when Paley was introduced).

61. Stiles to Christoph D. Ebeling, Feb. 20, 1795.

62. Ibid.

tion of the Greek Testament, and the three upper classes recited a divinity textbook only once a week, on Saturdays. At his accession Stiles found the sophomores and juniors reciting Vincent, the seniors Ames and Wollebius.[63] From the beginning he made Vincent (a much more elementary work than Ames or Wollebius) the seniors' text too, and in 1792 he reduced their recitations to once a month. In the following year sophomores and juniors recited no divinity.[64]

It should not be inferred from Stiles's reduction of the formal study of divinity that he had abandoned religious instruction at Yale. The students had prayers and a Bible reading in chapel twice daily, received a weekly ecclesiastical-history lecture, had their Saturday evening lectures on the Confession of Faith, and on Sunday spent sometimes as much as five or six hours in chapel, hearing morning prayers by the president, sermons from the professor of divinity before and after dinner, and at evening prayers a third sermon by a senior or resident bachelor. There were sermons by visiting preachers, sermons appropriate to the season, funeral sermons, thanksgiving sermons, fast-day sermons. Most of those by the professor of divinity fell into a four-year series which, taken together, comprised a complete exposition of Christian divinity. The series began with the characteristics of God (omnipotence, holiness, perfection, wisdom, trinity) and proceeded to creation, election, providence, the fall of man, Christ's atonement, and the processes of redemption.[65]

Although none of the changes in curriculum during his presidency could have been made without his consent, Stiles may not have originated all of them. He kept a judicious ear open to public criticism and the temper of his corporation; and he also allowed the tutors a large hand in determining what books they were to teach, perhaps from a realization that neither tutor nor student would profit from the recitation of a book in which neither was interested. In the assignment of outside reading he even seems to have permitted a program with which he did not wholly agree. In 1793, for instance, he noted, with

63. Thomas Vincent, *An Explicatory Catechism* (London, 1701); William Ames, *Medulla S.S. Theologiae* (Amsterdam, 1627); Joannes Wollebius, *Abridgement of Christian Divinity* (London, 1650).

64. *Lit. Diary*, 2, 314, 387–88; 3, 99 n.; "Memoranda: Yale College," Feb. 4, 1792. In 1759 Stiles favored replacing Ames with "Hucheson's or some other piece on moral Philosophy" (to Francis Alison, July 3, 1759). He may have looked on Paley, more than Vincent, as the substitute for Ames.

65. Stiles noted the subjects, passim in *Lit. Diary*, 2 and 3.

criticisms, the kinds of books prescribed for each class.[66] The freshmen read novels, plays, orations, speeches, and "nonsense"; the sophomores Rollin's ancient history, Robertson's Greece, and Shakespeare; the juniors Priestley (probably the *History of Electricity* already noted), Watts's *Astronomy*,[67] "a little phil.," belles lettres, and Rousseau's *Emile;* the seniors history, voyages, travels, and politics. Surviving student reading notes suggest a strong undergraduate interest in belles lettres. Shakespeare was the favorite dramatist, though not accorded quite the pre-eminence he has since achieved, and Laurence Sterne was the favorite novelist. Pope was still popular, and so were the polite essayists, especially Chesterfield. Among historians the students favored Robertson but also read Voltaire. He and Rousseau were the only representatives of the French Enlightenment.[68]

Stiles had mixed feelings about the popularity of belles lettres. He had explained to tutor John Lewis in 1775 that he had "an indifferent opinion" of poetry, dramatic writings, and novels but that he thought favorably of "the higher and more valuable Branches of the *belles lettres,* such as geography, history, speaking, and accurate composition in the *English language.*"[69] Time did not alter this opinion, and he was not happy about the freshmen reading novels and plays, which he thought a dubious way of improving their literary style. In spite of his approval of history, he thought the sophomores read it too soon, to the neglect of their mathematical studies. He also thought the undergraduate training deficient in languages, astronomy, and natural philosophy, and he wondered if it might not be better to spend some of the seniors' time on science instead of giving them such a heavy dose of political philosophy as he had been attempting.[70]

Stiles's criticism of his own program was typical of the man. He was fond of standing back from himself and looking at what he had done with a critical eye. But his criticisms also exhibit his willingness to allow healthy disagreement within the college. Not only did he

66. "Memoranda: Yale College," 1793.

67. Isaac Watts, *The Knowledge of the Heavens and the Earth Made Easy* (London, 1726).

68. Henry P. Dering, "Miscellany"; Simeon Baldwin, "Letter Book," 1781–82, Yale Univ. Lib.; John Cotton Smith, "College Notebooks and Diary," Conn. Hist. Soc. Further evidence will be found in the numerous student compositions preserved in the Yale Univ. Lib.

69. Stiles to John Lewis, Feb. 15, 1775.

70. "Memoranda: Yale College," 1793.

respect the tutors' wishes in assignments which he did not wholly approve, but he treated the students with the same respect. He was willing to let them make their own mistakes, as he had made his. In 1759, when President Clap removed from the library the sermons of Dr. Samuel Clarke (whose writings had started Stiles on the road to deism), Stiles had urged him to restore the volume, in the name of "that generous and equal Liberty for which Protestants and Dissenters have made so noble a Stand." Stiles admitted that "with this Liberty Error may be introduced." But without it "Truth may be extinguished." Deism, Stiles thought, could not be suppressed by hiding deistical writings. The only way to conquer it was "to come forth into the open Field and dispute the Matter on even Footing." [71]

In running the college himself Stiles did not falter from this creed. He was no friend of deism, nor for that matter of the New Divinity, but he did not take advantage of his position to impose his own views —he would have thought it futile to try—on either tutors or students. Instead, he tried to make his students think their own way through controversial questions. Although the recitation of assigned texts and the passive absorption of lectures were better designed to perpetuate traditional learning than to make students think for themselves, Stiles found in another part of the traditional curriculum the very medium he needed for the advancement of free inquiry.

At Yale, as at every university from the Middle Ages to the nineteenth century, an essential part of the weekly program was debating. On Mondays and Tuesdays the two upper classes gathered in the chapel to argue an assigned topic, the juniors before their tutor, the seniors before the president. The whole class prepared arguments, half in the negative, half in the affirmative, but presumably only a few students from each side were called upon to present them. After both sides had been heard, the president (or tutor) decided which had won, and sometimes gave a brief disquisition of his own on the subject.[72]

The disputations were of two kinds, forensic and syllogistic. The syllogistic, as in Stiles's undergraduate days, were in Latin, designed

71. Stiles to Clap, Aug. 6, 1759. See also Stiles to ——— Bennett, Sept. 14, 1759.

72. Stiles frequently recorded the subjects of disputations but seldom recorded his or the tutors' decisions, nor do surviving student notebooks often give his decisions, as a few notebooks do for his successor. See, for example, Abe C. Ravitz, ed., "Timothy Dwight's Decisions," *New Eng. Quart.*, 31 (1958), 514–19, and Theodore Dwight, Jr., *President Dwight's Decisions* (New York, 1833).

as exercises in the use of formal logic. Originally they occurred every Monday, but after 1782 Stiles reduced them to the first Monday in the month, and in 1789 gave them up altogether.[73] The forensic disputations were in English, took longer to deliver, and were more fun. They occurred every Tuesday and every Monday except the one reserved (until 1789) for syllogisms.

Before Stiles became president, the topics for both types of disputation were mostly old brain-teasers that every generation of Yale students had worked over: whether deception is ever lawful, whether polygamy is lawful, whether animals think, whether the human mind is always thinking, whether all human actions are voluntary, whether the Scriptures are divinely inspired, whether a promise extorted by force is binding, whether everything that happens is for the best, whether there are any innate ideas, whether man can sin while sleeping.[74] The difficulty with topics like these was that they presented issues so abstract or so remote from common experience that the arguments tended to be mere mental gymnastics. Students might get healthy exercise from wrestling with them, but nothing more.

When Stiles became president, he at first continued to use the old topics. Indeed, the first syllogistic topic he assigned was the one he had argued at commencement in 1746, "Jus Regum non est Jure divino haereditarium." [75] Throughout his presidency he used the old topics for syllogistic disputations, but in forensic disputes he set the students to arguing questions that brought the Yale curriculum almost painfully up to date. He made the students apply their history, political theory, and moral philosophy to the most controversial political questions of the time, varying the topics as public issues varied.

The first disputation of this kind came on April 6, 1779, when he had the seniors argue "Which [would be] the most just and eligible mode of Taxation for paying the Continental Debt, that founded on

73. *Lit. Diary*, 3, 47, 360; "Memoranda: Yale College," July 20, 1789. Stiles himself seems to have disapproved the action. He had told John Lewis (Feb. 15, 1775) that he had "no great opinion of *Logic*," but he evidently regretted the disappearance of any exercise that required the use of Latin. Latin, which had once been the official collegiate language was spoken less and less during the eighteenth century, and by 1793 Stiles thought that the students gave too little time to all languages: "Memoranda: Yale College," 1793.

74. These topics will be found in Stiles's own student notebooks and in those of Eleazar May (Yale 1752) and Jeremiah Day (Yale 1756), Yale Univ. Lib., and of Ammi Robbins (Yale 1760), Conn. Hist. Soc.

75. *Lit. Diary*, 2, 284.

Estates, or that on the *Number of Inhabitants,* or that on a Ratio and
Valuation compounded or constituted of both." [76] It was a question
the United States Congress had argued for some time without reaching agreement. On November 9, he sprang another of these questions:
"Whether the present War be lawful on the side of America." Since
New Haven contained a fair number of loyalists, the question would
not have been regarded there as purely academic. On March 28, 1780,
six weeks before Connecticut election day (and regularly thereafter
at this time of year) the seniors disputed "Whether it is for the public
Emolument that Representatives should be subject to and obliged
to act or vote according to the Instructions of their Constituents." Although he continued to use the old topics occasionally, he gradually
shifted the emphasis to new ones of this kind. One may trace the great
public issues of the period on both the national and the local scene
in the subjects he assigned:

> December 26, 1780: whether Vermont is, and of right ought to be a sep-
> arate and independent state.
>
> April 16, 1782: whether agriculture or commerce needs the most encourage-
> ment in the United States at present [Stiles thought neither; what needed
> encouragement was manufacturing].
>
> March 24, 1783: whether a standing army would be dangerous in America.
>
> April 28, 1783: whether it would be best to establish a general amnesty, and
> restore the refugee Tories to their estates and franchises.
>
> June 9, 1783: whether the army at disbanding have any just right to either
> half pay for life, or the commutation of five years.
>
> December 15, 1783: whether Congress ought to have more power and au-
> thority.
>
> April 19, 1784: whether the Institution of the Cincinnati will prove detri-
> mental to the public.
>
> March 20, 1786: whether depreciation ought in justice to be paid on the
> public securities.
>
> June 8, 1786: whether paper money is a benefit.
>
> February 20, 1787: whether the insurrection in the Massachusetts be justi-
> fiable.

76. This and the topics mentioned below will be found in the *Lit. Diary* at the
designated dates.

March 27, 1787: whether an emission of paper money would be advantageous to the state of Connecticut.

June 12, 1787: whether it would be good policy to pardon the Massachusetts Convicts.

June 19, 1787: whether the states acted wisely in sending delegates to the general convention now sitting at Philadelphia.

November 26, 1787: whether it is expedient for the states to adopt the new Constitution.

April 29, 1788: whether navigation of the Mississippi should be free.

February 10, 1789: whether a rotation in the public offices of government would be good policy in the United States.

June 9, 1789: whether it would be right to compel the unfederated states into the federal union.

Stiles did not shrink from debates that struck even closer to home than these. He had the seniors argue the ticklish question of whether laymen ought to be joined with ministers in the Yale corporation. When they rebelled against a new policy of making the July examination a real test of learning, he made them debate whether four years' residence at college should entitle a student to a degree regardless of his scholarship. When it looked as though a large number of students were going to leave college and study with Timothy Dwight, he had them debate whether a private (academy) education was preferable to a public (college) one. When they wanted to give or attend dramatic performances, he had them debate whether the theater ought to be encouraged.[77]

Disputations were the keystone of Stiles's curriculum. Through them he generated excitement, taught students to express themselves, made them rub against other minds with other views. Disputations assisted their digestion and absorption of assigned reading and lectures and taught them to ferret out supporting evidence from the books in the library.[78] Besides the topics drawn from current public issues,

77. *Lit. Diary*, 2, 545; 3, 210, 231, 260, 269, 315, 351.

78. Eli Whitney's record of disputations in 1790 and 1791 (Whitney Papers, Yale Univ. Lib.) gives citations of reading for several disputations. The books referred to included, besides Paley's *Moral and Political Philosophy* (recited by seniors), the following: William Robertson, *The History of the Reign of the Emperor Charles V* (3 vols. London, 1769); Charles Rollin, *The Ancient History of the Egyptians* (2d ed. 10 vols. London, 1738–40); John Gillies, *The History of*

Stiles had them debate such questions as whether Brutus was justified in killing Caesar, or whether Alexander, having conquered Thebes, had a right to the tribute which the Thessalonians paid the Thebans.[79] Frequently he assigned topics drawn from Daggett's or Wales's lectures in divinity, or ones which might clarify the students' thinking about deism, universal salvation, or other obnoxious but enticing alternatives to orthodox Christianity. Disputations also gave Stiles an opening to advance causes he favored: over and over, he framed propositions embodying the theme of religious tolerance. He also tried to help his students through some of the labyrinths of Christianity which had troubled him as a young man. No Yale student graduated during Stiles's presidency without having argued in some form during either his junior or senior year whether God is the efficient cause of sin and whether the Scriptures are of divine inspiration (argued sometimes as whether Christianity is of divine revelation).

Students occasionally spoke their arguments extemporaneously, but usually from notes. Although the notes were sometimes complete essays of 500 to 2,000 words, students received training in more formal speaking and writing from another traditional undergraduate exercise. Twice a week five or six students from each class delivered "declamations" (to their classmates or to the whole college after evening prayers) and handed the written composition to their tutor or to the president for criticism.[80] Declamations were commonly in English or Latin, occasionally in Greek, Hebrew, or French.[81] They usually ranged between 300 and 1,000 words, on general topics of the kind

---

Ancient Greece (2 vols. London, 1786); François Marie Arouet de Voltaire, *The Philosophy of History* (London, 1766); *Traité sur la tolérance* (Geneva, 1763); *The Philosophical Dictionary* (London, 1765); René Aubert de Vertot, *The History of the Revolutions That Happened in the Government of the Roman Republic* (2 vols. London, 1720).

79. *Lit. Diary*, *3*, 314, 318.

80. There are three boxes of declamations from the 1780s and 1790s in the Yale Univ. Lib. See also *The Laws of Yale College* (New Haven, 1774), p. 7; (1787), p. 9; (1795), p. 17. It is possible that students were also regularly assigned English compositions in addition to their declamations and disputations. See "Memoranda: Yale College," 1793.

81. Though French was not taught by the college, private masters offered instruction in New Haven, and students were allowed to study it, as Stiles himself did. *Lit. Diary*, *3*, 127; "Memoranda: Yale College," Dec. 14, 1784, Aug. 2, 1791; *American Mercury*, Jan. 12, 1795; Dyar Throop Hinckley, Diary, June 23, 1784.

that eighteenth-century polite essayists favored: generosity, conceit, indolence, wisdom, charity, benevolence, reputation, curiosity, matrimony. Here was an opportunity to display the style and polish that the vogue of belles lettres fostered. Student writing in all ages tends to be stilted; eighteenth-century students captivated by the baroque literary mannerisms of the time, often wrote their declamations in ridiculously elegant circumlocutions. In August 1785 Ebenezer Dutton (Yale 1787) began an essay this way: "The numerous objects which merit attention, the importance of discharging our respective functions in a becoming manner, render it indispensably necessary that we distribute our affairs in order and execute them in their proper season." In other words, "It is good to make hay while the sun shines," the title of Dutton's essay. Ezra Stiles, who could write with economy and precision, had reason to be skeptical about current literary fashions.

In the early years of Stiles's presidency, when classes were small, every student faced sooner or later the ordeal and honor of displaying his literary talents in some of the exhibitions of quarter days and commencement. As the classes grew larger, the honor was reserved for those who seemed most to merit it.[82] Other incentives to good scholarship were the several prizes and premiums awarded during the year. Under the terms of Dean Berkeley's bequest, the annual rent of his ninety-six acre Newport farm (a sum which rose from £33 6s. 8d. in 1782 to £44 10s. in 1792) was to be divided among three "scholars of the house," graduate students who showed proficiency in Latin and Greek. As provided by the will, the president and the senior Anglican minister of the state examined the candidates every May and, when less then three appeared qualified, expended the surplus income on Latin and Greek books for the authors of the best Latin declamations in each class. There were prizes from the bequest of Richard Salter, a former trustee, for the best Hebrew scholars. The tutors awarded special premiums of their own for the best declamations. From 1791 to 1795 a prize was given from funds provided by Noah Webster (1 per cent of the Connecticut royalties from his *Grammatical Institute*) for the best composition on belles lettres, ethics, or moral philosophy. Scholarship was also encouraged by the establishment in 1780 of a chapter of Phi Beta Kappa.[83]

82. "Memoranda: Yale College," Aug. 1, 1783.
83. Records of awards under the Berkeley, Salter, and Webster bequests were kept in separate volumes, now in the Yale Univ. Lib., which also contains the records

Stiles took an active interest in honoring the best scholars from each class, but he was equally concerned that every Yale student should maintain a respectable level of academic competence. In 1784, when the seniors proved deficient in syllogisms, he made them review Watts's *Logick*.[84] When the graduating class of 1788 forgot the Hebrew they had learned as freshmen, he gave them a review course.[85] In 1790 he made the seniors recite Cicero's *De oratore* for a time to improve their Latin pronunciation.[86] In the spring of 1794 he made all classes review geography.[87]

When Stiles became president, there seems to have been no system of grading or marking students in their daily work or in examinations. The examination given applicants for admission was a genuine (but easy) test of ability to read Latin, the rest mere formality. In 1762 Clap had introduced yearly examinations for all classes in September and May.[88] Although the innovation caused a student rebellion, there is no surviving evidence that examinations barred anyone from graduation.[89] A student, once admitted to college, could count on a degree as long as he spent his four years in residence and observed the college laws. The examinations, like the public exhibitions, were opportunities to show the proficiency of a few selected individuals who spoke for the class.

As president, Stiles shared with the tutors the task of examining candidates for admission. Occasionally he admitted an exceptionally well qualified student to advance standing in the sophomore or junior class.[90] But his entrance examination was not perfunctory. In 1788,

of Phi Beta Kappa and other undergraduate societies. The Phi Beta Kappa Society was as much a social as a scholastic society; but it enrolled only about a third of each class, and membership was regarded as an honor.

84. Dyar Throop Hinckley, Diary, Dec. 17, 1784.

85. *Lit. Diary*, 3, 167, 306 n. In 1793 Stiles failed all but one of the freshmen who volunteered for Hebrew: Thomas Robbins, Diary.

86. "Memoranda: Yale College," Apr. 9, 1790.

87. *Lit. Diary*, 3, 521–23.

88. Dexter, *Biographical Sketches*, 2, 777; *Lit. Diary*, 3, 232.

89. It is possible, however, that an occasional student had been barred. When four failed the examination in 1785 (see below) the corporation noted that it was "the first time for many years that any such instance has happened": Corporation Records, Sept. 14, 1785. I have been unable to discover a record of any previous instance.

90. "Memoranda: Yale College," Oct. 21, 1779; cf. Elijah Leonard to David Daggett, June 26, July 3, 1781, Daggett Papers, Yale Univ. Lib.; Stiles to ———— Strong, Mar. 3, 1794, Library of Congress.

for example, he refused admission to a son of the Honorable William Williams and thereby risked alienating a powerful politician and one of the few firm friends of Yale in the Connecticut Assembly.[91]

About examinations after admission Stiles had sterner ideas. He intended to transform Yale examinations into examinations. In July of 1784 the seniors were startled to find that the examiners quizzed them for two days instead of one and did not in the usual manner, as soon as the questioning was over, give their votes of approval.[92] Instead they retired to a room by themselves and there voted privately on each candidate. As it happened, they passed everyone, but by treating the examination seriously Stiles was imposing a real burden on the seniors. The examination covered not merely the work of their last year but virtually everything read or recited in four years of college, divinity and Hebrew excepted.

In the following year Stiles continued to tighten up. He had always participated in examining the lower classes, subjecting each in succession to a whole day of oral questioning. Each faculty member handled a different subject and they were as devoted as he to improving standards.[93] Not content to bask in the proficiencies of the diligent students, they probed the deficiencies of the slackers. To escape exposure boys took to leaving early for spring vacation, which followed the May examination. In 1785 Stiles transferred the examination to April, took attendance, and graded the fifty-eight students present, finding "20 Optimi, 16 2d Optimi, 12 Inferiores (Boni), 10 Pejores." [94] This was probably the first application of grades to students in the history of Yale. Stiles told them that "some had pass'd so poor examination, that they dishonoured themselves and College,—but he hoped that the mortification they must undergo, in seeing others so far above them, would spur them to closer application, that they may acquit themselves better at the next Examination." [95]

91. Stiles to William Williams, June 13, 1788.

92. *Lit. Diary*, 3, 129–30; "Memoranda: Yale College," July 21, 1784. Beginning in 1753, the examiners voted on each candidate "singly and by himself" but did so in his presence. In 1784 they "retired and voted upon Each Candidate privately and distinctly": Stiles, Journal of Activities as a Tutor.

93. Henry Channing to Simeon Baldwin, Dec. 20, 1786, Baldwin Papers.

94. "Memoranda: Yale College," Apr. 5–8, 1785; *Lit. Diary*, 3, 154. On May 2, 1787, Stiles recorded in his "Memoranda: Yale College" a grade for every student in each of nine subjects. The grades range from 2 to 6; the latter was evidently the highest grade given.

95. Dyar Throop Hinckley, Diary, Apr. 5, 1785.

At the July examination four seniors were judged unfit to receive a degree. In September the four were re-examined and again found unfit, but the tutors "after much deliberation, agreed not to recommend them from merit; but, it being a new thing and of course requiring caution . . . desired the President to recommend them to the corporation to have degrees *speciali gratia,* the day after Commencement." [96] The corporation granted the special degrees to three of the students; the fourth never showed up.[97] At the September examinations this year Stiles announced that hereafter the same standards would be applied to the other classes too, and "poor scholars must be put back to lower Classes." [98]

This policy had been adopted as early as 1762 at Princeton but was new at Yale.[99] Its principal effect was a greater attention to scholarship, but the students did not submit without an initial struggle. When college reassembled in the fall of 1785 the new examination policy was all the talk, and the dormitory lawyers were full of reasons why the president could not get away with this horrid innovation. On the day before the January vacation Stiles gave the seniors a trial run in an extra examination and held special recitations during the vacation for scholars who stayed in town.[100] By the end of the month some of those who had reason to fear the worst began to take refuge in flight to Harvard and Dartmouth. Stiles watched them go, not without concern but with a certain satisfaction as he reckoned their scholastic worth: Colt was "middling poor," Pumroy "nothing," Phelps "trifling," and so on.[101]

The spring examinations in 1786 were again held early (April 18–22), and after them undergraduate indignation broke out in riots of more serious proportions than the usual fracas with which students greeted the spring. Not quite daring to attack the president's house, which lay outside the college yard, the undergraduates broke the

96. "A Young Man's Journal of a Hundred Years Ago," New Haven Colony Hist. Soc., *Papers, 4* (1888), 207.

97. *Lit. Diary, 3,* 185, 189; Corporation Records, Sept. 14, 1785.

98. "Memoranda: Yale College," Sept. 8, 1785.

99. Francis L. Broderick, "Pulpit, Physics, and Politics: The Curriculum of the College of New Jersey, 1746–1794," *William and Mary Quarterly,* 3d ser., *6* (1949), 42–68.

100. *Lit. Diary, 3,* 206.

101. Ibid., p. 227 n. The document quoted here is not given in full and will be found in "Memoranda: Yale College," 1786.

windows of the tutors' chambers in the college and attempted, unsuccessfully, to break down the doors, "with the express purpose and
design of offering insult indignity and violence to the Persons of the
Tutors." Rioting went on from the twenty-sixth to the thirtieth, and
college did not really quiet down until the beginning of vacation on
May 6.[102]

Stiles had no intention of allowing the opposition to stop him. When
college convened again, several of the rioters had repented and disclosed the ringleaders. Two confessed their crime, and in accordance
with Puritan custom Stiles pardoned them. He rusticated three others
and expelled a fourth. These, together with the boys who had departed
for milder regimes, amounted to fourteen "martyrdoms to the cause
of poor scholarship." There was only one good scholar in the lot; the
rest were all "below par, and the most of them poverty itself." Stiles's
closing comment, echoed by many a dean and president, was "Happy
Purgation!" [103]

With this final reform Stiles could look at his college with pardon-
able pride. During the Newport years it had been a source of humiliation to see Yale brought ever lower in public esteem. In 1767 he had
suffered directly when a Yale junior, whom he recommended to his
friend John Winthrop for transfer to Harvard, was rejected as totally
unprepared.[104] Now he had turned the tables. Harvard had accepted
four of those who left him for "fear of having a Degree depend on
Merit." [105]

102. *Lit. Diary*, 3, 216–17; "Memoranda: Yale College," Apr. 18–May 9, 1786;
Minutes of a Meeting of the President and Tutors, June 21, 1786, Yale Univ. Lib.
103. See above, n. 101.
104. John Winthrop to Stiles, May 5, 1767.
105. See above, n. 101.

25

The Great Reconciliation

EZRA STILES was an intellectual, and he earned at Yale more intellectual than administrative success. His talent for governing students was good. His talent for conciliating students, tutors, parents, professors, and public was even better—and far too often relied upon by the corporation to mend damage they had done. But Stiles had no gift nor taste for manipulating people. When he wanted something done, his first thought was to do it himself, instead of arranging for someone else to do it. When the corporation starved the professor of natural philosophy into resigning, Stiles did not marshal supporters and fight back, nor did he fight to get another one appointed; instead he gave lectures in natural philosophy. When he thought Yale students should learn Hebrew, he did not wait for funds to endow a chair, he taught Hebrew.

Nevertheless, if Stiles made Yale in effect a one-man university, he made it a good one, and in the long run his intellectual success brought material success. It came, at first, in small amounts. Men who admired Stiles, both at home and abroad, contributed to the library, which had been depleted over the years not merely by normal attrition but also by losses incurred as the books were carted here and there to escape the danger of British raids. Dr. John Erskine, one of Stiles's Scottish correspondents, sent books regularly and persuaded other Scotsmen to do so.[1] Richard Price sent all his own works from England

1. *Lit. Diary*, 3, 235, 287, 306, 349, 408–09; Stiles to Erskine, Apr. 19, 1792; Erskine to Stiles, Sept. 15, 1794.

in 1784, and William Gordon, the historian, sent a parcel in 1786. Benjamin Franklin was another donor.[2] Perhaps in order to point up the library's needs, Stiles and the tutors in 1790 began a catalogue, which he published the next year. In spite of additions, it showed a total of only 2,700 books.[3] This was 100 more than in 1743 and 300 less than in 1755.[4] Although another few hundred volumes were available in the libraries of the Linonian Society and the Brothers in Unity, the college obviously needed more books.[5] Samuel Lockwood, the trustee who subscribed £100 for the philosophical apparatus, again responded to Yale's need. When he died in June 1791, he left an endowment of £336 14s. for replenishing the library. The annual income, though only £15, would purchase about thirty new books every year.[6]

Another trustee, Richard Salter, donated a 200-acre farm to the college, specifying that the annual rent (then £22) go toward the endowment of a professorship of Hebrew or toward undergraduate prizes for proficiency in the language. Salter was undoubtedly moved by Stiles's efforts to keep the subject alive, for he was himself a distinguished scholar in both Hebrew and Greek. Stiles arranged the gift in 1781 after ill health led Salter to retire from the corporation, but the transfer of property did not take place until his death, which occurred in 1787.[7]

The largest bequest during Stiles's presidency came from Daniel Lathrop, a Norwich physician who had made a fortune in trade. Dying

2. Manuscript notes by Stiles in the Yale copy of *A Catalogue of Books in the Library of Yale-College in New-Haven* (New Haven, 1755); *Lit. Diary*, *3*, 386; "Memoranda: Yale College," Nov. 15, 1786.

3. *Connecticut Journal*, July 21, 1790; Stiles, "Memoranda: Yale College," Aug. 4, 1790; *Catalogue of Books in the Library of Yale-College, New Haven* (New London, 1791). In 1787 Stiles had found 1,000 volumes in the Dartmouth library, 1,300 at Harvard: *Lit. Diary*, *3*, 283.

4. *A Catalogue of the Library of Yale-College in New Haven* (New London, 1743); *A Catalogue of Books in the Library of Yale-College in New-Haven* (New Haven, 1755).

5. In 1784 the Linonian Society had about 120 volumes; by 1794 it had about 450: manuscript catalogues of the books belonging to the society, Yale Univ. Lib.

6. *Lit. Diary*, *3*, 422–27. Books purchased by the Linonian Society in the 1780s, as recorded in the manuscript records, seldom cost more than 10s. a volume. On Feb. 20, 1795 Stiles wrote to Christoph D. Ebeling that the college library contained 3,000 books and the student libraries another 1,000.

7. *Lit. Diary*, *2*, 470, 533; *3*, 261.

childless in 1782, Lathrop left Yale £500. The college received half
of it in September 1787, the other half in March 1788.[8]

The total income from these legacies did not amount to more than
£70 or £75 annually, not enough to make much difference to the college budget.[9] But meanwhile Stiles's treasurer, James Hillhouse, took
advantage of changes in the securities market to make spectacular increases in the college's small capital funds. In 1777 the college had
pooled various legacies and sold enough land to get a working capital
of £1,230 to invest in certificates of the United States Loan Office.[10]
Because of the near-insolvency of the United States government, the
interest on this fund had depreciated to the vanishing point when
Hillhouse became treasurer in 1782. According to Governor Oliver
Wolcott, Hillhouse "never could do the most ordinary business in life,
without some chicanery," [11] but whatever chicanery he may have
exercised as treasurer of Yale was directed to Yale's interests. His
management, together with the rise in value of United States securities
brought about by the adoption of the Constitution and by Alexander
Hamilton's financial schemes, resulted by 1791 in an appreciation of
£770 in the value of the college endowment. In 1791 Hillhouse pulled
off another speculative coup. In May the corporation authorized him
to invest college funds in the new Bank of the United States, and he
purchased options on seven shares of stock, paying $25 each for them.
On August 10, Isaac Beers came to Stiles and offered $100 each for
them. The next day he went up to $170 and on the 12th to $175.
Stiles was in favor of holding out. He had heard that New York prices
were going as high as $280. Though he expected the bubble to burst
eventually, he thought that Yale might get as much as $250 and at
the least $200 a share. But Hillhouse favored playing it safe and took
the $175. Even at that price, he made $1,050 or £352 for the college
in three months' time.[12]

The interest on these funds and on the new legacies, the rents from
the farmlands owned by the college, and the charges to students gave
Yale a total annual income of about £1,175.[13] It was a small figure

8. Corporation Records, Sept. 12, 1787, Mar. 4, 1788.
9. *Lit. Diary*, 3, 427.
10. See above, Chap. 21.
11. Oliver Wolcott to Oliver Wolcott, Jr., May 21, 1796, Wolcott Papers, 5,
Conn. Hist. Soc.
12. *Lit. Diary*, 3, 425–28; Stiles, "Memoranda: Yale College," Aug. 10–13, 1791.
13. Ibid.

when compared with the £2,745 that Harvard had to spend,[14] but it was enough so that Stiles in 1791 could begin to think about appointment of another professor and construction of some much-needed buildings. His own salary (with an annual bonus allotted him by the corporation) amounted usually to £300 now, and Wales's to £200. At least £250 more should go to the tutors, who were currently underpaid. If another £250 were set aside for maintenance and contingencies, there would be approximately £100 left over annually.

The amount would fluctuate with farm rental values and student enrollment, and it was not enough salary to buy the kind of man Stiles wanted for a professor of mathematics and natural philosophy. Sacrificing present advantage for future gain, he decided that the major part of the college funds should be reinvested in deferred stock, which would yield an annual income of £150, beginning in 1801. Stiles thought that with the promise of £150 salary in 1801, an able man might be induced to accept the professorship of mathematics at £100 until then. He could annually raise that sum partly from student fees, partly from interest on undeferred stocks, and partly by liquidating some of those stocks each year.[15] But even while he juggled the figures to make Yale's slim resources yield another professor, he heard of the renewed possibility of obtaining funds from the only source that could give enough to make Yale a real university with a full professorial staff.

In the eighteenth century, as at most times in modern history, men looked to the state for support of enterprises clothed with a public purpose. Support did not necessarily mean direct payments of money; it might meant simply an exclusive right to collect from the public for certain services. The state might, for example, grant a monopoly of tolls to a company which undertook to build a needed bridge or canal or turnpike.[16] Connecticut had given Yale, in the charter of 1745, the right to grant degrees. There was nothing to prevent it from giving another college the same right, but in spite of efforts by the enemies of Yale, it did not. An act establishing a secondary school

14. *Connecticut Journal*, Mar. 2, 1791. But in spite of its relatively large endowment, Harvard's expenses were at this time outrunning its income; cf. Quincy, *History of Harvard*, 2, 238–57.

15. "Memoranda: Yale College," Aug. 15, 1791; *Lit. Diary*, 3, 426, 440. For the income from student fees see below, Appendix.

16. Oscar and Mary Handlin, *Commonwealth: A Study of the Role of Government in the American Economy: Massachusetts, 1774–1861* (New York, 1947).

at Plainfield in 1784 even carried a clause forbidding the trustees to make regulations inconsistent with the rights of Yale College.[17]

By preserving Yale's monopoly of collegiate education in Connecticut, the state gave the college a kind of support. But Stiles knew that other states were doing much more for higher education. Columbia, already assisted by the royal government before the Revolution, was given £2,552 by the new state government in 1784 and another £1,000, together with various parcels of land, in 1790.[18] In 1784 also Georgia granted 40,000 acres of public land to found and support the University of Georgia; [19] and Maryland endowed two colleges, St. John's at Annapolis and Washington College at Chestertown, with annual grants of £1,750 and £1,250 respectively.[20] Pennsylvania chartered Dickinson College in 1783 and Franklin College in 1787 and gave them 10,000 acres of land apiece.[21] North Carolina founded a state university in 1789 and gave it all arrears in taxes and other sums due the government for the years before 1783.[22] Massachusetts gave Harvard money regularly until 1786.[23] New Hampshire in 1789 gave 41,000 acres to Dartmouth.[24]

When he first became president, Stiles aspired for similar favors from Connecticut and did his best to cultivate friendly relations with the government. He knew old Governor Trumbull well and was also on cordial terms with Samuel Huntington, who took the governor's chair in 1786 and whose brother Enoch became a member of the corporation in 1780. Stiles regularly attended the annual election festivities at Hartford in May, simultaneously indulging his own sociability and promoting Yale's public relations by fraternizing with legislators and ministers from distant corners of Connecticut. While there,

17. L. W. Labaree, ed., *Public Records of the State of Connecticut for the Years 1783–1784* (Hartford, 1843), p. 406.

18. *Lit. Diary*, *1*, 439, 503; J. H. Van Amringe et al., *A History of Columbia University* (New York, 1904), pp. 63, 75.

19. *Lit. Diary*, *3*, 118; A. L. Hull, *A Historical Sketch of the University of Georgia* (Atlanta, 1894), p. 3.

20. Virgil Maxcy, ed., *The Laws of Maryland* (Baltimore, 1811), *1*, 482, 509.

21. J. H. Dubbs, *History of Franklin and Marshall College* (Lancaster, 1903), pp. 28–29; *The Statutes at Large of Pennsylvania from 1682 to 1801* (Harrisburg 1896–1915), *11*, 114; *12*, 222, 397.

22. Kemp P. Battle, *History of the University of North Carolina* (Raleigh, 1907), p. 9.

23. Quincy, *History of Harvard*, *2*, 248–49.

24. *American Mercury*, Mar. 16, 1789; *Laws of New Hampshire Including Public and Private Acts, Resolves, Votes, Etc.* (Concord, 1904–22), *5*, 396–97.

he presented any petitions the college had to lay before the Assembly and presided over the traditional election-day banquet. The high point of the day was the election sermon, in which a leading clergyman instructed the governor and the assembled legislators about the principles of politics. Stiles preached it in 1783, Joseph Huntington, another brother of the governor's, in 1784, and Professor Wales in 1785. They all took advantage of the occasion to urge that the government give financial support to the college.[25]

The Assembly always listened politely and ordered the sermons printed. But the members were unmoved by the appeals for help and continued to nourish the ancient grudge against Yale. When Stiles sought in 1780 to carry out his old plan of an American academy of arts and sciences, the Assembly would grant no charter of incorporation for fear, Stiles was told, that the institution might become an adjunct of the college.[26] When Yale faced extraordinary expenses and asked for help, the Assembly was usually cool. Though it did pay Stiles's moving costs from Portsmouth, it refused to help with Yale's debt to Milford (for taking their pastor, Samuel Wales, as professor of divinity).[27] In 1788 it rejected a petition to help repair the presidential house and another for some public lands in Kent.[28] In 1789 the corporation prepared a petition that reminded the Assembly of the bounty of other states to their colleges and asked for a grant of Connecticut's shadowy claim to a strip of land two miles wide on the northern border of Pennsylvania. Even this dubious favor was denied.[29]

The Assembly's refusal to help the college was dictated in part

25. Ezra Stiles, *The United States Elevated to Glory and Honor* (New Haven, 1783), pp. 93–94; Joseph Huntington, *God Ruling the Nations* (Hartford, 1784), p. 35; Samuel Wales, *The Dangers of Our National Prosperity* (Hartford, 1785), p. 34. On the clergy's annual banquet, see David McClure to Samuel McClintock, May 11, 1792, Yale Univ. Lib.

26. *Lit. Diary*, 2, 486–87. Nathan Strong to Stiles, Nov. 25, 1780, bound in manuscript Diary at July 28, 1780.

27. Corporation Records, Sept. 9, 1778, Apr. 18, 1782; Charles J. Hoadly, ed., *The Public Records of the State of Connecticut From May, 1778 to April, 1780* (Hartford, 1895), p. 137; *Lit. Diary*, 3, 284. The Milford church had objected so strenuously to parting with its pastor that the corporation voted the church £200, in compensation for the £300 fee which the church had paid Wales to induce him to settle with them.

28. Corporation Records, Mar. 4, May 5, 1788; *Lit. Diary*, 3, 317.

29. Corporation Records, May 14, 1789; Connecticut Archives, Schools and Colleges, 2d ser., 1, 51a.

by hard times. Connecticut farmers had undergone a long-range decline in prosperity during the later eighteenth century, and the sharp
depression which followed the Revolutionary War in all the states
did not lift in Connecticut until the 1790s.[30] People complained
steadily of high taxes and the scarcity of money. But depression had
not prevented other states from supporting their colleges. The obstacle in Connecticut was the same one that had blocked an accommo-
dation at the time when Stiles accepted the presidency. The Assembly,
backed by a rising anticlericalism among the people, had then refused
to give money unless the corporation should admit a balancing number of civilian Trustees. The corporation had refused, and Stiles had
not questioned their decision.

The 1780s saw an intensification of the anticlericalism that had
driven college and state apart. In spite of Stiles's great success at Yale,
he did not reverse the trend of the younger ministers toward the New
Divinity. By the 1790s the leaders of the movement claimed the
allegiance of more than half the existing ministers in the state and
virtually all the candidates.[31] But the New Divinity preachers were
no more successful than they had been earlier in carrying the people
with them. As the ministers spun out the fine thread of metaphysics,
their congregations grew cool and hostile, and complaints against the
clergy became ever more common.

In 1788 the clergy of the state, meeting in their general association,
issued a reprimand to the people for their neglect of public worship.[32]
The answers published in the newspapers showed the extent of popular disgust. "We have heard your animadversions," said one writer,
"upon our absence from Sabbath meetings, and humbly conceive if
you wish our attendance, you would make it worth our while to give
it. To miss of a sermon of the present growth, what is it but to miss of
an opiate? And can the loss of a nap expose our souls to eternal perdi-
tion?" [33] Another writer suggested that the clergy should be delighted
with the decline in church attendance. Was it not their doctrine that

30. Albert L. Olson, *Agricultural Economy and the Population in Eighteenth-
Century Connecticut* (New Haven, 1935); Labaree, *Public Records of Connecticut
from May 1789 through October 1792*, pp. xiv–xvi; L. W. Labaree and Catherine
Fennelly, *The Public Records of the State of Connecticut from May 1793 through
October 1796* (Hartford, 1951), pp. xxv–xxvi.

31. *Lit. Diary, 3,* 464.

32. *New Haven Gazette and Connecticut Magazine,* July 31, 1788.

33. Ibid., Oct. 9, 1788.

the condition of the unregenerate was hopeless, "so that our very prayers are abominable to God?" The ministers should regard as a sign of success the fact that families no longer prayed or went to church. People were simply acting on the doctrines that the ministers preached.[34]

Dissatisfaction with the Congregational clergy led people away from the church in various directions. The boldest became deists and derided the whole system of Calvinist Christianity, with its angry God, ridiculously moved by passion rather than reason. Others drifted toward denominations where the preaching was more intelligible or the ritual more satisfying. Baptists increased rapidly in the 1780s, and Anglicans, who were under a cloud during the Revolution, recovered and found a new strength in independence. In the 1790s Methodists invaded the state.[35] The Congregational clergy still received their salaries through the state tax collectors (the amount of the salary was determined by agreement between the minister and his congregation) but the law exempted from taxation dissenters who attended churches of other denominations. Such churches were entitled to support themselves by taxes in the same manner as the Congregational ones, but most of them preferred to subsist on voluntary contributions. There might therefore be an economic advantage in dissent, and it was commonly stated that men declared themselves Baptists simply to get out of church taxes and never bothered to attend that church at all. The effect of every desertion from the Congregational Church was to increase the financial burden of those who continued to attend, so that economic pressure in favor of dissent grew ever stronger.[36]

Under these circumstances the Congregational clergy, whether New Divinity or Old, looked to Yale as one institution which they could claim to be running successfully.[37] In 1778 probably a substantial number of ministers would have favored the addition of lay members to the corporation. In 1783 Stiles was told that only ten ministers in the state advocated it, and by 1792 even the most ardent of these,

34. *American Mercury*, Sept. 1, 1788.

35. Greene, *Religious Liberty in Connecticut*, pp. 38–360; Richard J. Purcell, *Connecticut in Transition, 1775–1818* (Washington, 1918), pp. 46–97.

36. *Acts and Laws of the State of Connecticut* (New London, 1784), pp. 21–22; Labaree, *Public Records* (1789–92), pp. 256, 311–13; *American Mercury*, Apr. 6, 1789; *Connecticut Courant*, Apr. 20, 1789; *Connecticut Journal*, Oct. 28, 1789.

37. David McClure to Samuel McClintock, May 11, 1792, Yale Univ. Lib.

Nathan Strong of Hartford, had become suspicious of the civilian push to get on the corporation.[38]

Attacks on the college, like those of the 1770s which demanded that it teach more practical subjects, were renewed periodically in the 1780s and 1790s, linked each time with anticlericalism. And now the force of republican simplicity and equality lent new strength to the arguments. The Yale curriculum, it was said, was well adapted to training clergymen: since clergymen served no useful purpose anyhow, it was appropriate for them to acquire useless knowledge. But the average man needed to be taught things that would help him fill his place in the new republic. "Idle speculation" was out of date.[39]

Stiles was willing to meet the critics part way. Some of his curricular changes—the dilution of the undergraduate dose of divinity, the virtual abandonment of syllogistic disputations—were probably prompted by public criticism that the program was overweighted with courses useful only to ministerial candidates. Nor was Stiles unsympathetic to the practical needs of a young republic. His disputation program and expanded English program, his introduction of history and political philosophy, his new textbooks, and his ambition for professorships in science, law, and medicine all demonstrated his eagerness to make Yale serve on as broad a front as possible. But he did not wish his college to abandon its primary responsibility, its dedication to learning for its own sake. Secular control might ultimately transform Yale into a trade school.

Stiles's fears were heightened by the development of Connecticut politics in the late 1780s and 90s, when economic depression speeded the scramble for public office. Membership in the General Assembly was not in itself lucrative, but the Assembly every year filled four or five hundred offices—justices of the peace, judges of the county courts, probate judges, and judges of the superior court—all of which entailed fees or salaries that brought the recipients a steady income. The Assembly also appointed and promoted militia officers, and judging from the regularity with which men used the titles of captain, major, and

38. *Lit. Diary*, 2, 534; 3, 9, 73, 451.
39. *New Haven Gazette* (Abel Morse), Mar. 2, 16, 1791. Ironically the argument in this essay was drawn largely (though without acknowledgment) from a book that Stiles had introduced at Yale the year before, Priestley's *Lectures on History* (see above, Chap. 24).

general, people set much store by them. The Upper House of the Assembly, usually called the Council, participated in all these appointments and in addition had authority by itself to appoint the sheriffs of the various counties.

The situation offered numerous opportunities for the organization of political factions. Various families and groups of families gained control of whole blocks of offices to which they clung as though by prescriptive right. Scandals were not unusual. In January 1789, for example, the state treasurer and the sheriff of Hartford County both resigned after it had been discovered that they were guilty of embezzling state taxes.[40]

The way in which their places were filled was revealing. The treasurer's office was elective, but as an interim appointment the Assembly chose Jedidiah Huntington of Norwich, a distant relative of the governor and son-in-law of former Governor Trumbull. Huntington was already judge of the Probate Court in Norwich and also sheriff of New London County.[41] A week later, by a vote of 4 to 3, the Council appointed Stephen Chester (Yale 1780) of Wethersfield as the new Hartford County sheriff.[42] Chester was the son of a Council member (John Chester, Harvard 1722), and the son-in-law of another (Stephen Mix Mitchell, Yale 1763), both of whom voted for him.[43] His mother was Jedidiah Huntington's sister. Another member of the council was Benjamin Huntington, a distant relative of Jedidiah. When, after less than a year, Jedidiah resigned as state treasurer to become federal collector of customs at New London, he also resigned as judge of the Norwich Probate Court and as sheriff of New London County. He was replaced in these offices by his brothers Andrew and Joshua.[44] Benjamin Huntington (Yale 1761) meanwhile went on to the United States House of Representatives.[45]

40. L. W. Labaree, *The Public Records of the State of Connecticut from May, 1785, through January, 1789* (Hartford, 1945), pp. 507, 543–47. Cf. *Lit. Diary*, 3, 338–39.

41. Labaree, *Public Records* (1785–89), pp. 507, 544.

42. Ibid., p. 547.

43. *Connecticut Courant*, Apr. 6, 13, 1789.

44. Labaree, *Public Records* (1785–89), p. 507; (1789–92), pp. 72, 545. On the Huntington relationships see E. B. Huntington, et al., *The Huntington Family in America* (Hartford, 1915).

45. Labaree, *Public Records* (1785–89), pp. 496–97.

The Huntington connection was more powerful than most but by no means unique,[46] and the virtual monopoly which a few families of this kind held on political appointments was extremely irksome to an aspiring group of able men who gained notoriety in the 1790s. There were a dozen or more of them, including Jonathan Ingersoll (Yale 1766), Pierpont Edwards (Princeton 1750), and David Daggett (Yale 1783) from New Haven, William Judd (Yale 1778) from Farmington, Ephraim Kirby and Uriah Tracy (Yale 1778) from Litchfield, Amasa Larned (Yale 1772) from New London, Elisha Hyde from Norwich, Zephaniah Swift (Yale 1778) from Windham, Moses Cleaveland (Yale 1777) from Canterbury, Jeremiah Halsey from Preston, and Philip Bradley from Ridgefield.

They had three things in common: they were young (most of them under forty); they were, or had been, members of the Assembly; and with the possible exception of Edwards they wanted higher offices than they had. Sooner or later most of them did attain high office, on either the state or the national level; but in 1791 they were young men in a hurry, and they had just discovered a common impatience toward those who occupied the positions above them. Meeting together of an evening after sessions of the Assembly in New Haven or Hartford, they decided to join forces in order to break into the upper ranks—a purpose in which they were quickly detected by the old guard, who dubbed them "The Nocturnal Society of Stelligeri." [47]

The Stelligeri had no perceptible political program to back their efforts to unseat the "old and steady folks," [48] but they skillfully capitalized on the prevalent anticlericalism. They were mostly lawyers,

46. See, for example, the list of officeholders related to Ursula Wolcott Griswold (1724–88) in E. E. Salisbury, "The Griswold Family of Connecticut," *Magazine of American History*, 11 (1884), 234–36.

47. *Litchfield Monitor*, Apr. 4, June 6, 1792; *American Mercury*, Mar. 26, Apr. 2, May 27, 1792; *Connecticut Courant*, Apr. 2, May 14, 21, 28, 1792; *Lit. Diary*, 3, 451; Itineraries, Vol. 6, May 8, 1792. Some of the Stelligeri had already tried their hands at political propaganda. Pierpont Edwards had attacked Roger Sherman the year before for consenting in Congress to a raise in pay for congressmen. Edwards' protégé, David Daggett, had pseudonymously attacked several Hartford politicians: *Connecticut Journal*, Sept. 8, 22, Oct. 13, 1790. See *American Mercury*, Nov. 22, Dec. 13, 1790; Connecticut Journal, Nov. 9, Dec. 15, 1790, Jan. 5, 1791.

48. The phrase is from a letter of Uriah Tracy to Charles Chauncy, May 19, 1792, Chauncy Papers, Yale Univ. Lib.

and lawyers still displayed the propensity to religious skepticism that Stiles had observed forty years earlier.[49]

The appearance of a new faction on the political scene was not an unusual occurrence in Connecticut politics, but the anticlerical bent of this one, together with the high degree of ability among its members, made Stiles uneasy about involving Yale in negotiations with the Assembly, where the Stelligeri were already powerful in the Lower House. The last thing he wanted was for the college to be caught in a political fight between ins and outs, especially where there was danger that anticlericalism might become an issue. But the Assembly, probably under prodding from the Stelligeri, took the initiative itself. In January 1791 Stiles recorded without comment the fact that the Lower House had appointed a "visitatorial Committee" of five to investigate the college.[50] Presumably the same motives that prompted the petitions of 1784 prompted this motion for investigation. But if the Stelligeri needed a pretext they could have cited—and undoubtedly did—"an unhappy Tumult at College" which Stiles laconically recorded a few days before the New Haven session of the Assembly adjourned.[51] Two of the Stelligeri, Swift and Tracy, were named to the visitation committee, and so was Asher Miller, a young Middle-

<hr/>

49. Pierpont Edwards, son of the elder Jonathan, was a notorious libertine and as free in theology as in morals. Daggett and Swift often indulged in sarcastic or irreverent comments on the clergy. See, for example, Daggett's *Oration* (New Haven, 1787); *Connecticut Courant*, May 30, 1791; *The Correspondent* (Windham, 1793). See also their correspondence in Daggett Papers, Yale Univ. Lib.

50. *Lit. Diary*, 3, 409; Connecticut Archives, Schools and Colleges, 2d ser. 1, 52a, Conn. State Lib.

51. *Lit. Diary*, 3, 409. The nature and cause of the tumult are nowhere stated, but it may have been part of a quarrel between students and administration that began in December over Stiles's dismissal of Elijah Waterman, a senior, for refusing to live in college. Waterman's classmates considered Stiles's action arbitrary and petitioned unsuccessfully in Waterman's favor. Although the tutors supported Stiles, they seem to have felt more sympathy for the boy than Stiles did. In the end, the corporation overruled Stiles and restored Waterman on March 8, 1791, "taking into View the Circumstances with which the case is attended at present." The circumstances may have been the attention Yale was receiving from the Assembly, where Waterman's father was a member. Many other Yale students, including four seniors who signed the petition for Waterman, also had fathers or uncles in the Assembly. Documents on the case are in the Yale Univ. Lib. There are also references in "Memoranda: Yale College," 1790–91, and Elizur Goodrich to Stiles, Feb. 3, 7, 1791.

town attorney, who may also have been one of the group.[52] When the
Upper House negatived the bill of appointment, Edwards and Swift
were sent to confer with them, but the opposition was unmoved and
the bill accordingly failed.[53]

In May 1791 an opportunity came to reopen the question of visitation when Governor Huntington recommended to the Assembly that
something be done to assist the college. Uriah Tracy reported on May
19 that "Yale College will again be bandied about as the subject was
most pathetically introduced by the Governors Speech." [54] Four days
later the Assembly appointed Tracy and Ingersoll, along with John
Chester of the Upper House, "to enquire into State of Yale College
as to Finance Expenditure and Government etc." [55]

This committee appears to have done nothing before September 12,
1791, when the Yale corporation adopted a resolution expressing
their readiness to furnish information.[56] Without appearing hopelessly
intransigent, the trustees could scarcely have avoided cooperating. It
was no more than they had done in 1778 and did not presuppose a
willingness to accept any alterations that might be suggested. When
the resolution was laid before the Assembly on October 28, 1791,
they appointed a new committee to carry on the investigation: Lieutenant Governor Oliver Wolcott and Stephen Mix Mitchell of the
Upper House, and Ingersoll, Tracy, and Miller of the Lower House.[57]

Stiles dreaded the outcome. The only development since 1778 that
might make an agreement more likely now than then was a change
in the composition of the corporation. In 1778 it had included four
New Divinity men: Warham Williams, Stephen Johnson, Samuel
Lockwood, and Timothy Pitkin. Now there were only two: Pitkin
and Levi Hart, who replaced Lockwood in 1791. And Hart, who had
always been noted for moderation anyhow, was thought to be moving
away from the principles of his New Divinity preceptor, the great
Joseph Bellamy. The other new members—there had been only six
in all since Stiles's accession—were Old Lights: Enoch Huntington,

52. Miller's membership may be inferred from a letter of William Judd to David
Daggett, Feb. 24, 1792, Daggett Papers, Yale Univ. Lib.

53. Connecticut Archives, Schools and Colleges, 2d ser., *1*, 52a.

54. Tracy to Charles Chauncy, May 19, 1791, Chauncy Papers, Yale Univ. Lib.

55. Journals of the House of Representatives, May 23, 1791, Conn. State Lib.

56. Corporation Records, Sept. 12, 1791.

57. Connecticut Archives, Schools and Colleges, 2d ser., *1*, 53a; Labaree, *Public
Records* (1789–92), pp. 334–35.

Josiah Whitney, David Ely, Nathan Williams, and Hezekiah Ripley. The New Divinity leaders had been much annoyed at the selections. In 1788 Stiles spent a stormy evening in West Hartford with two New Divinity ministers, Nathan Perkins and Nathan Strong, who complained bitterly of the recent elections of Whitney and Ely.[58] Whitney they found especially objectionable because he had been a strong opponent of President Clap and had studied theology with the Arminian minister of Springfield, Robert Breck. It was even said that Stiles would rather choose an Arminian than a New Divinity man.[59] In 1792 Strong told Stiles that the college was "obnoxious to above half the Ministers because Corporation don't choose New Divinity men; that such men as Mr. Smalley and Dr. Edwards ought to come in—that Mr. Hart lately elected has been 2 or 3 years getting off of New Divinity and has become one on whom they begin not to rely." [60] But Strong and Perkins were both extremists and possibly ambitious to be trustees themselves. Stiles thought the new members were well chosen: whatever their theologies, they were moderates. They would therefore be more ready than some of their predecessors would have been to accept a reasonable proposal if the Assembly should make one.

That the Assembly's proposals would be reasonable, however, seemed to Stiles highly improbable. After a conference with the Assembly's committee in January and another in early May, he was more apprehensive than ever. They went over the college's financial accounts and discussed the need for more dormitory space, library books, and professors; but he received the impression that the Assembly "would never do much in Money Matters or giving Funds or endowing Professorships, even if the College was altered to their Minds. They would make the Scholars support the Instructors." [61] Moreover, the committee had made it pretty clear, or so it seemed to Stiles, that they would not be content with an addition to the corporation of civilian members fewer in number than to constitute a majority. The Stelligeri wished to go even further and make all the members civilians: they "intend to have the Corporation Y.C. annually chosen by Assembly as the Judges of the Superior Court—and have College

58. *Lit. Diary*, 3, 317.
59. Ibid.
60. Ibid., p. 451.
61. Ibid., p. 454, cf. pp. 8–9.

Int. a Source of parliamenteering yearly as all other Officers." [62]

The thought of Yale turned into a new field for political patronage was more than Stiles could stomach. He told himself that the Stelligeri would be unable to swing the Assembly to so radical a proposal; what was more likely was that the Assembly, after the committee reported, would suggest an ex officio membership in the Yale corporation for the governor and Council. Since there were twelve councilors and ten trustees, the latter would be outnumbered and thus lose control of the college almost as completely as if the whole board were civilians. [63]

Stiles would have been willing to accept an addition of civilians amounting to a minority of the whole, and so, he believed, would most of the ministers on the existing corporation. This they would do in the interests of good will, even though they had "no pecuniary expectations" from the Assembly. He therefore spent a good deal of time on his annual election trip to Hartford (May 9 and 10, 1792) in feeling out the sentiments of the legislators. In particular he queried three (identified only as Mr. M———, Mr. S———, and Mr. C———) who had always been deep in the scheme for bringing in civilians. To each of them he put the question whether a corporation composed equally of civilians and ecclesiastics would satisfy them. They all said it would. But when he proposed a board composed two-thirds of ministers and one-third of civilians, each of them said no. "Thus," he concluded, "I see, that after all the Talk and Negotiating nothing will give radical Satisfaction, but such a Mutilation as is a Total Abolition and Surrendery of the College Constitution, and wresting it out of the Hands of Ministers into the Hands of Civilians." If such an alteration took place, it would "bring the deistical and mixt Characters hereafter ascending into the Council [the Stelligeri, for example] to such a Controll and Influence in this Institution as to neutralize and gradually to annihilate the Religion of the College, and so to lower down and mutilate the Course of Education, and model it to the Tast of the Age, as that in a few years we shall make no better Scholars than the other Colleges, or the Univ. of Oxford and Cambridge." [64]

Stiles knew that the corporation would join him in resisting such an alteration, and he worried about the effect their resistance would

62. Ibid., p. 451.
63. Ibid., p. 455.
64. Ibid., pp. 452–56.

inevitably have. Whatever proposal the Assembly made, its rejection by the corporation "would be converted into Obloquy against the College and increase the Offence and Disgust of the Civilians." [65]

Stiles returned from Hartford, then, expecting the worst. He did not learn what sort of report the Assembly's committee turned in or what action was taken on it until the evening of June 1, when he answered a knock on his door and found his treasurer, James Hillhouse (recently elected to Congress) with James Davenport (Yale 1777) of the Upper House and John Davenport (Yale 1770) of the Lower House. The three had just come from Hartford. Hillhouse handed him a copy of the committee's report, together with an act of the Assembly passed as a result of it. [66]

Stiles was astonished by what he read. The report of the committee was more favorable than he could have hoped. The college, it appeared to the committee, was well run. They had found "that the Severity of the antient Freshman Discipline is almost done away; and that the literary exercises of the respective Classes have of late Years undergone considerable Alterations, so as the better to accomodate the Education of the Undergraduates to the present State of Literature." They also found the treasury "in a much better condition than we apprehended," but not so much better but what it could use some assistance from the state. [67]

As Stiles moved on to the "Act for Enlarging the Powers and increasing the Funds of Yale College," he could scarcely believe what he read. The state was turning over arrears in taxes that amounted certainly to eight or nine thousand pounds and perhaps to as much as twelve. This was even more than other states had done, and the condition was simply the addition to the corporation of the governor, lieutenant governor, and six senior councilors. The addition would give the civilians more than one-third of the members but less than a majority; and the civilians were to take no part in elections to replace vacancies among the ministerial members. [68]

Stiles was overjoyed. "This is a grand and liberal Donation," he wrote in his Diary, "and a noble Condescension, beyond all Expecta-

65. Ibid., p. 455.
66. Ibid., p. 457.
67. Connecticut Archives, Schools and Colleges, 2d ser., *1*, 57. The report is also transcribed in the Corporation Records.
68. Labaree, *Public Records* (1789–92), pp. 392–94.

tion! Especially that the Civilians should acquiesce in being a Minority in the Corporation. *It will do.*" [69]

By the time the corporation met on June 26 to consider the offer, Stiles had had the opportunity to canvass many of the ministers in the state to see if they thought it would do. He later estimated that at least 136 of them (out of 168) did. In the corporation itself only Nathaniel Taylor of New Milford was unwilling to say yes when the ballot was taken at 6 P.M. on the 27th; and on the next morning Taylor gave in and made it unanimous.[70]

Stiles was keenly aware of the historic significance of the occasion. It meant that the forty-year quarrel between Yale and the state government had ended with victory for Yale. Though he did not say it in so many words, he knew that the state had capitulated largely because of the success that he had brought to the college. Those who complained of the dogmatism and narrowness of the clergy had learned to except Yale's president and to close their denunciations with "I wish there were more Doctor Stiles's." [71] The moderation of the Assembly's proposal was a vote of confidence in the gentle doctor as well as in his college, but Stiles himself concluded merely that the legislators were "heartily tired out of a 40 years storming against it and finding they could not kill it, as it had got good Reputation and about £1200 per ann. Revenue and could subsist." He thought the legislators had also been somewhat ashamed of the fact that neighboring states were doing great things for higher education, while Connecticut neglected a college that stood high, perhaps foremost, in reputation throughout the country.[72] Nevertheless, the donation had been wholly unexpected. The committee of the Assembly, he heard, would even have recommended a grant without the addition of civilians to the corporation. Though the Assembly had insisted on the addition, the terms were still so surprisingly liberal that Stiles gave thanks to "him who turns the Hearts of men as the Rivers of Waters are turned and can make even Nations willing in a Day." [73]

69. *Lit. Diary*, 3, 457.
70. Ibid., pp. 459–66.
71. Stanley Griswold to Simeon Baldwin, Jan. 27, 1787, Baldwin Papers.
72. *Lit. Diary*, 3, 301, 461.
73. Ibid., p. 463. Stiles seems to have given no credit to the loyalty of Yale men, in achieving the result; but the committee, including the Stelligeri, were evidently more favorably disposed to Yale than the Assembly as a whole, and the members of the committee were all Yale graduates.

He realized that men like the Stelligeri, deistical, indifferent, or even hostile to religion, might ultimately rise to senior positions in the Council and so to membership in the corporation. But he counted on the ministers of the state to keep the people alert to the importance of a *"religious* as well as otherwise well informed Magistracy." [74] He realized too that his new professorships might be filled with men "obnoxious to me, and who will at length enterprize Mischief to me personally"—Timothy Dwight was all too popular with the existing senior councilors.[75] Nevertheless, Stiles rejoiced in the merger, for he knew it was the right thing for Yale. The college might at last become a university.

The Assembly's generosity came at an opportune time. Although Stiles had brought Yale safely through a revolutionary war and a storm of political intrigue, he had to combat in the 1790s a more subtle attrition. With the continuing spread of anticlericalism, the increasing popularity of free thought, and the gradual return of prosperity, young New Englanders felt themselves emancipated in a manner that no previous generation had.

The feeling affected especially those of sufficient wealth and intelligence to go to college. Yale was inundated by a crowd of boys who strove to outdo one another in Chesterfieldian urbanity. Some of them came from the new academies, where they had already acquired a superficial polish and a skill in evading academic discipline. Others, arriving in New Haven fresh from the farm, gaped at the unspeakably sophisticated creatures who had come the year before and as fast as possible made themselves over.[76]

New Haven, instead of frowning on the new fashions, suddenly became tolerant. The town that had sent a dancing master packing in 1782 shortly afterward harbored several, who advertised their assemblies in the newspapers.[77] The young bucks of college could be seen at them every week, practicing elegant gestures and sophomoric

74. *Lit. Diary, 3,* 465.
75. Ibid., pp. 463, 504–06.
76. The Thomas Mills Day Papers contain a variety of revealing letters between students at Yale and former schoolmates at the academy in Sharon during the 1790s. The popularity of Chesterfield is evident in student compositions. See also *American Mercury,* Feb. 10, 1794.
77. "Memoranda: Yale College," Feb. 19, 1789, June 14, 1792; *New Haven Gazette* (Meigs, Bowen, Dana), Nov. 18, 1784, Apr. 28, May 5, 1785; *Connecticut Journal,* Mar. 21, 1787, Mar. 18, 1789, Apr. 27, 1791.

wit. When not engaged in these maneuvers, they patronized the billiard parlors, which, though forbidden by law, did a thriving business. New Haven merchants offered the materials necessary for the standard uniform which every young buck aspired to wear: shoe and knee buckles were out, replaced by yards of black ribbon done up in bows; breeches were to be one-eighth inch smaller than the natural size of the body; hair must be powdered, frosted, and perfumed; and to be really proper one needed a watch chain adorned with jingling trinkets (no watch required), a tamboured shirt, and a cape of a different color from one's coat.[78]

Young gentlemen adorned in such finery found the quarters in Yale's crowded and decrepit old college insupportable, the close supervision of tutors and president uncomfortable, the plain meals at commons too common to bear. During the year 1789–90 discontent with the college food was greater than normal, and in November 1790, when the next academic year opened, 120 students, out of a total of 141, asked permission to "live out." The records do not show how many got it, but on March 7, 1791, Stiles recorded that there had been no commons since the preceding commencement. There is no further mention of commons in his Diary or in the corporation records for the next two years. During this time it is probable that large numbers of students boarded and roomed with families in the town.[79]

The better food and the heated dining room of a boarding house may have been salutary for student health, but the dispersion was bad for student morale and morals. Parents worried about the dangerous opinions their sons might imbibe. Ezekiel Williams of Wethersfield, for example, feared for his son Thomas (Yale 1794). "I hear with much uneasiness," wrote the father, "that you are gone to board at the Deistical Wetmores where the Mitchels lived last year and am ex-

78. *Connecticut Journal*, Sept. 12, 1792.

79. On May 20, 1793, Daniel Read, a New Haven musician and comb maker, wrote to a correspondent that it was the custom for students to eat in the college hall, but that "for two or three years past there has been no provision of that kind, and the Students have boarded in private families" (Daniel Read Letter Book, New Haven Colony Hist. Soc.). It has sometimes been assumed that commons did not operate again during Stiles's administration, but letters of Jeremiah Day (Yale 1795) indicate that he ate in the college hall during these years (Day to Thomas Day, Dec. 22, 1795, Apr. 6, 1798, Day Papers). In September 1794 it was voted that commons be set up at the end of vacation and that the steward should erect an addition to the college kitchen (Corporation Records).

ceding Loth my Son that you should be there a Day . . . you will be in Eminent danger of being Tainted with the hints he will thro' out (if only you see him at Table in meal Times) of his shocking Divinity." [80] Mr. Wetmore's divinity could scarcely have been more shocking than Ezekiel Williams' arithmetic—in 1788 Williams had been caught $3,000 short in his accounts as sheriff of Hartford County.[81] But the Connecticut Assembly, which dropped Williams as sheriff, shared his view of the bad company that students found in New Haven. In 1792 the Assembly's committee reported that half the students were living in private lodgings, where they formed "unprofitable, idle and vicious connexions." [82]

This had been a perennial complaint, for Yale had never had enough space to house all its students. And though New Haven offered no greater opportunities for iniquity than any other town of its size, college students had special talents for discovering bad company and small talents for resisting its attractions. The Assembly had therefore stipulated that $2,500 of the state grant be applied to a new building, so that the students could live together in their own community apart from the town. Accordingly, on October 25, 1792, the corporation approved plans for a four-story building 130 feet long by 30 feet wide, to be placed as a wing at the north end of the existing "college."

The decision was no sooner made than complaints about the proposed dimensions and location began to pour in. Stiles thought they deserved consideration and summoned a special meeting of the corporation for January 1, 1793.[83] Just before they met, he received a letter from James Hillhouse with a masterful plan for a new design and new location.[84] Hillhouse, attending Congress in Philadelphia, had consulted John Trumbull, son of the old governor. Trumbull had already won fame as a painter and was currently engaged on a portrait of Washington. He turned aside from it long enough to draw plans for a new college building of shorter and wider dimensions to match roughly the existing college. What was more important, Trumbull placed the building in line with the old one and with the chapel which was to be in the middle, so that the three would form a symmetrical

80. Ezekiel Williams to Thomas S. Williams, June 18, 1793, Yale Univ. Lib.
81. See above, n. 40.
82. See above, n. 67.
83. Corporation Records, Oct. 25, 1792, Dec. 4, 1792; *Lit. Diary*, 3, 480.
84. Hillhouse to Stiles, Dec. 24, 1792.

unit, facing the green. The old college (Connecticut Hall), which was only three stories, was to have the roof raised and another story added to bring it up to the level of the proposed new building.[85]

Trumbull and Hillhouse even foresaw a time "when New Haven shall become another Oxford" and provided plans for two more buildings to extend the line northward the full length of the college yard. These could be built as the need arose and the whole "whether partially or compleatly executed, would be in all its stages handsome." With the long vista across the green the buildings would make an impressive display. Indeed Trumbull thought "it would be difficult to find in America or in Europe a situation where such an extent of public Buildings can be seen to such advantage."

He was right. The scheme, when completely executed some years later, gave Yale, in what was called "the brick row," a handsome set of buildings. When the corporation saw the plan, they recognized its superiority at once and agreed to set the new college where Trumbull proposed, at the south end of the chapel, and to make it 40 × 100 feet.[86] Stiles laid the cornerstone on April 15 and, of course, made a ceremony of it, with an academic procession and a speech delivered from atop the stone. He rehearsed for his audience the history of Yale and of its previous buildings and somewhat ungraciously mentioned the zeal of the surrounding states in supporting education, a zeal which had "at length enkindled an Emulation in this." He concluded, however, with expressions of gratitude to the Assembly for making the building possible,

> which with the Philosophic Apparatus, Donations for increasing the public Library and other Literary Augmentations especially in the Auxiliary Glory of the amicable union of Civilians in the Government of the College and in the Provision of Funds for the Establishment of ample Professorships in the various Branches of Literature, all these give us reason with pleasure to anticipate the future distinguished figure and increasing Utility of this Institution among the Sister Universities of these States and of the World.[87]

85. The plans, in the Yale Univ. Lib., are reproduced in Anne S. Pratt, "John Trumbull and the Brick Row," *Yale University Library Gazette*, 9 (1935), 11–20.

86. Corporation Records, Jan. 1, 1793; *Lit. Diary*, 3, 482–83.

87. *Lit. Diary*, 3, 490–92.

The new building would double Yale's dormitory space and make it possible at last to require the great majority of students to live where the college authorities could keep an eye on them. Stiles, while tolerant of what he called "light horsicality," had always taken a firm view of college discipline. The rising tide of misdemeanors during the 1790s is faithfully reflected in the rising number of punishments and dismissals he dispensed.[88] One student who attended in these years recalled later that the president "seemed to all transgressing neophytes to have been uncommonly sedulous to carry out, to the letter, the whole collegiate code of laws." [89] Actually the neophytes, often in their early teens, did more than their share of transgressing. The majority of disciplinary cases was always in the freshman and sophomore classes. Stiles's rigor was exercised among them, as the same boy admitted, "con amore." [90] It was his practice to visit students in their rooms during study hours in order to "admonish the negligent, or vicious; applaud the studious; assist and encourage all." [91]

Parents, of course, were never satisfied and criticized the college sometimes for being too harsh, sometimes for not being harsh enough.[92] The corporation too, perhaps under parental pressure, weakened the president's hand by occasionally overruling his decisions.[93] To bring about a more consistent policy and an improved public understanding, Stiles and a committee of the corporation in September 1793 began to overhaul the college laws. But they had no means to counteract the effect of two serious epidemics in New Haven that twice broke up the college in 1794. The interruptions hindered Stiles's disciplinary campaign, because the continuity of college discipline and the good example of upperclassmen were important factors in transforming wild freshmen or sophomores into respectable members of the college community. First an epidemic of scarlet fever disrupted academic rou-

88. Recorded in "Memoranda: Yale College."

89. Sprague, *Annals, 1,* 146.

90. Ibid.

91. Holmes, *Life,* pp. 364–65. Stiles sometimes allowed himself to be persuaded by the tutors to a greater degree of leniency than he thought wise. *Lit. Diary, 3,* 13.

92. Harvard had the same problems of discipline and the same inconsistent public criticism. See the papers of Eliphalet Pearson in the Edwards A. Park Collection, Yale Univ. Lib., especially a letter of Apr. 28, 1789. Cf. *Connecticut Journal,* Dec. 25, 1794.

93. As in the Waterman case (above, n. 51); see also *Connecticut Journal,* May 11, 18, 1785.

tine and finally closed the college in April 1794. Stiles resumed classes for the summer term; but more than half the students stayed home, because by then New Haven was in the grip of a serious yellow-fever epidemic, which struck 160 persons and killed 63 of them. To give the plague a chance to subside, college opened three weeks late in the fall of 1794. Probably in order to make up for lost time, the corporation abolished the January vacation and turned down a student petition asking for its reinstatement. The result was discontent and unruliness, particularly among the sophomores, who were an unusually bad lot that year.[94]

Even the new dormitory, instead of curbing student misbehavior, at first aggravated it. As the building neared completion in the summer of 1794, the students among themselves devised a scheme of casting lots for first choice of rooms. Stiles had his own ideas about who should be located where, for by locating potential troublemakers with boys he knew to be reliable, he could forestall trouble. A former student, who knew him well, recalled his method: "If he found such as were young, in danger from the contagious influence of dissipated companions; he took care to locate them with those of maturer years, and more fixed characters. The idle he located with the diligent; the gay with the serious; the mercurial and turbulent, with the phlegmatic and the steady:—an arrangement, which contributed to individual benefit, and to general order."[95] Accordingly he refused to be bound by the student's lottery. Some of them seem to have regarded his refusal as a grievance.[96]

Stiles took in his stride the disciplinary complexities of these later years, knowing that other presidents were facing the same difficulties. At Harvard the faculty bewailed "the spirit of opposition and disorder" and "the many kinds of indecency" among the students.[97] In February, 1795 Stiles told Professor Eliphalet Pearson of Harvard about the recent tumults at Yale and added resignedly, "But we shall get along. I hope things are tranquil at Harvard."[98]

At the time when Stiles wrote this letter, improvement had already

94. Stiles to Eliphalet Pearson, Feb. 12, 1795; Thomas Robbins, Diary, Conn. Hist. Soc.

95. Holmes, *Life*, pp. 369–70.

96. Thomas Robbins, Diary.

97. John Kirkland to Eliphalet Pearson, March 2, 1793, Park Collection, Yale Univ. Lib.

98. Stiles to Eliphalet Pearson, Feb. 12, 1795.

begun at Yale. A series of rustications and expulsions got rid of the worst offenders, and the students themselves enlisted in the work of reformation by forming an undergraduate moral society. One of its first members, a junior, later recalled: "This year I think I got the most solid learning and science that I ever have in one year." [99] The taming of the wild bucks was under way.

With the new dormitory in operation and discipline recovering, Yale in 1794–95 was ready to reach for the academic goals that Stiles had had in view since he accepted the presidency. During the two years that followed reconciliation, the college had actually lost ground intellectually. Professor Wales suffered so marked a decline that he was able to preach only four times in 1792, and in 1793 not at all. In September of that year the corporation voted to replace him with the Reverend Joseph Lathrop of West Springfield, an Old Light on whom Stiles had conferred an honorary degree two years before. Unfortunately, Lathrop declined the office, and there was no immediate agreement on another candidate, perhaps because the man who received the second largest number of votes was Timothy Dwight.[100]

Agreement on a new professor of mathematics and natural philosophy was more easily reached. After the corporation had ousted Nehemiah Strong in 1781, Professor Samuel Williams of Harvard had made an unsuccessful try for Strong's job. He tried again when subscriptions for the new philosophical apparatus were solicited.[101] But self-nominating professors have always been suspect. The corporation turned a cold shoulder to Williams' proposals but did allow Stiles to hire a former tutor, Josiah Meigs, to give occasional lectures on natural philosophy in 1787. Meigs, who was publishing a newspaper at the time, found the lectures too much of a burden and abandoned them after six months. In 1794 he looked like the best candidate for the new chair. When Yale offered it to him, at a salary of £150, though without promise of permanency, he accepted and was inducted into office on December 4.[102]

99. Thomas Robbins, Diary.

100. *Lit. Diary*, 3, 504–06, 508. It took three ballots to reach a majority vote. On the last one, eight Old Light ministers and two civilian members voted for Lathrop, while the two New Divinity ministers, Pitkin and Hart, and four civilian members voted for Dwight. Even before Wales's resignation Stiles was convinced that no first-class successor was available. Stiles to William Williams, Aug. 15, 1793.

101. *Lit. Diary*, 3, 29–30, 259, 318–19.

102. Ibid., pp. 258–59, 275, 541, 548–49. For Stiles's favorable view of Meigs see Stiles to Copeland Stiles, Nov. 21, 1789, to Jesse Dewees, Oct. 28, 1790.

The next most urgent business on the Stiles agenda was enlargement of the library,[103] and then, as rapidly as the promised public funds became available, the appointment of other professors. But an increasing feeling of age reminded Stiles that he might not live to see the appointments made. He faced the prospect with equanimity. After the great reconciliation of 1792 he knew that time would effect his purpose without further assistance from him.

103. A list of books, divided into classes according to priority of need, was apparently drawn up, and at the meeting of Sept. 11, 1793, the corporation voted to authorize the purchase of the first class, but then reversed itself. The vote was crossed out and not repassed until more funds became available after Stiles's death.

26

Private Life of a President

·

EZRA STILES liked to watch things grow: his college, his mulberry trees, his children, himself. By the time he came to Yale, his youngest child was already ten and his oldest, twenty. He still kept track of their increasing pounds and inches and the number of times they read the Bible. But he could only watch in uneasy, unmeasuring wonder as they grew, inevitably, up.

Ezra Jr. followed his father's trail more closely than the others, but even he grew gradually out of reach. He was a tall, lanky boy, tall at least for a Stiles, at five feet nine. When the family moved from Dighton to New Hampshire, he transferred from Yale to Harvard for his senior year. That winter he decided on a career in the law and began to study with Judge William Parker of Portsmouth during the December vacation. After his father moved to New Haven, he read with Charles Chauncy, the Connecticut state's attorney; and when the family was dispersed after the raid on New Haven, he studied with the college treasurer, John Trumbull, probably in Watertown. In April 1780 he was admitted to the bar.[1]

Ezra Jr.'s few surviving letters disclose a boyish, self-deprecating humor that was at times a little frantic, as when he called himself a "notorious crazy Fellow" or "a frail lump of blustering mortality." [2] His father showed satisfaction with the boy's intellectual attainments but seems to have shared his uncertainty about the ultimate outcome.

1. *Lit. Diary*, 2, 201, 263, 307, 419–20.
2. Ezra Stiles, Jr., to David McClure, Feb. 17, 1778, Conn. Hist. Soc.

"Whether he is to be and prove a good or a bad Character in Life," the father wrote in 1780, "is with the Most High." [3]

As soon as he was admitted to the bar, Ezra Jr. wisely removed himself from his illustrious father's overshadowing presence and settled as an attorney in Westminster, Vermont. Politics was his real interest, and he gained an immediate success in it. He was back in Connecticut in three months' time acting as emissary for the Vermont government, to persuade Timothy Green, the New London printer, to move to Vermont. The next year he was one of a committee appointed by the legislature to supervise the printing of the state's paper money. When the printer's boy decided to print some for himself and the counterfeit bills were discovered, Ezra Jr. was accused of complicity. In New Haven Stiles heard of the matter with great distress, but his son was fully acquitted and returned to the legislature at the next election.[4]

Ezra Jr. had meanwhile married Sybil Avery, a Connecticut girl who had likewise moved to Westminster. She presented him with a daughter, Stiles's first grandchild, in April 1782. Stiles urged his son to have the infant baptized, but it had not been done by the following September when the couple visited New Haven. There, under her father-in-law's urging, Sybil joined the college church, and Stiles had the pleasure of holding the baby while Professor Wales baptized her as Elizabeth Hubbard.[5]

Ezra Jr.'s promising career was broken by sickness in 1783. On a trip to New York via New Haven in September he was thoroughly drenched in a storm and took cold. The cold was followed, on his return to New Haven, by severe rheumatic pains, which confined him to bed. In January 1784, like many ailing boys before him, he sailed south in search of a cure. The following August, in a one-room log cabin near Edenton, North Carolina, he died. Sybil had remained behind in Connecticut to bear another child, Emilia Harriot, who later accompanied her mother back to Vermont. Ezra Jr.'s other child, Elizabeth Hubbard, stayed with her grandfather, where a profusion of aunts attended her.[6]

3. *Lit. Diary*, 2, 418.

4. Ibid., pp. 425, 463, 544, 545. Henry Reed Stiles, *The Stiles Family in America: Genealogies of the Connecticut Family* (Jersey City, 1895), pp. 249–52.

5. *Lit. Diary*, 3, 23, 35–36.

6. Stiles to Mrs. Ezra Stiles, Jr., Oct. 27, 1783, Library of Congress; *Lit. Diary*, 3, 96, 104, 109, 133, 134, 255, 282, 355.

Isaac's career was much different from Ezra's. He was fourteen when he came to New Haven and ready for college the next year. He was not, like his brother, spared the embarrassment of attending college as the president's son. His father at this time was too poor to send him away or perhaps feared to do so. Isaac had a temperament that matched his red hair. He lacked the interest or patience for scholarship; and though he had a curiosity as lively as his father's, it was not to be satisfied from books. Stiles may have feared that he would get out of hand if he left home. He managed to get through four years of Yale but was evidently not altogether happy about it. On June 7, 1781, Stiles noted in his diary that Isaac, then in his sophomore year, was "desirous of leaving college." [7] He was persuaded to stick it out, but there was friction in the following year too, resulting in his expulsion from the Linonian Society for insolence to his brother members.[8]

After graduating in September 1783, Isaac went south. He may have had an early touch of the wanderlust that overtook him in later years. Though he intended ultimately to become a lawyer, he wanted, like many young northern college graduates, to sample plantation life as a tutor in some southern gentleman's family. But in two months he was back, after a stormy voyage in which he froze both feet.[9] He studied law in 1784, was admitted to the bar in 1785,[10] began practice in Tolland, Connecticut in 1786, and was home again in 1787. He served his father occasionally during the next few years in selling parcels of land in different parts of the state, but he was clearly not cut out for a legal career.[11] In 1790 he finally discovered that what he really wanted was the permanent restlessness of the sea. He shipped first on a coastal voyage to Maine, but soon was traveling all over the world, to Bristol, Lisbon, and around Cape Horn to the Falkland Islands. Twice he was shipwrecked and survived. Stiles received a letter from him dated at Philadelphia on April 21, 1795, which said that he was sailing the next day for Port au Prince. He was never heard from again.[12]

7. *Lit. Diary*, 2, 539.

8. Records of the Linonian Society, Apr. 5, 1782; *Lit. Diary*, 3, 15.

9. *Lit. Diary*, 3, 95, 99; Itineraries, 3, 609.

10. *Lit. Diary*, 3, 154.

11. Ibid., pp. 208, 210, 211, 287, 326, 335, 376; Isaac Stiles to Stiles, July 23, 1786.

12. *Lit. Diary*, 3, 397–566 passim.

To the five girls New Haven offered more than it could to their brothers. No one expected them to echo their father's erudition, but Stiles gave them every opportunity to learn. He had always been fascinated by brilliant women, from Abigail Sergeant to Catharine Macaulay; and he liked to encourage erudition in young ladies, as on the December afternoon that he spent in 1783 with the learned Lucinda Foot, twelve-year old daughter of the Reverend John Foot of Cheshire. At the end of the interview he handed her a solemn parchment certificate in Latin, testifying that sex alone prevented her from entering the Yale freshman class.[13] He often made his seniors debate whether women should be given the vote, the right to hold office, and equal opportunities in higher education. But Yale was not yet ready for co-education, and the Stiles girls, though sharing some of their father's interests and welcoming his instruction, were sensitive to what the world expected of them.

What the world expected of a president's daughter, as of any well-born young woman, was good manners, pleasant conversation, and, hopefully, beauty. What a well-born young woman asked in turn was what all young women have always asked—young men. New Haven was well supplied with them, all the right age and all eager to please the president. It was a delightful situation for a girl but one that might tempt her to play the adolescent too long. New Haven had the reputation of making girls so imperious and coquettish that no one would marry them.[14]

The Stiles girls, from most accounts, did not have beauty, but they made up for it by being petite and lively. They were all under five feet three, and the oldest, Betsy, was barely five feet. John Quincy Adams, who met her when she was thirty-one, described her as "a lady of great vivacity, entertaining conversation, and agreeable manners, but no great beauty." [15] All the same, the boys knocked often at the president's door. One fastidious young man, who complained of the scandalous clothes and "horribly bouncing" gait of another New Haven girl, found the Stileses "accomplished and refin'd." After an evening of singing and conversation with them he pronounced to his

13. Ibid., pp. 102–03.
14. See the letters of William Page, Jr., to Thomas Mills Day, Day Papers, Yale Univ. Lib.
15. Mass. Hist. Soc., *Proceedings*, 36 (1902), 458.

diary that "the exercise of a little more prudence" on their part would make them the best company on the continent.[16]

The principal imprudence of the Stiles girls probably lay in assuming a little too much academic rank by association. In 1782, when they shared a pew in the college church with the twenty-year-old bride of Tutor Josiah Meigs, they asserted their dignity by leaving the pew before her after services were over. Mrs. Meigs thought that a tutor's wife outranked a president's daughter (though Betsy, Kezia, and Emilia were all older than Clara Meigs) and refused thereafter to attend church.[17] Stiles did not record his own position on this delicate question, and since married tutors were a rarity, it did not arise again.

Whether because they enjoyed their situation so much or because nobody asked them earlier, none of the girls married until she was on the verge of becoming, by eighteenth-century standards, an old maid. Kezia was the first. She married Lewis Burr Sturges (Yale 1782) in 1784 when she was twenty-four and died a year later in childbirth.[18] Polly, the youngest, married Abiel Holmes (Yale 1783) in 1790, when she was twenty-three.[19] Emilia and Ruth did not marry until after their father's death, and Betsy not at all.[20]

Betsy's failure to marry was not for lack of opportunity. The Reverend David McClure asked for her in 1778 when the family was in Portsmouth. Stiles recorded the request in his Diary in Latin ("Rev. D. Macclure rogavit ut filiam sibi connubio darem") as though it embarrassed him, and did not say whether he or Betsy refused it.[21] Ezra Jr., however, gave it his blessing. "If you can keep Betsy," he wrote to McClure, "you have my consent and a thousand pounds per annum for your first Son when I am in possession of my Earldom." [22] In New Haven a talented young man, nearly five years her junior, fell in love with Betsy. St. John Honeywood, the orphan son of a

16. Diary of John Cotton Smith, Jan. 16, Mar. 12, 1783.
17. Elizur Goodrich to Simeon Baldwin, Dec. 28, 1782, Baldwin Papers.
18. *Lit. Diary*, 3, 143, 204–05.
19. Ibid., p. 401.
20. Emilia married Jonathan Leavitt (Yale 1785) in 1796, settled with him in Greenfield, Mass., and died in 1833. Ruth married the Rev. Caleb Gannett of Cambridge, Mass., in 1799, and died in 1800. Polly and Betsy both died in 1795, within six months of their father.
21. *Lit. Diary*, 2, 263.
22. Mar. 26, 1778, Yale Univ. Lib.

Massachusetts physician, was a constant visitor in the Stiles household. A charming quick-witted boy, he liked to assail the girls with verses or with pen or pencil sketches. One January day in 1781 he amused them by dashing off a little portrait gallery of the whole family, on a leaf of the president's diary.[23] Honeywood liked them all. He called Emilia his "Romantic Genius" and Polly the "Nymph of the irresistable Figure." But Betsy swept him off his feet. He was so smitten with her that for several years after graduation, while studying law in New York, he bombarded her with love letters and even tried to get a position as college tutor in order to be near her again. Betsy enjoyed his attentions but never capitulated.[24]

When Betsy was thirty-three, Emilia twenty-nine, and Ruth twenty-six, all unmarried, Stiles began to worry about what would become of them after his death. His career had not been lucrative. In his first years as president he had sunk heavily in debt.[25] As the enrollment and reputation of Yale rose, the corporation began giving him a bonus in addition to his regular salary, until by the 1790s he was getting about £300 a year, in addition to forty or fifty pounds annually of "degree money," the fees that students paid for their diplomas. By 1785 he managed to clear himself of debt and in 1791 was able to buy a house on Cherry Street for his daughters to live in after his death should evict them from the presidential house. He conveyed the Cherry Street house to Betsy, Emilia, and Ruth in a deed dated September 21, 1791, with a proviso that his granddaughter, Elizabeth Hubbard Stiles, should have the use of the southeast chamber until she was twenty-one and that Polly should have the use of a room during her lifetime if she should become a widow.[26]

As long as he was president, however, the girls stayed on at College Street, and Stiles enjoyed the succession of students that entered the large front room to pay court to them. Sometimes a young man

23. See Fig. 5. This is one of the leaves noted as missing in *Lit. Diary*, 2, 496. Given to the Yale Univ. Lib. in 1958 by Lewis Stiles Gannett.

24. Dexter, *Biographical Sketches*, 4, 219–22; Honeywood to Elizabeth Stiles, May 20, June 4, 1782, Mar. 7, July 5, Sept. 10, Nov. 3, 1785, Jan. 26, June 26, Oct. 11, 1786, Stiles Papers; Honeywood to Simeon Baldwin, Mar. 6, Nov. 5, 1785, Jan. 24, 1786, Baldwin Papers.

25. *Lit. Diary*, 2, 396, 484.

26. Ibid., 3, 189, 431. A copy of the deed is in the Stiles Papers. He apparently went into debt again to buy the house, but had paid all his creditors by the following February (1792). *Lit. Diary*, 3, 443.

5. The Stiles Family, 1781, by St. John Honeywood.

PRESIDENT STILES Ætat 59 1786

6. Ezra Stiles, age fifty-nine, 1786, by St. John Honeywood. Courtesy of Yale University Art Gallery.

who called to see the girls would find himself drawn aside by the president to hear strictures on Lord Kames or a disquisition on a newly discovered planet.[27] Indeed the father was as great an attraction as the girls. Stiles was the kind of man that everyone listens to. As one friend put it, "When he took leave of a company, all perceived a void, which their sociability could not fill up." [28] James Kent (Yale 1781, later chancellor of New York) four years after graduation, recalled the combination of erudition and warmth that enlivened a visit with the president: "He always excited my Affection from the softness of his Manners and the Goodness of his heart, but my Admiration used to be carried to a very high Pitch from my Idea of the Immensity of his Learning and his Researches as an Antiquarian. He has many fanciful Notions which I shall not undertake to refute nor to defend. But he is the ornament of the Age as a Scholar." [29]

Kent had doubtless listened to Stiles expound his most fanciful notion, that of the scholar's progress into the moral and intellectual world of eternity. But Kent and every other student who sat at the president's feet could remember also the encyclopedic knowledge and the darting insight. On those evenings in the great front room, on excursions into the country with an admiring band of tutors, in chance conversations and formal lectures, Stiles talked away the books he should have written. He probably did not regret the loss, for in spite of the long hours he spent in study, his insatiable curiosity reached out for people as much as facts. In the pages of his Diary he collected both, impaling personalities with a few words. The shrewdness of his observations shows how closely he watched and how much he enjoyed the company even of those with whom he disagreed.

Often when students called at his house, they found him occupied with more distinguished visitors, who were equally enthralled. New Haven in those years was a way station connecting New England with the rest of the United States. Travelers trooped through in an unending procession, and no one of consequence thought it proper to leave without a visit to America's most successful college and a call upon its learned president. Most of them found the visit worth while but not always what they expected. When in September 1779, Baron Steuben brought La Luzerne, the French Ambassador, to call, Stiles

27. Diary of John Cotton Smith, Feb. 9, 1783.
28. Holmes, *Life*, quoting John Devotion, p. 352.
29. Kent to Simeon Baldwin, Sept. 16, 1785, Baldwin Papers.

found him "not a great Character," and gave most of his attention to one of his secretaries, François de Barbé-Marbois, whom he took to task because France did not give more religious liberty to the Huguenots.[30] New Englanders going to and from the United States Congress frequently stopped to chat and gave Stiles the latest reports of what was going on in Philadelphia or in their home states. Samuel Adams told him about American foreign affairs, Ira Allen about Vermont, and his old Rhode Island friend, General Nathanael Greene, about military operations.[31] Henry Marchant spent the night and reminisced about old days in Newport.[32] Thomas Jefferson called on his way to embark for France in 1784, and Stiles plied him with questions about William and Mary College, after which they discussed the latest developments in natural philosophy.[33]

Though visitors called to learn his views, Stiles had a gift for making them do much of the talking. Jefferson told him about the enormous bones dug up near the Ohio River, but did not discover until someone else told him later that Stiles had long been interested in these and other large bones found in the Hudson Valley. Jefferson at this time believed that the bones belonged to some animal which might still be living in the forests of the far west, and the size of the bones furnished him with a convenient answer to the charge of the French naturalist, Buffon, that the American continent produced only diminutive specimens of every animal. When Jefferson wrote to Stiles for further ammunition to use against Buffon, he received a supply of heavy artillery that even he was unwilling to use. The bones, Stiles thought (following his grandfather's view), belonged not to a mammoth or an elephant, but to a species of giant men who had once roamed the American forests! [34]

Visitors from beyond the mountains told Stiles about other curiosities there. From several he heard of the mounds at Muskingum, now covered with forest, and he found out as much as possible about these traces of America's ancient civilization, maintaining at the same time a lively correspondence with other scholars about the rock in-

30. *Lit. Diary*, 2, 370–72.
31. Ibid., pp. 291, 349.
32. Ibid., p. 344.
33. Ibid., 3, 124–26.
34. Ibid., p. 127; Julian P. Boyd, ed., *The Papers of Thomas Jefferson* (Princeton, 1950–), 7, 304, 312–17.

scriptions at Dighton and various other places.[35] Peter Pond, back in Connecticut after seventeen years in the Pacific Northwest, told him about the Indians there, and in 1793 seven Indians from the Mississippi Region, standing before him in long black hair and feather headdresses, assured him that the story of white "Welsh" Indians in that region was false. Stiles introduced them to Jonathan Edwards Jr., who from his days at Stockbridge knew a little of the Indian languages of western New England. After talking with them, Edwards concluded that their language resembled that used by the Indians he had known.[36]

Visitors who called during the college vacation were not likely to find the president at home. Immediately after commencement and as soon as classes ended for the vacations in January and May, he was on his horse and away, usually to Newport, for until 1786 the church there did not give up their claim to him. In September 1779 he used his vacation to visit the scattered members of his congregation. Newport was still occupied by the British, and two of their men of war rode at anchor in the harbor. But from Tower Hill across Narragansett Bay he was able to look through a telescope (perspective glass) at his house and church, still standing, though many houses had been destroyed. On the way home he preached at Providence and found that nearly half his flock had managed to get there to hear him. By the following spring vacation the British had evacuated Newport, and he enjoyed a poignant reunion with about two-thirds of his people in their desecrated meetinghouse. The British had run up a chimney in the middle of the building and demolished the pews and seats but left the pulpit intact. The returning church members pulled down the chimney and brought in enough benches and tables to produce the semblance of pews, so that Stiles was able to conduct divine services on Sunday, May 21, "tho' with a Pleasure intermixt with tender Grief." The next day the church met and approved his conduct in accepting the presidency of Yale, agreed to his continued absence during the war, but refused to dissolve their ties with him: they would continue to regard him as their pastor, though they might employ sub-

35. *Lit. Diary*, 3, 215–17, 304, 381–82; S. H. Parsons to Stiles, Apr. 27, 1786, Oct. 10, 1789; Noah Webster to Stiles, Jan. 20, Oct. 22, Dec. 13, 1787; John Smith to Stiles, July 25, 1789; Samuel Williams to Stiles, Mar. 8, 1782; James Winthrop to Stiles, July 31, 1782, Jan. 4, 1784.

36. *Lit. Diary*, 3, 488.

stitutes in his absence. He stayed for the following Sunday, when he baptized two children, one named Ezra Stiles Bissel in his honor and the other William Ellery Channing, who would eventually honor himself, though not in a cause that Ezra Stiles could have approved.[37]

Three days later, with heavy heart, he had to leave his lovely island and return to the thankless life of a president. Newport was in ruins, nearly three hundred houses destroyed, "but with Nehemiah," he wrote, "I could prefer the very dust of Zion to the Gardens of Persia, and the broken Walls of Jerusalem to the Palaces of Sushan. I rode over the Island and found the beautiful Rows of Trees which lined the Roads, with sundry Coppices or Groves and Orchards cut down and laid waste: but the natural Beauties of the Place still remain. And I doubt not the place will be rebuilt and excede its former splendor." [38]

Thereafter until 1786, with the exception of the year 1784, when he visited Princeton to receive honorary degrees as Doctor of Divinity and Doctor of Civil and Canon Laws, he spent every May and September vacation in Newport. If he had not loved the island so much, and if there had been good candidates to take his place, he might have persuaded his people to relinquish him sooner. But the condition of religion in Newport was much the same as in New Haven. Samuel Hopkins, whom Stiles still admired as a man but despised as a theologian, had fulfilled the predictions which Charles Chauncy and Chauncy Whittelsey made when he came to Newport: he had preached away most of his congregation by insisting on the peculiar tenets of the New Divinity. Stiles did not want his people subjected to such absurd and wicked doctrines as, for example, "that an Unconverted Man had better be killing his father and mother than praying for converting Grace," or "that true Repentance implies a Willingness and desire to be damned for the Glory of God." [39] But what could the people do? Candidates for the ministry were scarce, and the abler ones all leaned toward the New Divinity if they did not actually profess it. When the Newport church finally hit upon William Patten, a young Dartmouth graduate, Stiles was not altogether pleased, for upon hearing him preach and talking with him, Stiles detected "a covert New Divinity Man," a suspicion borne out some years later when Patten

37. Ibid., 2, 374, 425–26.
38. Ibid., p. 427.
39. Ibid., pp. 504–05.

confessed that he had got himself in hot water with the congregation by preaching infant damnation.[40]

With Patten's ordination, at which he gave the charge but declined to preach the sermon, Stiles's obligations to the Newport church were at an end. Thereafter he still returned from time to time—he could not bear to stay away for long—but usually now he spent his vacations in shorter trips around Connecticut (inspecting the college-owned farms and collecting the rents) or in an occasional longer expedition, which might take him 500 miles and more into Pennsylvania, upstate New York, Vermont, and New Hampshire, looking up correspondents he had never met, former students and friends. Once he stopped to talk old times with Abigail Dwight. Always he carried a pencil and a folded quarto sheet of paper tucked in his pocket, to record the local statistics and curiosities—the number of rings on a tree stump, the number of members in a church, the recollections of the oldest inhabitants, the opinions of the minister.[41]

In 1782, when visiting Rhode Island, Stiles stopped at Providence to call on Mary Checkley, the thirty-seven-year-old widow of an old acquaintance, William Checkley. He had called there before but this time, her friends noted, the two sat talking together late and seriously for two nights.[42] In August Stiles began writing cryptic Latin passages in his Diary with regard to M.C., whose initials he inscribed in Hebrew.[43] On September 4, "after earnestly looking up to the throne of Grace for the Direction of unerring Wisdom," he sent her "a letter of great Importance," and as soon as commencement was over, hurried off to Providence again himself. On October 17 they were married and eleven days later began a leisurely return to New Haven.

Their friends, following a pleasant custom of the time, escorted them in five chaises as far as Patuxet, where ten years earlier the *Gaspée* had burned. Here the company dined, then parted, and the newlyweds journeyed on a short distance to the house of Governor William Greene in Warwick, one of Stiles's regular stopping places. At Bolton, Connecticut, five days later, they ran into the first division

40. Ibid., 3, 185, 189, 212–13, 219; Patten to Stiles, Nov. 23, 1789.

41. Stiles kept these notes of "itineraries" together and later bound them into a total of six volumes.

42. Achsah Hitchcock to Enos Hitchcock, May 27, 1782; Hitchcock Papers, R.I. Hist. Soc.

43. *Lit. Diary*, 3, 35.

of the French army lumbering through town with 300 wagons, on the way to Providence. In the evening General Rochambeau visited them; and the next day on the way to Hartford they pulled up while 1,500 troops of the second division marched past, followed by 200 more wagons. Finally, on November 8, after a visit with John Hubbard at Meriden, they reached North Haven. There the ministers of New Haven and other friends awaited them in a dozen carriages and, as the sun set, the jubilant company escorted the bride to the "very agreeable Assembly" that had gathered to meet her in her new home.[44]

She seems to have fitted easily into the new environment. Elizur Goodrich, a tutor, reported that she was "a fine woman—diligent in business prudent in Oeconomy—sensible—polite in Company. Dignity and gracefulness unite in her Conduct and person." [45] In the January vacation Stiles packed her into a sleigh and took her to visit his friends around the state. After their return she described the experience to a Providence friend:

> The Day before yesterday Vacacion ended   We have spent three weeks very agreably   My good Man gave up his whole time in riding about the Country to see his friends and to shew his W——e   our Last tour was to Meradon at Brother Hubbards and Dr. Dana's at Wallingford (who by the way inquired after your Honour)   We feasted from house to house and made our selves merry (not fuddled) with agreable senseble Chit Chat (indeed I have a very different Opinion of people this way from what I had before I came this way) I dont see but that they are as Chearful and agreable as those we have been used to—We return'd the Day before yesterday and every thing was very Clever and very Agreeable and very Chearful   Brother Hubbard and Wife with us, and all in high Glee When Oh Dear the Slay tiped Over and we all got spilt my Dearry thought so much of his Wifey that no body thought of the Horsy who took a start and never stoped till it had got three miles—a slay in Company took us up but it spoiled our ride for that Day for tho no body was hurt yet it frightened me beyond measure   we rid the 13 miles in the Slay that took us up and left the runaway

44. Ibid., pp. 36, 44–45.
45. Elizur Goodrich to Simeon Baldwin, Nov. 27, 1782, Baldwin Papers.

7. Ezra Stiles, age sixty-seven, 1794, by Reuben Moulthrop. Courtesy of Yale University Art Gallery.

Slay to be brought hoom by some Lads that was Coming to Collage nothing I belive would have got me into it again except the Dr had insested on riding in it himself, I belive I should took my Chance with him.[46]

Mary was a little dismayed at the profusion of visitors who passed through her door and sometimes lingered longer than she might have wished. "Next thursday," she wrote in 1783, "we expect the Governor to spend a few weeks with us. The Assembly Sets here (but Sub Rosa I wish his Excellency had chose some other Lodgings) but no matter our family is Like the Old Womans [with] constant coming and going." [47] She did not let inconveniences bother her. Friends who had known her in Providence found without surprise that in a very short time she had the Stiles household well in hand and was "perfect mistress of the house." [48] But neither her husband nor her stepdaughters complained of her government. Indeed, in an effort to adjust her own life to her husband's, she even let Stiles teach her Hebrew.[49]

The new Mrs. Stiles brought her husband no new children, and to most of his contemporaries Stiles seemed more a grandfather than a bridegroom. He was often ill, and so near-sighted that a daring senior could sometimes cut classes by getting another to say "adsum" for him when the roll was called. Stiles himself watched with an almost morbid fascination the signs of age creeping upon him. In 1779 his horse had fallen with him, and he landed on his face, knocking out one of his front teeth. A few weeks later another dropped out. Though he was scarcely fifty-two, he was struck by this sign of approaching dissolution. By 1788, when he was sixty, he had only two teeth left, and his shrunken face made him look even older than his years. The great wig he wore whenever he stepped outside and the velvet cap with which he replaced it when sitting in his study both added to the appearance of antique decay.[50]

If ever appearances deceived, however, these did. During his years as president of Yale Stiles's energies were at their peak. As his body

46. Mary Checkley Stiles to Enos Hitchcock, Feb. 6, 1783, Hitchcock Papers.
47. Mary Checkley Stiles to Enos Hitchcock, Oct. 3, 1783, Hitchcock Papers.
48. Royal Flint to Enos Hitchcock, Mar. 18, 1783, Hitchcock Papers.
49. *Lit. Diary, 3,* 315.
50. Ibid., *2,* 379, 390; *3,* 291, 317; C. P. Lathrop, *Black Rock,* pp. 38, 42; Sprague, *Annals of the American Pulpit, 1,* 476–79.

progressed toward the grave, his mind continued its undiminished vigor. While he ran his college and family, acquired a new wife, and cared for his church, he still kept sacred his omnivorous curiosity. With a zest amounting to passion he continued to absorb every kind of information that came his way. Just as he had paced off the streets of Newport, measured them, mapped them, and numbered the houses and their occupants, so he attacked New Haven. In the winter of 1780 when the snow lay four feet deep in the woods and even the salt water was frozen solid, he took advantage of the ice to survey the harbor and measure it with a six-rod line, employing a tutor and five seniors as his chainmen.[51] At other times he made maps to trace the development of the town, enumerated the houses as he remembered them when he was in college, quizzed the oldest inhabitants to get estimates of the numbers in earlier days, and led students through the streets to count the existing buildings.[52]

The aurora borealis, which he had first observed as a boy from his bedroom window in North Haven, appeared in unusually spectacular displays during the 1780s. With Professor Strong he made measurements of its altitude and deluged friends all over New England with letters asking for similar measurements so that the dimensions of the phenomenon might be determined by triangulation. Unfortunately most of them were not equipped with the simple instruments necessary to give precision to their observations, but he at least was able to assure himself that the distances were of terrestrial rather than astronomical proportions.[53]

Once he had the college in order, his devotion to growing silkworms also reasserted itself. With a number of other enthusiasts he formed a company dedicated to spreading the growth of silk. After accumulating twenty ounces of mulberry seeds, he divided them into parcels of about 4,000 seeds each and sent them in 1789 to some ninety Connecticut ministers with instructions for planting. If the minister did not wish to undertake the task, he could arrange for someone else to do it. At the end of three years the planter was to distribute a quarter of his trees gratis to twenty or thirty families. The other three-quarters he could keep for himself. Stiles looked forward to four or five mil-

51. *Lit. Diary*, 2, 411–14.
52. Ibid., 3, 13–17, 238.
53. Stiles to James Madison, Feb. 15, 1781. Stiles made extensive notes and records of auroras in his Diary, most of which have been omitted from the printed version.

lion trees spread over Connecticut, with an annual silk production worth £100,000 sterling.[54] However extravagant this prediction, silk culture in Connecticut gave promise of being more successful than his earlier experiment in Newport. In 1790, before his nurseries were operating, devotees in the town of Northford produced enough raw silk to make 400 yards of cloth. To Stiles it must have seemed that his faith was well placed.[55]

His interest in Hebrew never diminished. He continued to study the Old Testament in the original and in 1794 came near to writing a book on the subject. To Sir William Jones, the great English orientalist, he explained his views in a book-length letter, a copy of which he actually prepared for publication but never sent to the printer.[56] In the same year, when Christoph Ebeling, the German geographer, asked him for information about Connecticut, he wrote him a brief history of the colony in eighty-six pages.[57] During his years as president he also learned French. After six months' study he could handle a hundred pages in an evening and began to read Racine and Voltaire. Later he took up Italian.[58]

As always, his curiosity was undiscriminating. He wanted to know everything. But the accumulation of intellectual furniture had never got in the way of his intellectual growth. As his teeth fell out and the students contemplated his great age, he was still growing—and much faster than most of them knew.

54. *Lit. Diary*, 3, 324, 350–51; notes folded into manuscript "Observations on Silk Worms and the Culture of Silk."

55. *Connecticut Courant*, May 9, 1791. According to John Trumbull, the painter, silk culture continued to thrive in some parts of Connecticut during the first part of the nineteenth century. In 1841 the people of Mansfield sold $50,000 worth of silk, grown on the mulberry trees planted in the 1790s. *The Autobiography of Colonel John Trumbull*, ed. Theodore Sizer (New Haven, 1953), p. 183.

56. Stiles to Jones, Jan. 8, 1794.

57. Stiles to Ebeling, Feb. 20, 1795.

58. *Lit. Diary*, 3, 127, 142–43, 147, 152, 338.

27

A Yale Jacobin

As president of Yale, Stiles never ceased to regard himself as a minister of the gospel. In his first years of office he preached almost as regularly in the college chapel or in nearby churches as he had during his pastorate at Newport.[1] He seems not to have doubted the propriety of doing so, even after 1786, when his final severance from his Newport congregation left him without any official church connections at all. He also continued to offer both baptism and communion, though such practices by unattached ministers had once shocked him.[2] When he preached for New Divinity ministers, as he often did, he sometimes even baptized children whom the regular minister refused to.[3] Everyone else looked on him as a minister too: he was frequently called upon to visit and pray with the sick in New Haven, and students sometimes came to him with their religious problems instead of going to the professor of divinity.[4]

When he took charge of the college church between the death of Daggett and the appointment of Wales, he introduced two practices that he had begun at Newport: the reading of a passage of Scripture and the administration of communion in the presence of the entire

1. In 1779 he preached the "equal" to 30 sabbaths (i.e. 60 sermons) in 1780 30, in 1781 37, in 1782 30, in 1783 29 or 30, in 1784 26. After 1784 the numbers dropped off. Stiles usually recorded the figures in his Diary, but Dexter has not always printed them.

2. Stiles had changed his earlier views by 1777: *Lit. Diary*, 2, 219.

3. Ibid., 3, 145, 440, cf. pp. 434–35.

4. Ibid., pp. 77, 181.

congregation.[5] He pointedly noted the fact when Wales abandoned the latter practice at his first communion service.[6] Although he did not interfere with Wales's management of the church, neither did he feel himself bound by it. In May 1785, when the college church refused to send a delegate to the ordination of James Noyes in Wallingford (because the Wallingford church was under censure by the consociation) Stiles attended in his own right and delivered a prayer during the laying on of hands.[7]

Stiles's theological views in his later years were the outgrowth or continuation of his earlier ones. He insisted as always on the supremacy of the Scriptures over all interpretations of them and emphasized the fact that Christ himself had treated the Old Testament as inspired.[8] That alone, he maintained, was sufficient reason for Christians to do likewise. In meeting the deists, they should take the offensive and proclaim their faith without resort to elaborate apologies. "We have gone too far," he said, "in undertaking to show the *reason* of every revealed doctrine; and in conceding and giving up everything we cannot explain." [9] If it came to the point where Christianity must rest on reason, there was scarcely a doctrine, he thought, that would survive. Resurrection, immortality of the soul, the last judgment, the trinity, atonement, predestination, original sin, regeneration—all, apart from the testimony of revelation, must appear conjectural and problematic. These doctrines must be taught directly from the Bible, with a "thus saith the Lord," and not "thus saith revealed reason." [10]

Stiles advanced more insistently now a view which he had formerly expressed privately, that the way to bring sinners to Christ was not to declaim upon the sweet reasonableness of Christianity but to frighten them with the terrors of hell:

> How far *reasoning* upon the equity, justice and holiness of God's law, and the rewards of virtue, may operate upon hearts blind to the beauties of it, I must leave. But I rather judge that towards awakening, alarming and exciting the attention of sinners, the

5. Ibid., 2, 485, 492.

6. Ibid., 3, 29.

7. Ibid., pp. 158–60.

8. Ibid., pp. 511, 513.

9. *A Sermon Delivered at the Ordination of the Reverend Henry Channing* (New London, 1787), p. 12.

10. Ibid., pp. 13–14.

principal and most pungent addresses are to be taken from other sources; from the *terrors of the world to come,* from the vengeance of an incensed deity, and from the gracious invitations of the merciful Jesus. Human language with the strongest metaphors, cannot go to excess in describing the awful horrors of eternal damnation, and the certain fearful looking for of divine vengeance, which assuredly awaits the ungodly and finally impenitent. Let these therefore be displayed, together with the odious nature of that moral character which incurs so tremendous a punishment. Should sinners realizing their danger, be pricked to the heart, and cry out, what shall we do to be saved; let them first be led to see their helpless state and the justice of their condemnation, in the perfection and holiness of the divine law:—and then let them be addressed with the gracious invitations of the divine Jesus.[11]

These sentiments, delivered in 1787 at the ordination of Henry Channing, one of his students, did not mean that Stiles had himself become a hell-fire preacher. He did not have the temperament for it. Nor had he capitulated to the New Divinity. On the contrary, his opinion of it, in private at least, became ever more bitter. The adherents of the New Divinity were as bad as the deists, he thought, in insisting upon their own feeble reasoning. Instead of preaching the great central truths of Christianity, they harped incessantly upon the peculiar conclusions (their private *Eurekas,* Stiles called them) which they thought they had deduced logically from those truths.[12]

Stiles's own exploration of theology, which he loved to study (though he never considered it a substitute for Scripture), led him more and more in these years to Dionysius the Areopagite.[13] Dionysius, with his mystical and all but incomprehensible jargon, would at first

11. Ibid., p. 16.

12. *Lit. Diary,* 3, 273–75, 286, 343–44, 374–78, 384–85; Stiles to William Williams, Aug. 15, 1793.

13. He had bought a copy in 1771 and at once became an admirer: *Lit. Diary,* 3, 470; Stiles to Abigail Dwight, Feb. 7, 1772, to Thomas Wright, Apr. 10, 1775, to Samuel Wilton, Apr. 13, 1775. Stiles's views on Dionysius are expressed at length in a "Dissertation to prove the authenticity of the works ascribed to Dionysius." This is appended to a translation by Stiles of two letters of Dionysius. He evidently intended the letters and the dissertation for posthumous publication, for he has written on the cover of the manuscript, "By EZRA STILES D.D. LLD. late President of YALE COLLEGE in Connecticut."

sight appear unlikely to arouse the enthusiasm of a man with Stiles's taste for religious simplicity; but Stiles found in him two qualities to admire: a reverence for Scripture and an insistence that God is ultimately incomprehensible, so that whatever words men employ to describe him must fall short of His perfection. Though Dionysius himself attempted a description, he emphasized that words were only symbols of something inexpressible.

Such a theology accorded well with the idea of human progress in knowledge which Stiles first outlined in his paper on the universe while a tutor at Yale. The human mind was incapable of perceiving directly the perfections of God, but it might perceive much through symbol, and thus prepare for the superior vision which would become possible after the human frame was sloughed off and the soul advanced upward in the scale of being. "At present," Dionysius argued, "we employ (so far as in us lies) appropriate symbols for things Divine and then from these we press on upward, according to our powers." Hereafter we would be able to reach much higher and participate "in an union transcending our mental faculties, and there, amidst the blinding blissful impulsions of His dazzling rays, we shall, in a diviner manner than at present, be like unto the heavenly Intelligences." [14]

This vision was so delightfully congenial to Stiles that in his later years he read Dionysius almost as regularly as he read the Scriptures. Dionysius had another merit too: he opposed the unitarian degradation of Christ to a mere human being. Socinianism and unitarianism, while not yet respectable in New England, were making progress. Dionysius, along with Origen, whom Stiles also came to admire, gave such arguments for the divinity of Christ as all but deprived Him of any human character. This too was a heresy (monophysitism), but Stiles does not seem to have discerned any danger in Dionysius and welcomed him for the way in which he disposed of unitarianism.

While he had no use for unitarianism or deism, Stiles continued to regard all denominations of Christians with catholic approval. All were marred by attachment to dubious principles; they all failed to see that absolute certainty in theological matters was impossible of human attainment, but all or almost all subscribed to the essential truths of Christianity and could help a man find his way to God. He still thought the Congregationalists were closer to the apostolic model

14. C. E. Rolt, trans., *Dionysius the Areopagite on the Divine Names and the Mystical Theology* (London, 1920), p. 58.

than any other group, and the Presbyterians next to them; but as the New Divinity claimed more and more New Englanders, he looked to the Dutch Reformed churches as possibly a more secure stronghold "for the Conservation of the pure Theology." [15] Though he still distrusted the Anglicans, he acknowledged, like the old Puritans whom he emulated, that the Anglican church, in spite of its corruptions, was a true church. On one of his trips to Newport when Rebecca Marchant, Henry's wife, decided to give up Anglicanism, Stiles admitted her to his own church without further examination.[16] The Lutherans, too, though even more deluded than the Anglicans, were true Christians. When he read in the newspapers of the death of Henry Melchior Muhlenberg, the eminent Lutheran minister, in 1787, he wrote in his diary this characteristic comment:

> He was doubtless an excellent Character; and a Proof that Lutherans, tho' deniers of Election and Predestination in the Calvinistic Sense, and holding Consubstantiation, and some other Peculiarities differing from us, yet at the same time being sound in the Doctrines of the Trinity, Regeneration, and Justification by Christ's imputed Righteousness, and living a holy Life, may arrive at the Realms of Bliss. And yet I suppose, Mr. West, Dr. Edwards, Dr. Bellamy, Mr. Smally, Mr. Dwight, Mr. Judson, Mr. Niles, Mr. Tullars, Mr. Trumbull North Haven, Mr. Hopkins, Mr. Emmons, Mr. Austin, Mr. Robinson &c would refuse to receive Communion in a Lutheran Church, or admit a holy and a regenerated Lutheran to Communion in the Congregational Churches, without leading them first to make profession of the Faith de novo and as if coming from Gentilism. But I renounce this limited Charity, which shuts out of our Churches more subjects of the celestial Kingdom than it admits.[17]

15. Stiles to Eilardus Westerlo, Sept. 13, 1788, in Thomas E. V. Smith, *The City of New York in the Year of Washington's Inauguration* (New York, 1889), pp. 128–29. When the Connecticut General Association of ministers resumed its former connection with the Presbyterians of the middle states, Stiles at last participated. But this time the union consisted only in the sending by each group of a few nonvoting delegates to the meetings of the other group: *Lit. Diary, 3,* 431, 496–97; Holmes, *Life,* pp. 312–14; Stiles to Ebeling, Feb. 20, 1795.

16. *Lit. Diary, 3,* 162–63.

17. Ibid., p. 286.

Even the Quakers, who had sinned politically as well as theologically in Stiles's eyes, came in for a share of his charity. One Adna Heaton, a Quaker who had become convinced that his church was wrong in denying the sacraments, sought Stiles's advice about persuading other Quakers to this view. Stiles in answer advised him against seeking so radical a reform:

Altho' I firmly believe that Jesus Christ instituted *Water Baptism* and the *Sacramental Supper,* and think they ought to be universally observed in the Church: yet I have a far higher opinion of *practical Virtue* and the *spiritual Exercises* of the divine Life, than I have of the Importance of these Ordinances— especially as I doubt not they will be very generally upheld all over Christendom; altho' our Christian Brethren the Friends should continue to omit them. Your Denomination hold the *Divinity and Atonement* of Christ, and Pardon as founded in his Atonement, as is apparent in Fothergills Sermons and Barcklay's Writings: They hold the *Influences and Indwelling of the Spirit* to guide direct sanctify and fit us for Heaven; they hold the principles of Integrity and Righteousness, and pure and sublime Morals of the Gospel and these with me are the weightier matters of our holy Religion. He that is right in these Things, and in these Things conscientiously serves God, will not be rejected because, with his fellow Christians in general, he does not feel the Necessity of outward Ordinances.

As to the highest most essential and most important principles of Religion, I think we are not to temporize, nor to confer with flesh and Blood, but to risque the Consequences with our dearest Connexions and Friends. But we are not to magnify the inferior Matters of Religion, of which however we may be persuaded, into Things of this Moment.[18]

Stiles did not confine his charity to pen and paper but freely offered his friendship and respect to men whose theology he rejected. He was often seen at New Haven's Second Church, where Jonathan Edwards Jr. could always be counted on for a strong dose of New Divinity. He attended Christmas services with the New Haven Anglicans and was on friendly terms with their minister Bela Hubbard. While he

18. Heaton to Stiles, Nov. 3, 1792. Stiles to Heaton, Dec. 10, 1792.

thought none of the Connecticut Anglican ministers outstanding in abilities, he gave one of them, Richard Mansfield, an honorary degree in 1792 and considered him a "worthy good man." [19]

There were limits, however, to Stiles's tolerance. He never quite overcame his earlier distrust of the Anglicans. When the once-dreaded bishop became a reality in 1785 in the person of Samuel Seabury (Yale 1748), Stiles and other Congregationalists bristled. They knew that Seabury could never gain temporal powers in an independent America, but they took pains to let him know, at every opportunity, that they considered themselves his ecclesiastical equals. Since he called himself Bishop of Connecticut, they voted in General Association that all ministers were entitled to be called bishop and should so address one another. When he appeared at Yale commencement, his fellow churchmen thought his rank should entitle him to a special seat, but Stiles treated him like any other clergyman.[20]

The Anglicans struck back in public attacks on Stiles not only for his treatment of Seabury but also for his compelling Anglican students to attend chapel. They ridiculed his views on Presbyterian and Congregational ordination.[21] Stiles made a point of not answering.[22] He thought it bad policy for Christians to be attacking each other when faced with an enemy that threatened them all. And he had become convinced that there was such an enemy. The growth of infidelity was so great in the 1780s and 1790s that Stiles found himself reconsidering some of the ideas about church and state that he had developed at a time when he thought that deism was on the way out.

In Connecticut every man was taxed for the support of a Congregational minister, unless he could prove that he attended a church of another denomination. If no such church existed in his neighborhood, he could not escape supporting the Congregational minister. This was a grievance to atheists and deists, who objected to paying for other men's superstitions, and to Baptists and Anglicans, who objected to

19. *Lit. Diary*, 3, 235, 474.

20. Ibid., p. 173; *American Mercury*, Apr. 20, 1795; Holmes, *Life*, p. 370; William Gordon to Stiles, Oct. 25, 1785, New Haven Colony Hist. Soc.; Joseph Willard to Stiles, Oct. 5, 1785.

21. John Bowden, *A Letter from John Bowden . . . to the Reverend Ezra Stiles* (New Haven, 1788), and *A Second Letter from John Bowden* (New Haven, 1789); *Lit. Diary*, 3, 311, 351.

22. Benjamin Trumbull to George Gillmore, Aug. 7, 1790, Yale Univ. Lib.; Holmes, *Life*, p. 351.

the favor shown the Congregationalists. Probably most residents of Connecticut were Congregationalists, but the dissenting minorities rightly complained of discrimination, and they joined the attacks of the infidels against all state support of religion.[23]

In Rhode Island, Stiles had been impressed by the way religion flourished without support from the state, and he had looked forward to the day when such complete separation of church and state would take place throughout America. By 1783 he had decided that the day of total separation needed postponing. He still believed that every man should be free to believe or not, and to go to Christ by any path he chose. And to the end of his life he looked at the future, confident that "the more christianity is attacked, the more firmly it stands, with an increasing and growing strength, not on power, not on the support of temporalities, or civil government, generally more fatal than beneficial, but on the calm, and weighty, and irresistible convictions of truth." [24] Nevertheless, Stiles was less confident in these years about the immediate prospects of Christianity. Infidelity was advancing; the number of young men entering the ministry was too few to fill the vacant pulpits; and religion seemed to be declining everywhere, in Rhode Island even more rapidly than in Connecticut.[25] Under these circumstances Stiles came out for governmental support to religion and failed to condemn the favored position that the Connecticut law gave to his own denomination.[26]

While Stiles thus moved a step backward in his views of the relation between church and state, he pushed beyond most of his contemporaries—indeed beyond most of his descendants—in his understanding of civil liberty.

During the years at Newport, when Stiles owned a slave himself, he and Samuel Hopkins had found common ground in a scheme to educate Negroes as missionaries and send them back to Africa.[27] Stiles continued to think this a laudable project after the war,[28] but he had meanwhile become more interested in helping the Negroes in America.

23. Purcell, *Connecticut in Transition*, chap. 2; Greene, *Development of Religious Liberty in Connecticut*, chaps. 12, 13.

24. Ezra Stiles, *A History of Three of the Judges of King Charles I* (Hartford, 1794), p. 316.

25. *Lit. Diary*, 2, 389, 402–04; 3, 147, 266; *Connecticut Gazette*, Apr. 2, 1790.

26. *The United States Elevated to Glory and Honor*, pp. 69–90.

27. Stiles to Charles Chauncy, Dec. 8, 1773, and to John Rodgers, July 15, 1774.

28. Stiles to John Erskine, Aug. 29, 1788.

Before coming to New Haven, he had freed his own slave (who later with his family followed Stiles to New Haven and became his paid servant), but the contradiction of slavery in a country dedicated to freedom still troubled him. He was confident that slavery would ultimately disappear, but he decided in 1790 that he should help it do so. In that year he and a number of other Connecticut ministers and patriots formed a society "for the promotion of freedom and for the relief of persons unlawfully holden in bondage." [29] The members, with Stiles as president, enrolled the names of Negroes born after March 1, 1784, who by Connecticut law would be entitled to freedom at the age of twenty-five. They also voted to inquire into violations of any other laws regarding slavery and to find out whether any persons in the state were illegally held in bondage. Slavery at the time seemed to be a relic of tyranny that must disappear, whether in the North or the South, when confronted by the moral determination of responsible citizens.

Less than four years later Stiles recorded in his Diary a visit from a former student, just returned from a trip to Georgia, where he had been staying at Mulberry Grove, the plantation of Catharine Greene, widow of General Nathanael and an old friend of Stiles's Rhode Island days: "Mr. Whitney brot to my house and shewed us his Machine, by him invented for cleaning Cotton of its seeds." [30] Stiles thought it "a curious and very ingenious piece of Mechanism." It did not occur to him that it would help to render meaningless his calculations about the imminent disappearance of slavery.

If Stiles could have foreseen the future of slavery in America he would have been saddened, but it would have taken more than this to dampen his confidence in the triumph of liberty. The Revolution had given him a vision of a new and powerful force that, whatever setbacks it might receive, would ultimately establish or restore human freedom all over the world. The force had first revealed itself at Lexington and Concord, but it had greater implications for peace than for war. It was the power of an informed and independent common people, the power of what we would call—though he did not—democracy.

Before his confidence in the British constitution had been shaken

29. *Connecticut Courant,* Sept. 20, 1790. Some of the records of the Society are in the Simeon Baldwin Papers.

30. *Lit. Diary,* 3, 516.

by the succession of events leading to the Revolution, Stiles had supposed that a constitutional monarchy of the British type could furnish
the surest protection for liberty. Now he was equally sure that no
monarchy was proof against the corruption that had overtaken Great
Britain. If God furnished the ruler with wisdom and virtue, monarchy
might be the best form of government, as it assuredly was among the
angels. But God did not provide earthly rulers with such talents. He
had not given them even to Moses. It was, therefore, folly to trust
any one man. The only safety was in numbers.

These ideas were not wholly new, even to Stiles. As early as 1766
when Benjamin Gale had proposed reinterpreting the Connecticut
charter so as to reduce popular control, Stiles had given his opinion
"frankly and fully for the most popular Elections." He told Gale
that he would rather see the House of Representatives larger in number and the franchise wider.[31] At the time Stiles had not pursued his
thoughts further. The Revolution gave him the impetus to do so;
and when his friend Governor Trumbull asked him to preach the
Connecticut Election Sermon in 1783, he was able to give his audience
a glimpse into the future of American democracy.[32]

Much of his speech was conventional to the occasion: magistrates
should protect religion and nourish the springs of learning. Ministers
should display "charity, union, and benevolence." These were important matters, but Stiles's main theme was something larger: the
future glory of the United States. He predicted an expanding population that would fill the continent and send ships all over the world
to return with untold riches. The source of this prosperity, the virtue
which would make the United States the envy and model of every
nation in the world, was liberty, liberty supported by an informed
and independent people. For Stiles the great philosopher of the Revolution was not John Locke but James Harrington. Proceeding from
Harrington's premise that political power must rest on economic
power, he pointed out that in America, and particularly in New England, property was widely distributed among the people. Here, therefore, as in Harrington's fanciful country of Oceana, the most successful
form of government must be republican. The country, of course, was
too large for the people to rule themselves in a pure democracy, but
they did choose their own rulers in annual elections.

31. Stiles to Gale, Oct. 1, 1766. See above, Chap. 16.
32. *The United States Elevated to Glory and Honor* (New Haven, 1783)

This, Stiles proudly proclaimed, was something new: in every other country the government lay beyond the immediate control of the people, "but a DEMOCRATICAL polity for millions, standing upon the broad basis of the people at large, amply charged with property, has not hitherto been exhibited." [33] In such a system, he thought, tyranny was impossible, for the people would not oppress themselves. Temporary evils there might be. The people might err in choosing rulers; good men once chosen might grow corrupt. But at the next election the people could remedy the situation. "Herein," said Stiles, "we far surpass any ¬tates on earth. We can correct ourselves, if in the wrong." [34] In this system liberty was secure as it had never been before, and for just that reason the system must endure.

Throughout his sermon Stiles struck an exultant note that had been missing in New England for more than a hundred years before the Revolution; and in so doing he joined hands again with the Puritans, who had looked upon themselves as leaders of the world. Their immigration to New England proved in the end to be a retreat rather than an advance, but for a generation they were ahead of the world, not behind it. They were a city set on a hill; God had sifted a whole nation to find them and plant them in this new world where all might look and imitate. Somehow the scheme had gone awry. The evangelical fires had burned out, and the world had looked the other way. In bewilderment their children could only blame themselves, and year after year the ministers poured out their Jeremiads until they almost seemed to enjoy it. [35]

With the coming of the Revolution a new excitement began to grow in New England, an excitement which in the beginning only a man of Stiles's breadth could appreciate and articulate. Suddenly he saw that the Puritan dream was coming to life, not quite in the Puritans' terms but in terms of his own enlightened Puritanism. While old Charles Chauncy kept complaining to him of the iniquity of the times, and Benjamin Gale deplored everything that had happened since 1765, Stiles saw that all America had become, once more, a city set upon a hill. As he addressed Governor Trumbull, the Council, and the representatives who he knew would deny him what he wanted for Yale, he was not really talking to them at all. He was talking over

33. Page 17.
34. Page 23.
35. See Miller, *Errand into the Wilderness*, pp. 1–15.

their heads to the world that lay three thousand miles over the water. America, he was saying, had not merely conquered George III; America had conquered monarchy. America was the future of Europe. In the coming years, as American ships carried the flag around the globe, the power of freedom would everywhere become apparent. American freedom and American purity of religion would set the world such an example that people would never again be content to sit quietly under tyranny. Let monarchs beware.

To Ezra Stiles, then, the birth of the American nation signalized also the birth of a new and wonderful liberty which would alter the world. In the remaining years of his life he saw his expectations confirmed. Because he had complete confidence that grievances could be redressed in a republic through the normal channels of government, he felt no sympathy for Shays's Rebellion. Nor was he alarmed by it. The danger, he assured Washington at the outbreak of the disturbance, was "doubtless magnified at a Distance." [36] When the Constitutional Convention was summoned in 1787 he thought the action a little premature: more experience was needed before the independent states could perfect a constitution. But he thought the resulting document a good one, in spite of the danger that the president might turn into a king, and he considered his friends in Rhode Island to be utterly mad when they refused for a long time to accept it.[37]

The success of the new government under Washington, whom he admired as much as other Americans did, was no more than Stiles had expected. What gave him the greatest thrill was not the success of American democracy at home but its impact abroad. With mounting excitement he watched the French people wrest power from their king and assert their rights as men. The power of freedom, first demonstrated in America, was exerting itself even more rapidly than he had anticipated, and he saw with satisfaction that the other kings of Europe were filled with alarm. As they joined together to put out the terrible fire of liberty, Stiles was not worried about the outcome. "The War of Kings," he called it, "or the Conflict of Royal Aristocracy with Republicanism, which will terminate in establishing the Republic of France, and the Republic of Holland decollated of its Statholder, and the Restitution of the Cortes of Spain—: and the Inoculation of

36. *Lit. Diary*, 3, 267–68; Stiles to Washington, Nov. 9, 1786, Feb. 7, 1787, Washington Papers, Library of Congress.

37. *Lit. Diary*, 3, 293–96, 358.

Germany, the Baltic Kingdoms, and all Europe with the epidemical contagion of Liberty the Rights of Man! And ultimately the Tameing, the Moderation and Amelioration [of] all the European Governments." [38]

Fifty years later, David Daggett could still remember vividly the enthusiasm with which Stiles greeted French success. Daggett had met the president on the street one day.

"Have you heard the glorious news?" cried Stiles.

"What news Mr. President?"

"The French have entered Holland—they have planted the Tree of Liberty before the Stadtholders palace. They will plant it before the palaces of all the princes of Europe. The people will live under its shade—I rejoice at it—I am a democrat—Yea, I am a Jacobin— I glory in the name!" [39]

Stiles followed every move in the War of Kings, never losing his confidence that the French Revolution was a triumph for liberty. On July 9, 1794, he affirmed his faith in an extraordinary letter to an old friend at Newport:

> I joyn with you in rejoycing in the Success of France against the combined Army, and in feeling humbled but not discouraged at their Repulses and Defeats. When the Tories are elevated the Friends of Liberty are depressed, when they are dejected we are elevated. But we are never discouraged. . . . Farewell Despotism, farewel Monarchy, farewel Aristocracy! It is time for you to give way to the mild and just Government of Liberty and Laws and the Rights of Man. From the first Moment of Commencement of Hostilities at Lexington I never had a doubt of the success of american Liberty—from the first moment of commencement of the struggle in france, particularly from the seizing and conducting the King a Prisoner from Versailles to Paris by Fayette, I have never entertained the least desponding Doubt of the final and ultimate glorious Triumph of Liberty in France. But I believe there must be more Use of the *Guillotine* yet. As I believ it has hitherto been exercised with *great Justice* in general, so there is remaining much more hurtful and poisonous Weeds to be mown down in the Field of Liberty, before Right

38. Ibid., p. 490.

39. David Daggett, New Haven Sixty Years Ago and Since, manuscript written in 1841, Yale Univ. Lib. Daggett thought, incorrectly, that Stiles later repudiated the French Revolution. Cf. Stiles to Joel Barlow, March 20, 1793.

Liberty and Tranquillity can be established. What fine Work England makes of it? Tossing away a hundred Thousand Men and 150 Million Debt to loose America and perhaps 20 Thousand Men and 50 Million more to fight the Cause of Kings and hasten their Downfall and Ruin? Providence makes Men, makes Kingdoms and States instrumental in accomplishing Events directly contrary to their Intentions and most vigorous Pursuits. The Kings could not take a more effectual step to loose their Crowns than to combine in Hostility against France.[40]

The letter is signed "Ezra Stiles an unchanged Son of Liberty." The reason for the signature and for the defiant tone of the letter are not far to seek. When the French Revolution began in 1789, most Americans joined Stiles in greeting it as an outgrowth of their own struggle. But the execution of Louis XVI early in 1793 led a great many to change their minds. This, they felt, was going too far: depose a king, yes; cut off his head, no. The French Revolution had got out of hand and threatened a total subversion of law and order. The Jacobinical societies which had precipitated the movement and which had spread to America would result in a multiplication here of the bloody scenes under way at Paris.[41] David Daggett, while listening to Stiles sing the glories of French democracy, was getting letters of a different character from Stiles's former students. "God alone can tell," wrote John Cotton Smith, the future governor of Connecticut, "what will be the consequence of complete success on the side of the French—universal anarchy I expect throughout Europe.—and even America if the infernal designs of our Democratic societies are carried into effect." Smith too thought there should be more use of the guillotine: "the first use I would make of it would be to sacrifice indiscriminately every member of every democratic junto upon this continent."[42] Newspapers rang with similar denunciations, and occasional defenses, of the French.[43] Americans were divided, and some of the ablest men in the country gave support to what Stiles could only regard as the cause of tyranny.

Before the split began, Stiles had already decided to enlist his

40. Stiles to Jacob Richardson, July 9, 1794.

41. Eugene P. Link, *Democratic-Republican Societies 1790–1800* (New York, 1942), pp. 175–209.

42. Smith to Daggett, July 21, 1794, Daggett Papers, Yale Univ. Lib.

43. Charles D. Hazen, *Contemporary American Opinion of the French Revolution* (Baltimore, 1897), pp. 253–78.

learning, in an appropriately learned manner, in the cause of liberty. He had long been interested in the history of the three judges who participated in condemning Charles I to death and fled to New England upon the restoration of Charles II. For years he had been gathering information about them, as he did about so many things, feeling a sympathy with them and their cause. They were, after all, the protagonists in the most daring action that the old Puritans undertook. At least one of them, John Dixwell, was buried in New Haven, and Stiles had often paused at the grave as he strolled across the green of an evening. In the fall of 1792, Aedanus Burke, chief justice of South Carolina and an ardent Whig, wrote to him proposing the erection at Yale of a monument to the regicides who, he said, had fought in the 1640s the same fight that the Americans took up in 1775.[44] Perhaps Stiles had talked with him about the regicides when Burke called at the college library the preceding August.[45] Stiles was enthusiastic about the proposal and at once began to prepare plans for the monument, which would proclaim at large the right of a people to judge their king.

In composing the inscription Stiles found it necessary to make further inquiries and researches; and before the project could be carried out, he found himself writing a historical memoir of the men, devoted in large part to the question of where they were buried. The composition, which he wrote between January 25 and April 27, 1793, represents Stiles at his worst.[46] It is a tedious hodgepodge of fact and fancy, compounded mainly out of dim recollections by old men and women of things their grandfathers had told them fifty years before.

Before he finished writing it, news reached America of the execution of Louis XVI; and as he read the comments in the newspapers, Stiles began to realize that tyrannicide had somehow ceased to be wholly respectable in America. The men whom he revered and whose story he had tried so painstakingly to reconstruct might no longer be accepted in America as the heroes they were. As he saw more and more of his friends turn against the French Revolution, he felt impelled to write a defense of tyrannicide, a defense which would vindicate the

44. Burke to Stiles, Sept. 20, 1792.
45. *Lit. Diary*, 3, 471.
46. *A History of Three of the Judges of King Charles I*. See Stiles to Mrs. Lydia Watkins, Dec. 20, 1792, to Mrs. Elvira Lothrop, March 16, 1793, to John Ewing, Nov. 18, 1794.

execution not only of Charles I but also of Louis XVI, a defense that would help people to realize that democracy is the only safe companion for liberty.

He wrote it at white heat in the summer of 1793 and appended it to his historical account of the regicides.[47] It was not an orderly performance, flying as it did from one great theme to another, but it was the finest thing that Stiles ever wrote, the distillation of his enlightened Puritanism, a glowing expression of his faith in democracy. Beginning as a justification of the regicides, it affirmed not merely that a people have a right to judge their rulers but that civil rights and liberty cannot permanently endure in conjunction with hereditary sovereignty or aristocracy, "that the perpetuity of the one must be attended with the ultimate downfall and extirpation of the other." [48] The people, in other words, were their own best rulers. Unhampered by kings and aristocrats, they could construct "a rational government and policy, on such plain and obvious general principles, as would be intelligible to the plainest rustic . . . And whatever the Filmers and Acherlys may say, the common people are abundantly capable and susceptible of such a polity." [49]

In condemning the Filmers and Acherlys, Stiles was tilting not against dead Englishmen but rather against the living Americans who wanted a government by the rich and well born. "The common people," he was now convinced, "will generally judge right, when duly informed. The general liberty is safe and secure in their hands. It is not from deficiency of abilities to judge, but from want of information, if they at any time as a body go wrong. Upon information from an abundance of enlightened characters always intermixt among them, they will ultimately always judge right, and be in the end the faithful guardians and support and security of government." [50]

Precisely because the common people would judge right, every monarch and aristocrat feared them. The Jacobin societies struck terror in the kings and nobility of Europe, because the governments there, outside the new France, had become "so corrupt and oppressive, as that they cannot stand before a well formed system of revolutionary societies." The United States government, on the other hand, was a

47. Pages 207–339.
48. Page 208.
49. Page 262.
50. Pages 274–75.

government by the people and had no reason to fear popular societies. The men who wished to suppress such societies were the real enemies to liberty and good government, because "there is no alternative between their right to assemble, and the abolition of liberty. Extinguish this right . . . and the people are slaves." [51]

The people must be free to assemble even for the purpose of overthrowing the government, for only by free assembly, free discussion, free inquiry could they reach the truth that makes men free. If the government had popular support, any attempt by a minority to overthrow it would fail. If it lacked support, then popular societies would be a means of altering it for the better.

> Why should despotism and oppression be entailed to subsequent generations? Why is it not just that the ages of tyranny should be succeeded by the ages of liberty? Under the obstinate and persevering opposition of the reigning powers this emancipation cannot be made but by the people. This must commence, as I have said, in popular societies, connected, spreading and growing up into a general popular exertion. . . . The enterprise is arduous, but combined national enthusiasm in the cause of liberty is of great and awful force. All Europe is ripening with celerity for a great revolution; the aera is commencing of a *general revolution*. The amelioration of human society must and will take place. It will be a conflict between Kings and their subjects. This war of Kings, like that of Gog and Magog, will be terrible. It will, for there is no other way, it will commence and originate in voluntary associations among subjects in all kingdoms. Eluded supplications and petitions for liberty, will be followed by armaments for the vindication of the rights of human nature. The public ardor will be kindled, and a national spirit and exertion roused, which undiscouraged, unsubdued by many defeats, will ultimately carry all before it.[52]

Stiles hid his eloquence under a bushel by publishing it at the close of his bewildering historical memoirs of the judges. There is no hint on the title page that the book contains a 130-page polemic in favor of human rights. As a result, few readers have plowed through the antiquarian beginning to find it. It deserves, nevertheless, to stand

51. Ibid.
52. Page 282.

with the writings of Jefferson, Barlow, and Paine as one of our noblest early expressions of the democratic idea.

Stiles assigned the profits of the book to the education at Yale of a descendant of the judges.[53] The first copy was bound on Betsy's birthday, April 17, 1795.[54] She was thirty-seven, Stiles himself sixty-seven and still as busy as ever, listening to senior recitations and disputations, writing his eighty-six page letter to Ebeling, studying English constitutional history, visiting a new cotton factory, and rejoicing over the French capture of Amsterdam and the abdication of the Stadt-holder. He called himself an unchanged Son of Liberty, but he was only half right: his love for liberty had never faltered, but neither had it stood still. His admiration for British constitutional monarchy had grown to a belief in democracy, just as his rational persuasion of the existence of God had grown to a faith surpassing knowledge, just as his reverence for the Puritans of New England had grown to a vision of democratic America as a new city set on a hill. His mind never stopped grasping at the next idea until a bilious fever struck him on May 8, 1795. Four days later he ceased to grow.

53. *Connecticut Journal*, May 27, 1795.
54. *Lit. Diary*, 3, 562.

Appendix

Enrollment and Quarter Bills 1778–94

The following table gives the total number of students enrolled at Yale at the opening of the academic year in November, together with the total of bills due from students during that year. In no year was the total number enrolled ever present at one time. The number of students actually on campus usually reached a maximum in December, but even then about 10 per cent or more were absent for one reason or another. The quarter bills covered tuition, study rent, fines levied for absences or for misbehavior, charges for broken glass and for sweeping, and "contingent charges," a fixed fee that was not connected with any service. The total bills for the year do not show an exact correlation with the number of students enrolled in November, because of changes in enrollment during the year. Varying numbers of new students were admitted during the course of every year, while others dropped out.

Year	Number of Students	Quarter Bills (Lawful Money) £ s. d.
1778	124	500
1779	139	614 13 6
1780	153	824 2 4
1781	224	1,114 2 8
1782	250	1,163 14 2
1783	265	1,236 14 9
1784	252	1,177 15 4
1785	201	992 13 10
1786	174	842 9 7
1787	139	707 15 1
1788	125	696 5 11
1789	131	770 18 4
1790	141	778 17 8
1791	143	789 6 8
1792	?	784 3 8
1793	136	847 12 11
1794	143	?

A Note on the Stiles Papers

EZRA STILES was an indefatigable note-taker. Wherever he went, he carried folded quarto sheets and was perpetually jotting down facts, fancies, diagrams, maps, extracts from books and newspapers, expenditures, calculations, conversations, and observations on every subject that came to mind. He carefully preserved the sheets and sewed or bound them together later. He sometimes used blank notebooks for special topics, but since he could never bear to see paper without writing on it, he was likely to make observations on, say, Hebrew or Arabic, college business or domestic economy in the unoccupied spaces of a notebook otherwise devoted to silk culture or astronomy. Besides keeping a diary which ran to fifteen volumes from 1769 to 1795, he made separate journals of his itineraries and a separate record of temperatures. He filled the margins of his almanacs with records of events. When he had the time, he made and kept copies of the letters he wrote. Letters that came to him he preserved, and if the writer had left large blank spaces, he was likely to fill them with his own jottings.

By his own reckoning he had in 1785 twenty-four bound quarto volumes of manuscripts;[1] in 1787 he recorded twenty-six bound quarto volumes and as many more folio and quarto manuscripts unbound.[2] On December 16, 1788, he recorded a total of thirty-four volumes of manuscripts bound, three of which were letters from other persons, the rest his own writing.[3] In his will, dated September 16, 1793, he gave "my Trunk of Manuscripts to Isaac; and my Cabinet of Manuscripts containing 30 or 40 Volumes according to an annexed List, to the care of the Revd. Abiel Holmes of Cambridge, to be by him kept for ten years and ten years after my decease to be deposited with the Archives of Yale College, and to be lodged and always kept in the Presidents House."[4] The annexed list reads as follows:

Ms Given to the Archives of Yale College
4 or more Vol 4to Itineraries fr 1760 to 1790 and onwds
14 or more Vol. 4to Lity Diary fr 1769 to 1793 and onwds

1. Marginal notation in almanac in Foote donation (see below).
2. Itineraries, *4*, 171
3. *Lit. Diary* 3, 336
4. Probate Records, Connecticut State Library, Hartford.

    5 or more Vol. 4to Thermo Register fr 1763 to 1793 and onwds

    1 V. 4to List of N. Engld Chhs and Pastors for first 150 years

    2 or more Vol. 4to Miscellanea, Letters &c

    1 Vol 4to on Culture of Silk

    1 Vol. 4to Heb. and Arab. Lett. Rabbi Karigal &c.

    1 Vol. 4to Extracts fr. Mss of Gov. Winthrop and others

    1 Fol Vol. bound

    <u>1 Do</u>   Do in Parchment

    31

    8 Fol. Mss unbound

    6 Vol. 4to unbound

    1 Vol my Election Sermon printed 1783

    1 Vol. all my Sermons &c printed 8vo

Holmes took advantage of his ten-year custody of the manuscripts to write *The Life of Ezra Stiles* (Boston, 1798). In 1805 the cabinet of manuscripts went to Yale College, where Timothy Dwight was president.

According to Stiles's will, the cabinet was to be kept in the president's house, but it appears that Dwight placed them in the "Old brick college [Connecticut Hall] southeast end" along with the old orrery constructed by Joseph Badger and "other rubbish." That, at any rate, is where Stiles's daughter Emilia found them, the cabinet door hanging on one hinge and the lock broken, when she visited New Haven.[5] Emilia had married Jonathan Leavitt Jr. (Yale 1785) on April 21, 1796, and lived in Greenfield, Mass. She felt a fierce pride in her father and probably shared his feelings about Dwight. She was so outraged by the treatment of the manuscript cabinet, that she did not trust herself to speak to Dwight about it. In 1818, after Jeremiah Day succeeded to the presidency, she wrote him about Dwight's neglect of the manuscripts.[6]

Day brought the manuscripts to his house and reported back to Emilia: "I do not find that any of them are missing except the history of the New England churches, which I learned from the Librarian of college has been loaned. In the extract from the will are mentioned 6 vol. quarto and 8 vol. other manuscripts unbound. The 6 quarto volumes I find *bound*. This has probably been done, since

5. Emilia Leavitt to Jeremiah Day, June 2, 1818, Yale Univ. Lib.; to Ezra Stiles Gannett, Sept. 13, 1832, letter in possession of Lewis Stiles Gannett, West Cornwall, Conn.

6. At the same time she suggested that he look into another matter. At Abiel Holmes's house in Cambridge she had seen a snuffbox of Elihu Yale, which her father had deposited in the Yale archives. She referred Day to an entry in her father's diary for May 1, 1788, recording this fact. "You will please to *find* such an entry," she wrote, "and *without* useing my *name*, you *will find* the *box* in Dr. Holmes's hands, *where I saw it* last January. *It is time* it *was placed* in Yale College Archives." Emilia Leavitt to Day, June 2, 1818.

the will was written, and at one time, as the binding of all of them is the same. The unbound manuscripts are stitched in 13 parcels; but some of them are too small to be called volumes." Besides the manuscripts mentioned in Stiles's will, Day found "a small bundle of letters and papers, loosely tied together," three diplomas in tin cases, and a volume of manuscripts of Stiles's grandfather, Edward Taylor (containing the poems published in this century).[7]

Emilia had a good idea where the manuscript history of the New England churches might have gone: President Dwight, she thought, had probably used it, and so, perhaps, had Benjamin Trumbull, who wrote a history of Connecticut and a history of the United States. Trumbull, she discovered, had passed on all his papers to Abiel Holmes, who was teaching ecclesiastical history at Harvard. "I think," she wrote to Day in 1818, "Dr. Holmes has them."[8] Holmes's papers, which wound up after his death in the Massachusetts Historical Society, include a volume of manuscript notes by Stiles on church history, but they are crude and undigested. It is possible that the volume referred to was the list of New England churches and their successive pastors, now among the Stiles Papers at Yale.

The Stiles Papers remaining at Yale from the original bequest include forty-four bound volumes and twenty-eight unbound volumes or collections of papers (some sewn, with paper wrappers) labeled either by Stiles or by subsequent keepers of the collection as follows:

Bound Volumes (quarto except where otherwise indicated)

> Literary Diary 1769–1795 (15 vols.)
> Itineraries 1760–1794 (6 vols.)
> Thermometrical Register 1763–1795 (6 vols.)
> List of New England Churches and Pastors
> Miscellanea 1755–58
> Miscellanea 1758–62
> Silk
> Hebrew and Arabic
> Extracts from MSS
> Letters (folio)
> Letters (5 vols. numbered 2, 3, 4, 6, 7)
> Variety
> Extracts 1760–65
> Orations
> Notebook 1744–50
> Extracts from John Winthrop's MS History of New England (also contains
>   extracts from other books and MSS)

7. Day to Emilia Leavitt, July 25, 1818, Day Papers, Yale Univ. Lib.
8. Emilia Leavitt to Day, Sept. 3, 1818, Day Papers, Yale Univ. Lib.

Unbound Volumes and Collections (*quarto except where otherwise indicated*)

> Notebook 1744–50 (mostly astronomy and geometry)
> Notebooks 1744–45 (two, octavo)
> Notebook 1745–46
> Notebook 1744 (surveying)
> Comets 1758 (three notebooks)
> Miscellaneous Notes 1745–46, 1763–67 (folio)
> Miscellaneous Notes 1760–62 (folio)
> Memoirs 1766, 1767
> Transit of Venus 1769
> Memoirs and Extracts 1763
> Stamp Act Notebook
> Memoirs on Ancient History and Geography
> Memoir of Robert Sandeman
> Hebrew (two notebooks)
> Observations on the Comet 1769
> Variety (contains part of Literary Diary for 1776)
> Letters (6 vols. numbered 2, 3, 4, 5, 9, 10)
> Memoranda: Yale College (a separate volume for every academic year, but the one for 1792–93 is missing)
> Sermons (numerous, of various dates, octavo. One large collection sewn together is labeled Sermons on Publick Thanksgivings and Publick Fasts)

Several items in the above lists do not appear to be in the list appended to the will, and several volumes mentioned in the will are not now at Yale. Of the ten folio volumes listed in the will only three survive. Moreover, the numbers on the volumes of letters show that volumes 1 and 5, at least, are missing from the bound volumes and 1, 6, 7, and 8, at least, from the unbound. The whereabouts of these is unknown. Either Stiles had lent them to friends before his death and they were never returned, or else they have been lost or stolen since then.[9]

Besides the manuscripts bequeathed to Yale, Stiles left a trunk of manuscripts to his son Isaac. Isaac was never heard from after his father's death and presumably died at sea. He was still assumed to be living in 1797, for he was assigned part of Betsy's estate in that year. By 1802 he was presumed dead and part of his estate had been assigned to Ezra Jr.'s children, Elizabeth Hubbard and Harriet Emilia.[10] Emilia's husband, Jonathan Leavitt, had become their legal guardian, and probably

9. Stiles evidently lent a volume to Jedidiah Morse in 1794: Stiles to Morse, Feb. 18, 1794. Vol. 6 of the bound volumes of letters has a note in the front cover by Abiel Holmes saying that it was not in the cabinet when the papers came to him and had probably been lent to Jeremy Belknap, from whose family Holmes later received it.

10. I.e. Emilia Harriot. Probate Records, Connecticut State Library, Hartford.

the trunk of manuscripts came into the possession of Emilia or of Ruth, the only two surviving children. The contents may have been distributed, but the bulk of the manuscripts must have gone eventually to Ruth's son, Ezra Stiles Gannett. From him they came into possession of his grandson, Lewis Stiles Gannett, now of West Cornwall, Connecticut. In 1940 Mr. Gannett gave most of his manuscripts to the Yale University Library. They included sixteen letters by Ezra Stiles, about fifty letters to him, and several small, unbound but sewn volumes, among them the following:

> Memoirs of the Family of Stiles
> Memoirs and Anecdotes of the Life of the Reverend Isaac Stiles
> Family Constitutions
> Birthday Reflections 1767–1793
> Account Books 1755–59 (six notebooks)
> Receipts 1755–1771
> Notebook 1750
> Sermons of Isaac Stiles (eight notebooks)
> Sermons of Ezra Stiles (eighteen notebooks)

Mr. Gannett made further donations of miscellaneous papers in 1958 and 1959. He retains a number of books from Stiles's library with manuscript annotations, and several almanacs, also annotated.

In 1931 a group of letters and papers totaling forty-eight items was presented to the Library by Mrs. Edward S. Harkness and was published (Isabel M. Calder, ed., *Letters and Papers of Ezra Stiles*, New Haven, 1933). These were purchased from the late Dr. A. S. W. Rosenbach, and it is not clear whether they came originally from the bequest to Yale or from the trunk given to Isaac.

Another donation was made in 1955 by Mrs. William Roe, including letters of St. John Honeywood to Betsy Stiles and some nineteenth-century letters of Emilia Stiles Leavitt.

In 1960 after the present work had been sent to the publishers, Mrs. Katharine D. Foote of Ridgewood, New Jersey, gave the Library a group of papers including several heavily annotated almanacs, a college notebook, and a valuable four-page autobiographical note entitled "Series of Occurrences in My Life." Occasional Stiles letters have been purchased by the Library from dealers.

The Stiles Papers have been heavily used by scholars working on a wide variety of topics, and the condition of some of the bound volumes has become critical. Stiles's habit of folding letters for binding and then sewing through the middle of them has resulted in a certain amount of damage along that fold, while the continual turning of leaves has so frayed the edges that some words have been completely lost. In order to prevent their further destruction the Yale Library has removed the bindings of several volumes of letters and has distributed the contents into separate folders. The documents most in need of it have been repaired, and others will be treated as time and funds permit. In order to avoid confusion in referring to particular items, I have not identified documents by the volume in which they are located, except in the case of volumes that will be kept intact, such as the Itineraries or the Literary Diary. Instead, I have identified by date and in the case of letters also by the name of the author and recipient.

In preparation for the present work, I had most of the Stiles Papers microfilmed. Exclusive of the Literary Diary, Itineraries, and Thermometrical Register, they occupy ten reels averaging about 1,000 frames each with two pages to a frame. My wife, Helen M. Morgan, calendared the films, with a separate file card for each frame. When these cards were arranged in chronological order, it became apparent that the great bulk of the Papers came from the years before Stiles's accession to the presidency. For the years after his accession, the only important body of material is contained in the Diary and in the briefer journals of his official actions, entitled "Memoranda: Yale College." There are comparatively few letters to or from Stiles in the 1780s and 1790s.

It seems unlikely that Stiles wrote or received fewer letters in this period or that he failed to preserve them. Probably most of them were among the volumes mentioned in the will that are now missing. Some may also have been deliberately destroyed. Pages have been cut or torn from the Literary Diary of the 1780s and 1790s at several points. In some cases they may have been removed by members of the family for sentimental reasons. The pages containing St. John Honeywood's gallery of sketches were evidently kept by Ruth or by one of the other girls. Lewis Stiles Gannett found them among his papers and restored them in 1958.[11] Another page was evidently removed because it contained a copy of a letter of George Washington to Stiles. It was restored in the Harkness donation.[12]

But a number of pages have obviously been removed by someone who found them damaging to himself, to his friends, or to the author. From the context it is apparent that some of these, at least, concerned Timothy Dwight. In one volume, where Stiles has made a brief table of contents in the fly leaves, even the subject of the missing pages has been eradicated from the table.[13] At another point an entry, which evidently had to do with Dwight's academy, has been eradicated beyond the power of ultra-violet light or infra-red photography to recover a coherent text.[14]

Franklin B. Dexter, who edited the Literary Diary for publication in 1901, surmised that Stiles himself had removed the missing pages because he found his

11. Reproduced in Fig. 5. See *Lit. Diary*, 2, 496 n.

12. *Lit. Diary*, 2, 532. Isabel M. Calder, ed., *Letters and Papers of Ezra Stiles* (New Haven, 1933), pp. 48–49.

13. Vol. 11 of the manuscript Diary. The missing pages are those noted in *Lit. Diary*, 2, 565 n. and 568 n.

14. *Lit. Diary*, 2, 538 n.

own vehement remarks about Dwight embarrassing.[15] But Holmes, in his *Life*, quotes a passage from the Diary that is not now present and evidently came from one of the missing pages.[16] Holmes may have removed the pages himself before passing the manuscripts to Yale, for fear that Dwight (in whose house they were supposed to be lodged) might see them and find them offensive. It may also be that Dwight removed them after they got there. But so might any number of other people. In 1843 Henry Stevens Jr. made copious extracts from the Diary, which are now in the Library of Congress. None of the extracts includes any of the missing passages.

Their absence has made it extremely difficult to unravel the story of Stiles's relationship with Timothy Dwight and Yale's relationship with the people of Connecticut. No extensive body of Dwight papers survives anywhere, and there are few Stiles papers in any public repository outside the Yale Library. The only important group outside Yale are the Record Books of the Second Congregational Church at Newport, Rhode Island, now in the Newport Historical Society. Other repositories have only occasional disconnected letters.

In hope of understanding some of the matters that have been removed from the Literary Diary and perhaps from other Stiles manuscripts at Yale, I have examined every collection of eighteenth-century Connecticut papers I could discover, the most extensive being in the Connecticut Historical Society and the Yale University Library. The results have been disappointing. In hundreds of letters between Yale graduates I have found only a few cryptic hints of the difficulties that estranged the community from Yale during the 1780s. I have pieced these hints together with Stiles's own remaining comments in the Literary Diary and with material from newspaper articles and pamphlets, to reconstruct as accurate a picture as possible, but I am painfully aware that much remains hidden.

Except where otherwise indicated, the documents referred to in the notes are in the Stiles Papers at Yale. I have not ordinarily differentiated the more recent accessions among the Papers from those in the original bequest.

Franklin B. Dexter, Assistant Librarian of Yale 1869–1912, edited and published Stiles's Literary Diary in three volumes (*The Literary Diary of Ezra Stiles*, New York, 1901). He also published a selection of his other papers and of his letters received (*Extracts from the Itineraries and Other Miscellanies of Ezra Stiles . . . with a Selection from His Correspondence*, New Haven, 1916). In citing the Diaries I have always cited Dexter's edition, except where the entry was omitted by Dexter. My quotations may differ slightly from the version in Dexter, because I have checked them from the original, expanding abbreviations but maintaining the original punctuation and orthography. Dexter's edition maintains a high level of accuracy. Its omissions are mainly of astronomical observations

15. Ibid., pp. 529, 530.
16. Holmes, *Life*, pp. 273–75.

and of extracts from books and newspapers. Occasionally there are capricious omissions: Dexter sometimes included routine notations, say, of who preached a sermon, or what the weather was; sometimes he omitted them. His edition of the *Itineraries and Miscellanies* is much less inclusive, and I have accordingly cited it less frequently.

Although I have lamented the loss of Stiles Papers for the 1780s and 1790s, there remains more in the papers and more to the man than I have been able to convey in the pages of this book.

Index

(Note: Ezra Stiles is abbreviated throughout as ES)

Stiles, Ezra (*E.S.*) (*continued*)
200, 219; *A Sermon Delivered at the Ordination of the Reverend Henry Channing*, 445–46; *The United States Elevated to Glory and Honor*, 181, 409, 451, 453–55; *A History of Three of the Judges of King Charles I*, 451, 458–61
Stiles, Mrs. Ezra. *See* Hubbard, Elizabeth
Stiles, Ezra, Jr., 126, 277, 280, 309; and invasion of New Haven, 332, 334; career, marriage, and death of, 429–30; letter to David McClure, 433; estate of, 468
Stiles, Isaac (father of ES), 125, 127, 181, 469; and ES, 1–19, 45, 60, 85–86, 94, 114; as student at Yale, 3, 16, 18, 36–37, 48, 49, 65; and Great Awakening, 22–41; preaches election sermon, 39–41; and North Haven church, 11–12, 18–19, 60–61, 199; Arminianism of, 63–64; opposes consociation, 198–99
Stiles, Isaac (son of ES), 126, 277, 308; at Yale, 332, 366, 431; career and death, 431, 468; MSS bequeathed to, 465, 468
Stiles, Mrs. Isaac. *See* Taylor, Kezia
Stiles, Job, 94
Stiles, John, 3–4, 9
Stiles, Kezia (Mrs. Lewis Burr Sturges), 126, 277, 280, 308, 433
Stiles, Mary (Polly, Mrs. Abiel Holmes), 126, 277, 308, 433–34
Stiles, Ruth (Mrs. Caleb Gannett), 126, 277, 309, 433, 469
Stiles, Ruth (sister of ES), 94
Stiles, Sarah, 126
Stillingfleet, Edward, 16
Stockbridge, Mass., 80–88, 437
Stoddard family, 10
Stoddard, Solomon, 24, 171, 175, 313; view of baptism, communion, and church membership, 61, 185–86, 373
Stonington, Conn., 208, 278, 309
Stratford, Conn., 110
Street, Nicholas, 181
Street, Samuel, 181
Strong, Nathan, 314, 412, 417

Strong, Nehemiah, 329, 337, 442; ousted from professorship, 339–41, 351, 352, 427; and "Parnassus" articles, 349, 351, 352; in petition against Yale, 354
Students, in Yale College: numbers of, 104, 318, 328, 359, 463; unruly behavior by, 36–37, 44–45, 97–100, 294, 367–68, 402–03; discipline of, 43–44, 47, 97–100, 326, 368–71, 419, 425–27; manners and customs of, 43–47, 369–73, 421–23; clubs of, 320, 365–66, 399, 405, 431; expenses of, 327, 463; petitions by, 345 n., 346–47, 353–54, 390
Sturges, Jonathan, 355
Sturges, Lewis Burr, 433
Sugar Act, 220, 224, 226
Surinam, 132
Susquehanna Company, 125
Swift, Zephaniah, 414, 415, 416

Tailor, Mr. *See* Taylor, John
Talmud, 144
Taunton, Mass., 284, 296
Taunton River, 279–80
Taylor, Edward, 4–5, 126, 467
Taylor, Eldad, 5, 127
Taylor, John, 67; *Scripture Doctrine of Original Sin*, 64, 87 n.
Taylor, Kezia (Mrs. Isaac Stiles), 1, 4–5, 10
Taylor, Nathaniel, 297–98, 306, 420
Taylor's Wharf (Newport), 116
Tea Act, 263
Technologia, 48–51, 54–56, 381–82
Temperature, ES' studies in, 134–36
Tennent, Gilbert, 26, 29–30
Throat distemper, 11
Thurston, Edward, 155
Tillotson, John, 16
Tindal, Matthew, 67; *Christianity as Old as the Creation*, 166
Todd, Jonathan, 63–64, 147
Tolland, Conn., 431
Tories, 221, 240, 278–79
Torrev, Joseph, 181
Touro, Isaac, 142
Townsend, Christopher, 155
Townshend Act, 256
Tracy, Uriah, 414, 415, 416